Communication
Yearbook
20

BRANT R. BURLESON, Editor
ADRIANNE W. KUNKEL, Editorial Assistant

Communication
Yearbook
20

 Published Annually for the
International Communication Association

SAGE Publications
International Educational and Professional Publisher
Thousand Oaks London New Delhi

For information address:

SAGE Publications, Inc.
2455 Teller Road
Thousand Oaks, California 91320
Phone: 805-499-0721
E-mail: order@sagepub.com

SAGE Publications Ltd.
6 Bonhill Street
London EC2A 4PU
United Kingdom

SAGE Publications India Pvt. Ltd.
M-32 Market
Greater Kailash I
New Delhi 110 048 India

Printed in the United States of America

Library of Congress: 76-45943

ISBN 0-7619-0686-X

ISSN 0147-4642

This book is printed on acid-free paper.

97 98 99 00 01 02 10 9 8 7 6 5 4 3 2 1

Acquiring Editor: Margaret Seawell
Editorial Assistant: Renée Piernot
Production Editor: Astrid Virding
Production Assistant: Karen Wiley
Typesetter/Designer: Andrea D. Swanson/Dick Palmer
Indexer: Cristina Haley
Cover Designer: Ravi Balasuriya
Print Buyer: Anna Chin

CONTENTS

THE INTERNATIONAL COMMUNICATION ASSOCIATION

The International Communication Association (ICA) was formed in 1950, bringing together academicians and other professionals whose interests focus on human communication. The Association maintains an active membership of more than 2,800 individuals, of whom some two-thirds are teaching and conducting research in colleges, universities, and schools around the world. Other members are in government, the media, communication technology, business, law, medicine, and other professions. The wide professional and geographic distribution of the membership provides the basic strength of the ICA. The Association is a meeting ground for sharing research and useful dialogue about communication interests.

Through its Divisions and Interest Groups, publications, annual conferences, and relations with other associations around the world, the ICA promotes the systematic study of communication theories, processes, and skills.

In addition to *Communication Yearbook,* the Association publishes the *Journal of Communication, Human Communication Research, Communication Theory, A Guide to Publishing in Scholarly Communication Journals, ICA Newsletter,* and the *ICA Membership Directory.*

For additional information about the ICA and its activities, contact Robert L. Cox, Executive Director, International Communication Association, P.O. Box 9589, Austin, TX 78766; phone (512) 454-8299; fax (512) 454-4221; e-mail icahdq@uts.cc.utexas.edu

Editors of the *Communication Yearbook* series:

Volumes 1 and 2, Brent D. Ruben
Volumes 3 and 4, Dan Nimmo
Volumes 5 and 6, Michael Burgoon
Volumes 7 and 8, Robert N. Bostrom
Volumes 9 and 10, Margaret L. McLaughlin
Volumes 11, 12, 13, and 14, James A. Anderson
Volumes 15, 16, and 17, Stanley A. Deetz
Volumes 18, 19, and 20, Brant R. Burleson

INTERNATIONAL COMMUNICATION ASSOCIATION
EXECUTIVE COMMITTEE

President
Stanley A. Deetz,
Rutgers University

President-Elect
Peter Monge, *University of*
Southern California

Immediate Past-President
Charles R. Berger, *University*
of California, Davis

Finance Chair
Akiba A. Cohen, *Hebrew University*
of Jerusalem

Executive Director
Robert L. Cox, *ICA Headquarters*

BOARD OF DIRECTORS

Members-at-Large
Joseph N. Cappella, *University*
of Pennsylvania
Christine Ogan, *Indiana University*
Esther Thorson, *University of Missouri*

Student Board Members
Adrianne W. Kunkel, *Purdue University*
Michele M. Strano, *University of*
Pennsylvania

Vice Presidents and Division Chairs

Information Systems
James B. Stiff, *University of Kansas*

Interpersonal Communication
James P. Dillard, *University of*
Wisconsin—Madison

Mass Communication
Joseph G. Turow, *University of*
Pennsylvania

Organizational Communication
Katherine Miller, *University of Kansas*

Intercultural/Development Communication
John K. Mayo, *Florida State University*

Political Communication
Wolfgang Donsbach, *University of Dresden*

Instructional/Developmental Communication
Katherine E. Rowan, *Purdue University*

Health Communication
Peter G. Northouse, *Western Michigan*
University

Philosophy of Communication
Anne Balsamo, *Georgia Institute of*
Technology

Communication and Technology
Leah A. Lievrouw, *University of*
California, Los Angeles

Feminist Scholarship
Jay F. Morrison, *University of*
Alaska, Fairbanks

Language and Social Interaction
Wendy Leeds-Hurwitz, *University of*
Wisconsin—Parkside

Special Interest Groups

Popular Communication
Barbie Zelizer, *Temple University*

Public Relations
Lynn Zoch, *University of South Carolina*

Communication Law and Policy
John Soloski, *University of Iowa*

Council of Communication Libraries
Susan G. Williamson, *University of*
Pennsylvania Library

Visual Communication
Robert L. Craig, *University of St. Thomas*

Gay, Lesbian, and Bisexual Studies
Lisa Henderson, *University of Massachu-*
setts

CONSULTING EDITORS

The following individuals helped make possible this volume of the *Communication Yearbook* by providing insightful reviews of papers and proposals. The editor gratefully acknowledges these scholars for the gifts of their time and wisdom.

EDITOR'S INTRODUCTION

Last year, *Communication Yearbook* inaugurated a new format. Beginning with Volume 19, *CY* became exclusively an outlet for state-of-the-art literature reviews. *CY* had, of course, always included some literature reviews among the mix of essays, commentaries, and research reports published in Volumes 1-18. However, ongoing changes in the publication landscape recently made it both possible and desirable to narrow *CY*'s mission to that of a literature review series. The reasons for the change in format are detailed in my introduction to *CY19*.

The current volume, *CY20,* is thus the second in the series to reflect the new format. *CY20* contains 10 outstanding literature reviews that summarize key developments in numerous areas of the communication discipline. Each of the chapters in this volume has undergone a rigorous development and revision process, including at least two rounds of peer review. The resulting works provide authoritative treatments of their subject matters and constitute resources that members of the scholarly community will be able to rely upon for many years.

Editing this collection of papers has made the varied contributions of a good literature review especially vivid to me. First and foremost, the good literature review contains a wealth of factual information. That is the primary purpose of a literature review, of course—to synthesize what is known about a particular topic so that it becomes possible to state what is the case and what remains to be determined. Good reviews organize information and answer questions. In so doing, they teach us how to think about an area of study, what questions are important, how those questions can be addressed fruitfully, what we know about a topic, and what we yet need to learn. Good literature reviews make for fascinating reading; they confirm hunches, explode illusions, resolve disputes, reveal inconsistencies, formulate new puzzles, and articulate agendas for the future. These are the familiar and important functions of the literature review—but good reviews do even more.

Good literature reviews focus on questions of enduring significance and, in so doing, help us refine our sense about those issues that matter and those that do not. To sustain research over a lengthy period—in some cases, several decades—the questions addressed must transcend contemporary notions regarding the intellectually trendy and fashionable. Questions lying at the core of some of the reviews in *CY20* include the following:

- How does television affect both U.S. society and other cultures?
- How does what counts as "news" get constituted as such?
- How is "public opinion" formed, and what effects does it have?
- How are attitudes affected by persuasive messages, and how is the reception of persuasive messages affected by attitudes?

- What factors influence participation in decision-making groups, and what are the effects of different levels of participation?
- What are the effects of anxiety on communication, and how can social anxiety be remedied?
- How does the social environment shape the child's development of social and communication competencies?

These questions clearly possess lasting import. They stand as models of questions worth pursuing and, as such, should inspire students and researchers to reexamine the significance of the issues they are currently exploring.

Good research reviews also help readers to develop a historical perspective on the topics examined in the reviews, on the research process, and on the discipline as a whole. Research is not a frozen body of technique and findings, but rather a living (and lively!) process that continuously interacts with features of a world that is itself an ongoing evolutionary process. Good reviews provide readers with a solid sense of how research areas develop over a period of years. The good review, like the reviews offered in this volume, helps us see how key questions unfold and get transformed over time; how innovations and concepts and method reshape an area; how external social, political, and economic factors establish contours within which research areas develop; how the accumulation of findings resolves old issues while posing new riddles; and how each generation of scholars appropriates a research tradition from it forebears, acts on and modifies that tradition, and then passes the modified tradition on to its progeny.

It is well understood that literature reviews are an invaluable asset for theory construction and development: Reviews summarize facts that theories must be capable of predicting, or at least explaining. What may be less well appreciated is that literature reviews often represent powerful exercises in theory development. The good review does not merely catalog research findings, but rather organizes and integrates those findings. Sometimes, existing theories provide the framework for the integrative synthesis of findings. Often, however, the authors of a review discover that no current theory is capable of assimilating the available findings, and so to accomplish their objectives, they must elaborate a fresh conceptual framework. The models and conceptual frameworks articulated to organize research findings frequently constitute new theories, at least in nascent form. So, whereas all of the chapters in *CY20* review important theories and research findings, several also constitute significant and original theoretical statements.

Good reviews exhibit a variety of virtues other than those mentioned above, but rather than my detailing these here, it is far better that readers discover them directly by examining the reviews in *CY20*. Briefly, here is what readers can look forward to in these 10 reviews.

Cultivation theory, developed by George Gerbner and his colleagues at the University of Pennsylvania more than 20 years ago, has emerged as one of the most prominent—and controversial—research paradigms in the study of mass communication. In essence, cultivation theorists assert that the content of the mass media, especially television, shapes how people perceive the world. Because the reality depicted in much television programming departs in important ways from the actual nature of the world, people who watch a lot of TV supposedly acquire a colored or distorted view of the world. A large body of empirical findings pertinent to the claims of cultivation theory have accumulated during the past 20 years. Michael Morgan and James Shanahan, two of the leading exponents of this approach, explicate cultivation theory, provide a narrative history of the development of this paradigm, review numerous criticisms and extensions of the theory, and present a meta-analysis of the results of studies empirically assessing the cultivation effect. On the basis of their meta-analysis, Morgan and Shanahan conclude that there is a small but reliable effect for cultivation: Amount of TV viewing accounts for about 1% of the variance in people's perceptions of the world. Morgan and Shanahan develop a case that the cultivation effect is socially significant despite its small size. Although this review certainly will not put an end to the controversy surrounding cultivation theory, it should help to move the debate to new and more productive issues.

The social and theoretical significance of small effect sizes is also an important issue in Michel Elasmar and John Hunter's meta-analytic review of the impact of foreign TV viewing on domestic audiences. Critics have long argued that the export of U.S. television programming represents a form of cultural imperialism that often harms the indigenous cultures of importing nations. As Elasmar and Hunter point out, this argument assumes that foreign TV programs have substantial influence on the beliefs, attitudes, values, and behaviors of domestic audiences. To assess this assumption, the authors carry out a careful meta-analytic examination of studies assessing the impact of foreign TV exposure. They conclude that there are reliable, if small, associations between the amount of foreign programming consumed and relevant cognitions and behaviors. But how important are these small associations? The first two chapters in *CY20* raise critical questions about the degree of social and theoretical significance that should be accorded small effect sizes.

Vickie Shields offers a narrative review and intellectual history of gender and advertising research. For more than 30 years now, researchers have examined how men and women are portrayed in advertising, questioning how these portrayals influence media consumers. Shields charts the evolution of this research, from early content-analytic studies to contemporary inquiries that utilize a variety of structuralist, semiological, and feminist methods. Shields's history nicely details how the changing values and political commitments of scholars have led to modifications in research agendas, methods, and practices.

How does what counts as "news" get constituted? Much of the research addressing this question has focused on the routines, practices, and values of reporters and the organizations for whom reporters work. But Glen Cameron, Lynne Sallot, and Patricia Curtin point out that the traditional focus on reporters is insufficient, because news sources—especially public relations practitioners and their clients—often set the agenda for the news media. Indeed, Cameron and his colleagues review evidence showing that up to 50% of contemporary news content is influenced by professional public relations practitioners. Consequently, our understanding of how the news is produced must encompass several aspects of the relationship between reporters and news sources, particularly public relations practitioners. Cameron and his associates develop a model that both organizes findings on source-reporter relations and suggests directions for future theory development and empirical research.

Among the oldest questions in the communication discipline are those concerning public opinion—its nature, its sources, and its effects. Carroll Glynn revisits many of these classic issues in the process of outlining a new model of public opinion as a normative opinion process. Reviewing research from a variety of disciplines, Glynn describes how public opinion emerges from interactions between individuals' actual opinions and their perceptions of others' opinions. Glynn's is a dynamic view, emphasizing the processual, evolutionary character of public opinion. Glynn suggests that conceptualizing public opinion as a social norm has some distinct advantages for theory development. Moreover, she demonstrates that her framework is capable of assimilating and organizing a considerable amount of the vast literature on public opinion.

Although persuasion researchers have been familiar with the "attitude" construct for a long time, in recent years many have turned away from this concept, questioning both its status as a target of persuasive efforts and its utility as a predictor of behavior change. David Roskos-Ewoldsen suggests that the abandonment of the attitude construct has been premature; he argues that it still has much to offer to persuasion researchers if they ask the appropriate questions. In developing this thesis, Roskos-Ewoldsen summarizes recent research on "attitude accessibility," the notion that some attitudes are more accessible from memory than are others. Attitude accessibility is important in persuasion study for at least two reasons. First, Roskos-Ewoldsen reviews research showing that attitude accessibility differentially influences the processing and impact of persuasive messages. Second, persuasive messages can be designed to enhance or prime the accessibility of important attitudes. Roskos-Ewoldsen thus offers a convincing case for refurbishing, rather than discarding, the attitude construct in persuasion research.

Joseph Bonito and Andrea Hollingshead present a comprehensive review of research on the determinants and effects of participation in small decision-making groups. These authors develop a model of five factors that influence the degree to which individuals participate during the course of group discussions, including member attributes, group characteristics, task features, communication technologies, and temporal constraints. They also review research examining how participation affects various outcomes, including individuals' cognitions, groups' actions, and social interactions. Bonito and Hollingshead's model proves an effective device for integrating the substantial findings on group participation generated by the disciplines of communication, sociology, and social psychology. The authors also demonstrate that their model has important implications for theory construction regarding group participation.

Miles Patterson and Vicki Ritts take on the daunting task of reviewing the voluminous literature on social and communicative anxiety. These authors first synthesize research examining associations among the dozen or so most popular instruments used in studying trait-based social anxiety. Patterson and Ritts conclude that these instruments appear to be measuring the same thing— a finding that will be reassuring to most students of this topic, but will prove disconcerting to some. The authors then carry out a meta-analytic review of research examining the effects of social anxiety on a wide range of physiological, cognitive, and behavioral measures. The meta-analysis reveals that there are large effects for social anxiety on numerous cognitive and behavioral variables. Patterson and Ritts follow up their meta-analysis with a lengthy narrative review that explores connections among the physiological, cognitive, and behavioral manifestations of social anxiety. This review will be an invaluable resource for scholars interested in social anxiety, communication apprehension, and similar topics.

How does the social environment affect the development of social and communicative competencies in children? Craig Hart, Susanne Olsen, Clyde Robinson, and Barbara Mandleco begin to tackle this difficult, but vital, issue by elaborating a broad-based model of the proximal, distal, and personal factors influencing the development of varied social skills during childhood. The authors then use this model to organize the findings of existing research, showing how the effects of proximal factors (e.g., parenting styles) on children's competencies vary as a complex function of both personal factors (e.g., a child's temperament) and distal factors (e.g., the family social support system). This is a powerful model—one that not only integrates a large and diverse literature, but, more important, helps us understand how the competencies of the individual emerge from complex interactions among personal characteristics, social experiences, and cultural structures.

In the volume's final chapter, Michael Monsour examines an important but understudied relationship: cross-sex friendship. Over the past century, changing social and cultural factors have made cross-sex friendship an increasingly common and important social form. However, research on this relationship type began only about 20 years ago and did not really "take off" until about 10 years ago. Still, a significant body of findings has been developed over the past decade, and this literature is in need of review. Monsour argues that the character and functions of cross-sex friendship differ across phases of the life cycle, so he takes a life-span developmental approach to reviewing the literature. Like all social relationships, cross-sex friendships are created and maintained through the communicative activities of the participants. Hence, throughout his review, Monsour emphasizes the issues involved in cross-sex friendships that will benefit most from the contributions of communication scholars in the future.

ACKNOWLEDGMENTS

This is the last volume of *CY* that I will edit, so I want to take this opportunity to thank publicly some of those who have made this task manageable, rewarding, and, I hope, fruitful. It is not possible to mention by name all those who have contributed to the substance of my volumes of *CY*—those who have suggested ideas or authors, those who have submitted proposals and papers, and those who have reviewed the submissions I have received— but all of these persons have been important. In a very real sense, the *CY* volumes are community projects, so it is fitting that I acknowledge and thank the community of communication scholars for its cooperation in producing these volumes.

The Department of Communication and School of Liberal Arts at Purdue University provided me with the time and many of the material resources needed to edit this series of volumes. At Purdue, some very special people have helped in some very special ways. I have been blessed with two of the finest editorial assistants anyone could have; my heartfelt thanks go to Adrianne Kunkel and Tammy Bergland for all they have done. Carolyn Parrish and Beverly Robinson provided excellent secretarial services over the past 3 years. I came to rely on many of my colleagues at Purdue for speedy and insightful reviews. Three of them—John Greene, Kathy Rowan, and Glenn Sparks—were especially helpful at many points in editing these volumes.

I did most of the editing for *CY20* during a sabbatical leave, which I spent at the University of Illinois at Urbana-Champaign. My special thanks go to David Swanson, head of the Department of Speech Communication at the University of Illinois, for providing me with space and resources that assisted in the production of this volume. I also thank my many friends at U of I for their personal and professional support during the past year.

The staff at Sage Publications has been most cooperative in assisting with the redesigned *CY.* In particular, I want to thank Alex Schwartz for helping to realize many of the changes associated with the new *CY* format, Astrid Virding for her outstanding production work, and Sara McCune for her continuing support of this series.

During the past year, ICA President Charles Berger provided useful advice about the redesign of *CY.* Joseph Cappella and Linda Putnam, chairs of the ICA Publications Committee, provided support and good advice throughout my editorial tenure. Finally, ICA Executive Director Bob Cox has been a reliable source of advice, assistance, and aid.

For the most part, I've enjoyed my circuit around the track. I am now pleased to pass the editorial baton into the skilled hands of my successor, Michael Roloff.

Brant R. Burleson
Champaign, Illinois

CHAPTER CONTENTS

1 Two Decades of Cultivation Research: An Appraisal and Meta-Analysis

MICHAEL MORGAN
University of Massachusetts, Amherst

JAMES SHANAHAN
Cornell University

This chapter presents a theoretical review and meta-analysis of cultivation research. The authors examine the roots of cultivation analysis, as developed by George Gerbner and colleagues, and review the progress made in cultivation research since its inception in the 1970s. They also review some of the critiques that have been made of cultivation theory over the years and provide their own critical review and responses. They then offer a meta-analysis of empirical findings from 20 years of cultivation research. This meta-analysis shows an average cultivation effect of .09. Much, but not all, of the variation in cultivation findings reported in the literature can be attributed to sampling error alone. Yet, although the authors tested a variety of hypothetical moderator variables, they found no specific moderator variables. The analysis suggests that many theoretical arguments tend to fade into the background when the corpus of cultivation findings is viewed from a meta-analytic perspective.

CULTIVATION analysis, pioneered by George Gerbner, is a well-known research paradigm for thinking about and studying the impacts of mass communication (Gerbner, 1973). Cultivation research examines the extent to which cumulative exposure to television contributes to viewers' conceptions of social reality, in ways that reflect the most stable, repetitive, and pervasive patterns of images and ideologies that television (especially entertainment programming) presents (Morgan & Signorielli, 1990). Cultivation research is concerned with what it means to grow up and live in a symbolic environment where television tells most of the stories to

AUTHORS' NOTE: The order of authorship of this chapter is alphabetical.

Correspondence and requests for reprints: Michael Morgan, Department of Communication, Machmer Hall, University of Massachusetts, Amherst, MA 01003; e-mail mmorgan@comm.umass.edu

Communication Yearbook 20, pp. 1-45

most of the people, most of the time (Gerbner, Gross, Morgan, & Signorielli, 1994).

It has been about 20 years since the first cultivation findings were published (Gerbner & Gross, 1976). Since that time, many studies have explored, enhanced, critiqued, dismissed, or defended the conceptual assumptions and methodological procedures of cultivation analysis. In 1986, Bryant noted that cultivation was one of only three topics covered in more than half of the "mass media and society" courses offered at U.S. colleges and universities. He even quipped that studies of cultivation seem "almost as ubiquitous as television itself" (p. 231).

Although cultivation analysis was once closely identified with the issue of violence, over the years researchers have looked at a broad range of topics, including sex roles, aging, political orientations, environmental attitudes, science, health, religion, minorities, and occupations. Replications have been carried out in Argentina, Australia, Brazil, Canada, China, England, Hungary, Israel, the Netherlands, Russia, South Korea, Sweden, Taiwan, and other countries.

The results of these studies have been many, varied, and sometimes counterintuitive. Although there is some disagreement in the field of communication regarding the validity of cultivation findings, cultivation theory is arguably among the most important contributions yet made to general public understanding of media effects. Certainly, it is among the few approaches that have contributed to the public policy debate surrounding the impacts of television. As Newhagen and Lewenstein (1992) put it, "Despite criticism, the theory persists, perhaps because the social implications of the idea that a mass medium can define our culture [are] too important to dismiss" (p. 49).

Cultivation has indeed been a highly controversial approach. Although some detailed reviews have appeared (Hawkins & Pingree, 1982; Potter, 1993), no one has yet attempted to undertake a systematic, empirical assessment of what has grown into a massive body of research. In order to advance the debate, we offer here both a theoretical appraisal and a meta-analysis of the published cultivation literature.

Meta-analysis—"the statistical integration of the results of independent studies" (Mullen, 1989, p. 1)—is becoming increasingly important in the reanalysis of communication findings (Allen, Emmers, Gebhardt, & Giery, 1995; Herrett-Skjellum & Allen, 1996; Kim & Hunter, 1993). Meta-analysis has an advantage over the traditional narrative review: It provides an estimate of how much of the variation in results observed across studies simply reflects sampling error (Hunter & Schmidt, 1990). That is, we can see how much of the difference in reported cultivation findings is "real" after the variation due to sampling error is accounted for. If any "real" variation is left, we can then determine if results vary across different types of samples, different dependent areas, different analytic strategies, and so on.

Accordingly, we used the technique of meta-analysis to guide us through this assessment of cultivation theory and findings. Taken together, reanalysis of theory and criticism and meta-analysis of data provide a unique way to look at the accomplishments of cultivation research in its first 20 years.

THEORETICAL REVIEW

Cultural Indicators

Cultivation analysis is one component of the long-term, ongoing research program called Cultural Indicators. The concept of a cultural "indicator" was developed to complement economic and social indicators, and to provide a barometer of important cultural issues. In the United States, the focus has been on television, because TV is the country's most pervasive cultural institution and most visible disseminator of cultural symbols. Other media, however, can be studied as indicators of cultural patterns and trends (Rosengren, 1984).

As conceived by Gerbner (1969), Cultural Indicators uses a three-pronged research strategy. The first, called *institutional process analysis,* investigates the systemic pressures and constraints that affect how media messages are selected, produced, and distributed. The second, called *message system analysis,* quantifies and tracks the most stable, pervasive, and recurrent images in media content, in terms of the portrayal of violence, minorities, gender roles, occupations, and many other issues. The third, called *cultivation analysis,* explores the extent to which television viewing contributes to audience members' conceptions about the real world.

Cultural Indicators research began with a profile of television violence in the 1967-1968 program season for the National Commission on the Causes and Prevention of Violence, and continued with support from the Surgeon General's Advisory Committee on Television and Social Behavior in 1972. The cultivation analysis phase began with a national probability survey of adults during the early 1970s in a study funded by the National Institute of Mental Health (Gerbner & Gross, 1976). Many other agencies and foundations have supported the project over the years.

Each year since 1967, researchers have content analyzed a week-long sample of U.S. network television drama in order to delineate selected features and trends in the overall world that television presents to its viewers. In the 1990s, this analysis has been extended to include the Fox television network, "reality" programs, and various cable channels. Through the years, message system analysis has focused on the most pervasive content patterns that are common to many different types of programs but characteristic of the system as a whole, because these hold the most significant potential lessons that television cultivates. The specific questions used in cultivation analysis should be based on the overarching content patterns revealed by message system analysis, although this has not been the case in all studies.

The Development of Cultivation Theory

It is difficult to discuss cultivation theory without giving a sense of the controversy that has developed around the research. The theoretical roots of cultivation theory have at times been obscured in a thicket of debate and colloquy, charges and countercharges, attack and retort. This has been manifested in an ever-widening spiral of conceptual and analytic refinements from many quarters, as well as in some hearty doses of atheoretical tinkering. From our perspective, over the years, researchers have too often oversimplified the notion of cultivation and yet have both complicated and distorted its methodology. In the final analysis, of course, science is about debate, and we argue here that 20 years of progress and contention in research now give us an ideal perspective from which we may make some larger claims.

Gerbner's original conception of cultivation was a break from conventional academic discourse about the social and cultural implications of mass communication. His goal was to develop an approach to mass communication distinct from the then-dominant paradigm of persuasion and propaganda research and to escape the scientism and positivism of the "effects" tradition. This meant dispensing with formal aesthetic categories and conventional concerns about style and artistic quality, along with questions of high culture versus low culture, selective exposure, and idiosyncratic readings and interpretations. It was not that Gerbner denied the existence or importance of these concerns and phenomena, but rather that he sought to go beyond them.

This required a reworking of the traditional methodological tactics that had been used to assess "effects." In general, early mass communication research focused on prediction and control, with a clear-cut criterion for an effect: some *change* in attitude or behavior following exposure to some message. Gerbner's early writings critiqued this, as he developed models of the communication process that distinguished it from purely persuasive exchanges (see, e.g., Gerbner, 1958). Rather than seeing communication research as a way to achieve a specific practical aim (e.g., selling soap, winning votes, improving public health), he saw it as a *basic cultural inquiry.* Above and beyond its communicative "power," he argued, any message is a socially and historically determined expression of concrete physical and social relationships. Messages imply propositions, assumptions, and points of view that are understandable only in terms of the social relationships and contexts in which they are produced. Yet they also reconstitute those relationships and contexts. Messages thus sustain the structures and practices that produce them.

Communication, according to Gerbner, is "interaction through messages," a distinctly human (and humanizing) process that both creates and is driven by the symbolic environment that constitutes culture. The symbolic environment reveals social and institutional dynamics, and because it expresses social patterns it also cultivates them. This, then, is the original meaning of *cultivation*—the process within which interaction through messages shapes and sustains the terms on which the messages are premised.

Mass communication—the mass production of the symbolic environment—implies cultural and political power: the power to create the messages that cultivate collective consciousness. But this is a two-sided process: The right to produce messages stems from social power, but social power can be accrued through the right to produce messages. This confounds simplistic notions of "causality" and is a significant reason many "causal" critiques of cultivation have missed the point.

Cultivation is, most of all, about the cultural process of storytelling. Gerbner often quotes Scottish patriot Andrew Fletcher's observation, "If a man were permitted to make all the ballads, he need not care who should make the laws of a nation." That is, it matters crucially who gets to tell the stories, and whose stories do not get told.

Much of what we know and think we know comes not from personal experience but from the stories we hear. In earlier times, the stories of a culture were generally told face-to-face by members of a community, parents, teachers, or the church. Today, storytelling is in the hands of global commercial interests that in effect operate outside the reach of democratic decision making. The great cultural stories of mythology, religion, legends, education, art, science, laws, fairy tales, and politics are increasingly packaged and disseminated by television. The narrative world we are inhabiting and (re)creating is one designed according to marketing strategies.

The impacts of stories are not hypodermic. Uncovering aggregate and implicit patterns in mass-produced messages "will not necessarily tell us what people think or do. But [it] will tell us what most people think or do something about and in common" (Gerbner, 1970). The messages set the hidden but pervasive boundary conditions for social discourse, wherein cultural ground rules for what exists, what is important, what is right, and so on, are repeated (and ritualistically consumed) so often that they become invisible. The model for cultivation is "enculturation," not persuasion.

Therefore, "cultivation is what a culture does," because "culture is the basic medium in which humans live and learn" (Gerbner, 1990, p. 249). Culture is a "system of stories and other artifacts—increasingly mass-produced—that mediates between existence and consciousness of existence, and thereby contributes to both" (p. 251). As our most pervasive and widely shared storyteller, television is likely to play a crucial role in the cultivation of common beliefs, values, and ideologies.

Cultivation Assumptions

Early research on media effects typically focused on the impacts of single programs or messages in the short term, usually based on experimental designs. The novelty of the cultivation approach was that it put aside the question of effects at the program level and concentrated on the level of the story system. The emphasis on *overall exposure* to television, regardless of genre, channel, or program type, is what is most unusual and important about cultivation analysis. It has also perhaps been its most nagging and persistent point of contention among critics.

It is not that cultivation theory simplistically asserts that "all programs contain exactly the same messages," although that is a straw argument sometimes attacked. Cultivation theory does not deny that programs differ, that viewing can be selective, that variations in channels and genres exist, or that any of these are important. It just sees these as separate issues, as separate research questions, distinct from the questions explored through cultivation analysis.

Focusing primarily on selectivity and diversity (values privileged by the pluralist ideology of print culture) can blind us to subtle commonalities underlying superficially different program types. To focus only on specific types of programs is to risk losing sight of what is most significant about television as a *system* of messages. Whatever impacts specific programs may have are not meaningless, but they are analytically distinct from the consequences of cumulative exposure to the total world of television.

There may well be some "heavy viewers" who watch nothing but shopping channels, travel documentaries, golf tournaments, or weather forecasts (and this sort of viewing is now possible), but cultivation theory assumes that most regular and heavy viewers will, over time, watch "more of everything." Even in a 100-channel universe, the programs attracting large, heterogeneous groups of viewers are narrative in nature. As narratives, different genres of fictional programs tend to manifest complementary—although, of course, not invariant—basic features. It is obvious that one will see more representations of police, crime, and violence on action/adventure shows than on most other types of shows, but potential lessons about safety, vulnerability, and the law are not limited to such programs, and it is precisely the overall contribution of these lessons with which cultivation research is concerned.

A researcher may find that exposure to police/action shows contributes more to images of violence than does overall viewing, or that viewers seem to learn more about doctors from medical shows than from overall viewing (or from game shows or from sports, and so on). In such an event, we could say that television does not in fact cultivate any global image. But, as Newhagen and Lewenstein (1992) point out, looking at the isolated effects of different program types is problematic, because viewers may not define genres in the same way as do researchers, and also because bizarre and nonsensical associations can emerge. There is a danger of reaching such trivial and irrelevant, though potentially true, conclusions, as "Heavy viewing of the Home and Garden Channel 'cultivates' awareness of when to plant different bulbs."

From the point of view of the cultivation of relatively stable and common images, what counts most is the total pattern of programming to which communities are exposed over long periods of time. The pattern of settings, casting, social typing, actions, and related outcomes cuts across most program types and viewing modes and defines the world of television—a world in which many viewers live so much of their lives that they cannot avoid absorbing or dealing with its recurrent patterns.

These assumptions have been challenged by those who point to "obvious" differences between various program types, and by the proliferation of alternative delivery systems, such as cable TV and the VCR, that seem to provide an enormous expansion in diversity and choice. Yet these developments have been accompanied by *decreased* diversity in ownership and greater concentration and commercialization of production and control, with little evident diversification in programming. In our own investigations into the impacts of new technologies, we predicted and found that VCRs, cable TV, and other devices mainly serve as delivery vehicles for the same system of messages for heavy viewers (Morgan & Shanahan, 1991a). More recent research is bearing us out in this regard: New technologies do not radically threaten the "integrity" of the message system (Eastman & Newton, 1995). In fact, they may strengthen it.

In sum, no matter what impact exposure to genre X may have on attitude Y, cultivation theory argues that important consequences of television cannot be found only in terms of exposure to isolated fragments of the whole. The cultivation project is an attempt to say something about the more broad-based, ideological consequences of a commercially supported cultural industry celebrating consumption, materialism, individualism, power, and the status quo along lines of gender, race, class, and age. None of this denies the fact that some programs may contain some messages more than others, or that these messages may change somewhat over time.

In the following sections we summarize the earliest cultivation studies and examine some of the major critical issues that have appeared over the years. Not every cultivation study can be described here, of course (more than 300 have been published), but we take a close look at some of the most significant and most often cited studies and critiques and the issues they raise. Following that, we present the methodology and results of our meta-analysis.

Early Findings

In 1976, Gerbner and Gross presented data that showed that heavy viewers were more likely than light viewers to give "television answers" to survey questions about law enforcement, trust, and danger. They used "forced-choice" questions for which one response, called the "TV answer," was slanted in the direction of the world of television (as revealed by the message system data), with the alternative slanted more in the direction of "reality."

For example, 1970 U.S. Census data showed that 1% of all working males had jobs in law enforcement and crime detection; in the world of television, that figure was 12% (Gerbner et al., 1977). So respondents were asked whether the proportion of males so employed was 5% (the TV answer) or 1%. The hypothesis was that if television viewing cultivates assumptions about the facts of life that reflect the medium's most recurrent portrayals, then heavy viewers should be more likely than light viewers to choose the higher number. Sure enough, 50% of the light viewers, compared with 59% of the heavy viewers, said 5% (Gerbner & Gross, 1976). This difference—here, 9 percentage points—is referred to as the *cultivation differential* and is interpreted as indicating the difference that television viewing makes to a particular attitude or belief.

In another early example, message system data showed that almost two-thirds of the characters in network television programs were involved in violence each week. In contrast, 1970 census data showed .32 violent crimes per 100 persons (Gerbner & Gross, 1976). When asked if the number of people involved in violence each week was "closer to 1 in 10" or "closer to 1 in 100," 39% of light viewers but 52% of heavy viewers gave the TV answer (1 in 10). Similar patterns were found in terms of trust: When asked if most people can be trusted, 48% of light viewers but 65% of heavy viewers chose the response "You can't be too careful."

The validity of "forced-error" questions, for which neither of the options offered is necessarily correct, has been questioned (e.g., Potter, 1994, finds them "curious" and "puzzling"), yet such measures have a long and respected pedigree in social psychology (Hammond, 1948). Campbell (1950) argues that they reveal systematic biases in ways that reflect "the essential practical meaning of attitude" (p. 19).

It was recognized from the start that statistical controls were essential to sustain the inference that these patterns could be taken as evidence of cultivation: "The obvious objection arises that light and heavy viewers are different prior to—and aside from—television. Factors other than television may account for the difference" (Gerbner & Gross, 1976, p. 191). The most important of these were demographic factors that influence both viewing levels and social conceptions, such as social status (education level, occupational prestige, and income), age, sex, and race, and other media use; many other controls have been thrown into the mix over the years.

Therefore, these same percentage comparisons between light and heavy viewers were made *within* more homogeneous subgroups. Cultivation differentials were compared for, say, those with and without a college education, males versus females, and younger or older respondents. In most cases, the results were not affected very much by the implementation of controls; the baselines of the dependent variables were higher or lower in different subgroups, and some groups showed weaker or stronger associations, but the general patterns persisted.

These apparently (and deceptively) straightforward patterns were soon to unleash a veritable firestorm of criticism, controversy, and confusion. Every aspect of measurement, coding, sampling, controls, question wording, scaling, and more was to come under intense scrutiny. In hindsight, it appears that cultivation theory was striking some remarkably sensitive nerves. The stridency of some of the critics was extremely high, given that cultivation researchers were, at this early stage, advancing some rather tentative and almost commonsensical propositions. With the benefit of 20 years, we can now see that this was as much a political phenomenon as anything else. Cultivation theorists were attacking the political basis of mainstream American media sociology (along with the prevailing wisdom about the "effects" of violence and how they should be studied, as well as long-cherished beliefs about the importance of selectivity, genre differences, and variations in individuals' interpretations), and many people did not like that. Thus, cultivation research, perhaps inevitably, politicized the debate on media effects.

Subsequent studies added secondary analyses of national surveys and convenience samples of adolescents, including panel studies, and began to focus on other issues besides violence. In all cases, the most fundamental questions revolved around social power. This point was often lost in the debates that were soon to come (and it continues to be lost in many contemporary critiques). Not only do those with power in society control the production and distribution of cultural stories, but the stories they tell express and reproduce (i.e., cultivate) specific patterns of power in material ways. Whether the issue at hand was violence, sex role stereotypes, aging, occupations, or anything else, the real concern was with whether television helps maintain a power hierarchy marked by an unequal distribution of resources, opportunities, and security, differentiated by gender, race, and other key markers of "difference." Critiques that attack cultivation research on methodological issues alone can deflect attention away from these larger issues of social power and cultural policy.

Although some critics have accused cultivation theorists of exaggerating television's impact, Gerbner, Gross, Jackson-Beeck, Jeffries-Fox, and Signorielli (1978) were careful "not to assert that television alone is responsible or necessarily decisive, only that it makes a contribution" to perpetuating an unequal social power hierarchy (p. 194). Important to this argument, the very notion of "causality" was explicitly rejected, as were models of "effects" that are more appropriate to experiments in the physical or biological sciences, which assume lawlike, stimulus-response models.

Still, the preponderance of associations reported in the early studies remained statistically significant even under controls. These studies emphasized that cultivation associations held up across a wide variety of subgroups, yet they also acknowledged the obvious fact that "television makes somewhat different contributions to the perspectives of different social groups" (Gerbner et al., 1978, p. 206). These clear variations in the size (and sometimes in the direction) of cultivation differentials, along with questions over the ways in which controls were applied, would soon become springboards for fierce controversies. We next deal with some of these critiques.

CRITIQUES

A "Humanistic" Critique

Newcomb (1978) started the ball rolling with what he called a "humanistic" critique of cultivation, based in part on perceived differences between quantitative and qualitative approaches. In effect, Newcomb anticipated some of the concepts and processes that concern contemporary cultural studies and semiotics researchers in terms of the "polysemy" of media texts as sites where hegemonic meanings are enacted, negotiated, resisted, or opposed. The issues he raised remain important to communication research today.

Newcomb argued that violence has had many symbolic meanings in U.S. history and culture, and that all viewers do not interpret acts of violence in the same way. He defended the value of in-depth analysis of individual programs against the Cultural Indicators focus on aggregate patterns. He emphasized *differences*—in contexts, in programs, in viewers—that mean that no program, much less all programs, can have a single invariant meaning that is unproblematically and "correctly" perceived by all audience members. That is, he questioned whether viewers would "get" the message that Gerbner and Gross (1976) claimed they should from exposure to television violence.

A moment of reflection on our own personal experiences with media texts will doubtless reveal that Newcomb's basic position is correct. Symbols are complex, and the meanings we construct as we interact with them are multiplicitous, unpredictable, and slippery. Nevertheless, there is nothing in Newcomb's view that contradicts the basic precepts of cultivation theory. To say that audiences' interactions with media texts are diverse is not to deny that there may be important commonalities as well. To explore those commonalities, as cultivation theorists do, is not to negate the differences; similarly, the examination of differences need not (and, arguably, cannot) deny the possibility of shared meanings in a culture. To privilege *only* the fact of polysemy is to risk removing any vestige of articulatory or determinational power from the text—and thereby to render culture impotent as well. The common argument that cultivation assumes a "passive" viewer cannot be substantiated.

In response to Newcomb, Gerbner and Gross (1979) justified their focus on the broad similarities that cut across program types by arguing that programs are more like formulaic, market-driven, assembly-line products than like uniquely crafted works of individual expressive artists. Most of all, they pointed out, the relationships observed between amount of viewing and various beliefs are precisely the test of whether the patterns and meanings inferred from message data are indeed absorbed by viewers. The relative statistical weakness of cultivation relationships is, of course, itself a proof of the operation of individual readings. Cultivation theory does not assert that every act of violence observed on television means the same thing to every viewer.

Potter (1994) has more recently reiterated Newcomb's argument by asking how cultivation researchers can "be confident that their designated television world answer has taken into account all the factors" that influence viewers' inferences from television content (p. 11). Although cultivation research attempts to account for a variety of other variables, the evidence is simply assessed in the *degree* to which heavy viewers are more likely to give responses that are demonstrably emphasized in the television world. Taking "all the factors" into account is both impossible and beside the point.

Ultimately, then, "Newcomb's big question, 'what does violence mean to the respondents' is not only irrelevant but distracting" (Gerbner & Gross, 1979, p. 227). Individual programs and variations in interpretation are interesting and valuable things to study, but cultivation research tries to illuminate broad patterns across large groups of people. The key distinction is not "humanism" versus "social science," or even "qualitative" versus "quantitative"; more simply, it is macro versus micro.

A Challenge From Britain

Around the same time Newcomb made his critique, Wober (1978) published the results of British research that failed to replicate what he called the "paranoid effect of television." Yet the apparent lack of evidence for cultivation in Wober's data may reflect important cultural and structural differences between the United States and Great Britain; British heavy viewers saw less violence than did U.S. light viewers (Pingree & Hawkins, 1981), and the institutional controls of British television ensured a more diversified and balanced flow of media messages that were not driven entirely by commercial interests (Wober & Gunter, 1988). Thus, Wober's work may actually strengthen the case for cultivation in the U.S. context, because exposure to a message system less dominated by violence indeed should not cultivate a heightened sense of apprehension and mistrust.

Questions have been raised about the validity of Wober's dependent measures (Neville, 1980), but there is a further problem that may also have been at work in his findings. His survey, sponsored by the Independent Broadcasting Authority, was apparently presented to respondents as one dealing with "attitudes to broadcasting." Gerbner and his colleagues have always been extremely careful not to introduce "television" in any way before asking respondents about their conceptions of social reality (Gerbner & Gross, 1976; Gerbner et al., 1994). Television is never mentioned until the viewing measures are reached late in the survey. Any explicit prior mention of television may subtly invoke some of the medium's images in respondents' minds when they answer the social reality questions, or may sensitize them to the purposes of the study. Either way, the data may be contaminated.

Indeed, experimental research has found clear evidence of demand artifact problems that affect the results when television viewing measures appear first in a survey, or when the title of the survey mentions television (Shrum, Wyer, & O'Guinn, 1994). Many studies make this mistake and thereby put the integrity of their data at risk. For example, Rubin, Perse, and Taylor (1988) told respondents that their study "concerned television viewing and communication with others" (p. 129). Weaver and Wakshlag (1986) started off their questionnaire with a television viewing diary. Many of Potter's analyses come from a survey titled "Estimations of TV and Society" (e.g., Potter, 1991b). The validity and import of such contaminated data, regardless of what they may suggest about cultivation, may be reduced accordingly. This is one dimension we explore in our meta-analysis below as a possible moderator of cultivation results.

Spuriousness or Specification?

Another major critique was Doob and Macdonald's (1979) study of the role of neighborhood crime rates in the cultivation process. This may be "the most widely cited research challenging the cultivation hypothesis" (Tamborini & Choi, 1990, p. 168). Yet the study's actual findings are usually misrepresented, and, in a manner ironically reminiscent of cultivation itself, the more often the misleading account of the study's findings is repeated, the more taken for granted the received (and incorrect) conclusion becomes.

Doob and Macdonald's hypothesis is conceptually appealing. Perhaps, they reasoned, people who live in high crime and/or urban areas tend to be more afraid because of where they live, and hence spend more time indoors, watching television. Accordingly, they sampled four areas of metropolitan Toronto: high crime/city, high crime/suburb, low crime/city, and low crime/suburb. If the relationship between television exposure and perception of violence is due to neighborhood crime level, then "within neighborhoods . . . the effect should be substantially reduced or eliminated" (Doob & Macdonald, 1979, p. 171).

Respondents were given newspaper listings of all available TV programs and asked which ones they had watched during the previous week. (This question came first in the interview, again raising the possibility of contamination.) Then respondents were asked 34 closed-ended questions dealing with a variety of perceptions of crime, violence, and danger. Factor analysis isolated nine of these items as measuring "fear of crime." Overall, the fear of crime index and the television exposure measure were significantly correlated ($r = .18$, $p < .01$). The correlations varied widely across neighborhoods, however, as shown in Table 1.1.

Doob and Macdonald emphasized that the average of the four correlations was only .09, and concluded that "there is essentially no relationship between

TABLE 1.1
Within-Neighborhood Correlations
of Television Viewing and "Fear of Crime" Index

	High Crime	Low Crime
City	.24* (N = 83)	.06 (N = 71)
Suburb	.16 (N = 69)	−.09 (N = 77)

SOURCE: Data from Doob and Macdonald (1979).
*p < .05.

media usage and fear of crime when the effect of neighborhood is removed"
(p. 173). Yet the average of the four correlations does not represent a partial
correlation of amount of viewing and fear of crime with the effects of
neighborhood "removed." These data do not show a "spurious" association;
if they did, the relationships would be essentially zero in all four areas.
Instead, they show a specification. The correlation is magnified in the high
crime/city area; it is essentially the same in the high crime/suburban area as
it is in the overall sample, but fails to reach significance because of the greatly
reduced sample size.

Gerbner, Gross, Morgan, and Signorielli (1980a) interpreted this finding
as "resonance." They proposed that television's messages about violence may
be most congruent, and thus "resonate," with the everyday reality of those
who live in high crime areas. They asserted that this "double dose" of
messages may amplify cultivation. There may be other explanations (as we
will see below), but the point for now is that Doob and Macdonald did not
find that neighborhood crime rates account for the relationship between
amount of viewing and fear of crime. Instead, neighborhood may have
moderated the relationship.

Also, Doob and Macdonald's fear of crime index included only 9 of the 34
questions asked. They also found that for 14 of the remaining 25 items,
correlations remained significant or comparable in magnitude even when
averaged across the four areas. These other items dealt more with perceptions
of the prevalence of crime than with personal fear. Thus, the results for these
other items go sharply against the usual version of the study's findings, even
using the authors' own criterion of averaged correlations. It should also be
noted that this study took place in Toronto, so its relevance to the United
States is uncertain. In sum, whatever this intriguing and innovative study did
show, it should be clear that it did not demonstrate that neighborhood crime
rates render cultivation patterns spurious.

Measurement Artifacts

One other study from the 1970s should be mentioned, because it points to
some methodological problems that have plagued more recent efforts. Fox

and Philliber (1978) examined how television viewing contributed to perceptions of affluence in a sample of 595 adults. The rationale was that, given that television overrepresents wealth and high-status occupations, heavy viewers could be expected to overestimate the degree of affluence in society.

Respondents answered open-ended questions asking "how many Americans out of 100" own a luxury car, belong to a country club, can afford a built-in swimming pool, and so on. Heavy viewers gave higher estimates of affluence, but the association was eliminated by social status controls, especially education. Fox and Philliber concluded that, with social class taken into account, television does not influence perceptions of affluence.

There are two problems with Fox and Philliber's study. First, they measured amount of viewing by asking, "On the average, how many evenings a week do you watch TV at least one hour?" (p. 107). This is a very weak measure, if only because it provides no way to differentiate between "regular" and "heavy" viewers. Someone who watches for 4 hours a night, 6 days a week would be classified as a medium viewer, whereas someone who watches 1 hour every night would be classified as heavy.

More troubling is the nature of their dependent variables, which were based on open-ended percentages. The items are clearly reliable—they produce a Cronbach's alpha of .85—but their validity is dubious. Unpublished Cultural Indicators documents describing data from a 1978 telephone survey of 355 adults suggest that to ask people such open-ended percentage questions is to ask for trouble. Respondents were asked to estimate what proportion of the population is made up of children, the elderly, nonwhites, teachers, police, and so on, as well as what percentages of the population fit into each of four income categories (a total of 12 items). The resulting matrix of 66 correlations revealed a striking pattern: All of the coefficients were positive and sizable (more than 50 exceeded .30), and only three were not significant. If people were responding in a valid way to the manifest content of these items, then few of them would be related. Yet estimates of the percentages of the population composed of "teachers" and "police" correlated at .71, and estimates of "children" and "judges" correlated at .42. Even the correlation between estimates of the percentages in the lowest and highest income levels was .36.

These distinct estimates may simply tap a tendency to give consistently high (or low) responses to open-ended percentage items. (And they do so quite reliably; the alpha for these 12 items was .87—even higher than Fox & Philliber's.) That is, these kinds of measures may reflect little more than the systematic tendency of respondents to exaggerate proportions that are elicited by open-ended questions. People with less education respond with higher percentages across the board; so do heavy viewers. It is therefore quite reasonable (and unremarkable) that controlling for education eliminated the relationship of such variables with amount of viewing.

This artifact might have been apparent if Fox and Philliber had also asked about how many Americans out of 100 are on welfare, receive food stamps, can't pay the rent, and so on. Indeed, Shrum, O'Guinn, Semenik, and Faber (1991) found that viewing was positively related both to estimates of the percentage of Americans who are millionaires and to estimates of the percentage who earn less than $15,000 a year.

The fact that discrete, independent open-ended percentage items are so highly intercorrelated suggests that such measures have low to no validity, yet many studies have used them (e.g., Carveth & Alexander, 1985; Potter, 1986, 1988, 1991c; Potter & Chang, 1990). Potter (1994) explicitly endorses them, and refers to Fox and Philliber's items as an example of "good scaling"; ignoring their weak validity, he assumes that the internal homogeneity of the seven items mean they are "a consistent measure of an underlying factor of perceptions of affluence" (p. 14). Most recently, Carlson (1993) has directly adopted Fox and Philliber's measure, with predictable results: a highly reliable index (alpha = .87) and failure to support the cultivation hypothesis for affluence. Using a forced-choice scale to measure support for "capitalist values," however, Carlson did find support for cultivation.

These (and other) critiques from the 1970s are still, well into the 1990s, often cited as having provided definitive disconfirmation of the cultivation hypothesis. Yet, as the foregoing summary discussion demonstrates, these efforts had as many (or more) conceptual, methodological, and analytic drawbacks as the studies they are alleged to refute. We are not playing fast and loose with double negatives here; pointing out the limitations and flaws in these critiques does not, by implication, necessarily lend greater credence to those studies that produced evidence supportive of cultivation. Rather, our point is simply that the case against cultivation is not convincingly made by these studies.

The Early 1980s

Building on the momentum generated by the regular publication of cultivation findings in annual violence profiles, along with the critiques discussed above, the 1980s brought many replications, attacks, and rejoinders. There were some independent confirmations and extensions (Bryant, Carveth, & Brown, 1981; Buerkel-Rothfuss & Mayes, 1981; Haney & Manzolati, 1981; Volgy & Schwartz, 1980). There was also some "friendly" criticism, offered by researchers who were generally sympathetic to cultivation research but who felt it could benefit from some theoretical and methodological modifications (Hawkins & Pingree, 1980, 1981; Slater & Elliott, 1982).

Then came the well-known reanalyses by Hughes (1980) and Hirsch (1980, 1981) of NORC data that had been analyzed and reported by Gerbner et al. in their Violence Profiles 8 and 9 (Gerbner et al., 1977, 1978). Hirsch's reanalyses in particular led to fierce, occasionally acrimonious, prolonged battles. The controversies consumed literally hundreds of pages of scholarly journals; the repercussions were felt at academic conferences and even spilled over into such popular media as *Time* magazine. The conflicts produced significant new issues and questions for cultivation analysis, many of which are still being developed and pursued (see Tapper, 1995).

The central points of contention revolved around questions of spuriousness and controls. For the most part, cultivation analyses had implemented controls by examining associations between amount of viewing and attitudes within subgroups, one at a time. That is, the results were presented for males, older people, those with less education, and so on, separately. There were some exceptions (e.g., partial correlations with multiple simultaneous controls were used as early as Violence Profile No. 8; Gerbner et al., 1977). But the majority of results were presented in simple cross-tabular form, controlling for one "third" variable at a time.

The scarcity of multiple controls was a problem, but did not reflect any attempt to misportray data. The presentation of data in subgroups was emphasized because it is simple, informative, and illustrates clearly the relative baselines and "effect sizes" (i.e., cultivation differentials) across subgroups. As Potter (1991c) notes, simple percentages can reveal patterns that multivariate coefficients can obscure. They do not tell the whole story, of course, but they are highly useful for portraying the general contours of relationships.

Nevertheless, it is quite understandable that researchers took another look at the publicly available NORC surveys, trying out other techniques and manipulations on the data and bringing in other dependent variables and controls. At around the same time, Hughes, Hirsch, the Cultural Indicators research team, and others (e.g., Stevens, 1980) were independently finding that many of the relationships reported earlier using NORC data looked quite different under multiple controls.

The various reanalyses clearly showed that the application of multiple simultaneous controls tended to reduce or eliminate relationships that held up in subgroups examined one at a time. (Hughes also brought in additional controls, such as church attendance, club membership, and hours worked per week.) The general interpretation was that it was insufficient to report that a given relationship held up under controls applied one at a time; it could be that each individual control explained only a small portion of the apparent relationship, and all controls applied together would make an association disappear. This is in fact what the reanalyses purported to show, and it led some investigators to conclude that cultivation relationships were spurious, mere artifacts of covariation of demographic controls with both amount of viewing and dependent variables.

Yet that conclusion applies only to a particular sample as a whole, and not to relationships that may persist within subgroups. As Hawkins and Pingree (1982) note, such controls "may mislead us by removing relationships that are conditional on third variables" (p. 236). This was the essence of Gerbner et al.'s rebuttal to these reanalyses: Simply, if an overall relationship disappears under multiple (or even single) controls, that does not mean that there are no nonspurious and theoretically meaningful associations within specific subgroups (Gerbner et al., 1980a, 1980b, 1981a, 1981b, 1981c). Thus, "wholesale controlling can obfuscate potential conditional relationships" (Hawkins & Pingree, 1982, p. 246).

The discovery that relationships may persist in certain subgroups even where they disappear under multiple controls for a sample as a whole had profound conceptual and analytic implications for cultivation theory, and ultimately led to important refinements and enhancements. The most central of these was the idea of "mainstreaming." Briefly, it was observed that differential cultivation associations across subgroups often took on a particular pattern, such that the relationship held up for the subgroup that "otherwise" (i.e., as light viewers) was least likely to give the "television answer." For example, under controls, less educated people showed no relationship between amount of viewing and scores on the "mean world" index of interpersonal mistrust; their scores were high regardless of amount of viewing. But a significant relationship persisted for those with more education, even under multiple simultaneous controls. Among heavy viewers, the impact of education was reduced, and the responses of people with more education "converged" with the responses of those with less education.

The mainstreaming idea fit the view of cultivation as a "gravitational," rather than unidirectional, process. The angle and direction of the "pull" depends on the location of groups of viewers and their lifestyles with reference to the center of gravity, the "mainstream" of the world of television. The enormous diversity of potential subgroups and their differential relevance for specific dependent variables makes it difficult, if not impossible, to predict a priori where and when mainstreaming will occur (Cook, Kendzierski, & Thomas, 1983). This is not necessarily a problem, as some have argued (Tapper, 1995), because general mainstreaming expectations can be formulated and tested in specific areas (Gerbner et al., 1982, 1994; Morgan, 1986; Morgan & Shanahan, 1995; Shanahan, 1995; Signorielli & Morgan, 1990).

Mainstreaming is not the only potential interaction pattern (Gerbner et al., 1981a, 1994), but it is by far the most commonly observed. It has been found in studies dealing with political orientations in the United States (Gerbner et al., 1982) and in other countries (Morgan & Shanahan, 1995; Piepe, Charlton, & Morey, 1990), as well as in studies of sex role stereotypes, interpersonal mistrust, health, science, and many other issues (Gerbner et al., 1994).

These developments show that cultivation is a more complex process than it may have appeared at first. Clearly, the critiques contributed to this theoretical refinement. Yet the fact that meaningful conditional associations can be found even when an overall relationship disappears goes a long way toward resolving most of the major objections raised by these reanalyses. A variety of other criticisms and concerns have been voiced, however, by these and by more recent studies; some of these are discussed briefly below.

The "Nonlinearity" of Cultivation Patterns

Both Hughes and Hirsch reported that the relationships they examined were "nonlinear" under controls. Hirsch went even further and broke out the usual light/medium/heavy viewing scheme into two additional categories—nonviewers (those reporting "zero hours" on "an average day") and extreme viewers (those watching more than 8 hours a day). He found that the nonviewers were often more alienated, anomic, and fearful than were the light viewers, whereas the extreme viewers were less so than the heavy viewers.

At first glance, this appears to contradict dramatically the cultivation prediction of a generally monotonic pattern across all viewing levels. Yet both of the "extreme" groups are small (about 4% of the sample); Hawkins and Pingree (1982) noted that they "are unusual enough that they probably differ from other groups on possibly relevant third variables" (p. 235). Moreover, Gerbner et al. (1981a) conducted tests for linearity on the same variables Hirsch used, across Hirsch's own viewing categories; 17 of the 22 tests showed significant linear trends, and only 1 showed significant nonlinearity. Thus, Hirsch's analysis does not clearly show that cultivation relationships are indeed nonlinear. If the extreme groups are eliminated—a practice that some statisticians recommend should be done routinely (Hunter & Schmidt, 1990, p. 207)—then the associations become even stronger for the remaining 90%+ of the NORC respondents.

Potter (1991b) also claimed to show that cultivation relationships are nonlinear, based on data from 308 adolescents. He divided the viewing distribution in various ways, such as into an even three-way split (the method preferred by Gerbner et al.), into quintiles, into stanines (nine equal-sized groups), and so on. He looked at the means of the dependent variables at each viewing level and ran correlations within each viewing group. He then regressed the dependent indices on demographics and various transformations of the viewing measure (the square, the square root, the log, and so on). He found that the magnitude of association varied within the different subgroups, and claimed that this showed a nonlinear association.

We believe it is misleading to compute correlations within quintiles and stanines because, with $N = 308$, each stanine represents at most about 34 cases. Such small samples are certain to produce unstable coefficients, and Potter made no correction for curtailment of variance (and variance for viewing is especially highly restricted within nine levels of viewing groups).

This study raises important issues about how television viewing should be handled as a variable, but it used a questionable measure of exposure. Potter generally asked adolescents how many hours a week they watch programs in each of 12 or so different genres. Asking respondents how many hours per week they do certain things seems like a fairly demanding task, especially when the researcher's program categories are imposed upon them (Newhagen & Lewenstein, 1992).

Overall exposure measures such as these, however, can be expected only to indicate relatively more or less exposure to television. Variations in question wording, response options, and the ages of persons in the sample all produce different distributions and mean that the numbers of actual hours reported are not relevant. That is why Gerbner et al. have consistently divided the sample into three groups of roughly equal size regardless of the actual cutoff points. Contrary to Potter's assertion that the "theorists feel free to alter cut points at will across studies" (p. 570), using the same cutoff points for all samples would be impractical and indefensible.

Potter further questions why respondents are put into viewing categories at all, arguing that more powerful tests can be conducted if the data are kept in continuous form. The whole point of categorization is to illustrate the nature of the relationship, including baselines, in ways that correlational statistics cannot reveal (an argument also made by Potter, 1991a). He also implies that correlations are computed with the trichotomized exposure measure (Potter, 1994, p. 27); this would indeed be a problem if it were true, but it is not. Cultivation analysts may examine the simple percentage patterns within subgroups, but more rigorous multivariate techniques are applied to the continuous data.

It is important to examine the data both ways, because, strictly speaking, correlations should not be used with television viewing in the first place; even though it is measured as a ratio-level variable, it is usually not distributed normally. As Potter (1991b) notes, his viewing measure "would probably be better treated as a categorical variable from a statistical point of view because the distributions do not meet the assumptions of normalcy" (p. 574). Examination of grouped patterns and more rigorous multivariate analysis of continuous data both have definite advantages and disadvantages; each clarifies some issues and obscures others.

The key conceptual problem with Potter's argument (and, in some ways, Hirsch's) stems from trying to read a level of precision into the viewing measures that cannot possibly be sustained. Potter's manipulations and conclusions assume that measures of viewing are perfectly reliable, with no error variance whatsoever. Of course, this is an unwarranted assumption.

Volgy and Schwartz (1980) note that many of their "medium" viewers (determined by the number of hours of viewing reported) also indicated watching a lot of specific programs; they suggest that this group may include both "real" medium and many "real" heavy viewers. Cultural Indicators' analyses of a 1979 national sample showed that 15% of those claiming to be "nonviewers" also listed "watching television" as one of their favorite leisure activities.

Further slippage is evident in the 1993 General Social Survey, which asked respondents how often they watch specific types of programs ("TV dramas and sitcoms," "world or national news," and "programs shown on public television") in addition to the regular question on hours of viewing. The data for the 61 self-proclaimed "nonviewers" (3.8% of the sample; total $N = 1,586$) are intriguing. Less than a third of these "nonviewers" actually said they "never watch" any of the three types of programs. Close to one in five (18%) said they watch dramas or sitcoms at least several times a month. A third of the "nonviewers" said they watch PBS at least a few times a month. More than half said they watch the news that often, and 13% said they watch the news every day!

All this makes "dose-specific" linearity tests such as Potter's insupportable, as they imply a level of precision that the measures cannot justify. Rough approximations of general patterns are all that cultivation analysis assumes or requires. We want to know if it's warm or cold, not if it's 68 degrees or 69 degrees. The relationship cannot be that tightly calibrated given available measurement techniques.

To be sure, nonmonotonic associations do appear in the cultivation literature (as do associations of no direction), but there is no evidence to date that such patterns are either common or important. And Potter (1991b, 1993) offers no conceptual guidance as to what we might make of this allegedly nonlinear pattern. What does it mean? Hawkins and Pingree (1982) argue that curvilinear relationships "demand further explanation—not the simple negation of the original simple hypothesis" (p. 236). Tapper (1995) has proposed a model wherein such patterns might be explained, but that model awaits empirical test. So far, however, no reason to expect cultivation to be nonlinear has been proposed, nor has any explanation of such patterns, when observed, been offered.

Summary

Cultivation was conceived as a critical social theory, not as a methodological exercise. Efforts to provide greater specificity and precision have helped sharpen the analysis, but often seem to result in observers' losing track of the real social significance of it all. We suggest that, after 20 years, researchers put aside their quibbles to focus critically on the social role of television. After all, if this research is to be important in the long term, it must be able to show whether television "means" anything and, if so, what. In this regard, the meta-analysis presented below will let us see if there are any substantive differences in the findings reported by Gerbner et al. and those given by independent investigators and critics.

In the past two decades, cultivation has advanced theoretically. Although the idea of mainstreaming is perhaps the most noticeable development, cultivation research has moved from a fairly "provincial" examination of violence effects to a more sophisticated paradigm for a variety of dependent variables in different cultures, countries, and contexts. This discussion has by no means covered all of the major developments and challenges in the field. In particular, we have not discussed international cultivation analysis, the implications of new technologies, research on cognitive processes underlying cultivation, the role of perceived reality, or a host of related and difficult questions (see Hawkins & Pingree, 1982, 1990; Morgan & Signorielli, 1990).

Our main point here is that the considerable variety of cultivation findings needs to be examined more systematically. Therefore, we feel a need to move from a narrative review (always open to problems of subjectivity) to a theoretically driven meta-analysis. Our purpose is to provide an overview of the achievements of 20 years of cultivation research and to provide a benchmark for future developments in the field.

META-ANALYSIS

Rationale and Design

Although theoretical overviews and detailed assessments of the evidence have appeared (Hawkins & Pingree, 1982; Ogles, 1987; Potter, 1993), no one has previously undertaken a meta-analysis of the body of cultivation data. Herrett-Skjellum and Allen (1996) recently performed a meta-analysis of television and sex role perceptions that includes some of the same studies meta-analyzed here. Their results—indicating a small positive effect—are relevant to cultivation, although they do not interpret their data from the cultivation perspective.

Perhaps the greatest justification for meta-analysis is that it takes some of the "subjectivity" out of the review process. Cultivation research has been portrayed in different ways, depending upon the academic and political commitments of those doing the reviewing. Given the divergences, one wonders whether the commentators are reading the same studies. Although we do not assume that a mere aggregation of results will somehow automatically provide "truer" evidence of effects, our data do let us look at cultivation in a more systematic way than previous reviews have allowed.

Meta-analysis corrects for many pitfalls of the traditional narrative literature review; for example, the risk of making Type II errors is rampant when the reviewer simply counts up the number of significant findings reported (Hunter & Schmidt, 1990). Meta-analysis can shed much-needed light on bodies of work that might otherwise be characterized as showing "inconsistent results."

In meta-analysis, each observed result is assumed to be a random sampling from a distribution whose mean represents the "true" effect. The analysis thus gives a better estimate of that true effect, adjusted for sample size, than does any individual study. But meta-analysis does more than that. The cumulated data are examined to see if the set of relationships is homogeneous (using the terminology of Mullen, 1989), or to see how much of the observed variation in results across studies reflects sampling error (using the terms of Hunter &

Schmidt, 1990). If the findings are heterogeneous, or if there remains much unexplained variance after sampling error has been removed and other adjustments have been made, then the meta-analyst can conduct a theory-driven investigation of the variables that might have moderated the observed effects. (In what follows, we use the term *effect* strictly in a statistical sense, and we stress that cultivation does not imply effects in the sense of stimulus-response causality.)

Study Selection

We began with the regularly updated, comprehensive bibliography of cultivation studies that have been published since 1976. This is available either from the Cultural Indicators project or from on-line databases such as Comserve and various communication-related World Wide Web pages. Further computer and bibliographic searches turned up no additional citations. From this list of more than 300 publications, we built a database of studies that (a) tested a relationship between amount of exposure to television (however measured) and a dependent variable that could be thought of as providing a "television answer" and (b) specifically adduced or criticized cultivation theory as an explanation of the results. Some studies that met these criteria could not be included for other reasons.

Some studies that are highly supportive of cultivation theory were excluded because they did not use the respondent as the unit of analysis. For example, Morgan (1983) found that subgroups more victimized on television showed stronger evidence of cultivation and in another study observed mainstreaming in an erosion of diversity across regions of the United States (1986); Rothschild (1984) used the peer group as the unit of analysis. Other studies touched on relevant issues but did not present relevant data that could be coded (e.g., Reep & Drambot, 1989, investigated how viewers' evaluations of selected characters vary according to gender, exposure to certain shows, and so on).

Research design was another factor. Almost all cultivation studies are survey based. There are experimental tests of cultivation relationships or experimental manipulations of cognitive variables, but these deal with short-term phenomena and hence do not really estimate cultivation processes.

Thus, we included only survey-type cultivation studies, which are by far the most common, and ignored the small handful of relevant experiments (for some examples, see Bryant et al., 1981; Shapiro, 1991; Tan, 1979; Wakshlag, Viol, & Tamborini, 1983; Zillman & Wakshlag, 1985).

In some cases there was no way to determine theoretically what the "television answer" should be. We coded all studies in which it was possible to make some reasonable connection to cultivation theory without straining credulity beyond the breaking point. This was, of course, a close judgment call in some cases; in general, we erred as much as possible on the liberal side, to favor inclusiveness. For some studies, however, simply no plausible expectations for cultivation relationships could be inferred; for example, Gunter and Wober (1983a) examined perceptions of personal risk from lightning, flooding, heart disease, nuclear attack, road accidents, food poisoning, and so on, and Potter (1986) looked at estimates of the percentages of deaths due to accidents, cancers, pneumonia, and heart disease. Without any evidence that television represents these dangers in any particular way, it was impossible to code the results according to whether or not they fit what cultivation would predict.

Only published studies were included, thus data from many unpublished conference papers, dissertations, and reports were excluded. It might be argued that this favors studies with "larger" results, given that nonsignificant findings often go unpublished in some fields; in the case of cultivation, however, that seems extremely unlikely, as journals have shown no apparent reluctance to publish studies that claim to debunk cultivation theory. This also keeps our analysis more evenhanded. We had access to many unpublished reports that Gerbner et al. have produced (Violence Profile technical reports, grant reports, and others). These contain large amounts of supportive data, but we have no way to balance these with any comparable amount of unpublished data from other sources that may (or may not) be contrary. Thus, data that have not been "published" in the conventional sense were not included. This also facilitates replicability.

No studies were eliminated simply for being methodologically "weak," or because of the way the independent variable of TV exposure was measured. This variable has taken many diverse forms, including self-reports of viewing hours (per day, per week, "yesterday," or for different times of the day), frequency of viewing specific programs or types (on ordinal scales), number of programs seen, and diary measures (see Potter, 1994, for a discussion of the many techniques that have been employed). It would be inappropriate to exclude studies based upon their measurement of the independent variable, because that disagreement itself represents an important part of the cultivation literature. Thus, we included any relevant operationalizations of viewing in order to determine meta-analytically if measuring television exposure in different ways has any different consequences.

Data Cumulation

Normally in meta-analysis, the individual study is treated as the unit of analysis, with each independent study (or independent data set) contributing a single finding—that is, a single estimate of effect size—to the cumulative data set that is then meta-analyzed. Many studies, of course, present multiple findings—for example, they may use several measures of a single construct—that are not always independent. In these cases, meta-analysts tend to choose one finding to "represent" a particular study or to average the correlations presented, so that each datum in the meta-analysis constitutes an "independent" test. (Violation of the assumption of independence does not affect the estimate of the effect size, but it does affect both the observed variance of effects and the estimate of variance expected by sampling error; Hunter & Schmidt, 1990, p. 480.)

Cultivation research raises the problem of multiple findings to an extreme. Cultivation studies almost never report a single "effect" (e.g., an F test or a correlation); it is usual to find many dozens of correlations, or gammas, or ANOVA means tests, or the like, in a single paper. Our selection criteria yielded a set of 82 published studies, and these contained a total of 5,633 different findings. This very high number of multiple (and nonindependent) findings is a result of three factors, and three different solutions were required to accomplish a meaningful independent cumulation across studies.

First, some studies contain multiple measures of dependent variables. Some studies combine a set of variables into an index of some sort (e.g., the three-item "Mean World Index"), but sometimes individual items are analyzed separately. When the different dependent variables were intended to be measures of a single underlying dimension or factor, the results were simply averaged. This is the least problematic situation, although because of lessened reliability, the estimate of effect size derived from this average is smaller than would be obtained from the same variables if they were combined in index form (Hunter & Schmidt, 1990, p. 456).

Second, many studies present numerous partial correlations, often first order; almost 40% of the 5,633 findings we coded are partials. In some studies, for example, partial correlations between amount of viewing and some dependent variable or index are presented controlling for sex, education, income, age, other media use, and more—first singly and then simultaneously. These are obviously not independent tests, but averaging them is not an appropriate way to handle the problem. Meta-analysis typically needs to be done on zero-order effect estimations; it is not advisable to use partial correlations or beta coefficients, because the different estimates of effect size then become noncomparable (Hunter & Schmidt, 1990, p. 502). Therefore, we did not cumulate any partials (or betas), and instead analyzed only simple associations.

This raises a problem in cultivation research, however, where there are significant concerns with spuriousness. This problem is partly ameliorated by addressing the third reason for the high number of nonindependent findings, which is that cultivation data are so often analyzed separately within various subgroups. That is, contingency (cross-tab) associations are typically presented for males and females, younger and older respondents, and so on. This has been an important technique, for instance, in the analysis of mainstreaming. But because these are overlapping groups (i.e., the same people count in more than one subgroup), the tests are not independent. It would not make any sense to average all these separate subgroups, because the result would then be equal to the overall data for the sample as a whole.

Therefore, we decided to conduct meta-analyses not only for overall samples, but also separately within demographic subgroups. Of the large numbers of subgroups that have been examined in the literature, we chose for simplicity's sake to focus only on three key demographic markers: gender, education, and age (although our larger data set includes data for other subgroups). That is, after we cumulated and analyzed the data for entire independent samples as a whole, we also carried out separate meta-analyses for males, females, more and less educated respondents, and those of different age groups. These are not independent tests across subgroups (e.g., females versus people with high education); rather, they are independent between each exclusive demographic division (e.g., male versus female). Although this is not standard meta-analytic procedure, it seems justifiable and reasonable given the nature of cultivation data and the need to examine subgroup variations in ways other than as moderator variables. (It does not, of course, deal with the issue of multiple simultaneous controls, which we address separately.)

Further Reductions and Modifications

As should be clear, cultivation research presents a bewildering variety of data about widely divergent issues, obtained using very different methods and measures, from many distinct samples, subjected to diverse statistical procedures, and with little consistency in the kinds of information reported (e.g., reliability estimates, standard deviations). Some studies report findings from several different data sets; some report results of more than one distinct study. And some data sets used studies reported in numerous publications. All this means that further modification and paring down were required before meta-analysis could be done.

For one thing, there is no single dependent variable in the cultivation literature; a wide variety of topical areas have been explored. Therefore, to keep things at a reasonable level of complexity, we focus only on cultivation findings in three areas: (a) violence (including fear and the mean world syndrome), (b) sex roles, and (c) political beliefs and orientations. Cultivation studies of images of aging, minorities, religion, occupations, science, health, the family, and other topics await their own meta-analyses.

We did not code findings reported without a specific coefficient. For example, authors often state something to the effect that "the data shown in Table X were relatively unchanged when Variable Y was applied as a further control." In such cases, with no data explicitly given, nothing was coded. Also, we did not code data that were summarized but not explicitly presented; for example, Gerbner et al. (1981a), Morgan (1984), and Morgan and Shanahan (1992b) together present tables summarizing almost 1,500 correlations, but because they do not give the actual coefficients, nothing was coded.

Beyond correlations, some cultivation studies have used ANOVA to examine mean differences on some dependent variable across light, medium, and heavy viewers. Formulas do exist to transform these kinds of data to an equivalent r coefficient, but unfortunately the published studies rarely contain the information (e.g., variance) necessary to do this. Therefore, no findings based on mean differences across viewing groups were included.

Cultivation research often uses gamma—about 30% of the 5,633 total findings are gammas. These are roughly conceptually comparable to Pearson correlations, though they are based on ordinal data; for a discussion of some computational advantages of gamma, see Nelson (1986). Extensive searching and consulting provided no guidance on how to transform a gamma to an r, so we developed our own formula through a modified Monte Carlo simulation. We calculated both rs and gammas of TV viewing with 100 randomly selected variables from the 1994 NORC General Social Survey. Gamma and r were highly correlated ($r = .946$). We calculated a variety of linear, nonlinear, and polynomial regression equations, and in every case it turned out that gamma, and gamma alone, accounted for more than 90% of the variance in r; no other transformation or variable added more than .0014% to the explained variance. Thus, we used the obtained regression formula ($r = .6024 *$ gamma $- .0032$) to achieve an approximate but satisfactory transformation of gamma to r.

Instrument

In most meta-analyses, the data-gathering instrument is not of paramount importance because only a few discrete bits of information are gathered from each study. In our study, however, we were ambitious about the sorts of information we wished to collect. Our instrument was therefore fairly extensive. Much information was coded on each of the 5,633 findings (although here we focus mainly on the independent, cumulated data).

For each study, we recorded relevant identifying information (author, year of publication, and journal) and noted the date(s) when the data were collected (some studies report data gathered over multiple years). Next, we coded how television viewing was measured in each study. We also coded how data were collected (mostly phone interview, questionnaire, or personal interview). Also coded were the dependent variable, the independent variable, and the subgroup (if any) the result applied to.

For each finding we recorded degrees of freedom and/or the N of the finding. In many cases we were forced to estimate these, due to inconsistencies in data reporting. Where we could make a justifiable estimate (from other information in the study), we did so. In some cases, there was not enough information to make such estimates. We also recorded the significance of each finding (although Hunter & Schmidt, 1990, do not think that significance is very important), often estimating significance level based only on asterisks presented in summary tables.

Also, we coded the sample's country of origin and the general nature of the sample. This allows us to differentiate between, for example, convenience samples of undergraduates and national probability samples of adults, and indicates the comprehensiveness and age focus of the sample from which the data emerged.

As we extracted the findings from each included study and further condensed the database during cumulation, we interacted continuously to ensure quality of data entry. Independent coders were not used because of the highly specialized nature of interpreting cultivation findings. Although this leaves a few possibilities for coding bias, we feel it helps ensure a more accurate data set. It is important to note that this was more of a transcribing process than a data coding exercise. Moreover, as Hunter and Schmidt (1990) remind us, it is "well known that meta-analysts do not make errors" (p. 262).

Results

Meta-Analysis of Cultivation Findings

As we have noted, cultivation studies present difficulties in terms of data independence. Although our overall data set includes 5,633 pieces of information about cultivation, our meta-analyses used significantly reduced and averaged data sets for the purpose of conforming to standard meta-analytic procedures (generally following Hunter & Schmidt, 1990; and Mullen, 1989).[1]

Our first analysis selected all findings that were (a) "overall" findings (dealt with an entire set of data); (b) about one of the three dependent areas of violence, sex roles, or political orientations; and (c) measured as Pearson rs (or as gammas transformed to rs). This yielded 52 independent samples (from a somewhat smaller number of actual "studies," some of which use multiple samples) that could contribute to our overall meta-analysis.

All overall coefficients from each sample, after conversion to the metric, were weighted and averaged to produce a single r for that sample. These averaged coefficients were then weighted by the average sample N for each sample (some findings from individual samples had different Ns), and averaged once more to produce the estimate of the average effect size.

Our analysis shows that the average overall effect size for cultivation studies is $r = .091$, $K = 52$. This confirms what most observers have assumed about cultivation: Its effect size tends to be small. Table 1.2 presents the results for this and all of our meta-analyses.

Hunter and Schmidt (1990) say that if at least 75% of the observed variance of the mean effect size across studies can be attributed to sampling error, or if the mean effect size is at least two standard deviations larger than zero, then the "true" effect can be assumed to be "always positive," no matter what any specific single study might suggest. With our data, following their formulas, the variance expected from sampling error alone (.000926) is nearly 40% of the actual observed variance (.002321). Thus, a good deal of the discussion about variation and replicability in cultivation has been a phantom—about

TABLE 1.2
Summary Statistics for Meta-Analyses

Analysis	K	Average Effect	% Variance From Error	χ^2	$SD \times 2$
Overall	52	.091	39	127.5***	.096
Dependent variables					
violence	32	.103	40	77.1***	.106
sex roles	14	.102	48	28.1**	.092
politics	27	.077	45	58.6***	.080
Gender					
females	26	.110	91	27.7	.084
males	26	.109	54	46.3**	.112
Education level					
lower	22	.082	40	54.2***	.108
higher	22	.088	96	22.2	.078
Age					
young	8	.064	78	11.1	.124
adolescent	9	.080	100	8.7	.085
young adult	13	.121	35	32.97***	.137
middle adult	13	.107	100	9.0	.065
older	13	.083	58	20.39	.108
Research groups					
core	31	.088	31	99.2***	.096
other	21	.100	75	29.7	.095
Independent variable					
overall viewing	45	.096	31	141.2***	.105
other	16	.076	48	32.4**	.115
Sensitization to independent variable					
yes	8	.117	83	9.2	.127
no	33	.095	51	61.3***	.102
don't know	11	.103	85	12.4	.081
Measurement of independent variable					
daily hours	34	.090	30	108.9***	.097
other	18	.092	94	18.5	.089
Sample size					
small	22	.136	61	34.1*	.149
large	30	.085	37	78.9***	.080

*$p < .05$; **$p < .01$; ***$p < .001$.

40% of the differences in cultivation findings that have been reported across different investigators, areas, and methods can be dismissed as merely reflecting sampling error.

This is a "bare-bones" meta-analysis finding. If the effect size estimates could be corrected for such factors as attenuation due to unreliability of measurement and range restrictions (e.g., some samples have narrower viewing distributions than others), then the figure would be higher than 40%. Unfortunately, the information required to make these adjustments is almost never given in published articles. Thus, we can say that 40% is a conservative estimate: At least 40% of the reported variation in cultivation data is due to sampling error.

Still, we cannot conclude from this that cultivation results are "always positive." The overall mean effect size (.091) is very nearly, but not quite, twice the size of the standard deviation (SD = .048; doubled, it equals .096). Also, we do not have a "homogeneous" set of findings, as indicated by the chi-square approach suggested by Mullen (1989; χ^2 = 127.5 df = 51, p < .001). Given that the results display heterogeneity, moderator variables are likely to be at work in the cultivation oeuvre. The remainder of our analysis is devoted to the exploration of theoretically meaningful moderator constructs.

We performed moderator analyses by meta-analyzing separate subsets of the data for theoretically meaningful variables that might generate any differences in cultivation results obtained across studies. If a variable moderates our overall finding, we should discover different effect sizes in the examined subgroups, and the variance of effect size (minus sampling error variance) within each data substratum should be less. We can measure the variance of effect size again using Hunter and Schmidt's formula. If variance is mostly due to sampling error in each subgroup of studies, then we have probably discovered an important moderator variable. In such a case, the observed effects will also be different. Thus, if each data group in a comparison shows low remaining variance of effect size (more than 75% explainable by sampling error), we can conclude that the variable is likely to be a true moderator. In Table 1.2 we present these estimates for each variable analyzed. We also present a doubled standard deviation for each analysis, to show whether an effect can be considered "always positive."

We examined a variety of variables, but none proved to be a moderator. First, we examined whether the dependent variable explained the observed heterogeneity of results. For this analysis, we separately meta-analyzed groups of studies based upon whether they dealt with violence, sex roles, or politics (note that our sample of studies on sex roles differs from that of Herrett-Skjellum & Allen, 1996, because their meta-analysis was not an assessment of cultivation studies). Published studies that dealt with more than one dependent area were treated as independent data sets, for the purposes of comparing effects across variables. Because some studies do deal with multiple dependent areas, there are more than 52 data points in this comparison. (Again, see Table 1.2 for a summary of the results.)

We found an average effect size of .077 with political beliefs as a dependent variable (K = 27). Here, about 45% of the variance in the magnitudes of the associations was explainable through sampling error (χ^2 = 58.60, df = 26, p < .001). Again, there is significant variance in this body of studies, though it is interesting to note a somewhat lower average coefficient.

Meta-analyzing 14 sex role studies, we found an average effect size of .102 (essentially the same as Herrett-Skjellum & Allen's finding of .101). For this group, 48% of the observed variance in effects can be attributed to sampling error ($\chi^2 = 28.19$, $df = 13$, $p = .008$). Herrett-Skjellum and Allen also found significant heterogeneity in their sample of sex role studies, without a clear moderator.

Finally, on the issue of violence, we found an average effect size of .103 ($K = 32$). With 40% of the variance explained by sampling error, we again conclude that these studies display heterogeneity ($\chi^2 = 77.1$, $df = 31$, $p < .001$). Thus, despite some differences in effect size (political associations seem to be somewhat weaker than those for violence and sex roles), the focus of the dependent variable is apparently not a moderator of cultivation.

We also thought that demographic subgroups, so important to cultivation analysis, might function as moderator variables. First, we performed an analysis on findings about males and females. This analysis ($K = 26$) showed little difference. Both females and males showed an average effect size of about .11. The observed effects remained heterogeneous for males, with about 54% of the variance explained by sampling error ($\chi^2 = 46.32$, $df = 25$, $p < .01$). However, the findings for females were rather more consistent across the studies, with 91% of the observed variance due to sampling error ($\chi^2 = 27.73$, $df = 25$, $p = .33$). The evidence of cultivation for females is thus more consistent across than that for males, though on average it is about the same size. Thus, gender itself is not a moderator (because the variance remained heterogeneous for males), although we can say that there is no need to search in the future for moderators of cultivation among females as a group.

We also investigated whether education level (or parental education, for children and adolescents) functions as a moderator. Low-education subgroups show a slightly lower average effect size ($r = .081$, $K = 22$), with a good deal of heterogeneity of effect (40%, $\chi^2 = 54.28$, $df = 21$, $p < .001$). High-education subgroups show a marginally higher effect ($r = .089$), but with most of the variance in effect due to sampling error (96%, $\chi^2 = 22.22$, $df = 21$, $p = .38$). Thus, the cultivation effect for higher education groups is more consistent across studies, though education does not moderate the overall relationship.

We next examined age subgroups as potential moderators. Cultivation studies have been conducted across the spectrum of age groups, facilitating a fairly comprehensive set of comparisons. Younger children show a some-what smaller effect size ($r = .064$, $K = 8$), and these studies are homogeneous with respect to effect size (78% of the variation in effect size being attribut-able to sampling error). Adolescents also show a smaller effect size ($r = .080$, $K = 9$), with no variation across studies remaining after sampling error is removed. Young adults show a higher effect ($r = .121$, $K = 13$), but there is heterogeneity of effect for this group (37% of variance in effect size from sampling error). Middle-aged adults show a larger-than-average effect size ($r = .107$, $K = 13$), with no heterogeneity in the variance (less variance than that expected from sampling error). The effect size drops off for older adults ($r = .083$, $K = 13$), with lesser heterogeneity of variance (58% of variance in magnitude of effect size due to sampling error; Table 1.2 shows the statistics for all age subgroups). Thus, despite some interesting patterns that future research might explore, we conclude that age does not moderate the cultivation relationship.

Because demographic subgroups do not explain all cultivation variance, we also examined study characteristics as potential moderators. Under this logic, variation in the methods of various studies may cause different results.

Further Analyses

One prominent issue in cultivation research is that many studies have been carried out by a group including and associated with Gerbner, Gross, Morgan, and Signorielli (who conducted many of the original cultivation studies in the 1970s and 1980s). This group includes individuals who attended the University of Pennsylvania as graduate students as well as persons who later came into contact with members of the original team in such places as the University of Massachusetts and the University of Delaware. However, cultivation research has also been carried out by many outside this core group, including critics, friendly amenders, and so on. We were interested in whether results differed across these groups, given that methods have differed and have been the focus of critical discussion.

Studies reported by the core (i.e., Gerbner) group had an average effect size of $r = .088$ ($K = 31$). The large N (more than 43,000) of this group meant that not much variance was explained by sample error (about 30%, $\chi^2 = 99.2$, $df = 32$, $p < .001$), which suggests that moderator variables are operating within this group of studies. Yet studies conducted by researchers outside of the core group showed a higher average effect ($r = .100$) with homogeneous variance (75% of variance in effect size explainable by sampling error, $\chi^2 = 29.77$, $df = 20$, $p = .07$). It is interesting and unexpected that results reported by researchers associated with Gerbner et al. would show a much wider diversity of effect sizes, and that variations in results reported by others can be interpreted as merely a function of sampling error. Nevertheless, this particular study characteristic is not moderating the cultivation relationship.

Another issue is the measurement of the independent variable. A point of some contention has been whether overall viewing or specific program measures should be used. Although we think there are important theoretical reasons to use overall viewing as the independent variable, in meta-analytic terms we find less difference than one might imagine. Those studies that used the normal method (exposure) converged on an average effect size of .096. Those using all other methods averaged a smaller effect size of .076. Both groups displayed heterogeneity of variance of effect size. It would appear that the argument that specific program exposure is a better measure simply does not hold up. More important, this is not, by itself, a moderator for the entire body of cultivation work.

As we have noted, in some studies respondents have been informed that the survey in which they are participating have to do with perceptions of television, or the instruments have measured TV exposure prior to social reality perceptions. Do these practices in fact contaminate the data and produce different effects? Such studies tend to produce slightly higher effect sizes ($r = .117$, $K = 8$). Studies that do not make this error converge on an effect size of .095 ($K = 33$). A group of studies for which we had no information about this issue fell in the middle ($r = .103$, $K = 11$). The studies conducted without informing respondents about the nature of the studies had the highest "real" variance, at around 50%. In contrast, in studies that gave potentially sensitizing instructions to respondents and in those that gave no information on this point, the variance in reported effect sizes seems to stem almost entirely from sampling error. Thus, because we do not see homogeneity of variance in each group of studies, we must conclude that potential contamination is not a true moderator.

Some studies use daily hours of viewing to estimate exposure; others use weekly exposure measures, checklists, and a variety of other ways. Studies using daily hours as an exposure measure averaged .09 in effect size ($K = 34$, with heterogeneous variance of effect size, $\chi^2 = 108.9$, $df = 33$, $p < .001$). Studies using other measures averaged .092 (though these results show almost no remaining variance in effect size beyond that due to sampling error, $\chi^2 = 18.5$, $df = 17$, $p = .35$). The data show that effect sizes derived from daily hour estimates do not differ much from the others, again putting to rest a rather contentious discussion. However, the consistency of nondaily hour estimates of viewing should be explored. Many of these studies used smaller sample sizes, which plays some role in the expected variance, because results from smaller studies are more subject to sampling error.

In fact, perhaps the widest differences are observed when sample sizes are compared. Larger random and representative samples are obviously preferred to smaller convenience samples. The reason for this can be seen when we meta-analyze small ($N < 600$) samples, which produce an average effect of .136, and larger ($N > 600$) samples, which produce an average effect of .085. Both large and small sample groups display some heterogeneity of variance for effect size, so this cannot be considered a true moderator variable, though the pattern is quite interesting from a descriptive perspective: A greater percentage of the variation in effects observed in small sample studies can be attributed to sampling error alone (61%, versus 37% for large sample studies).

In all of these comparisons—by dependent area, by demographic subgroup, and by study design features—we have seen cases in which the variance in observed effects can be explained by sampling error alone for one particular group of studies. In no cases, however, has the variance turned out to be homogeneous for all subsets within a given comparison of studies, which means that none of them can be considered as a moderator of variations in cultivation. Still, one tendency is worth noting. Studies that have stuck closer to the original design of the investigation—that is, studies conducted by those associated with Gerbner, studies that use larger samples, and studies that make sure not to sensitize respondents to the purposes of the research—all tend to produce somewhat smaller estimates of cultivation. It is interesting that the findings produced by researchers and methods most connected to Gerbner have been, in a meta-analytic sense, more conservative than those of the critics and others, who have sometimes used smaller and less representative samples. Again, however, these patterns are merely descriptive and suggestive, as no true moderator emerges from our analysis.

DISCUSSION

This study had a straightforward aim: to assess the findings of cultivation analysis using the tools and standards of meta-analysis. The evidence points to a mean overall effect size of approximately $r = .09$, with some small variation under different conditions. In most cases within groups of studies, the mean effect size is very close to the doubled standard deviation. The smallest coefficient applied to younger children ($r = .071$), but this was based on relatively few studies ($K = 9$); the largest coefficient emerged from studies using smaller ($N < 600$) sample sizes ($r = .136$, $K = 22$). In this section, we discuss the implications of this estimated effect size and mention various questions raised by our findings.

Some would argue that such a small average effect means that the cultivation relationship, although perhaps "true," is too trivial to be meaningful. It might be argued that the proportion of variance explained is so small ($r^2 = .01$ or less) that we cannot imbue amount of television viewing with any predictive or explanatory power. Yet the principles of meta-analysis make it clear that reliance only on r^2 leads to distorted underestimates of the practical and theoretical significance of how variables are related in the real world (Hunter & Schmidt, 1990, p. 199). In a specific application of this principle, Herrett-Skjellum and Allen (1996) used "binomial effect size display" to demonstrate how a comparably small effect size estimate ($r = .101$) can actually indicate far-reaching contributions of television viewing to sex role perceptions. Their point is that even small correlations can be very predictive at the more extreme ends of distributions.

On another level, it would be astonishing—and suspicious—to find statistically large effects from television viewing. Very few people in this society do not accumulate substantial exposure to television over the years, comparable messages are disseminated by other media, and light and heavy viewers live in the same general culture. The forces that shape our beliefs are many and varied; television is just one. As Gerbner et al. have repeatedly argued over the years, television is by no means the most powerful influence on people, but it is the most common, the most pervasive, the most widely shared.

Gerbner et al. have also argued that the *size* of an effect is less important than its *direction* and the nature of its steady contribution (see Gerbner et al., 1994). They have pointed out that "small effects" make the difference in a tight struggle. A single percentage point increase in television ratings is worth many millions of dollars in advertising revenue; many elections are won or lost by a few percentage points, and a global temperature change of a few degrees can lead to profound climatic upheavals. A difference of a few points often signals a landslide, a market takeover, or an epidemic, and it certainly tips the scale of any closely balanced choice, vote, or other decision.

Any pervasive, mainstream message system expresses, constitutes, and reproduces complex layers of general cultural patterns and contexts, against and through which many *particular* controversies and issues are filtered and shaped. Thus, the *global* attitudes, beliefs, and orientations cultivated by television, even if the difference viewing makes is statistically slight, can have diverse and specific social repercussions.

A 1% shift over time due to television in perceptions of real-world violence can help inform the background debate on particular issues. The ongoing political debates about television violence, for instance, show that the public readily accepts the notion that social violence is a difficult enough issue that it may require society to take steps that some see as censorship (e.g., introduction of the V chip) and that political authorities are the ones who should play such a censoring role. In other words, the ongoing cultivation of fear of violence has established a social baseline such that the assumption that violence can be corrected by proper authorities is widely accepted, even despite the paradox that television itself is implicated as a culprit.

This further relates to Gerbner et al.'s arguments that a fearful population may be more willing to accept repressive measures and hard-line solutions that promise to provide "security," regardless of the threat such measures may pose to civil liberties. The promotion of capital punishment, the institution of mandatory sentencing laws, and greater public spending on prisons than on education are only some of the results of policies built on fear, retribution, and authority. Television, of course, does not "cause" such policies, but it contributes to a political and cultural climate in which they are sustainable.

Similarly, in slow but steady ways, cultivation means that long-term, regular exposure to television's dramatic portrayals contributes to and helps reproduce our ideologies of individualism and consumerism; perceptions of the roles of women, children, and the family; notions of progress, technology, equality, and opportunity; and images of different groups of people. These in turn reflect and define the cultural climate from which actions and policies draw meaning; they subtly keep some values and perspectives alive while marginalizing or neglecting others. Bit by bit, the long-term accumulation of small changes and the maintenance of "common sense" can have far-reaching implications for many disparate realms of social policy.

Further, small changes in the direction hypothesized by cultivation may be seen as the narrowing of views among otherwise divergent social groups. Although our meta-analytic data do not address mainstreaming directly, one of the most profound consequences of cultivation may be the narrowing of differences that otherwise could have been much wider. Thus, a 1% difference in perceptions of violence can also be indicative of restriction in differences of perception that would have been wider without the contribution of television.

Thus, a systematic pattern of even small but consistent differences between light and heavy viewers may be of great consequence. That is why Gerbner et al. argue that a slight but pervasive (e.g., generational) shift in the cultivation of common perspectives may alter the cultural climate and upset the balance of social and political decision making without producing statistically large effects or changing observable behavior.

Moreover, ours is a bare-bones meta-analysis of observed correlations, correcting for sampling error only. (The high total combined sample size implies that our correction for sampling error is highly accurate; Hunter & Schmidt, p. 93.) Our estimated effect size is uncorrected for attenuation (measurement unreliability) and range restriction. Taking these into account requires knowing the means, standard deviations, and reliabilities, and having a correlation matrix of all relevant variables, but this information is rarely available in published cultivation articles. Our inability to make these statistical corrections has two specific consequences: The mean effect size is an *underestimate,* and the standard deviation of that effect size over studies is an *overestimate* (Hunter & Schmidt, 1990, pp. 156, 198). In other words, we can say that the "true" correlation *is larger than* .091, and the proportion of observed variation in cultivation studies due to sampling error alone *is larger than* 40%.

Although much of the difference in reported cultivation findings across studies represents nothing more than sampling error, the set of overall observed effects remains heterogeneous; the evidence indicates that moderators do exist. Yet we were not able unambiguously to detect any moderators. In most cases, the proportion of variance due to sampling error was fairly high, though in a few demographic cases (females, young adults, those with more education) we can say that *all* observed variation in findings probably stems from sampling error alone. Sampling error also seems to account fully for variation in cultivation found in studies done by those *not* connected with Gerbner and his associates, in studies using nondaily measures of viewing, and in studies that may have contaminated their data by mentioning television to respondents before measuring attitude.

Methodological characteristics produced some small differences in effect size estimates, such that researchers who are associated with Gerbner and/or use more "orthodox" methods tend to produce more conservative estimates of cultivation. But the study characteristics examined did not suggest clear evidence of any specific moderators at work. This means that although our data do suggest that there *are* moderators in cultivation research, we have not been able to determine what they might be. This is also what Herrett-Skjellum and Allen (1996) found in their meta-analysis of television and sex role perceptions. Of course, moderator analysis generally suffers from low statistical power, especially when the number of studies is small; real moderating influences may go undetected (Hunter & Schmidt, 1990, p. 88). As the number of cultivation studies accumulates, future meta-analyses might uncover moderators operating where we have not.

It should be noted that our data do not completely address what has been a very sticky controversy in cultivation research, and that is the question of whether the observed relationships are spurious. That question is less easily answered with existing techniques for meta-analysis, which work from simple estimates of effect size. Still, it is worth noting that although the average effect sizes examined within the key demographic subgroups defined by gender, education, and age did vary somewhat, the patterns did not reveal any suggestion of spuriousness. The separate meta-analyses for males and females even showed *higher* mean effect sizes ($r = .11$) than overall, suggesting that gender may somehow suppress rather than moderate the effect. The generally curvilinear (inverted-U) pattern of effect size over the life cycle was an intriguing and unexpected finding, and future cultivation research should explore this (although, again, this is not a moderator).

Nevertheless, the within-subgroup meta-analyses do not fully resolve the question of spuriousness. The patterns in the full data set shed some light on this question. (Violation of the assumption of independence affects observed variance, but it does not affect estimated effect size; Hunter & Schmidt, 1990, p. 480.) The average of the 1,302 simple rs (and gammas converted to rs) in the full data set is .092—the same as the mean r for the 52 fully independent estimates. And the mean of the 1,911 *partials* is very similar—in fact, it is even slightly higher ($r = .095$). Thus, the data and the techniques available suggest that cultivation is resilient to a wide variety of single and multiple controls. Still, we hope that as meta-analysis advances it becomes possible to take into account coefficients such as betas and partials (Hunter & Schmidt, 1990, p. 502).

The assertion that cultivation patterns are resilient to controls is a bold one, given the arguments various critics have made about spuriousness, and also given how much time Gerbner et al. have devoted to explaining manifest variations in susceptibility to cultivation across subgroups. Yet Hunter and Schmidt (1990) argue that to try to explain variations in observed results (across studies or across subgroups) without using meta-analysis is to invite massive Type II error and capitalization on chance.

How does this play out with respect to subgroup variations? Let's revisit Doob and Macdonald's (1979) data as an example. Recall from Table 1.1 that Doob and Macdonald found widely different correlations between viewing and fear in four different areas defined by crime levels. They found that the average of the four correlations was .09 (a coefficient that should be familiar by now) and concluded that a correlation of that size was too small to matter. Gerbner et al. looked at the differences between the correlations (differences that were significant) and claimed to find "resonance" due to the enhanced relationship in high crime urban areas.

Doob and Macdonald's error was in their assumption that averaging the four correlations would amount to controlling for neighborhood—that is, that the average was comparable to a partial. When those four correlations are meta-analyzed, we see that more than 80% of their variance can be explained simply by sampling error! That is, it is highly likely that those four correlations—although they may look very different to the naked eye—all come from a homogeneous distribution of effects whose mean is .091. If they differ only because of sampling error, however, then Gerbner et al.'s interpretation of resonance may also be misleading, a result of capitalization on chance. This must remain an open question for now, one that is complicated by the fact that Gerbner et al. did find the correlations to be significantly different in a conservative test.

This analysis also does not address issues of mainstreaming. Given the extremely common finding of mainstreaming patterns, it seems less likely that this too could reflect mere capitalization on chance. The fact that we found a slightly higher (and more homogeneous) effect size for more educated respondents is quite consistent with the idea of mainstreaming, given that it is so often the more educated heavy viewers who "converge toward" the outlooks of those with less education. Future researchers should try to develop a meta-analysis of data designed to assess the existence of mainstreaming.

There are numerous other important issues that we could not deal with here. There are, for example, differences between individuals' perceptions of the amount of violence in society in general and their own personal risk of being victimized (Gerbner et al., 1981a; Hawkins & Pingree, 1982; Sparks & Ogles, 1990; Tyler & Cook, 1984; Wakshlag et al., 1983). For the purposes of our meta-analysis, we lumped images of violence, fear, "mean world" views, and so on all together under "violence." As more studies on these subdimensions accumulate, it will become easier to see if these kinds of differences act as moderators of cultivation.

Neither did we differentiate between "first-order" and "second-order" measures, as that is a dimension more relevant to studies that explore the cognitive processes underlying cultivation (Hawkins & Pingree, 1990; Potter, 1988, 1991a). Some extremely useful work is currently going on that provides strong clues about how cultivation "works" on a cognitive level (e.g., Shrum & O'Guinn, 1993). Future work in this area may even lead to better understanding of how mainstreaming and other variations occur.

The findings presented here only begin to scratch the surface of the full body of cultivation analysis and the issues it raises. But given our review of the theory and methods of cultivation research and the results of our meta-analysis, we would like to emphasize the necessity to move "forward." We interpret our data as a kind of closing chapter in the methodological conflicts of the past 20 years, and as the opening chapter in a new book. Certainly not all of the issues are resolved, but, taken as a whole, the data show that cultivation theory has amply demonstrated the nature, importance, and resilience of its findings.

For the cultivation researcher, the key question is not necessarily what happens within people's minds, and the focus should not stray too far from culture or from the institutional structures (political, economic, and legal) that support the continued dominance of specific types of message systems. Thus, cultivation research should reclaim its critical roots. Also, although we do not recommend that cultivation researchers abandon their reliance on quantitative methodology, we believe that the time is now ripe for the examination of some different "processes" in cultivation. Perhaps, for example, fruitful connections could be made between theories of narrative and cultivation. Given that recent communication research is increasingly taking account of the importance of narrative, and given that cultivation itself implies a narrative account of enculturation, it seems reasonable that cultivation tests can begin to theorize and examine relationships between cultivation findings and forms of narrative.

This implies whole new possible connections with rhetorical and critical cultural studies; if these various approaches are seen as complementary rather than as a zero-sum game over contested terrain, many important new syntheses may be advanced. The spirit of cultivation research of the past would suggest a hybrid approach, in which narrative theories can be hooked to the cart of cultivation methodology, providing more specific accounts of cultivation processes. Our understanding of cultivation could also benefit from ethnographic work within subgroups (personal, work, and family), providing data that large-scale surveys are less able to detect.

Looking back over 20 years, it is clear that Gerbner's work established a theoretical paradigm of enormous elegance and usefulness. There are many other tasks still facing cultivation researchers (see Morgan & Signorielli, 1990, for a partial list). Expanded internationalization of the work is continuing. The results of cultivation are being converted to social action, under the auspices of the cultural environment movement, led by Gerbner. Every quarter, new studies appear; some rehash old trivialities and others break new ground. Most important, the basic task of cultivation research is still to keep track of the cultural indicators that are relevant to social policy making: Until television disappears from the scene, there will always be a need to theorize and measure its impacts. As technologies and policies inevitably change (or go in circles), the ongoing interplay of cultivation theory and data will continue to provide critical insights into the choices we can make about the kind of culture in which we wish to live.

NOTE

1. Tables that summarize the data we meta-analyze are available from the authors.

REFERENCES

Note: Asterisks indicate studies included in the meta-analysis.

Allen, M., Emmers, T., Gebhardt, L., & Giery, M. (1995). Exposure to pornography and acceptance of rape myths. *Journal of Communication, 45*(1), 5-26.
*Armstrong, B., & Neuendorf, K. (1992). TV entertainment, news and racial perceptions of college students. *Journal of Communication, 42*(3), 153-176.
*Berman, D., & Stookey, J. (1980). Adolescents, TV and support for government. *Public Opinion Quarterly, 44,* 330-340.
*Bosompra, K. (1993). TV, sexual behavior and attitudes towards AIDS: A study in cultivation analysis. *Africa Media Review, 7*(3), 35-62.
*Bouwman, H. (1984). Cultivation analysis: The Dutch case. In G. Melischek, K. E. Rosengren, & J. Stappers (Eds.), *Cultural Indicators: An international symposium* (pp. 407-422). Vienna: Verlag der Osterreichischen Akademie der Wissenschaften.
Bryant, J. (1986). The road most traveled: Yet another cultivation critique. *Journal of Broadcasting & Electronic Media, 30,* 231-235.
Bryant, J., Carveth, R., & Brown, D. (1981). Television viewing and anxiety: An experimental examination. *Journal of Communication, 31*(1), 106-119.
*Buerkel-Rothfuss, N., & Mayes, S. (1981). Soap opera viewing: The cultivation effect. *Journal of Communication, 31*(3), 108-115.
Campbell, D. (1950). The indirect assessment of social attitudes. *Psychological Bulletin, 47,* 15-38.
*Carlson, J. (1985). *Prime time law enforcement: Crime show viewing and attitudes toward the criminal justice system.* New York: Praeger.
*Carlson, J. (1993). Television viewing: Cultivating perceptions of affluence and support for capitalist values. *Political Communication, 10,* 243-257.
*Carveth, R., & Alexander, A. (1985). Soap opera viewing motivations and the cultivation process. *Journal of Broadcasting & Electronic Media, 29,* 259-273.
*Choi, J., & Tamborini, R. (1988). Communication-acculturation and the cultivation hypothesis: A comparative study between two Korean communities in the U.S. *Howard Journal of Communication, 1*(1), 57-74.
Cook, T., Kendzierski, D., & Thomas, S. (1983). The implicit assumptions of television research: An analysis of the 1982 NIMH report on television and behavior. *Public Opinion Quarterly, 47,* 161-201.
*Doob, A., & Macdonald, G. (1979). Television viewing and fear of victimization: Is the relationship causal? *Journal of Personality and Social Psychology, 37,* 170-179.
Eastman, S., & Newton, G. (1995). Delineating grazing: Observations of remote control use. *Journal of Communication, 45*(1), 77-95.
*Fox, W., & Philliber, W. (1978). Television viewing and the perception of affluence. *Sociological Quarterly, 19*(1), 103-112.
Gerbner, G. (1958). On content analysis and critical research in mass communication. *AV Communication Review, 6,* 85-108.
Gerbner, G. (1969). Toward "Cultural Indicators": The analysis of mass mediated message systems. *AV Communication Review, 17,* 137-148.

Gerbner, G. (1970). Cultural Indicators: The case of violence in television drama. *Annals of the American Academy of Political and Social Science, 388,* 69-81.

Gerbner, G. (1973). Cultural Indicators: The third voice. In G. Gerbner, L. Gross, & W. Melody (Eds.), *Communications technology and social policy* (pp. 555-573). New York: John Wiley.

Gerbner, G. (1990). Epilogue: Advancing on the path of righteousness (maybe). In N. Signorielli & M. Morgan (Eds.), *Cultivation analysis: New directions in media effects research* (pp. 249-262). Newbury Park, CA: Sage.

*Gerbner, G., & Gross, L. (1976). Living with television: The Violence Profile. *Journal of Communication, 26*(2), 173-199.

Gerbner, G., & Gross, L. (1979). Editorial response: A reply to Newcomb's "humanistic critique." *Communication Research, 6,* 223-230.

*Gerbner, G., Gross, L., Eleey, M., Jackson-Beeck, M., Jeffries-Fox, S., & Signorielli, N. (1977). TV Violence Profile No. 8: The highlights. *Journal of Communication, 27*(2), 171-180.

*Gerbner, G., Gross, L., Jackson-Beeck, M., Jeffries-Fox, S., & Signorielli, N. (1978). Cultural indicators: Violence Profile No. 9. *Journal of Communication, 28*(3), 176-207.

*Gerbner, G., Gross, L., Morgan, M., & Signorielli, N. (1980a). The "mainstreaming" of America: Violence Profile No. 11. *Journal of Communication, 30*(3), 10-29.

Gerbner, G., Gross, L., Morgan, M., & Signorielli, N. (1980b). Some additional comments on cultivation analysis. *Public Opinion Quarterly, 44,* 408-410.

*Gerbner, G., Gross, L., Morgan, M., & Signorielli, N. (1981a). A curious journey into the scary world of Paul Hirsch. *Communication Research, 8,* 39-72.

Gerbner, G., Gross, L., Morgan, M., & Signorielli, N. (1981b). Final reply to Hirsch. *Communication Research, 8,* 259-280.

Gerbner, G., Gross, L., Morgan, M., & Signorielli, N. (1981c). On the limits of "The limits of advocacy research": Response to Hirsch. *Public Opinion Quarterly, 45,* 116-118.

*Gerbner, G., Gross, L., Morgan, M., & Signorielli, N. (1981d, May/June). Scientists on the TV screen. *Society,* pp. 41-44.

Gerbner, G., Gross, L., Morgan, M., & Signorielli, N. (1982). Charting the mainstream: Television's contributions to political orientations. *Journal of Communication, 32*(2), 100-127.

*Gerbner, G., Gross, L., Morgan, M., & Signorielli, N. (1984). Political correlates of television viewing. *Public Opinion Quarterly, 48,* 283-300.

*Gerbner, G., Gross, L., Morgan, M., & Signorielli, N. (1986). Living with television: The dynamics of the cultivation process. In J. Bryant & D. Zillman (Eds.), *Perspectives on media effects* (pp. 17-40). Hillsdale, NJ: Lawrence Erlbaum.

*Gerbner, G., Gross, L., Morgan, M., & Signorielli, N. (1994). Growing up with television: The cultivation perspective. In J. Bryant & D. Zillman (Eds.), *Media effects: Advances in theory and research* (pp. 17-41). Hillsdale, NJ: Lawrence Erlbaum.

*Gerbner, G., Gross, L., Signorielli, N., & Morgan, M. (1980). Aging with television: Images on television drama and conceptions of social reality. *Journal of Communication, 30*(1), 37-47.

*Gerbner, G., Morgan, M., & Signorielli, N. (1982). Programming health portrayals: What viewers see, say and do. In D. Pearl, L. Bouthilet, & J. Lazar (Eds.), *Television and behavior: Ten years of scientific progress and implications for the 80's: Vol. 2. Technical reviews* (pp. 291-307). Rockville, MD: National Institute of Mental Health.

*Gross, L. (1984). The cultivation of intolerance: TV, blacks and gays. In G. Melischek, K. E. Rosengren, & J. Stappers (Eds.), *Cultural indicators: An international symposium* (pp. 345-363). Vienna: Verlag der Osterreichischen Akademie der Wissenschaften.

*Gross, L., & Jeffries-Fox, S. (1978). What do you want to be when you grow up, little girl? In G. Tuchman, A. K. Daniels, & J. Benet (Eds.), *Hearth and home: Images of women in the mass media* (pp. 240-265). New York: Oxford University Press.

*Gross, L., & Morgan, M. (1985). Television and enculturation. In J. Dominick & J. Fletcher (Eds.), *Broadcasting research methods* (pp. 221-234). Boston: Allyn & Bacon.

Gunter, B., & Wober, J. M. (1983a). Television viewing and public perceptions of hazards to life. *Journal of Environmental Psychology, 3,* 325-335.

*Gunter, B., & Wober, J. M. (1983b). Television viewing and public trust. *British Journal of Social Psychology, 22,* 174-176.

Hammond, K. (1948). Measuring attitude by error choice: An indirect method. *Journal of Abnormal and Social Psychology, 43,* 38-48.

Haney, C., & Manzolati, J. (1981). Television criminology: Network illusions of criminal justice realities. In E. Aronson (Ed.), *Readings about the social animal* (pp. 125-136). San Francisco: Freeman.

*Hawkins, R., & Pingree, S. (1980). Some processes in the cultivation effect. *Communication Research, 7,* 193-226.

*Hawkins, R., & Pingree, S. (1981). Uniform content and habitual viewing: Unnecessary assumptions in social reality effects. *Human Communication Research, 7,* 291-301.

Hawkins, R., & Pingree, S. (1982). Television's influence on social reality. In D. Pearl, L. Bouthilet, & J. Lazar (Eds.), *Television and behavior: Ten years of scientific progress and implications for the 80's: Vol. 2. Technical reviews* (pp. 224-227). Rockville, MD: National Institute of Mental Health.

Hawkins, R., & Pingree, S. (1990). Divergent psychological processes in constructing social reality from mass media content. In N. Signorielli & M. Morgan (Eds.), *Cultivation analysis: New directions in media effects research* (pp. 35-50). Newbury Park, CA: Sage.

*Hawkins, R., Pingree, S., & Adler, I. (1987). Searching for cognitive processes in the cultivation effect. *Human Communication Research, 13,* 553-577.

Herrett-Skjellum, J., & Allen, M. (1996). Television programming and sex stereotyping: A meta-analysis. In B. R. Burleson (Ed.), *Communication yearbook 19* (pp. 157-185). Thousand Oaks, CA: Sage.

*Hirsch, P. (1980). The "scary world" of the nonviewer and other anomalies: A reanalysis of Gerbner et al.'s findings on cultivation analysis. *Communication Research, 7,* 403-456.

Hirsch, P. (1981). On not learning from one's own mistakes: A reanalysis of Gerbner et al.'s findings on cultivation analysis, part II. *Communication Research, 8,* 3-37.

*Hoover, S. (1990). Television, religion, and religious television: Purposes and cross purposes. In N. Signorielli & M. Morgan (Eds.), *Cultivation analysis: New directions in media effects research* (pp. 123-140). Newbury Park, CA: Sage.

*Hughes, M. (1980). The fruits of cultivation analysis: A re-examination of the effects of television watching on fear of victimization, alienation, and the approval of violence. *Public Opinion Quarterly, 44,* 287-302.

Hunter, J. E., & Schmidt, F. L. (1990). *Methods of meta-analysis: Correcting error and bias in research findings.* Newbury Park, CA: Sage.

*Kang, J., & Morgan, M. (1988). Culture clash: US TV programs in Korea. *Journalism Quarterly, 65,* 431-438.

*Kiecolt, J., & Sayles, M. (1988). TV and the cultivation of attitudes toward subordinate groups. *Sociological Spectrum, 8,* 19-33.

Kim, M., & Hunter, J. (1993). Attitude-behavior relations: A meta-analysis of attitude relevance and topic. *Journal of Communication, 43*(1), 101-142.

*Matabane, P. (1988). Television and the black audience: Cultivating moderate perspectives on racial integration. *Journal of Communication, 38*(4), 21-31.

*Morgan, M. (1982). Television and adolescents' sex-role stereotypes: A longitudinal study. *Journal of Personality and Social Psychology, 43,* 947-955.

Morgan, M. (1983). Symbolic victimization and real-world fear. *Human Communication Research, 9,* 146-157.

*Morgan, M. (1984). Heavy television viewing and perceived quality of life. *Journalism Quarterly, 61,* 499-504.

Morgan, M. (1986). Television and the erosion of regional diversity. *Journal of Broadcasting & Electronic Media, 30,* 123-139.
*Morgan, M. (1987). Television, sex-role attitudes and sex-role behavior. *Journal of Early Adolescence, 7,* 269-282.
*Morgan, M. (1990). International cultivation analysis. In N. Signorielli & M. Morgan (Eds.), *Cultivation analysis: New directions in media effects research* (pp. 225-248). Newbury Park, CA: Sage.
*Morgan, M., & Rothschild, N. (1983). Impact of the new TV technology: Cable TV, peers, and sex-role cultivation in the electronic environment. *Youth & Society, 15,* 33-50.
*Morgan, M., & Shanahan, J. (1991a). Do VCRs change the TV picture? VCRs and the cultivation process. *American Behavioral Scientist, 35,* 122-135.
*Morgan, M., & Shanahan, J. (1991b). Television and the cultivation of political attitudes in Argentina. *Journal of Communication, 41*(1), 88-103.
*Morgan, M., & Shanahan, J. (1992a). Comparative cultivation analysis: Television and adolescents in Argentina and Taiwan. In F. Korzenny & S. Ting-Toomey (Eds.), *Mass media effects across cultures* (pp. 173-197). Newbury Park, CA: Sage.
*Morgan, M., & Shanahan, J. (1992b). Television viewing and voting 1975-1989. *Electoral Studies, 11,* 3-20.
*Morgan, M., & Shanahan, J. (1995). *Democracy tango: Television, adolescents, and authoritarian tensions in Argentina.* Cresskill, NJ: Hampton.
*Morgan, M., Shanahan, J., & Harris, C. (1990). VCRs and the effects of television: New diversity or more of the same? In J. Dobrow (Ed.), *Social and cultural aspects of VCR use* (pp. 107-123). Hillsdale, NJ: Lawrence Erlbaum.
Morgan, M., & Signorielli, N. (1990). Cultivation analysis: Conceptualization and methodology. In N. Signorielli & M. Morgan (Eds.), *Cultivation analysis: New directions in media effects research* (pp. 13-34). Newbury Park, CA: Sage.
Mullen, B. (1989). *Advanced BASIC meta-analysis.* Hillsdale, NJ: Lawrence Erlbaum.
Nelson, T. (1986). Basic programs for computation of the Goodman-Kruskal gamma coefficient. *Bulletin of the Psychonomic Society, 24,* 281-283.
Neville, T. (1980). *Television viewing and the expression of interpersonal mistrust.* Unpublished doctoral dissertation, Princeton University.
Newcomb, H. (1978). Assessing the Violence Profile of Gerbner and Gross: A humanistic critique and suggestion. *Communication Research, 5,* 264-282.
Newhagen, J., & Lewenstein, M. (1992). Cultivation and exposure to television following the 1989 Loma Prieta earthquake. *Mass Comm Review, 18,* 49-56.
*O'Keefe, G. (1984). Public views on crime: TV exposure and media credibility. In R. Bostrom (Ed.), *Communication yearbook 8* (pp. 514-535). Beverly Hills, CA: Sage.
Ogles, R. (1987). Cultivation analysis: Theory, methodology, and current research on television-influenced constructions of social reality. *Mass Comm Review, 14,* 43-53.
*Ogles, R., & Sparks, G. (1994). Question specificity and perceived probability of criminal victimization. *Mass Comm Review, 20,* 51-61.
*Passuth, P., & Cook, F. (1985). Effects of TV viewing on knowledge and attitudes about older adults: A critical reexamination. *Gerontologist, 25,* 69-77.
*Perse, E. (1990). Cultivation and involvement with local television news. In N. Signorielli & M. Morgan (Eds.), *Cultivation analysis: New directions in media effects research* (pp. 51-70). Newbury Park, CA: Sage.
*Perse, E., Ferguson, D., & McLeod, D. (1994). Cultivation in the newer media environment. *Communication Research, 21,* 79-104.
*Pfau, M., Mullen, L. J., Diedrich, T., & Garrow, K. (1995). Television viewing and public perceptions of attorneys. *Human Communication Research, 21,* 307-330.

*Piepe, A., Charlton, P., & Morey, J. (1990). Politics and television viewing in England: Hegemony or pluralism? *Journal of Communication, 40*(1), 24-35.

*Pingree, S. (1983). Children's cognitive processes in constructing social reality. *Journalism Quarterly, 60,* 415-422.

*Pingree, S., & Hawkins, R. (1981). U.S. programs on Australian television: The cultivation effect. *Journal of Communication, 31*(1), 97-105.

*Potter, J. (1986). Perceived reality and the cultivation hypothesis. *Journal of Broadcasting & Electronic Media, 30,* 159-174.

*Potter, J. (1988). Three strategies for elaborating the cultivation hypothesis. *Journalism Quarterly, 65,* 930-939.

*Potter, J. (1991a). Examining cultivation from a psychological perspective: Component subprocesses. *Communication Research, 18,* 77-102.

*Potter, J. (1991b). The linearity assumption in cultivation research. *Human Communication Research, 17,* 562-583.

Potter, J. (1991c). The relationship between first- and second-order measures of cultivation. *Human Communication Research, 18,* 92-113.

Potter, J. (1993). Cultivation theory and research: A conceptual analysis. *Human Communication Research, 19,* 564-601.

Potter, J. (1994). Cultivation theory and research: A methodological critique. *Journalism Monographs, 147,* 1-35.

Potter, J., & Chang, I. (1990). Television exposure measures and the cultivation hypothesis. *Journal of Broadcasting & Electronic Media, 34,* 313-333.

Reep, D., & Drambot, F. (1989). Effects of frequent television viewing on stereotypes: "Drip drip" or "drench"? *Journalism Quarterly, 66,* 542-556.

*Reimer, B., & Rosengren, K. E. (1990). Cultivated viewers and readers: A life-style perspective. In N. Signorielli & M. Morgan (Eds.), *Cultivation analysis: New directions in media effects research* (pp. 181-206). Newbury Park, CA: Sage.

Rosengren, K. E. (1984). Cultural indicators for the comparative study of culture. In G. Melischek, K. E. Rosengren, & J. Stappers (Eds.), *Cultural indicators: An international symposium* (pp. 11-32). Vienna: Verlag der Osterreichischen Akademie der Wissenschaften.

*Rothschild, N. (1984). Small group affiliation as a mediating factor in the cultivation process. In G. Melischek, K. E. Rosengren, & J. Stappers (Eds.), *Cultural indicators: An international symposium* (pp. 377-387). Vienna: Verlag der Osterreichischen Akademie der Wissenschaften.

*Rothschild, N., & Morgan, M. (1987). Cohesion and control: Relationships with parents as mediators of television. *Journal of Early Adolescence, 7,* 299-314.

*Rubin, A., Perse, E., & Taylor, D. (1988). A methodological examination of cultivation. *Communication Research, 15,* 107-134.

*Shanahan, J. (1993). Television and the cultivation of environmental concern: 1988-1992. In A. Hansen (Ed.), *The mass media and environmental issues* (pp. 181-197). Leicester, England: University of Leicester Press.

*Shanahan, J. (1995). Television viewing and adolescent authoritarianism. *Journal of Adolescence, 18,* 271-288.

Shapiro, M. (1991). Memory and decision processes in the construction of social reality. *Communication Research, 18,* 3-24.

Shrum, L. J., & O'Guinn, T. C. (1993). Processes and effects in the construction of social reality. *Communication Research, 20,* 436-471.

Shrum, L. J., O'Guinn, T. C., Semenik, R. J., & Faber, R. J. (1991). Processes and effects in the construction of normative consumer beliefs: The role of television. *Advances in Consumer Research, 18,* 755-763.

Shrum, L. J., Wyer, R. S., & O'Guinn, T. C. (1994). *Cognitive processes underlying the effects of television consumption.* Unpublished manuscript, Rutgers University.

*Signorielli, N. (1989). Television and conceptions about sex roles: Maintaining conventionality and the status quo. *Sex Roles, 21,* 341-360.

*Signorielli, N. (1990). Television's mean and dangerous world: A continuation of the Cultural Indicators perspective. In N. Signorielli & M. Morgan (Eds.), *Cultivation analysis: New directions in media effects research* (pp. 85-106). Newbury Park, CA: Sage.

*Signorielli, N. (1991). Adolescents and ambivalence toward marriage. *Youth & Society, 23,* 121-149.

*Signorielli, N. (1993). Television and adolescents' perceptions about work. *Youth & Society, 24,* 314-341.

*Signorielli, N., & Lears, M. (1992a). Children, television and conceptions about chores: Attitudes and behaviors. *Sex Roles, 27,* 157-170.

*Signorielli, N., & Lears, M. (1992b). Television and children's conceptions of nutrition: Unhealthy messages. *Health Communication, 4,* 245-258.

Signorielli, N., & Morgan, M. (Eds.). (1990). *Cultivation analysis: New directions in media effects research.* Newbury Park, CA: Sage.

*Singer, J., Singer, D., & Rapaczynski, W. (1984). Family patterns and TV viewing as predictors of children's beliefs and aggression. *Journal of Communication, 34*(2), 73-89.

*Slater, D., & Elliott, R. (1982). Television's influence on social reality. *Quarterly Journal of Speech, 68*(1), 69-79.

*Sparks, G., & Ogles, R. (1990). The difference between fear of victimization and the possibility of being victimized. *Journal of Broadcasting & Electronic Media, 34,* 351-358.

Stevens, G. (1980). *TV and attitudes of fear and alienation.* Unpublished master's thesis, Annenberg School for Communication, University of Pennsylvania.

Tamborini, R., & Choi, J. (1990). The role of cultural diversity in cultivation research. In N. Signorielli & M. Morgan (Eds.), *Cultivation analysis: New directions in media effects research* (pp. 157-180). Newbury Park, CA: Sage.

*Tan, A. (1979). TV beauty ads and role expectations of adolescent female viewers. *Journalism Quarterly, 56,* 827-831.

Tapper, J. (1995). The ecology of cultivation: A conceptual model for cultivation research. *Communication Theory, 15,* 36-57.

Tyler, T., & Cook, F. (1984). The mass media and judgments of risk: Distinguishing impact on personal and societal level judgments. *Journal of Personality and Social Psychology, 47,* 693-708.

*Umble, D. (1990). Mennonites and television: Applications of cultivation analysis to a religious subculture. In N. Signorielli & M. Morgan (Eds.), *Cultivation analysis: New directions in media effects research* (pp. 141-156). Newbury Park, CA: Sage.

*Volgy, T., & Schwartz, J. (1980). Television entertainment programming and sociopolitical attitudes. *Journalism Quarterly, 57,* 150-155.

Wakshlag, J., Viol, V., & Tamborini, R. (1983). Selecting crime drama and apprehension about crime. *Human Communication Research, 10,* 227-242.

*Weaver, J., & Wakshlag, J. (1986). Perceived vulnerability to crime, criminal victimization experience, and television viewing. *Journal of Broadcasting & Electronic Media, 30,* 141-158.

*Weimann, G. (1984). Images of life in America: The impact of American TV in Israel. *International Journal of Intercultural Relations, 8,* 185-197.

*Wober, J. M. (1978). Televised violence and paranoid perception: The view from Great Britain. *Public Opinion Quarterly, 42,* 315-321.

*Wober, J. M., & Gunter, B. (1982). Television and personal threat: Fact or artifact? *British Journal of Social Psychology, 21,* 239-247.

Wober, J. M., & Gunter, B. (1988). *Television and social control.* New York: St. Martin's.

*Zemach, T., & Cohen, A. (1986). Perception of gender equality on TV and in social reality. *Journal of Broadcasting & Electronic Media, 30,* 427-444.

Zillman, D., & Wakshlag, J. (1985). Fear of victimization and the appeal of crime drama. In D. Zillman & J. Bryant (Eds.), *Selective exposure to communication* (pp. 141-156). Hillsdale, NJ: Lawrence Erlbaum.

CHAPTER CONTENTS

2 The Impact of Foreign TV on a Domestic Audience: A Meta-Analysis

MICHEL G. ELASMAR
Boston University

JOHN E. HUNTER
Michigan State University

The impact of cross-border communication has long been of special interest to international communication scholars and policy makers. In this chapter the authors use meta-analytic procedures to investigate the size of the effects of cross-border television. The results of this study reveal that, overall, cross-border TV has very weak effects on viewers. This result contradicts cultural imperialism critics, who contend that foreign television has strong and negative impacts on viewers. The effects of foreign TV are usually assumed to be from TV to the audience members. This chapter, however, raises the possibility that the effects found are not only very weak, but could be due to some other factors that may be influencing the audience to seek and view foreign TV programs.

INTERNATIONAL communication as a topic of study encompasses many issues that have been vigorously debated over the years. Chief among these issues are dependency as related to imported media, media imperialism, international media and sovereignty, and the international flow of information. Although each of these topics can be studied distinctly, they all share a common concern about messages crossing between countries. This concern is based on the tacit assumption that imported messages have negative impacts on audiences in the importing countries.

Although large bodies of literature have been written about various aspects of international communication, few authors have directly addressed the issue of cross-border TV impact. The majority of those who have addressed this topic directly have approached it from a theoretical, conjectural, or speculative

Correspondence and requests for reprints: Michel G. Elasmar, Communication Research Center, Boston University, 640 Commonwealth Avenue, Boston, MA 02215; e-mail elasmar@bu.edu

Communication Yearbook 20, pp. 47-69

perspective. Unfortunately, many of the papers they have produced can be characterized as tirades or diatribes. Among the most emotional of these have been works expressing fear that local populations will be contaminated by exposure to immoral and exploitative foreigners.

In this chapter we investigate the topic of the cross-border impact of TV using a more objective and less normative approach. We propose to use meta-analytic procedures to analyze the current body of literature about cross-border TV. The general research question of this endeavor is, What are the empirical findings on the effects of cross-border TV?[1] More specific research questions include the following: What is the average effect size of cross-border TV across studies? What does the size of the average effect of cross-border TV mean to international communication scholars?

The outcomes of this study should be practically useful for those engaging in international communication policy debates. However, the analyses reported here also have theoretical implications. Cross-border TV exposes domestic audience members to individuals from distant lands depicted in television program content. In many cases, such mediated encounters may be the only contact domestic audience members will ever have with these imported characters. The imported characters are often from different societies, cultures, traditions, and nations. Thus, any effects stemming from exposure to such characters are of interest to researchers studying the social psychology of intergroup relations, intercultural communication, and international relations.

Although it is not within the scope of this chapter to provide a comprehensive review of qualitative essays that have been written about the impact of cross-border TV, in the following section we highlight the key arguments concerning this topic.

CONCEPTUALIZING THE IMPACT OF FOREIGN TV

During the past few decades, the presence of foreign programs in domestic television schedules has been seen by most observers as a source of national ills. Other observers, however, contend that the impact of such a presence is either negligible or unknown.

Foreign TV: A Source of National Ills

Lee (1980) summarizes the various concerns expressed about imported TV programs as follows: (a) The programs will make products manufactured in cities intensely attractive and encourage their consumption; (b) in many locales, audience members will be greatly frustrated because they cannot obtain or afford most of what these TV programs depict; and (c) the values embodied in these programs will influence the value structures of audience members. This last concern is the basis of one of the most intense accusations against imported TV: It is an instrument of cultural imperialism (Schiller, 1969). Cultural imperialism (CI) is said to be "a verifiable process of social influence by which a nation imposes on other countries its set of beliefs, values, knowledge and behavioral norms as well as its overall style of life" (Beltran, 1978a, p. 184). According to Goonasekara (1987), cultural imperialism is an effect stemming from the documented flow of television programs from Western countries into Third World television schedules. Advocates of CI theory claim that in "the face of this media invasion, the indigenous cultures of the Third World disintegrate consistently and without resistance" (Goonasekara, 1987, p. 11). Hadad (1978) argues that industrialized countries use international television as a tool to extend their domestic commercial activities. He contends that "the best way to achieve this goal is by launching a 'cultural invasion' of developing nations" (p. 19). This fear of domination has even influenced how some observers perceive the importation into Latin America of *Sesame Street,* a U.S. educational program for children. Goldsen and Bibliowicz (1976) contend that *Plaza Sesamo,* the Spanish-language version of the series, will "lay down an important part of the cultural scaffolding that Latin American children will build on. [It will] expose the continent's children to a massive cultural assault whose consequences are incalculable" (p. 125). Herbert Schiller (1991), the main proponent behind the idea of cultural imperialism in the 1960s, still believes that "the global preeminence of American cultural products is being not only maintained but extended to new locales" (p. 22).

Foreign TV: Limited or Unknown Effects

In contrast to those who view foreign TV as a source of cultural domination are those who contend that it has either negligible or unknown effects. For instance, Tracey (1985) asserts that those who support the notion that foreign TV is a source of cultural domination "have tended to study company reports, rather than the realities of individual lives" (p. 45). Taking the individual viewer into consideration, Browne, as early as 1967, explained the hurdles that prevent foreign TV from having a controlled impact on individuals in a domestic setting:

> Experience should have already taught us that there is no universal visual language, any more than there is universal spoken or written language . . . [which means that] if one picture is indeed worth a thousand words, those words will not mean the same thing to everyone. (p. 206)

According to Salwen (1991), foreign TV cannot be viewed as a direct cause of individuals' losing their indigenous cultures: "At the very least, factors inherent within cultures . . . account for different responses to foreign media messages" (p. 36). Salwen, Tracey, and Browne all base their arguments on the notion of audience activity. That is, they contend that individual audience members are not passive receivers of television messages; rather, audiences actively choose among the many available messages. The concept of audience activity contradicts the thinking of those who believe that audiences exposed to foreign TV are helpless victims influenced by ruthless message designers— the notion that the audience is composed of active receivers does not convince those who fear cultural imperialism. Schiller (1991), for example, believes that "much of the current work on audience reception comes uncomfortably close to being apologetics for present-day structures of cultural control" (p. 25).

Aside from those who point out the difficulties foreign TV has in achieving effects, there are those who assert that we just don't know enough about the topic to make an assessment. Tracey (1985) notes that "we have barely begun to scratch the surface of understanding the function and consequence of TV as an international cultural process" (p. 50), and Lee (1980) observes that "research on the likely influences of alien television programs on the decline of traditional cultures and arts is inconclusive" (p. 103).

Some researchers have assessed the effects of foreign TV after carrying out narrative reviews of the existing literature. Yaple and Korzenny (1989), for example, assert that the studies conducted so far "have concluded that media effects across national cultural groups are detectable but relatively small in magnitude, and that . . . the environment, cultural situation, and context affect selectivity and the interpretation of content" (p. 313). After a similar narrative review of the literature, Hur (1982) concludes that "exposure to American television and film content by local populations has few cognitive and attitudinal effects, much less behavioral effects" (p. 546).

So far, researchers assessing the impact of foreign TV have done so in one of two ways: (a) by following a set of arguments heavily grounded in political ideology or (b) by carrying out a narrative literature review of selected studies. We propose to use a more objective methodology—meta-analysis— to assess the entire body of quantitative studies about the topic.

STUDY EXPECTATIONS

The various views held regarding the effect of foreign TV enable us to develop expectations about the results of our study. Concerning the concept that foreign TV programs embody a tool of cultural imperialism, we expect the following:

- The results of our meta-analysis will reveal that foreign television programs have strong effects on the domestic audience members who view them.

Concerning the concept that messages are received differently by various audience members, we expect the following:

- The results of our meta-analysis will reveal that the effects of foreign TV differ across audience types (age groups and other demographic factors).

In the following sections, we describe the methods used to locate and then analyze the studies, detail the findings of this endeavor, and present a discussion of the results and their implications.

METHOD

For purposes of this study, we define a *television impact* as any detected variation in an individual at the cognitive, attitudinal, affective, cultural, or behavioral level of analysis that is assumed to be attributed to foreign television consumption.[2] A *foreign* television program is defined as one that is (a) produced in a country different from that in which it is shown, regardless of how it arrived in the latter country (videotape, cable, importation, cross-border TV transmission, direct broadcast satellite), and (b) primarily designed for consumption by the audience of the country in which it was produced.[3] These first two criteria were established in order to distinguish the studies relevant to our research questions. Thus, not included in our analysis are international comparative investigations of domestic television effects (e.g., comparative cultivation studies) and research covering the impact of a message designed in Country A especially to influence the audience of Country B (i.e., propaganda and/or persuasion).

In addition, only empirical studies exploring the impact of a given Country A's television programs on individuals in Country B were selected.[4] In the case that not all hypotheses or relationships satisfied this requirement, only the hypotheses or relationships that did were summarized. Both published and unpublished manuscripts, recent or dated, were sought, and electronic database and manual index searches were conducted to generate potential study leads.[5] In addition, letters were sent to numerous research institutions around the United States asking for unpublished manuscripts about the topic.[6] Copies of all studies identified were then gathered, read, and summarized.

The Study Codebook

In order to describe the studies in a systematic manner, we developed a codebook to fit the specific needs of the analysis. Variables coded include year of study, year of publication, author's (or authors') country of affiliation, department of origin, study type, type of publication, study location, primary theory, sample type, and method. After all studies were coded, the data were entered into a computer and statistical software was used to generate descriptive statistics.

Quantification of Results

Meta-analysis is a general procedure for analyzing results across studies. In order to be useful, a study had to report results in some quantitative form. To enable comparison and synthesis of results across studies, the statistical report had to have the property that it could be recoded into a measure of the size of the effect. Only those studies with useful data are included in the meta-analysis portion of this report.

For our report, we coded the size of the effect as the correlation between foreign TV exposure and the dependent variable. Methods for computing correlations from various kinds of statistical reports are available in most textbooks on meta-analysis, such as that by Hunter and Schmidt (1990). Hunter and Schmidt also provide formulas for converting results from correlations into other measures of the size of the effect. The data transformation task was difficult with this particular group of studies because there was so much diversity in the methods of reporting findings.

The following coding rules were adopted for the effects on beliefs, behaviors, and knowledge: A correlation was coded as positive if exposure to imported TV led to an increase in an individual's beliefs, behaviors, or knowledge, regardless of whether these beliefs, behaviors, or knowledge would be regarded as positive or negative from a normative point of view. This was done because it is very hard to reach agreement on which beliefs, behaviors, or knowledge can be normatively considered positive or negative. For example, buying American products is a behavior that may be considered normatively positive by some and normatively negative by others. If a study reported that increases in U.S. TV consumption led to increases in the purchase of American products, we coded the correlation as positive in the meta-analysis, regardless of whether such buying behavior is considered normatively positive or negative. For attitudes, however, a correlation was coded as positive when exposure to foreign TV resulted in a positive attitude toward the country originating the program and as negative when it resulted in a negative attitude toward the originating country. It was fairly simple to distinguish between positive and negative attitudes based upon the wording of the attitude items. For example, a statement such as "I like the United States" expresses a positive attitude toward the United States. Thus, a positive correlation between scores on this item and scores on a U.S. TV exposure measure was coded as positive in the meta-analysis.

Meta-analysis can correct the effects of sampling error and other methodological imperfections and can determine the extent to which study results differ by more than sampling error. This is discussed in meta-analysis under the rubric of "heterogeneity." This is best done by estimating the standard

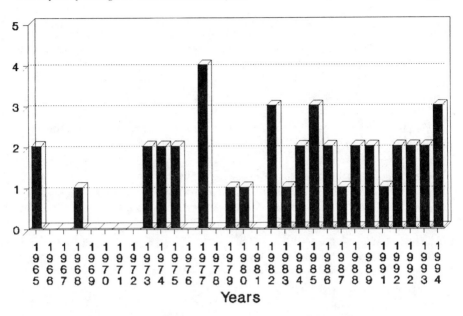

Figure 2.1. Foreign TV Impact Studies: Number of Studies Conducted by Year

deviation of the population values across studies. It is also possible to use a statistical significance test for homogeneity, though these tests sometimes do not work very well if the number of studies is small. The specific computational formulas used in our report are those of Hunter and Schmidt (1990).

RESULTS

The comprehensive search for literature spanned a time frame beginning with works published in 1960 and ending in January 1995 and located numerous articles addressing the topic of cross-border TV effects.[7] After a careful examination of the content of these articles, it was determined that the majority took a mostly critical approach to the topic at hand (examples include Beltran, 1978a, 1978b; Day, 1975; Dizard, 1965; Goldsen & Bibliowicz, 1976; Tracey, 1985). There were also numerous others that fit the category of international comparative TV effects (examples include Bouwman & Stappers, 1982; Hedinson & Windahl, 1982; Morgan & Shanahan, 1992; Straubhaar et al., 1992).

As the literature was being collected, sorted, and categorized, it became clear that quantitative studies examining the effects of foreign television on individuals are rare. After reading all articles obtained ($n = 177$), we found a total of 36 manuscripts to fit the basic criteria set at the start of this endeavor. Figure 2.1 shows the number of studies conducted by year. Few studies were published before 1970, but more studies have been published in recent years. In the 1960s there were 2, in the 1970s there were 5, and in the 1980s there were 18. Based upon this linear trend, we can project that a total of 28 studies will be done during the decade of the 1990s. The majority of the studies (55.6%) were published in academic journals.[8] Convention papers make up 22.2% of the total.

Many of the studies were not theory driven. In fact, 25% did not identify a primary theory from which hypotheses were formulated. The largest number of the investigations that were theory based relied on Gerbner's cultivation theory (recently reviewed by Morgan & Signorielli, 1990). Other theories informing the studies were as follows: cultural imperialism (11.1%), acculturation (6.7%), socialization (5.6%), dependency (5.6%), modernization (2.8%), and social learning (2.8%).

Most investigators relied on a group-distributed but self-administered survey method to collect data about individuals. Some researchers preferred to conduct door-to-door personal interviews by themselves (e.g., Oliveira, 1986) or with a few trained assistants (e.g., Veii, 1988) or by hiring a marketing firm (e.g., Skinner, 1984). Those studies that used the personal interview method accounted for 27.8% of the total, whereas those that used a mail survey accounted for 2.8%. Another 2.8% used a combination of methods. Of the 36 studies, 34 (94.4%) used a cross-sectional design, which means that the data were collected at only one point in time. The remaining 2 studies attempted to observe the effects of foreign TV on individuals over several years.

Countries Studied

The studies report results collected in 21 different countries or territories. Table 2.1 lists those countries and the number of studies for each. The number of instances is larger than the number of studies because some studies gathered data in more than one country.

Origin of Country of Content

The country of origin of the foreign television content analyzed in these studies was typically the United States ($n = 28$). The second most investigated foreign TV impact concerned programs of Canadian origin ($n = 6$). The impact of Mexican TV was investigated in a single study, and one of the research reports did not specify the origin of the foreign TV programming but merely indicated that it was not domestic (Zhao, 1989).

Classification of Audience Members

The majority of the studies (58.3%) focused upon the effects of foreign TV on students;[9] 22.2% focused upon the general population. That there were

TABLE 2.1
Locations of Cross-Border TV Impact Studies

Location	n
Australia	1
Belize	2
Native Canada	4
Nonnative Canada	5
China	3
Denmark	1
Finland	1
Iceland	2
India	1
Israel	1
Japan	3
Korea	4
Lebanon	1
Mexico	1
Namibia	1
Norway	1
Philippines	1
Russia	1
Sweden	1
Taiwan	3
Thailand	1
Trinidad	1
United States nonnative	2
Venezuela	1

only 8 general population studies conducted on this topic in 27 years is surprising. A few investigations looked at the impact of foreign TV on professionals (5.6%), and some even combined students and members of the general public in their samples (13.9%).

Because audiences differ in terms of sophistication, it is possible that the effects of foreign TV are different for different audiences. We coded each study as to audience so that we could check for such results.

Measurement of the Independent Variable

Ideally, each study should measure the exact extent to which each audience member is exposed to foreign TV. The studies varied in the quality of this measurement. Out of a total of 36 studies, 9 (25%) had no direct measure of the individuals' consumption of foreign TV. Instead, some investigators ($n = 7$) simply measured individuals' consumption of television in general (e.g., Werner, 1981), whereas others ($n = 2$) did not bother to assess even that variable (e.g., Tate & Trach, 1980). The former group of studies assumed that, because foreign programming was carried on a domestic TV station, an estimate of television exposure would yield an estimate of exposure to foreign programming. The latter studies assumed that if a leaning toward the United States on the part of audience members was detected, this indicated the impact of American TV programs present in the domestic TV broadcast schedule. The studies that did not clearly measure individuals' consumption of imported TV are not included in the meta-analysis section of this chapter.

The best of the 36 studies were the 27 investigations that did provide some measure of individual consumption of foreign TV. The researchers, however, differed in their measurement of foreign TV exposure and varied in their concern with content specificity. Some investigators measured exposure by assessing individuals' watching particular foreign TV genres, such as comedy, crime, or drama, on a domestic network (e.g., Pingree & Hawkins, 1981). Others measured exposure as the number of hours tuned in to a particular foreign TV network received domestically, regardless of the genres that individuals watched (e.g., Kang & Morgan, 1988). Still others measured exposure as the frequency of watching specific foreign TV programs (not genres) on a domestic network (e.g., Tan & Suarchavarat, 1988). Given the small number of studies at hand, we decided to consider all independent measures as being approximations of one another and best available estimates of foreign TV consumption.

Measures of the Dependent Variable

The researchers differed in how they assessed influence or impact. That is, they differed in both the number and the quality of their measurement of the dependent variables. After a qualitative assessment of the items, we coded the different dependent variables into five categories. The coding was carried out according to the following criteria.

Knowledge. The dependent variable assesses factual knowledge or information, such as the name of the U.S. president. Here a respondent's answer is contrasted with the true answer. The scoring choice is binary: 1 for true, 0 for false for each response. A correlation was coded positive if an increase in foreign TV consumption was associated with an increase in an individual's knowledge about the foreign country.

Beliefs. The dependent variable taps perception(s) or opinion(s), such as the perception of how wealthy Americans are. The variable here does not assess an individual's affect toward the topic but merely his or her perception or opinion. Here a person is asked what he or she thinks about a topic/object/place. In contrast to knowledge, beliefs are subjective. The researcher cannot assess them using a true/false scheme. Instead, researchers typically estimate the level of a respondent's agreement with the subjective belief in question. A correlation was coded positive if an increase in foreign TV consumption was associated with an increase in the level of beliefs about the foreign country, regardless of the normative evaluation of such beliefs.

Attitudinal. The dependent variable taps an affective belief, such as whether a person likes the United States. Here a person is asked how he or she feels toward a topic/object/place. Attitudes are distinguished from beliefs because whereas a person may strongly agree with a belief statement such as "Americans are wealthy," that person may hold a negative attitude toward Americans and may respond that he or she "doesn't like Americans at all." A correlation was coded as positive if an increase in foreign TV consumption was associated with a more positive attitude toward the foreign country.

Behavioral. The dependent variable assesses an individual's past action, such as past purchasing behavior. A correlation was coded positive if an increase in foreign TV consumption was associated with an increase in the purchasing of foreign goods.

Value. Values are beliefs that are known to be commonly held by a large proportion of a population. A belief is considered a value in Society A if that belief is known to be traditionally held by most individuals in Society A. Although societies may hold many values in common, this study considers to be of interest those values that differ between Society A and Society B. A difference exists when the value is present in Society A and not present in Society B. A difference also exists when a value is present in both Societies A and B but the views of individuals in Society A about the value in question are known to differ from the views of individuals in Society B. The dependent variable here typically assesses the respondent's position on particular issues that have been identified by the author of the study as different in the country receiving the message from those in the country sending the message. One example is the issue of "respect for the elderly." It is well-known that in Asian societies, in contrast with U.S. society, the elderly have traditionally been consistently revered. Asking a respondent in Korea to indicate his or her agreement with a statement such as "It is important to respect the elders in my family" functions as an assessment of that person's value for respecting the elderly in his or her family. A correlation was coded as positive if an increase in foreign TV consumption was associated with a preference for the values of the foreign country originating the message.

After coding the obtained articles, we found that beliefs were most often studied ($n = 11$), followed by values ($n = 7$), attitudes ($n = 6$), behaviors ($n = 2$), and knowledge ($n = 2$).

We analyzed each study to determine the effect size for each dependent variable measured in that study. The findings reported here are from those studies that provided either zero-order correlation coefficients in their results sections or some statistic that could be converted into correlation coefficients (e.g., F tests, t tests).[10] If a study had more than one measure of a given dependent variable, then the results were averaged across measures (Hunter & Schmidt, 1990). The individual study results for each of the five dependent variables are listed in Tables 2.2-2.6.

TABLE 2.2
The Impact of Foreign TV: Summary of Behavioral Effects

Author(s)	Sample[a]	Country	Behavior(s)	r
Oliveira (1986)	96	Colombia	use of American consumer products	.21
Kang & Morgan (1988)	226	Korea	wearing jeans	.24

a. Sample size corresponding to the specific relationship(s) is reported when available. Otherwise, total study sample size is reported.

TABLE 2.3
The Impact of Foreign TV: Summary of Knowledge-Based Effects

Author(s)	Sample[a]	Country	Knowledge	r
Payne (1978)	694	United States	knowledge of Canadian issues	.36
Payne & Caron (1982)	646	Canada	knowledge of U.S. issues	.09

a. Sample size corresponding to the specific relationship(s) is reported when available. Otherwise, total study sample size is reported.

TABLE 2.4
The Impact of Foreign TV: Summary of Value-Based Effects

Author(s)	Sample[a]	Country	Values	r
Tsai (1967)	160	Taiwan	general Western versus Eastern values	.08
Skinner (1984)	297	Trinidad	general U.S. values	.33
Kang & Morgan (1988)	226	Korea	Western versus traditional sex role values	.09
Zhao (1989)	990	China	general Western versus traditional values	.09
Wu (1989)	1,214	Taiwan	Western versus traditional sex role values	.06
Geiger (1992)	605	Venezuela	general U.S. versus Venezuelan values	.03
Chaffee et al. (1995)	1,862	China	general Western versus traditional values	.22

a. Sample size corresponding to the specific relationship(s) is reported when available. Otherwise, total study sample size is reported.

Meta-Analysis Results

For each dependent variable, we did an overall meta-analysis of the size of the effect. The results of these analyses are presented in Table 2.7, which gives the following key facts for each dependent variable: (a) the number of studies

TABLE 2.5
The Impact of Foreign TV: Summary of Attitudinal Effects

Author(s)	Sample[a]	Country	Attitude(s)	r
Tsai (1967)	598	Taiwan	attitudes toward U.S. and American cultural products	.13
Payne & Peake (1977)	39	Iceland	choice of U.S. to immigrate	.04
Payne (1978)	414	United States	attitudes toward Canada	−.10
Payne & Caron (1982)	646	Canada	attitudes toward the United States	.08
Oliveira (1986)	96	Belize	attitudes toward consumption of U.S. products	.42
Kang & Morgan (1988)	226	Korea	attitudes toward rock and roll	.12

a. Sample size corresponding to the specific relationship(s) is reported when available. Otherwise, total study sample size is reported.

TABLE 2.6
The Impact of Foreign TV: Summary of Belief-Based Effects

Author(s)	Sample[a]	Country	Belief(s)	r
Tsai (1967)	598	Taiwan	beliefs about Americans	.18
Payne (1978)	414	United States	various beliefs consistent with presentations on Canadian TV	−.01
Pingree & Hawkins (1981)	1,280	Australia	beliefs about the United States and Australia	.05
Skinner (1984)	297	Trinidad	beliefs about the United States	.25
Weimann (1984)	461	Israel	beliefs about the United States	.38
Tan & Suarchavarat (1988)	279	Thailand	beliefs about Americans	.07
Choi (1989)	222	Korea	beliefs about the United States	.05
Wu (1989)	1,214	Taiwan	beliefs about the United States	−.02
Ahn (1990)	705	Korea	beliefs about the United States	.13
El-Koussa & Elasmar (1995)	481	Lebanon	beliefs about the United States	.09
Elasmar & Akaishi (1995)	496	Japan	beliefs about the United States	.05

a. Sample size corresponding to the specific relationship(s) is reported when available. Otherwise, total study sample size is reported.

that measured that variable, (b) the total sample size across those studies, and (c) the average population correlation for those studies. The average population

TABLE 2.7
The Impact of Foreign TV: Meta-Analytic Results

Impact	K	N	Mean Rho	SD Rho	Low	High	χ^2
Behavior	2	322	.23	.00	.23	.23	00.07
Values	7	5,792	.15	.08	.05	.25	47.35*
Attitudes	6	2,019	.11	.08	.00	.21	20.77*
Beliefs	11	6,447	.09	.10	-.04	.22	75.59*
Knowledge	2	1,060	.19	.12	.04	.36	19.85*

*$p < .05$.

correlation is the generalized finding for the effect of foreign TV for the dependent variable.

Table 2.7 also presents several statistics that assess the extent to which findings differ across studies. First, there is the standard deviation of population correlations across studies. From that, high and low estimates can be computed, assuming that the results are normally distributed across studies. Finally, there is the statistical significance test for homogeneity; the chi-square test. Many believe that if the homogeneity test is not significant, then there is no meaningful evidence of variation across studies. However, when the number of studies is small, this significance test—like all significance tests—can have a very high error rate. Given that the number of studies is small in our case, we will focus instead on the standard deviation as the best measure of homogeneity.

Table 2.7 lists the findings by level of definiteness. *Definiteness,* in this case, refers to the relative homogeneity of the correlations for the dependent variable. The findings for studies of behavior ($r = .23$, $z = 4.36$, $p < .01$) show no evidence of variation in the size of the effect across studies. That is, both studies show the same level of effect for behavior. The effect is positive and statistically significant, though modest. Foreign TV increases the purchase of foreign products, especially clothing and other consumer products. Homogeneity, however, does not denote that a meaningful effect has been detected. A correlation of .23 means that foreign TV accounts for only 5% of the variance in audience buying behavior.

For the other four dependent variables, the average effect sizes are also positive, although there is variation across studies. The average correlations are as follows: for values, $r = .14$ ($z = 4.24$, $p < .001$); for attitudes, $r = .09$ ($z = 1.86$, $p > .05$); for beliefs, $r = .09$ ($z = 2.81$, $p < .01$); for knowledge, $r = .20$ ($z = 2.22$, $p < .05$).

Usually, interpretation of the average is better put off until a study is made of the cause for such variation. Thus, we did an analysis of potential causes of variation (moderators) for each of these four dependent variables.

TABLE 2.8
Moderator Analysis for Values: Sample Type

Moderator	K	N	Mean Rho	SD Rho	Low	High	χ^2
General population	4	3,754	.16	.08	.18	.27	31.97*
Students	3	1,600	.07	.00	.07	.07	00.21

*$p < .05$.

The moderator variable that we considered most likely to be relevant is that of audience segment, specifically age. Are older viewers either more or less likely to be influenced? In the case of knowledge, such a moderator analysis was not possible because only two studies had investigated a knowledge effect, and both had used adult audiences (see Table 2.3). For the three remaining dependent variables, we could classify most studies in terms of the type of sample used: student or general population. The two types were used as proxies for age.

Table 2.8 presents the moderator analysis for values. The mean effect size was .16 for the general population and only .07 for students. The results for student samples were homogeneous across studies. The results for the general population showed some variation ($SD = .08$) across studies, though it is virtually certain that all effects are positive. The mean effects suggest that foreign TV has less effect on the attitudes of young students than on adults, although the difference is not statistically significant ($z = 1.5, p > .05$).

Table 2.9 presents the moderator analysis for beliefs. The mean effect size was .12 for the general population and only .09 for students. The results for student samples were less homogeneous ($SD = .09$) than those for the general population ($SD = .07$). It is virtually certain, however, that all effects are positive. The mean effects would suggest that foreign TV has less effect on the beliefs of students than on those of adults, although the difference is not statistically significant ($z = .428, p > .05$).

Table 2.10 presents the moderator analysis for attitudes. The mean effect size was .12 for both the general population and students. The results for student samples were homogeneous across studies. The results for the general population showed some variation ($SD = .10$) across studies, though most results are positive. The mean effects suggest that for attitudes, there are no differences between adults and students ($z = .01, p > .05$).

We obtained similar results when we carried out a moderator analysis by grouping studies in terms of their geographic location. We considered the existence of other potential moderators (e.g., language), but the study characteristics did not permit their examination. In the following section we discuss the results of our meta-analysis and their implications.

TABLE 2.9
Moderator Analysis for Beliefs: Sample Type

Moderator	K	N	Mean Rho	SD Rho	Low	High	χ^2
General population	2	519	.16	.08	.06	.26	05.34*
Grade/ high school/ university	7	5,053	.06	.05	−.001	.13	20.51*

*$p < .05$.

TABLE 2.10
Moderator Analysis for Attitudes: Sample Type

Moderator	K	N	Mean Rho	SD Rho	Low	High	χ^2
General population	2	742	.12	.10	−.01	.25	09.94*
Grade/ high school	3	863	.12	.00	.12	.12	00.31

*$p < .05$.

DISCUSSION

The results of this endeavor reveal that empirical studies about the impact of foreign TV on a domestic audience are scarce. This result, by itself, is surprising, given the interest in this topic among policy makers and researchers. We found a total of 36 studies that met the most basic criteria set at the beginning of this research effort. Of these, 27 studies used direct measures of foreign TV exposure and were thus considered for the meta-analysis segment of this investigation. At the beginning of this endeavor, we identified two specific research questions and two expectations about our research results; we address these research questions and expectations below.

What Is the Average Effect Size
of Cross-Border TV Across Studies?

Our meta-analysis revealed weak, positive correlations between exposure to foreign TV and viewers' knowledge, attitudes, beliefs, values, and behaviors.

Although the correlations for behavior ($k = 2$) were homogeneous, the correlations for the other four dependent variables were not. This means that effect sizes differed across studies. Based upon the concept that a message will be received differently by various audience members, we had expected such variation. Because it is usually preferred to put off the interpretation of the average correlations until further investigation of this variation, we carried out a moderator analysis, and age was identified as a potential moderator. The moderator analysis, however, revealed that the effects of foreign TV on students did not significantly differ from the effects on general audiences.

Besides the existence of an audience segment moderator, however, there could also be other explanations for variations in the correlations obtained. Among such explanations are artifacts and study imperfections. Chief among such artifacts is measurement error. The fact that only a few studies reported reliability coefficients in their findings makes it impossible to assess the relative influence of measurement error on the homogeneity of the correlations. This is especially true in the case of the predictor variable "foreign TV consumption." In most cases a single estimate of this predictor was used, which makes it impossible to estimate the measurement error associated with this variable.

Perhaps there are true differences across studies. These differences could be attributed to real disparities across samples or real discrepancies due to an interaction between geographic location and the timing of a study. Such possibilities can be investigated when more studies become available to permit further breakdown of results along geographic and chronological lines.

What Does the Size of the Average Effect of Cross-Border TV Mean to International Communication Scholars?

Although the source of variation in effect size across studies is unexplained, the results of this meta-analysis reveal a pattern of positive correlations for all effect types. Assuming that the average correlation is the best available estimate of effect size across studies, these findings can be summarized as follows:

1. Exposure to foreign TV increases the purchase of foreign products, especially clothing and other consumer products. The size of this increase, however, is very small, because foreign TV accounts for only 5% of the variation in foreign product purchasing.
2. Overall, exposure to foreign TV increases the tendency of audience members to hold values similar to those present in the country producing the foreign message. The size of the increase, however, is very small, because foreign TV accounts for only 2% of the variation in audience values.
3. Overall, there is no statistically significant relationship between exposure to foreign TV and the likelihood that audience members will hold positive attitudes toward the country originating the foreign message.
4. Overall, exposure to foreign TV increases the strength of audience beliefs about the country originating the foreign message. The size of this increase, however, is very small, because foreign TV accounts for only .08% of the variation in beliefs. The reader needs to be cautioned that a positive correlation between

exposure to foreign TV and beliefs about the United States, for example, does not necessarily mean that exposure leads to positive beliefs about the United States. This is true because the belief type could very well be normatively negative (e.g., violent society). In this case the positive correlation indicates simply an increase in normatively negative beliefs. The distinction between normatively positive beliefs and normatively negative beliefs could not be made in this study because it is very difficult to achieve a consensus on what constitutes negative or positive beliefs from a normative point of view.

5. Overall, exposure to foreign TV increases audience knowledge about the country originating the message. The size of the increase, however, is very small, because foreign TV accounts for only 4% of the variation in knowledge.

Based on the concept that foreign TV programs embody a tool of cultural imperialism, we had expected our meta-analysis to reveal that foreign television programs have strong effects on the domestic audience members who view them. The results summarized above reveal that this is not the case. At most, foreign TV exposure may have a very weak impact upon audience members. This result contradicts the assertions of Herbert Schiller and his colleagues, who have long warned against the dangers of cultural imperialism. Given this assessment, the very weak and positive correlations obtained in our meta-analysis cannot be used to support the tacit assumption made by policy makers that imported messages have strong and negative impacts upon the audiences in the importing countries. Our results are more consistent with the prediction made by Browne (1967) and echoed by Salwen (1991) that the effects are most likely to vary. Our results are also consistent with the assessments made by Yaple and Korzenny (1989) and Hur (1982), who argue that the effects are either nonexistent or very weak.

Although we found a pattern of positive correlations in our meta-analysis, not only is the size of these correlations very small, but we can also question the assumption of directional causality embedded in the literature. It is unclear whether exposure to imported television leads to the effect types or whether the existence of these effects, due to some other variables, leads individuals to seek exposure to foreign TV.

A quick review of the theoretical frameworks utilized by the studies summarized in our meta-analysis reveals that all the theories identified are directional, with the arrow of causality pointing from TV to the individual. There is a very real possibility, however, that the arrow may actually point from the individual to the TV programs chosen by that individual. Television, after all, is not the only source of information about foreign countries. Family members (including those studying, working, or residing abroad), peers (including those who have family members abroad), religious leaders (including those affiliated with institutions abroad), dominant political ideologies within particular groups, as well as other factors, could very well influence viewers' attitudes, beliefs, knowledge, and behaviors. These, in turn, may influence exposure to or avoidance of foreign TV programs. In this case, the actual exposure would be influenced by knowledge, beliefs, attitudes, or behaviors, and not the other way around. Although this possibility is very real, it is not specifically addressed in any of the studies reviewed and is certainly not covered by any of the theoretical frameworks chosen by the researchers. Given the above reasoning, however, the very weak effects found in this meta-analysis could very well be indicative of the influence of existing knowledge, beliefs, values, or behaviors upon exposure to foreign TV programs.

The empirical studies in this area are apparently still at an early stage. The objective of this early research was to explore whether foreign TV has an impact. The use of standard media-impact theoretical frameworks across cultural contexts in the studies reviewed is indicative of this early research stage. The next stage needs to examine whether effects vary across subgroups along such cultural lines as differences in religion, language, or other cleavages within the cultural context being studied. This second stage will probably result in more culturally specific theories, which may enhance our understanding of the impact of foreign TV.

On the basis of our review of the studies composing this body of literature, we strongly recommend that researchers who conduct future studies do the following:

1. Clearly define predictor and criterion variables conceptually and operationally,
2. attempt to use similar predictor and criterion variables across studies and authors,
3. measure several controls to eliminate alternative explanation of results,
4. use multiple estimates for each variable, and
5. report reliability coefficients pertaining to each variable.

By providing a set of best available estimates for each effect type, we hope that this meta-analysis sheds light on the link between individuals' exposure to foreign TV and their attitudes, beliefs, values, behaviors, and/or knowledge. We also hope that the results of our meta-analysis, based upon the available body of literature, provide researchers with a solid background for future studies and inspire other researchers to carry out periodic updates of this analysis.

NOTES

1. This study is an extension and update of earlier work by Elasmar (1991, 1993), Elasmar and Straubhaar (1993), and Elasmar, Hunter, and Straubhaar (1995).

2. The findings of studies conducted about the impact of foreign TV on consumer behavior, for example, would yield information about the likely economic impact of foreign TV on local versus imported products.

3. The term *foreign TV* encompasses the term *cross-border TV*, as any television signal that is transmitted from Country A to Country B is foreign to Country B. We use the term *foreign TV*

here because it also encompasses television content that arrives in Country B from Country A through channels other than direct transmission, such as program importation or home video release. Because the effect of interest to this study is that of the TV program's origin, regardless of its mode of transmission, we use the term *foreign TV.*

4. The term *empirical* in this context is defined as systematic observations based upon the method of science (as opposed to the other methods of knowing identified by Kerlinger, 1986) and utilizing statistical analytic methods.

5. Database searches were performed using the Dialog information services. Databases searched were ERIC, PsycINFO, and Sociological Abstracts. The following indexes were searched manually: *Current Contents in the Social and Behavioral Sciences, Psychological Abstracts,* and *Sociological Abstracts.*

6. Letters were sent to mass communication departments known to conduct research on international communication during 1991. We are grateful to Professor Joseph Straubhaar of Brigham Young University, who helped carry out these contacts. In addition, from 1991 to 1994, the first author contacted researchers specializing in international communication at various professional conferences and asked for leads on unpublished studies about the topic at hand.

7. Whereas conference papers, theses, and dissertations were obtained through a multimethod search, our finding published articles depended on whether they were included in a database by early January 1995.

8. The possibility of bias toward significant findings is present in journal articles because journals tend to select for publication studies with effects over those without any effects. In this investigation we attempted to counter this possibility of bias by collecting unpublished studies, including master's theses and conference papers, that had not been subjected to a selection process that favors studies finding effects over those that do not.

9. This may limit the generalizability of the findings, as students may or may not be representative of the population at large.

10. Partial correlations or standardized regression coefficients were used as best available estimates when no zero-order correlation coefficients or any other convertible statistics were reported.

REFERENCES

Note: Asterisks indicate studies included in the meta-analysis.

*Ahn, Y. (1990). *Images of life in America: The relationships of Korean adolescents' U.S. television viewing and perceptions of American reality.* Unpublished master's thesis, Michigan State University, East Lansing.
*Barnett, G. A., & McPhail, T. L. (1980). An examination of the relationship of United States television and Canadian identity. *International Journal of Intercultural Relations, 4,* 219-232.
*Beattie, E. (1967). In Canada's centennial year, U.S. mass media probed. *Journalism Quarterly, 44,* 667-672.
Beltran, L. R. S. (1978a). Communication and cultural domination: USA-Latin American case. *Media Asia, 5,* 183-192.
Beltran, L. R. S. (1978b). TV etchings in the minds of Latin Americans: Conservatism, materialism and conformism. *Gazette, 24,* 61-85.
Bouwman, H., & Stappers, J. (1982). The Dutch violence profile: A replication of Gerbner's message system analysis. In G. Melischek, K. E. Rosengren, & J. Stappers (Eds.), *Cultural indicators: An international symposium* (pp. 101-125). Vienna: Verlag der Osterreichischen Akademie der Wissenschaften.

Browne, D. R. (1967). Problems in international television. *Journal of Communication, 17*(3), 198-210.

*Chaffee, S., Zhongdang, P., & Chu, G. (1995). *Western media in China: Audience and influence.* Paper presented at the annual meeting of the International Communication Association, Albuquerque, NM.

*Choi, J. (1989). *Use and effects of foreign television programming: A study of American armed forces television in Korea.* Unpublished doctoral dissertation, Michigan State University, East Lansing.

*Coldevin, G. O. (1976). Some effects of frontier television on a Canadian Eskimo community. *Journalism Quarterly, 53,* 34-39.

*Coldevin, G. O. (1979). Satellite television and cultural replacement among Canadian Eskimos. *Communication Research, 6,* 115-134.

*Coldevin, G. O., & Wilson, T. C. (1985). Effects of a decade of satellite television in the Canadian Arctic. *Journal of Cross-Cultural Psychology, 16,* 329-354.

*Day, P. (1975). Cultural imperialism in New Zealand. *Australian and New Zealand Journal of Sociology, 11,* 43-45.

Dizard, W. (1965). The political impact of television abroad. *Journal of Broadcasting, 9,* 195-214.

Elasmar, M. G. (1991). *Foreign TV impact: A systematic review of empirical studies.* Unpublished manuscript, Michigan State University, East Lansing.

Elasmar, M. G. (1993). *Analyzing the international direct broadcast satellite debate: Origins, decision-making factors and social concerns.* Unpublished doctoral dissertation, Michigan State University, East Lansing.

*Elasmar, M. G., & Akaishi, E. (1995). *The influence of American television on young Japanese females' beliefs about the United States.* Unpublished manuscript, Boston University.

Elasmar, M. G., Hunter, J. E., & Straubhaar, J. D. (1995). *Quantifying the size of the impact of foreign TV on a domestic audience.* Paper presented at the annual meeting of the Broadcast Education Association, Las Vegas, NV.

Elasmar, M. G., & Straubhaar, J. D. (1993). *Toward a meta-analysis of foreign TV effects research.* Paper presented at the annual meeting of the Speech Communication Association, Miami, FL.

*El-Koussa, H. H., & Elasmar, M. G. (1995). *The influence of U.S. TV programs on the perceptions of U.S. social reality among students in Lebanon.* Paper presented at the annual meeting of the Broadcast Education Association, Las Vegas, NV.

*Elliott, L. S. (1994). *Comparing cultural influences of U.S. and Mexican television in Mexico.* Paper presented at the annual meeting of the Association for Education in Journalism and Mass Communication, Atlanta, GA.

*Geiger, S. F. (1992). *Social reality in the Third World: The influence of American television on Venezuelan values.* Paper presented at the annual meeting of the International Communication Association, Miami, FL.

Goldsen, R. K., & Bibliowicz, A. (1976). Plaza Sesamo: "Neutral" language or "cultural assault." *Journal of Communication, 26*(2), 124-125.

Goonasekara, A. (1987). The influence of television on cultural values—with special reference to Third World countries. *Media Asia, 14,* 7-12.

*Granzberg, G. (1980). Psychological impact of television among Algonkians of Central Canada. In G. Granzberg & J. Steinbring (Eds.), *Television and the Canadian Indian* (pp. 321-359). Manitoba: University of Winnipeg.

Hadad, I. (1978). Media and international misunderstanding. *Phaedrus, 5,* 17-19.

Hedinson, E., & Windahl, S. (1982). Cultivation analysis: A Swedish illustration. In G. Melischek, K. E. Rosengren & J. Stappers (Eds.), *Cultural indicators: An international symposium* (pp. 204-227). Vienna: Verlag der Osterreichischen Akademie der Wissenschaften.

Hunter, J. E., & Schmidt, F. L. (1990). *Methods of meta-analysis: Correcting error and bias in research findings.* Newbury Park, CA: Sage.

Hur, K. K. (1982). International mass communication research: A critical review of theory and methods. In M. Burgoon (Ed.), *Communication yearbook 6* (pp. 531-554). Beverly Hills, CA: Sage.

*Kang, G. J., & Morgan, M. (1988). Cultural clash: Impact of U.S. television in Korea. *Journalism Quarterly, 65,* 431-438.

*Kapoor, S., & Kang, J. (1993). *Cultural effects of U.S. television programs in India and Korea.* Paper presented at the annual meeting of the Speech Communication Association, Miami, FL.

Kerlinger, F. N. (1986). *Foundations of behavioral research.* New York: Holt, Rinehart & Winston.

Lee, C. C. (1980). *Media imperialism reconsidered.* Beverly Hills, CA: Sage.

Morgan, M., & Shanahan, J. (1992). Comparative cultivation analysis: Television and adolescents in Argentina and Taiwan. In F. Korzenny & S. Ting-Toomey (Eds.), *Mass media effects across cultures* (pp. 173-197). Newbury Park, CA: Sage.

Morgan, M., & Signorielli, N. (1990). Cultivation analysis: Conceptualization and methodology. In N. Signorielli & M. Morgan (Eds.), *Cultivation analysis: New directions in media effects research* (pp. 13-34). Newbury Park, CA: Sage.

*Oliveira, O. S. (1986). Satellite TV and dependency: An empirical approach. *Gazette, 38,* 127-145.

*Payne, D. E. (1978). Cross-national diffusion: The effects of Canadian TV on rural Minnesota viewers. *American Sociological Review, 43,* 740-756.

*Payne, D. E., & Caron, A. H. (1982). Anglophone Canadian and American mass media: Use and effects on Quebecois adults. *Communication Research, 9,* 113-144.

*Payne, D. E., & Peake, C. A. (1977). Cultural diffusion: The role of U.S. TV in Iceland. *Journalism Quarterly, 54,* 523-531.

*Pingree, S., & Hawkins, R. (1981). U.S. programs on Australian television: The cultivation effect. *Journal of Communication, 31*(1), 97-105.

*Saito, S. (1994). *Television and perceptions of American society in Japan.* Paper presented at the annual meeting of the Association for Education in Journalism and Mass Communication, Atlanta, GA.

Salwen, M. B. (1991). Cultural imperialism: A media effects approach. *Critical Studies in Mass Communication, 8,* 29-38.

Schiller, H. I. (1969). *Mass communication and American empire.* Boston: Beacon.

Schiller, H. I. (1991). Not yet the post-imperialist era. *Critical Studies in Mass Communication, 8,* 13-28.

*Skinner, E. C. (1984). *Foreign TV program viewing and dependency: A case study of U.S. television viewing in Trinidad and Tobago.* Unpublished doctoral dissertation, Michigan State University, East Lansing.

*Snyder, L., Roser, C., & Chaffee, S. (1991). Foreign media and the desire to emigrate from Belize. *Journal of Communication, 41*(1), 117-132.

Straubhaar, J. D., Heeter, C., Greenberg, B. S., Ferreira, L., Wicks, R. H., & Lau, T. Y. (1992). What makes news: Western, socialist, and Third-World television newscasts compared in eight countries. In F. Korzenny & S. Ting-Toomey (Eds.), *Mass media effects across cultures* (pp. 89-109). Newbury Park, CA: Sage.

*Tan, A. S., Dong, Q., & Li, W. (1994). *American television and movies in China: Exploring socialization effects from a functional perspective.* Paper presented at the annual meeting of the Association for Education in Journalism and Mass Communication, Atlanta, GA.

*Tan, A. S., Gibson, T., & Fujioka, Y. (1993). *American television in Japan and Russia.* Paper presented at the annual meeting of the Speech Communication Association, Miami, FL.

*Tan, A. S., Li, S., & Simpson, C. (1986). American TV and social stereotypes of Americans in Taiwan and Mexico. *Journalism Quarterly, 63,* 809-814.

*Tan, A. S., & Suarchavarat, K. (1988). American TV and social stereotypes of Americans in Thailand. *Journalism Quarterly, 65,* 648-654.

*Tan, A. S., Tan, G. K., & Tan, A. S. (1987). American TV in the Philippines: A test of cultural impact. *Journalism Quarterly, 64,* 65-72, 144.

*Tate, E. D., & Trach, B. (1980). The effects of United States television programs upon Canadian beliefs about legal procedures. *Canadian Journal of Communication, 6,* 1-17.

Tracey, M. (1985). The poisoned chalice? International television and the idea of dominance. *Proceedings of the American Academy of Arts and Sciences, USA, 114,* 17-56.

*Tsai, M. (1967). *A study of the effects of American television programs on children in Formosa.* Unpublished master's thesis, Michigan State University, East Lansing.

*Veii, V. S. (1988). *Foreign television entertainment programs viewing and cultural imperialism: A case study of U.S. television entertainment programs viewing in Windhoek, Namibia.* Unpublished doctoral dissertation, Michigan State University, East Lansing.

*Weimann, G. (1984). Images of life in America: The impact of American TV in Israel. *International Journal of Intercultural Relations, 8,* 185-197.

*Werner, A. (1981). Television and attitudes toward foreign countries: A report on a survey on Scandinavian children. *Political Communication and Persuasion, 1,* 307-314.

*Wu, Y. K. (1989). *Television and the value systems of Taiwan's adolescents: A cultivation analysis.* Unpublished doctoral dissertation, University of Massachusetts, Amherst.

Yaple, P., & Korzenny, F. (1989). Electronic mass media effects across cultures. In M. K. Asante & W. B. Gudykunst (Eds.), *Handbook of international and intercultural communication* (pp. 295-317). Newbury Park, CA: Sage.

*Zhao, X. (1989). Effects of foreign media use, government and traditional influences on Chinese women's values. *Revue Europeenne des Sciences Sociales, 27,* 239-251.

CHAPTER CONTENTS

3   Selling the Sex That Sells: Mapping the Evolution of Gender Advertising Research Across Three Decades

VICKIE RUTLEDGE SHIELDS
Bowling Green State University

Advertising images pervade our everyday lives, bombarding us with snapshots of what we supposedly lack and what we need to fill the void. Images of idealized bodies, particularly female bodies, are some of the most dominant and pervasive messages produced by advertisers. Their pervasiveness has called forth popular and academic discourses foregrounding the crucial issue of how these images are implicated in the ongoing construction, negotiation, and maintenance of gender identities and social relationships between women and men. This chapter provides an intellectual history of gender advertising research across the past three decades by reviewing empirical and theoretical advances in the depiction, representation, and decoding of gender images in advertising. This evolution in intellectual work on gender and advertising reflects not only the historical location of academic research at different times and geographic locations, but also its often uneasy relationship to feminist politics. Finally, the current ferment in gender advertising research is discussed.

ADVERTISING is a key institution of socialization in modern/postmodern society (e.g., Ewen, 1976; Jhally, 1987; O'Barr, 1994; Schudson, 1984; Wernick, 1991). Fueled by the perennial struggle to market goods and services and by the development of a multimedia environment, advertising images increasingly pervade our everyday lives, bombarding us with snapshots of what we supposedly lack and what we need to fill the void. What we supposedly lack typically has more to do with the lifestyles,

AUTHOR'S NOTE: I thank Peter Shields, Brenda Dervin, and two anonymous reviewers for their thoughtful comments on earlier versions of this chapter.

Correspondence and requests for reprints: Vickie Rutledge Shields, Department of Telecommunications, Bowling Green State University, 322 West Hall, Bowling Green, OH 43403; e-mail vshield@bgnet.bgsu.edu looks, and aspirations advertisers seek to associate with the products they are trying to sell than with the inherent qualities and attributes of the products themselves (e.g., Jhally, 1987; Kellner, 1990; Leiss, Kline, & Jhally, 1986; Williamson, 1978). Almost from its inception, mass advertising has played a central role in perpetuating particular definitions—often in the form of stereotypes—of gender roles and gender relationships. Throughout the history of advertising, messages detailing the perfect female—her beauty, her societal roles, and her sexuality—have occupied a central role. These messages, used to sell everything from cosmetics to cars to beverages, provide prescriptions for how women should look and be looked at, how they should feel, and how they are expected to act. In short, these messages prescribe particular gender identities to which women should aspire. They also prescribe how men should relate to women.

An interdisciplinary interest in gender and advertising has reached ascendancy over the past 20 to 25 years. The academic fields of communication, journalism, sociology, anthropology, and women's studies all have offered theories and analyses of the relationship between gender and advertising in modern/postmodern societies. Broadly, the evolution in gender advertising research reflects many of the same trends as feminist theory across the social sciences and humanities. Inherent in this evolution has been a journey from a liberal conception of gender stereotyping (how women are treated unfairly and unequally) to a radical feminist conception (how men and women differ inherently and biologically), to a socialist feminist conception (how power structures hold inequities in place), to a discourse conception (how gender is created, maintained, and changed in discourse) (Dervin & Shields, in press). The evolution in intellectual work on gender and advertising over the past three decades reflects not only the historical location of academic research at different times and in different geographic locations, but also academic research's often uneasy relationship to the feminist political movement—a tension highlighted in this review.

My overall purpose in this review is to offer a new synthesis for communication scholars by mapping the evolution of gender and advertising research across the social sciences and humanities in the past three decades. More specifically, I offer an intellectual history that articulates the development of conceptual tools used in the analysis of gender images in advertising. I develop this intellectual history by reviewing empirical and theoretical advances in the depiction, representation, and decoding of gender images in advertising. The review concludes with a discussion of the current ferment in this area of research and directions for future study.

FOUNDING PERSPECTIVES

Serious scholarship on gender and advertising flourished in the 1970s (some influential work, such as Betty Friedan's *The Feminine Mystique,*

1963, precedes this date). In a climate of second-wave feminist politics, increasing support for an Equal Rights Amendment, and an increase in the number of female researchers in higher education, scholars in departments of mass communication, journalism, and marketing raced to produce empirical analyses of sex role stereotyping found in print and television. Through the use of content analysis, these scholars investigated questions pertaining to gender difference and inequality within the content of ads. This type of research fit in nicely with the empirical research paradigm already established in communication studies, while serving a political imperative (Rakow, 1986). In the midst of this flurry of content analysis research, Erving Goffman published his own empirical manifesto on the nature of advertising portrayals, titled *Gender Advertisements* (1976). Goffman, however, asked very different questions of his data than sex roles researchers asked of theirs, and he also employed a very different method for analyzing his results. Guided by the tenets of his chosen theoretical framework, symbolic interactionism, Goffman suggested that the most relevant questions we can ask of advertising are as follows: Of what aspects of real life do advertisements provide us a fair picture? What social effects do advertisements have upon the lives purportedly pictured in them?

The sex roles approach and Goffman's symbolic interactionist approach together provide the base of textual analysis upon which most other textual analyses of gender in advertising have been built, or against which researchers have reacted. An understanding of the origins and critiques of sex roles research on advertising portrayals provides a historical frame for an understanding of the impetus of current research. Further, and highly relevant to this study, the findings of sex roles research, invested with liberal feminist values, labels, and language, have filtered more readily into the popular discourses of our culture than virtually any other gender advertising research to date. Therefore, audience members are likely to employ the discourses made popular through sex roles research when interpreting the content and context of gender advertisements for themselves and in society.

Goffman's research was unique at the time for employing a method now labeled *semiotic content analysis.* Goffman's analysis focused on message structures across the entire discourse of print advertisements containing gender components. Goffman revealed patterns in messages about gender that, when repeated constantly and consistently, provide a picture of reality that seems natural and real. His work provides the base for textual analyses, to be reviewed later in this chapter, that are compatible with the tenets of semiotic content analysis and symbolic interactionism, such as poststructuralist and psychoanalytic approaches. Prominent feminist scholars concerned with gender and advertising, such as Jean Kilbourne, have built their highly persuasive and widely circulated findings on the nature of gender in advertising on Goffman's original categories (see Lazarus, 1987). Therefore, sex roles research and Goffman's original study on gender advertisements are presented here as the cornerstones of research on the nature of advertising portrayals of gender.

Sex Roles Research and Content Analysis

The research approach now referred to as *sex roles research* focuses on sex role stereotyping in advertising, both in print and on television. Through the use of content analysis, this approach sets out to show the inequality of male and female representation in advertising. Specifically, sex roles research has revealed that women in advertising are portrayed within restrictive categories, such as housewife or sex object, and that advertising reflects a false picture of women's real lives (see Courtney & Whipple, 1974).

In the early 1970s, the subfield of mass communication witnessed a surge in attention to sex role stereotyping in the mass media that peaked between 1971 and 1979. This rush to research the images of gender portrayal across the mass media can be attributed to at least three major factors. The first was the reemergence of feminist writing in the academy, spurred on by Betty Friedan's *The Feminine Mystique* (1963). Friedan was one of the first to raise pointed questions about the portrayal of women in women's magazines and the advertisements contained therein. She saw these images on "women's pages" not only as documentation to support her arguments, but as powerful shaping forces in the social fabric and a "critical moving force in creating for woman a view of her ideal self" (Courtney, 1983, p. 4).

Friedan found that the portrayal of women had changed considerably between the 1930s and the 1950s. In the late 1930s, "women were more likely to be portrayed in fiction as autonomous heroines seeking to fulfill their own personal goals, but as the forties progressed, the autonomous heroine gave way to the glorified housewife, praised and rewarded for her efforts to run the household and nurture others" (Courtney, 1983, p. 3). According to Friedan, advertising, perhaps even more than the magazines themselves, reflected (if not fostered and perpetuated) a limited lifestyle for U.S. women by portraying household care and the embodiment of the roles of ideal mother and wife as the ultimate goals for women. These roles constituted women's most creative opportunities.

Friedan's insights highlight a second factor driving the insurgence of sex roles research in the early 1970s. Advertising and print journalism received special attention because, more than ever, women were dominating many of the consumer groups targeted by advertisers; common sense dictated that the ways in which women viewed themselves in ads might have great impacts on the effectiveness of commercial marketing campaigns (Lundstrom & Sciglimpaglia, 1977; Morrison & Sherman, 1972; Wise, King, & Merenski, 1974; Wortzel & Frisbie, 1974). This research was concerned with advertising "effectiveness," examining whether, and under what conditions, more progressive, less stereotyped portrayals may be preferred to traditional ones. Of foremost concern was the measurement of causal relationships among women's heightened attitudes about "women's liberation," role portrayal, and product desirability. Several studies, for instance, hypothesized that women would view products more positively if the role portrayals offered in the advertising were those of women in jobs or careers (Wortzel & Frisbie, 1974).

Taken as a group, these studies resulted in inconclusive findings about segments of consumers who were more or less in favor of progressive role portrayals. Traditional roles are not displeasing to everyone, but do tend to irritate many consumer segments. One consistent finding that emerged from this research showed that "the sex of the product representative in the advertisement, the role portrayed, and the setting for the advertisement should match the product image" (Courtney, 1983, p. 98). Realism in advertising was important, therefore, whether the roles were more traditional or progressive in style.

Mainstream scholarship in gender and advertising has offered rich insight into the "messages" of advertising texts, beginning in the 1970s, through voluminous content analyses of sex roles and gender stereotyping.[1] Courtney and Lockeretz's (1971) content analysis of the portrayal of men and women in print advertising was one of the first and also one of the most widely cited and replicated research studies on the subject. These authors concluded that four general stereotypes of women existed across advertisements in eight major general-interest magazines in the years 1958, 1968, and 1978:

1. A woman's place is in the home.
2. Women do not make important decisions or do important things.
3. Women are dependent and need men's protection.
4. Men regard women primarily as sex objects. (cited in Courtney & Whipple, 1983, p. 7)

Television content analyses showed very similar results. These studies tended to report two main findings: (a) The prevalent female roles are maternal, housekeeping, and aesthetic; and (b) compared with men and boys, women and girls are seen less frequently, are shown to have different characteristics (less authoritative, decisive, powerful, rational), are housewives or in subservient, low-status occupations, and are depicted as less intelligent (Ferrante, Haynes, & Kingsley, 1988; Kimball, 1986; Lazier & Kendrick, 1993).

Studies charting progress in the images of women in advertising in the next few years also charted new problems. Wagner and Banos (1973) found that the percentage of women in working roles had increased, but that women in nonworking roles were being seen less in family settings and more in decorative capacities. Further, women were seldom depicted interacting with one another or making major purchases without a male also in the picture. Wagner and Banos concluded that stereotypes predating the women's movement remained and that advertising was not keeping up with the times in failing to portray realistically the diversity of women's roles (see also Belkaoui & Belkaoui, 1976).

Little attention was paid to male sex role portrayals in print ads at this time, with the exception of one major study replicating Courtney and Lockeretz's (1971) sample from a male standpoint (Wohleter & Lammers, 1980) and one minor study (Skelly & Lundstrom, 1981). These studies found that men were more likely to be shown working outside the home and to be involved in major purchases of expensive goods. All of these studies concluded that the roles of men and women in print advertisements had changed little over 20 years (Busby, 1975; Dominick & Rauch, 1972; Fejes, 1992).

In the 1980s and early 1990s, fewer sex roles studies of gender stereotypes in advertising were conducted than was the case in the 1970s. More recent empirical studies have investigated highly specialized areas, such as "women's adoption of the business uniform" (Saunders & Stead, 1986), sex role stereotyping of children on TV (Peirce, 1989), women in advertisements in medical journals (Hawkins & Aber, 1993), perception studies (Rossi & Rossi, 1985), achievement studies (Geis, Brown, Jennings, & Porter, 1984), and self-consciousness variables studies (Gould, 1987). Additional recent studies have examined cross-cultural or international perspectives on gender representation in advertising (see Furnham, 1989; Gilly, 1988; Griffin, Viswanath, & Schwartz, 1992; Mazzella, Durkin, Cerini, & Buralli, 1992).

Most recent sex roles research, however, has used the vast quantity of data collected over the past 15 to 20 years either (a) to advance theory on sex roles representation and the possible debilitating "effects" that stereotypical images can have for society or (b) to revisit the early research, replicating studies to see whether advertising images have progressed in the past 20 years (Whipple & Courtney, 1985). According to Lazier and Kendrick (1993), it is still important to study stereotypical portrayals of women because these portrayals are not only debilitating and demeaning, but they continue to be "inaccurate." Advertisements today "do not reflect the significant strides (both socially and statistically) made by women in the past two decades into the work force" (p. 201). Further, women are still not seen as decision makers for major purchases (although women actually make more family financial decisions than do men) and, finally, "by using outdated stereotypes, ads are simplistically ignoring the complexities of modern women's lives" (p. 201).

Lovdal (1989), in a study of 354 television commercials, replicated and extended the benchmark work of O'Donnell and O'Donnell (1978). Lovdal found that men are still dominant in advertising voice-overs and that men are portrayed in three times the variety of occupational roles as are women. Other recent research has found that men are more likely than women to be portrayed in independent roles; women are still portrayed primarily in a variety of stereotyped roles, such as wife, mother, bride, waitress, actress, and dancer (Bretl & Cantor, 1988; Gilly, 1988, Lazier & Kendrick, 1993). Even the

TABLE 3.1
Comparison of Female Portrayals in 1973 and 1986

| | Consciousness Scale for Sexism (%) | |
| | 1973 | 1986 |
Level	(N = 447)	(N = 530)
1. Put her down	27	37
2. Keep her in her place	48	35
3. Give her two places	4	3
4. Acknowledge equality	19	15
5. Nonstereotypic	2	11

SOURCE: Reprinted from Lazier and Kendrick (1993, p. 205).

feminist publication *Ms.*, whose editorial policy states that the magazine will not run advertising harmful to women, has not fared well under the scrutiny of content analysis (McCracken, 1993; McKinnon, 1995). In a study published in 1990, Ferguson, Kreshel, and Tinkham found that a substantial proportion of the advertising in *Ms.* promoted products considered harmful, such as cigarettes and alcohol. Further, although images of women in subordinate and decorative capacities had decreased, the number of ads depicting women as alluring sex objects was increasing.

In 1988, Lazier-Smith conducted research replicating three major studies by Pingree, Hawkins, Butler, and Paisley (1976), Goffman (1976), and Kilbourne (see Lazarus, 1987). In this study, Lazier-Smith replicated the method, categories, and procedures of Pingree and Hawkins's Consciousness Scale of Sexism and reapplied it, along with Goffman's sexist categories, to one full year of advertisements in *Ms., Playboy, Time,* and *Newsweek.* Lazier-Smith found no significant change between the 1970s analyses and representations in 1986. Some results of this study are presented in Table 3.1.

In updated research, Lazier and Kendrick (1993) report that preliminary results show a decrease in Level 1 (sex object/decoration/bimbo) portrayals. Further, "Goffman traits from the 1988 study did show some improvement, with three categories (relative size, function ranking, and family scenes) appearing so infrequently that they could be considered to no longer apply" (p. 205). However, the categories applying to women's subordination to men are still as prevalent.

Critiques of Sex Roles Research

The critics of sex roles research are many. However, perhaps the most important critiques to have an impact on the direction of research on gender and advertising have come from within feminist academe (Janus, 1977; Lott, 1981; Putnam, 1982; Steeves, 1987). These critics purport that not only do conceptual or operational flaws need analyzing in this research, the very assumptions underpinning these studies are of consequence—assumptions these critics call the *liberal feminist bias.*

Liberal feminism rests on assumptions inherent in liberal theory, which assumes that the state should act to assure equal opportunity for all in the pursuit of rational mental development. Liberal feminists focus their efforts on creating and changing laws that promote women's opportunities for professional success and intellectual growth, such as those concerning equal pay and employment (Shefer, 1990; Steeves, 1987). Liberal feminists believe that inequity is the result of irrational prejudice and can be eliminated through rational argument. Relying heavily on cognitive learning theories of modeling behaviors (see Tuchman, Daniels, & Benet, 1978), liberal feminists believe that "rational argument and legal struggle are effective in both increasing opportunities for women and in providing role models for adult women and for girls" (Steeves, 1987, p. 101). Equal opportunity, therefore, is possible within existing socioeconomic structures (Brown, 1990).

This bias shows up in the content analyses of sex roles in media described above. Although these studies suffer from an underdeveloped theoretical framework, they do stress the liberal ideal of increasing women's public visibility by criticizing traditional stereotypes (Janus, 1977; Putnam, 1982; Steeves, 1987). One of the major criticisms of this type of study is that content analyses such as these do not differentiate between form and content, and therefore fail to integrate the two levels of meaning into a common framework. Content analyses chart changes in form (for example, change from women in automobile ads wearing bikinis to women in such ads wearing business suits) without adequately addressing the little change in content. This kind of analysis offers a static picture in which an image is described in one moment in time (Janus, 1977). Further, the concept of "gender role" is troublesome, because is "flattens and homogenizes the meaning and evaluation of those experiences, as well as depoliticizes them" (Rakow, 1986, p. 15). Gender is not merely a demographic category; it "is a pervasive identity and set of self feelings that affect other social roles one might choose or be restricted from" (Rakow, 1986, p. 15).

The feminist critique of sex roles research is a valid one, themes of which I will take up later in this chapter. A more central critique for understanding communication processes, however, is offered by Sut Jhally (1987). Content analysis research of gender stereotyping in advertising places emphasis on the truth or falsity of representation, when in fact "advertisement images are neither false nor true reflections of social reality because they are in fact part of social reality" (p. 135). As such, advertising needs to be studied as a constituent part of our social reality, not as a distorted reflection of it. Therefore, emphasis must shift from questions of trueness or falseness to processes of "signification." This charge marks a theoretical and methodological shift in gender advertising research from analyses of manifest content to analyses of the "symbolic potential" of content.

Gender Advertising Ritualized

In the second approach to the study of gender and advertising, less emphasis is placed on the truth or falsity in representation of the larger society by ads; rather, the concern is with advertising's place as a part of society and, more specifically, its ability to "signify" or "communicate" to social actors. This second approach, called here the *ritualistic* perspective on gender and advertising, originated with Erving Goffman's *Gender Advertisements* (1976), a symbolic interactionist approach to "gender display."[2] Research conducted from this approach is most interested in how advertisements offer up ritualized "bits" of real gendered behaviors in order to offer a familiar picture of gender to consumers. Taken as a whole, however, or as a system of meaning, advertising, in fact, offers up a very distorted and hyperritualized picture of real gender relationships.

Goffman's *Gender Advertisements* (1976) was one of the first and is, to this day, one of the most influential textual analyses of the symbolic potential of advertising images. Goffman was intrigued by the signification (although Goffman would call it symbolism) of advertising images in their ability to look familiar, when on close inspection they portray a world that is really quite peculiar. Goffman's discussion of gender and advertising is based on a symbolic interactionist perspective on communication. For readers unfamiliar with Goffman's "ritual view" of gender in advertising, a brief explanation of the symbolic interactionist perspective may be helpful.

In a symbolic interactionist frame, at the heart of all interpretation is "meaning." When two individuals communicate, they do not do so through the sharing of identical meanings of the objects of the communication; instead, communication is achieved through an adequate level of common understanding. Each person in the interaction assigns meanings to the symbols used in the interaction. What is shared is an interaction of the ideas through the symbols used and the interpretations of those symbols. As Blumer (1969) notes, "Human beings act toward things on the basis of the meanings that the things have for them" (p. 86). Meaning constitutes an individual's reasons for action.

Thus, changes in how individuals see themselves and how they choose to behave evolve out of their interactions with others. These interactions are shaped by roles, or the communicators' social selves (Fisher, 1978, p. 174), and rules, or followable prescriptions that indicate what behavior is obligated, preferred, or prohibited in certain contexts (Shimanoff, 1980). The "generalized other" is representative of typical members of a culture or society with which the individual identifies him- or herself. The role-taking function allows the individual to align his or her behaviors with those of others within a social setting, and thus a social collectivity is organized that can perform identifiable actions.

Mass media are one way in which the prescribed roles and rules of a society get disseminated, and advertising plays a very large part in our experience of the mass media. In Goffman's (1976) view, advertisements offer highly stylized versions of "the other"—of social mores, definitions, attitudes, values, and behavioral tendencies whose meanings must be clear enough to be interpreted in an instant: "The task of the advertiser is to favorably dispose viewers to his product, his means, by and large, to show a sparkling version of that product in the context of glamorous events. The implication is that if you buy the one, you are on the way to realizing the other—and you should want to" (p. 26). For Goffman, the most relevant questions we can ask of advertising are as follows: Of what aspects of real life do advertisements provide us a fair picture? What social effects do advertisements have upon the lives purportedly pictured in them?

Goffman (1976) compares the "job" of the advertiser—to dramatize and make salient the worth of the product—to that of a society, in "infusing its social situations with ceremonial and ritual signs facilitating the orientation of participants to one another" (p. 27). Both must use limited resources to tell a story, both must transform the opaque into the easily readable. When studying gender in advertising, according to Goffman, the uncovering of sexual stereotypes is important, but not nearly as important as attending to how those who produce—and, for that matter, those who pose for—advertisements can "choreograph the materials available in social situations in order to achieve their end" (p. 27).

Central to Goffman's view of how gender operates in advertising is his notion of "gender display": "If gender be defined as the culturally established correlates of sex (whether in consequence of biology or learning), then gender display refers to conventionalized portrayals of these correlates" (p. 1). The key, then, to understanding how gender is communicated through advertisements lies in understanding the notion that advertisements present to us familiar ritualistic displays. Displays, however, in real life or in the world of advertising, can be, and are most likely to be, polysemic. More than one piece of cultural information may be encoded in a display. Further, once a display becomes well established and sequentialized—say, for example, the steps and gestures involved when a man opens a door for a woman—parts of the sequence can be taken out, bracketed. The stylization itself becomes the object of attention, the actor then having the ability to comment upon it. This is the process of "hyperritualization," according to Goffman: "Thus the human use of displays is complicated by the human capacity for re-framing behavior" (p. 3).

Partly because of this web of hyperritualization, individuals feel that gender accounts for some of the most deep-seated traits of human beings; femininity and masculinity are the prototypes of essential expression. Gender display, therefore, is something that can be expressed fleetingly and at the same time has the ability to characterize a person at the most basic level (Goffman, 1976, p. 7).

Advertisements, then, are actually "ritual-like bits of behavior which portray an ideal conception of the two sexes and their structural relationship to each other" (Goffman, 1976, p. 84). Actual gender expressions are artful poses, too. However, advertisements exist in a constant state of hyperritualization. Standardization, exaggeration, and simplification are found to an extensive degree in advertising. The gender displays in advertising are familiar because they show us rituals in which we engage in real life. However, advertisements further serve to conventionalize our conventions. Cut off from context and taken as a group, advertisements supply us with exaggerated distortions of a world with which we are intimately familiar.

Goffman lends empirical support for his arguments by suggesting six general categories of hyperritualizations that show up consistently throughout the more than 500 advertisements he analyzed. Under the title "The Feminine Touch," Goffman concludes that in advertising women, more often than men, are pictured using their fingers and their hands, whether to caress objects, cradle them, or outline their surfaces. Self-touching is also a feminine domain, indicating that the body is a precious and delicate object (pp. 29-31).

Further, Goffman concludes that advertisements rank the importance of individuals by the functions they perform, much as in real life. In his section headed, appropriately, "Function Ranking," Goffman explains that most often, if only one person is represented, it is a male who is pictured in an executive role. The hierarchy of functions is pictured both within and outside of occupational frames. In these depictions the male is the one executing the action, giving instruction, or overseeing the action. When instruction is depicted in advertising, generally, deference for the instructor on the part of the instructed is also shown.

Interestingly, when males are pictured in the traditional domain of female authority—namely, the home—three trends emerge. The first, and perhaps the best mirror of real life, is that the male is depicted as engaged in no contributing role at all, "in this way avoiding either subordination or contamination with the 'female' task" (Goffman, 1976, p. 36). The second is that the male is made ludicrous or childlike, therefore distancing the image from real life and preserving the male image of competence. Third, and most subtle, is that the male is pictured undertaking a task under the watchful eye of the female (pp. 36-37).

Perhaps most important to our concerns here is the category of hyperritualizations that Goffman calls "the ritualization of subordination." According to Goffman, a classic stereotype of deference is to lower oneself, in one way or another—to bow one's head, slump in one's posture, or sit or lie below another. Holding the body erect and the head high "is stereotypically a mark of unashamedness, superiority and disdain" (p. 40). Advertising embraces these conventions as if they were universal in value. Women and children seem be pictured sitting or lying on floors and on beds more than are men. Men also seem to be located higher than women in much advertising—drawing on our society's convention of elevating, quite literally, those of superior status, as in a courtroom setting, for example. Further, women, much more frequently than men, are pictured with one knee slightly bent—a convention of unpreparedness—and also in canting positions that can be read as acceptance of subordination. Women tend to smile more in ads than do men. Again, the smile can be read as a type of acceptance and as a mollifier of the male's activity or emotions.

Goffman's analysis forces the reader to reconsider the relationship between advertising and reality. As Leiss et al. (1986) note, "he also uncovers the assumptions underlying the interpretive codes buried in advertisements and the way advertising acts as an accomplice in perpetuating regressive forms of social relations" (p. 169). In all its familiarity, advertising does not merely reflect reality. Although it draws its materials from everyday life—from real gender displays, for instance—the bits of everyday life used are selected carefully and much is habitually omitted. By selecting some things to integrate continuously into the message system of advertising (a good example is the ideal female body image), ads create new meanings that are not necessarily found elsewhere.

Expanding Goffman's Analysis

Cultural critics of communication have attempted to build upon, as well as push beyond, Goffman's ideas of gender display. Taken in historical context, these new directions in theorizing are beginning to address more adequately how gender relations can be reproduced when viewed across time and symbolic conventions. Since the publication of *Gender Advertisements,* many scholars have expanded upon the concept of gender display in advertising and what these rituals communicate when viewed over and over again (Coward, 1982; Hay, 1989; Lazarus, 1987; Masse & Rosenbaum, 1988; Millium, 1975; Myers, 1982; Williamson, 1986; Winship, 1981, 1985). Two prominent themes have emerged in this body of work that are of particular relevance to this review. The first involves the "photographic cropping" (Millium, 1975) of female body parts to substitute for the entire body in advertising representations. The second theme is the active male versus the passive female in advertising representations.

One recurrent ritualization of considerable concern to cultural critics is the fragmentation of body parts in advertising. Women in advertising are very often signified in fragmented ways, by their lips, legs, hair, eyes, or hands. The "bit" stands for the whole, the sexualized woman (Winship, 1981, p. 25). Men, on the other hand, are less likely to be "dismembered" in this way in advertisements. Kilbourne, in particular, describes the cropping of photographs of women in advertising as one of the major elements that presents the female as dehumanized, as an object, a male fetish. This, she argues, contributes to a general climate of violence against women (see Lazarus, 1987). Treating the human as an object is the first step toward the legitimation of committing violence toward that person. Individual ads do not cause violence against women, but dehumanized gender displays across the discourse of advertising contribute to a callousness toward violence against women (see also Kuhn, 1985; Root, 1984).

In her analysis of the relationship between the positioning of hands and sexuality in advertising, Janice Winship (1981) brings together the theme of photographic cropping with a second theme, the public male and the domestic female. Male and female hands are part of an entire message system of social representation signifying appropriate gender behavior. In her analysis, Winship juxtaposes an ad depicting a man's hand holding an open pack of Rothman's cigarettes, the "World Leader," and an ad showing a woman's hand pouring a pitcher of Bird's Custard over a dessert, the caption reading, "home-made goodness." She points out that switching the hands in these two ads would disrupt the meanings:

> A woman's hand does not signify "world leader"; a man's hand does not signify "home-made." But as it is, the appropriately gendered hand allows us to key into familiar ideologies of masculinity and femininity. Those ideologies see "naturally" masculine or feminine, and the represented hand is "naturally" a man's or a woman's. (p. 30)

Kilbourne (in Lazarus, 1987) and Williamson (1986) make very similar points about the ideology of the active and "public" male and the passive, dependent, "domestic" female. Williamson names these divisions in representation the "male-work-social" and the "female-leisure-natural." Men are often positioned in very culturally specific and purposive poses and attire, such as in moments of working, conversing on the telephone, and conveying a commanding stare. Men are positioned as the consumers of the objects being advertised. Women, on the other hand, rarely have command of the stare, but are positioned in such a way that they are the object of the stare, the product to be consumed. "He needs the product with a drive that comes from his own masculinity, his activity at work [for example], while she needs the product to bring alive her universal femininity, which is represented as passive and completely separate from the social world" (Williamson, 1986, p. 105). He is society, culture, and she is "nature." Winship (1981) describes this odd mix of female subjectivity as passive, yet actively sexual:

> This ideology of sexuality in the ad context admits both to a passive, virginal and innocent sexuality—waiting for men, typified by the image of a young woman in long white robes and flowing blonde hair—and to an active experience of sexuality. However, the active experience of sexuality only takes place in a fetishistic mode. Women are invited by the ads to respond to themselves through the imagined fetishes of men—the tights/legs, the lipstick/lips which fragments or distortions of them stand for all their womanness. (p. 219)

Therefore, the fragmentation of female body parts in ads presents fetishes of sexuality that are seen as active, yet render the woman herself passive because the whole woman is only suggested, not represented.

The Codes and Subjects of
Gender Representations in Advertising

Many of the most illuminating studies of advertising images have employed some variation of semiotics or semiology (see Barthes, 1977, 1988; Leiss et al., 1986; Nichols, 1981; Williamson, 1978, 1986).[3] By treating the advertising image as a "text," semiotic analyses concentrate on the relationships between the ads' internal meaning structures as they relate to the larger cultural codes shared by viewers. Semiology's relationship to advertising is explained succinctly by Jhally (1987):

> Semiology is the study of signs, or more specifically the system of signs. A sign is something that has significance within a system of meaning and is constituted of two key elements: the signifier (the material vehicle) and the signified (the mental construct, the idea). The two elements are equally necessary and can be separated only analytically. . . . This is the difference between the signifier and the sign. A diamond as signifier is empty of meaning. The diamond as sign is full of meaning. . . . production produces commodities as signifiers while advertising produces them as signs. (p. 130)

For Roland Barthes (1974, 1977), advertising is a mythical structure in which any given advertisement has the ability to produce meaning at many different levels of signification. Barthes's essay "The Rhetoric of the Image" is considered essential for an understanding of the semiology of advertising.[4] Scholars such as Sut Jhally, Bill Nichols, and Judith Williamson have moved to refine and also expand Barthes's ideas in order to analyze the intertextuality of advertising as discourse. In other words, these authors are concerned with how individual advertisements are interdependent on one another, as well as the cultural codes brought by viewers, for meaning. Jhally (1987) explains: "In the semiotic tradition this is referred to as the utilization of *paradigmatic* structures of interpretation (which make use of resources outside the text) rather than strictly *syntagmatic* structures (based on a purely internal reading of the text)" (p. 140). The concept that unifies the different elements of the process of meaning construction is that of the *code*. A code is the store of experience upon which both the advertiser and the audience draw in their participation in the construction of "commodity meaning" (Jhally, 1987, p. 140).

Williamson's (1978) analysis of how advertisements can be "decoded" employs both semiotics and structuralism in order to explore the meaning structures of individual advertising images in relation to the larger structure of advertising "as currency." According to Williamson, advertising can be thought of as a "currency of signs." Advertising helps to invest commodities with value—not merely utility value, but value attached to an "image" or a "look." Williamson points out that advertisers invest their products with value by differentiating the images of their products from the images of other products in the same marketing categories. The value of an image, therefore, is dependent upon viewers' abilities to make references to the other products in a category.

Ads have the ability to signify to us when we know the cultural codes that allow us to reference what the signs replace. By bringing our own referent systems to the viewing, we complete the transfer of meaning, or "significance," to the commodity. Images of gender are highly structured cultural codes in U.S. society. The transfer of codes of sexuality is probably more widely accessible to more people than other cultural codes, and these codes are therefore continually recycled in the symbolic world of image production.

Williamson calls these systems of meaning from which we draw the tools to complete the transfer (from meaning to commodity) "referent systems." These constitute the body of knowledge from which both advertisers and audiences draw their materials. Mass media advertising, therefore, plays the role of mediator. "For the audience properly to decode the message (transfer meaning), advertisers have to draw their materials from the social knowledge of the audience, then transform this material into messages (encode), developing appropriate formats and shaping the content in order that the process of communication from audience be completed" (Jhally, 1987, p. 132). It is this point that separates the advertising image from other forms of artistic visual images. Unlike an artistic photograph, the advertising image is not the thing it represents, but instead a part of a referent system, dependent on the viewer's understanding and interpretation of the codes of advertising in general. Understanding this referent system requires an understanding of the larger cultural codes that the spectator brings to the viewing.

This method of decoding advertisements is based on the work of the French linguist Ferdinand de Saussure. Saussure (1956) tells us that in the English language we know the meaning of a thing by knowing what it is not. We know that C-A-T is not D-O-G. It is through the difference between the sound image of C-A-T and the sound image of D-O-G that each has meaning for us (Hawkes, 1977).[5] Based on this concept from Saussure, Williamson concludes that for the viewer, the value of a product depends more on what it is not than what it is.

For example, types of colognes, jeans, paper towels, and so on have very little significance of their own. Advertisements invest products with value by relating them to persons, objects, emotions, or images that already have value for us. Products not invested with such value through advertising are "generic." For instance, Hanes underwear is invested with value when it is differentiated from Jockey underwear. An advertisement featuring Michael Jordan wearing Hanes underwear is a sign that invests the underwear with the image associated with Michael Jordan. What is possibly signified is that rich, successful athletes wear Hanes underwear; Michael Jordan becomes the signifier.

It follows, therefore, that viewers give signs value through the recognition of what they replace. By transferring the significance of Michael Jordan to

Hanes underwear, we are acknowledging a value we place on the image of Michael Jordan. Of course, advertisers hope this is a positive value. However, whether positive or negative, this value differentiates Hanes underwear from Jockey or Fruit of the Loom underwear.

In order for this system of currency to have meaning for the viewer, the viewer must be able to associate the image of the product with a value that is in turn based on his or her own cultural codes. "Recognition," then, is the viewer's first level of involvement with the meaning of advertisements. The second level of involvement is the advertisement's ability to signify the viewer to him- or herself. Advertising insists that the viewer differentiate what kind of person he or she "is" in relation to a specific product. The product can then be exchanged for the quality of the person, as exemplified by "the Pepsi generation." If we drink Pepsi we are signified as something qualitatively different from those who drink Coke; and if we wear Calvin Klein jeans we are signified as different from the kind of person who wears Levi's 501 jeans (Shields, 1990).

Differentiation cannot be interpreted as a wholly overt and cognitively conscious process, however. Differentiation is often affective and sensual. Many fashion advertisements, for example, operate at a level of social significance that is once removed from the use value (utility) of the commodity being advertised. The sensuality of the image does not define the commodity so much as it differentiates the sensuousness of one commodity from the sensuousness of another.

This process of differentiation removed from use value is explored fully in the work of Haug (1987), who notes that differentiation is achieved through the process of "commodity aesthetics." Commodity aesthetics is the quality invested in certain advertisements that attempts to achieve semblance with our longings (desires) and not necessarily our needs. Because longings and desires are far more ambiguous than needs, semblance with the viewer's longings and desires operates at the visceral level of sensuality as well as at the cognitively conscious level of decision making. Perhaps the most pervasive means by which commodities are sensualized is through the use of sexuality-stimulating semblance. In advertising this semblance is achieved through sight.[6]

Haug draws upon a combination of semiotics and psychoanalysis to make the point that the general suppression of sexual drive accompanied by the semblance of sexual images in commodity aesthetics leads to a general sexualization through "sight." Sexuality then, takes on an exchange value all its own. It is an ambiguous discourse that can be visually attached to virtually any commodity in order to lend the commodity value. Therefore, when bikini-clad women appear in a commercial for Old Milwaukee beer, the relationship between the sexuality of the women and the commodity (beer) does not appear to be arbitrary. The sexuality of the women is a general exchange value lent in this case to the value of beer, but it could just as easily be lent to the value of an automobile or a brand of cigarettes.

Critiques of Semiology and Advertising Approaches

Haug's insights on the general exchange value of sexuality in Western societies are pivotal to an understanding of the naturalized association between sex and commodities. However, structural analyses such as those conducted by Haug, Williamson, and Nichols have been criticized for presenting "sexual semblance" as a gender-neutral or gender-equal phenomenon (see Shields, 1990). Feminist scholars of gender and advertising, in particular, argue that the sexual semblance of commodities is an appropriation (and in many cases a perpetuation) of dominant discourses and representations of gender in the larger society (Coward, 1982, 1985; Kuhn, 1985; Myers 1982, 1986; Warlaumont, 1993). Traditionally, it is the female body that has served as the object of sexual stimulation in advertising as well as most other mass-mediated forms. Although the male body is now also represented in this capacity, there is little confusion over which gender has traditionally occupied this dubious position in representation (Shields, 1990).

Annette Kuhn (1985) suggests that this cultural way of seeing the female form as the object of visual sexualization has very material and historical roots. She points out that "whenever we look at painted, drawn, sculpted or photographed images of women, it is important for us to remind ourselves that images of women have traditionally been the province and property of men" (pp. 10-11). The definitions of good photography and beautiful art have been conceived, owned, managed, and produced by males. Therefore, it is important to remember that the repetitious presentation of gender with which we are so familiar is the historical result of one gender's discretion.

John Berger (1972) expands on these ideas in explaining that the rise to prominence of the female nude in European oil painting depicts a turning point when women's bodies became the object of "the gaze." At the time, it was considered socially unacceptable to gaze at "nakedness," but it was quite a different matter to gaze upon "the nude." The nude is a form of high culture, the properties of which have come to define quality in aesthetics. The popularity of the nude was conceived and enjoyed within a particular material context. According to Berger, "In the art-form of the European nude, the painters and spectator-owners were usually men and the persons treated as objects, usually women" (p. 63). However, the codes of high-culture aesthetics seem to deny this materiality. The nude is not an iconic sign for female nakedness. The codes of high-culture aesthetics deny that the referent is the subject of the gaze; instead, "the nude" is objectified, a spectacle in its own right (Shields, 1990). The aesthetic "value" invested in the tradition of the nude in European oil painting has been instrumental, according to Berger, in molding the acceptable way of viewing women today.

Positioning the Gendered Subject

Another prominent approach to the study of gender and advertising is derived from psychoanalytic theories of language and visual images. A psychoanalytic approach to the study of media addresses how "the subject" is positioned by the text, whether the text is an advertisement, a film, or something else, and how male and female subjectivity are reproduced through language and image. The psychoanalytic perspective can be credited with giving scholars of gender advertising the theoretical tools to analyze the concept of the "male gaze" and the "voyeuristic gaze" encoded in photography and cinema. Further, feminist scholars of gender advertising have relied heavily on the construct of the "split consciousness" of the female subject to theorize how advertising works to encourage women to view themselves as objects to be improved upon for the male other, rather than to view themselves as subjects of their own femaleness.

The far-reaching influence of continental theories of structuralism and psychoanalysis for the study of representation, both in film studies and in still visual images, is immense. Perhaps the most influential figure in this movement is Jacques Lacan (1968, 1977). Lacan's contribution to psychoanalytic theory is a rereading of Freud that incorporates a theory of language, a theory of the symbolic. Closely associated with the semiology of Saussure and the ideological theories of Althusser, Lacan's theory of "the subject" uncovers the relationship between the unconscious and the symbolic. Lacan's "subject" provides the foundation for a materialist theory of subjectivity in social processes. Lacan analyzes the determinacy of language in the construction of the subject as it is imposed on the human subject in history and in ideological formations (Coward & Ellis, 1977).

Psychoanalysis as a theory of the human's emerging sexuality has been fiercely criticized for its degradation of the female, presenting her not for her difference in femaleness, but as her "lack of," and therefore inferiority to, maleness (or, more specifically, the penis). In this schema, female subordination in society is located in the structures through which sexual identity is acquired (the Oedipus complex) and in the immutable structures of the psyche (Burniston, Mort, & Weedon, 1978; Irigaray, 1985; Mitchell, 1975; Spivak, 1989). These critiques emerge, of course, in reaction to Freud's theory of the Oedipus complex. Lacan's rereading of Freud's Oedipus complex, what Lacan calls the "Oedipus phase," has, however, proved more palatable for feminist scholars in that it does not doom femininity to an essentialist subordinated position in society; rather, it provides, with startling accuracy, descriptions of patriarchy in process (see Benjamin, 1986; Rose, 1986).

Lacan's Oedipus phase is the process by which the baby becomes a sexed subject. When born, the infant is aware neither of itself as a distinct person nor of gender. However, when the child emerges in the symbolic from the imaginary, the harmony of dual relation in the imaginary is disrupted by a third relation: the Father, or the law (of culture).

In this schema, the figure of the father represents the fact that a wider familial and social network exists, and that the child must seek a position in that context.

The child must go beyond the imaginary identifications of the dual realm in which the distinction between "me/you" is always blurred, to take a position as someone who can designate himself as an "I" in a world of adult thirds. The appearance of the father thus prohibits the child's total unity with the mother, and . . . causes desire to be repressed in the unconscious. (Flitterman-Lewis, 1987, p. 178)

Possession of the phallus thus allows direct identification with the Father, whereas nonpossession does not. For Lacan, the phallus is a socially organized symbol of the difference between male and female; in patriarchal societies it is a symbol of male power and privilege.

Female Subjectivities

Lacan's conceptions of human subjectivity inform theories of representation as wide-ranging as film studies, advertising studies, and television criticism (see Flitterman-Lewis, 1987). Lacan's most noted theory in his later scholarship on representation, and which provides the base for gender studies of subjectivity, is his thesis in *Ecrits* (1977) on the "mirror stage." The mirror stage is the moment in time when the human baby enters into the world of the symbolic, leaving behind forever the world of "the real." According to Lacan, very early in its life the human baby becomes a subject by losing its direct relationship with the body of the mother. Its first binary oppositions experienced, here/gone, are much the same as the baby's first contact with the mirror, baby here/baby gone. Binary oppositions are, for Lacan, as they are for Saussure, the basic units of language, a system of difference. The result is the split subject—a subject constituted by "lack" of a unified ego.[7] The split subject emerges into language and an absolute separation is set up between the imaginary (binary oppositions: subject/mother, subject/ideal) and the symbolic (split subject in language and history; actual and variable symbolic structures).

Williamson (1978) suggests that advertisements attempt to represent to us the central object of our desire, the unified (but of course unattainable) self: "Ads set up, in your active relationship towards them, the fictional creation of an impossibly unified self: an 'Ego-Ideal' " (p. 65). They suggest that we can become the persons in the images in front of us. Advertising feeds off our desire for coherence and meaning, by at once alienating our identity and constituting us as one among many objects. We then make the exchange for images that give us back our own value.

Nowhere is this process more pronounced than in the offering to women of images of other women, particularly in advertising, but also in film and television. This concept of women being sold the ideal image of themselves is what has been described in cultural studies literature as the *split consciousness* of the surveyed female. In a patriarchal society, most representations of women connote "otherness," difference from the male norm (Kuhn, 1985). Females are the objects of the gaze, as opposed to the subjects of the gaze.

> The essential way of seeing women, the essential use to which their images are put, has not changed. Women are depicted in a quite different way than men—not because the feminine is different from the masculine—but because the "ideal" spectator is always assumed to be male and the image of the woman is designed to flatter him. (Berger, 1972, p. 64)

The male gaze connotes significantly more than mere voyeurism, however. It is a controlling gaze. "To possess the image of a woman's sexuality is, however mass-produced the image, also in some way to possess, to maintain a degree of control over the woman in general" (Kuhn, 1985, p. 11). Laura Mulvey (1975) further explains the concept of the gendered gaze:

> In a world ordered by sexual imbalance, pleasure in looking has been split between active/male and passive/female. The determining male gaze projects its fantasy onto the female figure, which is styled accordingly. In their traditional exhibitionist role women are simultaneously looked at and displayed, with their appearance coded for strong visual and erotic impact so that they can be said to connote to-be-looked-at-ness. (p. 16)

Rosalind Coward (1985) contends that the male gaze encoded in photographic images is an extension of how men view women in the streets. The naturalness of this way of seeing the female body follows from its pervasiveness in all arenas of female representation as well as experience. Put more simply, " 'men act' and 'women appear.' Men look at women. Women watch themselves being looked at. . . . The surveyor of women in herself is male: the surveyed female. Thus she turns herself into an object—and most particularly an object of vision: a 'sight' " (Berger, 1972, p. 47). The split consciousness of the surveyed female, then, is her embodiment of the object of the sight and simultaneously her awareness of being the object of the sight. It also allows for a way of seeing that seems natural in appeal to both male and female spectators. If aesthetic appeal of the female body is naturalized for both males and females, it also seems natural that the female body is represented as sexualized more than the male body.

These dominant "ways of seeing" are insidious throughout the discourse of advertising. However, as Kathy Myers (1982) notes, advertising images are constantly evolving and changing. Codes of image production are in a constant state of mutation. Advertisements, unlike most other mass media, absorb societal changes into their discourse quickly, appropriating and incorporating shifting cultural codes into images and text. Often this incorporation involves recirculating old stereotypes in new garb—advertisements for bras that offer "new freedom" and ads for cigarettes that suggest "You've come a long way, baby," for example. This type of advertisement may at first glance look "progressive" in its messages, when in fact it is simply recirculating traditional gender messages in new ways.

"The ability of the [advertising] media continually to create new meanings gives a certain instability to the image, which constantly threatens to escape the analytic categories or stereotypes within which we seek to contain it" (Myers, 1982, p. 89). For example, across the wide spectrum of photographic media, from family portraiture to soft- and hard-core pornography, conventions of poses, of pouts, of camera angles, of lighting, and so on are continuously shifting and overlapping.

Many fashion ads, for instance, borrow conventions from soft-core pornography (Coward, 1982, 1985; Kuhn, 1985; Myers, 1982).[8] Coward (1982) contends that the codes that categorize pornography are in no way confined there: "The direct look of the woman to the viewer, who identifies with the position of the camera, for example, pervades not only fashion magazines and advertising images but is also characteristic of portrait photography" (p. 16).

One of the major differences that separates fashion advertising from pornography, however, is the way in which the photograph positions its subject. Traditionally, the spectator of fashion advertising is positioned in such a way as to connect the pleasure of looking with the value of particular commodities. Unlike pornography, where the image is placed for instant gratification by the spectator, fashion advertising works to displace the spectator's instant satisfaction. The fashion image promises satisfaction upon obtaining "the look," and the look can (and must) be purchased.

What most advertisements "of" women give "to" women is the promise to enhance and improve their physical appearance by way of purchasing a product. However, this is rarely achieved through straightforward prescriptions; rather, it is achieved by offering the viewer a "look," a style. Advertisers offer up the power to achieve the look, "but unlike advertisements directed at men, this is not the power over people and things, but power of becoming the perfect 'sight' " (Root, 1984, p. 66). This type of power is limited. It is most often achieved through sexual display in place of subjectivity. Whereas male sexuality is traditionally defined as active, seeking, and decisive, female sexuality is defined as responsive and in a position to elicit a response from the male (Coward, 1985).

GENDERED DECODING

Scholarship theorizing "the female spectator" is growing rapidly, especially in feminist film and television criticism (Betterton, 1985; Bobo, 1988; Brown, 1989; Budge, 1989; Byars, 1988; Coward, 1982, 1985; Doane, 1982; Gamman, 1989; Gledhill, 1988; Gordon, 1984; Holland, 1983; Kaplan, 1983, 1988; Lewallen, 1989; McRobbie, 1984; Moore, 1989; Mulvey, 1989; Radway, 1984; Roach & Felix, 1989; Stacey, 1994; Van Zoonen, 1994; Waldman, 1989; Young, 1989). Scholarship on female spectatorship is interested in exploring beyond the entrapment presented by the concept of the "male gaze" to pose the following kinds of questions: How do women look at women? Are female looks at other women always about identification? Or do dynamics of fascination and difference have other, more progressive, resonances (Firat, 1994; Gamman & Marshment, 1989; Rapping, 1994; Stacey, 1994; Tseëlon, 1995; Van Zoonen, 1994)? Finally, in the case of many advertisements for commodities marketed to women, but in which the visual construction is for the pleasure of the male, how do these images "work" for women?

Narcissistic Damage

Traditionally, female pleasure in looking has been considered a form of narcissism. This theoretical position holds that woman is innately vain, finding pleasure in scrutinizing and assessing her outer image (Betterton, 1985; Coward, 1985). The result of this assessment is the need to mask the appearance in order to improve upon her personal beauty. One of the by-products of the pleasure of self-adoration is the need to gauge one's own beauty by assessing the beauty of others critically. The "others" referred to here are not only other real women, but also the women in the mass media. The flawless beauty of magazine cover girls and Hollywood screen goddesses set the standard for this assessment of feminine beauty. In real life, women work toward this standard as a goal of achievement, measuring their success by the reflection in the mirror and, more important, the attention gained from men as well as other women out in "public."

Coward (1985) contends that this explanation of women's pleasures in looking is extremely inadequate. Female pleasures in looking (at images of other women, for instance) have much deeper cultural roots than a psychologically based theory of female narcissism would suggest. Coward suggests that it is not self-love that leads to a woman's obsession with her own image, but actually a form of self-hate. She calls this form of feminine self-hate "narcissistic damage" (p. 80). Yes, women are fascinated with their own images, but not so much out of a sense of desire or pleasure as out of a sense of anxiety and urgency. In a highly visual and image-conscious society, a woman learns at a very early age that physical appearance is probably the most crucial way in which men form opinions about her worth. Therefore, feelings about appearance and self-image easily become mingled with feelings about security and comfort (p. 78). Absorption into the world of one's own image can be seen as a means of cultural survival, a bid for acceptance.

Given Coward's arguments, it follows that the female gaze can be theorized as doubly constrained—constrained as a lack (or absence) in the text of the visual image and constrained by convention in larger society. Women have been denied the control of the possessive gaze and are also denied the legitimate role of voyeur in public arenas. Males, therefore, possess not only the gaze, but the power that gaze imbues.

The ability to scrutinize is premised on power. Indeed the look confers power; women's inability to return such a critical and aggressive look is a sign of subordination, of being the recipients of another's assessment. Women, in the flesh, often feel embarrassed, irritated or downright angered by men's persistent gaze. But not wanting to risk male attention turning to male aggression, women avert their eyes and hurry on their way. (Coward, 1985, p. 76)

Further, Goldman (1992) explains that the power of the gaze in advertisements is invoked more by what ads conceal than by what they make visible:

These ads conceal diverse forms of terror experienced by women who objectify themselves. There is the mundane psychic terror associated with not receiving "looks" of admiration—i.e., of not having others validate one's appearance. A similar sense of terror involves the fear of "losing one's looks"—the quite reasonable fear that aging will deplete one's value and social power. A related source of anxiety involves fears about "losing control" over body weight and appearance. The neurotic obsession with body and food has become the scourge of young women. (p. 123)

This awareness of the relentlessness of the male gaze need not be confined to looks and stares from men on the streets. Other elements of the public domain can be equally persistent, such as the advertising images that surround the viewer in this society every day, almost everywhere. When women view photographic images, however, especially in magazines, they have a rare opportunity to look freely, not only at other women but at everyone on the pages. It is a kind of looking reserved for males on the street, but open to women in the limited arenas of visual consumption, such as in the viewing of photographs, watching films in a movie theater, and viewing soap operas (see Brown, 1989; Rosen, 1986). When a woman looks at a fashion magazine, she not only is allowed to look, she is allowed to stare, to assess and pass judgment on others instead of just herself (Coward, 1985, pp. 52-53).

The narcissistic theory of female pleasure in looking holds that the difference between the male and the female viewer of the image is that the male desires to possess the image, whereas the female identifies with the image. Coward argues that females do not so readily identify with the images they consume, but they too desire them, not as objects of possession, but rather as objects of emulation (see Shields, 1990). For women, the visual image presents clues for proper conduct that can open doors to happiness and fulfillment.

Narcissistic Damage and Discipline

Fulfilling the potential of ideal femininity in U.S. culture involves a constant focus on the body as the site of improvement and as the object of judgment—preparing it, painting it, trimming it, exercising it, feeding it, and even starving it. These beauty and "health" rituals are forms of self-imposed discipline. If not narcissism, however, where does the desire to self-discipline come from? In her analysis of the discourse of female weight reduction in American culture, Carole Spitzack (1990) examines the relationship between discourses of "women's health" as associated with thin bodies and discourses of "disease" associated with "weight" or fatness. These complementary discourses work with other numerous institutions and practices to encourage self-correction and therefore "liberation" for women—that is, liberation from the disease of fat resulting in "control" over one's health/beauty. Spitzack employs the insights of Michel Foucault to explain how power works through the penetrating cultural gaze, inciting the individual to impose discipline on the self:

> In his historical analysis of the relations between power and institutionalization of punishment, Foucault (1979) locates an important shift in disciplinary procedures which took place during seventeenth century practices. Corporeal forms of punishment, direct physical torture as means by which to underscore and make visible the power of government, was gradually replaced by an "optics" of power. The primary task of power was no longer to evidence its strength through physical brutality, but to establish, at countless points and through innumerable mechanisms, the surveillance of all who existed in its domain. The new mode of power is epitomized, Foucault suggests, in the architectural plans for the panopticon proposed by Jeremy Bentham (p. 200). Designed for use in prisons, the panopticon is a tower resting in the center of multiple stories of cells arranged in a circular fashion. At the back and front of each cell is a small window, allowing light to enter and illuminate each individually housed prisoner. The tower contains windows corresponding to cellular windows; due to the light entering from the back of each cell, guards in the tower cannot be seen by prisoners, but inmates are completely visible to guards. Each prisoner, Foucault writes, "is seen, but he does not see; he is the object of information, never the subject in communication . . . this invisibility is the guarantee of order." (p. 200)
>
> . . . In contemporary culture, Foucault writes, the panoptic scheme can be used whenever "one is dealing with a multiplicity of individuals on whom a task or particular form of behavior must be imposed" (p. 205). Power in the form of surveillance makes a demand on the individual to monitor the actions of the self, subjecting behavior to ever-greater examination, making visible each transgression, and punishing oneself for wrongdoing. Optical power is placed within the body of each person over whom it presides so that the individual "assumes responsibility for the constraints of power; he makes them play spontaneously upon himself; he inscribes in himself the power relation in which he simultaneously plays both roles; he becomes the principle of his own subjection" (pp. 202-203). In the final analysis, the body of each person is governed not by a visible and openly repressive power source, but by those individuals who have become wholly exposed to the inspecting gaze of power. (Spitzack, 1990, pp. 43-44)

It can be reasonably argued that women in Western cultures are individuals who have become wholly exposed to the inspecting gaze of power. Foucault's insights are therefore especially applicable to a discussion on the self-disciplining of female bodies. Most women have experienced being the object of information without being the subject in communication. For example, anytime a woman's worth is assessed solely on her appearance, she is the object but not the subject of a controlling gaze. Street harassment of women by men is an overt example of this. Further, the popular iconography of the female body in film, advertising, television, and so on is premised on the woman as object, but not subject in a communication arrangement. The prison guards of the controlling gaze in this arrangement are not men, per se, but the conspicuous invisibility of male bodies as the object of aesthetic pleasure and judgment in comparison to the completely exposed female body as aesthetic object. Coward (1985) suggests that the invisibility of men's bodies is needed for the control of women's bodies:

> Men's bodies and sexuality are taken for granted, exempted from scrutiny, whereas women's bodies are extensively defined and overexposed. Sexual and social meanings are imposed on women's bodies, not men's. Controlling the look, men have left themselves out of the picture because a body defined is a body controlled. (p. 229)

This explains one type of control, control over the body of the objectified female. However, the internalization of the panoptic logic insists that the woman must identify herself as the "principle of her own subjection, playing the roles of tower guard and prisoner simultaneously. She is spectator and spectacle, one who sees and is seen" (Spitzack, 1990, p. 45). Spitzack suggests that this arrangement is aided by an ideology of women's health that condones policing the body in order to reap the reward of "freedom" or "release" from the unhealthy fat body. In order to maintain the healthy liberated body, one must continuously discipline the body, policing its cravings and excesses, reprimanding self when discipline falters.

Women's weight and body shape constitute a prominent domain where the optics of power play out through and on women's bodies in contemporary American culture. Women's weight gain and weight loss invite two different kinds of gazes, both controlling, but one negative and one positive (see Myers & Biocca, 1992). Spitzack (1990) explains that part of the liberation discourse of dieting involves the diminishing of negative judgments. "Frequently, women describe body reduction as a means by which to undergo public scrutiny without fear of reprisals or self-condemnation" (p. 46). Weight loss is seen as a means to reduce negative judgments and at the same time become the object of approval. Weight loss can, however, invite an intensification of the woman as object, but not the subject, of communication arrangement. As she moves closer to the societal ideal of perfect body size, she invites more attention, not all positive or even wanted.

Recent literature on the body has focused on two closely related domains in which women are particularly self-surveilling: "exercise" and "diet" (Bordo, 1993; Chernin, 1986; Diamond, 1985; Featherstone, 1991; Morse, 1987-1988; Shefer, 1990; Spitzack, 1988, 1990; Turner, 1984; Wolf, 1991). Morse (1987-1988) argues that under the guise of physical and emotional health, aerobic exercise has become a magic tonic for women, staving off the processes of aging. As women age, they grow further from society's ideal of beauty and femininity. In this cultural way of seeing, a woman's value as a worker and sexual partner diminishes with age also. Morse explains that this devaluation of the woman through aging is matched by a cultural "neuteriza-tion" of the female identity. "To be old, tired, or unattractive is to be vulnerable to a kind of cultural extinction before death" (p. 21).

Actress/activist turned fitness guru Jane Fonda is attributed with creating the first credible link between beauty culture and obsessive weight loss by promoting a cardiovascular fitness regimen designed for women. Through this regimen of counting heartbeats, calories, and music rhythms, the female body can be transformed beyond thinness to an ideal of the "female physique" (Morse, 1987-1988, p. 23). Aerobics, like the cosmetics and fashion indus-tries, is now an integral part of commercial "beauty culture." Like other beauty industries, the "fitness industry" preys on the difference between the ideal fashion model and the natural tendencies of real women's bodies (to store more fat than men's bodies, for example). Also like other beauty industries, aerobics offers a "solution" to this difference, through disciplining the body in the name of fitness—the triumph of culture over nature (Diamond, 1985; Morse, 1987-1988; Wolf, 1991).

Morse (1987-1988) argues that aerobic exercise is situated at the intersec-tion of several competing discourses. It has been deemed the first feminist-sanctioned approach to weight loss. This approval, according to Morse, stems from the intrinsic properties of activity and movement in aerobic exercise, which run counter to long-prevailing notions of feminine passivity and stasis. Further, "the entree of exercise can be understood as an aid to weight loss and as part of the fitness movement as well as an expression of anxiety and as a potentially liberating antidote to it" (p. 24). Women can take charge of molding and sculpting their own bodies for societal display. Femininity is cultural.

The definition of the ideal female physique is cultural also, and has changed many times over the past century.[9] The voluptuous, wasp-waisted, rounded-hips physique epitomized by Marilyn Monroe in the 1950s gave way to the ultrathin waif of the 1960s epitomized by Twiggy. This dubious "never too thin" legacy stretched into the 1970s fashion world. The 1980s ushered in a new female physique complementary to aerobic exercise and activity. This curvaceous, muscular look, which is now most closely associated in its ideal form with supermodel Cindy Crawford, is the combination of cultural antithe-ses: "Thin and muscular, hard and curvaceous, it suggests power and yet a slender boyishness; furthermore those very muscles which empower are also the material of feminine curves" (Morse, 1987-1988, p. 25). Achieving this combination of attributes is difficult; it involves an investment of large amounts of time, money, and effort on "body work." The ultrathin look of the 1960s and 1970s could be achieved through starvation diets alone, but today, thinness without muscle tone falls short of the ideal feminine physique. The ideal must be achieved through a regimen of diet plus exercise. Even the naturally thin are no longer safe from weight-loss regimens. Thinness is no longer an immediate sign for fitness or health; these signs are found in the definition of body muscle and the glow of skin tone from a well-exercised body (or achieved artificially at the tanning salon).

The anxiety that women feel in American culture over the difference between the body they see promoted in advertising (and throughout the mass media) and the body they live in can often lead to types of self-surveilling and extreme discipline that fall outside societal parameters of "health" or even beauty. Societal pressures for women to conform to ideal body images presented throughout society are considered a prominent contributor to the onset of eating disorders in women, such as anorexia nervosa (self-starvation) and bulimia (bingeing and purging) (Bordo, 1993; Bruch, 1988; Chernin, 1986; Diamond, 1985; Hsu, 1990; Morse, 1987-1988; Shefer, 1990; Spitzack, 1990; Turner, 1984; Wolf, 1991; Zraly & Swift, 1990).[10] The multiple causes of such illnesses in individuals are complex; they include psychological and familial components as well as other major contributing factors. Although psychologists and therapists have been examining and treating these illnesses under these names for more than 20 years, popular and academic discourses have only recently begun to examine anorexia and bulimia in their sociological contexts, as biological reactions to cultural conditions.

Spitzack (1990) describes anorexia as "the body's triumph over dieting" (p. 12). For the anorexic, the weight loss effort is endless, even past the point of emaciation. Definitive of all anorexic behavior is the extreme need for control over the body. Many times this need to control one's own body comes in response to the body's violation by others, either emotionally or physically. Sometimes the anorexic is a victim of physical sexual abuse. In many of these cases the anorexic feels compelled to exorcise femininity (sexuality) from the body, reducing any signs of feminine curves, halting menstruation (see Turner, 1984), and shielding the shape of the body from the view of others with multilayered clothing (Bruch, 1988; Hsu, 1990; Zraly & Swift, 1990).

In other cases an overemphasis placed on body shape by parents, especially mothers, compels the anorexic to gain the parents' approval and at the same time gain control over her own body by starving it until acceptably thin (Bruch, 1988). These women are generally lavished with praise once initial weight loss is achieved, and often the craving for additional praise spurs them on to continue losing weight, no matter how thin they become. A similar response can happen when a child is continuously encouraged by parents to overeat. The anorexic's response is to gain control in the only arena in which she has complete power to do so (Spitzack, 1990)—she says no to the thing that her parents are insistent upon, and therefore asserts a type of control over her parents.

In still other cases, self-reports by anorexics reveal that their illness is the logical conclusion of narcissistic damage created and reproduced by the fashion, cosmetics, and fitness industries. Dr. Michael Strober, director of the Eating Disorder Center at UCLA's Neuropsychiatric Institute, stated in a recent magazine article that "a woman becomes anorexic because her soul has been battered by the unreasonable expectation that you can never be too thin and that fat—any fat—equals failure" (Lague & Lynn, 1993). For some women the self-surveilling gaze becomes overwhelming and, in turn, distorted. The anorexic can no longer gauge the image in the mirror against the ideal with any objectivity. No matter how thin the anorexic becomes, she still sees a fat, and therefore powerless, body in the mirror. In time, any plumpness of flesh on the body looks to her like unwanted fat, and she feels she must rid her body of it through starvation and exercise—the ultimate discipline.

Symbolic Annihilation

The preceding arguments have dealt directly with women's encounters with mass-mediated messages prescribing an often oppressive ideal female beauty. What if, however, one rarely sees representations of oneself in mass media to emulate? What if one's identity is deemed unworthy of representation in the dominant ideology of images? In media theory, such serious underrepresentation has been called *symbolic annihilation* (Gerbner & Gross, 1976; Tuchman et al., 1978). Symbolic annihilation refers to the most profound inequities in "the spectrum of mediated representations of social groups" (see Kielwasser & Wolf, 1992, p. 351). For example, until very recently, women and men of color were required to be fine featured, resembling the European ideal of beauty, in order to be represented in print or television advertising. Further, although gay men and lesbians are major actors (encoders) in the fashion and entertainment industries, representations of homosexual relationships are rarely made explicit in mainstream advertising. Both of these "minorities" suffer from similar types of symbolic invisibility (Dyer, 1984, 1988; Gillespie, 1993; hooks, 1992; Kielwasser & Wolf, 1992).

Feminist scholars such as Roach and Felix (1989) suggest that Americans live in a culture where the dominant gaze is not only male, but white. Up until the past decade or so, when representations of African Americans were not totally excluded they were stereotyped and ghettoized, presenting a spectrum from negative representations to no representations—placed outside "natural" and "beautiful" representation in advertising and positioned as "other." However, unlike the "exotic other" of the Hawaiian or Asian "girls" in suntan advertisements (see Williamson, 1986), African Americans are society's mun-

1967; Cantor, 1972; Courtney & Whipple, 1974; Culley & Bennett, 1976; Dominick
72; McArthur & Resko, 1975; Schuetz & Sprafkin, 1978).

ctionism suggests that the "I" and the "me" are two integrated aspects of the "self."
Fisher (1978), "The 'I' is the active portion of self capable of performing behaviors.
bodies within the self the concept of 'other'—social mores, definitions, attitudes,
behavioral tendencies" (p. 167). The "me" provides direction for the "I." The
cts as both the subject and object when in interaction with others, with the "me"
ppropriate action for the "I." This process of experience and interpretation is called
ion" (p. 167). Through the process of "taking the role of the other" an individual
ther's perspective of him- or herself. Further, the individual can assume the "stand-
rpretive processes) of others in order to define the self. This definition of self,
not always a result of how the individual is "actually" seen by others, but often is
how he or she "thinks" others see him or her. Often referred to as "referential
r Cooley's "looking-glass self" (Altman & Taylor, 1973; Berger, Gardner, Clatter-
ulman, 1976), this line of thinking goes further to suggest that individuals come to
ppraisals of others who are important to them. In other words, individuals interpret
pear to others and how others judge that appearance; they therefore respond to the
hey "think" others make.

iotics and semiology are often referred to as two names for the same science of signs.
emiotics is actually a part of the philosophy of Charles S. Peirce, later taken up in
Umberto Eco. Semiology, on the other hand, is the theory of Ferdinand de Saussure
rated upon in the work of Roland Barthes and Jacques Lacan. The work of Saussure,
d Lacan is heavily influenced by and intertwined with Freudian psychoanalysis,
heories of the unconscious. Peirce's semiotics does not address the unconscious, but
orates a theory of the referent.
hes rejects this notion of the transparent iconic sign. Much like Goffman, he rejects
that images are or could be iconic. Instead, images are signs whose meanings are
s. Barthes explains that an icon or an analogic code, lacking communicative proper-
e of resistance to meaning. Analogy is perceived as an inferior meaning. Advertising
sess linguistic properties; instead of a site that is resistant to meaning or that has only
ng, the image is polysemous, bearing an almost infinite chain of meanings.
Saussure, the sign is arbitrary. The sound image (meaning literally that we name
und) is equal to the signifier in contemporary semiology. Saussure refers to the
as we now think of it) as the "concept." Saussure's linguistic theory does not address
t. For Saussure, the meaning of representation is nothing more than another repre-
The sign does not "stand for" an object in general, but in very specific ways. See
1956).

course, many magazine advertisements now are attempting to arouse the level of the
olfactory as well as visual means. Many cologne ads are now heavily scented, and
scent becomes a part of every page of the magazine. Therefore, even if the reader
ot to attend to a cologne advertisement, there is an effect at the visceral level.
ving through the mirror stage does not constitute the baby as a unified ego (as in humanist
y or ego psychology). The unified ego is itself an ideology or a fantasy. Instead, he or she
ted by the "lack" or "absence" of an unmediated real. Because the subject lives in
culture, the symbolic, he or she is separated from the real. Central to Lacan's theory of
bjectivity is his distinction between the "unconscious" and the "preconscious." The
us, for Lacan, operates through a crude sliding of images, sounds, smells, and so on. It is
high affect—loves, needs, desires, and the like—that cannot tell the difference between
n and the hallucination of satisfaction. Language is structured in the unconscious. The
ous organizes subjectivity as a system of differences. It is a system with low affect attached
eeds, desires, and so on, and operates by displacing those emotions. The preconscious
kind of censor and discipline for the unconscious.

dane other (Fredrickson, 1988; Miles, 1989; Omi & Winant, 1986), "a blot on the cultural landscape" (Roach & Felix, 1989, p. 130). These cultural ways of seeing are changing, but very slowly.

DISCUSSION

Since the rash of sex roles research and Goffman's semiotic content analysis published in the 1970s, feminist scholars, in particular, have been instrumental in focusing their analyses of gender and advertising on the larger theoretical and epistemological debates bubbling up in feminist scholarship, the social sciences, and the humanities. For example, scholars such as Williamson and Coward have employed advances in film theory, psychoanalysis, and structuralism to analyze how gender subjectivities are positioned through advertising. The psychoanalytic perspective can be credited with giving scholars of gender advertising the theoretical tools to analyze the concept of the "male gaze" and the "voyeuristic gaze" encoded in most mass media in U.S. society. Further, feminist scholars of gender advertising have relied heavily on the construct of the "split consciousness" of the female subject to theorize how advertising works to encourage women to view themselves continuously as objects to be improved upon for the male other, rather than as subjects of their own femaleness.

However, the ferment in gender advertising research at present is in the area of "reception," or how gendered audience members interpret how these images "fit" with their everyday experiences. Recently, many feminist writers on female pleasures in looking, especially in film theory, have expressed growing discomfort with the limited range of female pleasures in looking that can be explored with the male gaze, woman-as-object frame (see Betterton, 1985; Doane, 1982; Kaplan, 1983; Mulvey, 1989; Pribram, 1988; Waldman, 1989). Many of these scholars contend that although the convention of the male gaze in visual images is a dominant convention in U.S. society, it is wrong to theorize that female spectatorship can be seen only as an activity that is dictated by the male gaze. Women have developed their own ways of looking that should not be defined through the masculine lens.

Both Rosemary Betterton (1985) and Diane Waldman (1989) argue that whereas one must be careful not to minimize or trivialize the power of dominant ways of seeing visual images, one must also be aware of the changing and evolving consciousness of many of the female spectators in question. According to Betterton, a result of this evolving consciousness is the ability of many female spectators to switch points of view between the position of surveyor (active, voyeuristic) and that of the surveyed (passive, narcissistic). This ability empowers the female spectator with the ability to take up a critical position of looking that is not traditionally masculine or feminine.

In looking at a glamour photo or a nude it is possible to be both fascinated and attracted by the image, and at the same time, be well aware of the difference between the image and our experience: just as in reading a romance or in watching a melodrama one can be swept up by, and yet recognize the seductive pull of fantasy. (Betterton, 1985, p. 10)

It is possible to both read "against the grain" and enjoy the pleasure of viewing. This ability, or need, is what is meant by "negotiating" with the text and is similar in conceptualization to Stuart Hall's notion of articulation:

The term negotiation implies the holding together of opposite sides in an ongoing process of give and take. As a model of meaning production, negotiation conceives cultural exchange as the intersection of processes of production and reception, in which overlapping but nonmatching determinations operate. Meaning is neither imposed or passively imbibed, but arises out of a struggle or negotiation between competing frames of reference, motivation and experience. (Gledhill, 1988, p. 68)

In the past, many feminist scholars would have considered female pleasure gained from a dominant oppressive text to be a naive reading and a sign of "preconsciousness" (see Kuhn, 1985). Without dismissing the possibility that this type of reading is still prevalent in U.S. society, feminist interviewers and ethnographers are beginning to discover the dynamics of ways of looking and reading that are both critical of and responsive to the particular representation or cultural form being investigated (see Shields & Dervin, 1993).

Waldman (1989) argues that once we begin to theorize about the possibilities of the critical and at the same time responsive female spectator, it is helpful to distinguish the positions that are "feminist" from those that are strictly "female." This ability to move between culturally defined male and female viewing positions is not the innate province of the female psyche, but is instead the result of a disruption in traditional ways of seeing that can be directly attributed to multiple feminist discourses in society. No longer can the female spectator be seen solely in the dualistic terms of the culturally emasculated (determined by the male gaze) or the culturally enlightened (empowered by the teachings of feminist scholarship). Instead, a female spectator's ability to be critical of the images from which she derives pleasure may be the product of her everyday cultural experiences.

A limited number of theories of male spectatorship seems to take an opposite stance. Whereas women are able to negotiate with images from their own experience, presenting its nuances and sensations, men, even at their most perceptive, seem to theorize about themselves, analyzing from the outside (Tolson, 1977). Betterton (1985) concludes that men too look critically, but within forms of culture made for and by men, they are less likely to be forced to negotiate the viewpoint. Further, they are less likely to choose to do so.

A few authors have commented on the r confines of their larger arguments (Dyer, 1982 and scholarship focusing on masculinity as a rise (see Boone & Cadden, 1990; Chapman baugh, 1990; Craig, 1992; Kervin, 1990; Nai One reason for a "lack" of theory on the ma female spectatorship may be the inherent ass will generally decode along the lines of the doi of the text. The representation is made for hir for negotiation or distance. The gaze encodec the decoder is a "natural" psychoanalytic fit subject position" in the text will parallel the re

This argument is what many feminist schola Barrett, 1987). Male audience members, like fei their own experiences, situational constraints, entations to the viewing. Feminist scholars su emphasize the need to resist viewing the differei as the only and most important divisions. Experi gender, such as class, race, education, and sexu important to investigate. Although the literature the fact that males and females will decode dif be taken to suggest that male decoding will be r

Future research in gender and advertising rece subtle distinctions, avoiding essentialist argumen rigorous investigations of where gender decoding situations, for example, where female and male dec within gender. For example, recent gay and lesbian spectatorship suggests that not only would lesbian ures in looking at women than would straight woi differences between lesbian pleasures in looking looking (Dyer, 1982, 1984, 1987; Gross, 1991; Kiel 1983; Stacey, 1989). Another scenario that could si within a gender might involve men who have had e and consciousness as opposed to men who have not

NOTES

1. Three general types of content analysis concentrating throughout this era: analyses of the types and frequencies of r TV dramas (Downing, 1974; Lemon, 1978; McNeil, 1975; Seeg 1974), analyses of women's and men's portrayals in magazine ac 1976; Courtney & Lockeretz, 1971; Dodd, Harcar, Foerch, & 1976; Poe, 1976; Sexton & Haberman, 1974; Skelly & Lundstroi Wohleter & Lammers, 1980), and analyses of gender portrayal:

& Schuman,
& Rauch, 19

2. Intera
According t
The 'me' en
values, and
individual a
indicating a
"self-indica
assumes and
points" (int
however, is
defined by
appraisal" (
buck, & Sc
reflect the a
how they ai
judgments

3. Sem
However, s
the work of
and is elab
Barthes, ai
especially
instead ela

4. Bar
the notion
polysemou
ties, is a si
images po
one meani

5. For
through s
signified (
the refere
sentation.
Saussure (

6. Of
sensual b
often the
chooses r

7. M
philosoph
is constit
language,
human su
unconscio
an area o
satisfacti
preconsc
to loves,
acts as a

8. "The central motif of most pornography is the presentation of women's bodies, or parts of them, for consumption by men. The woman will be positioned in front of the camera in a way designed to produce maximum arousal in the purchaser by making her body accessible to his gaze" (Root, 1984, p. 43).

9. Wolf (1991, p. 185) reports that in the 20 years after the start of the second wave of the women's movement, the average weight of Miss America plummeted and the average weight of *Playboy* Playmates dropped from 11% below national average in 1970 to 17% below it in 8 years. The average model, dancer, or actress is thinner than 95% of the U.S. female population.

10. Estimates of the percentage of American women suffering from eating disorders vary, mainly because of the secretive nature of the illnesses, especially in the case of bulimia. Wolf (1991) reports that the American Anorexia and Bulimia Association states that these illnesses strike a million American women every year; 30,000, it reports, also become emetic abusers. Each year, according to the association, 150,000 American women die of anorexia. Brumberg (1988) estimates the number of anorexics at 5% to 10% of all American girls and women. On some college campuses, she believes, one woman student in five is anorexic.

REFERENCES

Altman, I., & Taylor, D. A. (1973). *Social penetration: The development of interpersonal relationships.* New York: Holt, Rinehart & Winston.

Bardwick, J., & Schuman, S. (1967). Portrait of American men and women in TV commercials. *Psychology, 4*(4), 18-23.

Barrett, M. (1987). The concept of difference. *Feminist Review, 26,* 29-40.

Barthes, R. (1974). *Mythologies* (A. Lavers, Trans.). New York: Hill & Wang.

Barthes, R. (1977). *Image-music-text.* New York: Noonday.

Barthes, R. (1988). *The semiotic challenge* (R. Howard, Trans.). New York: Hill & Wang.

Belkaoui, A., & Belkaoui, J. M. (1976). A comparative study of the roles portrayed by women in print advertisements: 1958, 1969, 1972. *Journal of Marketing Research, 13,* 168-172.

Benjamin, J. (1986). A desire of one's own: Psychoanalytic feminism and intersubjective space. In T. de Lauretis (Ed.), *Feminist studies/critical studies* (pp. 78-101). Bloomington: Indiana University Press.

Berger, C. R., Gardner, R. R., Clatterbuck, G. W., & Schulman, L. S. (1976). Perceptions of information sequencing in relational development. *Human Communication Research, 3,* 29-46.

Berger, J. (1972). *Ways of seeing.* London: British Film Institute.

Betterton, R. (1985). How do women look? The female nude in the work of Suzanne Valadon. *Feminist Review, 19,* 3-24.

Blumer, H. (1969). *Symbolic interactionism: Perspective and method.* Englewood Cliffs, NJ: Prentice Hall.

Bobo, J. (1988). *The Color Purple*: Black women as cultural readers. In E. D. Pribram (Ed.), *Female spectators: Looking at film and television* (pp. 90-109). London: Verso.

Boone, J. A., & Cadden, M. (Eds.). (1990). *Engendering men: The question of male feminist criticism.* New York: Routledge.

Bordo, S. (1993). *Unbearable weight.* Los Angeles: University of California Press.

Bretl, D. J., & Cantor, J. (1988). The portrayal of men and women in U.S. television commercials: A recent content analysis and trends over 15 years. *Sex Roles, 18,* 595-609.

Brown, M. E. (1989). Soap opera and women's culture: Politics and the popular. In K. Carter & C. Spitzack (Eds.), *Doing research on women's communication* (pp. 161-190). Norwood, NJ: Ablex.

Brown, M. E. (1990). *Television and women's culture.* Newbury Park, CA: Sage.

Bruch, H. (1988). *Conversations with anorexics* (D. Czyzewski & M. A. Suhr, Eds.). New York: Basic Books.

Brumberg, J. J. (1988). *Fasting girls: The emergence of anorexia nervosa as a modern disease*. Cambridge, MA: Harvard University Press.

Budge, B. (1989). Joan Collins and the wilder side of women: Exploring pleasure and representation. In L. Gamman & M. Marshment (Eds.), *The female gaze: Women as viewers of popular culture* (pp. 102-111). Seattle: Real Comet.

Burniston, S., Mort, F., & Weedon, C. (1978). Psychoanalysis and the cultural acquisition of sexuality and subjectivity. In Women's Study Group, Centre for Contemporary Cultural Studies (Ed.), *Women take issue* (pp. 109-131). London: Hutchinson.

Busby, L. J. (1975). Sex-role research on the mass media. *Journal of Communication, 25*(4), 107-131.

Byars, J. (1988). Gazes/voices/power: Expanding psychoanalysis for feminist film and television theory. In E. D. Pribram (Ed.), *Female spectators: Looking at film and television* (pp. 110-131). London: Verso.

Cantor, M. G. (1972). Comparison of the tasks and roles of males and females in commercials aired by WRC-TV. In National Organization for Women (Ed.), *Women in the wasteland fight back: A report on the image of women portrayed in TV programming* (pp. 12-51). Washington, DC: National Organization for Women.

Chapman, R., & Rutherford, J. (Eds.). (1988). *Male order: Unwrapping masculinity*. London: Lawrence & Wishart.

Chernin, K. (1986). *The hungry self: Women, eating and identity*. London: Virago.

Clatterbaugh, K. (1990). *Contemporary perspectives on masculinity: Men, women, and politics in modern society*. Boulder, CO: Westview.

Courtney, A. E. (1983). *Sex stereotyping in advertising*. Lexington, MA: Lexington.

Courtney, A. E., & Lockeretz, S. W. (1971). A woman's place: An analysis of the roles portrayed by women in magazine advertisements. *Journal of Marketing Research, 8*, 92-95.

Courtney, A. E., & Whipple, T. W. (1974). Women in TV commercials. *Journal of Communication, 24*(2), 110-118.

Courtney, A. E., & Whipple, T. W. (1983). *Sex stereotyping in advertising*. Lexington, MA: Lexington.

Coward, R. (1982). Sexual violence and sexuality. *Feminist Review, 16*(11), 9-22.

Coward, R. (1985). *Female desires: How they are sought, bought and packaged*. New York: Grove.

Coward, R., & Ellis, J. (1977). *Language and materialism: Developments in semiology and the theory of the subject*. London: Routledge & Kegan Paul.

Craig, S. (Ed.). (1992). *Men, masculinity, and the media*. Newbury Park, CA: Sage.

Culley, J. D., & Bennett, R. (1976). Selling women, selling blacks. *Journal of Communication, 26*(4), 160-174.

Dervin, B., & Shields, V. R. (in press). Communications: Overview. In C. Kramarae & D. Spender (Eds.), *The women's studies international encyclopedia*. London: Simon & Schuster.

Diamond, N. (1985). Thin is the feminist issue. *Feminist Review, 19*, 45-65.

Doane, M. A. (1982). Film and the masquerade: Theorising the female spectator. *Screen, 23*(3-4), 74-87.

Dodd, D. K., Harcar, V., Foerch, B. J., & Anderson, H. T. (1989). Face-ism and facial expressions of women in magazine photos. *Psychological Record, 39*, 325-331.

Dominick, J. R., & Rauch, G. E. (1972). The image of women in network TV commercials. *Journal of Broadcasting, 16*, 259-265.

Downing, M. (1974). Heroine of the daytime serial. *Journal of Communication, 24*(2), 130-137.

Dyer, R. (1982). Don't look now: The instabilities of the male pin-up. *Screen, 23*(3-4), 61-74.

Dyer, R. (Ed.). (1984). *Gays and films*. New York: Zoetrope.

Dyer, R. (1987). *Heavenly bodies: Film stars and society*. New York: St. Martin's.

Dyer, R. (1988). White. *Screen, 29*(4), 44-65.

Ewen, S. (1976). *Captains of consciousness.* New York: McGraw-Hill.

Featherstone, M. (1991). The body in consumer culture. In M. Featherstone, M. Hepworth, & B. S. Turner (Eds.), *The body: Social process and cultural theory* (pp. 170-196). Newbury Park, CA: Sage.

Fejes, F. (1992). Masculinity as fact: A review of empirical mass communication research on masculinity. In S. Craig (Ed.), *Men, masculinity, and the media* (pp. 9-22). Newbury Park, CA: Sage.

Ferguson, J. H., Kreshel, P. J., & Tinkham, S. F. (1990). In the pages of *Ms.:* Sex role portrayals of women in advertising. *Journal of Advertising, 19*(1), 40-51.

Ferrante, C. L., Haynes, A. M., & Kingsley, S. M. (1988). Image of women in television advertising. *Journal of Broadcasting & Electronic Media, 32,* 231-237.

Firat, F. (1994). Gender and consumption: Transcending the feminine. In J. A. Costa (Ed.), *Gender issues and consumer behavior* (pp. 205-228). Thousand Oaks, CA: Sage.

Fisher, B. A. (1978). *Perspectives on human communication.* New York: Macmillan.

Flitterman-Lewis, S. (1987). Psychoanalysis, film, and television. In R. C. Allen (Ed.), *Channels of discourse: Television and contemporary criticism* (pp. 172-209). Chapel Hill: University of North Carolina Press.

Foucault, M. (1979). *Discipline and punish: The birth of the prison.* New York: Vintage.

Fredrickson, G. M. (1988). *The arrogance of race: Historical perspectives on slavery, racism, and social inequality.* Middleton, CT: Wesleyan University Press.

Friedan, B. (1963). *The feminine mystique.* New York: Dell.

Furnham, A. (1989). Gender stereotypes in Italian television advertisements. *Journal of Broadcasting & Electronic Media, 33,* 175-185.

Gamman, L. (1989). Watching the detectives: The enigma of the female gaze. In L. Gamman & M. Marshment (Eds.), *The female gaze: Women as viewers of popular culture* (pp. 8-26). Seattle: Real Comet.

Gamman, L., & Marshment, M. (Eds.). (1989). *The female gaze: Women as viewers of popular culture.* Seattle: Real Comet.

Geis, F. L., Brown, V., Jennings, J., & Porter, N. (1984). TV commercials as achievement scripts for women. *Sex Roles, 10,* 513-525.

Gerbner, G., & Gross, L. (1976), Living with television: The Violence Profile. *Journal of Communication, 26*(2), 173-199.

Gillespie, M. A. (1993, January). Mirror mirror. *Essence,* pp. 73-79.

Gilly, M. C. (1988). Sex roles in advertising: A comparison of television advertisements in Australia, Mexico, and the United States. *Journal of Marketing, 52,* 75-85.

Gledhill, C. (1988). Pleasurable negotiations. In E. D. Pribram (Ed.), *Female spectators: Looking at film and television* (pp. 64-89). London: Verso.

Goffman, E. (1976). *Gender advertisements.* New York: Harper & Row.

Goldman, R. (1992). *Reading ads socially.* London: Routledge.

Gordon, B. (1984). Variety: The pleasure in looking. In C. S. Vance (Ed.), *Pleasure and danger: Toward a politics of sexuality* (pp. 189-203). London: Routledge & Kegan Paul.

Gould, S. J. (1987). Gender differences in advertising response and self-consciousness variables. *Sex Roles, 16,* 215-225.

Griffin, M., Viswanath, K., & Schwartz, D. (1992). *Gender advertising in the U.S. and India: Exporting cultural stereotypes.* Minneapolis: University of Minnesota, School of Journalism and Mass Communication.

Gross, L. (1991). Out of the mainstream: Sexual minorities and the mass media. In M. A. Wolf & A. P. Kielwasser (Eds.), *Gay people, sex and the media* (pp. 19-46). Binghamton, NY: Harryton Park/Haworth.

Haug, W. F. (1987). *Commodity aesthetics, ideology and culture* (S. Brown & K. Kramer, Trans.). New York: International General.

Hawkes, T. (1977). *Structuralism and semiotics.* London: Methuen.
Hawkins, J. W., & Aber, C. S. (1993). Women in advertisements in medical journals. *Sex Roles, 28,* 233-242.
Hay, J. (1989). Advertising as a cultural text (rethinking message analysis in a recombinant culture). In B. Dervin, L. Grossberg, B. J. O'Keefe, & E. Wartella (Eds.), *Rethinking communication* (pp. 129-151). Newbury Park, CA: Sage.
Holland, P. (1983). The page three girl speaks to women, too. *Screen, 24*(3), 84-102.
hooks, b. (1992). Representing whiteness in black imagination. In L. Grossberg, C. Nelson, & P. A. Treichler (Eds.), *Cultural studies* (pp. 338-346). New York: Routledge.
Hsu, L. K. G. (1990). *Eating disorders.* New York: Guilford.
Irigaray, L. (1985). *This sex which is not one.* Ithaca, NY: Cornell University Press.
Janus, N. Z. (1977). Research on sex-roles in the mass media: Toward a critical approach. *Insurgent Sociologist, 7,* 19-31.
Jhally, S. (1987). *Codes of advertising.* London: Frances Pinter.
Kaplan, E. A. (1983). *Women and film: Both sides of the camera.* New York: Methuen.
Kaplan, E. A. (1988). Whose imaginary? The television apparatus, the female body and textual strategies in select rock videos on MTV. In E. D. Pribram (Ed.), *Female spectators: Looking at film and television* (pp. 132-156). London: Verso.
Kellner, D. (1990). Advertising and consumer culture. In J. Downing, A. Mohammadi, & A. Sreberny-Mohammadi (Eds.), *Questioning the media: A critical introduction* (pp. 242-254). Newbury Park, CA: Sage.
Kervin, D. (1990). Advertising masculinity: The representation of males in "Esquire" advertisements. *Journal of Communication Inquiry, 14*(1), 51-70.
Kielwasser, A. P., & Wolf, M. A. (1992). Mainstream television, adolescent homosexuality, and significant silence. *Critical Studies in Mass Communication, 9,* 350-373.
Kimball, M. M. (1986). Television and sex-role attitudes. In T. M. Williams (Ed.), *The impact of television: A natural experiment in three communities* (pp. 265-284). New York: Academic Press.
Kuhn, A. (1985). *The power of the image.* Boston: Routledge & Kegan Paul.
Lacan, J. (1968). *The language of the self: The function of language in psychoanalysis* (A. Wilden, Trans.). New York: Dell.
Lacan, J. (1977). *Ecrits: A selection* (A. Sheridan, Trans.). New York: W. W. Norton.
Lague, L., & Lynn, A. (1993, September 20). How thin is too thin? *People,* pp. 74-80.
Lazarus, M. (Producer & Director). (1987). *Still killing us softly: Advertising images of women* [Film]. Cambridge: Jean Kilbourne/Cambridge Documentary Films.
Lazier, L., & Kendrick, A. G. (1993). Women in advertisements: Sizing up the images, roles, and functions. In P. J. Creedon (Ed.), *Women in mass communication* (2nd ed., pp. 199-219). Newbury Park, CA: Sage.
Lazier-Smith, L. (1988). *The effect of changes in women's social status on the images of women in magazine advertising: The Pingree-Hawkins sexism scale reapplied, Goffman reconsidered, Kilbourne revisited.* Unpublished doctoral dissertation, Indiana University.
Leiss, W., Kline, S., & Jhally, S. (1986). *Social communication in advertising: Persons, products, and images of well being.* London: Methuen.
Lemon, J. (1978). Dominant or dominated? Women on prime-time television. In G. Tuchman, A. K. Daniels, & J. Benet (Eds.), *Hearth and home: Images of women in the mass media* (pp. 51-68). New York: Oxford University Press.
Lewallen, A. (1989). Lace: Pornography for women? In L. Gamman & M. Marshment (Eds.), *The female gaze: Women as viewers of popular culture* (pp. 86-101). Seattle: Real Comet.
Lott, B. (1981). A feminist critique of androgyny: Toward the elimination of gender attributions for learned behavior. In C. Mayo & N. M. Henley (Eds.), *Gender and nonverbal behavior* (pp. 171-180). New York: Springer-Verlag.
Lovdal, L. T. (1989). Sex role messages in television commercials: An update. *Sex Roles, 21,* 715-724.

Lundstrom, W. J., & Sciglimpaglia, D. (1977). Sex role portrayals in advertising. *Journal of Marketing, 41,* 72-79.

Masse, M. A., & Rosenbaum, K. (1988). Male and female created they them: The depiction of gender in the advertising of traditional women's and men's magazines. *Women's Studies International Forum, 11,* 127-144.

Mazzella, C., Durkin, K., Cerini, E., & Buralli, P. (1992). Sex role stereotyping in Australian television advertisements. *Sex Roles, 26,* 243-259.

McArthur, L. Z., & Resko, B. G. (1975). The portrayal of men and women in American television commercials. *Journal of Social Psychology, 97,* 209-220.

McCracken, E. (1993). *Decoding women's magazines: From* Mademoiselle *to* Ms. London: Macmillan.

McKinnon, L. M. (1995). *Ms.*ing the free press: The advertising and editorial content of *Ms.* magazine, 1972-1992. In D. Abrahamson (Ed.), *The American magazine: Research perspectives and prospects* (pp. 98-107). Ames: Iowa State University Press.

McNeil, J. C. (1975). Feminism, femininity, and television series: A content analysis. *Journal of Broadcasting, 19,* 259-269.

McRobbie, A. (1984). Dance and social fantasy. In A. McRobbie & M. Nava (Eds.), *Gender and generation* (pp. 130-161). London: Macmillan.

Miles, R. (1989). *Racism.* London: Routledge.

Millium, T. (1975). *Images of women: Advertising in women's magazines.* London: Chatto & Windus.

Mitchell, J. (1975). *Psychoanalysis and feminism: Freud, Reich, Laing and women.* New York: Vintage.

Moore, S. (1989). Here's looking at you, kid! In L. Gamman & M. Marshment (Eds.), *The female gaze: Women as viewers of popular culture* (pp. 44-59). Seattle: Real Comet.

Morrison, B. J., & Sherman, R. C. (1972). Who responds to sex in advertising? *Journal of Advertising Research, 12*(2), 15-19.

Morse, M. (1987-1988). Artemis aging: Exercise and the female body on video. *Discourse, 10*(1), 20-53.

Mulvey, L. (1975). Visual pleasure and narrative cinema. *Screen, 16*(3), 6-18.

Mulvey, L. (1989). *Visual and other pleasures.* Bloomington: Indiana University Press.

Myers, K. (1982). Fashion 'n' passion. *Screen, 23*(2-3), 89-97.

Myers, K. (1986). *Understains: The sense and seduction of advertising.* London: Comedia.

Myers, P. N., & Biocca, F. A. (1992). The elastic body image: The effect of television advertising and programming on body image. *Journal of Communication, 42*(3), 108-133.

Nakayama, T. K. (1994). Show/down time: Race, gender, sexuality, and popular culture. *Critical Studies in Mass Communication, 11,* 162-179.

Neale, S. (1983). Masculinity as spectacle. *Screen, 24*(6), 2-16.

Nichols, B. (1981). *Ideology and the image.* Bloomington: Indiana University Press.

O'Barr, W. M. (1994). *Culture and the ad: Exploring otherness in the world of advertising.* Oxford: Westview.

O'Donnell, W. J., & O'Donnell, K. J. (1978). Update: Sex-role messages in TV commercials. *Journal of Communication, 28*(1), 156-158.

Omi, M., & Winant, H. (1986). *Racial formation in the United States from the 1960s to the 1980s.* London: Routledge.

Peirce, K. (1989). Sex-role stereotyping of children on television: A content analysis of the roles and attributes of child characters. *Sociological Spectrum 9,* 321-328.

Pingree, S., Hawkins, R. P., Butler, R. P., & Paisley, W. (1976). Equality in advertising: A scale for sexism. *Journal of Communication, 26*(2), 193-200.

Poe, A. (1976). Active women in ads. *Journal of Communication 26*(2), 185-192.

Pribram, E. D. (Ed.). (1988). *Female spectators: Looking at film and television.* London: Verso.

Pronger, B. (1990). *The arena of masculinity.* New York: St. Martin's.

Putnam, L. (1982). In search of gender: A critique of communication and sex-roles research. *Women's Studies in Communication, 5,* 1-9.

Radway, J. (1984). *Reading the romance: Women, patriarchy, and popular literature.* Chapel Hill: University of North Carolina Press.

Rakow, L. (1986). Rethinking gender in communication. *Journal of Communication, 36*(4), 11-26.

Rapping, E. (1994). *Media-tions: Forays into the culture and gender wars.* Boston: South End.

Roach, J., & Felix, P. (1989). Black looks. In L. Gamman & M. Marshment (Eds.), *The female gaze: Women as viewers of popular culture* (pp. 130-142). Seattle: Real Comet.

Root, J. (1984). *Pictures of women: Sexuality.* Boston: Pandora.

Rose, J. (1986). *Sexuality in the field of vision.* London: Verso.

Rosen, R. (1986). Search for yesterday. In T. Gitlin (Ed.), *Watching television* (pp. 42-67). New York: Pantheon.

Rossi, S. R., & Rossi, J. S. (1985). Gender differences in the perception of women in magazine advertising. *Sex Roles, 12,* 1033-1039.

Saunders, C. S., & Stead, B. A. (1986). Women's adoption of a business uniform: A content analysis of magazine advertisements. *Sex Roles, 15,* 197-205.

Saussure, F. de. (1956). *A course in general linguistics* (W. Baskin, Trans.). London: Peter Owen.

Schudson, M. (1984). *Advertising, the uneasy persuasion: Its dubious impact on American society.* New York: Basic Books.

Schuetz, S., & Sprafkin, J. N. (1978). Spot messages appearing within Saturday morning television programs. In G. Tuchman, A. K. Daniels, & J. Benet (Eds.), *Hearth and home: Images of women in the mass media* (pp. 69-77). New York: Oxford University Press.

Seeger, J. (1974). Imagery of women in television drama: 1974. *Journal of Broadcasting, 19,* 273-281.

Sexton, D. E., & Haberman, P. (1974). Women in magazine advertisements. *Journal of Advertising Research, 14*(4), 41-46.

Shefer, T. (1990). Feminist theories of the role of the body within women's oppression. *Critical Arts, 5*(2), 37-54.

Shields, V. R. (1990). Advertising visual images: Gendered ways of seeing and looking. *Journal of Communication Inquiry, 14*(2), 25-39.

Shields, V. R., & Dervin, B. (1993). Sense-making in feminist social science research: A call to enlarge the methodological options of feminist studies. *Women's Studies International Forum, 16,* 65-81.

Shimanoff, S. B. (1980). *Communication rules: Theory and research.* Beverly Hills, CA: Sage.

Skelly, G. U., & Lundstrom, W. J. (1981). Male sex roles in magazine advertising, 1959-1979. *Journal of Communication, 31*(4), 52-57.

Spitzack, C. (1988). Body talk: The politics of weight loss and female identity. In B. Bate & A. Taylor (Eds.), *Women communicating: Studies of women's talk* (pp. 51-74). Norwood, NJ: Ablex.

Spitzack, C. (1990). *Confessing excess: Women and the politics of body reduction.* Albany: State University of New York Press.

Spivak, G. C. (1989). A response to the difference within. In E. Meese & A. Parker (Eds.), *The difference within* (pp. 207-220). Philadelphia: John Benjamin.

Stacey, J. (1989). Desperately seeking difference. In L. Gamman & M. Marshment (Eds.), *The female gaze: Women as viewers of popular culture* (pp. 112-129). Seattle: Real Comet.

Stacey, J. (1994). *Star gazing: Hollywood cinema and female spectatorship.* London: Routledge.

Steeves, H. L. (1987). Feminist theories and media studies. *Critical Studies in Mass Communication, 4,* 95-135.

Tedesco, N. (1974). Patterns in prime time. *Journal of Communication, 24*(2), 119-124.

Tolson, A. (1977). *The limits of masculinity.* London: Routledge.

Tseëlon, E. (1995). *The masque of femininity.* Thousand Oaks, CA: Sage.

Tuchman, G., Daniels, A., & Benet, J. (Eds.). (1978). *Hearth and home: Images of women in the mass media.* New York: Oxford University Press.

Turner, B. S. (1984). *The body and society: Explorations in social theory.* New York: Basil Blackwell.

Turow, J. (1974). Advising and ordering: Daytime, prime time. *Journal of Communication, 24*(2), 138-141.

Van Zoonen, L. (1994). *Feminist media studies.* Thousand Oaks, CA: Sage.

Wagner, L. C., & Banos, J. B. (1973). A woman's place: A follow-up analysis of the roles portrayed by women in magazine advertisements. *Journal of Marketing Research, 10,* 213-214.

Waldman, D. (1989). Film theory and the gendered spectator: The female or the feminist reader? *Camera Obscura, 18,* 80-94.

Warlaumont, H. G. (1993). Visual grammars of gender: The gaze and psychoanalytic theory in advertisements. *Journal of Communication Inquiry, 17*(1), 25-40.

Wernick, A. (1991). *Promotional culture: Advertising, ideology and symbolic expression.* New York: Russell Sage.

Whipple, T. W., & Courtney, A. E. (1985). Female role portrayals in advertising and communication effectiveness: A review. *Journal of Advertising, 14*(3), 4-8.

Williamson, J. (1978). *Decoding advertisements.* London: Methuen.

Williamson, J. (1986). Woman is an island: Femininity and colonization. In T. Modleski (Ed.), *Studies in entertainment: Critical approaches to mass culture* (pp. 99-118). Bloomington: Indiana University Press.

Winship, J. (1981). Handling sex. *Media, Culture & Society, 3*(3), 25-41.

Winship, J. (1985). "A girl needs to get street-wise": Magazines of the 1980s. *Feminist Review, 21,* 25-46.

Wise, G. L., King, A. L., & Merenski, J. P. (1974). Reactions to sexy ads vary with age. *Journal of Advertising Research, 14*(4), 11-16.

Wohleter, M., & Lammers, B. H. (1980). An analysis of male roles in print advertisements over a 20-year span: 1958-1978. In J. C. Olson (Ed.), *Advances in consumer research* (pp. 760-761). Ann Arbor, MI: Association for Consumer Research.

Wolf, N. (1991). *The beauty myth: How images of beauty are used against women.* Garden City, NY: Anchor.

Wortzel, L., & Frisbie, J. M. (1974). Women's role portrayal preferences in advertisements. *Journal of Marketing, 38,* 41-46.

Young, S. (1989). Feminism and the politics of power: Whose gaze is it anyway? In L. Gamman & M. Marshment (Eds.), *The female gaze: Women as viewers of popular culture* (pp. 173-187). Seattle: Real Comet.

Zraly, K., & Swift, D. (1990). *Anorexia, bulimia, and compulsive overeating: A practical guide for counselors and families.* New York: Continuum.

CHAPTER CONTENTS

4 Public Relations and the Production of News: A Critical Review and Theoretical Framework

GLEN T. CAMERON
LYNNE M. SALLOT
PATRICIA A. CURTIN
C. Richard Yarbrough Public Relations Laboratory, University of Georgia

Because the source-reporter relationship forms the focal point of news gathering, it is a significant topic in the media sociology literature. Most of the source-reporter literature, however, focuses on the routines and values of the reporter. In this chapter the authors argue that public relations often sets the agenda for news media simply because the source in source-reporter interaction is often either a public relations practitioner or a practitioner's client. A three-section model explaining the role and impact of public relations in the news-gathering and news dissemination process is presented and used to organize a review of the literature. The source-reporter relationship section of the model includes studies of mutual assessments and power dynamics. The organizational section contains studies of practices and values in public relations, including ethics and professional values such as routines and news values. The societal section of the model covers studies pertaining to information subsidies and other influences on news media agendas, such as marketing pressures. A summary assessment of the source-reporter literature concludes that too much of the scholarly research has been merely descriptive. Theoretical directions are suggested to enrich public relations research and our understanding of public relations practice.

IN recent years, a strong research tradition has developed in media sociological studies of mass communication—studies of the processes, routines, values, and social organization of news makers. A significant portion of the media sociology literature is devoted to source-reporter rela-

Correspondence and requests for reprints: Glen T. Cameron, C. Richard Yarbrough Public Relations Laboratory, Henry W. Grady College of Journalism and Mass Communication, University of Georgia, Athens, GA 30602-3018; e-mail gcameron@uga.cc.uga.edu

Communication Yearbook 20, pp. 111-155

tions. However, most of this literature focuses on the routines and values of the reporter, not of the source. By examining studies of the routines and values not of the news reporter, but of the news source, we seek a fresh perspective of particular value to public relations researchers and practitioners.

McCombs and Shaw's (1972) study of the 1968 U.S. presidential election introduced the concept of agenda setting—namely, that the media might not be successful in telling people what to think, but they do succeed in telling people what to think about. The media, then, are a determining factor in the issues up for public debate.

But who sets the agenda for the media? How do the media decide what issues are newsworthy and should be brought before the public everyday? As Hall (1973) notes, the process is not a transparent one:

> Journalists speak of "the news" as if events select themselves. Further, they speak as if which is the "most significant" news story, and which "news angles" are most salient are divinely inspired. Yet of the millions of events which occur every day in the world, only a tiny proportion, only a small fraction are actually produced as the day's news in the news media. (p. 181)

In this chapter we will argue that public relations often helps determine the day's news. Public relations sets the agenda for media simply because the source in source-reporter interaction is often either a public relations practitioner or a practitioner's client. Researchers have estimated that 25% to 50% of news content in the United States is influenced by public relations (Aronoff, 1976; Cutlip, Center, & Broom, 1994; Lee & Solomon, 1990; Sachsman, 1976; Sallot, 1990b), with some estimates running as high as 80%. The influence of public relations activity on news is so great that some have even suggested that issues suffering poor news coverage are those with "unskilled or no public relations" (Sandman, Rubin, & Sachsman, 1976, p. 266).

Because it is impossible for media gatekeepers to cover all events and issues, public relations practitioners serve a useful role for news media. At the same time, public relations efforts increase the probability that an event or issue will be covered, thereby achieving communication objectives for organizations. By focusing on studies of sources' attitudes, practices, and social impacts, we offer in this review not only a critical assessment of a school of public relations research, but insights about the practice of public relations.

A MODEL OF THE ROLE AND IMPACT OF SOURCES IN NEWS

Given the importance of public relations practice to the formation of news content and news agendas, it is no surprise that the impact and role of public relations have been the subject of at least 150 studies since the 1960s. These studies have spanned all qualitative and quantitative methods and have looked at topics ranging from effective "story pitching" to the hegemonic role of public relations sources in the information economy, from the ethics of public relations to power dynamics in source-reporter relationships.

The single element binding the literature is the public relations practitioner in his or her role as a news source. A source is defined as any person conveying information to a news reporter that can be used in a news story, thereby fulfilling one of many functions of public relations in organizations. Serving as a news source has implications for three distinct entities: the news reporter, the organization employing the public relations practitioner, and the news consumer. These three entities reflect relational, organizational, and societal domains of a basic model of news production. Central to the model is the relationship between the public relations person as news source and the reporter. The source functions within an organizational context, serving as boundary spanner between the organization and its publics, including the media. As news is produced, stories reach the third domain of the model, the news consumer, where societal impacts of public relations activity are considered.

The three domains of the model offer the framework for the literature review, as well as theoretical directions for future research. First, we review articles examining the source-reporter relationship. These articles fall into two groups:

1. *Mutual assessments:* studies that employ surveys to explore attitudes of reporters and sources toward each other
2. *Power dynamics in source-reporter relations:* studies that consider the adversarial relationship between reporters and sources in terms of power dynamics

We then examine the organizational domain of the model of practices and values in public relations. Portions of the research literature deal with what the public relations professional brings to his or her organization as background to any informational transactions that occur in the source-reporter relationship. Such antecedent factors are elements of the source's experience and worldview that are brought to bear on the source-reporter relationship within the organizational context.

1. *Ethics and professional values:* studies that formalize or evaluate source ethics and professional standards

Other aspects of the literature dealing with practices and values in public relations deal with both antecedent and coeval factors:

2. *Routines and practices of sources:* studies that document how sources do their media relations work
3. *News values and acceptance of source materials:* studies that identify and evaluate characteristics of effective source materials

Finally, we review the literature examining the societal impacts of news sources:

1. *Information subsidy:* studies and theoretical pieces that evaluate the impact of public relations on news agendas
2. *Marketing pressures:* studies that assess how budgetary pressures and profit motives affect source-reporter relations and hence the news "product"

In the second half of the chapter, which is based on a summary assessment of the source-reporter literature, we argue that too much of the scholarly work has been merely descriptive, particularly in the organizational and relational sections of the model. Future research must be better grounded in theories that afford parsimony and universality. Greater explanatory/predictive power is possible through theory testing than is typical of the periodic "snapshots" of current opinions and practices of sources and source contexts. The field should also gain a coherence and cogency currently lacking in the literature. To these ends, we close the chapter with suggestions regarding some theoretical directions that should enrich public relations research and our understanding of public relations practice.

LITERATURE REVIEW

The Source-Reporter Relationship

Public relations practitioners fulfill numerous functions in organizations, but one of their more visible and traditional functions is called *media relations*.[1] Practitioners attempt to relate their organizations' worldviews to reporters and in turn to relate reporters' questions and views to their organizations. In this boundary-spanning role between an organization and the news media (Wilcox, Ault, & Agee, 1995), a public relations practitioner serves as a buffer between the press and the organization's management (Dimmick, 1974). In the process, the practitioner's relationships with reporters can undergo tension and mistrust—this aspect of such relationships has made them the topic of numerous studies.

Mutual Assessments

A number of surveys have compared how journalists and public relations practitioners assess each other. Feldman (1961a, 1961b) was the first to conduct such a study, using a Likert-type attitude scale with pro and con statements.[2] Feldman's survey subjects were 746 city editors of newspapers and 88 officers of local Public Relations Society of America (PRSA) chapters across the country. Published accounts of his findings did not report statistics, only narrative interpretations. This inaugural study, like all subsequent studies in this vein, found discrepancies in the attitudes of the two groups on dimensions such as credibility, occupational status, and professionalism.

Two studies done in the 1970s to build on Feldman's work served as the basis for replication in the 1980s and 1990s. Aronoff's (1975) four-part study involved 48 Texas newspaper journalists and 26 area PR practitioners. In the first section, replicating Feldman's attitude survey, Aronoff found generally negative attitudes toward public relations by journalists and positive attitudes by practitioners, although "most public relations practitioners and many journalists acknowledge the contribution made by public relations to the process of news production" (p. 51). Replicating Feldman's earlier reports, Aronoff found that journalists view public relations practitioners as low in source credibility.

Aronoff (1975) also asked the journalists and practitioners in his sample to rank order their own news values and the perceived news values of their counterparts. News values rank ordered in this and similar studies typically included accuracy, interest to reader, usefulness to reader, completeness, prompt publication, and depiction of subject "in favorable light." Public relations practitioners' perceptions of journalists' news values were accurate and correlated highly with journalists' reported values, whereas journalists' perceptions of PR practitioners' reported values were highly inaccurate.

In addition, Aronoff (1975) used rank orderings by his subjects of 16 occupations to measure perceptions of status. The list included a public relations practitioner, journalist, architect, artist, banker, farmer, politician, and professor, among others. Journalists ranked themselves first and practitioners last. Practitioners ranked journalists third and themselves fourth, indicating perceptions of almost equal status.

To study the credibility of practitioners, Aronoff (1975) asked only the journalists to read and evaluate four feature stories: Half read stories attributed to fictional practitioners and half read stories attributed to fictional journalists. The journalists were then asked to evaluate the stories for writing quality, newsworthiness, interest, objectivity, originality, and style. They generally favored the stories attributed to journalists, and they considered PR practitioners to be low-credibility sources. Combining the findings with the attitude scale results, public relations practitioners were seen as highly motivated communicators with something to gain from acceptance of their messages. Journalists believed the self-interests of the public relations advocates interfered with their credibility.

Aronoff's survey, like all the replications reviewed below, suffers from a number of methodological weaknesses. Samples were drawn from professional society membership lists that may have represented relatively idealistic practitioners who were also perhaps better-trained and more ambitious practitioners than those who were not members of a professional society. One might conclude that attitudes of the larger PR practitioner population would be markedly different from those of the 10% to 20% of practitioners who join professional societies. Studies have tended to overgeneralize from this distinct sample.

The combined journalist-practitioner samples used in these studies have been small (fewer than 200 in all the surveys reviewed), and occasionally analyses have been based on even smaller subgroups within samples. Although socially desirable response sets concerning ethics, professional standards, news values, and mutual assessments were a distinct possibility, none of the studies describes attempts to measure this bias using scenario or projection questions or questionnaire designs employing progressive questions. Nor do any of the surveys in this group report inter-item reliability tests as a check for such concerns. Bearing in mind these methodological concerns, however, the studies offer many insights about source-reporter relations.

The second article serving as a progenitor of many subsequent studies was Jeffers's (1977) survey of the expectations that journalists and public relations practitioners have of each other. Jeffers developed a questionnaire with items focusing on skills, ethics, and cooperation-competitiveness.[3] The subjects were 51 newspaper journalists and 45 public relations practitioners in Ohio. For the ethics and skills items, subjects recorded their general perceptions of their counterparts, then answered again for members of the counterpart group with whom they had regular contact, and a third time for their own group.

Mark Twain once said, "Familiarity breeds contempt—and children." For journalists, familiarity with PR practitioners apparently breeds respect. For practitioners, however, familiarity with journalists breeds contempt. Jeffers found that the journalists in his study believed PR practitioners in general lacked ethics, but those with whom they had regular contact were significantly more ethical; the public relations practitioners evaluated the ethics of specific journalists as lower than those of journalists in general. Regarding skills and ethics, journalists had higher expectations of themselves than they had of either general or specific PR practitioners, whereas practitioners had slightly higher expectations of journalists in general than of themselves.

The journalists perceived their relationships with PR practitioners as slightly cooperative; the practitioners saw them as much more so. Again, the self-interests of public relations advocates hamper their credibility in the minds of journalists, at least until the individual journalist gets to know the individual practitioner. But increased contact between the two professional types does not change journalists' generally negative stereotypes of practitioners as a whole. Jeffers (1977) concludes that the "newsman/source relationship is not the adversary one suggested by conventional journalistic wisdom" (p. 306).

Brody (1984) found that generalizations of source-reporter antipathy are exaggerated. He surveyed 74 media gatekeepers and 38 members of a local PRSA chapter. As in the earlier studies, the public relations practitioners' perceptions of news media representatives were more positive than media gatekeepers' perceptions of practitioners. Ratings of their counterparts on items ranging from ethical behavior to writing skills, however, were uniformly high for both groups.

Swartz (1983) employed concepts of occupational sociology in a humanistic essay to study an undisclosed number of government press secretaries. He evaluated the tendency for journalists to progress through careers culminating in public relations practice. He notes that journalists and public relations practitioners have much in common, and that the differences are "based less upon the skills that each group uses than how each occupation is perceived by others" (p. 13). According to Swartz, journalists think of themselves as being above crass commercialism and hold a poor image of public relations. With the change from reporter to source comes a conflict of loyalties and a shift in commitments. Swartz points out that "side bets" such as buying a new house tend to accelerate the process of change and commitment to the new role. The government press secretaries Swartz studied experienced an inverse status passage when leaving reportorial jobs but justified the move as career advancement or culmination. This process of career and value change appears unidirectional: One becomes a product of the organizational culture and remains in it. Swartz concludes that journalists who work as press secretaries lose their credibility as journalists and are unable to return to the field because of these cultural images of the professions.

Like Aronoff, Kopenhaver, Martinson, and Ryan (1984) employed coorientation theory in analyzing mutual assessments by 47 Florida journalists and 57 PRSA members. The journalists and public relations persons agreed on which elements of news are most important, and the public relations persons accurately perceived the journalists' news values. But the journalists inaccurately perceived the stated positions of the public relations persons. Whereas the journalists expected that public relations news values would place "depicting the subject in a favorable light" as most important, public relations persons actually ranked this as least important. Largely replicating Aronoff's measure of professional status, Kopenhaver et al. found that journalists ranked themselves first and PR practitioners next to last. Practitioners ranked themselves fourth, as in the Aronoff study, but journalists ninth.

Kopenhaver (1985) published a second article from the same data set used by Kopenhaver et al., reporting that news values of the two groups were virtually identical but that their views toward public relations practice conflicted. The journalists viewed public relations practitioners as obstructionist and their news releases as publicity disguised as news. Kopenhaver calls for educators to avoid stereotyping public relations in a negative light and exhorts public relations practitioners to maintain practice consistent with the news values they claim to hold.

Stegall and Sanders (1986) used a Q-sort technique of 50 statements to replicate Kopenhaver et al.'s (1984) coorientation study. Six education reporters at newspapers of various sizes and eight public relations practitioners at different educational institutions participated. This study corroborates Kopenhaver et al.'s results; its main difference from earlier work is found in the identification of two distinct public relations practitioner profiles. First are those long-time practitioners who are idealistic, altruistic, and see themselves as journalists or communicators, with responsibility to society as well as the institution; second are those practitioners who see themselves as businesspeople first and journalists second, with first allegiance to the institution, and a marketing or promotional orientation. Generally, practitioners of the first type in Stegall and Sanders's study had values more closely aligned with those of the practitioners in Kopenhaver et al.'s study.

Two replications of Aronoff's work have drawn similar conclusions. Sallot's (1990b) sample included 66 PRSA members in South Florida, 53 PRSA members in metropolitan New York, 50 working journalist members of the Society of Professional Journalists (SPJ) in South Florida, and 35 working journalist SPJ members in metropolitan New York. Sallot argues that low valuations by journalists of PR practitioners' news values contributes to the low credibility journalists assign to practitioners. Carroll (1994) surveyed 83 journalists who cover education and 119 public relations practitioners representing colleges and universities across the country. Carroll found the reporters held negative opinions about the practitioners, ranked themselves higher in occupational status, and did not perceive the same news value orientations for practitioners as for themselves. The PR practitioners held higher opinions of themselves and their work than the journalists did, ranked themselves equal in occupational status to education writers, and had the same news value orientations as journalists.

These mutual assessment studies share an interesting pattern. Distrust and low esteem for public relations practitioners are more profound in the abstract than in the specific experience of journalists. Perhaps it "is hard to hate up close." Or perhaps a stereotype has been promulgated about public relations that does not reconcile with experience. Cline (1982) conducted a content analysis of 12 introductory mass communication texts to evaluate their portrayal of public relations. She found public relations stereotyped as less ethical, less professional, but better paying than journalism. The prevailing metaphor for public relations was prostitution.

Further evidence also suggests that college courses in journalism are anti-public relations. Another replication of Aronoff's work by Habermann, Kopenhaver, and Martinson (1988)—this one surveying 80 university faculty in news-editorial and public relations sequences nationwide—found that news-editorial faculty held only slightly less negative attitudes toward public relations than their professional counterparts. A survey by Pincus, Rimmer, Rayfield, and Cropp (1993) of 166 business, news, and sports editors' perceptions of PR practitioners indicated that editors who had completed college courses in public relations viewed public relations more positively than did editors who had not, presumably because such courses afford a better understanding of public relations.

In sum, education apparently has an impact on subsequent professional values. Textbooks and course content may be sources of generalized negative assessments of public relations. In practice or on specific evaluative points, however, the schism between journalists and practitioners is not so profound.

Two content analyses demonstrate a convergence of academic and journalistic stereotypes of public relations. In an analysis of the terms *public relations* and *PR* in 84 published press references, Spicer (1993) found that more than 80% of the time the terms were embedded in negative contexts. Disaster, distraction, and mere fluff accounted for 55% of all uses. Schmooze and hype accounted for 20%, and war accounts for 8%. Spicer's sample, however, was serendipitous, consisting of all print mentions sent to him over a 4-year period. Although some of the mentions occurred in cartoons, letters to editors, and other outside material, Spicer attributes all the meanings expressed to journalists. The results, therefore, must be viewed as perhaps more indicative of the larger cultural meaning of public relations than of specifically journalists' attitudes toward the profession.

Bishop (1988) found more innocuous tendencies in his content analysis of three newspapers. The term *public relations* was seldom mentioned in the press; *publicity,* however, was often used. Bishop concludes that journalists view public relations as equivalent to publicity, and this is how journalists tend to use the concept in their writing. Such a view makes sense given that the interaction between source and reporter usually has to do with publicity. However, journalists tend to be unaware that media relations is generally only one of many functions performed by public relations practitioners.

Turk (1985, 1986a, 1986b) offers an explanation of journalists' negative assessments of public relations that follows from typecasting public relations practitioners as publicists. Turk found that Louisiana journalists stated they had no distrust of public relations practitioners, yet preferred information dug up on their own over information from public relations sources. She suggests that the folklore of journalism emphasizes reportorial entrepreneurship and initiative. Furthermore, "in journalistic folklore there is a distrust, or mistrust, of public relations practitioners as biased 'flacks' engaged in puffery and manipulation of information, and indeed public relations practitioners themselves are indoctrinated to expect that attitude of distrust from journalists" (Turk, 1986a, p. 27).

This summary of journalistic folklore is supported by evidence from a study focusing on why such attitudes are held. Ryan and Martinson (1988) developed Likert-type attitude scales and surveyed 118 organization-affiliated PRSA members concerning antagonism between the two professions.[4] However, this study was more than a replication of earlier research that offered only a description of the relationship between source and reporter. Ryan and Martinson sought to analyze some of the reasons for the state of this relationship. In addition to citing blind prejudice as a cause, public relations practitioners reported unprofessional practices in public relations as contributing to negative reporter attitudes.

Ryan and Martinson's subjects were all public relations practitioners. Sallot (1990b) replicated Ryan and Martinson's work, but surveyed journalists as well as practitioners. The two groups agreed that journalists believe their work is more important to society than is public relations, which may account for some of the journalists' antagonism. The journalists also believed that PR practitioners bear part of the responsibility for journalists' negative attitudes because practitioners are responsible for policing the peripheral "bad apples." But the practitioners attributed journalists' negative attitudes toward public relations to the journalists' inflated views of their own status and their negative experiences with the few "bad apples" in public relations.

The practitioners also believed that journalists' dim view of public relations is not justified. The journalists blamed public relations practitioners for being unprofessional and insufficiently concerned about journalists' needs for clear, concise, accurate information and believed their negative attitudes were justified. Although some of the biases against public relations are unfair, they are widely accepted and stubbornly held.

Using a role theory perspective, Belz, Talbott, and Starck (1989) applied Q-methodology to four categories of roles—personal characteristics, rights, duties, and skills—to study cross-perceptions of journalists and practitioners. The authors derived 54 statements from journalism and public relations texts and professional codes. Subjects were 14 journalists from a variety of news media and with gatekeeping powers over public relations materials and 15 public relations practitioners who had media relations responsibilities. All subjects sorted the Q-statements twice: once according to perceptions of their own group's roles, then for the perceived roles of the other group. Order was randomized; statements were reshuffled between sortings. Attitudes between the two groups differed sharply about the role of public relations as well as specific issues such as freedom of the press, balance, objectivity, aggressiveness, protection of the public interest, withholding of information, diplomacy, previous experience, and ability to construct interesting messages. The journalists viewed public relations practitioners negatively for their role as advocates and for having hidden agendas, withholding information, and compromising ethics.

Power Dynamics in Source-Reporter Relations

Only two articles alluded to the question of power between source and reporter. Nicolai and Riley (1972) state that editorial gatekeepers occupy positions of power relative to public relations practitioners, "whose livelihoods depend on the decision-making power of editors to use their material" (p. 371).

In a brief article, Newsom (1983) provides a sketch of what could be called the adversary theory of the press. She begins by declaring that pressure groups receive more coverage than the institutions they attack. Parenti (1986), Gitlin

(1980), and others might beg to differ with this postulate. Newsom then explains her assertion by noting the following circumstances: Media technology enables direct, simple access; freedom of speech allows the use of pressure tactics (she gives no examples of pressure tactics, but one can assume that pseudoevents such as picketing would be an example). In these circumstances, Newsom seems to sympathize with the institutional victim, who is also constrained by the complexity of the problem from giving stock answers. The organization must retreat to silence and information suppression, leaving the public forum open to pressure groups. Newsom portrays pressure groups and the media as a combined force holding an unfair advantage over the public relations practitioner, although she cites Washington correspondent John B. Donovan's observation that the media adopt an adversarial position when dealing with a disagreeable administration, but the posture vanishes when the administration is agreeable. This article plays a trailblazing role in addressing the important issues of power and the adversarial function of the reporter.

Tangentially related to the concept of power may be job satisfaction and autonomy. In a survey of 395 journalists and 395 public relations practitioners in the San Francisco Bay Area, Olson (1989) found practitioners significantly more satisfied with their jobs, profession, salaries, and potential for career advancement. Although both groups showed significant correlations between job satisfaction and autonomy, journalists reported low levels of autonomy. Olson concludes that the comparatively lower levels of job satisfaction for journalists are a result of their lack of autonomy.

Practices and Values in Public Relations

Ethics and Professional Values

The literature on source ethics in source-reporter relations comprises two broad theoretical approaches. A majority of studies emphasizes professionalism as the means of codifying professional norms and standards. Much recent work employs general systems theory, either in a functional-structural approach to define standards or as a means of defining ethical standards for communication processes rather than decision outcomes.

Studies of professionalism have failed to find a strong sense of professional norms. Wright (1982) surveyed 72 accredited and 76 nonaccredited members of PRSA and compared responses on measures of professionalism, such as values and involvement in professional organizations. Although accredited practitioners scored higher, the level of professional orientation was still low.[5]

Codes of ethics are widely held to enhance images of professionalism (Hunt & Tirpok, 1993; Kruckeberg, 1993; Seib & Fitzpatrick, 1995; Wright, 1993). Studies of public relations codes of ethics, however, have criticized the codes for being either too rigid or too vague. Englehardt and Evans (1994), in an anecdotal overview, argue that a teleological approach is preferable because it would take into account situational and personal variances. Parsons (1993) suggests an alternative model for ethical decision making based on weighing and avoiding conflict among the individual, the organization, the profession, and society, but the model lacks normative force because avoidance of conflict is its only guide. Both studies note the problems inherent in trying to know and weigh consequences, and neither examines the effects that adoption of such systems over codes of ethics would have on perceived professionalism.

Sharpe (1986), in a prescriptive article, calls for operational definitions of the PRSA code standards to make them less vague and to give practitioners a buffer from management influence, to enhance the profession's credibility, and to provide professional accountability. Bivins (1993) specifically addresses the lack of development in the code of the concept of public interest, which he believes lies at the basis of professionalism. Both of these authors fail to examine the enforcement problems inherent in such development; breadth instead of specificity is a hallmark of codes because they cannot outline every situation or they risk creating ethical and legal pitfalls (Seib & Fitzpatrick, 1995). Because codes necessarily lack substance, Wright (1993) proposes that they serve the purpose of enhancing professionalism but are unenforceable and therefore not pragmatic solutions to ethical problems. Codes may slightly enhance public relations practitioners' reputations as sources with the media, but they do not provide concrete behavioral guidelines.

Scholars who have used coorientation theory to compare professionalism in public relations and journalism include Nayman, McKnee, and Lattimore (1977), who employed methodology similar to that used by Aronoff (1975) and Jeffers (1977). Nayman et al. found journalists and public relations practitioners to hold similar professional perspectives about expertise, autonomy, responsibility, and commitment to occupation and the public, but such similarities may have arisen because two-thirds of the public relations sample was made up of former journalists. The practitioners reported better pay and job satisfaction rates and emphasized the need to exert influence and hold more prestige-oriented jobs. Journalists were more team oriented and altruistic, and they complained about supervision; more than half of the journalists said they would consider public relations work if the price was right.

Ryan and Martinson (1991) surveyed 105 journalists and 105 PR practitioners to determine how members of each profession determined what constituted lying on the part of a source. Both groups defined telling untruths and denying rumors known to be true as lying; neither group believed refusing to comment or failing to tell the whole truth constituted lying on the part of a public relations practitioner. Ryan and Martinson conclude that the self-interest inherent in an advocacy role causes both journalists and public relations practitioners to view practitioners as less than forthright; thus, journalists do not view practitioners as serious sources.

In a historical essay, McBride (1989) criticizes this emphasis on coorientation theory and its ramifications for public relations ethics. Although Ivy

Lee, one of the earliest public relations practitioners, was a former journalist who worked within the journalist-in-residence model, McBride claims that Edward L. Bernays, the father of modern public relations, profoundly changed the nature of the profession by stressing its advocacy function. McBride believes that development of professional norms has stagnated at the earlier, journalistic stage, leaving a now persuasive profession locked into a dysfunctional journalistic ethic of objectivity to which it can never hope to conform and thus be perceived as ethical.

McBride concludes that because no professional norms have developed as an outgrowth of advocacy, practitioners lack direction when making ethical decisions, which results in ethical relativism. This conclusion is supported by the empirical work of Ryan and Martinson (1984), Olasky (1985), and Saunders (1989). Ryan and Martinson (1984) conducted a quasi-experiment using vignettes posing moral dilemmas with varying situations: public and nonprofit versus private and for profit. They found that varying the situational factors had no effect, despite professional folklore that corporate practitioners are less ethical than government or nonprofit practitioners. Respondents who were prepared to mislead the public did not blame management but recognized their personal responsibility for their actions. Overall, ethical relativism predominated: No majority response emerged because practitioners held no common guidelines on which to base their decisions.

In an article presenting findings from 50 interviews with middle- to upper-level practitioners in a major corporation, Olasky (1985) strongly condemns public relations as an adversarial, cynical profession that lacks ethical norms and makes manipulation of reporters a game. From the selected quotes presented, however, it is impossible to tell how representative these portrayals are of even the subjects interviewed at one corporation, much less the profession as a whole. Olasky's work leaves unexamined what variables (e.g., personal variables, such as educational background, age, and journalistic experience, and organizational variables, such as type and size of organization) predict abuses.

Saunders (1989) surveyed 95 members of the Florida Public Relations Association using open-ended questions to obtain their perceptions of professional ethics. Again, ethical relativism was evident: Almost 20% of respondents said they encountered no ethical dilemmas in their jobs, 62% were unsure when withholding information could be considered ethical, and many respondents were unsure when telling partial truths was allowable. Conversely, journalists may be held captive by public relations practitioners, who not only control access to news makers but also may create and control news. Practitioners often suffer divided loyalties between media "pounding them for not telling everything they know" and management pounding them "for telling too much" (Saunders, 1989, p. 26).

Although Olasky claims that persuasion can never be ethical (see Abend & Olasky, 1985), a position supported by Grunig (1992) in his recent theoretical work, the prevalent ethical relativism in the field has led Abend (Abend & Olasky, 1985), Nelson (1994), and McBride (1989) to make critical calls for an advocacy ethic based on social responsibility theory. Work on developing such an ethic has been limited; Barney and Black (1994) use political philosophy to sketch out the basis for such an ethic within a participatory democracy. Building from libertarian principles such as Milton's marketplace of ideas, they argue that within a democracy speech is protected to allow all voices to be heard: Advocacy is thus not only allowable but to be expected and encouraged. The obstacle to ethical public relations is authoritarianism, because it blocks free information flow. Such libertarianism is not unbounded, however; drawing on social contract theory, Barney and Black assert that public relations must abandon its advocacy role when it endangers the larger social interest. They do not, however, provide guidelines for determining when individual and societal goals are in conflict or any motivation for subsuming libertarian principles to those of social responsibility when they do conflict.

Whereas the studies mentioned above have built on the role of public relations in society to develop a professional ethic, Judd (1989) and Bivins (1987, 1989) have suggested a structural-functional approach based in systems theory. In humanistic essays, Bivins has proposed different ethical standards for the two major public relations functions: communication technician and communication manager. He equates the function of a communication technician with that of a courtroom lawyer, who functions as an advocate and whose loyalty to the cause forms the basis of ethical action. Communication managers, however, are akin to legal advisers, who must present an objective view and therefore should follow a codified set of rules to ensure fair representation. Bivins (1989, 1992) suggests an ethical decision-making hierarchy: Practitioners should first turn to deontological principles such as codes of ethics; if codes are unavailable or incomplete, practitioners should then turn to utilitarian principles.

Bivins's decision-making hierarchy, however, suggests professional norms can be separated from personal values and makes ethical judgments a matter of convenience. Wright (1989), who claims that professional and personal norms are related, used 50 Likert-scaled items from Crissman's moral value judgments inventory to investigate the ethical values of 105 American public relations practitioners, 104 Canadian practitioners, and 215 public relations students. Using a forced varimax rotated factor analysis, Wright identified six types of morality that influence ethical thinking: socioeconomic, religious, basic, puritanical, basic social responsibility, and financial. However, Wright does not report reliabilities of the measures and fails to explain how the initial 14 factors were collapsed to 6. Also lacking is an explanation of how these types of moralities might inform or define professional ethics. Shamir, Reed, and Connell (1990) have also studied the relationship of personal and professional ethics, using a mail survey of 198 PRSA members. These researchers found a significant correlation between personal and professional ethics, and they propose that the ethics practitioners bring with them into the profession will guide how they perform their job function; function does not define the ethic.

Judd (1989) found support for Bivins's adviser function in a survey of 100 practitioners in management roles. He found a significant positive correlation between socially responsible actions and participation in policy decisions, with 65% reporting that their first responsibility is to society. This result must be viewed with caution, however; both the telephone survey method and self-reports of ethical behavior invite courtesy bias from respondents. The respondents did indicate a need for greater professionalism; they did not believe they served as credible sources because their public image was low, ranking above only advertisers and car dealers. In a survey of PRSA members, Pratt (1991) also found that professionals ranked the public image of professional ethics as poor. A functional basis for ethical development, then, may be inadequate if a shared notion of the function is not widely held and may consequently reduce any motivation to conform to ethical standards. These approaches also leave larger normative questions unanswered; for example, a thieves' code of honor may be functionally adequate, yet it leaves unexamined the issue of whether thievery itself is a moral act.

Pearson's (1989a, 1989b, 1990) theoretical work examined the ethical constructs inherent in systems theory, building on Sullivan's work in the 1960s. Sullivan (1965a, 1965b) outlines three types of public relations values: technical, which he views as amoral; partisan, comprising commitment, loyalty, and trust in the organization; and mutual, comprising institutional obligations to the public based on principles of mutuality and rationality. Sullivan places the locus of public relations practitioners' ethical issues at the intersection of partisan and mutual values, similar to the siting of conflict between libertarian and social responsibility values in Barney and Black's (1994) work and in direct opposition to Bivins's (1989) removal of conflict by differentiating these two aspects of public relations work.

Pearson (1990) notes that Bivins's (1989) functionalist, separatist perspective emphasizes the strategic goal achievement aspects of systems theory. Pearson prefers a broader reading emphasizing relationships, which are the locus of ethics, and resituating ethics in the process of communication rather than in communication outcomes. Drawing on Habermas's (1979) communicative ethics, Pearson (1989a) outlines the structural characteristics of a communication system that promotes negotiation among equal and rational communicators, similar to Grunig's ideal model of public relations practice, the two-way symmetrical communication model.

Although the theoretical development of an ethics governing communication processes holds promise for public relations practice, pragmatic difficulties remain when the theory is applied to the area of media relations. The process is dependent on the application of the concepts of mutuality and autonomy, yet the source-reporter literature reviewed here suggests that reporters do not consider public relations sources as having power and status equal to reporters' own. Although a survey of practitioners, educators, and students by Newsom, Ramsey, and Carrell (1993) indicates that public relations sources believe they share responsibility with the media for media performance, a study by Wylie (1974) demonstrates that when dealing with public relations sources, journalists often consider themselves to be in a position of power, which they abuse. Unless this basic relational dynamic changes, Pearson's systems theory approach remains problematic for source-reporter relations.

Routines and Practices of Sources

We found only two media sociological studies in the tradition of Tuchman (1978), Gans (1979), and Altheide (1976) that concentrated on the perspective of the source. In the first of these studies, Gieber (1960) interviewed 25 sources representing civil rights agencies and 22 newspaper reporters nominated by the sources about perceptions of each other. Subjects judged 26 "local news events potentially productive of symbols relevant to civil rights and liberties" adopted from actual news stories in five newspapers (p. 77). Both groups saw themselves as communicators to a mass audience, but for both groups the mass audience proved secondary. Sources, using connotative symbols, acted primarily according to the needs of their agencies and their liberal community supporters, whereas reporters, preferring denotative symbols, responded primarily to the social structure and pressures of the newsroom. The fate of local news stories about civil rights and liberties was determined by the demands of the source's or reporter's primary reference group—agency/supporters or newspaper employer—not by the needs of the community's mass audience.

In the second study, Gieber and Johnson (1961) interviewed and observed elected and appointed government sources and newspaper reporters on a city-hall beat in suburban California. Anxious to promote community consensus and downplay controversy within a frame of reference of "city," the sources did not see the reporters as doing a good job for them, nor did they recognize the conflict between their dependency on and desire to control press coverage. In contrast, reporters operated from a frame of "beat," and clearly saw the conflicts between their idealized public protector role and the cooperation and collaboration that evolved with ever closer source relationships.

Media criticism and media sociological studies offer some further works on the routines and practices of sources, although in most cases the attention to sources is almost incidental to a focus on reporters and news media. Bagdikian (1963; cited in Rivers, Schramm, & Christians, 1980) drew on his own research and Senate committee hearings to reveal how "sophisticated" public relations sources "reach" journalists to "plant" their items to a "dismaying" extent. Bagdikian (1963) concludes:

It may be time for the executives of great news organizations to reconsider the role of public relations in the news. Public relations is useful, but it has taken over some editorial functions. That it would try to do this is inevitable and it must be said that public relations men are far clearer in their objectives than are editors and publishers. The PR men are bound to further the interests of their clients and they, at least, are doing what they are getting paid to do. They don't have the responsibility of editors and news executives, who arrogate to themselves a crucial and exalted position in American democracy and who insist that they exist and are paid primarily to protect the readers' interests in a fair presentation of significant news. (p. 29; quoted in Rivers et al., 1980)

In a similar vein, Sallot (1990a) identifies several instances when White House public relations sources released to the wire services carefully planned publicity photographs of then President Ronald Reagan astride a white steed, to bolster his popularity. She concludes that Reagan's handlers purposefully manipulated the president's image, linking his public persona with popular American myths, during periods when the president's popularity ratings dipped. Boorstin (1964) warns of the dangers of perceived exaggeration, insincerity, and cynicism when special interest groups, led formally or informally by persons charged with public relations functions, construct pseudo-events to gain publicity and impress others.

Gans (1979) found that the overriding concern when journalists use sources is efficiency. Because reporters have limited resources to gather the news, they depend on credible sources to supply information. Pragmatically, the more useful public relations sources are, the more favorably journalists view them. Gans called this relationship between journalists and their sources "a dance" in which the source generally takes the lead (p. 116) based on four source credibility factors: incentives, power, ability to supply suitable information, and geographic/social proximity.

In terms of incentive, most sources are eager for media exposure but may not have the right characteristics to succeed. The ability to supply suitable information is often based on a source's similarity to the reporter in socioeconomic status. Additionally, organizations that can supply "expert" witnesses are more likely to receive coverage. Finally, rural and low-income areas tend not to be covered because they lack geographic and social proximity.

Tuchman (1978) conducted participant observation work with reporters to determine how news is constructed. Her observations on sources are less detailed than those of Gans, although they roughly parallel his. She also notes that people with status serve as sources because they are viewed as inherently credible. The authority of their position gives them authority as sources.

A distinction must be drawn between studies of source diversity and studies of source credibility. As Strentz (1989) points out, there is a difference between reporting on sources and working with sources. For public relations practitioners trying to establish working relationships with reporters, the construct of source credibility is of greater concern. As sources, practitioners hope to establish themselves as credible purveyors of news items, not as news items in and of themselves. But as academic studies of the relationship between journalists and PR practitioners demonstrate, practitioners lack source credibility among journalists. These studies thus indirectly support the construct of source credibility outlined by Gans and Tuchman as dependent on perceived prestige and power.

Underscoring source credibility, Soley (1994) used content analysis to assess change in use of expert sources in selected news stories appearing in the *New York Times, Los Angeles Times,* and *Washington Post* in 1978 and 1990. He found that nearly twice as many expert sources were quoted in 1990 as in 1978, and that sources were more likely to be identified in 1990.

Using an elite theoretical model and network analysis, Reese and Danielian (1994) cataloged news sources appearing in October and November 1987 on a range of television network news and interview programs. Two or more sources appearing in the same program segment, speaking on the same issue, were coded as symmetrically linked. Clear patterns emerged with 27 groups from a 237-member pool. The largest group, the "Insiders," consisted primarily of senators, representatives, and present and past administration officials. Adding to the cohesion of the source group was the fact that many members made multiple appearances, resulting in a narrow expert source structure. Reese and Danielian suggest that this structure in part explains media convergence or consonance in coverage.[6] Similarly, Atwater (1989) suggests that shared news values and procedures for news gathering and presentation account for news consonance.

After analyzing 35 campaigns recognized for excellence by PRSA for their intent and success in generating news media convergence or consonance of coverage, however, Sallot (1992) found that 80% greatly exceeded or exceeded their objectives to create consonant publicity in the news media. She concludes that public relations is a primary precipitator of consonant news coverage, although public relations' influence on news content is rarely acknowledged.

We found no articles documenting the practice of public relations as the product of an organizational culture. However, we did find a few articles that examine the mediator tasks of public information officers with news media in scientific research organizations. Tichenor, Olien, Harrison, and Donohue (1970) found that 52% of a sample of scientists said their organizations had specific policies regarding reporting of research to the public and that a public information officer, higher administrator, or both handled such reports. Also, the scientists perceived such mediation to result in more accurate news coverage than would have been received otherwise.

Three other studies report less positive findings. Bassett, Davison, and Hopson (1968) found that although sociologists from six universities said researchers have an obligation to keep the public informed, they did not view public information officers as integral to the process. In a study of scientists at two Ohio universities, Dunwoody and Scott (1982) found that although 61% of the sample reported public information personnel acting as mediators in initiation of coverage about their work, there was no relationship between reliance on public information officers and attitudes toward media science coverage. Dunwoody and Ryan (1983) surveyed 287 scientists from a professional organization, and a majority reported that whereas public information officers make it easier for scientists to deal with journalists, such officers may hinder public understanding in some situations, and the scientists preferred direct contact with journalists.

Several articles offer tangential insights about the values and practices of public relations practitioners. Morton (1992-1993, 1993) has written two overview pieces, one addressed to journalists, the other to practitioners. She challenges Aronoff's (1976) findings, stating that writing style is a major factor in news release acceptance rates and that personal knowledge of the source does not matter. She notes that news releases are not as simply written as news stories; they average longer word use and more passive voice. She also distinguishes between proximity of source and localization of the release. Morton argues that Aronoff wrongly used source proximity as a major acceptance factor. Pointing instead to her work on "hometowners," she concludes that localization of a release is more important. Finally, she notes the need for reader relevance, suggesting that practitioners provide relevance through the concept of reader service; releases that contain information desired by readers will have the highest acceptance rates.

Part of the difference between Aronoff and Morton can be attributed to the operationalization of key terms in each study. Given her strict definition of acceptance as publication in substantially unaltered form, it stands to reason that Morton would find writing style to be a larger factor in use rates than does Aronoff. Morton's distinction between source proximity and story localization is one that Aronoff simply does not make, but it does add to a more precise understanding of how important personal contact is in getting publicity. Morton uses the distinction to question Aronoff's conclusion that an old boys' network exists that aids in publication of releases. Further work may sort out the relative importance of writing skill and source techniques to journalistic acceptance.

In a more theoretically based study, Grunig (1983) used his situational theory to categorize reporters as publics for source information. Canonical correlation revealed five types, with activist and apathetic types at the two extremes. Grunig also found that both personal interest and institutional constraints can determine the information-seeking habits of reporters. Discriminant analysis revealed characteristics typical of each type, facilitating source strategies in dealing with reporters.

Analyzing results of interviews with 19 journalists and 20 practitioners in Quebec City and Montreal, Charron (1989) drew on game theory to explore the development and status of journalism, recent evolution of public relations, and relations between journalists and practitioners. Relations are characterized as exchanges involving dimensions of conflict as well as cooperation, mediated by negotiation.

In light of the denigration in mass communication textbooks of public relations as a sellout profession made up of news manipulators (Cline, 1982), it is notable that sociological research on the traditions, mores, and routines of public relations practice presents a remarkably wholesome picture. A contradiction exists between the textbook depictions of insidious public relations practice and media sociological research that merits further work, with greater attention to the source's world of work.

News Values and Acceptance of Source Material

A major stream of research has centered not on the sources of news but on the materials sources produce. Researchers have examined the qualities of information subsidy materials, particularly news releases, to determine what factors improve acceptance rates.

Morton has conducted much of the research concerning news release acceptance rates, better operationalizing many of the constructs over time. The purpose of this stream of research is to aid practitioners in providing journalists with what they want, thereby increasing chances of publication. Aligning the news values of source and reporter helps public relations practitioners better serve the media.

In 1984, Morton conducted research on gatekeeper decisions about photographs accompanying news releases. Morton's (1986) study centered on whether the type of release (institutional, coming events, past events, consumer information, timely topics, features, and research stories) and the circulation size and frequency of publication of the paper affected acceptance rates. After coding and tracking 408 releases from a university information office, she found that circulation size had no significant effect on acceptance rates, but frequency of publication did. Weeklies and papers published twice weekly used more news releases than did dailies, with those publishing twice weekly using the most. The consumer information type of release was the most heavily used; releases about past events, features, and institutional releases were used the least. Morton concludes that the releases used had an element of reader service to them that the others lacked.

Morton (1988) then examined camera-ready copy produced by the same university information office and divided it into the same typology as above to determine how rates of publication and time until publication varied. She obtained self-reported use rates and actual use rates as determined by a clipping service. She found that editors tended to overreport their use rates, possibly exhibiting courtesy bias. Most uses were by small-circulation papers and papers with news staffs of three or fewer people. The most-used types of releases concerned timely topics (28%), research (18%), and consumer information (17%). Publication rates did not vary except for releases about past events, which were published more quickly than other releases when they were used. Morton concludes that camera-ready copy is convenient and effective for small papers with small staffs that are not equipped for electronic transmission of news releases.

Looking at Flesch readability assessments and acceptance rates of 181 releases from three institutions of higher education over 6 months, Warren and Morton (1991) found that simpler releases were used more often. Contrary to conventional wisdom that briefer is better, releases with longer paragraphs were used more than were releases with shorter paragraphs. However, the latter finding may be an anomaly, because the average difference between paragraph length of accepted and rejected releases was only four words.

Morton and Warren (1992b, 1992c) examined the effects of proximity of source and localization of story on acceptance rates. Press releases from the public relations office of a university were coded as general or customized for local news angle (releases with 45% or more of the copy customized were deemed "hometowners" and were not included in the sample). A clipping service then provided actual use rates for the state's daily and weekly papers. Use of a release was operationalized as publication in substantially unaltered form. Only 5% of general releases were used by 32% of the receiving papers, whereas 45% of the localized releases were used by 58% of the receiving papers. Localization, then, played a large role in acceptance rates. Geographic distance was not significant at the $p < .01$ level, but the authors note that at the $p < .05$ level it would have been.

The same authors conducted a separate study on "hometowners" to determine if the acceptance rate for these highly localized pieces was affected by picture inclusion, size of paper, and frequency of publication (Morton & Warren, 1992a). A sample of 196 hometown releases from a university information bureau was checked for essentially unedited media use. The authors found the overall use rate to be 36%. Inclusion of a picture diminished publication rates, even if the picture was not run. Publication rates were best for small- to medium-sized papers; very small and large papers tended not to run the release. In contrast to the findings reported by Morton (1986), frequency of publication had no effect on publication rates.

Much of the work reviewed above has been descriptive. Morton's (1986) conception of consumer-information-as-reader-service as a predictor of news release acceptance deserves more attention as an organizing concept. In Aronoff's (1975) work and in subsequent studies of journalists' versus practitioners' news values, practitioners have repeatedly rated reader interest lower in news value than have journalists. Morton's work suggests that practitioners should give reader interest more thought if they wish to improve acceptance rates for their material; the same is true for researchers.

In an early study, Harris (1961) surveyed 22 editors of industrial magazines and analyzed 1,553 rejected releases. He found that 90% of all releases received were rejected. Rejection rates were no different between releases produced by in-house departments and those produced by outside firms. The longer the release, the better chance it had of being rejected. Editors' main reasons for rejection were missing information, unclear focus, lack of time-liness, flooding from one source, poor writing, poor visuals, and lack of relevance. Qualities that led to acceptance were real information, clearly presented, with proper formatting and targeting. The editors said that they viewed a source as credible until they received too many poor releases from that source.

In a companion study to his survey of journalist and practitioner attitudes, Aronoff (1976) tracked all locally originating stories that ran at one newspa-per for one week. The source of each story was determined, and a public relations source was defined as material "originating from self-interested parties external to the news organization." For each piece of public relations material not used, gatekeepers at the paper completed a brief survey stating why it was rejected. Aronoff found that approximately half of all local origination stories that ran during the week came from public relations sources. Because of their brevity, however, they constituted only 25% of the newshole. Qualities that led to acceptance were proximity of source, brevity, and fewer competing items. The best acceptance rates were for brief releases from local sources known to the journalist. Aronoff places emphasis on this finding, noting that quality of writing was not a factor. The release was considered better if it appeared to be objective and of interest to readers. Of those releases rejected, 71% were judged not newsworthy, 19% were dupli-cate information, 5% were categorized as advertising, and 5% were rejected for stylistic or presentation deficiencies.

Martin and Singletary (1981) tracked the use of 199 releases from a state information office to determine how many were used verbatim, whether the subject or valence of coverage affected publication rates, and whether treat-ment varied among dailies, nondailies, and wire services. Of the 199 releases, almost 60% were run, but of all copies of the releases sent, only 11% were used. Verbatim use constituted 20%; the remainder were almost totally rewrit-ten. Nondailies were less likely to run releases, but when they did they usually ran them verbatim. There was no relationship between running a release verbatim and circulation size, contrary to the authors' expectations. If a wire service picked up a release, the placement rate was higher. Geographic distance from the source made no difference in placement rates. Valence of coverage did, however; if a release was negative, it was more likely to be used.

In a similar study, Walters and Walters (1992) used content analysis of a state agency's releases to determine the relationship between topic and place-ment rate; the impact of topic, timing, and location of first placement on subsequent placements; and the role of personal contact in placement success. During a 9-month period, 89% of all releases were placed. Success rates were highest for ceremonies and international affairs (100%) and lowest for administration/personnel (75%). Inclusion of a summary sheet helped placement rates for economics and finance, recreation and tourism, and science topics. Walters and Walters also found that pickup by a wire service increased placement rates, with the number of services picking up a release exponentially affecting its use rate. Topics picked up most frequently by wire services were science, health, and education. Smaller news staff equated with higher placement rates. Timeliness was also a factor, with transmittal by e-mail or fax leading to more placements.

Neuwirth, Liebler, Dunwoody, and Riddle (1988) examined the effects of electronic transmission on news release use. They tracked use of releases from a university information office in two newspapers over two time periods: pre-electronic transmission and post-electronic transmission. A use was counted even if significant rewriting was done, but a use was not counted if the release served only as a story idea or prompt. Overall use rate was 37%, declining slightly in the post-electronic transmission period. Of these, approximately one-third were substantially rewritten. Better publication rates occurred for releases with specific dollar amounts mentioned, greater numbers of people mentioned, or mentions of prominently affiliated groups. Overt pointing out of unique aspects of a story lessened publication rates. Electronic transmission of releases did aid in publication of timely stories and of longer stories. Electronically transmitted releases were also less likely to be edited, perhaps because editors had difficultly editing on-screen. Neuwirth et al. conclude that sources can retain greater control of information through electronic transmission. Because this research focused on new technology, however, follow-up work is necessary to see if, over time, editors have adjusted to on-screen editing.

Stocking (1985) also found that prominent group affiliation increased release acceptance rates. Using a content analysis of three newsmagazines and four newspapers over a one-year period, Stocking compared medical school mentions with the output of 55 medical schools' public information offices. She found no correlation between the amount of material released and the amount of coverage. Proximity also had no effect. Instead, coverage was related to research productivity and prestige, with Harvard Medical School receiving the most mentions. Stocking concludes that Harvard is inherently prestigious and therefore ultimately perceived as credible; thus, it is more frequently used as an information source.

Assessing elite sources in *Fortune, Business Week, Canadian Business,* and *Report on Business,* the two largest-circulation business magazines in the United States and in Canada, respectively, McShane (1995) found status, gender, and geographic source biases. Of 1,404 sources identified in 40 feature articles from each magazine during one year, senior executives were the most heavily relied upon and government officials the least. Women were severely underutilized as sources. Contrary to elite power theory, in the U.S. magazines a relatively higher percentage of sources were from the Mid-Atlantic region; sources from the Midwest and Southwest were underrepresented. The Canadian magazines relied heavily on sources from Ontario; Quebec and the Prairie regions were underrepresented.

One study attempted to assess the effect of self-monitoring of social presence and mode of information gathering on reporters' attribution of sources' motives to behave in particular ways. In an experiment with high school student journalists, Fredin (1984) looked for differences between journalists using interviews with actors or informational handouts and their own degree of self-monitoring on their assessments of sources' behavior. Results were inconclusive, possibly because of conceptual and empirical inconsistencies in Snyder's Self-Monitoring Scale and other methodological shortcomings (see, e.g., Briggs & Cheek, 1988).

Abbott and Brassfield (1989) used quantitative and qualitative methodology to determine whether print and broadcast gatekeepers differed in their criteria for accepting news releases. Gatekeepers at eight daily papers and five commercial television stations in central Iowa monitored all releases received over a given time period and marked use decisions and rationales on each; they were then interviewed about their decisions. The researchers found that the biggest factor affecting use was local application. The second major factor was significant interest; timeliness was third. Small television stations used the most releases and large stations used the least. Small newspapers and large stations had the lowest use rates overall. Newspapers that ran releases almost verbatim preferred longer releases; newspapers that used releases as story ideas preferred shorter releases. Whereas TV stations tended to have one gatekeeper who made all decisions, the gatekeepers at newspapers often asked for second opinions, and use was often determined by group decision.

Recent research by Berkowitz has concentrated on the acceptance of information subsidy material by the broadcast media. In a content analysis of network and local newscasts, like those who analyzed content of newspapers before him (Brown, Bybee, Wearden, & Straughan, 1987; Sigal, 1973), and like Soloski (1989), who employed participant observation at a local newspaper after him, Berkowitz (1987) found that most news originated with routine channels, such as press conferences and press releases, and that most sources used were affiliated with government.

Berkowitz and Adams (1990) used participant observation work, interviews, and content analysis of releases received to determine what affects use rates of releases at local television stations. Of 1,023 releases received, 78% were rejected. Business and government sources were discarded most frequently (about 83%); nonprofit and interest group sources were discarded the least (about 66%). City settings were preferred to national settings, and releases about planned events were more often used than was straight informational material. The authors conclude that many practitioners still employ a shotgun distribution approach that is ineffective. Local television stations prefer material that is contextually relevant, targeted, and of interest to the audience.

Berkowitz (1990) extended the above study, examining actual use rates for 391 releases that survived the first cut. Of these, 57.8% were actually aired. Releases concerning accidents and disasters, government and politics, and crime stories were most likely to be aired. Education, business and economics, and health and welfare stories did not fare as well. Berkowitz notes that the topics most often aired were the most concrete and required the least reporter time and expertise. The most important news factor was timeliness, followed by significance. The gatekeeping process at this later stage, unlike the initial one discussed by Berkowitz and Adams (1990), was a group activity. Of concern was the news mix; a balance was sought among story types. Planned events were considered the easiest to cover and were often included. National trends and perceived audience interest also were factors in selection of stories. As broadcast time neared, however, news releases were dropped in favor of emerging spot news. The overriding concern was logistics: News values often took a backseat to time constraints and other organizational factors.

Still working with the sample of 391 items that survived the first gatekeeping selection, Berkowitz (1991) performed a qualitative content analysis to determine the ranking of the following story selection factors: news judgment, resource constraints, information subsidies, and electronic technology. Because a qualitative coding methodology was used, coding categories were not always clear-cut, and intercoder reliability varied from .61 to 1.00. Given this limitation, however, Berkowitz found the following ranking in news selection: News judgment was first, followed by resource constraints. Electronic technology was not a factor, and information subsidies negatively correlated with use—in other words, public relations materials were seen as inherently not newsworthy. The design of this study is problematic, however; that Berkowitz divided information subsidies from news judgment in his initial coding scheme suggests that the design may have influenced the results. Although his findings concerning the lack of news value perceived in releases is suspect, what is of note is his finding that news values and resource constraints were the two most important factors in news selection. His recent work is, in fact, an effort to delineate how the relation between these two factors affects the news selection process.

Investigating how newspaper editors edited 60 releases issued by a major education and research-related state agency during a one-year period, Walters, Walters, and Starr (1994) found that stories based on releases were generally half as long as and easier to read than the releases themselves. These researchers conclude that syntax, as it relates to average word length and sentence word count, accounts for as much as 25% of placement success. They found few differences in editing between large and small newspapers, although large newspapers retained more key words and phrases, perhaps indicating greater attention to detail or fewer resource constraints, such as size of editing staff.

In what appears to be the latest in a stream of workweek-long "wastebasket" studies of press release usage,[7] Minnis and Pratt (1994) found that a Michigan weekly newspaper accepted 34% of press releases received. Of those releases, 57% had local content. An informal poll that found two-thirds of journalists "don't trust" public relations practitioners and 7 in 10 likened them to weasels (Hampson, 1991) made lively wire copy and received considerable media play. Nevertheless, those same journalists reported heavy use of public relations sources—81% of journalists responding indicated they need public relations practitioners, 38% said they get half their stories from PR practitioners, and 17% said they used PR sources in every story.

At the other end of the spectrum, Baxter (1981) used self-reports of 123 managing editors of daily newspapers to estimate that editors use only 9.2% of all releases received from public relations sources. Likewise, based on their survey of 102 journalists in two large metropolitan areas, Pfau and Gorham (1995) conclude that public relations materials, such as corporate press kits, have only marginal direct influence on journalists. However, these materials indirectly influence journalists' perceptions of the credibility of company spokespersons and exert a third-person effect, in which journalists perceive the materials to wield greater influence on their colleagues than on themselves.

Source materials traditionally have been print dominant, but new technologies are now being employed in public relations, and studies are emerging that examine video news releases (VNRs). In a survey of television journalists conducted by Frederick and Salmon (1991), respondents indicated that VNRs are an expedient way for television news directors to fill news time. Frederick and Salmon found that certain media routines and journalistic norms are more likely to affect VNR acceptance, including deadlines, newshole, staffing and budget, VNR format, and interest to local audience.

Cameron and Blount (in press) content analyzed 47 television news stories at 40 television stations generated by a video news release and conducted a survey of the stations' news directors ($n = 17$; 42.5% response rate). Their results suggest that production costs for a packaged VNR story may be wasted. News editors tended to use B-roll footage, sound bites from high officials, and footage from events such as press conferences—elements that reporters often cover in person. When the packaged VNR story was used, it was heavily edited or truncated. Contrary to popular wisdom, resource-poor stations did not make greater use of the packaged VNR story.

For the most part, release acceptance studies are descriptive, providing little opportunity for the drawing of generalizations. Although some contradictory findings occur, certain factors emerge that help predict use of information subsidies. One is source credibility. Personal knowledge of the source, acceptance of the story by the wire services, and prestige of the source all are factors that contribute to higher use rates. Resource constraints are also evident. Although circulation size is not in general a good predictor of use, size of news staff and size of newshole are. The smaller the news staff and the larger the newshole, the more material tends to be used.

Societal Impacts of News Sources

Much of the research addresses the relational and organizational aspects of the role played by public relations in the news process. However, the point of much source behavior is to influence the news content consumed by the public. A limited number of studies have examined how sources in news channels affect society.

Information Subsidy

Even when education and professional values lead to ethical practice, public relations can have hegemonic effects on society. Grunig (1987) quotes several practitioners who illustrate their awareness of the value to their organizations of subsidizing information for the media by becoming regular, reliable sources. They accomplish this largely by providing credible, ample, and polished information in the form of subsidies to reporters on a regular basis, thereby becoming routine sources.

Turk (1985, 1986a, 1986b, 1988) studied the influence of public relations on media content by reviewing the theory of agenda setting and then considering the agenda-setting function of the source as encompassed by Gandy's (1982) concept of information subsidy. Turk points out that just as journalists select from an array of sources and events to include in the news, sources likewise make selections. Sources can choose from a large pool of information and a wide array of techniques, with selection based on relative efficiency in producing influence. Mass media are typically the most important targets for this output.

Turk content analyzed news releases and news articles pertaining to six Louisiana government agencies and interviewed media gatekeepers about the releases. Her findings confirm that public relations practice has a moderate effect on the news agenda: At least some editorial priorities are being set through public relations efforts. Turk (1985) outlines the advantages of the process for practitioners:

> To the extent that their subsidies are used in media content, these practitioners have influenced the media agenda. And if they can influence the media's agenda, perhaps they also can influence public opinion and the public agenda, for most of what an organization's key publics know about it is mass-media created and disseminated. (p. 12)

However, more than half the stories about agencies contained no subsidized information, and most of the subsidy information used by the media was neutral. Media gatekeepers were active and influential, preferring their own resources for usable information, tending toward more critical content when they queried agencies for information, rejecting public relations attempts that were clearly persuasive, and fairly consistently judging the news value of the subsidized information.

Marketing Pressures

Berkowitz (1993) examined the business-journalism dialectic and the variable of job roles to determine influences on the news selection process. He hypothesized that news managers would be more business oriented and news gatherers would place more emphasis on journalistic news ideals. He surveyed television journalists at 12 stations in Iowa, receiving 43 usable questionnaires evenly split between news gatherers and news managers, for a response rate of more than 70%. Berkowitz found no real differences in how news was selected based on occupational roles within news organizations.

Cluster analysis, however, revealed three different groups that crossed occupational title lines: the business/programming group, which focused more on marketing considerations, such as formatting requirements and audience interests; the business/resources group, guided most in story selection by resource constraints; and the journalistic values group, which adhered to traditional news values in the news selection process. All three groups believed that newsworthiness was the ideal, but the two business-oriented groups thought the ideal did not function in practice. Those in the journalistic values group were more likely to belong to professional organizations, to have more job satisfaction, and to believe they turned out a better product. Berkowitz concludes that they are more socialized into journalism and thus are less driven by the business aspects of news production.

McManus (1990) performed qualitative and quantitative analyses of three local television news organizations to determine whether they used a profit-maximizing model of news discovery, defined as dependence on cheaper, passively obtained sources of news, or a model of professional news discovery, defined as sacrificing some profit to uphold the watchdog role of the media. McManus used participant observation and in-depth interviews to study three Western network affiliate stations of varying market sizes. All personnel were surveyed about the source of news and development of news stories on four different broadcast nights ($n = 239$; 87% response rate), and those broadcasts were also content analyzed. The results indicated that the stations studied depended highly on passively obtained information, much of it originating with newspaper copy, public relations personnel, and wire copy. Only at the largest station studied, which had greater financial resources, was any emphasis given to active surveying of the environment.

McManus (1990) concludes that local television news operations have for the most part capitulated their watchdog role and therefore their First Amendment protections, relying instead on passive, and therefore economically rational, means of news gathering. Such reliance, he warns, allows special interests to "take advantage of cost-conscious media to influence what the public learns. The proliferation of public relations efforts suggests that these special interests are eager to assume such influence" (p. 682).

Lasorsa and Reese (1990) content analyzed 167 stories citing 1,022 sources about the 1987 stock market crash appearing in October and November 1987 on the *CBS Evening News* and in *Newsweek,* the *New York Times,* and the *Wall Street Journal.* Contrary to expectations that the national media are alike in their messages, the researchers found that sources with different organizational affiliations delivered different messages about causes and effects of the crash in the different media. They also found that television relied more heavily on unattributed or easily accessible, routine sources, perhaps because of resource constraints. Differences in functions of the media may at least partially account for differences in messages, given that the *Wall Street Journal* primarily serves the financial community, whereas the *New York Times* informs the national elite across institutional sectors and network television and *Newsweek* appeals to mass audiences.

Kaniss (1991) used content analysis and participant observation studies to determine how local news is constructed at Philadelphia television stations and newspapers. Her study confirms the corporate influence theory: Newspapers, even those that are chain owned, are themselves local businesses with stakes in other local businesses. Publishers, therefore, are of necessity concerned with watching the bottom line and maintaining good relations with their local business associates. At newspapers, Kaniss found, "local news comes to look the way it does through a combination of the constraints and incentives set by newspaper management and the internalized professional and personal values of local reporters" (p. 71). Confirming the results of McManus's 1990 study, she concludes that when operating within managerial constraints designed to increase profit, reporters follow routinized news search procedures. News releases represent a steady stream of stories obtained with great economic efficiency. When combined with deadline pressures and financial constraints, this often means that the reporting angle on a story is limited to that presented in a release. At least initial stories, then, tend to be single source, with practitioners subsidizing the information flow.

A THEORETICAL FRAMEWORK

In considering the literature reviewed here, it becomes evident that atheoretical description and introspection about the field of public relations has prevailed. Limited theoretical work has been done concerning such public relations practice issues as information subsidy, source power, source and reporter roles, the third-person effect, and ethnography of reporters. In general, studies have been descriptive, lacking a theoretical basis that offers scholars, educators, and practitioners a parsimonious, generalizable explanation of source-reporter communication.

Research based on theory enhances understanding and helps to organize our knowledge about the role and impact of public relations in news. The three-part model of the role and impact of public relations on news offers a framework for the literature review, dividing the research into relational, organizational, and societal categories. Using this same model, we offer suggestions below for more theory-driven research in each of these categories.

Relational Research

The crux of the news-gathering process is the relationship between the source and the reporter. This is the transaction point for information that often becomes the news fare of the day. Because the transaction is interpersonal, the suggestions that follow include some domains of research in which the unit of analysis is the relationship, not the individuals composing it. We found a dearth of such analysis in the current literature, along with an absence of any use of theories of interpersonal communication.

Rules Theory

Rules research offers particular promise in source-reporter relational research. The theory, developed in pragmatic linguistics and applied to interpersonal relations and organizational communication, is readily adaptable to the question of appropriate media relations behavior by sources. Public relations textbooks and handbooks prescribe rules for appropriate behavior of practitioners in media relations (Cutlip et al., 1994; Grunig & Hunt, 1984; Howard & Mathews, 1985; Lesly, 1983; Seitel, 1995). These rules are largely based on traditions in the practice of media relations, not empirical testing. Rules research methodology bears exploration by public relations researchers interested in the culture of the source or the interaction of the source with the reporter. Rules theory involves the uncovering of communication rules as used in a given setting, with several techniques successfully employed (Cameron, 1983; Cushman & Pearce, 1977; Cushman & Whiting, 1972; Frentz & Farrell, 1976; Harré, 1974; O'Brian, 1978; Shellen & Bach, 1983; Shimanoff, 1980; Shockley-Zalabak & Morley, 1994; Toulmin, 1974).

Theories of Conflict in Relationships

Another area of model and theory building in interpersonal communication is the conflict literature. The concept of conflict offers particular promise for the understanding and perhaps even improvement of source-reporter relations. Hocker and Wilmot (1991) define conflict as "an expressed struggle between at least two interdependent parties who perceive incompatible goals, scarce resources, and interference from the other party in achieving goals" (p. 12). This definition encapsulates the communicative nature of conflict (expressed), the interdependence of parties in conflict (such as sources and reporters), and the perceived incompatibility of goals (reporter objectivity versus source desire for favorable coverage). For both the reporter and the source, resources are limited, if not scarce, and both parties have been found to view the other as interfering with smooth operation of the news process. The ingredients for hypothesis testing are ample, perhaps with an underlying emphasis on arriving at productive conflict management—parties who are "more willing to cooperate, able to have a more productive conflict . . . and more satisfied with the result" (Hocker & Wilmot, 1991, p. 38).

Power

Power is a mediating factor related to the conflict management process. In addition to affecting the intensity and extent of conflict in relationships, power affects other behaviors of sources and reporters. Gans (1979) found that sources have power to withhold information when the media desire that information. He notes that sources without power must create civil disturbances or have unusually dramatic stories to obtain coverage, which implies that marginalized groups will not receive "norm" coverage. For this reason, power is one of the most important factors in source-reporter relations meriting theory-driven research. The distribution of power between the source and the reporter is presented in Table 4.1 as a tool for conducting source-reporter research. Using this matrix, one could explore how source-reporter interactions might change depending on the conditions of each cell of the matrix. For example, low-power sources might be more likely to use pseudoevents as a means of obtaining coverage. Over time, this could lead to greater power and interactions with reporters as high-power sources dealing with high-power reporters.

According to Robinson (1977), high-power sources and high-power reporters enjoy a symbiotic relationship. However, if a source does not have significant activities and power outside the source-reporter relationship, the symbiotic may turn parasitic, as the media begin to usurp the functions and agenda of the source organization. Increasingly, the source may find itself making decisions based on the practice or expectations of the media. Robinson gives only one example, the decline of the party system in politics. Gitlin (1980) documents a second example in his study of the Students for a Democratic Society. Relations, then, can run a continuum from symbiotic to parasitic, depending on the source's ability to function effectively without the reporter. Research should include this third dimension, namely, the power of the source outside the relationship with the journalist.

Another aspect of the power concept is the bases of power and how these might differ for sources and journalists. French and Raven (1959) have

TABLE 4.1

Matrix of Source and Reporter Power (including an example in each cell)

Reporter Power	Source Power	
	High	Low
High	Sam Donaldson and President Clinton	60 Minutes's Mike Wallace and president of bogus charity
Low	student newspaper reporter and university president	fringe journalist and "save the snail" environmentalist

developed a widely used typology of five bases of power: coercive, reward, legitimate, expert, and referent. Alternatively, Hocker and Wilmot (1991) offer four power currencies that emphasize relational conflict: expertise, resource control, interpersonal linkages, and communication skills. Comparative validation of both models should go forward in the source-reporter context. Additionally, the efficacy of power bases or currencies in explaining source-reporter interaction would help teachers and practitioners to understand source-reporter dynamics. For example, do sources hold coercive power (e.g., freezing out reporters, pressuring their bosses, pulling advertising from papers)? If so, does its application work, both immediately and over time? Coercive power derives from the potential to punish, and French and Raven (1959) contend that over time it is counterproductive to a relationship. This is one of many testable suppositions in the theoretical literature on power in relationships. Other questions include the following: Does a news leak or an exclusive story confer reward power? Do reporters hold and use legitimate power by virtue of their position? What about certain sources? How fragile/robust is expert power in fields such as health and science?

Reporter Role

From the public relations perspective, we offer four broad role definitions as a basis for research: adversary contending against a duplicitous source threatening the free exchange of true information; judge of information presented by two or more contending source/advocates, such as political candidates; judge of news value of information from a single source; and advocate of a position in public contention between two competing camps. These four roles can be represented in a matrix as shown in Table 4.2.

One could examine the conditions under which each reportorial role is played out, and the effect each has on source behaviors. In this literature review, virtually all the studies discussed held an implicit view of the reporter as judge, mainly of news values. This may reflect the high esteem in which sources hold reporters as professionals, but certainly the other roles do occur. Research is lacking on how the myth of objectivity is reconciled with adversarial and advocacy roles for reporters. Sources may not recognize the conflict between simple reporting

TABLE 4.2
Roles Played by Reporters in Dealing With Single or Contending Sources
(including an example in each cell)

| Reporter Role | Number of Sources | |
	Single	Contending Advocates
Judge	product promotion	campaign coverage
Adversary	20/20 interview with chemical company president	editorial stance on an issue

and acting as an adversary against certain sources, instances in which the reporter is judge of the truth-value of information.

Other Relational Factors

Variables such as communication competence, negotiation skills, psychological type, listening, attractiveness, self-monitoring, communication apprehension, and compliance gaining are well-developed constructs in the interpersonal literature with effective research methods appropriate to theory. These constructs deserve consideration in bringing theory to bear upon the source-reporter relationship.

Organizational Research

Organizational research includes the study of the organization and organizational culture as factors in the news process. The news source is a key individual in the organization, bringing professional values, training, and socialization as a public relations practitioner to the boundary-spanning role served for the organization.

A Contingency Model of Accommodation in Public Relations

In looking at ways the organization affects models of public relations practice (its operating environment, its structure, its culture, its worldview), previous research has been relatively fruitless. Grunig and Grunig (1989) conclude that a wide array of organizational factors tested in numerous studies correlate only weakly with Grunig's four models of public relations practice. Cameron, Estes, and Sallot (1996) have developed an alternative to the four models, arguing for a continuum ranging from pure advocacy on behalf of the organization to pure collaboration with an external public.

The contingency model offers more than 80 factors arrayed into internal and external categories that affect the degree of accommodation a practitioner will adopt in dealing with a specific issue and a particular public at a given point in time. Cameron et al. (1996) conducted an initial test of the model based on 18 in-depth interviews with public relations practitioners. The welter of antecedent, moderating, and mediating factors in the model, the dynamic nature of the model, and the subtlety of a model allowing degrees of accommodation or symmetry with publics appealed to the interviewees. The model offers a structure for examining the wealth of factors that could affect how sources conduct media relations. In measuring behavior of practitioners, the model eliminates the categorical level of measurement inherent in discrete models of practice (e.g., Grunig's four models and Plowman et al.'s 1995 conception of five models of conflict resolution).

Ethics and Professional Standards for Sources

In a recent overview, Pratt (1994) divided the public relations ethics literature by method into empirical analyses and qualitative discourses, noting that both research methods are problematic. The qualitative discourses lack empirical grounding; the empirical studies invite courtesy bias through self-reports of ethical behavior. Pratt calls for more integrative work in the field to provide an overall theoretical framework with empirical support. These same criticisms apply to the narrower body of literature on source ethics. Many of the critical studies lack normative force, which could be supplied by a more complete grounding in classical ethical theory. These same studies often lack guidelines for pragmatic application, indicating a need for empirical study. Conversely, many of the empirical studies lack theoretical grounding and thus fail to extend development of a source ethics or provide direction for further study.

Most studies of professionalism concerning codes of ethics consist of qualitative discourses either attacking a rule deontology approach to professional ethics in favor of more teleological approaches or demanding greater specificity in codes to provide concrete guidelines. Empirical studies are needed to determine how often and to what extent codes are consulted, to what extent codes versus teleological approaches enhance professional image, and whether reporters are familiar with and respect public relations codes. Because of the problems noted by Pratt (1994) with self-reports of ethical behavior, behavioral studies would benefit from participant observation work. Tests of reporter knowledge and awareness studies would lend themselves to survey or experimental methods.

Coorientation theory centering on journalistic values has been overused in the study of source-reporter relations; McBride (1989) convincingly makes the point that public relations practitioners are not journalists and therefore will never be perceived as adhering to the same standards as journalists. One new area that has yet to be explored, however, is that suggested by the community press movement. Christians, Ferre, and Fackler (1993) have argued that the social responsibility theory of the press underlying journalistic ethics is inadequate. Their proposed communitarian model, with its emphases on community commitment, civic transformation, and mutuality in organizational culture, suggests more room for shared values between sources and reporters. Christians et al.'s study serves as a normative guide; much theoretical and empirical work remains to determine the model's utility.

Barney and Black's (1994) work provides a preliminary sketch of a larger theoretical framework of an ethics of persuasion, which to be fully developed could profit from incorporating recent work in the political liberalism tradition. The missing normative basis could be supplied through the incorporation of John Rawls's (1971, 1993) notions of distributive and procedural justice, which could then be tested empirically through observation and content analysis studies to determine whether true participatory democracy does guarantee unimpeded information flows and encourage competing voices. Conversely, postmodern political philosophy has emerged that questions the validity of political liberalism in a diverse modern society (see, e.g., Young, 1990). Given the trends in public relations toward multiculturalism and narrowcasting, postmodern political philosophy may provide a more congruent base from which to build an ethic of persuasion.

The structural-functional approaches suggest differing ethical standards for differing job functions, but the fit between personal and professional values remains problematic and understudied. As early as 1982, Wright noted that moral development theory, such as that of Kohlberg (see Jaska & Pritchard, 1994, chap. 4), could fill this gap, but little theoretical work has been done. Instruments that operationalize Kohlberg's work, such as the Defining Issues Test developed by Rest (1979, 1986), would provide a theoretically grounded empirical study of the relation of personal variables, such as age and education, to the development of professional norms. Given the increasing feminization of the public relations field, the work of Gilligan (1982), which suggests that women employ different ethical reasoning than that proposed by Kohlberg, should also be explored.

Pearson's work in general systems theory possesses theoretical robustness but lacks empirical testing and pragmatic application. Because it relies heavily on Grunig's two-way symmetrical model, it must be noted that in empirical tests, Grunig's model has been found to be normative only. Thus, although Pearson's thought provides the normative basis that many of the other approaches lack, participant observation, interviews, experiments, and surveys are needed to determine if the theory can be made pragmatic and under what conditions.

Such methods are being used to study professional standards in public relations. Cameron, Sallot, and Lariscy (1996) administered a survey instrument derived from 60 in-depth interviews to 598 public relations professionals across the nation and achieved a 42% response rate. Based on a review of literature and the interview phase of the study, 24 elements of professional performance were operationalized in the survey. Survey respondents assessed the extent to which a standard of professionalism currently exists for each of the 24 items. Respondents viewed ethical guidelines, accreditation, and writing/editing skills as enjoying well-established standards. Licensing, location of public relations on the organizational chart, and inclusion of public relations in the dominant coalition were viewed as most lacking in a standard of professional performance. The 24 items factored into eight dimensions. Assessments of professionalism along these eight factors differed significantly as a function of age, education, race, and both length of time and geographic region of practice of public relations. These researchers are also investigating effects of gender and culture on perceptions of professional standards among public relations professionals.

Societal Research

Third-Person Effects

Davison (1982) posits that we tend to overestimate the influence of mass communication on others. This effect is accentuated for experts, who judge themselves immune to effects that they expect occur among members of the less knowledgeable lay audience. The theory predicts that sources are more sensitive about how they are covered in the news, attributing more consequences to critical or incorrect coverage than are likely to occur among the audience. Additionally, sources face the same third-person effect from their superiors. Overreaction of their management or clients to news coverage, especially on technical subjects such as investor news or high-tech reporting, may be expected. Research in this area, informed by third-person theory, would shift the focus from traditional audience effects to effects of media messages on the source of the message.

Market-Driven Journalism

Little work has been done examining the relationship between market-driven journalism and source-reporter relations. Macroeconomic studies have been driven by Marxist critical study or by studies of the effects of industry concentration. In both cases, the focus has been on the resulting media content and not on the relationship between sources and reporters. For example, although Bagdikian's (1992) analysis of the effects of media ownership patterns in the United States on the news industry makes inferences about the pollution or enervation of news content by economic considerations such as advertising revenues, more study is needed to examine the mechanisms at work in converting economic will into media content.

In examining the source-reporter relationship from the source's perspective, participant observation and interview studies could explore the effects of source of corporate advertising and advertising budgets as a lever to obtain news coverage. Another variable of interest is the influence of the employer's economic clout in the communication industry on the public relations practitioner's behavior as a source. Investigative research, not survey analysis, is needed to determine whether sources working for companies with news conglomerates as subsidiaries attempt to use their connections to advantage.

Microeconomic studies have resulted in models of commercial news production (McManus, 1994), but empirical testing to date has been limited to a few studies of broadcast media. For PR practitioners, however, the print news release remains the most common tool of conveying information to the media: "Publicity in newspapers, day in and day out, forms the foundation of most information programs" (Cutlip et al., 1994, p. 281; see also Wilcox et al., 1995). More empirical testing of the model is needed, particularly in terms of print media, to determine whether public relations information subsidies are becoming more valued by journalists because of their economic worth. Preliminary studies indicate that in fact a backlash might be occurring, with journalists resenting economic dependence on sources and becoming more determined not to use those sources' material (Curtin, 1995).

The interplay of sociological and ideological factors in conjunction with economic factors remains understudied yet promises great heuristic value. In-depth interviews with reporters and sources, as well as participant observation work and content analyses tracking both information subsidy and media content flows, could help us to understand the interplay between these forces. Additionally, source and reader studies are necessary to determine whether microeconomic trends will signal an end to third-party credibility of news releases and thus force sources to use means other than media to achieve their goals.

Information Subsidy

More attention should be devoted to how sources' values, routines, and relations with reporters can affect both the media and public agendas. To some extent, the public relations practitioner surveys reviewed in the section above on mutual assessment are an attempt by public relations researchers to deal with the issue of distrust. The assumption in this work seems to be that distrust is unhealthy in the source-reporter relationship. But perhaps distrust is good for the practice of both journalism and public relations, and particularly salubrious for the informational marketplace. More sources are heard when reporters resist the temptation to use subsidized information. Likewise, verification of source information is more likely to occur when reporters approach sources with healthy skepticism.

Additional work using the information subsidy theory should prove informative in tracing effects of sources on reporters and for the broader issue of the co-opting of the news and public agenda. Further study must address how the free exchange of ideas suffers when information is readily available from sources who work expertly to maintain the best possible relations with the press. The other concern, equally important, involves the suppression of information by sources to penalize reporters, to manage crisis situations, to follow the advice of legal counsel, or to reify an authoritarian culture that suppresses ideas and issues. Distinct programs of research may be needed, each defining a different type of source-reporter relationship (information subsidy versus information suppression), to understand what does and does not appear before the court of public opinion.

CONCLUSION

By framing the impacts and roles of public relations in terms of relationships, organizational dynamics, and societal impacts, researchers may bring greater order to the study of public relations sources and the news agenda upon which they strive to have an effect. Within this framework, theory-driven research employing diverse and innovative methods will greatly enrich the literature.

NOTES

1. Indeed, some researchers argue that managing relationships of all kinds, not just media relations, is the essence of public relations (Pavlik, 1987).

2. Typical attitude scale statements in these studies include the following: "Public relations and the press are partners in the dissemination of news"; "The public relations practitioner does work for the newspaper that would otherwise go undone"; "Public relations practitioners often act as obstructionists, keeping reporters from the people they really should be seeing"; and "Public relations material is usually publicity disguised as news."

3. Jeffers' questionnaire included items such as "Newsmen are much more skilled than public relations practitioners"; "Public relations practitioners are about as ethical as newsmen"; "Cooperation between newsmen and public relations practitioners is usually detrimental to the public interest"; and "Intentionally or not, when newsmen use material supplied by public relations practitioners, they are helping the practitioners improve the images of their clients or organizations."

4. Items included "Many journalists' stereotypes of public relations persons are based on the negative experiences they have had with a few 'bad apples' "; "A general feeling among many journalists that their work is more important to society than public relations accounts for some of the antagonism journalists feel toward public relations"; "Many journalists' negative views of public relations are not justified by the facts"; and "The negative views many journalists express in surveys toward public relations are consistent with the views held by journalists I know."

5. Since this study was conducted, PRSA has elevated the requirements for accreditation, including making periodic reaccreditation mandatory. To be eligible for reaccreditation, professionals must now engage in regular continuing education.

6. *Consonance* here is defined as the concept of the repeated reporting of the same news story with a similar focus, "slant," or "spin" in multiple news media. Noelle-Neumann (1974; Noelle-Neumann & Mathes, 1987) considers news consonance one of the conditions leading to the "spiral of silence."

7. While on the faculty at the University of Wisconsin, Scott Cutlip directed unpublished master's theses constituting some of these "wastebasket" studies. Schabacker (1963) found that

public relations served as a news source for 10% to 51% of all news-editorial content of five Minneapolis media in one week; a partial replication of Schabacker's study by Sandquist (1976) found 9-46% of news content in four media in Milwaukee in one week was inspired by public relations releases.

REFERENCES

Abbott, E. A., & Brassfield, L. T. (1989). Comparing decisions on releases by TV and newspaper gatekeepers. *Journalism Quarterly, 66,* 853-856.

Abend, A., & Olasky, M. (1985). PR debate. *Business and Society Review, 54,* 93-94.

Altheide, D. L. (1976). *Creating reality: How TV news distorts events.* Beverly Hills, CA: Sage.

Aronoff, C. (1975). Credibility of public relations for journalists. *Public Relations Review, 1*(2), 45-56.

Aronoff, C. (1976). Predictors of success in placing news releases in newspapers. *Public Relations Review, 2*(4), 43-57.

Atwater, T. (1989). News format in network evening news coverage of the TWA hijacking. *Journal of Broadcasting & Electronic Media, 33,* 293-304.

Bagdikian, B. H. (1963, Fall). Journalist meets propagandist. *Columbia Journalism Review,* p. 29.

Bagdikian, B. H. (1992). *The media monopoly* (4th ed.). Boston: Beacon.

Barney, R. D., & Black, J. (1994). Ethics and professional persuasive communications. *Public Relations Review, 20,* 233-248.

Bassett, G., Davison, W. P., & Hopson, A. L. (1968). *Social scientists, university news bureaus, and the public: Some factors affecting the communication of social science information.* New York: Russell Sage.

Baxter, B. L. (1981). The news release: An idea whose time has gone? *Public Relations Review, 7*(1), 27-31.

Belz, A., Talbott, A. D., & Starck, K. (1989). Using role theory to study cross perceptions of journalists and public relations practitioners. In J. E. Grunig & L. A. Grunig (Eds.), *Public relations research annual* (Vol. 1, pp. 125-139). Hillsdale, NJ: Lawrence Erlbaum.

Berkowitz, D. (1987). TV news sources and news channels: A study in agenda-building. *Journalism Quarterly, 64,* 508-513.

Berkowitz, D. (1990). Refining the gatekeeping metaphor for local television news. *Journal of Broadcasting & Electronic Media, 34,* 55-68.

Berkowitz, D. (1991). Assessing forces in the selection of local television news. *Journal of Broadcasting & Electronic Media, 35,* 245-251.

Berkowitz, D. (1993). Work rules and news selection in local TV: Examining the business-journalism dialectic. *Journal of Broadcasting & Electronic Media, 37,* 67-81.

Berkowitz, D., & Adams, D. B. (1990). Information subsidy and agenda setting in local television news. *Journalism Quarterly, 67,* 723-731.

Bishop, R. L. (1988). What newspapers say about public relations. *Public Relations Review, 14*(2), 50-52.

Bivins, T. H. (1987). Applying ethical theory to public relations. *Journal of Business Ethics, 6,* 195-200.

Bivins, T. H. (1989). Ethical implications of the relationship of purpose to role and function in public relations. *Journal of Business Ethics, 8,* 65-73.

Bivins, T. H. (1992). A systems model for ethical decision making in public relations. *Public Relations Review, 18,* 365-383.

Bivins, T. H. (1993). Public relations, professionalism, and the public interest. *Journal of Business Ethics, 12,* 117-126.

Boorstin, D. J. (1964). *The image: A guide to pseudo-events in America.* New York: Harper & Row.

Briggs, S. R., & Cheek, J. M. (1988). On the nature of self-monitoring: Problems with assessment, problems with validity. *Journal of Personality and Social Psychology, 54,* 663-678.

Brody, E. W. (1984). Antipathy exaggerated between journalism and public relations. *Public Relations Review, 10*(4), 11-15.

Brown, J. D., Bybee, C. R., Wearden, S. T., & Straughan, D. M. (1987). Invisible power: Newspaper news sources and the limits of diversity. *Journalism Quarterly, 64,* 45-54.

Cameron, G. T. (1983). *A rules-based study of nurse-geriatric patient communication.* Unpublished master's thesis, University of Montana, Missoula.

Cameron, G. T., & Blount, D. (in press). VNRs and air checks: A content analysis of the use of video news releases in television newscasts. *Journalism and Mass Communication Quarterly.*

Cameron, G. T., Estes, A. A., & Sallot, L. M. (1996). *It's a matter of degree: A test of the contingency model of accommodation in public relations.* Manuscript in preparation.

Cameron, G. T., Sallot, L. M., & Lariscy, R. A. (1996). Developing standards of professional performance in public relations. *Public Relations Review, 22*(1), 43-61.

Carroll, R. A. (1994, August). *Journalists continue to express negative attitudes toward public relations practitioners.* Paper presented at the annual meeting of the Association for Education in Journalism and Mass Communication, Atlanta, GA.

Charron, J. (1989). Relations between journalists and public relations practitioners: Cooperation, conflict and negotiation. *Canadian Journal of Communication, 14*(2), 41-54.

Christians, C. G., Ferre, J. P., & Fackler, P. M. (1993). *Good news: Social ethics and the press.* New York: Oxford University Press.

Cline, C. (1982). The image of public relations in mass comm texts. *Public Relations Review, 8*(3), 63-72.

Curtin, P. A. (1995, August). *Market-driven journalism: Perspectives on the role of market pressures in the construction of news.* Paper presented at the annual meeting of the Association for Education in Journalism and Mass Communication, Washington, DC.

Cushman, D. P., & Pearce, W. B. (1977). Generality and necessity in three types of human communication theory: Special attention to rules theory. *Human Communication Research, 3,* 344-353.

Cushman, D. P., & Whiting, G. D. (1972). An approach to communication theory: Toward consensus on rules. *Journal of Communication, 22*(3), 217-238.

Cutlip, S. M., Center, A. H., & Broom, G. M. (1994). *Effective public relations* (7th ed.). Englewood Cliffs, NJ: Prentice Hall.

Davison, W. P. (1982). The third-person effect of communication. *Public Opinion Quarterly, 46,* 1-15.

Dimmick, J. (1974). The gate-keeper: An uncertainty theory. *Journalism Monographs, 37.*

Dunwoody, S., & Ryan, M. (1983). Public information persons as mediators between scientists and journalists. *Journalism Quarterly, 60,* 647-656.

Dunwoody, S., & Scott, B. T. (1982). Scientists as mass media sources. *Journalism Quarterly, 59*(1), 52-59.

Englehardt, E. E., & Evans, D. (1994). Lies, deception, and public relations. *Public Relations Review, 20,* 249-266.

Feldman, L. (1961a, July 22). City editor's image of PR man "blurred." *Editor & Publisher,* pp. 36-37.

Feldman, L. (1961b, October). The public relations man as city editors see him. *Quill,* pp. 16-18.

Frederick, E. R., & Salmon, C. T. (1991, May). *Using information subsidies: Inclusive and exclusive predictors of broadcast gatekeepers' acceptance of video news releases.* Paper presented at the annual meeting of the International Communication Association, Dublin.

Fredin, E. S. (1984). Assessing sources: Interviewing, self-monitoring and attribution theory. *Journalism Quarterly, 61,* 866-873.

French, J. R. P., & Raven, B. (1959). *Studies in social power.* Ann Arbor, MI: Institute for Social Research.

Frentz, T. S., & Farrell, T. B. (1976). Language action: A paradigm for communication. *Quarterly Journal of Speech, 62*, 333-349.

Gandy, O. H., Jr. (1982). *Beyond agenda setting: Information subsidies and public policy.* Norwood, NJ: Ablex.

Gans, H. J. (1979). *Deciding what's news: A study of CBS Evening News, NBC Nightly News, Newsweek, and Time.* New York: Vintage.

Gieber, W. (1960). Two communicators of the news: A study of the roles of sources and reporters. *Social Forces, 39,* 76-83.

Gieber, W., & Johnson, W. (1961). The city hall "beat": A study of reporter and source roles. *Journalism Quarterly, 38,* 289-297.

Gilligan, C. (1982). *In a different voice: Psychological theory and women's development.* Cambridge, MA: Harvard University Press.

Gitlin, T. (1980). *The whole world is watching.* Berkeley: University of California Press.

Grunig, J. E. (1983). Washington reporter publics of corporate public affairs programs. *Journalism Quarterly, 60,* 603-614.

Grunig, J. E. (Ed.). (1992). *Excellence in public relations and communication management.* Hillsdale, NJ: Lawrence Erlbaum.

Grunig, J. E., & Grunig, L. A. (1989). Toward a theory of the public relations behavior of organizations: Review of a program of research. In J. E. Grunig & L. A. Grunig (Eds.), *Public relations research annual* (Vol. 1, pp. 27-63). Hillsdale, NJ: Lawrence Erlbaum.

Grunig, J. E., & Hunt, T. (1984). *Managing public relations.* New York: Holt, Rinehart & Winston.

Grunig, L. A. (1987). Variation in relations with environmental publics. *Public Relations Review, 13*(1), 46-58.

Habermann, P., Kopenhaver, L. L., & Martinson, D. L. (1988). Sequence faculty divided on PR value, status and news orientation. *Journalism Quarterly, 65,* 490-496.

Habermas, J. (1979). *Communication and the evolution of society* (T. McCarthy, Trans.). Boston: Beacon.

Hall, S. (1973). The determination of news photographs. In S. Cohen & J. Young (Eds.), *The manufacture of news: A reader* (pp. 176-190). Beverly Hills, CA: Sage.

Hampson, R. (1991, September 10). *Survey gives journalists chance to write off PR people.* Associated Press wire story.

Harré, R. (1974). Some remarks on "rule" as a scientific concept. In T. Mischel (Ed.), *Understanding other persons* (pp. 143-184). Oxford: Basil Blackwell.

Harris, D. (1961, June). Publicity releases: Why they end up in the wastebasket. *Industrial Marketing,* pp. 98-100.

Hocker, J. L., & Wilmot, W. W. (1991). *Interpersonal conflict* (3rd ed.). Dubuque, IA: William C. Brown.

Howard, C., & Mathews, W. (1985). *On deadline: Managing media relations.* New York: Longman.

Hunt, T., & Tirpok, A. (1993). Universal ethics code: An idea whose time has come. *Public Relations Review, 19,* 1-11.

Jaska, J. A., & Pritchard, M. S. (1994). *Communication ethics: Methods of analysis* (2nd ed.). Belmont, CA: Wadsworth.

Jeffers, D. W. (1977). Performance expectations as a measure of relative status of news and PR people. *Journalism Quarterly, 54,* 299-306.

Judd, L. R. (1989). Credibility, public relations, and social responsibility. *Public Relations Review, 15*(2), 34-40.

Kaniss, P. (1991). *Making local news.* Chicago: University of Chicago Press.

Kopenhaver, L. L. (1985). Aligning values of practitioners and journalists. *Public Relations Review, 11*(2), 34-42.

Kopenhaver, L. L., Martinson, D., & Ryan, M. (1984). How public relations practitioners and editors in Florida view each other. *Journalism Quarterly, 61,* 860-865, 884.

Kruckeberg, D. (1993). Universal ethics code: Both possible and feasible. *Public Relations Review, 19,* 21-31.

Lasorsa, D. L., & Reese, S. D. (1990). News source use in the crash of 1987: A study of four national media. *Journalism Quarterly, 67,* 60-71.

Lee, M. A., & Solomon, N. (1990). *Unreliable sources.* New York: Carol.

Lesly, P. (1983). *Lesly's public relations handbook* (3rd ed.). Englewood Cliffs, NJ: Prentice Hall.

Martin, W. P., & Singletary, M. W. (1981). Newspaper treatment of state government releases. *Journalism Quarterly, 58,* 93-96.

McBride, G. (1989). Ethical thought in public relations history: Seeking a relevant perspective. *Journal of Mass Media Ethics, 4*(1), 5-20.

McCombs, M. E., & Shaw, D. L. (1972). The agenda-setting function of mass media. *Public Opinion Quarterly, 36,* 176-187.

McManus, J. (1990). How local television learns what is news. *Journalism Quarterly, 67,* 672-683.

McManus, J. (1994). *Market-driven journalism: Let the citizen beware?* Thousand Oaks, CA: Sage.

McShane, S. (1995). Occupational, gender, and geographic representation of information sources in U.S. and Canadian business magazines. *Journalism and Mass Communication Quarterly, 72*(1), 190-204.

Minnis, J. H., & Pratt, C. B. (1994, August). *Newsroom socialization and the press release: Implications for media relations.* Paper presented at the annual meeting of the Association for Education in Journalism and Mass Communication, Atlanta, GA.

Morton, L. P. (1984). Use of photos in public relations messages. *Public Relations Review, 10*(4), 15-22.

Morton, L. P. (1986). How newspapers choose the releases they use. *Public Relations Review, 12*(3), 22-27.

Morton, L. P. (1988). Effectiveness of camera-ready copy in press releases. *Public Relations Review, 14*(2), 45-49.

Morton, L. P. (1992-1993). Producing publishable press releases: A research perspective. *Public Relations Quarterly, 37*(4), 9-11.

Morton, L. P. (1993, May 8). Researcher finds complaints against press releases are justified. *Editor & Publisher,* pp. 52, 42.

Morton, L. P., & Warren, J. (1992a). Acceptance characteristics of hometown press releases. *Public Relations Review, 18,* 385-390.

Morton, L. P., & Warren, J. (1992b). News elements and editors' choices. *Public Relations Review, 18,* 47-52.

Morton, L. P., & Warren, J. (1992c). Proximity: Localization vs. distance in PR news releases. *Journalism Quarterly, 69,* 1023-1029.

Nayman, O., McKnee, B., & Lattimore, D. L. (1977). PR personnel and print journalists: A comparison of professionalism. *Journalism Quarterly, 54,* 492-497.

Nelson, R. A. (1994). Issues communication and advocacy: Contemporary ethical challenges. *Public Relations Review, 20,* 225-231.

Neuwirth, K., Liebler, C. M., Dunwoody, S., & Riddle, J. (1988). The effect of "electronic" news sources on selection and editing of news. *Journalism Quarterly, 65,* 85-94.

Newsom, D. A. (1983). Conflict: Who gets media attention and why? *Public Relations Review, 9*(3), 35-39.

Newsom, D. A., Ramsey, S. A., & Carrell, R. J. (1993). Chameleon chasing II: A replication. *Public Relations Review, 19,* 33-47.

Nicolai, R. R., & Riley, S. G. (1972). The gatekeeping function from the point of view of the PR man. *Journalism Quarterly, 49,* 371-373.

Noelle-Neumann, E. (1974). The spiral of silence: A theory of public opinion. *Journal of Communication, 24,* 43-51.

Noelle-Neumann, E., & Mathes, R. (1987). The "event as event" and the "event as news": The significance of consonance for media effects research. *European Journal of Communication, 2,* 391-414.

O'Brian, C. E. (1978). *A rules-based approach to communication within a formal organization: Theory and case studies.* Unpublished doctoral dissertation, University of Massachusetts, Amherst.

Olasky, M. N. (1985). Inside the amoral world of public relations: Truth molded for corporate gain. *Business and Society Review, 52,* 41-44.

Olson, L. D. (1989). Job satisfaction of journalists and PR personnel. *Public Relations Review, 15*(4), 37-45.

Parenti, M. (1986). *Inventing reality: The politics of the mass media.* New York: St. Martin's.

Parsons, P. H. (1993). Framework for analysis of conflicting loyalties. *Public Relations Review, 19,* 49-57.

Pavlik, J. V. (1987). *Public relations: What research tells us.* Newbury Park, CA: Sage.

Pearson, R. (1989a). Beyond ethical relativism in public relations: Coorientation, rules, and the idea of communication symmetry. In J. E. Grunig & L. A. Grunig (Eds.), *Public relations research annual* (Vol. 1, pp. 67-87). Hillsdale, NJ: Lawrence Erlbaum.

Pearson, R. (1989b). Reviewing Albert J. Sullivan's theory of public relations. *Public Relations Review, 15*(2), 52-62.

Pearson, R. (1990). Ethical values or strategic values? The two faces of systems theory in public relations. In L. A. Grunig & J. E. Grunig (Eds.), *Public relations research annual* (Vol. 2, pp. 219-234). Hillsdale, NJ: Lawrence Erlbaum.

Pfau, M., & Gorham, B. W. (1995, May). *Influence of public relations materials on journalists' attitudes and practices.* Paper presented at the annual meeting of the International Communication Association, Albuquerque, NM.

Pincus, J. D., Rimmer, T., Rayfield, R. E., & Cropp, F. (1993). Newspaper editors' perceptions of public relations: How business, news, and sports editors differ. *Journal of Public Relations Research, 5,* 27-45.

Plowman, K. D., ReVelle, C., Meirovich, S., Pien, M., Stemple, R., Sheng, V., & Fay, K. (1995). Walgreens: A case study in health care issues and conflict resolution. *Journal of Public Relations Research, 7,* 231-258.

Pratt, C. B. (1991). Public relations: The empirical research on practitioner ethics. *Journal of Business Ethics, 10,* 229-236.

Pratt, C. B. (1994). Research progress in public relations ethics: An overview. *Public Relations Review, 20,* 217-224.

Rawls, J. (1971). *A theory of justice.* Cambridge, MA: Harvard University Press.

Rawls, J. (1993). *Political liberalism.* New York: Columbia University Press.

Reese, S. D., & Danielian, L. H. (1994). The structure of news sources on television: A network analysis of "CBS News," "Nightline," "MacNeil/Lehrer," and "This Week with David Brinkley." *Journal of Communication, 44*(2), 84-107.

Rest, J. (1979). *Development in judging moral issues.* Minneapolis: University of Minnesota Press.

Rest, J. (1986). *Moral development: Advances in research and theory.* New York: Praeger.

Rivers, W. L., Schramm, W., & Christians, C. G. (1980). *Responsibility in mass communication* (3rd ed.). New York: Harper & Row.

Robinson, M. (1977). Television and American politics: 1956-1976. *Public Interest, 48,* 3-39.

Ryan, M., & Martinson, D. L. (1984). Ethical values, the flow of journalistic information and public relations persons. *Journalism Quarterly, 61,* 27-34.

Ryan, M., & Martinson, D. L. (1988). Journalists and public relations practitioners: Why the antagonism? *Journalism Quarterly, 65,* 131-140.

Ryan, M., & Martinson, D. L. (1991, August). *How journalists and public relations practitioners define lying.* Paper presented at the annual meeting of the Association for Education in Journalism and Mass Communication, Boston.

Sachsman, D. B. (1976). Public relations influence on coverage of environment in San Francisco area. *Journalism Quarterly, 53,* 54-60.

Sallot, L. M. (1990a). The man on a white horse: The presidency, persuasion and myth. *Florida Communication Journal, 18*(1), 1-8.

Sallot, L. M. (1990b, August). *Public relations and mass media: How professionals in the fields in Miami and New York view public relations effects on the mass media, themselves, and each other.* Paper presented at the annual meeting of the Association for Education in Journalism and Mass Communication, Minneapolis.

Sallot, L. M. (1992, May). *Mass media consonance: Proposing public relations as a factor.* Paper presented at the annual meeting of the International Communication Association, Miami, FL.

Sandman, P. M., Rubin, D. M., & Sachsman, D. B. (Eds.). (1976). *Media: An introductory analysis of American mass communications* (2nd ed.). Englewood Cliffs, NJ: Prentice Hall.

Sandquist, K. (1976). *Public relations and the news media: A comparative study of the utilization of public relations material by representative Milwaukee news media.* Unpublished master's thesis, University of Wisconsin—Madison.

Saunders, M. D. (1989). Ethical dilemmas in public relations: Perceptions of Florida practitioners. *Florida Communication Journal, 17*(2), 23-27.

Schabacker, W. (1963). *Public relations and the news media: A study of the selection and utilization of representative Milwaukee news media of materials emanating from public relations sources.* Unpublished master's thesis, University of Wisconsin—Madison.

Seib, P., & Fitzpatrick, K. (1995). *Public relations ethics.* Fort Worth, TX: Harcourt Brace.

Seitel, F. P. (1995). *The practice of public relations* (6th ed.). New York: Macmillan.

Shamir, J., Reed, B. S., & Connell, S. (1990). Individual differences in ethical values of public relations practitioners. *Journalism Quarterly, 67,* 956-963.

Sharpe, M. L. (1986). Recognition comes from consistently high standards. *Public Relations Review, 12*(4), 17-26.

Shellen, W. N., & Bach, B. (1983, May). *The language of disagreement: Judgments of dominant, equal, and submissive styles.* Paper presented at the annual meeting of the Western Speech Communication Association, Coeur d'Alene, ID.

Shimanoff, S. B. (1980). *Communication rules: Theory and research.* Beverly Hills, CA: Sage.

Shockley-Zalabak, P., & Morley, D. D. (1994). Creating a culture: A longitudinal examination of the influence of management and employee values on communication rule stability and emergence. *Human Communication Research, 20,* 334-355.

Sigal, L. V. (1973). *Reporters and officials.* Lexington, MA: D. C. Heath.

Soley, L. C. (1994). Pundits in print: "Experts" and their use in newspaper stories. *Newspaper Research Journal, 15*(2), 65-75.

Soloski, J. (1989). Sources and channels of local news. *Journalism Quarterly, 66,* 864-870.

Spicer, C. H. (1993). Images of public relations in the print media. *Journal of Public Relations Research, 5,* 47-61.

Stegall, S. K., & Sanders, K. P. (1986). Coorientation of PR practitioners and news personnel in education news. *Journalism Quarterly, 64,* 341-347, 393.

Stocking, S. H. (1985). Effect of public relations efforts on media visibility of organizations. *Journalism Quarterly, 62,* 358-366, 450.

Strentz, H. (1989). *News reporters and news sources: Accomplices in shaping and misshaping the news.* Ames: Iowa State University Press.

Sullivan, A. J. (1965a). Toward a philosophy of public relations: Images. In O. Lerbinger & A. Sullivan (Eds.), *Information, influence, and communication: A reader in public relations* (pp. 220-249). New York: Basic Books.

Sullivan, A. J. (1965b). Values in public relations. In O. Lerbinger & A. J. Sullivan (Eds.), *Information, influence, and communication: A reader in public relations* (pp. 412-439). New York: Basic Books.

Swartz, J. E. (1983). On the margin: Between journalist and publicist. *Public Relations Review, 9*(3), 11-23.

Tichenor, P. J., Olien, C. N., Harrison, A., & Donohue, G. (1970). Mass communication systems and communication accuracy in science news reporting. *Journalism Quarterly, 47,* 673-683.

Toulmin, S. E. (1974). Rules and their relevance for understanding human behavior. In T. Mischel (Ed.), *Understanding other persons* (pp. 185-215). Oxford: Basil Blackwell.

Tuchman, G. (1978). *Making news: A study in the construction of reality.* New York: Free Press.

Turk, J. V. (1985). Information subsidies and influence. *Public Relations Review, 11*(3), 1-14.

Turk, J. V. (1986a). Information subsidies and media content: A study of public relations influence on the news. *Journalism Monographs, 100.*

Turk, J. V. (1986b). Public relations' influence on the news. *Newspaper Research Journal, 7*(4), 15-27.

Turk, J. V. (1988). Public relations' influence on the news. In R. E. Hiebert (Ed.), *Precision public relations* (pp. 224-239). New York: Longman.

Walters, L. M., & Walters, T. N. (1992). Environment of confidence: Daily newspaper use of press releases. *Public Relations Review, 18,* 31-47.

Walters, T. N., Walters, L. M., & Starr, D. P. (1994). After the highwayman: Syntax and successful placement of press releases in newspapers. *Public Relations Review, 20,* 345-356.

Warren, J., & Morton, L. P. (1991). Readability and acceptance of public relations releases from institutions of higher education. *Communication Research Reports, 8*(2), 113-119.

Wilcox, D., Ault, P., & Agee, W. (1995). *Public relations: Strategies and tactics* (4th ed.). New York: Harper & Row.

Wright, D. K. (1982). Philosophy of ethics. *Public Relations Journal, 38,* 14-16.

Wright, D. K. (1989). Examining ethical and moral values of public relations people. *Public Relations Review, 15*(2), 19-33.

Wright, D. K. (1993). Enforcement dilemma: Voluntary nature of public relations codes. *Public Relations Review, 19,* 13-20.

Wylie, F. W. (1974). A common code of ethics. *Public Relations Journal, 30,* 14-15.

Young, I. M. (1990). *Justice and the politics of difference.* Princeton, NJ: Princeton University Press.

CHAPTER CONTENTS

5 Public Opinion as a Normative Opinion Process

CARROLL J. GLYNN
Cornell University

This chapter provides a review of literature related to the conceptualization of the expression of public opinion as a normative opinion process. Public opinion is described, in part, as an expression of the interaction between individuals' actual opinions and their perceptions of others' opinions. It also is seen as an indicator of social norms on particular issues. The literature review describes, in detail, group processes and social comparison, and explains the development of group norms as they relate to communication and public opinion. In addition, the author examines normative influences and the public opinion process by describing two types of norms that may affect the extent of normative influences on expressed opinion and the manner in which norms may be accepted by individuals. A description of the potential for integrating norms in current public opinion research is presented.

RECENT theoretical concerns in public opinion have forged a renewed interest in relationships between the individual and the group. A growing body of empirical research from diverse academic perspectives has investigated the relationship between the self and others as a major factor influencing the communication of the public's opinions and behavior (see Davison, 1983; Glynn, 1989; Granberg, 1984; Noelle-Neumann, 1984; Ross, Greene, & House, 1977; Tyler & Cook, 1984). Although a number of studies have investigated this relationship as an additional psychological variable, it most clearly marks the return to a conceptualization of public opinion as a combination of social and psychological processes (see Campbell, 1950; Eagly & Chaiken, 1993; Festinger, 1954; Glynn & McLeod, 1984; McKirnan, 1980; Price & Allen, 1990; Price & Oshagan, 1995; Schachter, 1951).

This chapter presents a review of literature related to the conceptualization of the expression of a public opinion as a *normative opinion process*: Public opinion is described, in part, as an expression of the interaction between individuals' actual opinions and their perceptions of others' opinions. It also is seen as an indicator of social norms on particular issues. In this model,

Correspondence and requests for reprints: Carroll J. Glynn, Department of Communication, 336 Kennedy Hall, Cornell University, Ithaca, NY 14853; e-mail cjg4@cornell.edu

Communication Yearbook 20, pp. 157-183

expressed public opinion represents a social norm: an opinion that is both appropriate and typical for the individual to hold. Individuals who hold opinions counter to the norm face the same constraints and difficulties as do individuals in other counternormative situations.

Conceptualizing public opinion as a norm may be an aid in the clarification of certain public opinion theories and in integrating recent research on public opinion. In order to orient the reader, I first present an overview that describes some characteristics and linkages among communication, reference groups, and social norms. In the second section, I expand these social perspectives through a review of the literature on group process and social comparison, describing the development of group norms as they relate to communication and public opinion. Following that, I examine normative influences on the public opinion process by describing two types of norms that may affect the extent of these influences on expressed opinion and the manner in which norms may be accepted by individuals. In the next section I describe two general characteristics of norms that affect expressed opinion. Finally, I describe the role of norms in current public opinion research, discuss some of the ways in which hypotheses related to norms and normative influences can be developed, and offer suggestions for future research on the normative opinion process.

COMMUNICATION, REFERENCE GROUPS, AND SOCIAL NORMS

Communication and Opinion Formation

The social and communicative nature of public opinion is a consistent thread running through the literature since the turn of the century (Cooley, 1902; Ross, 1901). Fifty years ago, Blumer (1946; cited in Price & Oshagan, 1995) suggested that public opinion arises when a group recognizes disagreement over some matter and subsequently engages in discussion and debate over the issue to determine an appropriate way of dealing with the problem. Years ago, Campbell (1950) pointed toward the insurmountable evidence within social psychology that social and individual sources combine in their influence on opinion expression.

Scholars across the social science disciplines recognize the importance of communication in attitude and opinion formation and change. For example, Roiser (1987) asserts that ideas, knowledge, and opinions are developed through the interaction of common sense and science: "Within commonsense, knowledge spreads in an informal, everyday manner via conversation and the mass media of communication, generating both the insights of common understanding and the mistakes of rumour and gossip" (p. 412).

Moscovici (1988) notes that we derive only a small fraction of our knowledge and information from the simple interaction between ourselves and the facts we encounter in the world. He states that most of our knowledge is supplied to us not by direct experience but by communication, which affects our way of thinking and creates new content through social representations. Moscovici's (1981, 1984) theory of social representations has received widespread attention in the European sphere of social psychology, but has received little theoretical or empirical attention in North America.

For Moscovici (1988), *social representations* refers to the ideas, thoughts, images, and knowledge that members of a collectivity share—"consensual universes of thought which are socially created and socially communicated to form part of a common consciousness" (Augoustinos & Innes, 1990, p. 215). According to this line of reasoning, social representations are the stock of common knowledge and information that people share in the form of commonsense theories about the social world. Through these representations, members of a society are able to construct social reality.

It is clear that communication's role is critical in every step of the public opinion process—the process begins and is modified, influenced, and maintained by communication. Communication becomes a particularly critical and pervasive component in investigating groups—a necessary component of public opinion. When one is dealing with relatively small groups and individual behavior within those groups, interactions may seem relatively clear and simple to monitor. As group size increases, individual variability increases and group norms become more difficult to enforce, requiring increasingly complex communication to maintain group affiliations (Nowak, Szamrej, & Latané, 1990).

Because of these conditions, communication and public opinion are "inextricably wed" (Zukin, 1981). For example, various forms of informal communication (such as hearsay, nonverbal communication, and rumors) can contribute to opinion expression outcomes. In addition, the public is largely dependent on the mass media for information about issues, actors, and institutions. Mass communications "have the advantage of being able to reach large numbers of people simultaneously, but even when they are not available the same effect may be achieved, although more slowly and with infinitely more difficulty, through person-to-person communication systems" (Davison, 1975, p. 106). As Davison (1975) points out, through intergroup communication (particularly mass communication), ideas that were originally developed as a result of interaction within face-to-face groups become available to large numbers of people who are not personally acquainted with each other.

Several researchers in communication recently have begun to link social psychological theories of group behavior to communication and public opinion processes (Glynn, 1989; Glynn, Ostman, & McDonald, 1995; Noelle-Neumann, 1977; Price & Allen, 1990; Price & Oshagan, 1995). A number of these perspectives focus on the role of reference groups in the public opinion process, paying particular attention to those aspects of the group that cannot exist at the individual level (e.g., conflict, consensus and norms) (Glynn et al., 1995; Glynn & Park, 1995; Price & Oshagan, 1995).

The literature in communication has been consistent with much of the social psychological literature in finding that people form attachments to reference groups and in-group/out-group distinctions quite easily through communicated content. In a study of social identification effects on group polarization, for example, Mackie (1986) found that simply labeling opinions as coming from a relevant in-group or out-group affected the evaluation of the representativeness of the information. In addition, when subjects in her experiment were focused on their group membership, group norms were perceived as more extreme, and polarization due to conformity to these extreme attitudes occurred. When these subjects were focused on their own individual performance, their attitudes shifted to a more neutral position on the issues.

Glynn and Park's (1995) analysis of survey data collected in six Canadian towns also supports the idea of in-group/out-group distinctions and the ease with which these distinctions are formed. These researchers found that in-group/out-group distinctions are formed on the basis of opinions on issues that would appear, on the surface, to be relatively noncontroversial. In their study, they found that people were able to distinguish in-group/out-group norms easily and that their distinctions led to sometimes bitter polarization effects. Such polarization was associated with frequency of communication between in-group and out-group members.

Price (1989) has developed a model of social identification and public opinion that suggests that when news articles emphasize group conflict, readers think about issues through their particular group perspectives, triggering a host of group processes (such as polarized differences and conformity to group norms). As Price notes, when conflict within a group occurs, "members try to alleviate it or control it through discussion, thereby restoring group consensus or creating a new consensus. Conflict among group members stimulates discussion, and, through it, opinion formation and change within the group" (p. 197).

Traugott and Price (1992) suggest that a similar effect occurred in the 1989 Virginia gubernatorial race. During that race, inaccurate results were obtained through personal interviews with white respondents, who invoked processes similar to in-group/out-group polarization by overemphasizing the amount of support the African American candidate would have.

The literature on communication and public opinion is thus consistent in documenting, through both survey and experimental approaches, the important role communication plays in invoking reference groups and group processes that have impacts on public opinion. I will examine some of these processes in more detail below.

Communication and Group Process

As many authors have observed, each person is simultaneously a member of numerous groupings and affiliations (Cooley, 1902; Sherif & Sherif, 1964).

These groupings and affiliations, generally known as *reference groups,* carry with them specific norms and values, acceptable and unacceptable behaviors.

Contemporary researchers in social psychology investigating such areas as small group processes, attribution theory, person perception, intergroup perception, assimilation-contrast phenomena, social identification, group conformity, reference groups, social comparison, and group polarization have explored important dimensions of social perception that are relevant to public opinion processes, but few have directly generalized or applied their research to public opinion processes. Instead, these scholars have focused their efforts on descriptions of small groups or on sweeping social change (see Levine, 1989; Moscovici, 1985).

Reference Groups and Social Norms

Unfortunately, despite their long history and extended use, there is no consensus about the explanatory and predictive value of social norms—nor is there consensus on a common definition of social norms. As Cialdini, Kallgren, and Reno (1991) note, there are, on the one hand, "those who see the concept as crucial to a full understanding of human social behavior (e.g., Berkowitz, 1972; McKirnan, 1980; Sherif, 1936). On the other hand are those who view the concept as vague and overly general, often contradictory and ill suited to empirical test (e.g., Krebs & Miller, 1985; Marini, 1984)" (p. 202).

Eagly and Chaiken (1993) suggest that a norm should be defined as a standard or rule that is accepted by members of a group, an approach in keeping with work by Kelley (1955) and Newcomb (1961). This definition of norm implies that each participant in a social interaction not only has a favorable attitude toward a particular regularity in behavior but also perceives that most other participants in the group hold this same attitude.

Research on social norms dates back to the late nineteenth and early twentieth centuries, when scholars measured the force of custom and tradition (Bagehot, 1869/1948; Sumner, 1906) or were concerned with mechanisms leading to influence and to compliance with the will of groups or individuals (Ross, 1901). In the 1920s, Ogburn (1922) formulated cultural lag as an explanation for social problems and Park (1928) explored the problems of developing a "viable self-conception" in the face of cultural conflict (see Turner, 1991). However, it is clear that for most of these researchers, the normative element was either inseparable from the idea of tradition or tradition and myth were seen as major control mechanisms, studied without the postulation of "any intervening system of norms" (Turner, 1991).

These conceptualizations and viewpoints changed following Sherif's (1936) research on the emergence of individual and group norms in connection with the autokinetic phenomenon. Sherif's research made important contributions to research on social norms and conformity, occurring at a time when scholars were "struggling to create a general theory of social norms from several disparate lines of development" (Turner, 1991, p. 77). Turner (1991) notes how Sherif's research turned attention away from the persistence and enforcement of norms to a focus on their emergence—where norms become dynamic and realistic. Sherif also examined the relationship of social norms to perception.

Asch's (1951) experiments also contributed to the literature on conformity and norm formation. They were designed to investigate situations that Asch considered less conducive to social influence because the stimuli presented were unambiguous. However, his results showed that more than a third of subjects would agree with obviously incorrect answers when the other members of their groups (confederates) gave the wrong answers.

Although Sherif's and Asch's experiments are often confused or blended together in descriptions, the two researchers clearly provide examples of two very different phenomena. In Sherif's (1936) experiments, the stimulus used was ambiguous, so that the norm established by confederates provided information about an objective reality. In Asch's (1951) experiments, the confederates were clearly providing judgments that were incorrect to the experimental subjects. In this case, the norms provided by confederates appeared to constitute a persuasive influence.

Other research sheds important light upon the conception of social norms. For example, functional perspectives emphasize the usefulness of social norms for society (Merton & Rossi, 1950). And Durkheim's (1894/1933) theory of collective representations provides important insight into social norms as well as social representations. Durkheim describes individual perceptions as being shaped by a group frame of reference whose "categories were compelling to the individual and were experienced as having a reality external to human perceptual or cognitive processes" (Turner, 1991, p. 80).

Due to the renewed popularity of Durkheim's and Sherif's works among contemporary sociological theorists, social norms are no longer thought of as only "behavioral" and no longer need to be linked simply to the order and predictability of behaviors. Some scholars now indicate that norms can exist not only for behaviors, but for attitudes, opinions, and tendencies to behave (see Glynn, 1989; Hogg, Turner, & Davidson, 1990; Jackson, 1965; Moscovici, 1988; Traugott & Price, 1992). Such liberalization of the conceptualization of norms should lead to sophisticated approaches to theory development, but few public opinion scholars have approached the study of the public's opinions with social norms as an active component in the process.

Clearly, Noelle-Neumann's (1977, 1984) work on the "spiral of silence" can be considered an exception. The general principle of spiral of silence theory is that individuals continually scan their social environments for clues related to majority and minority opinion on issues with which they are concerned. When they perceive that their opinions are gaining ground, this theory suggests, they will express their views confidently in public; when they perceive that their views are losing ground, they will be more reluctant to speak out in public.

Although, from a conceptual viewpoint, the spiral of silence is linked to the idea of norms and normative influences, Noelle-Neumann does not tie her theory explicitly to the literature on norms. However, several researchers have begun to make these links (Glynn, 1989; Glynn & McLeod, 1984; Price & Allen, 1990). In my own work on public opinion and norms (1989; Glynn & McLeod, 1984, 1985; Glynn & Ostman, 1988), I was originally concerned with testing the spiral of silence, but I have since become more concerned with the idea of perceptions of public opinion as a normative influence on opinion expression, having found considerable evidence that people are influenced by what they perceive to be the norm for public opinion.

Price's work (Price & Allen, 1990; Price & Oshagan, 1995; Price & Roberts, 1987) has been focused on the normative aspect of reference groups on opinion formation and change as well as on the distinctions between mass-mediated and interpersonal channels of social influence (Price & Roberts, 1987), both important considerations in research on norms and reference groups.

The Role of Reference Groups in Opinion Formation

It is a truism to suggest that norms need to be considered in conjunction with the reference groups with which they are concerned. However, it is difficult to describe the role of reference groups in the development and maintenance of social norms related to opinion expression. Sherif (1936) defines a reference group as any group that provides norms that are used by an individual as anchoring points in the structuring of the individual's perceptual field. Thus, reference groups (both positive and negative) provide "benchmarks" that the individual can use to "organize his/her perceived social world in a way that is personally meaningful" (Hall, Varca, & Fisher, 1986, p. 311).

Tajfel's (1969, 1972, 1982) notion of *social categorization* also has been used to explain how social norms aid in determining the ways people classify themselves and others in a behavioral setting as members of these distinct categories and reference groups (see also Price & Oshagan, 1995; Turner & Oakes, 1989). Social categorization research has shown that the simple act of classifying others into social categories is enough to provoke discrimination between in-group and out-group members. This classification also results in a variety of effects characteristic of group formation, including discriminatory in-group behavior, intragroup cohesion, and ethnocentric biases (Brewer, 1979; Turner, 1975, 1982, 1983).

When individuals classify themselves and others into categorical groups, there are perceptual effects: increased perception of differences between groups (polarization) and decreased perception of differences within groups (homogenization). As Kelley (1955) notes, when people classify themselves and others in this fashion, they tend to conform behaviorally to the norms of their groups. Tajfel has suggested two processes to account for these effects: *categorization* (Tajfel, 1969), in which the classification process leads to perceptual accentuation of intraclass similarities and interclass differences, and *social identity/intergroup comparison* (Tajfel, 1972; Turner, 1975), in which people seek positive distinctiveness for their groups (Turner & Oakes, 1989). Traugott and Price (1992) have used these notions to explain social desirability effects in a sample survey.

Turner (1985) modified social categorization theory and the related concept "social identity" to develop *self-categorization theory*, which departs from Tajfel's original formulation in its emphasis on the interrelationship of personal and social identity (see also Turner, 1987; Turner & Oakes, 1989). Self-categorization theory holds that people conform to positions perceived as normative for (or stereotypical of) their groups precisely because, in reflecting the agreement of similar others, such positions provide subjectively valid evidence about the external world (see Hogg et al., 1990; Turner, 1987).

Price (1989) suggests that news reports cue their recipients to think about the reported issues in terms of their particular group perspectives. These perspectives lead to polarized or exaggerated perceptions of group opinions, finally leading to expression of personal opinion consistent with the exaggerated perception of the group norm. Price interprets his data as indicating that media reports emphasizing group conflicts may play a role in the formation of public opinion.

Thus, in a manner similar to that suggested by Festinger's (1954) social comparison mechanisms, individuals appear to formulate and use group norms as a comparison base in justifying their own opinions. As an individual makes comparisons, he or she draws distinctions and differences between his or her own reference group and other comparison groups. A common result of such comparisons is group polarization.

Group Polarization

Self-categorization theory explains group polarization as conformity to a polarized norm that defines one's own group in contrast to other groups within a specific social context (Hogg et al., 1990). Under conditions that render an in-group psychologically salient, people conform to the in-group norm, the position perceived as most "consensual" (Hogg et al., 1990; Turner, 1987). In some circumstances, the group norm will be the position that is the average for the in-group distribution—the position that minimizes the differences between in-group members.

However, as Hogg et al. (1990) note, it is equally likely that the norm of the in-group will not be the group mean, but some other point in the distribution. According to Hogg et al., this occurs because groups do not exist in isolation, but in a wider social frame of reference that encompasses both in-groups and out-groups. The defining features of a group, its norms and stereotypes, not only characterize the in-group's qualities, but also distinguish the in-group clearly from relevant other groups, thus maximizing differences between in-groups and out-groups. The actual position of the in-group norm is a trade-off between minimization of intragroup differences and maximization of intergroup differences. The homogenization of group members' opinions becomes a part of the polarization effect as members seek to differentiate themselves from the out-group.

Thus, self-categorization theory explains polarization as a conformity phenomenon "in which individuals who identify with a group conform, through the process of self-categorization, to the local norm which best represents the group" (Hogg et al., 1990, p. 81). Glynn and McDonald (1994) have found polarization and resultant "exaggerated differences" to develop even between people who reside in different countries.

Social Comparisons

Group polarization can happen only when people make social comparisons. Leon Festinger (1954), probably best known for his theory of cognitive dissonance, was clearly an advocate of both social and psychological sources of influence. The first hypothesis advanced in his "social comparison theory" suggests that a human has a "drive to evaluate his opinions and his abilities" (p. 117). His second hypothesis suggests that when objective means of evaluation are unavailable, humans compare their opinions and abilities with the opinions and abilities of others. Additional hypotheses and corollaries of social comparison theory suggest that individuals select particular groups and particular members of groups as references for comparison, and that these comparisons are generally made on the basis of perceived similarity to these individuals.

Festinger's (1950, 1954) social comparison process suggests an important role for norms in that people turn to social reality to validate their beliefs when those beliefs are unsupported by clear-cut physical reality. As Festinger (1950) observes, "An opinion, a belief, an attitude is 'correct,' 'valid,' and 'proper' to the extent that it is anchored in a group of people with similar beliefs, opinions and attitudes" (p. 272). By 1954, Festinger had developed even stronger theories about our use of norms. He saw humans as having a basic need or drive to evaluate their beliefs and abilities and using one another for such evaluations whenever physical reality is too ambiguous to provide much guidance (Eagly & Chaiken, 1993).

Social comparison theory has received renewed attention in recent years (e.g., Goethals & Darley, 1977; Gorenflo & Crano, 1989; Orive, 1988), but has had little direct application in public opinion research. This is surprising, given the importance of perception of opinions in recent research and theory (see Glynn et al., 1995). However, a number of studies have investigated people's tendencies to monitor social distributions of opinion without the benefit of social comparison as a theoretical base. These studies have relied on several related public opinion hypotheses, such as the "third-person effect" or "pluralistic ignorance," or on the more elaborate spiral of silence, which depends upon people's ability to discern the trend of opinion.

Nisbett and Kunda (1985), for example, examined the accuracy of perceptions of the distribution of social attitudes and behaviors and found that, although there were a number of systematic biases, overall accuracy was "impressive." Shamir (1995) studied the information cues and indicators of the "climate of opinion" and found that people use different cues for assessing opinion distributions and opinion trends. In a study of pluralistic ignorance, Shamir (1993) found that, for salient issues, people can quite accurately assess majority and minority opinions. He suggests that people may use the political continuum as a surrogate distribution when direct information on others' opinions on an issue is scarce. Shamir finds both a "conservative bias" and a "liberal bias" in his research and suggests that the distinction is a reflection of social norms rather than an individual tendency to view others as more or less conservative than oneself. This suggestion echoes my own analysis of the conservative and liberal bias phenomenon (Glynn, 1989).

Matera and Salwen (1992) used Noelle-Neumann's theory of the spiral of silence as a base and developed a cross-cultural test of people's willingness to speak out on a controversial issue. They found that the best predictors of willingness to express one's opinion publicly were personal opinion and perceptions of others' opinions—findings consistent with Noelle-Neumann's spiral of silence hypothesis. In her analysis of third-person effects and the public expression of opinions, Mutz (1989) examined the role of perceptions of others' opinions as they relate to the formation of public opinion. She also found some support for Noelle-Neumann's contention that perception of the trend of opinion is a key factor in willingness to express one's own opinion.

Katz and Baldassare (1992, 1994) also used the spiral of silence as a base in analyzing the perception of opinion climates in relation to opinion expression during a presidential election. They found no relation in one study, but their second, more complex, analysis suggests support for the spiral of silence, especially when the popularity of one candidate was at its steepest decline. Eveland, McLeod, and Signorielli (1995) found that the perception of public support for the Persian Gulf War was a strong predictor of opinion expression, again supporting Noelle-Neumann's spiral of silence theory.

Types of Influence: Descriptive and Injunctive Norms

All of the studies reviewed in the previous subsection indicate the importance of social comparison to opinion formation. However, it is also clear that people use norms for different reasons. In fact, results of experiments such as those conducted by Sherif and Asch stimulated considerable work in the 1950s on the impacts group members have on each others' responses and on how people are influenced in social situations (Eagly & Chaiken, 1993). In keeping with the different aspects of the Sherif and Asch experiments, Deutsch and Gerard (1955) propose two distinctions in the influence of norms: normative influence and informational influence. These researchers define normative influence as "influence to conform to the positive expectations of another," whereas they define informational influence as the "influence to accept information obtained from another as evidence about reality" (p. 629). Eagly and Chaiken (1993) suggest that this distinction concerns the extent to which people communicate to one another (a) expectations about appropriate conduct or (b) evidence about the nature of reality. This distinction provides a clear link to MacLeod's (1951) formulation of social perception, and is very similar to distinctions made by Kelley (1955) in describing normative and comparative functions of reference groups.

Jones and Gerard (1967) suggest that the normative and informational influence components should be studied in terms of what they label effect dependence and information dependence. They suggest that humans' dependence on one another occurs in these two forms. *Effect dependence* refers to the reliance of one person on another for direct satisfaction of needs, which leads people to be concerned about how others evaluate them. *Information dependence* refers to the reliance of one person on another for information about the environment and possibilities for action (Eagly & Chaiken, 1993).

Cialdini, Reno, and Kallgren (1990) discuss the differences in the meaning of the word *norm* in academic usage (also see Shaffer, 1983): It is used to refer both to what is commonly done (normal) and to what is commonly approved or socially sanctioned (normative). Cialdini et al. (1991) develop the concept further, labeling norms that characterize the perception of what most people do as *descriptive* norms and norms that characterize the perception of what most people approve or disapprove as *injunctive* norms. To maintain consistency, I use the term *descriptive norms* here for those norms that have an informational function and *injunctive norms* to indicate those norms that have a sanctioning function.

Normative Influences, Descriptive Norms

As Cialdini et al. (1991) propose, descriptive norms motivate by providing evidence as to what will likely be effective and adaptive action ("If everyone is doing or thinking or believing it, it must be a sensible thing to do or think or believe"). In contrast, injunctive norms specify what ought to be done, or the "moral rules of the group" (Cialdini et al., 1991). In a sense, descriptive norms perform a kind of abstracting service for the senses.

Festinger's (1954) social comparison theory suggests an important role for descriptive norms in providing the comparison base by which individuals validate their opinions. Opinions that are normative for the group provide a validity check for individuals, because others (who were already judged to be similar to the individual) hold a particular opinion norm. According to Festinger, the opinion norm thus provides the closest thing to an "objective" measure of what is real, true, or the "correct" opinion to hold.

Normative Influences, Injunctive Norms

As noted above, injunctive norms are the perceptions of what most people approve or disapprove—perceptions of what is socially sanctioned. Injunctive norms are thus linked to the notion of "social desirability" in opinion research, which is based on the tendency of individuals to conform to social norms. An example of the role of injunctive norms is provided by Anderson, Silver, and Abramson (1988), who suggest that survey respondents often "exaggerate their conformity with socially approved norms":

> However well theoretical concepts are defined, survey questions are formulated and data are analyzed, the data are the product of an interview. The interview involves an interaction between interviewer and respondent in which the stimulus is not just the "question" as it is written in the survey booklet, but also the social context in which the question is asked. (p. 290)

Anderson et al. (1988) suggest that normative acquiescence comes into play when there is a perceived threat to polite conversation. Injunctive norms also are important in the presence of third parties. Aquilino (1993), for example, found that the presence of a spouse during an interview affected responses on perceptions of utility of marriage, estimates of spouse contribution to housework, and, for men, estimates of the probability of marriage dissolution. Anderson et al. (1988) found that when a third party was present during a social survey interview, respondents were more likely to be honest about whether or not they had voted than when they were interviewed alone. These findings suggest that when no one is present to say otherwise, people are more likely to report conforming to injunctive norms than when a third source is present who is likely to know that the person does not conform.

Public Compliance and Private Acceptance

The concepts of normative and informational influence have drawn attention to the distinction between public compliance with others' views and private acceptance (or internalization) of these views. Asch's (1951) results, for example, provide evidence that individuals may publicly *agree* with confederates' public statements, but not necessarily *believe* those statements. Thus, people may conform publicly without changing their attitudes. Eagly and Chaiken (1993) suggest that when influence is of an injunctive nature, social pressures may produce public agreement with other group members, but create little or no private acceptance.

Nail (1986) has distinguished four possibilities in the compliance/acceptance situation: (a) conforming privately and publicly (conversion), (b) conforming publicly but not privately (compliance), (c) conforming privately but not publicly (anticompliance), and (d) nonconformity at both private and public levels (independence). Thus, although many researchers use the term *conformity* to refer to public agreement, Nail's conceptualization suggests that this may not be an accurate label for what occurs. The idea of private and public aspects of conformity should have considerable interest for researchers in public opinion, and provides an important consideration for research on norm conformity: Expression of an opinion that is in keeping with a social norm does not necessarily indicate that behavior or even an individual's belief on the subject is consistent with what he or she has expressed.

In the literature related to communication and public opinion, little work has assessed directly the different implications of descriptive and injunctive norms or of public versus private acceptance. Price and Oshagan (1995), for example, make the descriptive/injunctive distinction but rely entirely on literature from psychology and social psychology in their explanation.

However, a number of studies have examined the concepts as they appear within public opinion perspectives. For example, Gonzenbach (1992) examines norm conformity not within the context of public/private acceptance, but as the first link in Noelle-Neumann's (1984) spiral of silence theory. Suggesting that pressure to conform is at the heart of Noelle-Neumann's definition of public opinion and the spiral of silence, Gonzenbach finds partial support for the conformity hypothesis as formulated by Noelle-Neumann. More directly concerned with public/private acceptance has been my own work on public opinion, in which I have focused on perceptions of others' opinions as a major force in my conceptualization of public opinion (Glynn, 1989; Glynn & Ostman, 1988; Glynn et al., 1995). My study of perceptions as a component (Glynn, 1989) suggests that public opinion itself includes perceptions of others' opinions, developing a set of possibilities that is similar in tone to that developed by Nail (1986).

NORM CHARACTERISTICS AFFECTING PUBLIC OPINION: INTENSITY AND CRYSTALLIZATION

Although previous references to norms have suggested an "either/or" condition, several researchers have attempted to describe characteristics of norms, so that variance in norm characteristics might be better used to develop hypotheses and suggest research directions. Public opinion researchers often are interested in what may happen when social norms are in flux or changing, and empirical research requires clearer explanation of norm characteristics to document those changes.

Jackson (1965) has described several variables characteristic of social norms related to behavior that may easily be related to norms of opinion expression. Two of these variables, norm intensity and norm crystallization, are important for the present discussion. *Norm intensity* refers to the amount of societal pressure to conform to the norm. In some societies, for example, certain norms may reflect intense moral pressure on the individual to conform to what is considered proper. Other norms may exist, but may reflect a combination of happenstance, coincidence, or social structure, with no moral overtones or pressure to conform. In the former case, the individual who violates the norm may receive severe social ostracism or physical punishment, whereas in the latter case people might see norm violation as odd, but perfectly acceptable. *Norm crystallization* refers to the idea that most norms allow a certain range of freedom for group members, and crystallization is equivalent to the dispersion or variance associated with the norm itself (Jackson, 1965). Applied to public opinion norms, crystallization refers to the range of opinions members of the group have available to them. If others know that their opinions are outside of the boundaries of that range, they will incur social disapproval.

When applied to public opinion research, the most important aspects of the workings of these two characteristics of norms are that crystallization should affect the range of freedom available to individuals when expressing their opinions within a group, whereas the intensity of the norm should reflect the amount of censure individuals would expect to feel from the relevant social group(s) if that range is violated.

In general, low-intensity norms should provide an atmosphere in which the individual feels less societal pressure to conform. High-intensity norms, on the other hand, should make individuals more concerned about group responses and how they "fit" within the group. Jackson's (1965) suggested relationships among norm intensity, norm crystallization, and behavior are incorporated into a tabular presentation in Table 5.1.

In low-intensity/low-crystallization situations, there is little guidance for the individual in the form of norms, and little concern about violation of the norm. Jackson (1965) suggests that, if both intensity and crystallization are low, norms on the topic may not even exist. In high-intensity/high-crystallization situations, the individual has a much narrower range of opinion responses available, and must risk much heavier censure for violating social norms.

Those issues that result in norms with intensity and crystallization in opposite conditions (high/low or low/high) also predict different response pressures. Low intensity coupled with high crystallization may indicate a topic that may not be considered very important—people seem to follow the norm, but may not care too much about the norm itself. The opposite case (high intensity and low crystallization) may indicate a situation in which a group is beginning to form around an issue or the group members are beginning to form opinions concerning an issue. Low crystallization suggests high variance in responses; high intensity suggests that the issue is volatile, stimulating deeply felt opinions. There may be a wide range of "acceptable" opinions, but because of the diversity of actual opinions, anyone who voices an opinion may find that someone holding an opposing view may be nearby.

TABLE 5.1
Some Expectations Related to
Normative Influences and Opinion Expression

Normative Influence		Opinion Expression
Intensity	Crystallization	Derivations
Low	Low	Norms may not exist;[a] no normative pressure[b] or reason for disowning projection.[c]
	High	Intense opinions may not be evident in calculation because of group members in disagreement;[a] members may not consider the topic very important.[a]
High	Low	Groups may be forming;[a] a wide range of opinions may be acceptable;[a] immediate environment or perception of opinion trend likely to determine disowning projection.[d, e, f]
	High	May suggest a narrow range for acceptable opinion;[a] if actual opinion differs from perception of others' opinions, disowning projection or silence likely,[c, d, e, f] except for "hard-core."[c, d]

NOTE: Superscripts indicate sources for the derivations.
a. Jackson (1965).
b. Fields and Schuman (1976).
c. Pettigrew (1965).
d. Noelle-Neumann (1977).
e. Glynn (1989).
f. Granberg (1984).

INTEGRATING CURRENT PERSPECTIVES
WITH THE NORMATIVE OPINION PROCESS

Beginning with social representations and moving through self-categorization and polarization, social psychologists have described social norms as an important, fundamental part of what are generally considered public opinion processes. These norms help define and orient us to our world by helping us to understand the opinions and behaviors of those we are close to, as well as the opinions of those in perceived out-groups. These norms also help to determine what our own opinions will be on issues relevant to us as well as to in-group and out-group members. That is, there is general agreement that individuals in a given society are aware of the views, opinions, behaviors, and so forth that are valued in that society and that they recognize that by being observed as adhering "to society's standards they will be rewarded by social approval or will avoid social disapproval from others" (Hogg et al., 1990, p. 90). Festinger's (1954) social comparison theory suggests a third major function for comparison of ourselves with others—the evaluation of what is "true," or the "best" opinion to hold—a manner of comparing similar others to ourselves and the use of that information in forming our own opinions.

Three Current Perspectives

A number of recent perspectives on public opinion and communication may profit from a reexamination of the literature on norms and normative influences. This section addresses three areas currently of interest in public opinion research: the spiral of silence, pluralistic ignorance, and false consensus. For each approach, I provide a description of how it might fit within a normative framework and how a normative framework might be used to clarify some basic propositions or suggest new directions for research.

The Spiral of Silence

Noelle-Neumann's (1984) work on the spiral of silence is among the best-known and most highly developed theories of the public opinion process. Although controversial, and receiving partial support in the research literature, the spiral of silence has generated considerable research and discussion during the past 20 years. As mentioned above, the general principle of spiral of silence theory is that individuals continually scan their social environments for clues related to majority and minority opinion on issues to determine whether or not to speak up or remain silent.

Noelle-Neumann's (1977, 1984) spiral of silence theory implies that people have a "quasi-statistical sense" that they employ in developing estimates of the opinions that appear to be gaining and losing ground. This notion would appear to fit quite nicely with Festinger's social comparison theory, which suggests that humans have a need to compare themselves with others. Additional work by Nisbett and Kunda (1985) has documented accurate perceptions of social distributions, and Shamir's (1993) study of pluralistic ignorance suggests that those perceptions may in fact be highly accurate and based on a number of modes of information.

It is clear that spiral of silence theory could profit considerably from a consideration of the literature on normative influences. For example, the theory does not consider reference groups used by the individual in assessing the impact of changes in majority support (although this has been suggested by Glynn & McLeod, 1984; Price & Oshagan, 1995; and Salmon & Kline, 1985).

In addition, research reviewed above indicates that a number of mechanisms such as group polarization and perception of group homogeneity are probably triggered in the polling situations often used to collect data testing the spiral of silence. If these processes are at work, we should see individuals' opinions polarizing as the questions are asked on perception of majority/minority opinions. This process might exaggerate any differences the individual perceived before the interview began, and the act of polling may contribute to an exaggerated perception of majority/minority differences (see Granberg, 1984).

Also, by providing reference groups in surveys (usually political parties), research on the spiral of silence may be investigating the behavior of methodological artifacts. Although a host of studies suggest that it is fairly easy to set up in-group/out-group distinctions, the study of political elections as far back as the Elmira study (Berelson, Lazarsfeld, & McPhee, 1954) suggests that other reference groups are important in election situations. A profitable tack that might be taken when investigating the spiral of silence would be to ascertain which reference groups are operant on particular issues, and then ascertain opinion and perception of majority opinion. Rather than a question of "majority/minority" opinion, the spiral of silence might be clarified through consideration of in-group/out-group opinion.

Another area of concern in the spiral of silence literature is the distinction between injunctive and descriptive norms. A perspective that considers the injunctive nature of the perception of majority opinion might offer some important insight into *how* opinions tend to gain or lose ground. That is, using the literature on conformity as a base, examining private and public acceptance of group norms may be useful for developing an understanding of the manner in which majority/minority opinion fluctuates over time. Noelle-Neumann's work is markedly silent on how these fluctuations occur (majority and minority opinions are conceptualized as fluctuating, with little explanation as to why), yet this aspect of her theory is ripe for investigation.

The idea of injunctive normative influence, clearly established in Asch's (1951) work, is predicated on the notion that there is social pressure to conform to the norm. Whether the power behind this pressure is related to fear of isolation is not clear through the normative influence literature, although a number of studies in communication have supported this idea through direct self-report of survey participants (Glynn & Park, 1995; Lasorsa, 1989). Still other researchers suggest that, rather than avoiding isolation by remaining silent, the converse—speaking out in public—is seen as providing certain benefits and may be a driving mechanism in some spiral of silence situations (Lasorsa, 1989; Salmon & Neuwirth, 1990; Taylor, 1982).

If, as is supposed, we all have a "quasi-statistical sense" that we use to ascertain the rise and fall of majority opinion, does this serve as a descriptive or injunctive norm? Gonzenbach (1992) interprets Noelle-Neumann as suggesting that the norm is injunctive—individuals use the information in complying with a perceived "acceptable" normative response or remain silent to avoid social isolation. Shamir (1993, 1995) has taken a somewhat different approach, investigating the information sources used in ascertaining majority opinion and opinion trends. Shamir's analysis suggests that there may be a descriptive norm operating here.

An interesting possibility for future research might be to consider Festinger's (1954) social comparison theory (suggesting that we have a need to validate our opinions against those of others) and the idea of the perception of majority opinion as a descriptive, rather than injunctive, norm. A test of the two competing explanations might do much to clarify some of the ambiguities in the spiral of silence literature.

Festinger's (1954) social comparison theory and its later variations (Goethals, 1976; Goethals & Darley, 1977) also suggest that individuals seek to maintain cohesion and unity in verifying opinions. One way in which social comparison theory might illuminate this aspect of the spiral of silence is to direct investigation toward cohesion and unity in relation to norm maintenance.

It may be a general characteristic of social norms that the evaluative tone is positive for public expression of majority opinion and negative for public expression of any opinion that invites discord. If that is true, fear of isolation need not be the primary driving force behind the spiral of silence, but may be a motivating factor in one respect—keeping the minority silent.

Jackson's (1965) model of norms offers other ideas. Jackson suggests that there is a certain range of acceptable behavior in regard to public expression, so that a very low frequency of expression is met with disfavor. In such a situation, the individual is seen as not contributing to general discussion. However, groups also disfavor a high frequency of expression, because the individual is seen as "hogging" the conversation. Applied to Noelle-Neumann's work, we might expect that there are benefits to expression in some situations. When one cares deeply about an issue there is a positive motivation for public expression and a norm with a positive expectation for public expression (Glynn & Park, 1995; Salmon & Neuwirth, 1990). A test of the spiral of silence using Jackson's ideas of norm intensity and crystallization might provide a clearer explanation of the conditions under which people will or will not express their opinions.

The characteristic norm for public expression may become more negative when public expression of minority opinion results in discord (e.g., expressing a "taboo" or politically incorrect opinion) or makes group disagreement become salient. Related to this area, a study by Price (1989) develops some expectations about the effects of communicating group conflict, and Jackson's (1975) refinement of his measurement model of norms develops the idea of normative power and conflict potential.

Pluralistic Ignorance

One of the most often cited areas of public opinion research, pluralistic ignorance has been studied under a number of different names with particular characteristics, including attributive projection, egocentric bias, illusory correlation, false uniqueness, and social projection (Allport, 1924; O'Gorman, 1976; Schanck, 1932; Taylor, 1982). The term *pluralistic ignorance* refers to a situation in which a minority position on an issue is incorrectly perceived to be the majority position, or vice versa.

Few studies have actually begun with the intention of studying pluralistic ignorance, if only because there is too little understanding of the causes or conditions of the phenomenon. As a result, researchers have yet to specify when pluralistic ignorance might be expected to occur (Glynn et al., 1995). Researchers are more likely to report pluralistic ignorance when they have found it in the investigation of some other aspect of social perception, and then attempt to extrapolate the causes for it in that particular situation (Fields & Schuman, 1976; Miller & McFarland, 1980; O'Gorman, 1976; Taylor, 1982).

Shamir (1993) attempted to study pluralistic ignorance by assessing actual and perceived opinion on five issues and then examining the characteristics of those issues in which there was pluralistic ignorance. However, he was unable to document pluralistic ignorance in those issues and was forced to examine conservative/liberal bias instead. He concludes that any perceptual bias that may be operating is highly contextual or situation specific.

Miller and McFarland (1980) suggest that embarrassment may be one of the key motivating factors behind pluralistic ignorance. They note that if individuals are inhibited from expressing their true opinions on issues, the result may be pluralistic ignorance.

Significantly, the two "classic" studies of pluralistic ignorance, conducted by Allport (1924) and Darley and Latané (1970), were both studies of a situation of public acceptance but private rejection of a norm (Glynn et al., 1995). This occurrence calls to mind an immediate interest in the application of the literature on public compliance and private acceptance, as well as Nail's (1986) discussion of four possibilities in the compliance/acceptance situation. These two classic studies fall under Nail's second situation (public, but not private, conformity), which he refers to as "compliance." It would be interesting to examine the frequency of occurrence of pluralistic ignorance in the other three cells of Nail's typology (described earlier) to develop a clearer understanding of the causes of pluralistic ignorance.

In addition to the application of conformity literature and Nail's (1986) typology to issues associated with pluralistic ignorance, a more careful theoretical explanation of pluralistic ignorance may be offered by the literature on group polarization. Eagly and Chaiken (1993) suggest that one explanation (offered by Stoner, 1961) may be that when people find that others express opinions more liberal (or conservative) than they had originally expected, the individuals will perceive this more extreme position as desirable and move their own expressions of opinion toward the desirable position. The initial misperception is then exaggerated through communication with other group members until a state of pluralistic ignorance occurs.

Tajfel's (1982) and Turner's (1975) social identity theory suggests another explanation for why certain issues are subject to pluralistic ignorance and others are not. According to social identity theory, polarization is amplified or exaggerated when information comes from a distinct social group. If that group is considered to be the in-group, people will conform to the exaggerated or "extremetized" norm. Mackie (1986) suggests three parts of the process that might account for pluralistic ignorance: social categorization of information sources, extremetization of their positions on the issue, and conformity to the group norm if that group is perceived as the in-group.

False Consensus

False consensus is the tendency for individuals to see their own opinions as relatively common and appropriate while seeing alternative opinions as uncommon and inappropriate (Ross et al., 1977). Schanck's (1932) study of false consensus was originally a study of norms, but many of the recent studies of false consensus have not involved the literature on norms or normative processes. Instead, these studies have examined psychological mechanisms that may be responsible for the effect, without considering the social aspects that may associated with its appearance (e.g., Gilovich, 1990; Gilovich, Jennings, & Jennings, 1983; Ross et al., 1977).

Explanations for false consensus effects generally rely on Allport's (1924) notion of social projection, and some interesting explanations have been offered for how the false consensus effect may occur. However, a coherent theory that might help explain *why* these effects occur has not yet been developed. Here again, Jackson's suggestion of norm characteristics of intensity and crystallization might prove invaluable for ascertaining the social conditions that may make the issue ripe for false consensus effects in a public opinion situation.

Orive (1988) attempted to go beyond traditional social projection explanations for false consensus and combined social comparison theory with projection explanations to generate predictions about how false consensus might occur. Orive found strong effects associated with the social comparison process, suggesting another potentially fruitful area of research. Further elaboration on the role of reference groups in generating false consensus phenomena is clearly a major possibility for future research.

A MODEL OF THE NORMATIVE OPINION PROCESS

To summarize, individual beliefs and attitudes do not develop in a social vacuum, but are influenced, shaped, contradicted, and reinforced by the expressed and implied opinions of others. Thus, *perceptions of others' opinions* involve those opinions perceived by the individual to be the prototypical opinions of a reference group. *Actual opinions* are those individual opinions that are privately held by the individual. The *normative opinion process* described in this chapter concerns the interplay of actual and perceived opinions operating within the context of social norms and normative influences.

To reiterate, the normative opinion process described here reflects individuals' own opinions and their perceptions and interpretations of what are "socially correct" opinions. That is, *expressed opinion* is conceptualized as an interaction between what an individual actually thinks and what he or she believes is an appropriate and normative response for relevant social groups. The normative opinion process model developed from this perspective arises also from a practical concern: Several studies have shown that certain factors will affect the relative contribution or weight of actual or perceived opinions in public opinion processes. How are we to understand public opinion dynamics without understanding these weightings?

The Range of Possibilities

If the normative opinion process results in expressed opinions that are a partial reflection of the perceived norm related to others' opinions, we should be able to generate predictions of expressed opinion based on the literature on public opinion and social norms. An illustration of these predictions is provided in Figure 5.1, which depicts the range of possible outcomes by juxtaposing actual opinion on an x-axis with perception of others' opinions on a y-axis. As can be seen, expressed opinion can take on a range of values in which each of the two components (actual opinion and perception of others' opinion) varies from weak to strong.

Expressed = Actual Opinion

Probably the most common outcome of the normative opinion process is represented by situations in which an opinion falls to the right of the diagonal line in Figure 5.1. That is, a typical topic of conversation may evoke little concern, little interest, or the norm may be such that a wide range of acceptable opinions are possible within a person's relevant social groups. In such a case, there is little reason not to express one's actual opinion, so the individual's actual opinion is the more heavily weighted component of the two. This typically would be the case when people are asked about such nonissues as their favorite color or favorite ice cream.

In terms of normative phenomena discussed above, such a situation suggests low-intensity norms related to the issue, or the "others" serving as a reference group for this particular issue may not be among the individual's reference groups—the individual may not consider him- or herself similar to the reference group, and so may not care what these others think. The dominance of actual opinion would also be evident when the individual is in a state of noncompliance or anticompliance.

Expressed = Perceived = Actual

In situations in which there are very strong normative influences, individual expression would not be expected to deviate from perceptions of what others think. The norm itself serves to constrain perceptions and perspectives on issues, so that contrary positions may not be considered viable options (e.g., issues such as working for a living, regular bathing, or driving while intoxicated).

Such strong norms would make it highly probable that all members of the relevant (i.e., influential or salient) social group being considered would tend to have essentially the same opinion on the issues—actual opinion might be the same as perceptions of others' opinion, and expressed opinions may be the same as actual opinions. In this case, actual opinion and perceptions of others' opinion would coincide, and, if graphed in the space of Figure 5.1, would be placed exactly on the diagonal line.

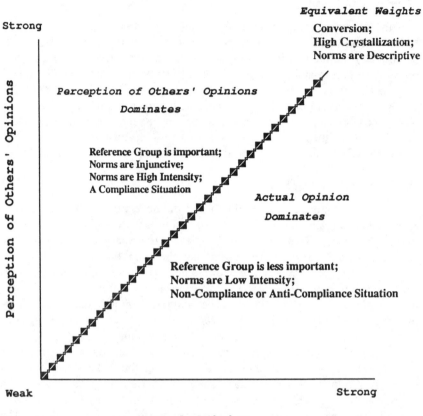

Figure 5.1. The Opinion Response Field: Expressed Opinion as a Function of Actual Opinion and Perception of Others' Opinions

Typical situations or issues in which such a situation might occur include those of conversion and high crystallization as well as those situations in which the norm related to others' opinions serves primarily a descriptive, rather than an injunctive, function.

Expressed ≠ Perceived ≠ Actual

However, public opinion scholars often are interested in opinions on controversial or emerging public issues, or in issues for which a norm may be changing (e.g., sensitive issues such as whether gays should be allowed in the military). In highly involving and controversial situations such as these, the individual should feel a pressure to conform to the perceived group opinion (Asch, 1951; Cameron, 1947; Fields & Schuman, 1976; Glynn, 1989; Noelle-Neumann, 1977).

When intense opinions are associated with issues, relevant social groups may exert a strong normative influence on an individual's opinion response. The immediate social environment (e.g., who is listening or watching) may have an important impact on expressed opinion. In some of these situations, individuals may be embarrassed, afraid, or hesitant to provide their actual opinions. In this case, there are three options: (a) to provide one's actual opinion, in spite of the fear of isolation (Noelle-Neumann, 1977); (b) to provide a more "acceptable" opinion (Asch, 1951; Cameron, 1947; Glynn, 1989; Pettigrew, 1965); or (c) to not provide an opinion on the issue (Glynn, 1989; Granberg, 1984; Noelle-Neumann, 1977).

If the individual provides a more "acceptable" opinion, expressed opinion will fall to the left of the diagonal line in Figure 5.1, indicating that perception of others' opinions is a stronger component of expressed opinion than is actual opinion (a compliance to the norm). Such might be the case when norms are injunctive, when the "others" are an important reference group, or when the issue reflects a high-intensity norm.

It is important to note that what is important for the current discussion is *not* the accuracy or inaccuracy of perception, but the *process* of providing the opinion. The accuracy or inaccuracy of perception is judged by the outcomes of the process, and does not indicate the process itself. Whether such a process produces a false consensus effect, pluralistic ignorance, or a spiral of silence is irrelevant for ascertaining whether or not the process is occurring, although such effects may be important for clarification or amplification of aspects of the process.

Assumptions and Enduring Issues

Public opinion studies typically deal with the aggregation of responses from individuals. These aggregations often are characterized by the assumption that individuals who have no obvious relation to each other "nevertheless behave in approximately the same way, either because they are identical or because they happen to be in an analogous situation" (Galam & Moscovici, 1991, p. 207). In public opinion research, even though the range of possible social groupings is endless, the relationships of respondents to others in the study typically are not considered—sample size and an approximation to random sampling are of paramount importance in assuring representativeness.

Unfortunately, what is left out, unavailable, and therefore unrepresentative in many public opinion studies is the social aspect of public opinion. By an odd twist of development of the field, the thing that is most social—public opinion—is deprived of its social character through the method employed to investigate it. The emphasis on the individual as the unit of analysis has led to development of a large literature focused on the individual without reference to those around him or her. The representative character of certain individual traits is emphasized, to the exclusion of a representative context. The emphasis on public opinion as an aggregation loses sight of public opinion as a norm in and of itself, and we lose sight of our social selves.

REFERENCES

Allport, F. H. (1924). *Social psychology.* Cambridge, MA: Riverside.

Anderson, B. A., Silver, B. D., & Abramson, P. R. (1988). Interviewer race and black voter participation. *Public Opinion Quarterly, 52,* 53-83.

Aquilino, W. S. (1993). Effects of spouse presence during the interview on survey responses concerning marriage. *Public Opinion Quarterly, 57,* 358-376.

Asch, S. E. (1951). Effects of group pressure upon the modification and distortion of judgments. In H. Guetzkow (Ed.), *Groups, leadership and men* (pp. 200-210). Pittsburgh: Carnegie.

Augoustinos, M., & Innes, J. M. (1990). Towards an integration of social representations and social schema theory. *British Journal of Social Psychology, 29,* 213-331.

Bagehot, W. (1948). *Physics and politics.* New York: Knopf. (Original work published 1869)

Berelson, B., Lazarsfeld, P. F., & McPhee, R. D. (1954). *Voting.* Chicago: University of Chicago Press.

Berkowitz, L. (1972). Social norms, feelings and other factors affecting helping and altruism. In L. Berkowitz (Ed.), *Advances in experimental social psychology* (Vol. 6, pp. 150-190). New York: Academic Press.

Blumer, H. (1946). Collective behavior. In A. M. Lee (Ed.), *New outlines of the principles of sociology.* New York: Barnes & Noble.

Brewer, M. B. (1979). In-group bias in the minimal intergroup situation: A cognitive-motivational analysis. *Psychological Bulletin, 86,* 307-324.

Cameron, N. (1947). *The psychology of behavior disorders.* Boston: Houghton Mifflin.

Campbell, D. T. (1950). Social attitudes and other acquired behavioral dispositions. In S. Koch (Ed.), *Psychology: A study of a science* (pp. 94-172). New York: McGraw-Hill.

Cialdini, R. B., Kallgren, C. A., & Reno, R. R. (1991). A focus theory of normative conduct: A theoretical refinement and reevaluation of the role of norms in human behavior. In M. P. Zanna (Ed.), *Advances in experimental social psychology* (Vol. 24, pp. 201-234). San Diego, CA: Academic Press.

Cialdini, R. B., Reno, R. R., & Kallgren, C. A. (1990). A focus theory of normative conduct: Recycling the concept of norms to reduce littering in public places. *Journal of Personality and Social Psychology, 58,* 1015-1026.

Cooley, C. H. (1902). *Human nature and the social order.* New York: Charles Scribner's Sons.

Darley, J. M., & Latané, B. (1970). Norms and normative behavior: Field studies of social interdependence. In J. Macaulay & L. Berkowitz (Eds.), *Altruism and helping behavior* (pp. 83-102). New York: Academic Press.

Davison, W. P. (1975). The public opinion process. In R. O. Carlson (Ed.), *Communications and public opinion* (pp. 103-118). New York: Praeger.

Davison, W. P. (1983). The third-person effect in communication. *Public Opinion Quarterly, 47,* 1-15.

Deutsch, M., & Gerard, H. B. (1955). A study of normative and informational social influence upon individual judgment. *Journal of Abnormal and Social Psychology, 51,* 629-636.

Durkheim, E. (1933). *The division of labor in society.* New York: Macmillan. (Original work published 1894)

Eagly, A. H., & Chaiken, S. (1993). *The psychology of attitudes.* Fort Worth, TX: Harcourt Brace Jovanovich.

Eveland, W. P., Jr., McLeod, D. M., & Signorielli, N. (1995). Actual and perceived U.S. public opinion: The spiral of silence during the Persian Gulf War. *International Journal of Public Opinion Research, 7,* 91-108.

Festinger, L. (1950). Informal social communication. *Psychological Review, 57,* 271-282.

Festinger, L. (1954). A theory of social comparison processes. *Human Relations, 7,* 117-140.

Fields, J., & Schuman, H. (1976). Public beliefs about the beliefs of the public. *Public Opinion Quarterly, 40,* 313-330.

Galam, S., & Moscovici, S. (1991). Towards a theory of collective phenomena: Consensus and attitude changes in groups. *European Journal of Social Psychology, 21,* 49-74.

Gilovich, T. (1990). Differential construal and the false consensus effect. *Journal of Personality and Social Psychology, 59,* 623-634.

Gilovich, T., Jennings, S., & Jennings, D. L. (1983). Causal focus and estimates of consensus: An examination of the false consensus effect. *Journal of Personality and Social Psychology, 45,* 550-559.

Glynn, C. J. (1989). Perception of others' opinions as a component of public opinion. *Social Science Research, 18,* 53-69.

Glynn, C. J., & McDonald, D. G. (1994). Exaggerated differences between nations. *Journal of Social Psychology, 134,* 131-134.

Glynn, C. J., & McLeod, J. M. (1984). Public opinion du jour: An examination of the spiral of silence. *Public Opinion Quarterly, 48,* 731-740.

Glynn, C. J., & McLeod, J. M. (1985). Implications of the spiral of silence theory for communication and public opinion research. In K. R. Sanders, L. Kaid, & D. Nimmo (Eds.), *Political communication yearbook* (pp. 43-68). Carbondale: Southern Illinois University Press.

Glynn, C. J., & Ostman, R. E. (1988). Public opinion about public opinion. *Journalism Quarterly, 65,* 299-306.

Glynn, C. J., Ostman, R. E., & McDonald, D. G. (1995). Opinions, perceptions and social reality. In T. Glasser & C. T. Salmon (Eds.), *Public opinion and the communication of consent* (pp. 249-280). New York: Guilford.

Glynn, C. J., & Park, E. (1995, May). *Reference groups, opinion thresholds and public opinion expression: A modification of the spiral of silence.* Paper presented at the annual meeting of the American Association for Public Opinion Research, Fort Lauderdale, FL.

Goethals, G. R. (1976). An attributional analysis of some social influence phenomena. In J. H. Harvey, W. J. Ickes, & R. F. Kidd (Eds.), *New directions in attribution research* (Vol. 1, pp. 291-310). Hillsdale, NJ: Lawrence Erlbaum.

Goethals, G. R., & Darley, J. M. (1977). Social comparison theory: An attributional approach. In J. M. Suls & R. L. Miller (Eds.), *Social comparison processes: Theoretical and empirical perspectives* (pp. 259-278). Washington, DC: Halstead-Wiley.

Gonzenbach, W. J. (1992). The conformity hypothesis: Empirical considerations for the spiral of silence's first link. *Journalism Quarterly, 69,* 633-645.

Gorenflo, D. W., & Crano, W. D. (1989). Judgmental subjectivity/objectivity and locus of choice in social comparison. *Journal of Personality and Social Psychology, 57,* 605-614.

Granberg, D. (1984). Attributing attitudes to members of groups. In J. R. Eiser (Ed.), *Attitudinal judgment* (pp. 85-108). New York: Springer-Verlag.

Hall, R. G., Varca, P. E., & Fisher, T. D. (1986). The effect of reference groups, opinion polls, and attitude polarization on attitude formation and change. *Political Psychology, 7,* 309-321.

Hogg, M. A., Turner, J. C., & Davidson, B. (1990). Polarized norms and social frames of reference: A test of the self-categorization theory of group polarization. *Basic and Applied Social Psychology, 11,* 77-100.

Jackson, J. M. (1965). Structural characteristics of norms. In I. D. Steiner & M. Fishbein (Eds.), *Current studies in social psychology* (pp. 301-309). New York: Holt, Rinehart & Winston.

Jackson, J. M. (1975). Normative power and conflict potential. *Sociological Methods and Research, 4,* 237-263.

Jones, E. E., & Gerard, H. B. (1967). *Foundations of social psychology.* New York: John Wiley.

Katz, C., & Baldassare, M. (1992). Using the L-word in public: A test of the spiral of silence in conservative Orange County, California. *Public Opinion Quarterly, 56,* 232-235.

Katz, C., & Baldassare, M. (1994). Popularity in a freefall: Measuring a spiral of silence at the end of the Bush presidency. *International Journal of Public Opinion Research, 6,* 1-12.

Kelley, H. H. (1955). Salience of membership and resistance to change of group-anchored attitudes. *Human Relations, 8,* 275-289.

Krebs, D. L., & Miller, D. T. (1985). Altruism and aggression. In G. Lindzey & E. Aronson (Eds.), *Handbook of social psychology* (3rd ed., Vol. 2). New York: Random House.

Lasorsa, D. L. (1989). Real and perceived effects of "Amerika." *Journalism Quarterly, 66,* 373-378.

Levine, J. M. (1989). Reaction to opinion deviance in small groups. In P. B. Paulus (Ed.), *Psychology of group influence* (Vol. 2, pp. 187-232). Hillsdale, NJ: Lawrence Erlbaum.

Mackie, D. M. (1986). Social identification effects in group polarization. *Journal of Personality and Social Psychology, 50,* 720-728.
MacLeod, R. D. (1951). The place of phenomenological analysis in social psychological theory. In J. H. Rohrer & M. Sherif (Eds.), *Social psychology at the crossroads* (pp. 215-241). New York: Harper.
Marini, M. M. (1984). Age and sequencing norms in the transition to adulthood. *Social Forces, 63,* 229-244.
Matera, F. R., & Salwen, M. B. (1992). Support for Radio Marti among Miami's Cubans and non-Cubans. *International Journal of Intercultural Relations, 16,* 135-144.
McKirnan, D. J. (1980). The conceptualization of deviance: A conceptualization and initial test of a model of social norms. *European Journal of Social Psychology, 10,* 79-93.
Merton, R., & Rossi, A. (1950). Contributions to the theory of reference group behavior. In R. Merton & P. Lazarsfeld (Eds.), *Studies in the scope and method of "The American soldier"* (pp. 40-105). New York: Free Press.
Miller, D. T., & McFarland, C. (1980). Pluralistic ignorance: When similarity is interpreted as dissimilarity. *Journal of Personality and Social Psychology, 53,* 298-305.
Moscovici, S. (1981). On social representations. In J. P. Forgas (Ed.), *Social cognition* (pp. 80-95). London: Academic Press.
Moscovici, S. (1984). The phenomenon of social representations. In R. Farr & S. Moscovici (Eds.), *Social representations* (pp. 3-70). Cambridge: Cambridge University Press.
Moscovici, S. (1985). *The age of the crowd.* Cambridge: Cambridge University Press.
Moscovici, S. (1988). Notes towards a description of social representations. *European Journal of Social Psychology, 18,* 211-250.
Mutz, D. (1989). Perceptions of others in the public opinion process. *International Journal of Public Opinion Research, 1,* 3-21.
Nail, P. R. (1986). Toward an integration of some models and theories of social response. *Psychological Bulletin, 83,* 603-627.
Newcomb, T. M. (1961). *The acquaintance process.* New York: Holt, Rinehart & Winston.
Nisbett, R. E., & Kunda, Z. (1985). Perception of social distributions. *Journal of Personality and Social Psychology, 48,* 297-311.
Noelle-Neumann, E. (1977). Turbulences in the climate of opinion: Methodological applications of the spiral of silence theory. *Public Opinion Quarterly, 40,* 143-158.
Noelle-Neumann, E. (1984). *The spiral of silence: Public opinion—our social skin.* Chicago: University of Chicago Press.
Nowak, A., Szamrej, J., & Latané, B. (1990). From private attitude to public opinion: A dynamic theory of social impact. *Psychological Review, 97,* 362-376.
Ogburn, W. F. (1922). *Social change: With respect to culture and original nature.* New York: Huebsch.
O'Gorman, H., with Garry, S. (1976). Pluralistic ignorance: A replication and extension. *Public Opinion Quarterly, 40,* 449-458.
Orive, R. (1988). Social projection and social comparison of opinions. *Journal of Personality and Social Psychology, 54,* 953-964.
Park, R. E. (1928). Human migration and the marginal man. *American Journal of Sociology, 33,* 881-893.
Pettigrew, T. F. (1965). Social psychology and desegregation research. In I. D. Steiner & M. Fishbein (Eds.), *Current studies in social psychology* (pp. 508-519). New York: Holt, Rinehart & Winston.
Price, V. (1989). Social identification and public opinion. *Public Opinion Quarterly, 53,* 197-224.
Price, V., & Allen, S. (1990). Opinion spirals, silent and otherwise. *Communication Research, 17,* 369-391.
Price, V., & Oshagan, H. (1995). Social-psychological perspectives on public opinion. In T. Glaser & C. T. Salmon (Eds.), *Public opinion and the communication of consent* (pp. 177-206). New York: Guilford.
Price, V., & Roberts, D. F. (1987). Public opinion processes. In C. Berger & S. Chaffee (Eds.), *Handbook of communication science* (pp. 781-816). Newbury Park, CA: Sage.
Roiser, M. (1987). Commonsense, science and public opinion. *Journal for the Theory of Social Behaviour, 17,* 411-431.

Ross, E. A. (1901). *Social control: A survey of the foundations of order.* New York: Macmillan.

Ross, L., Greene, D., & House, P. (1977). The "false consensus effect": An egocentric bias in social perception and attribution processes. *Journal of Experimental Social Psychology, 13,* 279-301.

Salmon, C. T., & Kline, F. G. (1985). The spiral of silence ten years later. In K. R. Sanders, L. Kaid, & D. Nimmo (Eds.), *Political communication yearbook* (pp. 3-30). Carbondale: Southern Illinois University Press.

Salmon, C. T., & Neuwirth, K. (1990). Perception of opinion "climates" and willingness to discuss the issue of abortion. *Journalism Quarterly, 67,* 567-577.

Schachter, S. (1951). Deviation, rejection and communication. *Journal of Abnormal and Social Psychology, 46,* 190-207.

Schanck, R. (1932). A study of a community and its groups and institutions conceived of as behaviors of individuals. *Psychological Monographs, 43*(2, Whole No. 195).

Shaffer, L. S. (1983). Toward Pepitone's vision of a normative social psychology: What is a social norm? *Journal of Mind and Behavior, 4,* 275-294.

Shamir, J. (1993). Pluralistic ignorance revisited: Perceptions of opinion distributions in Israel. *International Journal of Public Opinion Research, 5,* 22-39.

Shamir, J. (1995). Information cues and indicators of the climate of opinion: The spiral of silence in the Intifada. *Communication Research, 22,* 24-53.

Sherif, M. (1936). *The psychology of social norms.* New York: Harper.

Sherif, M., & Sherif, C. W. (1964). *Reference groups: Exploration into conformity and deviation of adolescents.* New York: Harper.

Stoner, J. A. F. (1961). *A comparison of individual and group decisions involving risk.* Unpublished master's thesis, Massachusetts Institute of Technology.

Sumner, W. G. (1906). *Folkways.* Boston: Ginn.

Tajfel, H. (1969). Social and cultural factors in perception. In G. Lindzey & E. Aronson (Eds.), *Handbook of social psychology* (Vol. 3, pp. 30-45). Reading, MA: Addison-Wesley.

Tajfel, H. (1972). Experiments in a vacuum. In J. Israel & H. Tajfel (Eds.), *The context of social psychology* (pp. 45-55). London: Academic Press.

Tajfel, H. (1982). The social psychology of intergroup relations. *Annual Review of Psychology, 33,* 1-39.

Taylor, D. G. (1982). Pluralistic ignorance and the spiral of silence: A formal analysis. *Public Opinion Quarterly, 46,* 311-335.

Traugott, M. W., & Price, V. (1992). Exit polls in the 1989 Virginia gubernatorial race: Where did they go wrong? *Public Opinion Quarterly, 56,* 245-253.

Turner, J. C. (1975). Social comparison and social identity: Some prospects for intergroup behavior. *European Journal of Social Psychology, 5,* 5-34.

Turner, J. C. (1982). Towards a cognitive redefinition of the social group. In H. Tajfel (Ed.), *Social identity and intergroup relations* (pp. 15-40). Cambridge: Cambridge University Press.

Turner, J. C. (1983). Some comments on "The measurement of social orientations in the minimal group paradigm." *European Journal of Social Psychology, 13,* 351-367.

Turner, J. C. (1985). Social categorization and the self-concept: A social cognitive theory of group behavior. In E. J. Lawler (Ed.), *Advances in group processes* (Vol. 2, pp. 77-122). Greenwich, CT: JAI.

Turner, J. C. (1987). *Rediscovering the social group: A self-categorization theory.* Oxford: Basil Blackwell.

Turner, J. C., & Oakes, P. J. (1989). Self-categorization theory and social influence. In P. B. Paulus (Ed.), *Psychology of group influence* (2nd ed., pp. 233-278). Hillsdale, NJ: Lawrence Erlbaum.

Turner, R. H. (1991). Some contributions of Muzafer Sherif to sociology. In D. Granberg & G. Sarup (Eds.), *Social judgment and intergroup relations* (pp. 75-88). New York: Springer-Verlag.

Tyler, T. R., & Cook, F. L. (1984). The mass media and judgments of risk: Distinguishing impact on personal and societal level judgments. *Journal of Personality and Social Psychology, 47,* 693-708.

Zukin, C. (1981). Communication and public opinion. In D. Nimmo & K. R. Sanders (Eds.), *Handbook of political communication* (pp. 359-390). Beverly Hills, CA: Sage.

CHAPTER CONTENTS

6 Attitude Accessibility and Persuasion: Review and a Transactive Model

DAVID R. ROSKOS-EWOLDSEN
University of Alabama

For a number of reasons, communication scholars have neglected the attitude construct. However, recent research on the cognitive basis of attitudes has thrived. This research suggests that the abandonment of the attitude construct may be premature. A complete understanding of how persuasive messages are processed and the effectiveness of attempts at social influence necessitates a reconsideration of the utility of attitudes. This chapter reviews research on an important aspect of the construct: attitude accessibility. Attitudes that are highly accessible from memory are likely to influence the allocation of attention and the degree of message elaboration, result in selective information processing, and influence behavior. Mechanisms by which persuasive messages may make attitudes accessible are discussed, and a model of the transactive relationship between persuasion and attitude accessibility is proposed.

COMMUNICATION scholars have produced an abundance of research on social influence over the past 20 years. However, this research has primarily studied the use of compliance-gaining behaviors in interpersonal communication (Burgoon & Miller, 1990; Kellerman & Cole, 1994; Seibold, Cantrill, & Meyers, 1985). At the same time, the study of attitudes and attitude change has essentially disappeared from the pages of communication journals (Burgoon, 1989; Seibold, 1993). The decline in the study of attitudes by communication scholars occurred for a number of reasons, including the apparent inability of attitudes to predict behavior, conceptual ambiguities as to what constitutes an attitude, and problems in the methodologies used to study

AUTHOR'S NOTE: I would like to thank Beverly Roskos-Ewoldsen, Mark Klinger, Lori Melton McKinnon, Russ Fazio, Brant Burleson, and two anonymous reviewers for their comments and discussions during the preparation of this chapter.

Correspondence and requests for reprints: David R. Roskos-Ewoldsen, University of Alabama, College of Communication, Box 870172, Tuscaloosa, AL 35487-0172; e-mail droskos-@ua1vm.ua.edu (the hyphen is part of the address)

Communication Yearbook 20, pp. 185-225

attitudes (Greenwald, 1989; Larson & Sanders, 1975; Miller & Burgoon, 1978). In this chapter I argue that the abandonment of the attitude construct is premature. Recent advances in our understanding of attitudes demonstrate the important role that attitudes play in how messages are processed and in the outcomes of persuasion attempts (Dillard, 1993; Seibold, 1993).

This revival of attitude research is in part a result of the study of the cognitive foundations of attitudes. Research and theorizing on attitudes has taken on a decidedly cognitive focus (McGuire, 1986). Recent research has explored the influence of attitudes on the allocation of attention (Roskos-Ewoldsen & Fazio, 1992b), information processing (Fazio, Roskos-Ewoldsen, & Powell, 1994; Lord, Ross, & Lepper, 1979), memory (Pratkanis, 1989; Roberts, 1985; Roskos-Ewoldsen, Franks, & Roskos-Ewoldsen, 1996), and reconstructive memory (Ross & Conway, 1986), as well as the cognitive representation of attitudes (Fazio, 1986; Judd, Drake, Downing, & Krosnick, 1991; Pratkanis, 1989). Likewise, recent models focusing on the processing of persuasive messages, such as Petty and Cacioppo's (1986) elaboration likelihood model (ELM), Chaiken, Liberman, and Eagly's (1989) heuristic-systematic model (HSM), and Stiff's (1986; Stiff & Boster, 1987) elastic capacity model of persuasive cue processing, clearly have a strong social-cognitive flavor.

The advances in attitude theory guided by a cognitive approach suggest that attitudes play a central role in how persuasive and social influence messages are processed and the likely impacts of persuasive messages. Specifically, the accessibility of an attitude from memory plays an integral role in when attitudes are likely to influence attention, perception, and behavior (Fazio, 1989; Fazio & Roskos-Ewoldsen, 1994; Fazio et al., 1994). In this chapter, I review and discuss the implications of social-cognitive research for our understanding of persuasion. I first explore the model of attitudes that this research is based upon, and then consider the impact of accessible attitudes on the processing of persuasive messages. Specifically, accessible attitudes function by influencing whether a persuasive message is attended to, the degree of message processing, biased perception of the message, and subsequent decisions and behavior that are responses to the message. In the third section I address the mechanisms by which attitudes may become more accessible from memory, in hopes of identifying how persuasive messages might affect attitude accessibility. Finally, I offer a transactive model of persuasion and attitude accessibility.

ATTITUDE ACCESSIBILITY

The research on attitude accessibility stems from a view of attitudes derived from the process model of the attitude-behavior relationship (Fazio, 1986, 1989, 1990a, 1993, 1995; Fazio, Chen, McDonel, & Sherman, 1982; Fazio,

Powell, & Herr, 1983; Fazio, Sanbonmatsu, Powell, & Kardes, 1986), which is based on network models of memory (see Anderson, 1983; Greene, 1984a; Smith, 1994).[1] Network models assume that information is represented in memory as nodes. A node is posited to become activated in memory when a sufficient amount of activation is present to bring the node above its activation threshold. In addition, nodes that are associated in some manner are connected via associative pathways. For example, a concept will be related to attributes of that concept (e.g., "bird" will be related to "feather"), superordinate categories ("bird" to "animal"), and supraordinate categories ("bird" to "robin"). These associative pathways are important because they allow activation to spread from an activated node to other related nodes. Within a network model of memory, attitudes can be viewed as associations in memory between the attitude object and the individual's evaluation of the object. For example, most people would have a negative evaluation connected to the node for "cockroach." Thus, when cockroach is activated, activation would spread to the associated concept of "yuck."

An additional assumption of network models of memory stipulates that the strength of the associative pathways in memory varies as a function of the relatedness of any two nodes. Nodes that are highly related are assumed to be connected by stronger pathways (Anderson, 1983; Wyer & Srull, 1989). The strength of the association between two objects determines how accessible those two objects are in relation to one another, with stronger associations resulting in higher levels of accessibility of one object in relation to the other. For example, the belief that former President Reagan is conservative may automatically come to mind whenever one thinks of Ronald Reagan. On the other hand, there are situations in which people may have knowledge of an object, but the knowledge is only weakly associated with the object. The information that Reagan was once a registered Democrat may be available in memory for a given individual, but only weakly associated with his or her memorial representation of Reagan. Information that is easy to retrieve from memory is said to be highly accessible, whereas information that is difficult to retrieve is low in accessibility. Likewise, the association between an object and the evaluation of that object can also vary. This associative strength between the object and its evaluation has been observed to act as a determinant of the likelihood that the evaluation will be automatically activated from memory upon the individual's encountering the attitude object.

This view of varying associative "strength" allows for the consideration of the attitude/nonattitude continuum (Bargh, Chaiken, Govender, & Pratto, 1992; Fazio, 1986, 1989; Fazio et al., 1986; Roskos-Ewoldsen & Fazio, 1992b). At the nonattitude end of the continuum is the case of the individual not possessing any a priori evaluation of the object stored in memory. For example, if you were asked how well you like Tibetan food, you may have to think extensively about Tibetan food and its likely attributes before deciding whether you probably would like Tibetan cuisine. As one moves along the continuum, an evaluation is available in memory and the strength of the association between the object and the evaluation increases. As the strength of association between the object and the evaluation increases, the probability that the attitude will be activated upon observation of the attitude object increases. At the upper end of the continuum is the case of the well-learned association. In this instance, the strength of the association between the attitude object and the evaluation of the object is sufficiently strong that the evaluation is capable of being activated automatically from memory upon mere observation of the attitude object.[2] Most people have very strong associative pathways between "cockroach" and "yuck," with the result that the "yuck" response is accessed spontaneously from memory when they see a cockroach. Importantly, the "yuck" response occurs upon mere observation of the cockroach, without any intention to determine whether the cockroach is good or bad. In this instance, the attitudinal response occurs *automatically.*

A number of studies have established that subjects' attitudes toward given words can be automatically accessed from memory upon mere observation of the words or objects (e.g., Bargh et al., 1992; Fazio, 1993; Fazio et al., 1986; Greenwald, Klinger, & Liu, 1989; Roskos-Ewoldsen & Fazio, 1992b). Using a standard priming paradigm, several of these studies have demonstrated that attitude-evoking primes facilitated how quickly research participants made like/dislike judgments of targets of the same valence as the prime. Upon mere observation of the attitude-eliciting object (i.e., the prime), an individual's attitude was activated from memory, without any intention on the part of the individual. In addition, when there was enough time for controlled processes to operate, the controlled processes attenuated the automatic priming effects (Fazio et al., 1986).

OPERATIONALIZATION OF ATTITUDE ACCESSIBILITY

The research methodologies used to study attitude accessibility draw heavily from cognitive psychology, including the use of reaction time procedures to measure the accessibility of attitudes from memory (Bargh et al., 1992; Bassili, 1993; Berger & Mitchell, 1989; Fazio et al., 1986; Houston & Fazio, 1989; Powell & Fazio, 1984; Roskos-Ewoldsen & Fazio, 1992b; Yi, Phelps, & Roskos-Ewoldsen, 1995). When reaction time measures are used, research participants are presented with the name or picture of an object (i.e., the attitude probe) on a computer screen and asked to indicate whether they like or dislike the depicted object. Of interest is the latency with which participants respond to the attitude probe. It is assumed that attitude accessibility has an inverse relation with reaction time: As attitude accessibility increases, reaction time becomes quicker. (For a more detailed discussion of methodological and statistical issues involved with the use of reaction times to measure attitude accessibility, see Fazio, 1990a.)

When *manipulating* attitude accessibility, it is important to remember that attitudes can be made either temporarily or chronically more accessible from memory. For example, presenting an item for judgment will temporarily increase the activation of related concepts. As a result, when "nurse" precedes "doctor" in a list, the response to "doctor" is faster than when "doctor" is preceded by "bread." Presumably, upon presentation the concept "nurse" is activated in memory and activation spreads from nurse to related concepts such as "doctor." The activation that spreads from nurse to doctor increases the accessibility of the concept "doctor"; however, the energy dissipates relatively quickly (Anderson, 1983, 1990; Higgins, Bargh, & Lombardi, 1985; compare Srull & Wyer, 1979). In contrast, chronically accessible constructs are assumed to have lower activation thresholds to begin with, and consequently they are relatively easy to activate from memory. If an individual frequently makes the attribution that a friend is clumsy, the concept "clumsy" will, with time, become a chronically accessible attribute of that friend.

As an aside, attitudes that are chronically accessible from memory are going to operate in a functional manner more frequently than attitudes that are temporarily made accessible because chronically accessible attitudes are consistently likely to be activated when cued by the environment. However, attitudes that are temporarily primed from memory can also operate in a functional manner (Fazio et al., 1983). Nevertheless, attitudes that are less accessible from memory are less likely to operate in a functional manner because they either require some priming event or must be cued by the environment in a "stronger" manner.

In the attitude realm, repeated attitude judgments of an object appear to increase the chronic accessibility of the attitude toward that object from memory (Fazio, 1995; Fazio et al., 1986; Powell & Fazio, 1984; Roskos-Ewoldsen & Fazio, 1992b). The effect of repeated attitude judgments is found whether subjects make the same attitude judgment several times (Fazio et al., 1986) or make multiple judgments using different evaluative scales (e.g., like/dislike, good/bad, pleasant/unpleasant; see Downing, Judd, & Brauer, 1992; Houston & Fazio, 1989; Powell & Fazio, 1984; Roskos-Ewoldsen & Fazio, 1992a). Although in some contexts (e.g., person perception;, Srull & Wyer, 1979; Wyer & Srull, 1989) making repeated judgments only temporarily primes a construct, making repeated *attitude* judgments has long-term effects on the accessibility of the attitude from memory (Fazio, 1995; Roskos-Ewoldsen & Fazio, 1992b).

The typical technique used to increase the accessibility of an attitude temporarily involves a priming paradigm. A temporary increase in the accessibility of the attitude toward another object results when that object is immediately preceded by another object with a highly accessible attitude (Bargh et al., 1992; Fazio, 1993; Fazio et al., 1986). For example, if a reaction time task had found that an individual has a highly accessible positive attitude toward "kind," presenting the word "kind" (prime) immediately prior to the presentation of the word "basketball" (target) would temporarily increase the accessibility of that individual's attitude toward basketball. However, priming effects increase the accessibility of the target word's attitude only if the prime and target words have the same valenced attitudes. Presenting a countervalenced attitude as a prime word has no effect on the accessibility of the prime word's attitude.

THE INFLUENCE OF ACCESSIBLE ATTITUDES
ON THE PROCESSING OF PERSUASIVE MESSAGES

The hypothesis that attitudes serve various functions was originally proposed nearly 40 years ago (Katz, 1960; Smith, Bruner, & White, 1956). Of particular interest is the knowledge function, which posits that attitudes guide how we interpret and understand our world (Allport, 1935; Katz, 1960). Katz (1960) explains that "people need standards or frames of reference for understanding their world, and attitudes help to supply such standards" (p. 175). Likewise, Allport (1935) argues:

> Attitudes determine for each individual what he will see and hear, what he will think and what he will do. To borrow a phrase from William James, they "engender meaning upon the world"; they draw lines about and segregate an otherwise chaotic environment; they are our methods for finding our way about in an ambiguous universe. (p. 806)

According to Allport, attitudes serve this knowledge function by influencing attention, perception, and behavior. The knowledge function is distinct from other attitude functions because *all* attitudes potentially provide a frame to aid our understanding of the world (Dillard, 1993; Fazio, 1989; Petty, Priester, & Wegener, 1994; Tesser & Shaffer, 1990). On the other hand, whether an attitude serves, for example, utilitarian or value expressive function is closely tied to the nature of the attitude object (Dillard & Witte, 1993; Shavitt, 1989). In other words, attitudes toward certain kinds of objects are likely to serve a utilitarian function (e.g., our attitudes toward coffeemakers or refrigerators) because those objects are used (not used) due to their pragmatic nature. In contrast, attitudes toward other kinds of objects are likely to serve a value expressive function (e.g., class rings or university T-shirts) because those objects are used (not used) because of what they say about the person who uses (does not use) them. In each case, not all attitudes serve these types of functions.

If attitudes do, in fact, act as a frame of reference through which we see the world, then an individual's attitudes should certainly influence if, how, and to what extent that individual processes a persuasive message. Below, I review research that suggests that accessible attitudes serve the knowledge function. As a consequence, accessible attitudes have important implications for the outcome of social influence attempts. Specifically, accessible attitudes may influence whether messages are attended to, how elaborately the messages are processed, whether the messages are processed in an attitudinally consistent manner, and the long-term consequences of the messages' outcome on behavior.

Influence of Attitudes on Attention

Individuals interact in a complex social world. As a result, people must select which stimuli, out of myriad potential stimuli, receive attention. Though the cognitive system is capable of processing great quantities of information, the mechanism of selective attention enables the system to focus upon and adequately process specific information within our complex and diverse world (Kahneman & Treisman, 1984).

A number of theorists have argued that attention is an important component in the persuasive process (Eagly & Chaiken, 1993; Kruglanski, 1989; McGuire, 1968; Rhodes & Wood, 1992; Sherman, 1987). The basic reasoning is that unless an individual attends to a persuasive message, it is unlikely that the message will have any impact on his or her attitudes. However, little research has tested this assumption (Eagly & Chaiken, 1993; Rhodes & Wood, 1992). In addition, although ELM and HSM identify factors that influence *how much* we attend to a message (Chaiken et al., 1989; Petty & Cacioppo, 1986; Stiff, 1986), there has been relatively little research on factors that influence what *attracts* our attention or when we are likely to pay attention to a message.

A functional system should, through some mechanism, direct its attention to stimuli that it likes or dislikes (Roskos-Ewoldsen & Fazio, 1992b). Thus, attitudes could serve an orienting function because they direct attention to attitude-evoking objects. Research by Erdelyi and Appelbaum (1973) suggests that attitude-evoking items may influence the allocation of attention. In this study, Jewish participants were briefly exposed to a display of a swastika, the Star of David, or an outline of a window surrounded by eight items. The research participants recalled significantly fewer of the remaining objects when the Star of David or the swastika was the central item. Presumably, the Star of David and the swastika, both attitude-evoking objects for Jewish participants, attracted attention. However, the research participants were instructed to focus their attention on the critical items (e.g., the swastika or the Star of David), which makes it difficult to ascertain whether the items *attracted* attention. Further, rather than attracting attention, the swastika or the Star of David may have disrupted the processing of the display.

An important question concerns whether *all* attitudes serve an orienting function. Several theorists have proposed that affective responses may precede cognitive responses (e.g., Kitayama & Howard, 1994; Zajonc, 1980), in which case the attitude toward an object may be activated from memory at an early stage in the processing of the visual field. Once the attitude is elicited, attention may be oriented to the attitude-eliciting object so that ultimately the stimulus receives sufficient processing for the individual to report having noticed the presence of the object. Thus, attitudes that are activated from memory could play a role in the allocation of attention, thus serving the orienting function.

Recent research has found that accessible attitudes do serve an orienting function. Roskos-Ewoldsen and Fazio (1992b) found that items that were noticed during the brief presentation of a visual display had more accessible attitudes than those items that were not noticed. This finding held whether attitude accessibility was measured using a reaction time task (Experiment 1) or manipulated by a frequency of judgment task (Experiment 2). In a separate experiment that afforded a stricter test concerning whether attitude-evoking objects attract attention, the participants' task involved determining, as quickly as possible, whether target items were present in a display. The research participants learned through instruction and practice trials that the targets would appear only in certain positions within the display, and, in order to complete the task as quickly as possible, they should ignore the items located in the other, distracter positions. The presence of affect-laden distracters interfered with the participants' ability to search the display efficiently, indicating that the affect-laden objects attracted subjects' attention, even though they were told to ignore those positions.

The finding that objects toward which an individual has accessible attitudes are more likely to attract that individual's attention has important implications for persuasion research. We are constantly bombarded by numerous persuasive messages. Obviously, if a persuasive message is going to influence our attitudes, we must attend to that message at some level. Little research has been conducted on why our attention is attracted to certain messages and not to others. In part, this lack is a consequence of the use of the captive audience. Most important, the Roskos-Ewoldsen and Fazio (1992b) research on the orienting function of attitudes indicates that as the accessibility of an individual's attitude toward the topic of a message increases, there should be a corresponding increase in the likelihood that the person's attention will be attracted to the message.

However, there has been an important limitation to the research on the orienting function of attitudes for persuasion scholars. This research has used stimuli consisting of pictorial representations of objects. Extrapolation of these results to verbal materials is somewhat risky. Nevertheless, the processes that underlie the orientation of attention to attitude-evoking pictures should be the same as the processes involved in the allocation of attention to verbal (propositional) information. Thus, an important component, possibly the *first* component, of the persuasion process may be mediated by the accessibility of people's attitudes toward the topic(s) dealt with in the message.

Influence of Attitude Accessibility on
the Elaborative Processing of Persuasive Messages

Attitude accessibility influences not only the orienting of attention, but
how much attention is involved in the processing of a message. In two
experiments, Wu and Shaffer (1987) manipulated whether research participants' attitudes toward two brands of low-calorie peanut butter were based
on direct experience (tasting the peanut butter) or indirect experience (verbal
appeals). Previous research had demonstrated that attitudes based on direct
experience are more accessible from memory than are attitudes based on
indirect experience (Fazio et al., 1983; Fazio & Zanna, 1981). Participants in
the peanut butter experiment whose attitudes were based on indirect experience were more susceptible to peripheral cues (source credibility), whereas
participants whose attitudes were based on direct experience were influenced
more by the strength of the arguments in the message.

The indirect experience subjects were evidently processing the message in
a peripheral manner, whereas direct experience subjects relied on elaborative
processing of the message's content (Wu & Shaffer, 1987). This result suggests that the accessibility of the individual's attitude toward the topic of the
message influences the manner in which the message is processed. The
finding that people with more accessible attitudes toward the topic of a
message are more likely to process the content of a persuasive message
critically makes sense when one considers that when an individual is presented with a message concerning an attitude-evoking topic, the activation of
that attitude will result in an affective reaction to the message. This affective
reaction should act as a marker that this is an important topic, which will
motivate the person to process the message centrally. More recent research
supports Wu and Shaffer's (1987) interpretation of their findings (Fabrigar,
Wegener, Priester, & Petty, 1995; Priester, Fabrigar, Wegener, & Petty, 1994).
For example, individuals with accessible attitudes toward vegetarianism are
more sensitive to variations in the strength of the arguments in a pro-vegetarian
message. Of course, sensitivity to the strength of the arguments that appear
in a message is one of the indicants of elaborative processing of the message
(Petty & Cacioppo, 1986).

The attitude toward the topic of the message is not the only attitude that
can influence how the message is processed. A series of experiments has
demonstrated that message recipients with more accessible attitudes toward
the source of a message were more persuaded by a message attributed to the
source than were subjects with less accessible evaluations of the source
(Roskos-Ewoldsen & Fazio, 1992a). There are three possible explanations for
the role of accessible attitudes toward the source in persuasion. Increasing
the accessibility of a source's likability may have resulted in (a) biased central
processing of the message, (b) an increased likelihood of using a "likability
heuristic" (Eagly & Chaiken, 1993), or (c) an enhanced motivation to process

the message centrally (Booth-Butterfield & Gutowski, 1993; Heesacker, Petty, & Cacioppo, 1983). A related experiment found that as the accessibility of the source's likability increased, research participants were more likely to process critically a message attributed to that source (Roskos-Ewoldsen, Bichsel, Hill, & Hoffman, 1995). Hence, it appears that accessible attitudes toward any number of features associated with a message may increase the likelihood that the message will be centrally processed. In other words, an affective reaction to the topic of the message, or any significant feature of that message, should lead to a judgment that this is an important message and motivate systematic processing of the message content.

Two explanations have been proposed for why accessible attitudes toward the topic of a message might lead to central processing of that message (Fabrigar et al., 1995). First, as just argued, the affective reaction that results from the activation of the attitude toward the topic may signify that this is an important topic and motivate central processing (Wu & Shaffer, 1987). Second, accessible attitudes may be an indicant of accessible knowledge toward the topic (Wood, 1982), and the accessibility of the knowledge enables the message recipient to process the message critically. However, the results of the Roskos-Ewoldsen et al. (1995) experiment support the motivational explanation because it is unlikely that the accessibility of the source's likability would influence the accessibility of knowledge about the topic of the message.

This research on attitude accessibility and elaborative processing of messages provides evidence that attitude accessibility plays an important role in the processing of persuasive messages. Individuals will allocate more attention to the processing of the message when they have highly accessible attitudes toward the topic of the message or some feature of the message, such as the message's source. Further research is needed to explore exactly how attitude accessibility influences the processing of persuasive messages. For example, the activation of an attitude may influence the amount of attentional resources that are available for processing the persuasive message (Stiff, 1986; Stiff & Boster, 1987). Thus, two basic components of the persuasive process—attention to and the degree of processing of a persuasive message—are influenced by attitudes. More important, attitude accessibility is an important moderator of this process. To the extent that individuals have highly accessible attitudes toward the object of the persuasive message, the more likely it is they will attend to and systematically process the message.

Influence of Accessible Attitudes on
the Biased Perception of Persuasive Messages

The crux of the knowledge function is the assumption that attitudes influence perception (Katz, 1960; Smith et al., 1956). In a classic illustration of the influence of attitudes on perception, Lord et al. (1979) demonstrated that as attitude extremity increased, so did the magnitude of biased interpretations

TABLE 6.1
Correlations Between Attitudes and Perception
for High and Low Accessible Attitudes

| | Attitude Accessibility | |
Experiment	Low	High
Fazio & Williams (1986)		
first presidential debate	.45	.56
vice presidential debate	.49	.62
both debates	.51	.67
Houston & Fazio (1989)[a]		
Experiment 1	.13	.54
Experiment 2	.08	.58

a. These correlations are the average correlations across three measures of subjects' perception.

of attitudinally relevant information. Based on the attitude/nonattitude continuum, attitudes that are more accessible from memory should also result in more biased processing of information. Initial support for the accessibility hypothesis was found in a study focusing on people's attitudes toward the two presidential candidates (Reagan and Mondale) in the 1984 election (Fazio & Williams, 1986). Of concern was whether people's attitudes influenced their perceptions of who won the first presidential debate and the vice presidential debate between Bush and Ferraro. The accessibility of people's attitudes toward the two presidential candidates was measured using a reaction time task at a shopping mall during June and July 1984. As one would expect, people who liked Reagan perceived Reagan and Bush as winning their respective debates, and people who liked Mondale perceived Mondale and Ferraro as winning their respective debates. More important, the study found that attitude accessibility was an important moderator of the biasing effect of attitudes. Specifically, as attitude accessibility increased, subjects' perceptions of who won the debates was increasingly biased by their attitudes (see Table 6.1). Interestingly, the effect of attitude accessibility was much more pronounced for the vice presidential debate than for the presidential debate. This finding is explained by the fact that, whereas Mondale was perceived as the clear winner of the first presidential debate, the vice presidential debate was much more of a toss-up. Thus, when the outcome of the debate was more ambiguous, attitudes had a significantly greater biasing effect on perceptions of who won the debates.

Judgments of who won a vice presidential debate are rather subjective. Do accessible attitudes result in biased processing when the information is perceived as more "objective"? To test this possibility, Houston and Fazio (1989) replicated a study by Lord et al. (1979) that involved judgments of the relative merit of two scientific studies on the deterrent effect of capital punishment. Replicating the earlier results, subjects judged the counterattitudinal "objective" information as less valid and convincing than the corresponding proattitudinal "objective" information. However, subjects with highly accessible attitudes showed substantially more biased processing of the messages (see Table 6.1). This finding held true whether attitude accessibility was measured with a reaction time task (Experiment 1) or a frequency of judgment task was used to manipulate attitude accessibility (Experiment 2). Thus, even "objective" scientific evidence is susceptible to biased processing as a result of highly accessible attitudes.

These results have several important implications for the study of persuasion. First, this research suggests that highly accessible attitudes may put severe constraints on the effectiveness of counterattitudinal persuasive campaigns (Sherman, 1987). When individuals have highly accessible attitudes, they are likely to process information in a biased manner, which will make any attempts at persuasion difficult. On the other hand, the research by Houston and Fazio (1989) suggests that proattitudinal messages may be judged as much stronger and more persuasive by subjects with highly accessible attitudes. However, attempting to change highly accessible attitudes may not be as hopeless as these studies would seem to suggest. In all of these studies, accessible attitudes were more likely to result in biased processing when the information was ambiguous and open to multiple interpretations. When information is less ambiguous, accessible attitudes appear to exert proportionately less influence on how the information is interpreted. In addition, as will be discussed later, when people are highly motivated and given sufficient opportunity, they can "override" the effects of highly accessible attitudes and consider information in a less theory-driven manner (Fazio, 1990a; Jamieson & Zanna, 1989; Sanbonmatsu & Fazio, 1990; Schuette & Fazio, 1995).

A second implication of this research is that if persuaders want to bring about long-term attitude change, they should not only attempt to change/reinforce their audiences' attitude, but also try to make the attitude more accessible from memory. If a persuader is effective in creating accessible attitudes in the audience, the attitudes should be resistant to counterattack, because the attitudes should influence how later information is interpreted (Fazio & Williams, 1986; Sherman, 1987). Indeed, several studies have demonstrated that accessible attitudes are very stable across time (Grant, Button, & Noseworthy, 1994; Hodges & Wilson, 1993). In the past, persuasion research focused on *changing* the valence or extremity of attitudes. However, persuasive messages that increase the accessibility of attitudes without changing the valence or extremity of attitudes may be just as important (Dillard, 1993).

Influence of Accessible Attitudes on the Consequences of Persuasive Messages: The Attitude-Behavior Relationship

Despite some notable early failures to find a correspondence between attitudes and behavior (Corey, 1937; LaPiere, 1934), a major impetus for the study of attitudes was the almost axiomatic assumption that attitudes predict behavior (see, most notably, Allport, 1935; Doob, 1947). However, the apparent inability to find a strong relationship between attitudes and behavior almost led to the demise of attitude research in the early 1970s (Wicker, 1969). Fortunately, the apparent failure of attitudes to predict behavior stimulated a new round of research that identified factors influencing *when* and *how* attitudes predict behavior (Fazio & Roskos-Ewoldsen, 1994; Zanna & Fazio, 1982).[3]

The initial research on attitude accessibility revolved around the issue of whether attitudes can influence behavior. A number of studies found that attitudes that are highly accessible from memory are more likely to predict behavior than are attitudes that are not accessible from memory (for general reviews, see Fazio, 1986, 1990a; Fazio & Roskos-Ewoldsen, 1994). The basic idea is that an attitude can affect behavior only if the attitude has been activated from memory. Hence, attitudes that are more accessible from memory are more likely to be activated and to influence the behavioral process.

Typically, social situations are characterized by ambiguity because there are many potential interpretations of these situations. How a situation is perceived plays an integral role in how people respond to that situation (Latané & Darley, 1970). Consequently, any factor biasing how an individual interprets a situation should influence how the individual responds to the situation. As discussed earlier, attitudes exert a profound influence on the interpretation of ambiguous information (Fazio et al., 1994; Fazio & Williams, 1986; Houston & Fazio, 1989). This biased interpretation allows attitudes to affect how persons respond to situational cues. For example, when someone sees a cockroach, he or she typically perceives the situation as repulsive. Once the interpretation of the situation is colored by attitudes, the behavior within the situation is likely to be consistent with the attitude(s) that influenced the interpretation of that situation. When the presence of a cockroach results in the person's perceiving the situation as repulsive, the person should act accordingly, by calling an exterminator, using bug spray, or stepping on the cockroach. However, in those situations where the individual does not have an accessible attitude from memory, salient features of the situation are more likely to influence behavior (Fazio, Powell, & Williams, 1989).

This basic idea underlies the process model of the attitude-behavior relationship (Fazio, 1986). A modified version of the process model appears in Figure 6.1. When an attitude toward some object is activated from memory, that object attracts attention. Once attention is attracted to that object, the attitude influences the perceptions of the attitude object. For example, if I walk by an ice cream store and my positive attitude toward ice cream is activated from memory, I will view the ice cream as a positive feature of the situation. As a consequence, I should see this as a positive situation. Thus, the attitudinally consistent perception of the attitude object (ice cream)

Attitude ⟶ Orienting of ⟶ Selective ⟶ Selective ⟶ Behavior
Activation   Attention   Perception   Perception of
                            of the   the Situation
                            Object

Figure 6.1. Modified Version of the Original Process Model of the Attitude-Behavior Relationship (Fazio, 1986)

TABLE 6.2

Correlations Between Attitudes and Behavior From
Select Experiments for High and Low Accessible Attitudes

Experiment	Attitude Accessibility	
	Low	High
Fazio et al. (1982)	.29	.48
Fazio & Williams (1986)[a]	.72	.88
Berger & Mitchell (1989)[b]	.47	.71
Fazio et al. (1989)[c]	.50	.62
Branscombe & Deaux (1991)	.18	.62

a. These data are from the subjects who voted in the election. For all respondents, the correlations were .64 and .82 in the low and high accessibility conditions, respectively.
b. These correlations are extracted from a figure and are approximate.
c. These authors used three levels of attitude accessibility in their analysis of the attitude-behavior correlation. The correlation between attitude and behavior for the moderate attitude accessibility condition was .54.

should influence my general reaction to the situation. The model maintains that attitudes influence behavior through their influence on the perception of social situations. Of course, other factors can influence both how the situation is defined and behavior within that situation.[4]

A number of studies have found that highly accessible attitudes are more predictive of behavior than are attitudes that are less accessible from memory. Table 6.2 presents the correlations between high and low accessible attitudes and behavior from those studies where these correlations were presented. For example, in the 1984 presidential voting study, attitude accessibility moderated the strength of the correlation between the townspeople's attitudes toward Reagan and Mondale and their voting behavior (Fazio & Williams, 1986). People with highly accessible attitudes showed a very strong correspondence between their attitudes and their voting behavior ($r = .88$). However, people with identical attitudes as measured by a semantic differential, but whose attitudes were less accessible from memory, display significantly lower attitude-behavior correspondence ($r = .72$). In a replication of this study, Bassili (1993) found that attitude accessibility was an important moderator of the attitude-behavior relationship in a study of the 1990 Ontario provincial election. The role of attitude accessibility in the attitude-behavior relationship has been demonstrated in other correlational and experimental studies involving product choice (Berger & Mitchell, 1989; Fazio et al., 1989; Woodside & Trappey, 1992), environmental behaviors (Manfredo, Yuan, & McGuire, 1992; Smith, Haugtvedt, & Petty, 1994), and feminist behaviors (Branscombe & Deaux, 1991).[5]

Earlier in this chapter, I noted that one reason communication scholars reduced their research on attitudes was the lack of correspondence between attitudes and behavior (Larson & Sanders, 1975; Miller & Burgoon, 1978). However, the research on attitude accessibility suggests that accessible attitudes do indeed predict behavior. Attitudes that are accessible from memory can have a major influence on behavior. If communication scholars are interested in the relationship between communication and behavior, an important area for them to study is attitude accessibility.

Another reason communication scholars reduced research on attitudes is that attitudes were considered to be ephemeral. In the 1984 presidential election study, attitude accessibility was measured 4 to 5 *months* before the election (Fazio & Williams, 1986). Indeed, the highly accessible attitudes appeared to be very resistant to change. There are several reasons this might be the case. First, as discussed earlier, accessible attitudes bias how information is interpreted. Thus, threats to the attitude can be dealt with easily through biased processing. Second, recent research has found that people are more satisfied with decisions that are based on high, as opposed to low, accessible attitudes (Fazio, Blascovich, & Driscoll, 1992). Thus, not only are individuals more likely to act consistently with highly accessible attitudes, they are also more likely to be satisfied with their decisions that are based on accessible attitudes.

Attitude Accessibility and the Processing of Persuasive Messages

McGuire's (1968) six-step model of persuasion provides a useful heuristic for summarizing the impact of accessible attitudes on the persuasion process (see Table 6.3). McGuire maintains that persuasion is a probabilistic function of six stages. First, the persuasive message has to be *communicated* to the message recipient. The message recipient has to then *attend* to and *comprehend* the message. If the message arguments are convincing to the recipient, the individual will *yield* to the message and attitude change will result. Then, the new attitude must be *retained* to influence subsequent *behavior.* Although there are several problems with simple linear process models of persuasion (see Eagly & Chaiken, 1993), one can see in Table 6.3 that McGuire's model highlights the various places where attitude accessibility has impacts on the persuasion process.

Currently, there are no available data suggesting that attitude accessibility influences whether or not a message will be communicated. On the other hand,

TABLE 6.3
The Impact of Accessible Attitudes on the Persuasion Process
as Highlighted by McGuire's 6-Stage Model of Persuasion

Stage in McGuire's Model of Persuasion	Influence of Increased Attitude Accessibility
1. Communicate	no known impact
2. Attention	more likely to attend to message
3. Comprehension	increased elaborative processing of message
4. Yielding	
proattitudinal	accommodation of message
counterattitudinal	discounting of message
5. Retention	attitude resistant to change
6. Behavior	attitude more predictive of behavior

attitude-evoking objects do attract attention (Roskos-Ewoldsen & Fazio, 1992b). A person should be more likely to have his or her attention drawn to messages that are attitude-evoking. Whether a person will continue to listen to a persuasive message after his or her attention has initially been attracted is a separate issue. However, if the message recipient has an accessible attitude toward some feature of the message (e.g., the topic of the message, the source of the message), then the recipient should be more likely to elaborate critically on the content of the message (Fabrigar et al., 1995; Priester et al., 1994; Roskos-Ewoldsen et al., 1995; Wu & Shaffer, 1987).

The issue of primary importance to many persuasion scholars is whether the message recipient will yield to the message's arguments. When the topic is an attitude-evoking one for the message recipient, yielding is unlikely if the message is counterattitudinal because the content of the message will be discounted (Fazio & Williams, 1986; Houston & Fazio, 1989). On the other hand, if the message is proattitudinal, then the message should be augmented and should act to strengthen an already strong attitude. Because accessible attitudes act to minimize the threat of counterattitudinal messages, retention of accessible attitudes has been demonstrated to be very high (Fazio & Williams, 1986; Grant et al., 1994; Hodges & Wilson, 1993). Finally, we know from a number of studies that as an attitude increases in accessibility, the attitude is more likely to influence behavior (Fazio, 1986; Fazio & Roskos-Ewoldsen, 1994).

INCREASING THE ACCESSIBILITY OF ATTITUDES

Research on persuasion and social influence has traditionally focused on changing the extremity or valence of attitudes. However, given the functionality of accessible attitudes, research on social influence should begin to focus on how to make attitudes more accessible from memory. As Dillard (1993) notes, "Enhancement of attitude accessibility may be as important to applied persuasion efforts as changing the evaluation itself" (p. 93). The change in focus from attitude change to increasing the accessibility of attitudes could result in some intriguing shifts in the study of persuasion. For example, research may find an attitude's accessibility can increase without any changes in the extremity or valence of the attitude. In the past, research where there was no attitude change would be interpreted as producing a null result. However, this research may still have important implications because of changes in the accessibility of the attitude from memory.

Research on attitude accessibility has found that attitudes based on direct experience with the attitude object are more accessible from memory (see Fazio et al., 1983; Fazio & Zanna, 1981). Likewise, as discussed earlier, making repeated attitudinal judgments of an object increases the accessibility of the attitude toward that object (see Fazio et al., 1986; Houston & Fazio, 1989; Powell & Fazio, 1984; Roskos-Ewoldsen & Fazio, 1992b). Consistent with this research, repeatedly viewing a commercial has been shown to result in more accessible attitudes (Berger, 1992; Berger & Mitchell, 1989). Notwithstanding this research, little is known about the processes that underlie attitude accessibility and, hence, the manner in which attitudes become accessible (Bargh et al., 1992; Fazio, 1995; Smith, 1994). In addition, little research has explored the influence of message factors on attitude accessibility.

On the other hand, several cognitive and social-cognitive theories, as well as a number of studies, have explored the cognitive mechanisms by which other types of social constructs, such as personality traits or stereotypes, become accessible from memory (for general reviews, see Anderson, 1983, 1990; Higgins & King, 1981; Smith, 1994; Wyer & Srull, 1989). Based on the empirical literature and the cognitive and social-cognitive theories dealing with construct accessibility, several mechanisms that should increase the accessibility of attitudes have been identified: expectations, cognitive elaboration, recency, and frequency of activation.[6] The potential influence of each of these mechanisms on attitude accessibility is discussed in turn below. In addition, specific message strategies that may influence attitude accessibility via the identified mechanisms are explored in the discussion of the general mechanisms.

Expectations

Bruner (1957) was the first to argue that expectations can influence accessibility. For example, if a prospective student has the stereotype that all professors are liberal, that student is likely to categorize ambiguous behaviors of professors as liberal. Specifically, when an individual believes that there is an increased probability of encountering a particular instance of a category (e.g., liberal professor), the likelihood the person will use that category to interpret information will increase. In other words, if an individual perceives the *need* to use a particular category because that category reflects his or her anticipations, the accessibility of that category will increase in readiness to be used. Expectation-based accessibility is most commonly studied in the domain of stereotypes, where research has explored how stereotypes (expectations) influence how ambiguous information is encoded.

Research within the domain of attitudes suggests that expectations can play a role in increasing the accessibility of attitudes, but in a different manner than within the study of stereotypes. In particular, when an individual anticipates future evaluative encounters with an object, the individual will develop a more accessible attitude toward that object. In other words, if the person anticipates that the attitude will be functional in the future, that individual will develop a more accessible attitude than will the person who does not anticipate needing the attitude in the future (e.g., "This is the only time I will encounter object X"). Research has demonstrated that when subjects expected to make attitudinal judgments of a novel object in the future, they formed attitudes spontaneously when they initially encountered that object (Fazio, Lenn, & Effrein, 1984). In addition, the attitudes of those subjects who spontaneously formed attitudes were more accessible as measured through reaction times than were the attitudes of subjects who had the same experience with the novel object but who had not been led to believe they would be asked to express their attitudes (see also Fazio, 1990b; Fazio et al., 1992). Thus, the expectation that one would later "need" an attitude resulted in the spontaneous formation of an attitude.

At one level, spontaneous attitude formation seems far removed from persuasion. However, from a practical standpoint, persuasion researchers are often criticized because standard attitude measures are insensitive to whether the measured attitude is "real" or is simply expressed as a response to an attitude query. For example, when listening to low-involving persuasive messages, research participants may not form attitudes toward the topic of the message until they complete the dependent measures of the experiment that explicitly ask for attitudinal responses. Understanding when attitudes are spontaneously formed would help us to understand when attitudes are actually stored in memory versus when they are responses to a measurement scale.

In addition, one of the basic postulates of the elaboration likelihood model is that central processing should result in attitudes that are more accessible from memory (Petty & Cacioppo, 1986). A study by Rennier (1989) supports this hypothesis. In this study, subjects developed more accessible attitudes in response to reading personally relevant messages than they did in response to messages that were not personally relevant. The research on spontaneous attitude formation suggests one mechanism by which central processing should result in more accessible attitudes. A cornerstone of central processing involves the personal relevance of the message. Personally relevant messages generally motivate message recipients to expend the necessary effort to process the messages critically. In those situations where an individual does not have an attitude (or a well-developed attitude), appeals to the personal relevance of the topic, and hence the necessity of holding an attitude on that topic, should induce spontaneous attitude formation.

Comparative advertising may constitute another situation in which spontaneous attitude formation occurs. Comparative advertising involves explicit comparisons of a product with a competitor's product. Research in this area has been mixed in terms of the effectiveness of such advertising. However, comparative advertising may motivate people to form attitudes spontaneously because of the explicit evaluative comparison of one brand to a successful (and, hence, probably liked) brand. Comparative advertisements have been found to increase the accessibility of attitudes toward a new product more than noncomparative advertisements that contained the same information about the new product (Yi, Phelps, & Roskos-Ewoldsen, 1995).

Cognitive Elaboration

Network models of memory assume that when a node is activated from memory, activation spreads along the associative pathway from that node to related nodes. One implication of this assumption is that the accessibility of a construct can be increased because of its relation to other constructs within the associative network. If Node A is connected to a large number of nodes, whenever any of those other nodes is activated, A will become more accessible from memory because of the spread of activation from the activated node to A. Assuming all else is equal, the more nodes A is connected to, the greater the likelihood that one of those nodes will be activated and result in A's being more active. Thus, the architecture of the network can lead to an increase in the accessibility of Node A because A is connected to a large number of nodes. In addition, this mechanism increases the frequency with which Node A is activated, and, as will be discussed, frequent activation increases the accessibility of a construct from memory.

The structure of the cognitive network has been found to influence the accessibility of attitudes from memory. Initially, attitudes that are judged to be important by individuals also tend to be more accessible from memory (Krosnick, 1989). This increase in accessibility is probably due to elaboration, because, as Krosnick speculates, important attitudes are probably linked to a number of beliefs and attitudes (see Judd & Krosnick, 1989).[7] As a result, the attitude can be activated via the spread of activation from a number of different associative links. More direct evidence concerning the spread of activation between attitude nodes comes from research on the expression of attitudes toward political issues. This research demonstrated that recent expression of attitudes toward political issues that are associatively linked to a target political issue facilitated subjects' response latencies when they were queried about their attitudes toward that target issue (Judd et al., 1991; Tourangeau, Rasinski, & D'Andrade, 1991).

This research implies that the context in which a persuasive message is received may have significant impacts on how likely it is the message will be attended to and processed. Specifically, to the extent that contextual factors, including the persuasive message itself, activate attitudes or beliefs that are relevant to the message (or part of the message), attitudes relevant to the message topic will be activated from memory. As discussed earlier, if the attitude toward the topic of the message or some feature of the message (e.g., the source of the message) is accessed from memory, the message will more likely be attended to and elaboratively processed.

In addition, this systematic, elaborative processing of a message's content has been hypothesized to result in more accessible attitudes from memory (Chaiken et al., 1989; Petty & Cacioppo, 1986; Sherman, 1987). Specifically, the greater cognitive "work" involved in central processing should result in better-integrated attitudes (Chaudhuri & Buck, 1995) that are more accessible from memory. However, only one published study has tested the effect of central processing on attitude accessibility. Kardes (1988) found that when subjects were highly involved *and* the conclusion of advertisement was *implicit,* the resulting attitude was more accessible than in the low-involving conditions or when involvement was high but the conclusion was explicitly provided by the message (see also Stayman & Kardes, 1992). Interestingly, the conclusion of the advertisement was equally accessible from memory in the explicit conclusion conditions and the high involvement/implicit conclusion condition. Thus, it is not the accessibility of knowledge, per se, that results in more accessible attitudes. Rather, the elaborative processing that was required to ascertain the conclusion in the implicit conclusion condition increased the accessibility of the attitude from memory.

Also, although it did not explicitly test the effect of elaborative processing on attitude accessibility, research conducted in the early 1960s on learning theoretic approaches to attitudes found evidence that message factors influenced the speed with which subjects expressed their agreement with opinion statements (Weiss, Chalupa, Gorman, & Goodman, 1968; Weiss, Rawson, & Pasamanick, 1963).[8] Specifically, strong arguments presented after an opinion statement resulted in significantly faster response latencies than did weak arguments (Weiss et al., 1963, 1968). Although the effect of message factors on persuasion suggests that central processing was occurring, care must be taken in using this research to support the contention that central processing results in more accessible attitudes. First, research participants in these studies were probably not centrally processing the arguments, because the topics were neither personally relevant to the subjects nor topics the subjects likely knew much about (e.g., the reorganization of the British House of Lords and the greatness of a thirteenth-century Turkish general). Second, Weiss and Pasamanick (1964) were not able to replicate the effect of argument strength on the speed with which subjects could agree with the opinion statements.

Fear Appeals

The study of fear appeals has been a major concern of persuasion scholars since the 1950s (Boster & Mongeau, 1984; Dillard, 1994; Witte, 1995). The theories that have dominated the study of fear appeals can be separated roughly into two paradigms, one focusing on motivation and the other on cognitions. Early on, fear was considered to be a psychological drive that motivated individuals either to take action to reduce the threat that produced the fear or to act in a self-protective manner to minimize the threat (e.g., defensive avoidance; Hovland, Janis, & Kelley, 1953). Later, in the 1970s, the study of fear appeals became more cognitive and focused on how individuals appraise threats and their ability to deal effectively with threats (Leventhal, 1970; Rogers, 1983).

Theorizing on fear appeals treated the motivation and cognitive theories as distinct approaches to the study of fear-based persuasion, and little theoretical integration across these two paradigms occurred. One exception is the extended parallel process model (EPPM), which broadened Leventhal's (1970) parallel response model by incorporating many of the theoretical components of the earlier motivational approaches (Witte, 1992, 1994, 1995). Specifically, EPPM maintains that when receiving a fear appeal, people engage in two appraisal processes: perceived threat appraisal and perceived efficacy appraisal. Perceived threat appraisal involves judging the severity of the danger and one's susceptibility to the danger. Perceived efficacy appraisal incorporates judgments of the efficacy of the proposed response and self-efficacy judgments (e.g., "Can I carry out the proposal?"). If the perceived threat appraisal results in an at-risk judgment and the efficacy appraisal suggests the individual can respond to the threat, the individual should be motivated to accept the proposed action to decrease the danger to him- or herself. However, if the person judges the threat as real but does not feel that the proposed action can be effectively carried out, fear will result and will motivate the individual to undertake defensive processes, such as avoiding future information on the topic or derogating the source of the information.

Attitude accessibility may provide another explanation of fear-based persuasion that has both motivational and cognitive components. Specifically, fear appeal messages may be successful because they enhance the accessibility of the receiver's attitude from memory. There are several reasons to hypothesize why fear appeals should affect attitude accessibility. First, the threat appraisal process should result in elaborative processing of the message's content because of the nature of threat appeals. Successful threat appeals incorporate both the danger of the threat and the individual's susceptibility to the threat (Witte, 1993; Witte, Stokols, Ituarte, & Schneider, 1993). These two components of the threat appeal should motivate the individual to elaborate the message's content critically (Chaiken et al., 1989; Petty & Cacioppo, 1986). However, recent research suggests that only individuals with high anxiety will elaboratively process high fear appeal messages (Hale, Lemieus, & Mongeau, 1995). Second, threat appeals tend to rely on the use of highly personalized language (Witte, 1992, 1993), and research has demonstrated that the use of personalized language increases the motivation for individuals to process persuasive messages elaboratively (Burnkrant & Unnava, 1989).

Given the large amounts of information that are required for successful high fear appeal messages (e.g., information suggesting the severity of the threat, the personal nature of the threat, the efficacy of the proposal, and self-efficacy), elaborative processing of the message's content should result in an elaborate and accessible memory trace. Unfortunately, no published studies have tested the impact of fear appeal messages on attitude accessibility.

Inoculation

McGuire's (1964) inoculation theory was one of the earliest attempts to explore attitude resistance. Inoculation theory maintained that attitudes could be made more resistant to attack by subjecting them to weak attacks (a refutational defense) than by exposure to information that defended the attitudes (a supportive defense). Exposure of attitudes to weak attacks was hypothesized to allow people holding those attitudes to develop defenses against stronger attacks. In more cognitive terms, a refutational defense allows a person to develop an elaborative network of supportive beliefs to defend the attack from counterattitudinal information. As a result, inoculation should be successful because it enables people to counterargue counterattitudinal messages better. Though research does not support the counterarguing explanation of inoculation (Benoit, 1991), a number of studies have demonstrated that inoculation increases the resistance of attitudes to counterattitudinal attacks (Benoit, 1991; Burgoon, Pfau, & Birk, 1995; Pfau, 1992; Pfau & Burgoon, 1989; Pfau, Kenski, Nitz, & Sorenson, 1990).

Inoculation may operate by making attitudes more accessible from memory. Clearly, both refutational and supportive defense strategies should result in a more elaborative network of beliefs in relation to the attitude. This elaborative network may increase the accessibility of the attitude from memory. As earlier research has demonstrated, accessible attitudes are resistant to change in the same manner that inoculated attitudes are presumed to be resistant (e.g., Fazio & Williams, 1986; Houston & Fazio, 1989). Unfortunately, none of the research on inoculation has measured the effects of inoculation strategies on attitude accessibility. Future research should address the potential role that attitude accessibility plays in conferring resistance to counterattitudinal messages via inoculation.

Two-Sided Messages

The relative persuasiveness of one- versus two-sided messages is another domain where attitude accessibility may play a key role in the persuasion process. Generally, two-sided messages are more persuasive than one-sided messages (Burgoon, 1989). In addition, two-sided refutational messages appear to be moderately more persuasive than two-sided nonrefutational messages (Allen, 1991, 1993; Hale, Mongeau, & Thomas, 1991; O'Keefe, 1993). Again, two-sided messages should result in more elaborative memory traces than one-sided messages, because they provide more information about the topic of the messages. In addition, a two-sided message that directly refutes the opposing arguments should result in an even more elaborative trace because the interrelationship between the two positions is made more explicit than in a nonrefutational two-sided message. This elaborative processing should increase the accessibility of the resulting attitudes from memory. Support for the idea that two-sided messages result in greater elaboration has been reported by Hale et al. (1991). They found that message elaboration mediated the influence of message-sidedness on persuasion. However, as with the research on inoculation, no research on message-sidedness has measured the effects of one-sided, two-sided nonrefutational, and two-sided refutational messages on attitude accessibility.

Evidence

In an extensive review of the research on evidence, Reinard (1988) concludes that evidence increases the persuasive impact of a message (see also Reynolds & Burgoon, 1983). Furthermore, Reinard hypothesizes that evidence will result in more attitude change if the message is centrally processed. As already discussed, central processing should increase the accessibility of attitudes from memory. The addition of evidence should result in an even more accessible attitude, for several reasons. First, the evidence should become part of the belief structure supporting the attitude. Providing evidence to support the beliefs should result in a more integrated and elaborate structure than if no evidence is supplied. Second, evidence should result in beliefs that are perceived as more diagnostic than beliefs that are not supported by evidence. Fazio (1995) has hypothesized that diagnostic evidence should result in more accessible attitudes.

Recency of Activation

A number of studies have found that the more recently a concept has been activated in memory, the more accessible that construct is from memory. As discussed earlier, most models of memory assume that when a concept is activated from memory, the activation will slowly dissipate unless the concept is reactivated. Thus, concepts that have been recently activated will temporarily be more accessible from memory (Anderson, 1983, 1990). Generally, the activation is thought to dissipate relatively quickly (Higgins et al., 1985).

The studies on attitude priming provide evidence that recently activated attitudes can be made temporarily more accessible from memory and influence the processing of subsequently presented information (Bargh et al., 1992;

Fazio et al., 1986, 1993; Greenwald et al., 1989). In each of these studies, the presentation of an attitudinally laden noun (e.g., *gold* or *handgun*) facilitated research participants' judgments of whether evaluatively congruent adjectives were good/bad (e.g., *excellent* or *horrible*). Presumably, the recent presentation of an attitude-evoking object primed the congruent attitude response. The heightened activation of the attitude allowed participants to respond to congruently valenced adjectives more quickly because less energy was necessary to activate the response. However, this priming effect dissipates relatively quickly (Fazio et al., 1986), which suggests that recent activation of attitudes should have little impact on the persuasive process. Within the paradigms used by these researchers, recent presentation of an attitude-evoking prime resulted in the brief activation of an attitude, perhaps for only 550 to 600 milliseconds (Franks, Roskos-Ewoldsen, Bilbrey, & Roskos-Ewoldsen, 1995). Thus, priming effects appear to dissipate too quickly to affect the persuasion process. However, these studies dealt with priming using a very specific task, and research procedures that have more closely approached a persuasive context have shown priming effects on the *judgment* of ambiguous information after a much longer delay (Fazio et al., 1983).

Language Intensity

A voluminous literature exists on the effects of language intensity on attitude change (Aune & Kikuchi, 1993; Bradac, Bowers, & Courtright, 1979; Burgoon, 1989; Burgoon & Chase, 1973; Burgoon & King, 1974; Hamilton, Hunter, & Burgoon, 1990; Hamilton & Stewart, 1993; Perloff, 1993). Generally, language intensity has an impact on attitude change; however, the relationship is complex. The impact of language intensity depends on the expectations of the message recipient (Burgoon, 1989), the similarity between the language intensity of the source and that of the recipient (Aune & Kikuchi, 1993), and receiver anxiety (Hamilton et al., 1990). In addition, language intensity influences judgments of the message source and the arguments contained in the message (Hamilton et al., 1990; Hamilton & Stewart, 1993; McEwen & Greenberg, 1970).

Attitudinal priming might offer a potential explanation for the effect of language intensity on persuasion. For example, god- and devil-terms (Weaver, 1953) such as "the evil empire" and "freedom of press" are clearly attitudinally laden. Perhaps god-terms, devil-terms, and other forms of intense language act as attitude-evoking primes that result in the biased processing of later information. This would indicate that the use of words or phrases that represent concepts toward which individuals have highly accessible attitudes could "color" the interpretation of later information.

Organization of the Message

The research on how information is organized within a persuasive message has focused on either whether the message is organized or how various types of organizational patterns influence persuasive outcomes (Burgoon, 1989). Generally, organized messages are better retained and more persuasive (Burgoon, 1989; Eagly & Chaiken, 1993). However, studies on how to organize the arguments within a message suggest that the order of arguments has no appreciable effect on persuasive outcomes (O'Keefe, 1990; Perloff, 1993). A recent experiment on question order in surveys provides evidence for the effect of recently activated attitudes and beliefs on people's attitudes (Tourangeau, Rasinski, Bradburn, & D'Andrade, 1989). In this research, a phone survey was conducted on people's attitudes toward various social issues (e.g., abortion, aid to the Nicaraguan Contras). In a subsequent survey, the same respondents were again asked about their attitudes toward the same social issues. However, prior to being asked about these issues, the respondents were asked questions that were consistent with either the pro or con side of the issue. For example, for the abortion issue, people were asked questions about either women's rights (e.g., comparative worth laws) or religion (e.g., the influence of religion). Questions on comparative worth laws should make general beliefs about women's rights more accessible and should influence respondents to be more favorable toward abortion, whereas just the opposite should occur with the religion question. This is the pattern of results that was obtained. Respondents' attitudes were influenced by the biasing questions, despite the fact that these questions dealt with the target issue only at a very general level. Interestingly, the biasing effects of the questions were stronger when these questions were temporally closer to the target items, which indicates that the effects of these priming questions faded with time. These results show that apparently unrelated topics that are discussed earlier in the persuasive message may influence respondents' attitudes toward later issues in the message.

Frequency of Activation

A common finding is that the more frequently a category is primed, the more accessible that category will be from memory (Higgins et al., 1985; Smith, 1994; Srull & Wyer, 1979). The analogy of a neural synapse helps to explain the effects of frequent activation of a construct (Higgins et al., 1985). The activation of a neuron is either all or none. However, the length of time that the neuron is "active" is a function of the frequency or duration of stimulation. Thus, the more frequently a neuron is activated, the longer that neuron will remain active. Research provides support for this model of the effects of frequency on concept priming (Higgins et al., 1985). Thus, frequent priming appears to increase the accessibility of a construct temporarily.

Earlier in this chapter, in the discussion how to manipulate attitude accessibility, I presented evidence of the influence of repeated attitude judgments on attitude accessibility (Downing et al., 1992; Fazio et al., 1986; Houston & Fazio, 1989; Powell & Fazio, 1984; Roskos-Ewoldsen & Fazio, 1992a,

1992b). The question remains as to how generalizable these results are beyond a lab setting where participants are required to make repeated attitude judgments. Support for the generality of these findings is provided by Berger and Mitchell's (1989) research on repeated exposure to a persuasive message. In their study, subjects' repeated viewing of a commercial about a candy bar resulted in more accessible attitudes toward that candy bar. In addition, the accessible attitudes that resulted from repeated viewings of the commercial were more predictive of subsequent behavior (see also Weiss, 1967; Weiss et al., 1968; Weiss & Pasamanick, 1964). Likewise, in a study where research participants were required to make short speeches about their feelings on a topic, the more times participants were asked to express their attitudes, the more accessible their attitudes were from memory (Downing et al., 1992).[9]

Frequent activation of a construct also results in increases in the chronic accessibility of constructs (Shiffrin, 1988). The effect of repeated attitudinal judgments discussed above appears to influence the chronic accessibility of attitudes inasmuch as the effects of repeated expression of one's attitude on the accessibility of the attitude has been detected 2 weeks after the repetition manipulation (Fazio, 1995; see also Roskos-Ewoldsen & Fazio, 1992b).

There are several factors that limit the influence of frequent judgments on the accessibility of an attitude. First, the repeated judgments must be consistent with one another. Roskos-Ewoldsen and Franks (1991) found a strong relationship ($r = .68$) between how consistently an attitude is expressed and the accessibility of that attitude (see also Bargh et al., 1992). Second, a general finding in the literature on the development of automatic processes is that each successive judgment has less influence on the accessibility of that item from memory (Shiffrin, 1988). This general rule appears to hold for attitudes as well, in that attitude accessibility increases more between one and three repeated attitudinal judgments than it does between three and six repeated judgments (Powell & Fazio, 1984). Finally, for frequency of activation to have an effect on attitude accessibility, it is necessary for an attitude judgment to occur (Berger, 1992; Fazio et al., 1984; Maio & Olson, 1995). The discussion on the effects of expectations on attitude accessibility highlights some instances when individuals are likely to make spontaneous judgments. However, the conditions under which people spontaneously make attitude judgments should be explored so that we can better understand how attitudes can be made more accessible in more natural settings.

How Does One Change Highly Accessible Attitudes?

Based on the research on attitude accessibility, one might conclude that humans are mindless automatons whose behaviors are driven by accessible attitudes. The change agent need only increase the accessibility of an individual's attitude to exert control over that individual. Though I would maintain that accessible attitudes are functional, obviously humans are not mindless, and the influences of accessible attitudes are controllable. To understand how accessible attitudes can be countermanded, it is important to note that human behavior is influenced by both reflective introspection and more spontaneous cognitive processes (e.g., accessible attitudes or other heuristic processes).

To reflect the different antecedents of spontaneous and reflective social behavior, the MODE (*m*otivation and *o*pportunity as *de*terminants of processing) model of attitudes was developed (Fazio, 1990a). The MODE model maintains that whether an individual's social behavior is deliberative or spontaneous depends on whether that person is motivated and has the opportunity to deliberate before acting. An important type of motivation concerns our desire not to reach a mistaken conclusion—our "fear of invalidity" (Kruglanski, 1989). In some instances it is much more important to avoid making a bad decision (e.g., deciding which job offer to accept) than it is in other situations (e.g., deciding what flavor of ice cream to purchase). When people have a high fear of invalidity they are much more likely to process the available information carefully so as to make an accurate decision. If a persuader can heighten the target's fear of invalidity, the target is much more likely to process information in a systematic, as opposed to peripheral, manner, and attitudes should have less impact on message processing. Of course, simply motivating individuals does not guarantee that they will engage in deliberative processing. In addition, individuals must be given ample opportunity to consider their decisions. Recent research suggests that when people are highly motivated and given sufficient opportunity, they can override the effects of highly accessible attitudes and consider information in a more "objective" manner (Berger, 1992; Fazio, 1990a; Sanbonmatsu & Fazio, 1990; Schuette & Fazio, 1995). However, this research has dealt with how to limit the effects of accessible attitudes and not how to change accessible attitudes.

There has been no research published on how to change highly accessible attitudes. In fact, little research has been conducted on how to change any type of highly accessible construct. One line of research suggests that the accessibility of a construct will decrease across time if the construct is not activated (Grant & Logan, 1993). However, attitude-evoking objects attract attention (Roskos-Ewoldsen & Fazio, 1992b), which increases the probability that the attitude will be activated from memory, and this activation will operate to maintain the attitude's accessibility from memory. Simply ignoring an accessible attitude in hopes that its accessibility will decrease across time seems unlikely to succeed and is impractical. In addition, it is difficult to make direct attempts to persuade an individual with a highly accessible attitude because the accessible attitude biases how the individual processes information (Fazio et al., 1994; Fazio & Williams, 1986; Houston & Fazio, 1989). In fact, accessible attitudes are perfect examples of the homeostatic nature of attitudes (Cacioppo, Petty, & Geen, 1989) in that they operate in a manner that protects or maintains attitudes at their current steady state.

Two general strategies may be available for changing highly accessible attitudes. First, persuasion attempts may be made to try to create new attitudes that will override the influence of previous accessible attitudes. Any behavior can be represented at different levels of abstraction (Dillard, 1990; Wegner & Vallacher, 1986). For example, assume that the goal of the persuasion attempt is to decrease risk-taking behaviors among sexually active teenagers. If these teens have accessible negative attitudes toward condom use, the goal of the persuasive campaign may be to create accessible positive attitudes toward the more abstract behavior of practicing safe sex. However, this will be a difficult process. Attempting to create a new attitude will almost certainly involve activating the already accessible attitude. The activation of the existing attitude will serve to reinforce the accessibility of that attitude. In addition, the activated attitude will influence how information is processed—especially if that information is ambiguous. In addition, even if the persuasive campaign is successful, and an accessible positive attitude toward safe sex is developed, it is uncertain whether this attitude would "override" the negative attitude toward condom use or whether the individual would, instead, have an ambivalent attitude toward safe sex and condom use.

A second strategy for changing accessible attitudes would involve attempting to change the content of a highly accessible attitude. Unfortunately, little is known about the mental representation of highly accessible attitudes (Franks et al., 1995), so it is difficult to speculate on how one could change the content of such an attitude. Clearly, motivational factors must play a role in any attempt to persuade an individual with a highly accessible attitude. When facing an audience with highly accessible attitudes that are counter to the proposed position, the MODE model indicates that a persuader will need to focus on increasing the audience's motivation in order to limit the biasing effects of highly accessible attitudes (Schuette & Fazio, 1995).

A second implication of the MODE model is that attempts to influence an individual's behavior demand an analysis of whether the behavior is likely to be spontaneous or deliberative. In terms of the attitude-behavior relationship, the MODE model suggests that attitude accessibility exerts an influence on behavior when individuals are engaged in more spontaneous actions. In more deliberative settings, models such as Fishbein and Ajzen's (1975) theory of reasoned action do a better job of predicting the attitude-behavior relationship (Fazio, 1990a; Fazio & Roskos-Ewoldsen, 1994; Sanbonmatsu & Fazio, 1990).

A MODEL OF ATTITUDE ACCESSIBILITY

The research on persuasion and message effects typically focuses on the impact of some element of the message on beliefs, attitudes, or values. As a result, attitudes have traditionally been one of the dependent variables of choice. However, the research on attitude accessibility suggests that it should

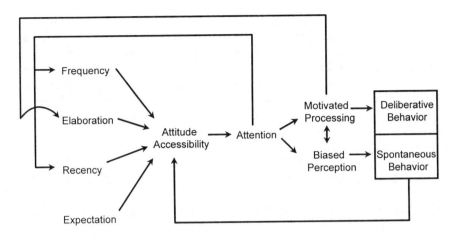

Figure 6.2. Preliminary Model of the Transactive Relationship Between Persuasion and Attitude Accessibility

be one of the dependent *and independent variables* of choice. Persuasion scholars need to focus on both how messages influence attitudes (i.e., attitude accessibility as dependent variable) and how attitudes influence attention to, and processing of, the message (i.e., attitude accessibility as independent variable). In this section, I develop a preliminary model of the transactive nature of persuasion and attitude accessibility. The model highlights both how persuasion can increase attitude accessibility and the effects of accessible attitudes on persuasion, with feedback loops incorporated to highlight the transactive nature of these processes. It is important to note that advances in cognitive psychology over the past two decades have demonstrated the limitations of flowchart models of cognitive and social-cognitive phenomena (Smith, 1994). However, flowchart models still serve useful functions. They provide a holistic view of the relationships among the variables in the domain of study. In addition, these models often are helpful for identifying nonobvious relationships. Finally, a flowchart model can provide a useful heuristic for identifying weak links in a hypothesized model.

A preliminary model of the transactive nature of persuasion and attitude accessibility is proposed in Figure 6.2. The left-hand part of the model highlights the factors that are hypothesized to influence attitude accessibility. Based on the earlier discussion, the two factors that should be of greatest interest to persuasion scholars are frequency of activation and cognitive elaboration. Recency of activation involves a temporary increase in accessibility. Likewise, expectation probably plays a greater role in attitude formation than in the development of accessible attitudes.

The right-hand part of the model focuses on the consequences of accessible attitudes. Once an accessible attitude is developed, the attitude influences how attention is allocated (Roskos-Ewoldsen & Fazio, 1992b). Attitude-evoking objects that are present in the environment should be more likely to attract attention. In addition, based on the research on attitude priming (Bargh et al., 1992; Fazio, 1993; Fazio et al., 1986), one would anticipate that those features of the object that are congruent with the attitude should be activated. For example, when one's attention is attracted to an ice cream stand because of an accessible positive attitude toward ice cream, the positive features of ice cream should be salient. Careful reflection may be necessary to identify the negative features of ice cream (e.g., calories or fat grams).

After an attitude-evoking object has attracted attention, there are details of the model that need to be developed further. Clearly, the activated attitude will influence how information relevant to that object is processed. Accessible attitudes are likely to bias how information is interpreted, and this bias will be greater as the information becomes more ambiguous (Fazio et al., 1994; Fazio & Williams, 1986; Houston & Fazio, 1989). However, other research suggests that the affective reaction associated with the activation of an attitude motivates people to process information in the environment critically (Fabrigar et al., 1995; Priester et al., 1994; Roskos-Ewoldsen et al., 1995; Wu & Shaffer, 1987). The incongruity between critical processing of information and biased processing of information can be resolved through the acknowledgment that critical processing is not necessarily bias-free processing. Both ELM and HSM acknowledge that systematic processing of a message may well involve biased processing of that message (Chaiken et al., 1989; Petty & Cacioppo, 1986; Petty et al., 1994). This relationship between systematic processing and biased processing is highlighted in the model by the arrow connecting motivated processing and biased perception.

However, acknowledging the potentially biased nature of central processing does not entirely solve this apparent incongruity. Recall that when people are motivated by a fear of invalidity, they are able to overcome the biasing effects of accessible attitudes (Schuette & Fazio, 1995). At this point in time, the research on attitude accessibility suggests three conclusions about the effects of accessible attitudes on information processing:

1. Accessible attitudes bias information processing.
2. Accessible attitudes motivate critical processing of information.
3. When motivated, people can, but do not necessarily, override the biasing effects of accessible attitudes.

The question is, How can accessible attitudes bias information processing *if* activation of attitudes motivates critical processing and critical processing can overcome the effects of accessible attitudes? One possibility is that the nature of the motivation that is evoked by the activation of an accessible attitude is different from the motivation that is aroused through the manipulation of fear of invalidity. The activation of an accessible attitude probably affects motivation to process a message because the activation of the attitude indicates that this topic is important to the individual. Thus, the individual is motivated to process the message because of topic importance. However, Schuette and Fazio (1995) created a motivation for research participants to be accurate. Specifically, the subjects in their high fear of invalidity condition were instructed that a blue-ribbon panel of scientists had evaluated the relative merits of the research they were about to read. Furthermore, the participants were told that after they had evaluated the research, they would meet with a group of students and their evaluations of the study would be compared with the experts' evaluation of the study. Schuette and Fazio found that motivation involved a strong impression management component that is probably not involved when people are motivated to process a message because of personal topic importance. Clearly, more research is needed on how, and under what circumstances, accessible attitudes promote biased processing of information, motivated processing of information, and biased motivated processing of information.

The impact of accessible attitudes on the interpretation of the environment presumably influences behavior. Within the process model of the attitude-behavior relationship (Fazio, 1986), attitudes influence behavior because they "color" how situations are perceived. As noted in an example used earlier, when an individual sees a cockroach, the situation is defined as noxious because of the activation of a negative attitude toward the cockroach. This interpretation of the situation should then guide how the individual acts within that context. Thus, attitudes influence behavior because they bias perception of the situation. Attitudes also influence behavior through motivated processing. Recall that Fazio's (1990a) MODE model maintains that when people are motivated, attitudes predict behavior through the processes outlined in Fishbein and Ajzen's (1975) theory of reasoned action.

Interestingly, accessible attitudes may influence behavior through two very distinct processes. When accessible attitudes result in biased perception, they can influence behavior because the attitudes influence the interpretation of the situation as outlined in Fazio's (1986, 1990a) process model. However, when accessible attitudes result in motivated processing, they can influence behavior through more introspective processes, as outlined in Fishbein and Ajzen's (1975) theory of reasoned action. In this manner, accessible attitudes might influence both spontaneous and deliberative behaviors. Importantly, however, accessible attitudes would exert these influences through different processes. In the case of spontaneous behaviors, accessible attitudes exert their influence in a manner outlined in the process model (Fazio, 1986). For more deliberative behaviors, accessible attitudes might act as the motivational impetus that results in attitudes influencing behaviors, as outlined by Fishbein and Ajzen (1975).

Finally, it is important to note that accessible attitudes operate to maintain their accessibility. The activation level of chronically accessible constructs can fade with time (Grant & Logan, 1993). However, the consequences of accessible attitudes should provide a feedback loop to aid in maintaining the accessibility of the attitude. When the activation of an accessible attitude influences the allocation of attention, attitudinal processing occurs, which should help maintain the accessibility of the attitude through frequent and recent activation (Roskos-Ewoldsen, Franks, & Roskos-Ewoldsen, 1996). Also, when the activation of an accessible attitude motivates elaborative processing, the motivated processing should result in a more elaborative memory trace, which will maintain or enhance the accessibility of the attitude. Finally, several studies have found that attitudes based upon direct experience with the attitude object are more accessible from memory than are attitudes based on indirect experience (Fazio & Zanna, 1981). However, how behavior influences the accessibility of an attitude from memory is unclear. Behavior could create an expectation that the attitude will be functional in the future, causing the attitude to be developed spontaneously. On the other hand, behavior could result in a more elaborative memory trace because the behavioral information will be stored in memory as episodic memory traces. Because it is unclear how behavior influences attitude accessibility, this feedback loop is left unspecified.

This model is a very simple first step toward the development of a more detailed theory of attitude accessibility. Nevertheless, even this simple model highlights the complexities that face researchers interested in attitudes, attitude accessibility, and behavior. Even though there are a number of important questions that still need to be answered, the existing research on attitude accessibility clearly highlights the importance of the construct of attitude accessibility for the understanding of attitudes and persuasion.

CONCLUSIONS

To paraphrase Kelman's (1974) review of the attitude-behavior relationship, attitudes are alive and well, and *should be* gainfully employed in the study of persuasion. The study of attitudes has undergone a resurgence. One reason for this renewed interest in attitudes involves recent advances in our understanding of the cognitive foundations of attitudes. Attitudes provide a framework that assists in the interpretation and understanding of an otherwise disorganized world and, accordingly, influences how people act. However, the research on attitude accessibility suggests that, though all attitudes have the potential to be functional, those attitudes that are highly accessible from memory are more likely to be functional in any particular setting.

The research on attitude accessibility indicates that communication scholars may have been premature in banishing the attitude construct. Instead of asking whether or not attitudes influence behavior, perception, and so forth, communication scholars would have been well served by asking *under what conditions* and *by what processes* attitudes function (Zanna & Fazio, 1982). Clearly, attitudes do not begin to explain all, or maybe even substantial proportions, of the variance in social behavior. However, the fact that attitudes do not *always* predict behavior or influence perception does not mean that they *never* influence behavior or perception. Rather, the nature of the attitude, as well as other factors, influences the attitude's functional value.

It is time for a resurgence of research on persuasion and attitude change by communication scholars. Most notably, what communication, as a discipline, has to offer this research tradition is an understanding of the manner in which social influence processes may increase the accessibility of attitudes from memory. In addition, research is needed on how to counter the biasing effects of highly accessible attitudes (Fazio et al., 1994; Fazio & Williams, 1986; Houston & Fazio, 1989). How is a persuader to overcome the biasing effects of highly accessible attitudes? Likewise, is it possible for a persuader to moderate the influence of accessible attitudes on behavior? Can motivational factors mediate the role of well-learned attitudes? Questions such as these need to be answered before we can develop a complete understanding of the factors that potentially mediate the influence of accessible attitudes.

The study of attitudes has progressed significantly since communication scholars abandoned this concept in the late 1970s and early 1980s. The cognitive approach to the study of attitudes has a promising future. If the communication disciplines are to understand social influence fully, we must return to the study of attitudes. Further, attitude accessibility is an important area of research for communication scholars. Indeed, communication scholars have much to offer in the development of a more complete understanding of the cognitive underpinnings and functional values of attitudes.

NOTES

1. This discussion draws heavily from John Anderson's (1983) ACT* network model of memory. However, given the level of discussion in this chapter, most network models would make the same predictions. In fact, Smith (1994) has argued that attitude accessibility could be handled within a production system framework. This points to one of the limitations of current theorizing about attitude accessibility. Specifically, as Greene (1984b) notes, a cognitive theory needs to specify both how information is represented and how it is processed within the cognitive system. Current models of attitude accessibility do not present a complete cognitive theory of attitudes because they lack specificity as to how attitudes are processed.

2. Because this terminology is sometimes cumbersome, I shall often refer to objects toward which a given individual possesses such highly accessible attitudes as "attitude-evoking" or "attitude-activating" objects.

3. Results of a recent meta-analysis by Kim and Hunter (1993) indicate that a strong relationship exists between attitudes and behavior. These authors further argue that their meta-analysis results negate the necessity of such constructs as attitude accessibility to explain the

attitude-behavior relationship. However, it is simplistic to assume that theoretical models of the attitude-behavior relationship are, as a consequence, unnecessary. Simply demonstrating that attitudes *predict* behavior does not advance our understanding of *how* attitudes influence behavior. Furthermore, another recent meta-analysis found that attitude accessibility is an important moderator of the attitude-behavior relationship (Kraus, 1995).

4. Fazio's (1986) model includes the influence of norms on behavior. Obviously, social norms influence behavior. However, the relative influence of norms within the Fazio process model has not been explored and so is not included in this modified model. In addition, the original model did not include the step concerning orienting of attention. This step is added to the modified process model because the object must be attended to before perception can be biased in an attitudinally congruent manner.

5. One published experiment failed to find that highly accessible attitudes are more predictive of behavior than are low accessible attitudes. Doll and Ajzen (1992) studied the formation of attitudes toward a novel video game. They found that attitude accessibility did not moderate the relationship between attitudes and behavior. However, there is an important limitation to this study in that the subjects' attitudes toward the video game were not very accessible from memory. The mean reaction times for most experimental conditions were more than 4,000 milliseconds. These reaction times clearly fall outside the range of high (or even moderately) accessible attitudes (Bargh et al., 1992; Franks et al., 1995). It appears that Doll and Ajzen were not studying attitudes that were highly accessible from memory.

6. Higgins and King (1981) also proposed that motivation would increase the accessibility of social constructs from memory. For example, when a person is hungry, he or she is more likely to order items in terms of food-related categories (Bruner, 1957). However, within the domain of attitudes, motivation will not be considered as a separate determinant of accessibility because, as will be discussed, motivation plays a key role in several of the other factors that influence accessibility. At this time, any *unique* role of motivation in increasing the accessibility of attitudes from memory is difficult to quantify. Higgins and King also proposed that salience could influence accessibility. However, the relation between salience and accessibility is not clear and will not be discussed in this chapter (see Perloff, 1993; Shedler & Manis, 1986).

7. In addition, attitudes can be judged as important *because* they are accessible from memory. Roese and Olson (1994) demonstrated that attitudes that were made more accessible through a repeated judgment manipulation were later judged to be more important.

8. Weiss and his colleagues were actually testing a version of Hull's learning theory (Weiss, 1967, 1968; Weiss et al., 1963, 1968; Weiss & Pasamanick, 1964). Weiss hypothesized that strong arguments are more reinforcing than weak arguments and thus should result in more instrumental conditioning of the attitude response.

9. Downing et al. (1992) argue that repeated attitude expression results in more extreme attitudes, which are also more accessible from memory. If this is the case, there is a potential confounding of attitude accessibility and attitude extremity. A number of studies have found a moderate correlation between attitude accessibility and attitude extremity (Bargh et al., 1992; Fazio & Williams, 1986; Houston & Fazio, 1989; Judd et al., 1991; Powell & Fazio, 1984). However, a number of studies also have found no effect of repeated expression on attitude extremity (Fazio, 1995; Houston & Fazio, 1989; Powell & Fazio, 1984; Roskos-Ewoldsen et al., 1995; Roskos-Ewoldsen & Fazio, 1992a, 1992b). In addition, all of these studies found that attitude accessibility and attitude extremity have independent effects on behavior, perception, and attention.

REFERENCES

Allen, M. (1991). Meta-analysis comparing the persuasiveness of one-sided and two-sided messages. *Western Journal of Speech Communication, 55,* 390-404.

Allen, M. (1993). Determining the persuasiveness of message sidedness: A prudent note about utilizing research summaries. *Western Journal of Speech Communication, 57,* 98-103.

Allport, G. W. (1935). Attitudes. In C. A. Murchison (Ed.), *Handbook of social psychology* (Vol. 2, pp. 798-844). Worcester, MA: Clark University Press.

Anderson, J. R. (1983). *The architecture of cognition.* Cambridge, MA: Harvard University Press.

Anderson, J. R. (1990). *The adaptive character of thought.* Hillsdale, NJ: Lawrence Erlbaum.

Aune, R. K., & Kikuchi, T. (1993). Effects of language intensity similarity on perceptions of credibility, relational attributions, and persuasion. *Journal of Language and Social Psychology, 12,* 224-237.

Bargh, J. A., Chaiken, S., Govender, R., & Pratto, F. (1992). The generality of the automatic attitude activation effect. *Journal of Personality and Social Psychology, 62,* 893-912.

Bassili, J. N. (1993). Response latency versus certainty as indexes of the strength of voting intentions in a CATI survey. *Public Opinion Quarterly, 57,* 54-61.

Benoit, W. L. (1991). Two tests of the mechanisms of inoculation theory. *Southern Communication Journal, 56,* 219-229.

Berger, I. E. (1992). The nature of attitude accessibility and attitude confidence: A triangulated experiment. *Journal of Consumer Psychology, 1,* 103-123.

Berger, I. E., & Mitchell, A. A. (1989). The effect of advertising on attitude accessibility, attitude confidence, and the attitude-behavior relationship. *Journal of Consumer Research, 16,* 269-279.

Booth-Butterfield, S., & Gutowski, C. (1993). Message modality and source credibility can interact to affect argument processing. *Communication Quarterly, 41,* 77-89.

Boster, F. J., & Mongeau, P. (1984). Fear-arousing persuasive messages. In R. N. Bostrom (Ed.), *Communication yearbook 8* (pp. 330-375). Beverly Hills, CA: Sage.

Bradac, J. J., Bowers, J. W., & Courtright, J. A. (1979). Three language variables in communication research: Intensity, immediacy, and diversity. *Human Communication Research, 5,* 257-269.

Branscombe, N. R., & Deaux, K. (1991). Feminist attitude accessibility and behavioral intentions. *Psychology of Women Quarterly, 15,* 411-418.

Bruner, J. S. (1957). On perceptual readiness. *Psychological Review, 64,* 123-152.

Burgoon, M. (1989). Messages and persuasive effects. In J. J. Bradac (Ed.), *Message effects in communication science* (pp. 129-164). Newbury Park, CA: Sage.

Burgoon, M., & Chase, L. J. (1973). The effects of differential linguistic patterns in messages attempting to induce resistance to persuasion. *Speech Monographs, 40,* 1-7.

Burgoon, M., & King, L. B. (1974). The mediation of resistance to persuasion strategies by language variables and active-passive participation. *Human Communication Research, 1,* 30-41.

Burgoon, M., & Miller, G. R. (1990). Paths. *Communication Monographs, 57,* 152-160.

Burgoon, M., Pfau, M., & Birk, T. S. (1995). An inoculation theory explanation of the effects of corporate issue/advocacy advertising campaigns. *Communication Research, 22,* 485-505.

Burnkrant, R. E., & Unnava, H. R. (1989). Self-referencing: A strategy for increasing processing of message content. *Personality and Social Psychology Bulletin, 15,* 628-638.

Cacioppo, J. T., Petty, R. E., & Geen, T. R. (1989). Attitude structure and function: From the tripartite to the homeostasis model of attitudes. In A. R. Pratkanis, S. J. Breckler, & A. G. Greenwald (Eds.), *Attitude structure and function* (pp. 275-309). Hillsdale, NJ: Lawrence Erlbaum.

Chaiken, S., Liberman, A., & Eagly, A. H. (1989). Heuristic and systematic information processing within and beyond the persuasion context. In J. S. Uleman & J. A. Bargh (Eds.), *Unintended thought* (pp. 212-252). New York: Guilford.

Chaudhuri, A., & Buck, R. (1995). Affect, reason, and persuasion: Advertising strategies that predict affective and analytic-cognitive responses. *Human Communication Research, 21,* 422-441.

Corey, S. M. (1937). Professed attitudes and actual behavior. *Journal of Educational Psychology, 28,* 271-280.

Dillard, J. P. (1990). Self-inference and the foot-in-the-door technique: Quantity of behavior and attitudinal mediation. *Human Communication Research, 16,* 422-447.

Dillard, J. P. (1993). Persuasion past and present: Attitudes aren't what they used to be. *Communication Monographs, 60,* 90-97.

Dillard, J. P. (1994). Rethinking the study of fear appeals: An emotional perspective. *Communication Theory, 4,* 295-323.

Dillard, J. P., & Witte, K. (1993). Possessions theory of persuasion: An examination of its basis and range. *Communication Studies, 44,* 188-199.

Doll, J., & Ajzen, I. (1992). Accessibility and stability of predictors in the theory of planned behavior. *Journal of Personality and Social Psychology, 63,* 754-765.

Doob, L. W. (1947). The behavior of attitudes. *Psychological Review, 54,* 135-156.

Downing, J. W., Judd, C. M., & Brauer, M. (1992). Effects of repeated expressions on attitude extremity. *Journal of Personality and Social Psychology, 63,* 17-29.

Eagly, A. H., & Chaiken, S. (1993). *The psychology of attitudes.* Fort Worth, TX: Harcourt Brace Jovanovich.

Erdelyi, M. H., & Appelbaum, A. G. (1973). Cognitive masking: The disruptive effect of an emotional stimulus upon the perception of contiguous neutral items. *Bulletin of the Psychonomic Society, 1,* 59-61.

Fabrigar, L. R., Wegener, D. T., Priester J. R., & Petty, R. E. (1995, May). *The impact of attitude accessibility on cognitive elaboration of persuasive messages.* Paper presented at the annual meeting of the Midwestern Psychological Association, Chicago.

Fazio, R. H. (1986). How do attitudes guide behavior? In R. M. Sorrentino & E. T. Higgins (Eds.), *The handbook of motivation and cognition: Foundations of social behavior* (pp. 204-243). New York: Guilford.

Fazio, R. H. (1989). On the power and functionality of attitudes: The role of attitude accessibility. In A. R. Pratkanis, S. J. Breckler, & A. G. Greenwald (Eds.), *Attitude structure and function* (pp. 153-179). Hillsdale, NJ: Lawrence Erlbaum.

Fazio, R. H. (1990a). Multiple processes by which attitudes guide behavior: The MODE model as an integrative framework. In M. P. Zanna (Ed.), *Advances in experimental social psychology* (Vol. 23, pp. 75-109). Orlando, FL: Academic Press.

Fazio, R. H. (1990b). A practical guide to the use of response latency in social psychological research. In C. Hendrick & M. S. Clark (Eds.), *Research methods in personality and social psychology* (Vol. 11, pp. 74-97). Newbury Park, CA: Sage.

Fazio, R. H. (1993). Variability in the likelihood of automatic attitude activation: Data re-analysis and commentary on the paper by Bargh, Chaiken, Govender, and Pratto. *Journal of Personality and Social Psychology, 64,* 753-758.

Fazio, R. H. (1995). Attitudes as object-evaluation associations: Determinants, consequences, and correlates of attitude accessibility. In R. E. Petty & J. A. Krosnick (Eds.), *Attitude strength: Antecedents and consequences* (pp. 247-282). Mahwah, NJ: Lawrence Erlbaum.

Fazio, R. H., Blascovich, J., & Driscoll, D. M. (1992). On the functional value of attitudes: The influence of attitude accessibility upon the ease and quality of decision-making. *Personality and Social Psychology Bulletin, 18,* 388-401.

Fazio, R. H., Chen, J., McDonel, E. C., & Sherman, S. J. (1982). Attitude accessibility, attitude-behavior consistency, and the strength of the object-evaluation association. *Journal of Experimental Social Psychology, 18,* 339-357.

Fazio, R. H., Lenn, T. M., & Effrein, E. A. (1984). Spontaneous attitude formation. *Social Cognition, 2,* 217-234.

Fazio, R. H., Powell, M. C., & Herr, P. M. (1983). Toward a process model of the attitude-behavior relation: Accessing one's attitude upon mere observation of the attitude object. *Journal of Personality and Social Psychology, 44,* 723-735.

Fazio, R. H., Powell, M. C., & Williams, C. J. (1989). The role of attitude accessibility in the attitude-to-behavior process. *Journal of Consumer Research, 16,* 280-288.

Fazio, R. H., & Roskos-Ewoldsen, D. R. (1994). Acting as we feel: When and how attitudes guide behavior. In T. C. Brock & S. Shavitt (Eds.), *Psychology of persuasion* (pp. 71-94). Boston: Allyn & Bacon.

Fazio, R. H., Roskos-Ewoldsen, D. R., & Powell, M. C. (1994). Attitudes, perception, and attention. In P. M. Niedenthal & S. Kitayama (Eds.), *The heart's eye: Emotional influences in perception and attention* (pp. 197-216). Orlando, FL: Academic Press.

Fazio, R. H., Sanbonmatsu, D. M., Powell, M. C., & Kardes, F. F. (1986). On the automatic activation of attitudes. *Journal of Personality and Social Psychology, 50*, 229-238.

Fazio, R. H., & Williams, C. J. (1986). Attitude accessibility as a moderator of the attitude-perception and attitude behavior relations: An investigation of the 1984 presidential election. *Journal of Personality and Social Psychology, 51*, 505-514.

Fazio, R. H., & Zanna, M. P. (1981). Direct experience and attitude-behavior consistency. In L. Berkowitz (Ed.), *Advances in experimental social psychology* (Vol. 14, pp. 161-202). Orlando, FL: Academic Press.

Fishbein, M., & Ajzen, I. (1975). *Belief, attitude, intention, and behavior: An introduction to theory and research*. Reading, MA: Addison-Wesley.

Franks, J. J., Roskos-Ewoldsen, D. R., Bilbrey, C. W., & Roskos-Ewoldsen, B. (1995). *Testing models of attitude accessibility*. Manuscript submitted for publication.

Grant, M. J., Button, C. M., & Noseworthy, J. (1994). Predicting attitude stability. *Canadian Journal of Behavioural Science, 26*, 68-84.

Grant, S. C., & Logan, G. D. (1993). The loss of repetition priming and automaticity over time as a function of degree of initial learning. *Memory and Cognition, 21*, 611-618.

Greene, J. O. (1984a). A cognitive approach to human communication: An action assembly theory. *Communication Monographs, 51*, 289-306.

Greene, J. O. (1984b). Evaluating cognitive explanations of communicative phenomena. *Quarterly Journal of Speech, 70*, 241-254.

Greenwald, A. G. (1989). Why are attitudes so important? In A. R. Pratkanis, S. J. Breckler, & A. G. Greenwald (Eds.), *Attitude structure and function* (pp. 1-10). Hillsdale, NJ: Lawrence Erlbaum.

Greenwald, A. G., Klinger, M. R., & Liu, T. J. (1989). Unconscious processing of dichotically masked words. *Memory and Cognition, 17*, 35-47.

Hale, J. L., Lemieus, R., & Mongeau, P. A. (1995). Cognitive processing of fear-arousing message content. *Communication Research, 22*, 459-474.

Hale, J. L., Mongeau, P. A., & Thomas, R. M. (1991). Cognitive processing of one- and two-sided persuasive messages. *Western Journal of Speech Communication, 55*, 380-389.

Hamilton, M. A., Hunter, J. E., & Burgoon, M. (1990). An empirical test of an axiomatic model of the relationship between language intensity and persuasion. *Journal of Language and Social Psychology, 9*, 235-255.

Hamilton, M. A., & Stewart, B. L. (1993). Extending an information processing model of language intensity effects. *Communication Quarterly, 41*, 231-246.

Heesacker, M. H., Petty, R. E., & Cacioppo, J. T. (1983). Field dependence and attitude change: Source credibility can alter persuasion by affecting message-relevant thinking. *Journal of Personality, 51*, 653-666.

Higgins, E. T., Bargh, J. A., & Lombardi, W. (1985). Nature of priming effects on categorizing. *Journal of Experimental Psychology: Learning, Memory, & Cognition, 11*, 59-69.

Higgins, E. T., & King, G. (1981). Accessibility of social constructs: Information-processing consequences of individual and contextual variability. In N. Cantor & J. F. Kihlstrom (Eds.), *Personality, cognition, and social interaction* (pp. 69-121). Hillsdale, NJ: Lawrence Erlbaum.

Hodges, S. D., & Wilson, T. D. (1993). Effects of analyzing reasons on attitude change: The moderating role of attitude accessibility. *Social Cognition, 11*, 353-366.

Houston, D. A., & Fazio, R. H. (1989). Biased processing as a function of attitude accessibility: Making objective judgments subjectively. *Social Cognition, 7*, 51-66.

Hovland, C. I., Janis, I. L., & Kelley, H. H. (1953). *Communication and persuasion: Psychological studies of opinion change*. New Haven, CT: Yale University Press.

Jamieson, D. W., & Zanna, M. P. (1989). Need for structure in attitude formation and expression. In A. R. Pratkanis, S. J. Breckler, & A. G. Greenwald (Eds.), *Attitude structure and function* (pp. 383-406). Hillsdale, NJ: Lawrence Erlbaum.

Judd, C. M., Drake, R. A., Downing, J. W., & Krosnick, J. A. (1991). Some dynamic properties of attitude structures: Context-induced response facilitation and polarization. *Journal of Personality and Social Psychology, 60,* 193-202.

Judd, C. M., & Krosnick, J. A. (1989). The structural basis of consistency among political attitudes: Effects of political expertise and attitude importance. In A. R. Pratkanis, S. J. Breckler, & A. G. Greenwald (Eds.), *Attitude structure and function* (pp. 99-128). Hillsdale, NJ: Lawrence Erlbaum.

Kahneman, D., & Treisman, A. (1984). Changing views of attention and automaticity. In R. Parasuraman & D. R. Davis (Eds.), *Varieties of attention* (pp. 29-60). Orlando, FL: Academic Press.

Kardes, F. R. (1988). Spontaneous inference processes in advertising: The effects of conclusion omission and involvement on persuasion. *Journal of Consumer Research, 15,* 225-233.

Katz, D. (1960). The functional approach to the study of attitudes. *Public Opinion Quarterly, 24,* 163-204.

Kellerman, K., & Cole, T. (1994). Classifying compliance gaining messages: Taxonomic disorder and strategic confusion. *Communication Theory, 4,* 3-60.

Kelman, H. C. (1974). Attitudes are alive and well and gainfully employed in the sphere of action. *American Psychologist, 29,* 310-324.

Kim, M. S., & Hunter, J. E. (1993). Attitude-behavior relations: A meta-analysis of attitudinal relevance and topic. *Journal of Communication, 43,* 101-142.

Kitayama, S., & Howard, S. (1994). Affective regulation of perception and comprehension: Amplification and semantic priming. In P. M. Niedenthal & S. Kitayama (Eds.), *The heart's eye: Emotional influences in perception and attention* (pp. 41-65). San Diego: Academic Press.

Kraus, S. J. (1995). Attitudes and the prediction of behavior: A meta-analysis of the empirical literature. *Personality and Social Psychology Bulletin, 21,* 58-75.

Krosnick, J. A. (1989). Attitude importance and attitude accessibility. *Personality and Social Psychology Bulletin, 15,* 297-308.

Kruglanski, A. W. (1989). *Lay epistemics and human knowledge: Cognitive and motivational biases.* New York: Plenum.

LaPiere, R. T. (1934). Attitudes vs. actions. *Social Forces, 13,* 230-237.

Larson, C., & Sanders, R. (1975). Faith, mystery, and data: An analysis of "scientific" studies of persuasion. *Quarterly Journal of Speech, 61,* 178-194.

Latané, B., & Darley, J. M. (1970). *The unresponsive bystander: Why doesn't he help?* New York: Appleton-Century-Crofts.

Levanthal, H. (1970). Findings and theory in the study of fear communications. In L. Berkowitz (Ed.), *Advances in experimental social psychology* (Vol. 5, pp. 119-186). Orlando, FL: Academic Press.

Lord, C. G., Ross, L., & Lepper, M. R. (1979). Biased assimilation and attitude polarization: The effects of prior theories on subsequently considered information. *Journal of Personality and Social Psychology, 37,* 2098-2109.

Maio, G. R., & Olson, J. M. (1995). The effect of attitude dissimulation on attitude accessibility. *Social Cognition, 13,* 127-144.

Manfredo, M. J., Yuan, S. M., & McGuire, F. A. (1992). The influence of attitude accessibility on attitude-behavior relationships: Implications for recreation research. *Journal of Leisure Research, 24,* 157-170.

McEwen, W. J., & Greenberg, B. S. (1970). The effects of message intensity on receiver evaluations of source, message and topic. *Journal of Communication, 20,* 340-350.

McGuire, W. J. (1964). Inducing resistance to persuasion: Some contemporary approaches. In L. Berkowitz (Ed.), *Advances in experimental social psychology* (Vol. 1, pp. 191-229). Orlando, FL: Academic Press.

McGuire, W. J. (1968). Personality and attitude change: An information-processing theory. In A. G. Greenwald, T. C. Brock, & T. M. Ostrom (Eds.), *Psychological foundations of attitudes* (pp. 171-196). Orlando, FL: Academic Press.

McGuire, W. J. (1986). The vicissitudes of attitudes and similar representational constructs in twentieth century psychology. *European Journal of Social Psychology, 16,* 89-130.

Miller, G. R., & Burgoon, M. (1978). Persuasion research: Review and commentary. In B. D. Ruben (Ed.), *Communication yearbook 2* (pp. 29-47). New Brunswick, NJ: Transaction.

O'Keefe, D. J. (1990). *Persuasion: Theory and research.* Newbury Park, CA: Sage.

O'Keefe, D. J. (1993). The persuasive effects of message sidedness variations: A cautionary note concerning Allen's (1991) meta-analysis. *Western Journal of Communication, 57,* 87-97.

Perloff, R. M. (1993). *The dynamics of persuasion.* Hillsdale, NJ: Lawrence Erlbaum.

Petty, R. E., & Cacioppo, J. T. (1986). *Communication and persuasion: Central and peripheral routes to attitude change.* New York: Springer-Verlag.

Petty, R. E., Priester, J. R., & Wegener, D. T. (1994). Cognitive processes in attitude change. In R. S. Wyer, Jr., & T. K. Srull (Eds.), *Handbook of social cognition: Vol. 2. Applications* (pp. 69-142). Hillsdale, NJ: Lawrence Erlbaum.

Pfau, M. (1992). The potential of inoculation in promoting resistance to the effectiveness of comparative advertising messages. *Communication Quarterly, 40,* 26-44.

Pfau, M., & Burgoon, M. (1989). Inoculation in political campaign communication. *Human Communication Research, 15,* 91-111.

Pfau, M., Kenski, H. C., Nitz, M., & Sorenson, J. (1990). Efficacy of inoculation strategies in promoting resistance to political attack messages: Application to direct mail. *Communication Monographs, 57,* 25-43.

Powell, M. C., & Fazio, R. H. (1984). Attitude accessibility as a function of repeated attitude expression. *Personality and Social Psychology Bulletin, 10,* 139-148.

Pratkanis, A. R. (1989). The cognitive representation of attitudes. In A. R. Pratkanis, S. J. Breckler, & A. G. Greenwald (Eds.), *Attitude structure and function* (pp. 71-98). Hillsdale, NJ: Lawrence Erlbaum.

Priester, J. R., Fabrigar, L. R., Wegener, D. T., & Petty, R. E. (1994, May). *Message elaboration as a function of manipulated attitude accessibility.* Paper presented at the annual meeting of the Midwestern Psychology Association, Chicago.

Reinard, J. C. (1988). The empirical study of the persuasive effects of evidence: The status after fifty years of research. *Human Communication Research, 15,* 3-59.

Rennier, G. A. (1989). The strength of the object-evaluation association, the attitude-behavior relationship, and the elaboration-likelihood model of persuasion. *Dissertation Abstracts International, 50*(04), 907A. (University Microfilms No. DA89-15339)

Reynolds, R. A., & Burgoon, M. (1983). Belief processing, reasoning, and evidence. In R. N. Bostrom (Ed.), *Communication yearbook 7* (pp. 83-104). Beverly Hills, CA: Sage.

Rhodes, N., & Wood, W. (1992). Self-esteem and intelligence affect influenceability: The mediating role of message reception. *Psychological Bulletin, 111,* 156-171.

Roberts, J. V. (1985). The attitude-memory relationship after 40 years: A meta-analysis of the literature. *Basic and Applied Social Psychology, 6,* 221-241.

Roese, N. J., & Olson, J. M. (1994). Attitude importance as a function of repeated attitude expression. *Journal of Experimental Social Psychology, 30,* 39-51.

Rogers, R. W. (1983). Cognitive and physiological processes in fear appeals and attitude change: A revised theory of protection motivation. In J. T. Cacioppo & R. E. Petty (Eds.), *Social psychophysiology: A sourcebook* (pp. 153-176). New York: Guilford.

Roskos-Ewoldsen, D. R., Bichsel, J., Hill, J., & Hoffman, K. (1995, May). *How does the accessibility of source likability influence persuasion?* Paper presented at the annual meeting of the Midwestern Psychology Association, Chicago.

Roskos-Ewoldsen, D. R., & Fazio, R. H. (1992a). The accessibility of source likability as a determinant of persuasion. *Personality and Social Psychology Bulletin, 18,* 19-25.

Roskos-Ewoldsen, D. R., & Fazio, R. H. (1992b). On the orienting value of attitudes: Attitude accessibility as a determinant of an object's attraction of visual attention. *Journal of Personality and Social Psychology, 63,* 198-211.

Roskos-Ewoldsen, D. R., & Franks, J. J. (1991). [Attitude accessibility norms]. Unpublished data.

Roskos-Ewoldsen, D. R., Franks, J. J., & Roskos-Ewoldsen, B. (1996). *The influence of attitude processes in remembering.* Manuscript submitted for publication.

Ross, M., & Conway, M. (1986). Remembering one's own past: The construction of personal histories. In R. M. Sorrentino & E. T. Higgins (Eds.), *Handbook of motivation and cognition: Foundations of social behavior* (pp. 122-144). New York: Guilford.

Sanbonmatsu, D. M., & Fazio, R. H. (1990). The role of attitudes in memory-based decision making. *Journal of Personality and Social Psychology, 59,* 614-622.

Schuette, R. A., & Fazio, R. H. (1995). Attitude accessibility and motivation as determinants of biased processing: A test of the MODE model. *Personality and Social Psychology Bulletin, 21,* 704-710.

Seibold, D. R. (1993). [Review of the book *The psychology of attitudes*]. *Communication Theory, 3,* 267-271.

Seibold, D. R., Cantrill, J. G., & Meyers, R. A. (1985). Communication and interpersonal influence. In M. L. Knapp & G. R. Miller (Eds.), *Handbook of interpersonal communication* (pp. 551-611). Beverly Hills, CA: Sage.

Shavitt, S. (1989). Operationalizing functional theories of attitude. In A. R. Pratkanis, S. J. Breckler, & A. G. Greenwald (Eds.), *Attitude structure and function* (pp. 311-337). Hillsdale, NJ: Lawrence Erlbaum.

Shedler, J., & Manis, M. (1986). Can the availability heuristic explain vividness effects? *Journal of Personality and Social Psychology, 51,* 26-36.

Sherman, S. J. (1987). Cognitive processes in the formation, change, and expression of attitudes. In M. P. Zanna, J. M. Olson, & C. P. Herman (Eds), *Social influence: The Ontario Symposium* (Vol. 5, pp. 75-106). Hillsdale, NJ: Lawrence Erlbaum.

Shiffrin, R. M. (1988). Attention. In R. C. Atkinson, R. J. Hernstein, G. Lindzey, & R. D. Luce (Eds.), *Stevens' handbook of experimental psychology: Vol. 2. Learning and cognition* (pp. 739-811). New York: John Wiley.

Smith, E. R. (1994). Procedural knowledge and processing strategies in social cognition. In R. S. Wyer, Jr., & T. K. Srull (Eds.), *Handbook of social cognition: Vol. 1. Basic processes* (pp. 99-151). Hillsdale, NJ: Lawrence Erlbaum.

Smith, M. B., Bruner, J. S., & White, R. W. (1956). *Opinions and personality.* New York: John Wiley.

Smith, S. M., Haugtvedt, C. P., & Petty, R. E. (1994). Attitudes and recycling: Does the measurement of affect enhance behavioral prediction? *Psychology & Marketing, 11,* 359-374.

Srull, T. K., & Wyer, R. S., Jr. (1979). The role of category accessibility in the interpretation of information about persons: Some determinants and implications. *Journal of Personality and Social Psychology, 37,* 1660-1672.

Stayman, D. M., & Kardes, F. R. (1992). Spontaneous inference processes in advertising: Effects of need for cognition and self-monitoring on inference generation and utilization. *Journal of Consumer Psychology, 1,* 125-142.

Stiff, J. B. (1986). Cognitive processing of persuasive message cues: A meta-analytic review of the effects of supporting information on attitudes. *Communication Monographs, 53,* 75-89.

Stiff, J. B., & Boster, F. J. (1987). Cognitive processing: Additional thoughts and a reply to Petty, Kasmer, Haugtvedt, and Cacioppo. *Communication Monographs, 53,* 250-256.

Tesser, A., & Shaffer, D. R. (1990). Attitudes and attitude change. *Annual Review of Psychology, 41,* 479-523.

Tourangeau, R., Rasinski, K. A., Bradburn, N., & D'Andrade, R. (1989). Belief accessibility and context effects in attitude measurement. *Journal of Experimental Social Psychology, 25,* 401-421.

Tourangeau, R., Rasinski, K. A., & D'Andrade, R. (1991). Attitude structure and belief accessibility. *Journal of Experimental Social Psychology, 27,* 48-75.

Weaver, R. (1953). *The ethics of rhetoric.* Chicago: Henry Regnery.

Wegner, D. M., & Vallacher, R. R. (1986). Action identification. In R. M. Sorrentino & E. T. Higgins (Eds.), *Handbook of motivation and cognition: Foundations of social behavior* (pp. 550-582). New York: Guilford.

Weiss, R. F. (1967). A delay of argument gradient in the instrumental conditioning of attitudes. *Psychonomic Science, 8,* 457-458.

Weiss, R. F. (1968). An extension of Hullian learning theory to persuasive communication. In A. G. Greenwald, T. C. Brock, & T. M. Ostrom (Eds.), *Psychological foundations of attitudes* (pp. 109-145). New York: Academic Press.

Weiss, R. F., Chalupa, L. M., Gorman, B. S., & Goodman, N, H. (1968). Classical conditioning of attitudes as a function of number of persuasion trials and argument (UCS) strength. *Psychonomic Science, 11,* 59-60.

Weiss, R. F., & Pasamanick, B. (1964). Number of exposures to persuasive communication in the instrumental conditioning of attitudes. *Journal of Social Psychology, 63,* 373-382.

Weiss, R. F., Rawson, H. E., & Pasamanick, B. (1963). Argument strength, delay of argument, and anxiety in the "conditioning" and "selective learning" of attitudes. *Journal of Abnormal and Social Psychology, 67,* 157-165.

Wicker, A. W. (1969). Attitudes versus actions: The relationship of verbal and overt behavioral responses to attitude objects. *Journal of Social Issues, 25,* 41-78.

Witte, K. (1992). Putting the fear back into fear appeals: The extended parallel process model. *Communication Monographs, 59,* 329-349.

Witte, K. (1993). Message and conceptual confounds in fear appeals: The role of threat, fear, and efficacy. *Southern Communication Journal, 58,* 147-155.

Witte, K. (1994). Fear control and danger control: A test of the extended parallel process model (EPPM). *Communication Monographs, 61,* 113-134.

Witte, K. (1995). Generating effective risk messages: How scary should your risk communication be? In B. R. Burleson (Ed.), *Communication yearbook 18* (pp. 229-254). Thousand Oaks, CA: Sage.

Witte, K., Stokols, D., Ituarte, P., & Schneider, M. (1993). Testing the health belief model in a field study to promote bicycle safety helmets. *Communication Research, 20,* 564-586.

Wood, W. (1982). Retrieval of attitude-relevant information from memory: Effects on susceptibility to persuasion and on intrinsic motivation. *Journal of Personality and Social Psychology, 42,* 798-810.

Woodside, A. G., & Trappey, R. J., III. (1992). Finding out why customers shop your store and buy your brand: Automatic cognitive processing models of primary choice. *Journal of Advertising Research, 32*(6), 59-78.

Wu, C., & Shaffer, D. R. (1987). Susceptibility to persuasive appeals as a function of source credibility and prior experience with the attitude object. *Journal of Personality and Social Psychology, 52,* 677-688.

Wyer, R. S., Jr., & Srull, T. K. (1989). *Memory and cognition in its social context.* Hillsdale, NJ: Lawrence Erlbaum.

Yi, H., Phelps, J., & Roskos-Ewoldsen, D. R. (1995). *The influence of comparative advertising and amount of information on attitude accessibility.* Manuscript submitted for publication.

Zajonc, R. B. (1980). Feeling and thinking: Preferences need no inferences. *American Psychologist, 35,* 151-175.

Zanna, M. P., & Fazio, R. H. (1982). The attitude-behavior relation: Moving toward a third generation of research. In M. P. Zanna, E. T. Higgins, & C. P. Herman (Eds.), *Consistency in social behavior: The Ontario Symposium* (Vol. 2, pp. 283-301). Hillsdale, NJ: Lawrence Erlbaum.

CHAPTER CONTENTS

7 Participation in Small Groups

JOSEPH A. BONITO
University of Arizona

ANDREA B. HOLLINGSHEAD
University of Illinois

This essay reviews the literature on participation in small groups. Studies are distinguished as concerned with (a) identifying social or psychological factors that are assumed to be responsible for distributions of speaking opportunities in groups or (b) assessing the effect of participation hierarchies on group process and outcomes. Five general classes of antecedents are identified: member, group, and task characteristics; technology; and time. Three types of participation effects are also identified: individual- and group-level effects and effects on interaction. Two general criticisms are provided: First, a theory of participation is needed that specifies the role of antecedents on participation and how such antecedents play a role in participation outcomes; second, studies of participation should consider the role of discourse in the distribution of opportunities to speak. Suggestions for future research are offered.

S MALL group communication scholars often work under the premise that interaction is consequential for group outcomes. Gouran, Hirokawa, Julian, and Leatham (1993), for instance, suggest that discussion serves three functions essential to effective decision making. First, discussion is the vehicle by which members distribute and pool information. As work on information pooling has indicated, groups that carefully consider relevant information about all possible alternatives during discussion will make better decisions than those that do not (e.g., Hollingshead, 1993; Stasser, Taylor, & Hanna, 1989; Stasser & Titus, 1985). Second, errors in judgment may be identified and addressed by members. Third, discussion provides the opportunity for persuasion; it is the primary means by which individuals may be influential. Interaction is the *sine qua non* of group communication research because it is through communication practices that a group arrives at particular decisions.[1]

Correspondence and requests for reprints: Joseph A. Bonito, University of Arizona Communication, Bldg. #25, Room 209 Tucson, AZ 85721-0025; e-mail j-bonito@Barbara.comm.Arizona.edu; or Andrea B. Hollingshead, Department of Speech Communication, University of Illinois, 702 S. Wright Street, No. 244, Urbana, IL 61801; e-mail hollings@uiuc.edu

Communication Yearbook 20, pp. 227-261

Crucial to effective performance is participation. Researchers have long been interested in describing, predicting, and explaining the conditions under which group members contribute to discussion, for it is the group's communication patterns and practices that often determine the quality of outcomes. It has been well documented that participation is uneven and that such disparities have identifiable effects on group outcomes (e.g., McGrath, 1984). Understanding the conditions under which certain patterns of participation among members emerge and the potential effects of those patterns in different group contexts will inform other work on group processes, such as social influence, leader emergence, information pooling, and decision development.

Research on participation may be characterized along the two dimensions represented in Figure 7.1. The first consists of the antecedent conditions of participation, or those factors that influence how opportunities to speak are distributed within groups. These factors include group characteristics, member characteristics, task characteristics, technology, and time. The second dimension is the consequences of participation, that is, the effects that various distributions of participation have on a group and its members. There are three distinct categories of effects. The first is the effect of an act of participation on the cognitions of those who hear it (including the speaker, who, we assume, is monitoring his or her speech); we call this $effect_c$. This is an individual-level effect that reflects how an act of participation has changed how the hearer or speaker thinks, for example, about the group's decision, the group's progress, and/or its members. Second, participation has group-level effects ($effect_g$), such as the quality of group performance. Third, an act of participation affects subsequent acts by other members ($effect_i$). Work on conversational coherence (e.g., Craig & Tracy, 1983; Grice, 1975; Sanders, 1987), as well as conversation analysis (Levinson, 1983; Nofsinger, 1991; Schegloff, 1988), has provided ample evidence that social actors orient their talk to the discourse that has preceded it. A given act limits, at least to a certain degree, the options of the next speaker (see Jacobs, 1985). In addition, the effects of interaction are consequential for subsequent participation. A particular act produced by a speaker affects who may speak next (Sacks, Schegloff, & Jefferson, 1978).

It is important to note that no single piece of research addresses all the components presented in Figure 7.1. In fact, most studies concentrate on either antecedent or consequent conditions. Figure 7.1 represents a conceptual framework for studying and understanding participation in groups. It also is used as the organizing scheme for this review. In the next two sections, we present the scope of the review and define the construct of participation. We then discuss the antecedents and consequences of participation. We end with a general critique of past scholarship that includes considerations for future research on participation in small groups.

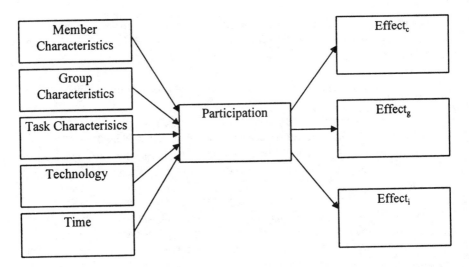

Figure 7.1. Conceptual Framework for Literature on Participation in Small Groups

DEFINING THE SCOPE OF THE LITERATURE REVIEW

Research on participation in small groups spans many disciplines, including speech communication, psychology, sociology, and organizational behavior. Although these are all concerned with different aspects of participation, they do have in common several features that allow us to focus our review. The first criterion for inclusion in this review is that studies must be concerned with the *number* of acts each group member contributes to discussion. Such studies assume that differential participation is consequential for group processes and outcomes and that understanding why such differentiation occurs provides important information about group process. They are generally not concerned with the *type* of act produced in discussion (see Burke, 1974; Leik, 1965) and assume, much like Hayes and Meltzer (1972), that the amount of time a group member speaks has an effect on group process that is independent of what he or she says.

The second criterion for inclusion is the unit of analysis. Only studies that examine participation patterns of individuals are reviewed. Studies that attempt to model behavior in groups as a function of individual differences on some set of variables are included, as well as those that track an individual's amount of participation throughout discussion. This review excludes studies that examine group processes at the group level of analysis, for example, group decision development (Poole, 1983a, 1983b; Poole & Roth, 1988a, 1988b) and most research from the functional perspective (for a review, see Gouran et al., 1993). Although both are concerned tangentially with participation, their primary purpose is to explain more global or systemic features of group interaction, irrespective of what each individual contributes to it.

The third and last criterion for delimiting the literature on participation in groups concerns the type of group analyzed. Balkwell (1994) provides a set of four scope conditions that serve as benchmarks here:

1. The group is small enough for face-to-face interaction to occur among all its members.
2. The group convenes for the purpose of accomplishing shared and well-defined goals.
3. There are shared standards for success and failure in achieving these goals.
4. Group members consider it both necessary and proper to take each other's contributions into account as they pursue their objectives. (pp. 122-123)

These scope conditions restrict our review to analyses of problem-solving and decision-making groups. The majority of empirical studies of problem-solving and decision-making groups are conducted with zero-history experimental groups that convene only for the purposes of the study and are then debriefed and disbanded. However, some researchers have examined participation processes in natural groups (e.g., Sigman, 1984) or experimental groups that have several meetings over a period of time (e.g., Clark & Schaefer, 1989). These scope conditions exclude studies of participation in nontask therapy and encounter groups, in which participation is viewed as therapeutic, a means for boosting an individual's self-esteem or improving a family's cohesiveness.

PARTICIPATION DEFINED

There is no general definition of *participation* extant in the literature. It is understood by the way it is operationalized and measured to refer to a verbal contribution to discussion.[2] In this regard, an act of participation is similar to what discourse and conversation-analytic literatures refer to as a *turn at talk*, defined by Edelsky (1993) as "an on-record speaking . . . behind which lies an intention to convey a message that is both referential and functional" (p. 207). A turn at talk may be a short, one-word utterance (e.g., "No") or it may be much longer, for example, a narrative or story (Goodwin, 1984). The length of most turns in normal, unregulated interaction tends to fall somewhere between these two extremes.

Some studies equate an act of participation with a turn (e.g., Parker, 1988; Stasser & Taylor, 1991; Stephan & Mishler, 1952), whereas others do not. Bales, Strodtbeck, Mills, and Roseborough (1951) and Burke (1974) define an act as a simple subject-predicate combination. Thus, one person's turn may contain several acts. Hoffman and Maier (1979) define an act as a statement or series of statements that are solution oriented. Any statement that does not address an aspect of the solution is uncoded; it is not an act (Hoffman & Maier, 1979, p. 19).[3] Bottger (1984) and Dabbs and Ruback (1987) used a time-based approach; Bottger was concerned with only the amount of time a given member spoke, whereas Dabbs and Ruback in several of their analyses examined contributions to discussion every quarter second.

Regardless of how an act is defined and/or measured, the objective is usually the same: to understand how differences in participation occur within and across groups as well how differences in participation affect group outcomes. Tsaí (1977) notes that differences in measurement of participation do not mitigate the robustness of the finding that opportunities to speak are differentially allocated within groups. His study used three measures of participation, and all yielded essentially the same finding: Participation in groups is differentiated. In the following sections, beginning with member attributes, we will consider antecedent conditions of participation, those factors that presumably contribute to differences in participation within groups.

ANTECEDENTS OF PARTICIPATION IN SMALL GROUPS

Member Attributes

A common approach for researchers studying participation has been to look at the effects of personality characteristics on individual participation. Although researchers have had some success at predicting participation by referring to some aspect of a group member's personality, the effects are typically not large and are likely to be moderated by other factors (Shaw, 1971).

Bass, Wurster, Doll, and Clair (1953) and Shaw (1959) found a positive correlation between participation and ascendancy (the desire or wish of an individual to be prominent in group situations). Bass, McGehee, Hawkins, Young, and Gebel (1953) found participation to be positively correlated with sociability. Other research has found positive correlations between intelligence and a group member's "activity" (e.g., Bass, Wurster, et al., 1953; Zeleny, 1939). Markel, Bein, Campbell, and Shaw (1976) showed the need for inclusion to be positively associated with speaking time. McGrath (1984) noted that seating position is associated with participation: Low participators tend to sit at the periphery of meeting areas, whereas high participators sit at more prominent positions (e.g., the head of the table).

The effects of communication-specific member characteristics on participation also have been examined. McCroskey and Richmond (1988), for instance, argue that participation in groups is affected by communication apprehension, or the degree to which individuals experience or feel anxious about speaking to other people in particular situations. Although communication apprehension is most commonly associated with public speaking situations, it applies to other contexts as well (Daly & McCroskey, 1984). McCroskey and Richmond (1988) found that individuals who scored high on communication apprehension (i.e., were more anxious about speaking in group situations) were less likely to participate in group discussion than were those who scored low.

Koomen and Sagel (1977) and Willard and Strodtbeck (1972) argue that people differ with regard to how quickly they provide contributions to discussions when opportunities present themselves. Latency of verbal response (LVR) is defined as the pause a speaker takes before responding to some sort of prior action (i.e., a verbal or nonverbal participation). People with short LVR times are more likely to participate simply because they gain control of the floor by virtue of their ability to speak quickly after the floor becomes available. However, findings suggest that LVR is associated with participation only in "competitive" situations; overall, the correlation between LVR and participation is weak (Koomen & Sagel, 1977).

Other researchers have hypothesized that group members differ regarding interaction and receiving proclivities. Interaction propensities are usually inferred from observed frequencies of participation. In general, the numbers of contributions to and from each member are represented in a linear equation, with each of the parameters representing interaction propensities (Keller, 1951). Leik (1967), for example, has developed several models that include propensity to initiate acts, type of act, and coalition formation. Other scholars have endeavored to develop mathematical models that fit observed rates of participation (Coleman, 1960; Horvath, 1965; Kadane & Lewis, 1969; Kadane, Lewis, & Ramage, 1969; Keller, 1951; Leik, 1965).

It is important to note that personality characteristics are not strongly correlated with and do not accurately predict an individual's behavior within a group. Davis (1992), for example, argues that individuals' preferences for particular solutions or courses of action may be exaggerated or moderated by group processes; an individual may vote for a "risky" solution during or after discussion even though his or her initial preference reflects a more conservative plan. Group processes might have a similar effect on the relation between participation and personality characteristics. For example, on a complex task, experts might be more active participators than nonexperts who were found to be "loquacious" prior to discussion (for more on this issue, see Bales, 1950, 1970). This may also explain why many mathematical models of interaction propensities do not fit observed frequencies of participation very well (Goetsch & McFarland, 1980). A person's propensity to speak is affected by the group he or she is in and what it is trying to accomplish (Leik, 1965). These considerations are not reflected in most models of participation that include personality characteristics.

Group Characteristics

One of the main assumptions in research on group characteristics is that differences in participation are a function of composition. A person's place in a group is relative to the places of the other members who constitute it. For example, a person low in status in one group may be high in status in another. Thus, examining a group's composition allows a better understanding of how opportunities to participate are distributed. Composition may be investigated in a variety of ways (for a review, see Moreland & Levine, 1992).

Research on participation and group composition is largely concerned with status, which we will discuss first. We will then consider the effects of culture and group size on participation.

Status

Status is perhaps the most frequently studied group characteristic relevant to participation. Status is "a characteristic around which differences in cognitions and evaluations of individuals or social types of them come to be organized" (Berger & Zelditch, 1977, p. 5). In other words, status embodies those characteristics that lead people to think about others in terms of who they are and what they can do relative to the task. Such characteristics include, but are not limited to, race, gender, and age. Differences among group members on one or more of these characteristics are assumed to lead to differences in participation: "Observable inequalities in the structure of social interaction are then understood as consequences of the emergence of status characteristics" (Berger & Zelditch, 1977, p. 5).

Most research on the effects of status on participation is unified by expectation states theory (EST), which argues that group members form expectations about themselves and their fellow interactants and that these expectations are responsible for the development of participation hierarchies.[4] According to the theory, expectations are derived from diffuse status characteristics (Berger, Cohen, & Zelditch, 1966), or the way in which status markers identify how an individual might perform on a given task. Expectations, then, are "beliefs about how actors with a given state of a given status characteristic will behave in appropriate situations" (Berger et al., 1966, p. 33). Because EST assumes that participation is guided by performance expectations, it follows that group members make estimations about the usefulness of potential contributions by other group members and compare them with what they themselves might usefully add to discussion (Berger & Conner, 1969). Differences in expectations related to status lead participants to acquire and allocate speaking turns differentially, with those perceived as high in status taking more opportunities to speak than those perceived as low in status. Berger and Zelditch (1977) note: "If Smith comes to believe that Jones has higher ability and that therefore Jones can be expected to be right about things more than Smith himself, Smith is likely to wait for Jones to act, hence has fewer opportunities than Jones" (p. 19).

In sum, expectation states theory seeks to explain behavior by examining the relation between status and expectations, and more specifically how the latter affects what one will do and when one will do it in a given interaction. Expectations are formed as interlocutors evaluate one another on a variety of task-related or social characteristics. It is assumed that these expectations enable each member to predict how the other will perform on a given task. Importantly, a group member is likely to contribute if he or she expects that another may perform a desired behavior poorly or not at all; conversely, a member may decide not to contribute if he or she feels that another member is better able to participate effectively. Such expectations form a hierarchy in which contributions of some actors are viewed as more valuable than contributions of others.

Some EST research on participation operationalizes status in terms of gender. In fact, many studies (Balkwell, 1991, 1994, 1995; Skvoretz, 1988; Skvoretz & Fararo, 1996; Smith-Lovin, Skvoretz, & Hudson, 1986) have used the same data set (from Smith-Lovin et al., 1986), in which gender composition was systematically manipulated for six-person groups. Although it is generally true that men talk more than women in mixed-sex small groups (Moreland & Levine, 1992), most of the predictions based on calculations derived from various expectation states postulates did not fit the data well. Skvoretz (1988), for example, tested six different models of participation, all of which had different assumptions of the effect of status on how opportunities to speak are distributed among group members. He concludes that status as measured by gender is an inaccurate predictor of participation in small groups.

There are several explanations for this finding. Skvoretz (1981) and Smith-Lovin et al. (1986) both suggest that there are subgroup divisions within particular status groups; for example, status hierarchies may develop within gender groups, a point made earlier by Nowakasowa (1978), who developed a mathematical representation of participation in groups that reflects the influence of factions on participation. Balkwell (1991, 1995) believes that the poor fit of models is due to estimation error and use of inadequate statistical tools. Balkwell (1995) argues that some of the major tenets of EST might also be problematic and calls for a reassessment of some aspects of the theory. He shows that models with weaker assumptions about the role of gender in developing and maintaining status differences produce more accurate predictions of participation rates. In other words, the role of gender in the development of status hierarchies, especially as characterized by Fisek, Berger, and Norman (1991), might be overemphasized.

The effect of other status characteristics on participation has been investigated. Skvoretz (1981) looked at differences in participation for members of a hospital advisory board and found that high-status members (e.g., surgeons and administrators) spoke more frequently than did low-status members (e.g., nurses). Bloom (1980) observed that higher-status nurses spoke more than lower-ranked ones. Pauchet (1982), in a study of a university teaching and research council, found that higher-ranked members (e.g., full professors) spoke almost twice as much as members of lower ranks (e.g., associate and assistant professors). Unranked members (e.g., staff and students) spoke infrequently. In a study by Tammivara (1982), students who were acknowledged as having higher reading abilities were found to be more likely to participate in other class activities. Finally, Conner (1977) produced evidence showing that differences in competence led to status differences among members, creating a differentiated participation structure.

Several problems exist in the EST research paradigm. The first concerns problems with the data used by EST researchers. Skvoretz and Fararo (1996) contend that the models developed by EST researchers are more complex than the data. The data, usually frequency counts of the number of contributions of each member, are not sensitive to the processes described in theories of participation (e.g., Berger, Fisek, Norman, & Zelditch, 1977; Fisek et al., 1991). Higher-quality databases would reflect the content of discussion, so that researchers could better determine how participation relates to phases of discussion, as well as how and to whom opportunities to participate are directed by group members (Skvoretz & Fararo, 1996).

Another problem is that empirical examinations of EST, in operationalizing status in terms of gender, assume that actors develop performance expectations based on sex differences (Meeker, 1994). However, Tannen (1993) argues that the relation between language and gender is ambiguous and that deriving relative power from what representatives of a particular gender category say is problematic. She asserts that particular linguistic forms may mark either power differences or solidarity (i.e., feelings of unity). For example, interruptions are viewed by some as indices of power in gender talk; men tend to interrupt more than women and, hence, are said to have more power over them in particular interactions. Tannen argues that not all interruptions are about power; some are about collaboration (see Goodwin, 1987)— that is, they are used to complete particular utterances or narratives and have the effect of increasing solidarity, or reducing power differentials. As Tannen (1993) notes, "Attempts to understand what goes on between women and men in conversation are muddled by the ambiguity of power and solidarity" (p. 183). Gender, then, offers an inadequate basis for operationalizing status; it is difficult to predict just when power differentials will develop because language may minimize rather than exacerbate them.

In sum, status does affect the distribution of turns in group discussion, but not all types of status are equally influential. For example, gender does not appear to be as important as occupational prestige in accounting for differences in participation within groups. In addition, EST research suffers from deficiencies in its databases. Balkwell (1995) and Skvoretz and Fararo (1995) have begun to address these issues in an attempt to provide a better fit between theories of participation and data.

Culture

Only a few studies have addressed the relation between culture and participation in groups. We will discuss two of these. In general, the assumption is that amount of participation is associated with or may be predicted by cultural differences among a group's members. In a study conducted at a Canadian university, Kirchmeyer (1993) compared the amount of contributions of minorities (defined as persons not of European ancestry, e.g., Asian, Indian) with the contributions of majorities (defined as persons of European ancestry) to discussion. Her results revealed that minorities contributed less frequently to discussion than did majorities. In addition, she found that minority status was positively associated with femininity (defined as yielding, sensitive, loyal, and so on) and negatively associated with communication competence. In turn, communication competence was positively associated and femininity was negatively associated with contributing to discussion.

Strodtbeck (1980), in a study of power and participation in husband-wife interaction, found differences across cultures in the relation between participation and influence. The general assumption regarding influence and participation is that people who talk more during discussion are usually more influential (see the section below on effect$_c$). However, Strodtbeck found that not all cultures exhibit this pattern, and that some marital partners are more influential even though they talk less. Thus, the rate at which one speaks in husband-wife interactions and the influence one exerts are subject to cultural influences.

Group Size

Group size is an important factor in the distribution of participation (Bales & Borgatta, 1953; Bales et al., 1951; Coleman, 1960; Stephan & Mishler, 1952). McGrath (1984), in a review of group interaction studies, noted that, across small groups of all sizes, the most active group member contributes approximately 43% of all turns in discussion, the next most active member 23%, the next about 17%, and so on. However, disparities in participation tend to be minimized in smaller groups, whereas differentiation in participation increases as groups increase in size. Table 7.1 shows that as group size increases, the proportion of acts contributed by the most active member, relatively speaking, remains constant, whereas other members contribute proportionately fewer acts. For example, in groups with 3 members, the most active member contributes 44.4% of the acts, whereas the least active member contributes 23%. In groups with 10 members, the most active member contributes 42.6% of the acts, whereas the least active member contributes 2.8%. Group size then affects how acts are distributed among group members.

Moreland and Levine (1992) offer several explanations for this phenomenon. First, larger groups tend to develop status systems, and such systems are responsible for particular distributions of speaking opportunities (see the discussion above). Second, satisfaction of some members decreases as groups become larger, a finding that suggests members are more likely to become alienated from the group and, as a consequence, make fewer contributions to

TABLE 7.1

Proportion of Contributions to Discussion as a Function of
Individual Rank and Group Size (in percentages)

Rank in Group	Group Size							
	3	4	5	6	7	8	9	10
1	44.4	32.9	46.1	43.1	43.2	39.8	49.1	42.6
2	32.6	27.3	22.0	18.8	15.2	16.6	19.0	12.0
3	23.0	22.7	15.6	14.2	11.9	12.6	7.6	10.0
4		17.1	10.5	11.1	9.9	9.9	5.3	9.1
5			5.8	7.5	8.6	8.6	4.9	6.0
6				5.6	6.3	5.5	4.1	5.3
7					5.0	4.2	3.8	5.0
8						2.7	3.7	3.7
9							2.5	3.3
10								2.8

SOURCE: Coleman (1960, p. 49).

discussion. Finally, members feel more efficacious in smaller groups; they feel that their contributions play a part in the group's decision. Some members in larger groups feel less efficacious and are less likely, therefore, to offer contributions to groups.

Task

An important issue regarding participation in small groups is whether the task on which a group is working affects participation patterns. The few studies that have been conducted on the task participation problem provide evidence that tasks do affect participation distributions. For example, Dabbs and Ruback (1987) studied patterns of turn taking in three different types of groups, using data from three earlier studies (Dabbs & Ruback, 1984; Dabbs, Ruback, & Evans, 1987; Ruback, Dabbs, & Hopper, 1984) of get-acquainted, brainstorming, and problem-solving groups, respectively. Dabbs and Ruback (1987) assumed that vocal activity in groups is typically confined to particular subgroups, especially dyads. They compared reciprocity correlations—that is, sequential associations (for one lag)—between the contributions of all possible pairs of speakers for each type of group.

Dabbs and Ruback (1987) computed a pooled reciprocity correlation for all three groups ($r = .42$, $p = .001$). This finding indicates that there is some order to group discussion such that certain pairs of speakers "control" discussion; in some cases, a particular member's contribution makes another member's contribution in the next turn more or less likely. In addition, the correlations for all three groups were significant, with $r = .27$, .40, and .62 for problem-solving, brainstorming, and get-acquainted, respectively ($p <$

.001 for each). Reciprocity correlations for get-acquainted groups differed significantly from those of both problem-solving and brainstorming groups ($z = 4.22$ and 2.84, respectively; $p < .01$). This finding suggests that discussion in get-acquainted groups is somewhat more patterned than that in problem-solving or brainstorming groups.

Two possible explanations have been suggested for differences in participation patterns among the three groups. Dabbs and Ruback (1987) offer a tentative explanation by stating that get-acquainted groups, "being least restrained by task demands, allowed most freedom for subjects to respond to others who had responded to them" (p. 151). Conversely, participation in problem-solving and brainstorming groups is task oriented; members make contributions as necessary to complete a task. A second explanation concerns the types of communication that are likely to occur in each group. Although Dabbs and Ruback's analysis ignores the content of discussion and, as a consequence, the communication practices of each of the groups is unknown, one may speculate about the interactional foci of each. Research on the communication processes at work when people endeavor to acquire information about one another suggests that becoming acquainted is accomplished largely through interactive strategies, such as interrogation, self-disclosure, and relax-the-target techniques (C. R. Berger & Kellerman, 1994). These techniques require that addressees respond to the people who produce them; they are, by definition, patterns of interaction that make the responses of certain individuals more or less likely during group discussion. However, the primary goal of discussion in problem-solving and brainstorming groups is to perform a tangible task, not social information acquisition. Because the group is oriented to the task, messages are more likely to be directed to the group rather than to any specific individual. This is especially true in brainstorming groups, where the purpose is to generate or "throw out" as many ideas as possible. In addition, Bales et al. (1951), Stephan (1952), and Stephan and Mishler (1952) all studied decision-making groups and found that many—in some cases, most—contributions are addressed to the group as a whole. Because acts in problem-solving and brainstorming groups are not necessarily addressed to any particular individual, patterning is less likely to occur.[5]

Communication Technologies

Many studies have revealed that groups interacting via computer have more equal participation among members than do groups interacting face-to-face (e.g., Clapper, McLean, & Watson, 1991; Daly, 1993; Dubrovsky, Kiesler, & Sethna, 1991; George, Easton, Nunamaker, & Northcraft, 1990; Hiltz, Johnson, & Turoff, 1986; McLeod, 1992; Rice, 1984; Siegel, Dubrovsky, Kiesler, & McGuire, 1986; Straus & McGrath, 1994; Zigurs, Poole, & DeSanctis, 1988). This general finding has been labeled the "participation equalization effect." The general explanation for the effect is that people feel less inhibited when interacting through a computer network as a result of the reduction in social cues that provide information regarding status in the group. Because people communicating electronically are less aware of social differences, they feel a greater sense of anonymity and detect less individuality in others (Sproull & Kiesler, 1991).

It is important to note some common elements across this set of studies. All were conducted during single experimental sessions in laboratory settings, with ad hoc groups made up of students. It is also important to note that this finding was observed across a variety of communication technologies or group support systems (see McGrath & Hollingshead, 1993, for a classification of group support systems).

Several studies showed no evidence of the participation equalization effect in computer-mediated groups (Lea & Spears, 1991; McLeod & Liker, 1992; Spears & Lea, 1992; Watson, DeSanctis, & Poole, 1988; Weisband, 1992; Weisband, Schneider, & Connolly, 1995). To what can we attribute these seemingly contradictory findings? One possible explanation is that status differences among members within the groups may have been differentially salient across studies.

Some studies experimentally controlled the status of participants within the group, with mixed results. Dubrovsky et al. (1991) discerned that when groups made controversial decisions through a synchronous computer conferencing system, patterns of participation and influence among members in mixed-status groups were more nearly equal in a computer-supported context than in a face-to-face context. The researchers conclude that the reduction of status cues led low-status members to feel less inhibited and to participate relatively more in a computer-mediated discussion than in a face-to-face discussion. However, Spears and Lea (1992) and Hollingshead (1996) observed that when member identities were known or were visually available, status differences persisted even in a computer-mediated setting. Weisband et al. (1995) sought to identify the underlying mechanisms regarding the participation equalization effect of computer mediation. They uncovered no evidence of the effect when the group members were clearly identified in unequal status groups. High-status members talked more and were perceived as contributing more to the final decision than were low-status members. When status labels were hidden and low-status members were in the majority, status differences in participation were slightly reduced, though not eliminated, but status differences in influence virtually disappeared. Weisband et al. conclude that status labels and the impressions formed from those labels have a larger impact on participation and influence than do communication media.

More recently, questions have arisen concerning whether the participation equalization effect is merely an artifact of the pragmatic and technical demands of the communication medium and of the experimental studies that have reported it (Spears & Lea, 1994; Weisband et al., 1995). The participation equalization effect observed in computer-mediated groups may be an indication of how the medium reduces the baseline of each member's partici- pation rather than how the medium leads to increased participation of low- status members during the group discussion (McGrath & Hollingshead, 1994; Spears & Lea, 1994).

It takes more time to type a message on a computer network than it does to say that same message verbally. In the experiments cited above, the computer sessions were at least as long as the face-to-face sessions; however, the amounts and rates of communication in the computer-mediated settings were much lower. Another possible technological explanation for greater egalitarian participation patterns in computer-mediated settings is that electronic group members have the ability to participate without interruption, because turn taking is not a norm in a computer-mediated environment (Weisband et al., 1995).

As noted previously, most empirical studies reporting the participation equalization effect have been conducted with ad hoc groups of students in laboratory settings (Hollingshead & McGrath, 1995). Even though status differences have been controlled in several studies, the experimental status manipulations have been relatively minor and may not apply in organizations in which status differences are much larger and have organizational conse- quences (Spears & Lea, 1994). These studies, with few exceptions, were each run during only one session. Longitudinal research in different communica- tion environments has indicated that performance and process differences between face-to-face and computer-mediated groups disappear relatively quickly over sessions (Hollingshead, McGrath, & O'Connor, 1993; Walther, Anderson, & Park, 1994), which suggests that a participation equalization effect observed initially in a computer-mediated context may be ephemeral.

Time

McGrath (1990) argues that small group researchers do not devote enough attention to the effects of time on group processes. Research on participation is no exception: Most studies ignore the effects of time on how and when members contribute to discussion. However, studies that have investigated the participation-time relation have found that participation structures change as groups mature.

Contractor and Seibold (1993), in a series of computer simulations de- signed to assess how groups appropriate and use group decision support systems (GDSS), found that participation patterns change over time. Their model makes two major assumptions about the dynamics of participation: First, groups develop norms for appropriating GDSS systems, and awareness of such norms influences the degree to which members contribute to discus- sion; second, expertise with the task and expertise with GDSS affect both participation and the development of norms within the group.

Contractor and Seibold's (1993) simulations began with a baseline model in which awareness of norms and experience with GDSS were low and increases in task experience and GDSS facility over time were moderate. This model revealed that the level of participation increased rapidly during the beginning of discussion but then leveled off after members developed and became aware of norms of appropriation. Other models with different assumptions regarding initial levels of expertise and GDSS facility showed that different communication patterns emerged. For example, extensive training in GDSS technology produced relatively consistent cycles in which members spent some time frequently communicating, but, in other cases, communicated less frequently. Thus, patterns of communication changed as a function of the dynamic interaction between time and the development and awareness of norms.

Clark and his colleagues examined changes in participation patterns across multiple discussion sessions (Clark & Schaefer, 1989; Clark & Wilkes-Gibbs, 1986; Isaacs & Clark, 1987). Their work on reference in conversation shows that the nature of participation changes as a function of how experts and novices learn to collaborate on a task. They demonstrate that, over time, experts and novices coordinate their contributions to discourse in order to accommodate differences in knowledge. For example, on a matching task (Isaacs & Clark, 1987), expert "directors" instructed novice "matchers" to arrange pictures of New York City in a particular order. The task was repeated five times. On the first trial, most of the experts realized that the novices were unaware of the proper names of the structures and places in the photographs. The experts then tended to use descriptions as a way to complete the task. However, over the six trials, novices were able to learn many of the proper names of the items in the pictures. The result was that, by the sixth trial, experts and novices alike were better able to coordinate their contributions to the task such that it was completed in fewer words and with more proper names; collaboration on the task was more efficient. Isaacs and Clark (1987) suggest that

> in conversation . . . making a successful reference requires the coordinated participation of both speaker and addressee, and the two do not take the process as complete until they reach the mutual belief that the addressee has understood it to a criterion sufficient for current purposes. (p. 35)

The criterion for understanding changes as actors become more familiar with each other and the task over time. As the nature of understanding changes, so do the number and kind of contributions each makes to discussion. This is true not only for familiarity with a task, as in Clark's case, but also for groups that meet over many sessions to work on different problems. McGrath (1984), for example, in a review of the group development literature, noted that patterns of interactional content at the group level of analysis change across discussion sessions. Although that research does not fit our criteria for inclusion in this review, it lends support to the proposition that time (over sessions) changes the conditions under which group members contribute to discussion.

CONSEQUENCES OF PARTICIPATION IN SMALL GROUPS

Effects of Participation on Individual Cognitions (Effect$_c$)

Participation affects how members think about their group and the people in it. In this section we report on research that addresses the relation between participation and perceptions of influence, leadership, and several affective measures.

Participation and Influence

A central assumption regarding participation is that high participators are more influential than low participators during discussion. In other words, a group's decision is more likely to reflect the suggestions and opinions of high participators. Empirical results are consistent with this claim; participation and influence are highly associated (Bottger, 1984; Hoffman, Burke, & Maier, 1965; Riecken, 1958). However, there are several moderating conditions that require further discussion.

Strodtbeck (1980) found that cultural differences are responsible for the relation between influence and speaking time. Bottger (1984) argues that finer distinctions should be made regarding types of influence and their relation to participation. He found that the number of contributions to discussion was highly correlated with perceived influence, or the reported degree of influence across group members. However, actual influence, the degree to which the group decision reflected a given subject's suggestions, although moderately correlated with participation, was strongly associated with expertise. Expertise was moderately associated with participation; people with greater task-related ability tended to speak more during discussion. Littlepage and Silbiger (1992) observed that group performance and the ability to recognize expertise in groups were positively associated. Thus, groups in which participation and expertise were positively associated and recognized by members were more likely to make superior decisions than were those groups in which participation and expertise were not or were negatively correlated.

Participation and Leadership

There is substantial evidence to suggest that amount of participation is consequential for how leadership develops or emerges in small groups (Stein & Heller, 1979). In general, the member who speaks the most is rated or identified by other group members as the group's leader (Dabbs & Ruback,

1984; Dabbs et al., 1987; Ginter & Lindskold, 1975; Jaffe & Lucas, 1969; Ruback et al., 1984; Sorrentino & Boutillier, 1975; Stein & Heller, 1979). However, there are several conditions that qualify or even vitiate the generalization that group members tend to perceive high participators as leaders.

A central issue for participation and leadership concerns the relation between the amount of speaking and what is said. Are perceptions of leadership solely the result of speaking time, or is there an effect of what a person says on how he or she is perceived in group discussion? Jaffe and Lucas (1969) used confederates in one of two ways to ascertain the relation between speaking and leadership. Confederates were instructed either to "dominate" discussion by speaking frequently but without providing solution-relevant information or to speak infrequently while making half of their contributions "correct." Jaffe and Lucas discovered that high participators were more likely than low participators to be ranked as leaders. These findings were moderated by two other factors. First, the researchers discovered that "perceptive" subjects were more likely to rank high- *and* low-participating confederates as leaders rather than any of the other group members. Second, the order of experimental manipulations affected ratings of leadership. Jaffe and Lucas used the same confederate in each of the participation roles across two discussion sessions with the same group. They varied the order of the confederate's participation in one of two ways, high/low or low/high, and aggregated the leader rankings across sessions. The results indicated that confederates who were high participators in the first session but low participators in the second were less likely to be rated as leaders than were confederates whose order of participation was reversed. However, correlations for amount of speaking and leader choice showed that low-participating confederates were more likely to be chosen as leader in the second session—that is, if they had been high participators in the first session. Jaffe and Lucas conclude that once a person has been established as the dominant speaker in the group hierarchy, this affects how group members react to him or her in subsequent sessions.

Sorrentino and Boutillier (1975) argue for a fundamental difference between quality and quantity of participation. Quantity of participation is likely to be perceived by group members as an indication of motivation, whereas quality of participation is an indicator of ability. Furthermore, these authors suggest that quantity of interaction is a more accurate reflection of leadership, because motivation provides a clear indication of a group member's intentions—for example, that he or she cares about the group enough to make contributions to discussion that facilitate group process. Sorrentino and Boutillier suggest that ability is indicative of task-specific information, but does not indicate a concern with group process itself.

In an experimental situation similar to that used by Jaffe and Lucas (1969), Sorrentino and Boutillier (1975) found that high participators, regardless of the quality of their contributions, were ranked as more competent, more confident, more interested in discussion, and more influential than were low participators. High-quality participators—that is, confederates who supplied only task-relevant communication—were perceived as more competent, more influential, and contributing more to the group's goal than were low-quality participators. Sorrentino and Boutillier also investigated how participation affects perceptions of task and socioemotional leadership ability. They found that only quantity of participation was significant in both areas; the interaction of quality and quantity was found to be significant for socioemotional leadership. Although quality of participation is important for some perceptions of leadership, quantity of participation—and the underlying attributions of motivation associated with it—seems to be the best predictor of leadership.

Ginter and Lindskold (1975) determined that rate of participation is an accurate predictor of leadership under certain conditions. They argue that the relation of perceptions of leadership and rate of participation are moderated by task-related expertise and task ambiguity. They found that high and low participators who were identified as experts were equally likely to be rated as leader. In the nonexpert condition, only high participators were more likely to be ranked as leader. Moreover, when task ambiguity was low, nonexpert high participators *and* expert low participators were less likely to be perceived as leader. Ginter and Lindskold conclude that, in the absence of task-related ability on ambiguous or demanding tasks, high participators fill the leadership void "until a more tangible basis for selection emerges" (p. 1089), but that in nondemanding or unambiguous tasks, the value of expertise diminishes.

Dabbs, Ruback, and their colleagues examined participation and leadership from a slightly different perspective (Dabbs & Ruback, 1984, 1987; Dabbs et al., 1987; Ruback et al., 1984). They were concerned with how particular structures of discourse—specifically, interruptions, overlapping speech, and length of pause—are distributed among group members. They assumed that these discourse structures are related to how leaders emerge in group discussion. Dabbs and Ruback (1984), Dabbs et al. (1987), and Ruback et al. (1984) discovered that amount of talking was positively associated with perceptions of leadership. Concerning more specific features of discourse, Dabbs and Ruback (1984) and Dabbs et al. (1987) showed that perceptions of leadership were positively correlated with speaking within one's own turn (i.e., not interrupting when another turn is in progress) and negatively correlated with overlapping turns. Ruback et al. (1984), moreover, observed that leaders spent more time orienting the group toward speaker transition; more of their turns involved speaker exchange than did turns of other group members.

Participation and Affect

Differentiated participation structures affect how group members think and feel about the group and about each other. In general, the more one speaks during group discussion, the more likely one is to perceive the group and the process of discussion positively (McGrath, 1984). The inverse applies to low participators. Those who speak infrequently during discussion tend to perceive the group and its processes negatively. In several studies, rate of speaking was positively associated with liking; those who spoke more were better liked than those who spoke infrequently (Dabbs & Ruback, 1984, 1987; Dabbs et al., 1987; Ruback et al., 1984). Ruback et al. (1984) and Dabbs and Ruback (1984) noted that individuals in groups with undifferentiated participation structures felt that their groups had more spirit.

The association between participation and affect is not consistent across studies and tends to be moderated by other factors. For example, Hoffman et al. (1965) found that total participation was not significantly associated with satisfaction with influence or satisfaction with solution. Interestingly, in their study, total participation was significantly associated with attempted influence and actual influence; the more an individual participated, the more likely he or she was to influence the group's direction. Given this result, it is not surprising to learn that actual influence was positively correlated with both satisfaction with solution and influence attempts.

Effects of Participation on Group-Level Phenomena (Effect$_g$)

Several studies have assessed the relation between participation structures and group performance. The general question concerns equal participation: Do groups with undifferentiated participation perform better than groups in which opportunities to participate are stratified? In theory, groups with equalized participation make better-quality decisions because each member's perspective is brought to bear on the problem. In practice, equalized participation is useful when certain conditions are met. The effectiveness of equalized participation is dependent on the interaction of contextual factors, including the following: commitment; superiors' decision-making styles; subordinates' skills, knowledge, and experience; and organizational climate. As Yetton and Crawford (1992) note: "Participation is *only* effective when matched with the nature of subordinates, the nature of the task, and the nature of the decision problems faced. If these contingencies are not heeded, the generally positive effects of participation may not occur" (p. 95; emphasis added).

Research provides some evidence supporting Yetton and Crawford's (1992) assertion. Gastil's (1993) case study of a grocery co-op revealed that opportunities to speak were equally distributed although not everyone took advantage of those opportunities. In the end, Gastil concludes that the group's patterns of participation allowed it to produce sound decisions that reflected all members' interests. The nature of a co-op, with decentralized decision making and relatively equal status among members, seemed to necessitate equal participation in order for it to function optimally.

Experimental studies suggest that equal participation is not always associated with effective group performance. Littlepage and Silbiger (1992), using a task in which groups answered 20 multiple-choice questions, uncovered no significant differences in performance across groups with differentiated and undifferentiated participation structures. Less direct evidence appears in studies on participative decision making, in which participation constraints have been imposed on group members. Latham and his colleagues discovered that, in many cases, participation by subordinates in goal-setting meetings did not improve their performance (Dossett, Latham, & Mitchell, 1979; Latham & Marshall, 1982; Latham, Mitchell, & Dossett, 1978; Latham & Steele, 1983).

Latham and associates' experimental paradigm compared different participation conditions. Managers were instructed to pursue meetings in one of several ways: *assigned goals,* in which the manager tells the subordinate what is expected of him or her; *participative* condition, in which the manager works with and seeks feedback from the subordinate in determining goals; or *do best,* in which the subordinate is encouraged to set his or her own goals. Most productivity gains occurred in the assigned goals condition; subordinates performed better when they were provided with goals by their superiors. However, Latham et al. (1978), in a study conducted in an engineering firm, found that *participative* decision making increased performance over *do best* and control groups. These findings suggest that allowing subordinates an equal voice in decision making does not always increase productivity.

Effects of Participation on Interaction (Effect$_i$)

Differences in rates of participation among group members can change as discussion progresses. Fisek and Ofshe (1970) noted that approximately half of their experimental groups changed participation rates during the course of discussion. Some groups began with relatively undifferentiated participation but subsequently moved toward a state of differentiation. This pattern, however, was not characteristic of all groups. Some displayed differentiation as early as the first minute of discussion and maintained it throughout. As an explanation, Fisek and Ofshe suggest that status might be responsible for both interactional trajectories. In the first case, early contributions by each member may have revealed his or her ability regarding the task at hand, and subsequent turns were allocated on the basis of this perceived ability. In the latter case, some aspect of status may have been salient to each of the members prior to or immediately after the start of discussion, and turns were allocated accordingly.

Another explanation of the effects of past participation on future interaction is provided by a number of researchers concerned with turn-by-turn analyses of discussion and with the process by which participation hierarchies develop in groups (Dabbs & Ruback, 1984, 1987; Dabbs et al., 1987; Parker, 1988; Ruback et al., 1984; Stasser & Taylor, 1991). This research addresses the structure of participation, defined as patterns of vocal activity over time (Dabbs & Ruback, 1987).

The results from this body of research are interesting and useful, suggesting that one can predict patterns of speakers in group discussion: "Knowing who has the turn at turn t helps tell us who will have the turn at $t + 1$" (Dabbs & Ruback, 1987, p. 149). Moreover, Parker (1988) found that the person who produced a turn at time t is likely to speak again at time $t + 2$. In other words, in four-person groups, speaker A would produce the first and third turns, speaker B the second; speakers C and D would be silent. This pattern is represented as ABA.[6] Parker discovered that 61% of the turns produced by group members were of this pattern; he concludes that group discussion is dominated by patterns of dyadic interaction—dyads tend to hold the floor in group interaction.[7]

What happens at the conclusion of the ABA pattern? Parker (1988) identifies four possible events or floors that occur with certain likelihoods following the original pattern: continued floor, broken floor, regain floor, and nonfloor. Continued floors maintain the sequence of speakers (e.g., ABAB); broken floors introduce a new speaker into the pattern (e.g., ABAC); regain floors either reestablish a previous floor or establish a new one; nonfloors display no obvious patterns of speakers. Figure 7.2 shows the transitional probabilities for, as well as the percentages of, turns that occur within each floor type. In general, groups are likely to stay in or return to some sort of floor state, that is, some predictable pattern of two speakers. Discussion, then, is not characterized by random distribution of speaking opportunities.

Stasser and Taylor (1991) extended Parker's (1988) results to six-person groups. They detected patterns of speakers and floors in their data that were consistent with Parker's. In addition, they conducted a computer simulation showing that participation was intermittent; people tended to speak in "waves," that is, they speak frequently at some points in the discussion and not at all in others. However, this may not be true of all members. Dabbs and Ruback (1987), for instance, observed that members who spoke infrequently at the beginning of the interaction were less likely to participate as the discussion continued.

Burke's (1982, 1986) work has shown that activities change the nature of participation, because on occasion, making certain contributions becomes redundant or unnecessary. Burke studied instruction giving across four media (face-to-face, telephone, audiotape, and writing). Participants were divided into two groups, the first consisting of experts trained in the assembly of a toy water pump and the second made up of novices who were instructed by the experts, via one of the four media, to assemble the pump.

Of interest here are the findings in the face-to-face condition. Burke (1982) found that experts modified their instructions as a function of the process of the assembly. Many novices were able to fit together parts of the pump *before* or during the expert's instruction. Thus, the experts began to supply instructions as a function of the novices' behavior. In some cases, instruction was not required; in others, only partial instruction was necessary; and in yet

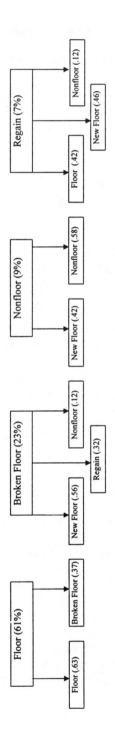

Figure 7.2. Transitions of Floor States in Parker's (1988) Data

NOTE: Percentages in parentheses refer to the proportion of turns produced with a floor state. Decimals in parentheses refer to the conditional probability of a floor state occurring from a previous one.

others, complete instructions were essential to the assembly of particular parts. In sum, of all the knowledge an expert had available about the pump assembly, only a subset of it was relevant, and its relevance was determined by the nature of the activity. If the activity did not make relevant an instruction, then the instruction was unlikely to be supplied.

SUMMARY AND CONCLUSIONS

In general, opportunities to speak in group discussion are differentially allocated and acquired by group members. Antecedents of participation structures and their effects are summarized below.

Participation structures are affected by several antecedent conditions, including the following:

- Some personality characteristics seem to affect participation distributions, but they have been examined as independent of an individual's role or position in the group.
- Group structure, most notably the distribution of status, allows group members to develop performance expectations about each other. These expectations lead the group to allocate speaking opportunities to members who are perceived as better able to make useful contributions to discussion.
- A number of studies have found evidence of a participation equalization effect in computer-mediated groups, although recent work has cast doubt on the validity and generalizability of that effect.
- Participation is also affected by time, especially when group members have the opportunity to develop an understanding of the task and what each member can contribute to it.

Differential distributions of participation affect various group outcomes. These include the following:

- Those who speak frequently are more likely to be perceived as influential, ranked as leader, and liked by other group members.
- Group performance is affected by participation structures, but the relation is dependent on contextual factors. In some cases groups are more effective when participation is equalized or when normally silent members are encouraged to contribute. However, in other cases, performance is improved if certain members are allowed to provide more contributions to discussion.
- Participation affects how subsequent discussion occurs. Interaction is dominated by dyadic exchanges in which sets of two actors are in control of discussion for some period of time. In addition, some dyads are more likely than others to hold the floor for a given period of time. Thus, one may predict patterns of participation over the course of several exchanges.

We offer below two general criticisms of research on participation in small groups as well as some suggestions for future research.

A Call for Theory

Studies of participation would profit from better grounding in theoretical principles addressing the social, psychological, and cognitive mechanisms of group process. With the exception of expectation states, much of the literature on participation is without theoretical basis. The relation between participation and particular antecedents or consequences is largely unspecified, or, if it is, the process that underlies it is incorrect or unrealistic (McGrath, 1984, pp. 164-165). This is especially true of mathematical models that, on the surface, accurately predict rates of participation by various group members. Such models gloss the process of participation and are accurate only because the process they presume to measure is actually correlated with the "real" underlying process: "The value of a mathematical model as a basis for describing and predicting the phenomenon (in this case, the distribution of participation in a group) does not rest entirely on the validity of the processes hypothesized as underlying the phenomenon" (McGrath, 1984, p. 164; italics omitted).

There are several directions future research may take in investigating the relations among participation, antecedents, and consequences. First, theory and research ought to develop a dynamic model of participation, focusing on how particular antecedent conditions affect participation structures, and on how such structures affect group outcomes. One opportunity in this area is the relation of tasks and participation. Research by Dabbs and Ruback (1987), discussed above, has shown that participation patterns are affected by task considerations. However, Dabbs and Ruback's explanation of this phenomenon is limited because there is no underlying theory that systematically documents task characteristics and how participation is affected by them.

Hirokawa's (1990) approach might be useful here. Hirokawa argues that there are three task dimensions. The first, task structure, specifies the relation between a task's goal and the path to achieving it. Tasks may be simple or complex, depending on the difficulty of the means-end path. The second dimension is the information requirement, that is, the relation between group members and the information needed to solve a problem. In some cases information is equally distributed, whereas in others it is centralized in one person. In addition, some information requires group-level processing (i.e., critical examination through discussion), whereas in other situations, information may demand less processing. The third dimension of tasks is the evaluation demand, or the means by which groups determine whether or not a particular solution is viable. Some tasks, for example, have clear and objective criteria by which a solution may be judged, whereas others have more ambiguous solution criteria.

Hirokawa (1990) uses these task dimensions to show how they affect group process. For example, simple tasks require less coordination, in which case the solution and the process used to produce it are dependent not on discussion but on other variables exogenous to discussion (e.g., status and group size). Complex tasks require that a group critically examine its information through discussion. Group outcomes, in this case, depend on the process of discussion in addition to, or perhaps in place of, "input" variables. In general, whenever the task produces complexity, ambiguity, or equivocality, discussion is assumed to be the determining factor in how a group performs.

Although Hirokawa's (1990) classification of task dimensions does not directly address how tasks affect participation, Ginter and Lindskold (1975) have shown that task ambiguity affects perceptions of leadership of high participators (see the discussion above). When tasks are not ambiguous, high participators are less likely to be perceived as leaders than in those situations where task ambiguity is high. Thus, there is evidence that the dimensions Hirokawa describes do matter for participation outcomes.

A second avenue for future research on participation antecedents and outcomes is to investigate how differences in relevant cognitions affect participation patterns and consequences. For example, work by Bottger (1984), Littlepage and Silbiger (1992), and Ginter and Lindskold (1975) has shown that expertise plays a role in several participation outcomes. People who participate more tend to be more influential, but this finding is moderated by expertise: One need not participate frequently in order to be influential if one is known to be an expert or displays task-relevant expertise during discussion. However, the role of expertise in the development of participation structures is largely unknown. What are the conditions under which experts participate more frequently than nonexperts? What are relevant displays of expertise? What is the relation between ascribed status (e.g., gender, rank, or age) and earned status (i.e., influence acquired as a function of making useful contributions to discussion)?

A third avenue for research on participation antecedents and outcomes concerns the effects of time on participation. For example, research should address how deadlines affect group processes. Brilhart and Galanes (1995) note that groups impose more structure on their meetings when they have little time in which to complete a task. This implies that opportunities to contribute are constrained by the amount of time group members have to work. In addition, research needs to address how interaction changes over the course of discussion. Some studies address time in terms of sequences of speakers (see the section on effects$_i$ above), but such time frames are very short and do not permit assessment of how participation changes as meetings progress (see Fisek & Ofshe, 1970). Finally, longitudinal studies are necessary to determine whether or not participation patterns change over the course of several meetings. Contractor and Seibold's (1993) computer simulations have demonstrated that values and norms change as groups members become more

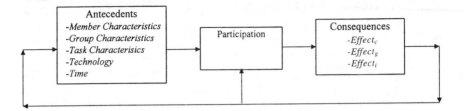

Figure 7.3. Conceptual Framework for Future Research on Participation in Small Groups

familiar with each other and the task on which they are working. Empirical research ought to investigate how changes in group norms change over time and how such changes affect opportunities to participate.

Regardless of the paths researchers choose to pursue the investigation of group participation, it is important that they remember that the relations among participation, its antecedents, and its outcomes are dynamic. Figure 7.3 shows that outcomes, antecedents, and participation constitute a feedback loop such that an individual's experience with particular group situations, tasks, and technologies has an impact on starting points for subsequent involvement in groups. Moreover, outcomes affect the development of participation structures within meetings. For example, a member who grows dissatisfied with his or her role in the group's participation structure within a particular meeting might change when and how he or she contributes to discussion as the meeting progresses. This dynamic element of participation is virtually overlooked in research on group interaction and should be included in future models of group processes.

What Role for Discourse?

Research on participation has not sufficiently attended to the role of discourse in the process of distributing turns in interaction. There are three general areas where discourse might play a role in participation. The first concerns the process by which turns are allocated in interaction. Sacks et al. (1978) specify two main methods of turn allocation: current speaker selects next speaker and other selection. In the first case, a current speaker specifies in some manner who the next speaker should be, for example, by proper name or pronominal reference (e.g., "What do you think, John?"). Current speakers may also use nonverbal methods to delimit future speakership. Kalma (1992) reports that all members of his three-person groups employed "prolonged gazes," that is, looked at another member during and after the turn in progress was completed. The person to whom the utterance and prolonged gaze were directed spoke next approximately 70% of the time. In the second method of turn allocation, no next-speaker designation is made and a kind of competition for the floor exists; usually the first person to speak is allowed to continue speaking. The upshot of this is that not all turns in discussion afford equal access to the floor. One type of turn specifies who should speak next, the other does not.

Because floor allocation is controlled by interactants themselves (Goffman, 1981; Levinson, 1988; Nofsinger, 1991) and not some outside agency (i.e., are not specified in advance by a set of rules; for an exception, see Larrue & Trognon, 1993), future research should investigate the circumstances under which certain turns are allocated to certain members as well as when and how other members take turns when the floor is open. Social actors have motivations, both personal and interactional, for allocating turns to specific others rather than leaving the floor open. For example, performance expectations (Meeker, 1994) may shape how methods of turn taking are allocated in group discussion. As discussion progresses, certain members may be explicitly given more turns because they have displayed task-relevant competence. Others, if they wish to speak, must wait to respond to those turns in which no next speaker is selected. Again, the important issue here is that certain turns offer differential probabilities regarding next speakers; models and theories of participation need to incorporate these features of turn taking.

A second area in which discourse should play a role in participation concerns how the content of discussion contributes to the development of participation hierarchies. What people say in discussion is relevant to what has preceded it (Sanders, 1987). One candidate is O'Keefe and Shepherd's (1987) analysis of topic initiation and how it shapes subsequent turns at talk by placing participants in particular interaction roles. For example, an actor produces an argument or statement that initiates a new topic (e.g., "I wish you'd be more considerate to my friends"). Common responses to this type of utterance are rebuttals or agreements (Alderton & Frey, 1983; Frey & Alderton, 1984; Seibold, McPhee, Poole, Tanita, & Canary, 1981). For this particular issue, the actor who began the exchange is the initiator, the other the respondent. What each actor does during the course of the exchange is dependent on his or her interactional role. Although O'Keefe and Shepherd's (1987) analysis is restricted to dyads, it should be a useful tool for analyzing participation in groups of three or more.[8] In group interaction, these roles of initiator and respondent should label who, over the series of subsequent turns, is expected to participate and how. Thus, future research should examine how exchanges (or other interactional phenomena) place members in particular topic-relevant participation roles.

A third area in which discourse plays a role in participation concerns the relations among member cognitions, group structure, and participation. It is generally assumed that member cognitions and group structure affect the distribution of participation, and that such distributions shape subsequent cognitions and group structures (see Figure 7.1). But these distributions of actions are actually messages, and messages differ regarding their effects on hearers (D. O'Keefe, 1990). In fact, some messages have limited impact on individual cognitions or social structures (Sanders, 1989). In other words, some utterances change how group members think about each other and the group, whereas others do not. In terms of expectation states, not all contributions to discussion affect performance expectations, which, as noted above, are assumed to affect to whom subsequent turns in discussion are awarded. Future research, then, should identify which utterances are consequential for how social actors think about subsequent participation. Identifying "critical incidents" in discussion that lead to changes in subsequent participation would allow researchers to understand more clearly the relation between interaction and cognition in group discussion.

These criticisms suggest that models of participation should be concerned with understanding how discussion and the people involved in it are responsible for distributing and acquiring opportunities to speak in group discussion. The reasons people speak when they do are complicated and are related to the topics or issues they are pursuing as well as to the people who constitute the group. New theories of participation are needed that describe the relations among group members, discourse, and turn allocation in group discussion.

NOTES

1. Pavitt (1993) suggests that the role of communication in aiding prediction of group outcomes is unclear. In many cases, group outcomes are accurately predicted by "input" variables, that is, factors external to discussion (e.g., personality, distribution of initial solution preferences, and informational demands of the task); not much is gained by examining how interaction influences the cognitions of groups as they work toward a solution. Although it is true that the role of communication in *predicting* group outcomes is ambiguous, we agree with Pavitt (1993) that every matter particular to discussion, including preference displays and information pooling, is accomplished via communicative means, and, in that sense, communication is *consequential* for the quality of decision making.

2. Nonverbal contributions to discussion are not considered here because they are virtually ignored in the literature. Some notable exceptions include Bales, Strodtbeck, Mills, and Roseborough (1951), Bales (1970), and Kalma (1992).

3. Hoffman et al. (1965) used this definition in their study of participation and influence. They found that the correlation between the time an individual spoke (i.e., total participation) and the number of solution acts contributed by that individual was quite high ($r = .92$). Thus, even though their definition might ignore some of a group's process, it seems to be a reasonable estimate of an individual's total participation.

4. For a more complete description and analysis of expectation states theory, especially as it relates to group processes, see Knottnerus (1994).

5. It should be noted that Dabbs and Ruback (1987) were unable to compare contributions made to the group across all three conditions because their method focused on only the amount of time subjects spoke and the order of speakers. No attempt was made to establish addressees for messages at the group or individual level. Thus, their analysis was limited to sequential ordering of speakers and time spent communicating.

6. Parker (1988) argues that this pattern is more or less likely for particular group members. For example, ABA might be more likely to occur than ACA; B and C differ regarding how likely they are to hold the floor with A.

7. The term *floor,* as Edelsky (1993) points out, has no clearly defined or consistent usage across a variety of literatures. Parker (1988) uses it in the most conventional sense: the time during which interactants produce discourse to which others are oriented. This definition has been challenged, most notably by Edelsky (1993), Hayashi (1991), and Morganthaler (1990), on the grounds that there are different ways in which social actors orient to the production of discourse. Parker's use of the term is aligned with the competitive model of floor; people compete for speaking time such that winners get to speak and losers remain silent. An alternate model is the collaborative floor, in which speakership is not perceived as a zero-sum game but as jointly produced. Thus, more than one speaker may hold a floor at a given time; both are perceived as having produced sets of messages.

8. Berg (1967) has offered an analysis of themes in groups that is based only on task- and relationship-oriented issues. Such schemes ignore important facets of interaction, especially the relation between what is talked about (i.e., the topic) and what group members have to contribute to it. The method proposed here is topic relevant, and the discourse roles of initiator and respondent are dependent on how a topic is pursued by the person who initiated it as well as the responses to it by other group members.

REFERENCES

Alderton, S., & Frey, L. (1983, July). *A content analytic scheme for the processual study of argumentation in decision-making groups.* Paper presented at the Third Summer Conference on Argumentation, Alta, UT.

Bales, R. F. (1950). *Interaction process analysis.* Reading, MA: Addison-Wesley.

Bales, R. F. (1970). *Personality and interpersonal behavior.* New York: Holt, Rinehart & Winston.

Bales, R. F., & Borgatta, E. F. (1953). Interaction of individuals in reconstituted groups. *Sociometry, 16,* 302-320.

Bales, R. F., Strodtbeck, F. L., Mills, T. M., & Roseborough, M. E. (1951). Channels of communication in small groups. *American Sociological Review, 16,* 461-468.

Balkwell, J. W. (1991). From expectations to behavior: An improved postulate for expectation states theory. *American Sociological Review, 56,* 355-369.

Balkwell, J. W. (1994). Status. In M. Foschi & E. J. Lawler (Eds.), *Group processes: Sociological analyses* (pp. 119-148). Chicago: Nelson-Hall.

Balkwell, J. W. (1995). Strong tests of expectation-states hypotheses. *Social Psychology Quarterly, 58,* 44-51.

Bass, B. M., McGehee, C. R., Hawkins, W. C., Young, P. C., & Gebel, A. S. (1953). Personality variables related to leaderless group discussion. *Journal of Abnormal and Social Psychology, 48,* 120-128.

Bass, B. M., Wurster, C. R., Doll, P. A., & Clair, D. J. (1953). Situational and personality factors in leadership among sorority women. *Psychological Monographs, 67*(Whole No. 366).

Berg, D. M. (1967). A descriptive analysis of the distribution and duration of themes discussed by task-oriented small groups. *Speech Monographs, 34,* 172-175.

Berger, C. R., & Kellerman, K. (1994). Acquiring social information. In J. A. Daly & J. M. Wiemann (Eds.), *Strategic interpersonal communication* (pp. 1-32). Hillsdale, NJ: Lawrence Erlbaum.

Berger, J., Cohen, B. P., & Zelditch, M., Jr. (1966). Status characteristics and expectation states. In J. Berger, M. Zelditch, Jr., & B. Anderson (Eds.), *Sociological theories in progress* (Vol. 1, pp. 29-46). Boston: Houghton-Mifflin.

Berger, J., & Conner, T. L. (1969). Performance expectations and behavior in small groups. *Acta Sociologica, 12,* 189-198.

Berger, J., Fisek, M. H., Norman, R. Z., & Zelditch, M., Jr. (Eds.). (1977). *Status characteristics and social interaction: An expectation-states approach.* New York: Elsevier.

Berger, J., & Zelditch, M., Jr. (1977). Status characteristics and social interaction: The status-organizing process. In J. Berger, M. H. Fisek, R. Z. Norman, & M. Zelditch, Jr. (Eds.), *Status characteristics and social interaction: An expectation-states approach* (pp. 3-87). New York: Elsevier.

Bloom, J. R. (1980). Status characteristics, leadership consensus and decision-making among nurses. *Social Science and Medicine, 14,* 15-22.

Bottger, P. C. (1984). Expertise and air time as bases of actual and perceived influence in problem-solving groups. *Journal of Applied Psychology, 69,* 214-221.

Brilhart, J. K. & Galanes, G. J. (1995). *Effective group discussion* (8th ed.). Madison, WI: William C. Brown/Benchmark.

Burke, J. A. (1982). *An analysis of intelligibility in a practical activity.* Unpublished doctoral dissertation, University of Illinois, Urbana-Champaign.

Burke, J. A. (1986). Interacting plans in the accomplishment of a practical activity. In D. G. Ellis & W. A. Donohue (Eds.), *Contemporary issues in language and discourse processes* (pp. 203-222). Hillsdale, NJ: Lawrence Erlbaum.

Burke, P. J. (1974). Participation and leadership in small groups. *American Sociological Review, 39,* 832-843.

Clapper, D. L., McLean, E. R., & Watson, R. T. (1991). An experimental investigation of the effect of group decision support on normative influence in small groups. In J. I. De Gross, I. Benbasat, G. DeSanctis, & C. M. Beath (Eds.), *Proceedings of the Twelfth International Conference on Information Systems* (pp. 273-282). New York: Association for Computing Machinery.

Clark, H. H., & Schaefer, E. F. (1989). Contributing to discourse. *Cognitive Science, 13,* 259-294.

Clark, H. H., & Wilkes-Gibbs, D. (1986). Referring as a collaborative process. *Cognition, 22,* 1-39.

Coleman, J. S. (1960). The mathematical study of small groups. In H. Solomon (Ed.), *Mathematical thinking in the measurement of behavior* (pp. 7-149). Glencoe, IL: Free Press.

Conner, T. L. (1977). Performance expectations and the initiation of problem solving attempts. *Journal of Mathematical Sociology, 5,* 187-198.

Contractor, N. S., & Seibold, D. R. (1993). Theoretical frameworks for the study of structuring processes in group decision support systems. *Human Communication Research, 19,* 528-563.

Craig, R. T., & Tracy, K. (Eds.). (1983). *Conversational coherence.* Beverly Hills, CA: Sage.

Dabbs, J. M., Jr., & Ruback, R. B. (1984). Vocal patterns in male and female groups. *Personality and Social Psychology Bulletin, 10,* 518-525.

Dabbs, J. M., Jr., & Ruback, R. B. (1987). Dimensions of group process: Amount and structure of group interaction. In L. Berkowitz (Ed.), *Advances in experimental social psychology* (Vol. 20, pp. 123-169). San Diego, CA: Academic Press.

Dabbs, J. M., Jr., Ruback, R. B., & Evans, M. S. (1987). Grouptalk: Patterns of sounds and silence in group conversation. In A. W. Siegman & S. Feldstein (Eds.), *Nonverbal behavior and communication* (2nd ed., pp. 501-520). Hillsdale, NJ: Lawrence Erlbaum.

Daly, B. (1993). The influence of face-to-face versus computer-mediated communication channels on collective induction. *Accounting, Management and Information Technology, 3*(1), 1-22.

Daly, J. A., & McCroskey, J. C. (Eds.). (1984). *Avoiding communication: Shyness, reticence, and communication apprehension.* Beverly Hills, CA: Sage.

Davis, J. H. (1992). Some compelling intuitions about group consensus decisions, theoretical and empirical research, and interpersonal aggregation phenomena: Selected examples, 1950-1990. *Organizational Behavior and Human Decision Processes, 52,* 3-38.

Dossett, D. L., Latham, G. P., & Mitchell, T. R. (1979). Effects of assigned versus participatively set goals, knowledge of results, and individual differences on employee behavior when goal difficulty is held constant. *Journal of Applied Psychology, 64,* 291-298.

Dubrovsky, V. J., Kiesler, S., & Sethna, B. N. (1991). The equalization phenomenon: Status effects in computer-mediated and face-to-face decision making groups. *Human-Computer Interaction, 6,* 119-146.

Edelsky, C. (1993). Who's got the floor? In D. Tannen (Ed.), *Gender and conversational interaction* (pp. 189-227). New York: Oxford University Press.

Fisek, M. H., Berger, J., & Norman, R. Z. (1991). Participation in hetero- and homogeneous groups: A theoretical integration. *American Journal of Sociology, 97,* 114-142.

Fisek, M. H., & Ofshe, R. (1970). The process of status evolution. *Sociometry, 33,* 327-357.

Frey, L., & Alderton, S. (1984, November). *Studying small groups processually: Some promising themes, schemes, and other means.* Paper presented at the annual meeting of the Speech Communication Association, Chicago.

Gastil, J. (1993). *Democracy in small groups.* Philadelphia: New Society.

George, J., Easton, G., Nunamaker, J., & Northcraft, G. (1990). A study of collaborative group work with and without computer-based support. *Information Systems Research, 1,* 394-415.

Ginter, G., & Lindskold, S. (1975). Rate of participation and expertise as factors influencing leader choice. *Journal of Personality and Social Psychology, 32,* 1085-1089.

Goetsch, G. G., & McFarland, D. D. (1980). Models of the distribution of acts in small group discussion. *Social Psychology Quarterly, 43,* 173-183.

Goffman, E. (1981). *Forms of talk.* Philadelphia: University of Pennsylvania Press.

Goodwin, C. (1984). Notes on story structure and the organization of participation. In J. M. Atkinson & J. Heritage (Eds.), *Structures of social action* (pp. 225-246). Cambridge: Cambridge University Press.

Goodwin, C. (1987). Forgetfulness as an interactive resource. *Social Psychology Quarterly, 50,* 115-131.

Gouran, D. S., Hirokawa, R. Y., Julian, K. M., & Leatham, G. B. (1993). The evolution and current status of the functional perspective on communication in decision-making and problem-solving groups. In S. A. Deetz (Ed.), *Communication yearbook 16* (pp. 573-600). Newbury Park, CA: Sage.

Grice, H. P. (1975). Logic and conversation. In P. Cole & J. Morgan (Eds.), *Syntax and semantics 3: Speech acts* (pp. 41-58). New York: Academic Press.

Hayashi, R. (1991). Floor structure in conversation. *Journal of Pragmatics, 16,* 1-30.

Hayes, D. P., & Meltzer, L. (1972). Interpersonal judgments based on talkativeness: Fact or artifact? *Sociometry, 35,* 538-561.

Hiltz, S. R., Johnson, K., & Turoff, M. (1986). Experiments in group decision making, 1: Communications process and outcome in face-to-face vs. computerized conferences. *Human Communication Research, 13,* 225-252.

Hirokawa, R. Y. (1990). The role of communication in group decision-making efficacy: A task contingency perspective. *Small Group Research, 21,* 190-204.

Hoffman, L. R., Burke, R. J., & Maier, N. R. F. (1965). Participation, influence, and satisfaction among members of problem solving groups. *Psychological Reports, 16,* 661-667.

Hoffman, L. R., & Maier, N. R. F. (1979). Valence in the adoption of solutions by problem-solving groups: Concept, method, and results. In L. R. Hoffman (Ed.), *The group problem solving process* (pp. 17-30). New York: Praeger.

Hollingshead, A. B. (1993). *Information, influence, and technology in group decision making.* Unpublished doctoral dissertation, University of Illinois, Urbana-Champaign.

Hollingshead, A. B. (1996). Information suppression and status persistence in group decision making: The effects of communication media. *Human Communication Research, 23,* 2.

Hollingshead, A. B., & McGrath, J. E. (1995). The whole is less than the sum of its parts: A critical review of research on computer-assisted groups. In R. A. Guzzo & E. Salas (Eds.), *Team effectiveness and decision making in organizations* (pp. 46-78). San Francisco: Jossey-Bass.

Hollingshead, A. B., McGrath, J. E., & O'Connor, K. M. (1993). Group task performance and communication technology: A longitudinal study of computer-mediated vs. face-to-face work groups. *Small Group Research, 24,* 307-333.

Horvath, W. J. (1965). A mathematical model of participation in small groups. *Behavioral Science, 10,* 164-166.

Isaacs, E. A., & Clark, H. H. (1987). References in conversation between experts and novices. *Journal of Experimental Psychology: General, 116,* 26-37.

Jacobs, S. (1985). Language. In M. L. Knapp & G. R. Miller (Eds.), *Handbook of interpersonal communication* (pp. 313-343). Beverly Hills, CA: Sage.

Jaffe, C. L., & Lucas, R. L. (1969). Effects of rates of talking and correctness of decisions on leader choice in small groups. *Journal of Social Psychology, 79,* 247-254.

Kadane, J. B., & Lewis, G. (1969). The distribution of participation in group discussions: An empirical and theoretical reappraisal. *American Sociological Review, 34,* 710-722.

Kadane, J. B., Lewis, G., & Ramage, J. G. (1969). Horvath's theory of participation in group discussions. *Sociometry, 32,* 348-361.

Kalma, A. (1992). Gazing in triads: A powerful signal in floor apportionment. *British Journal of Sociology, 31,* 21-39.

Keller, J. B. (1951). Comments on "Channels of communication in small groups." *American Sociological Review, 16,* 842-843.

Kirchmeyer, C. (1993). Multicultural task groups: An account of the low contribution level of minorities. *Small Group Research, 24,* 127-148.

Knottnerus, J. D. (1994). Expectations states theory and the analysis of group processes and structures. In J. D. Knottnerus & C. Prendergast (Eds.), *Current perspectives in social theory: Recent developments in the theory of social structure* (Suppl. 1, pp. 49-74). Greenwich, CT: JAI.

Koomen, W., & Sagel, P. K. (1977). The prediction of participation in two-person groups. *Sociometry, 40,* 369-373.

Larrue, J., & Trognon, A. (1993). Organization of turn-taking and mechanisms for turn-taking repairs in a chaired meeting. *Journal of Pragmatics, 19,* 177-196.

Latham, G. P., & Marshall, H. A. (1982). The effects of self-set, participatively set and assigned goals on the performance of government employees. *Personnel Psychology, 35,* 399-404.

Latham, G. P., Mitchell, T. R., & Dossett, D. L. (1978). Importance of participative goal setting and anticipated rewards on goal difficulty and job performance. *Journal of Applied Psychology, 63,* 163-171.

Latham, G. P., & Steele, T. P. (1983). The motivational effects of participation versus goal setting on performance. *Academy of Management Journal, 26,* 406-417.

Lea, M., & Spears, R. (1991). Computer-mediated communication, de-individuation, and group decision making. *International Journal of Man-Machine Studies, 34,* 283-301.

Leik, R. K. (1965). Type of group and the probability of initiating acts. *Sociometry, 28,* 57-65.

Leik, R. K. (1967). The distribution of acts in small groups. *Sociometry, 30,* 280-299.

Levinson, S. C. (1983). *Pragmatics.* Cambridge: Cambridge University Press.

Levinson, S. C. (1988). Putting linguistics on a proper footing: Explorations in Goffman's concepts of participation. In P. Drew & A. Wooten (Eds.), *Erving Goffman: Exploring the interaction order* (pp. 161-227). Boston: Northeastern University Press.

Littlepage, G. E., & Silbiger, H. (1992). Recognition of expertise in decision-making groups: Effects of group size and participation patterns. *Small Group Research, 23,* 344-355.

Markel, N. N., Bein, M. F., Campbell, W. W., & Shaw, M. E. (1976). The relationship between self-rating of expressed inclusion and speaking time. *Language and Speech, 19,* 117-120.

McCroskey, J. C., & Richmond, V. P. (1988). Communication apprehension and small group communication. In R. S. Cathcart & L. A. Samovar (Eds.), *Small group communication: A reader* (5th ed., pp. 405-419). Dubuque, IA: William C. Brown.

McGrath, J. E. (1984). *Groups: Interaction and performance.* Englewood Cliffs, NJ: Prentice Hall.

McGrath, J. E. (1990). Time matters in groups. In J. Galegher, R. Kraut, & C. Egido (Eds.), *Intellectual teamwork: Social and technological foundations of cooperative work* (pp. 23-61). Hillsdale, NJ: Lawrence Erlbaum.

McGrath, J. E., & Hollingshead, A. B. (1993). Putting the "group" back into group support systems: Some theoretical issues about dynamic processes in groups with technological enhancements. In L. M. Jessup & J. S. Valachich (Eds.), *Group support systems: New perspectives* (pp. 78-96). New York: MacMillan.

McGrath, J. E., & Hollingshead, A. B. (1994). *Groups interacting with technology.* Thousand Oaks, CA: Sage.

McLeod, P. L. (1992). An assessment of the experimental literature on the electronic support of group work: Results of a meta-analysis. *Human-Computer Interaction, 7,* 257-280.

McLeod, P. L., & Liker, J. K. (1992). Electronic meeting systems: Evidence from a low structure environment. *Information Systems Research, 3,* 195-223.

Meeker, B. F. (1994). Performance evaluation. In M. Foschi & E. J. Lawler (Eds.), *Group processes: Sociological analyses* (pp. 95-117). Chicago: Nelson-Hall.

Moreland, R. L., & Levine, J. M. (1992). The composition of small groups. In E. J. Lawler, B. Markovsky, C. Ridgeway, & H. Walker (Eds.), *Advances in group processes* (Vol. 9, pp. 237-280). Greenwich, CT: JAI.

Morganthaler, L. (1990). Who's got WHAT floor? *Journal of Pragmatics, 14,* 537-557.

Nofsinger, R. E. (1991). *Everyday conversation.* Newbury Park, CA: Sage.

Nowakasowa, M. (1978). A model of participation in group discussion. *Behavioral Science, 23,* 209-212.

O'Keefe, B. J., & Shepherd, G. J. (1987). The pursuit of multiple objectives in face-to-face persuasive interactions: Effects of construct differentiation on message organization. *Communication Monographs, 54,* 396-419.

O'Keefe, D. J. (1990). *Persuasion: Theory and research.* Newbury Park, CA: Sage.

Parker, K. H. C. (1988). Speaking turns in small group interaction: A context-sensitive event sequence model. *Journal of Personality and Social Psychology, 54,* 965-971.

Pauchet, C. (1982). Speaking time during the university teaching and research council's meetings [CD-ROM]. *Revue-Française-de-Sociologie, 23,* 275-282. Abstract from: Sociofile

Pavitt, C. (1993). Does communication matter in social influence during small group discussion? Five positions. *Communication Studies, 44,* 216-227.

Poole, M. S. (1983a). Decision development in small groups II: A study of multiple sequences in group development. *Communication Monographs, 50,* 206-232.

Poole, M. S. (1983b). Decision development in small groups III: A multiple sequence model of group decision development. *Communication Monographs, 50,* 321-342.

Poole, M. S., & Roth, J. (1988a). Decision development in small groups IV: A typology of group decision paths. *Human Communication Research, 15,* 323-356.

Poole, M. S., & Roth, J. (1988b). Decision development in small groups V: Test of a contingency model. *Human Communication Research, 15,* 549-589.

Rice, R. E. (1984). Mediated group communication. In R. E. Rice & Associates (Eds.), *The new media: Communication, research, and technology* (pp. 129-154). Beverly Hills, CA: Sage.

Riecken, H. W. (1958). The effects of talkativeness on ability to influence group solutions to problems. *Sociometry, 21,* 309-321.

Ruback, R. B., Dabbs, J. M., Jr., & Hopper, C. H. (1984). The process of brainstorming: An analysis with individual and group vocal parameters. *Journal of Personality and Social Psychology, 47,* 558-567.

Sacks, H., Schegloff, E. A., & Jefferson, G. (1978). A simplest systematics for the organization of turn-taking for conversation. In J. Schenkein (Ed.), *Studies in the organization of turn-taking for conversation* (pp. 7-55). New York: Academic Press.

Sanders, R. E. (1987). *Cognitive foundations of calculated speech.* Albany: State University of New York Press.

Sanders, R. E. (1989). Message effects via induced changes in the social meaning of a response. In J. Bradac (Ed.), *Message effects in communication science* (pp. 165-194). London: Sage.

Schegloff, E. A. (1988). Goffman and the analysis of conversation. In P. Drew & A. Wooten (Eds.), *Erving Goffman: Exploring the interaction order* (pp. 89-135). Boston: Northeastern University Press.

Seibold, D. R., McPhee, R. D., Poole, M. S., Tanita, N., & Canary, D. J. (1981). Argument, group influence, and decision outcomes. In G. Ziegelmueller & J. Rhodes (Eds.), *Dimensions of argument: Proceedings of the Second Summer Conference on Argumentation* (pp. 663-692). Annandale, VA: Speech Communication Association.

Shaw, M. E. (1959). Some effects of individually prominent behavior upon group effectiveness and member satisfaction. *Journal of Abnormal and Social Psychology, 59,* 382-386.

Shaw, M. E. (1971). *Group dynamics: The psychology of group behavior.* New York: McGraw-Hill.

Siegel, J., Dubrovsky, V. J., Kiesler, S., & McGuire, T. W. (1986). Group processes in computer-mediated communication. *Organizational Behavior and Human Decision Processes, 37,* 157-187.

Sigman, S. J. (1984). Talk and interaction strategy in a task-oriented group. *Small Group Behavior, 15,* 33-51.

Skvoretz, J. (1981). Extending expectation states theory: Comparative status models of participation in *n* person groups. *Social Forces, 59,* 752-770.

Skvoretz, J. (1988). Models of participation in status-differentiated groups. *Social Psychology Quarterly, 51,* 43-57.

Skvoretz, J., & Fararo, T. J. (1996). Status and participation in task groups: A dynamic model. *American Journal of Sociology, 101,* 1366-1414.

Smith-Lovin, L., Skvoretz, J. V., & Hudson, C. G. (1986). Status and participation in six-person groups: A test of Skvoretz's comparative status model. *Social Forces, 64,* 992-1005.

Sorrentino, R. M., & Boutillier, R. G. (1975). The effect of quantity and quality of verbal interaction on ratings of leadership. *Journal of Experimental Social Psychology, 11,* 403-411.

Spears, R., & Lea, M. (1992). Social influence and the influence of the "social" in computer-mediated communication. In M. Lea (Ed.), *Contexts of computer-mediated communication.* London: Harvester-Wheatsheaf.

Spears, R., & Lea, M. (1994). Panacea or panopticon? The hidden power in computer-mediated communication. *Communication Research, 21,* 427-459.

Sproull, L. S., & Kiesler, S. (1991). *Connections: New ways of working in the networked organization.* Cambridge: MIT Press.

Stasser, G., & Taylor, L. A. (1991). Speaking turns in face-to-face discussion. *Journal of Personality and Social Psychology, 60,* 675-684.

Stasser, G., Taylor, L. A., & Hanna, C. (1989). Information sampling in structured and unstructured discussions of three- and six-person groups. *Journal of Personality and Social Psychology, 57,* 67-78.

Stasser, G., & Titus, W. (1985). Pooling of unshared information in group decision making: Biased information sampling during discussion. *Journal of Personality and Social Psychology, 48,* 1467-1478.

Stein, R. T., & Heller, T. (1979). Empirical analysis of the correlations between leadership status and participation rates reported in the literature. *Journal of Personality and Social Psychology, 37,* 583-596.

Stephan, F. F. (1952). The relative rate of communication between members of small groups. *American Sociological Review, 17,* 482-486.

Stephan, F. F., & Mishler, E. G. (1952). The distribution of participation in small groups: An exponential approximation. *American Sociological Review, 17,* 598-608.

Straus, S., & McGrath, J. E. (1994). Does the medium matter? The interaction of task type and technology on group performance and member reactions. *Journal of Applied Psychology, 79,* 87-97.

Strodtbeck, F. L. (1980). *A study of husband-wife interaction in three cultures.* New York: Arno.

Tammivara, J. S. (1982). The effect of task structure on beliefs about competence and participation in small groups. *Sociology of Education, 55,* 212-222.

Tannen, D. (1993). The relativity of linguistic strategies: Rethinking power and solidarity in gender and dominance. In D. Tannen (Ed.), *Gender and conversational interaction* (pp. 165-188). New York: Oxford University Press.

Tsai, Y. (1977). Hierarchical structure of participation in natural groups. *Behavioral Science, 22,* 38-40.

Walther, J. B., Anderson, J. F., & Park, D. W. (1994). Interpersonal effects in computer-mediated interaction: A meta-analysis of social and antisocial communication. *Communication Research, 21,* 460-487.

Watson, R., DeSanctis, G., & Poole, M. S. (1988). Using a GDSS to facilitate group consensus: Some intended and unintended consequences. *Management Information Systems Quarterly, 12,* 463-478.

Weisband, S. P. (1992). Group discussion and first advocacy effects in computer-mediated and face-to-face decision making groups. *Organizational Behavior and Human Decision Processes, 53,* 352-380.

Weisband, S. P., Schneider, S. K., & Connolly, T. (1995). Electronic communication and social information: Status salience and status differences. *Academy of Management Journal, 38,* 1124-1151.

Willard, D., & Strodtbeck, F. L. (1972). Latency of verbal response and participation in small groups. *Sociometry, 35,* 161-175.

Yetton, P., & Crawford, M. (1992). Reassessment of participative decision-making: A case of too much participation. In F. Heller (Ed.), *Decision-making and leadership* (pp. 90-111). Cambridge: Cambridge University Press.

Zeleny, L. D. (1939). Characteristics of group leaders. *Sociology and Social Research, 24,* 140-149.

Zigurs, I., Poole, M., & DeSanctis, G. (1988). A study of influence in computer-mediated group decision making. *Management Information Systems Quarterly, 12,* 625-644.

CHAPTER CONTENTS

8 Social and Communicative Anxiety: A Review and Meta-Analysis

MILES L. PATTERSON
University of Missouri-St. Louis

VICKI RITTS
St. Louis Community College-Meramec

This chapter provides a comprehensive review and meta-analysis of the empirical research on social and communicative anxiety. First, in laying the groundwork for their review, the authors show that there is considerable evidence that a variety of different scales of trait social and communicative anxiety are highly correlated and, consequently, appear to be measuring a common construct. In order to assess the relationships between social anxiety and various physiological, behavioral, and cognitive measures, the authors conducted a meta-analysis of the empirical studies. The results of the meta-analysis indicate consistently large effects of social anxiety on a wide variety of cognitive and behavioral measures, but somewhat smaller effects on physiological measures of arousal. A substantive review of this literature supplements the meta-analysis, examining the links between social anxiety and specific physiological, behavioral, and cognitive reactions. Finally, the authors discuss contrasting theoretical explanations relating trait social anxiety, physiological arousal, behavior, and cognitive reactions to the experience of social anxiety.

I N recent years, the topic of social and communicative anxiety has been the focus of extensive empirical research. Previous reviews of this literature have emphasized selected aspects of this research, such as different test measures of (e.g., Leary, 1982), cognitions related to social and communicative anxiety and (e.g., Cheek & Melchior, 1990) specific manifestations of social anxiety, such as dating anxiety (Hope & Heimberg, 1990).

The primary purpose of this chapter is to provide a meta-analysis and comprehensive review of the empirical research on social and communicative anxiety. In addition to the meta-analysis and substantive review, we also

Correspondence and requests for reprints: Miles L. Patterson, Department of Psychology, University of Missouri, 8001 Natural Bridge Road, St. Louis, MO 63121-4499.

Communication Yearbook 20, pp. 263-303

examine the dynamics underlying the experience of anxiety in interactions. This review focuses specifically on the physiological, behavioral, and cognitive correlates of social and communicative anxiety. Because a number of different scales have been used to measure social and communicative anxiety, our first concern is to determine if these various scales are, in fact, measuring a common construct.

SCALE MEASURES OF
SOCIAL AND COMMUNICATIVE ANXIETY

Although there are a number of different theoretical approaches to social and communicative anxiety (Buss, 1980; Leary, 1983c; McCroskey, 1977, 1984; Schlenker & Leary, 1982; Trower & Gilbert, 1989), the most general description of the construct is as follows: the anxiety precipitated by social situations, or by the prospect of being in such situations. As Leary (1991) emphasizes, the focus is on the subjective reaction or feeling component, even though social anxiety may also be accompanied by distinct behavioral reactions.

Most scale measures of social and communicative anxiety focus on the disposition or trait that identifies the habitual tendency to experience anxiety in social situations (Leary, 1983c, pp. 28-30; McCroskey, 1977). Presumably, trait social or communicative anxiety is the relatively enduring, cross-situational, individual difference variable that predisposes people to experience state anxiety in specific social circumstances. Thus, individuals who are dispositionally anxious do not always experience state anxiety and, conversely, individuals who are dispositionally nonanxious may sometimes experience state anxiety. Nevertheless, when both state and trait measures are assessed, the two are highly correlated (e.g., Booth-Butterfield & Gould, 1986; S. Daly, 1978). Theories differ, of course, on the specific mechanisms mediating the experience of social and communicative anxiety and on the importance of and links among physiological, cognitive, and behavioral components. These different mechanisms will be examined more closely later.

A number of different terms are used to refer to the experience of anxiety in social settings, including *shyness, communication apprehension, reticence, evaluation anxiety, dating anxiety, social-communicative anxiety,* and *interpersonal anxiousness.* Although these terms are not synonymous, all involve some aspect of social and communicative anxiety (Daly & Stafford, 1984; Leary, 1982, 1983a, 1986a, 1990; Leary & Kowalski, 1993).

Table 8.1 provides a summary of the studies reporting correlations among eight commonly used measures of social and communicative anxiety: the Social Avoidance and Distress Scale (Watson & Friend, 1969), the Fear of Negative Evaluation Scale (Watson & Friend, 1969), the Social Anxiety Subscale of the Self-Consciousness Scale (Fenigstein, Scheier, & Buss, 1975), the Interaction Anxiety Scale (Leary, 1983b), the Cheek and Buss Shyness

TABLE 8.1
Correlations Between Common Social Anxiety Measures

	SAD	FNE	SCS-SA	IAS	CB-SHY	PRCS	SRS
FNE	.71[a]						
	.50[h]						
	.51[m]						
	.46[s]						
	.64[g]						
	.59[b]						
	.65[u]						
SCS-SA	.74[d]	.65[t]					
IAS	.52[n]	.41[k]	.78[k]				
	.73[k]	.64[p]	.78[h]				
	.75[h]	.52[h]	.78[o]				
	.71[o]	.32[l]					
		.32[m]					
		.44[o]					
		.55[q]					
CB-SHY	.70[n]	.51[h]	.72[c]	.69[n]			
	.77[h]		.47[q]	.88[k]			
				.88[l]			
				.88[o]			
				.83[q]			
PRCS	.63[d]	.37[e]		.63[i]			
	.44[e]						
SRS	.72[h]	.45[h]		.78[h]	.79[h]		
	.76[r]						
PRCA	.54[d]					.88[d]	.68[i]
							.76[j]

NOTE: SAD = Social Avoidance and Distress Scale (Watson & Friend, 1969), FNE = Fear of Negative Evaluation (Watson & Friend, 1969), SCS-SA = Social Anxiety Subscale of the Self-Consciousness Scale (Fenigstein et al., 1975), IAS = Interaction Anxiety Scale (Leary, 1983b), CB-SHY = Cheek and Buss Shyness Scale (Cheek & Buss, 1981), PRCS = Personal Report of Confidence of a Speaker (Paul, 1966), SRS = Social Reticence Scale (Jones & Russell, 1982), PRCA = Personal Report of Communication Apprehension (McCroskey, 1978). Superscripts indicate the sources of the figures in the table.
a. Arkowitz et al. (1975).
b. Beidel et al. (1993).
c. Cheek (1982).
d. J. A. Daly (1978).
e. Deffenbacher et al. (1986).
f. Edelmann (1990).
g. Johnson et al. (1992).
h. Jones et al. (1986).
i. Kelly (1982).
j. Kelly and Keaton (1992).
k. Leary (1983b).
l. Leary (1987).
m. Leary (1991).
n. Leary et al. (1986).
o. Leary and Kowalski (1993).
p. Leary and Meadows (1991).
q. Miller (1995).
r. Montgomery et al. (1991).
s. Morris et al. (1981).
t. Schlenker and Leary (1982).
u. Strauman and Higgins (1988).

Scale (Cheek & Buss, 1981), the Personal Report of Confidence of a Speaker (Paul, 1966), the Social Reticence Scale (Jones & Russell, 1982), and the Personal Report of Communication Apprehension (McCroskey, 1970, 1978, 1982; Richmond & McCroskey, 1992). These scales usually focus on trait or dispositional anxiety, but they can be modified to assess state anxiety.

Although some of the scales shown in Table 8.1 emphasize affective aspects of anxiety, whereas other scales measure both affective and behavioral components, the correlations indicate that the various scales are highly related. With the exception of Watson and Friend's (1969) Fear of Negative Evaluation scale, all of the measures are moderately to highly ($.44 < r < .88$) correlated with one another. Thus, in spite of the considerable range of labels and measures, the moderate to high correlations across scales suggest that there is substantial convergence in what is actually being assessed (Anderson & Harvey, 1988; J. A. Daly, 1978; Jones, Briggs, & Smith, 1986; Kelly, 1982; Leary, 1983c). Consequently, in the remainder of this chapter we simply use the term *social anxiety* to refer to this characteristic.

Furthermore, from an empirical standpoint it appears to make little difference which scale is used (Leary, 1991). For this reason, we will not be distinguishing among the various scales of social anxiety. Nevertheless, as Leary (1983a, 1991) notes, some measures are more appropriate than others for particular research purposes, and researchers should select their measures based on the goals of their studies. In the next section, we begin our review of the correlates of social anxiety with a description of the meta-analysis of social anxiety effects on physiological, cognitive, and behavioral reactions.

META-ANALYSIS

Meta-analysis is a statistical procedure that combines independent results across studies to obtain an estimate of the overall strength of the relationship between variables. In this case, our goal was to provide a quantitative assessment of the strength of the relationship between social anxiety and various physiological, behavioral, and cognitive measures.

Literature Search

The literature search was conducted on studies published between 1968 and the end of 1994 using the following sources in communication and psychology: COMINDEX, *Communication Abstracts, Index to Journals in Communication,* PsycINFO, PsycLIT, *Psychological Abstracts, Wilson Indexes,* ERIC, and *PsychFirst.* In conducting the literature search, the following key words were used: social anxiety, shyness, communication apprehension, reticence, interpersonal anxiety, evaluation apprehension, dating anxiety, and socio-communicative anxiety. In addition, the most recent issues of relevant journals were searched through the first few months of 1995. Finally, the reference sections of the articles we found were also examined for additional studies that might be included.

Analysis

The meta-analysis was accomplished in two steps. First, in the studies with the appropriate summary statistics, the overall effect size (d; Cohen, 1977) was calculated for social anxiety on each of the dependent measures. The mean and the variance of the effect size estimates were calculated for each of the dependent measures. Next, the expected variance due to sampling error was subtracted from the observed variance, using the procedure outlined by Hunter, Schmidt, and Jackson (1982, 1990). For studies in which no differences were found but the appropriate statistics were not reported and d could not be computed directly, d was estimated as equal to zero.

Results

Table 8.2 identifies the general response category (physiological, behavioral, and cognitive), the total number of effect size tests and subjects, and their associated weighted grand mean ds. Within each general category, the specific response measures, the number of effect size tests for each measure, the total number of subjects, and the average d values are presented. Across all of the measures, there were 380 effect tests involving over 38,000 subjects.

The majority of studies represented in Table 8.2 did not examine gender differences in social anxiety. For the few specific measures on which there were enough tests to make gender comparisons (verbal output, negative thoughts, negative self-ratings, and evaluations by others), the average d values were virtually identical for males and females. Consequently, gender comparisons are not included in the table.

The most obvious characteristic of the values in the table is that, with two exceptions (heart rate and self-attribution), all of the specific ds represent large effect sizes (Cohen, 1977). (The articles from which the effect sizes were computed are identified in the reference section with asterisks.)

Physiological correlates. In the meta-analysis of the physiological correlates, the single effect size on blood pressure was combined with those on heart rate. The effect sizes for the smaller group of studies on blushing were averaged separately. From Table 8.2 it is clear that the relationship between social anxiety and blushing ($d = .99$) was stronger than that between social anxiety and heart rate ($d = .55$).

Behavioral correlates. Because several specific measures had too few effect size values to be reliable, related measures were combined to form new categories. First, measures of speech disfluencies and self-manipulation, characteristic of increased arousal, were combined to form an arousal-mediated behavior category ($d = .86$). Second, verbal output and initiating conversation

TABLE 8.2
Effect Sizes of Social Anxiety on
Physiological, Behavioral, and Cognitive Measures

Measure	k^a	Total N	Mean d^b
Physiological responses	(28)	(2,203)	(.77)
heart rate	23	1,535	.55
blushing	5	668	.99
Behavioral responses	(120)	(11,205)	(.88)
arousal-mediated behaviors	23	1,445	.86
verbal involvement	40	3,346	.81
nonverbal involvement	26	1,769	.99
avoidance of others	20	3,673	.89
protective self-presentation	11	972	.85
Cognitive responses	(232)	(27,195)	(1.05)
self-focus	9	677	1.26
negative thoughts	34	4,153	1.18
negative self-ratings	78	9,436	.90
evaluation apprehension	19	2,505	.83
self-efficacy	35	3,760	1.56
evaluation by others	27	3,407	1.11
self-attribution	14	1,513	.66
irrational beliefs	8	1,074	1.00
memory effects	8	670	.99

NOTE: Cumulative values for general categories are shown in parentheses.
a. k is the number of effect size tests.
b. According to Cohen (1977), effect sizes from .20 to .50 may be described as small, from .50 to .80 as moderate, and greater than .80 as large.

were combined to form a verbal involvement measure ($d = .81$). Third, gaze and distance measures were combined into the category of nonverbal involvement ($d = .99$). Next, measures of relationships and avoidance of encounters were combined into an avoidance of others category ($d = .89$). Finally, measures of cautious self-description, similarity, conformity, and innocuous sociability were identified as a protective self-presentation category ($d = .90$). It is interesting that, although the behaviors represented here are quite diverse, the range of mean effect sizes was relatively small (.81 to .99).

Cognitive correlates. With only one exception, large effect sizes were also found for all of cognitive dependent measures. A few specific results might be highlighted here. The largest effect size was for self-efficacy ($d = 1.56$) and the smallest for self-attribution ($d = .66$). Effect sizes for the remaining measures ranged from $d = .83$ (evaluation apprehension) to $d = 1.26$ (self-focus).

Summary

The results of the meta-analysis clearly show that social anxiety is more strongly related to the cognitive measures than to the behavioral and physiological measures. This pattern suggests that a variety of negative self-focused cognitions may be at the core of social anxiety. Nevertheless, some caution is warranted because both trait and state measures of social anxiety and the various cognitive correlates of social anxiety are all assessed by self-report measures. That is, these self-report measures share a common method variance that is necessarily absent in the relationships between social anxiety and the behavioral and physiological correlates (Campbell & Fiske, 1959). Thus, the results reported here may overestimate the true strength of the relationship between social anxiety and the various cognitive measures.

In the next section, we go beyond these quantitative estimates in an attempt to understand the specific relationships of social anxiety to the physiological, cognitive, and behavioral measures. This substantive review will, in turn, facilitate a consideration of theoretical alternatives linking dispositional social anxiety to state social anxiety and its manifestation in physiological, cognitive, and behavioral reactions.

PHYSIOLOGICAL CORRELATES OF SOCIAL ANXIETY

Anxiety is often accompanied by arousal of the sympathetic nervous system, resulting in increases in heart rate, respiration, blood pressure, perspiration, and/or muscle tension (Beck & Emery, 1985; Behnke, 1971). Apparently, anxious people experience more arousal in interactions because they often anticipate negative outcomes in the encounters (Anderson & Coussoule, 1980; Beatty, 1984; Behnke & Beatty, 1981; McCroskey, 1984). Furthermore, anxious individuals who report physiological arousal in social situations fear (often without justification) that their physiological reactions will be seen by others and this may, in turn, heighten their social anxiety (McEwan & Devins, 1983; Nichols, 1974).

Research on the relationship between social anxiety and physiological arousal has typically employed one or more of the following measures: (a) heart rate, (b) blood pressure, and (c) blushing. The usual procedure for investigating the physiological responses of socially anxious individuals involves the subject's interacting with a partner, in most cases an opposite-sex confederate, in either a structured or an unstructured interaction. The moderate size effect of social anxiety on heart rate and blood pressure ($d = .55$) is one indication of greater autonomic arousal in anxious than in nonanxious individuals (e.g., Beidel, Turner, & Dancu, 1985; Booth-Butterfield, 1987; Bruch, Gorsky, Collins, & Berger, 1989; Edelmann, 1991; Turner, Beidel, & Larkin, 1986). Nevertheless, almost one-half of the studies we found (10 of 23) cited no effect of social anxiety on heart rate.

The results of the meta-analysis indicate that increased social anxiety is strongly related ($d = .99$) to blushing (e.g., Amies, Gelder, & Shaw, 1983; Cheek & Watson, 1989; Edelmann & Skov, 1993; Fatis, 1983; Leary & Kowalski, 1993). Individuals rarely, if ever, blush when they are alone (Leary & Meadows, 1991). Blushing tends to arise when individuals are objects of undesired social attention (Leary, Britt, Cutlip, & Templeton, 1992) and are concerned about the evaluative judgments and reactions of others (e.g., Buss, 1980; Castelfranchi & Poggi, 1990; Darwin, 1872/1955; Edelmann, 1987).

For example, Leary and his colleagues (Leary & Kowalski, 1993; Leary & Meadows, 1991) found that an individual's propensity to blush was highly correlated with scores on the Interaction Anxiety Scale (Leary, 1983b) ($r =$ .51) and the Fear of Negative Evaluation Scale (Watson & Friend, 1969) ($r =$ .48), both measures that emphasize evaluative concerns in social settings. Because chronic blushers are often aware of their propensity for blushing, they are also concerned with others' reactions to their blushing (Edelmann, 1987; Leary et al., 1992). In fact, this fear of blushing can be a prevalent and psychologically debilitating condition in and of itself (Edelmann, 1990).

Although social anxiety is typically accompanied by one or more indicators of physiological arousal (e.g., heart rate, blood pressure, and blushing) and behavioral signs of anxiety (e.g., fidgeting), the research is not completely consistent. For example, in a series of role-playing studies by Monti and his colleagues, social anxiety was not found to be related to heart rate (Ahern, Wallander, Abrahms, & Monti, 1983; Monti, Boice, et al., 1984; Monti, Kolko, Fingeret, & Zwick, 1984; Monti, Wallander, Ahern, Abrahms, & Munroe, 1983). Nevertheless, the absence of effects in these studies may simply be a product of using role-playing methodology rather than actual interactions.

The absence of a relationship may also reflect the complexity in the psychophysiology of the responses and inconsistencies in the ways individuals interpret such responses (Jones et al., 1986; Leary, 1983c). In addition, Lacey (1967) has suggested that "differential fractionation" may account for the dissociation between heart rate measures and other indicators of autonomic arousal. Specifically, heart rate deceleration may occur in otherwise stimulating circumstances if the related cognitive processing involves selective attention rather than cognitive elaboration.

BEHAVIORAL CORRELATES OF SOCIAL ANXIETY

The behavioral concomitants of social anxiety identified in Table 8.2 can be grouped into the following categories: (a) arousal-mediated behaviors, (b) verbal and nonverbal involvement, (c) avoidance of others, and (d) protective self-presentations (Leary, 1982, 1983c). The results of the meta-analysis indicate that the effects of social anxiety on all of these behavioral reactions are similarly strong (d range = .81 to .99).

Arousal-Mediated Behaviors

The arousal-mediated behaviors are presumably the overt manifestations of sympathetic activation and signal to others that the individual is nervous

(Leary, 1982, 1983c). People who are chronically socially anxious typically show one or more of the following patterns: (a) speaking less fluently (Borkovec, Stone, O'Brien, & Kaloupek, 1974; DePaulo, Dull, Greenberg, & Swaim, 1989; Freimuth, 1976; Johnson & Glass, 1989; Mulac & Sherman, 1975; Pelias & Pelias, 1988), (b) stuttering (Fatis, 1983; Ragsdale, 1976), (c) speaking with a quivering voice (Monti, Boice, et al., 1984; O'Hair, Cody, & Behnke, 1985; Pearson & Turner, 1984), (d) repeating speech (Jordan & Powers, 1978; Ragsdale, 1976), and (e) initiating more frequent pauses (Asendorpf, 1992; Booth-Butterfield & Booth-Butterfield, 1986; Cappella, 1985; Dow, Biglan, & Glaser, 1985; Pilkonis, 1977) or pauses at inappropriate times (Fischetti, Curran, & Wessberg, 1977; Peterson, Fischetti, Curran, & Arland, 1981). In one study, no differences were found in the pausing behavior of socially anxious and nonanxious females who interacted with a same-sex confederate (Alden, 1987).

Precisely how anxiety interferes with speaking is not completely understood. Leary (1983c) offers three different explanations. First, speech disfluencies may result from the individual's preoccupation with the source of the threat (e.g., audience or interaction partners). This preoccupation with the audience presumably makes it difficult for the actor to focus and concentrate on what he or she is saying. A second explanation runs counter to the first. That is, the effect of anxiety on speech may result from too much self-focused attention. Individuals who pay too much attention to what they are saying, or are going to say, may be unable to attend to situational cues. In turn, this causes speech disfluencies. Both of these opposing hypotheses are based on cognitive and attentional processes and do not necessarily posit an arousal-mediated mechanism.

It is possible, however, that arousal may direct attention either to the audience or to the self. Leary's third explanation is that anxiety and the accompanying arousal interfere with normal breathing, which, in turn, results in shorter, faster respiration and causes speech disfluencies such as stuttering. This does not necessarily account for the pause differences typically found, unless the pauses serve to facilitate taking a breath.

The few studies that have been conducted on self-manipulative behaviors have found conflicting results. First, Pilkonis (1977) found no significant differences in the self-manipulative behaviors of shy and nonshy males and females in unstructured interactions with opposite-sex confederates. In contrast, Cheek and Buss (1981) and Burgoon and Koper (1984) found that shy females in same-sex interactions engaged in more self-manipulative behaviors. Two studies by Monti and his colleagues obtained similar results with shy males in opposite-sex interactions (Monti, Boice, et al., 1984; Monti, Kolku, et al. 1984).

Verbal and Nonverbal Involvement

This section reviews the negative effects of social anxiety on affiliation in terms of two important categories in Table 8.2: verbal and nonverbal involvement. Although affiliation is one of the most basic human tendencies, socially anxious individuals report decreased interest in affiliating with others (Alden & Phillips, 1990). The most commonly cited behavioral correlate of social anxiety is decreased verbal output (e.g., Beidel, Borden, Turner, & Jacob, 1989; Borkovec, Fleischman, & Caputo, 1973; Evans, 1993; Lederman, 1983). In addition to speaking less in interactions, socially anxious individuals are less likely to initiate conversations with others (e.g., Cheek & Buss, 1981; Dodge, Heimberg, Nyman, & O'Brien, 1987; Glasgow & Arkowitz, 1975; Hall & Goldberg, 1977). Not initiating conversations protects socially anxious individuals by not drawing them into social encounters that precipitate anxiety.

A similar pattern is present in the nonverbal involvement of individuals, where the largest behavioral effect of social anxiety was found ($d = .99$). For example, initiating gaze toward others signals a desire to interact and later helps to regulate the flow of communication (Argyle & Dean, 1965; Exline & Fehr, 1978; Kendon, 1967). Because gaze is associated with a desire to affiliate, it is not surprising that socially anxious individuals report that they avert their gaze while engaged in conversations (Clevenger & King, 1961; Farabee, Holcom, Ramsey, & Cole, 1993; Fatis, 1983; Hill, 1989; Lord & Zimbardo, 1985). The behavioral evidence supporting such gaze avoidance is particularly characteristic of opposite-sex interactions (e.g., Booth-Butterfield & Booth-Butterfield, 1986; Conger & Farrell, 1981; Heimberg, Madsen, Montgomery, & McNabb, 1980; Iizuka, 1994), but it can also be seen in same-sex interactions (e.g., Asendorpf, 1992; Burgoon & Koper, 1984) and in small group interactions (Modigliani, 1971). In a few studies, no differences were found in gaze as a function of social anxiety (Alden, 1987; Cappella, 1985; Glasgow & Arkowitz, 1975) or differences were found only for males in opposite-sex interactions (Garcia, Stinson, Ickes, Bissonnette, & Briggs, 1991; Pilkonis, 1977).

Gaze aversion apparently serves two functions for socially anxious individuals (Leary, 1983c). First, by decreasing gaze, the socially anxious individual decreases the probability that others will initiate a conversation with him or her. Second, gaze aversion allows a degree of psychological withdrawal without actually leaving the interaction. Reducing gaze may allow socially anxious individuals to avoid unwanted social interactions, but it can create other difficulties. Because people typically like others who gaze at them (LaFrance & Mayo, 1978), the gaze avoidance of socially anxious individuals results in less favorable impressions (Leary, 1983c). Compared with nonanxious individuals, socially anxious individuals are often judged more negatively by others (e.g., Jones & Carpenter, 1986).

Physical distance is another nonverbal behavior that affects the flow of communication. For example, appropriate interaction distances between individuals can contribute to gaining information, regulating the interaction, and expressing intimacy (Patterson, 1983). The closer one person approaches another, the more the situation demands communication. Thus, because socially anxious people interact at greater interpersonal distances (Carducci & Webber, 1979; Haemmerlie, 1983; Patterson, 1973, 1977; Pilkonis, 1977), communication can suffer.

Avoidance of Others

Decreasing verbal participation, reducing gaze, and interacting at greater distances allow socially anxious individuals to disengage partially from social interactions yet remain in the encounters. Socially anxious individuals may totally disengage by withdrawing from social encounters or attempting to avoid them altogether (e.g., Asendorpf, 1986; Cheek & Watson, 1989; Dodge et al., 1987; McCroskey, 1976, 1984; Phillips, 1968; Samter & Burleson, 1984).

Physical withdrawal from anxiety-producing situations is often the preferred course, because the anxious individual is completely removed from the aversive encounter (Schlenker & Leary, 1985). Total withdrawal, however, is not always possible. Another consequence of this pattern of avoidance is that socially anxious individuals have fewer social relationships with others (e.g., Arkowitz, Hinton, Perl, & Himadi, 1978; Hansson, 1986; Jones & Russell, 1982; Maroldo, 1981; Monroe & Borzi, 1988; Richmond & McCroskey, 1985, 1992; Zakahi, Jordan, & Christophel, 1992).

Social anxiety not only limits interpersonal contacts, but also produces other negative consequences. For example, people who are socially anxious in opposite-sex interactions tend to be less sexually experienced, report more sexual dysfunction, and express greater apprehension about sex (Barlow, 1986; Leary, 1983c; Leary & Dobbins, 1983). Furthermore, the behavior of socially anxious people is often seen as disinterest, superiority, or snobbishness; consequently, anxious individuals are judged to be unfriendly (Cheek & Buss, 1981; Jones & Carpenter, 1986). If such impressions are common, it is understandable that social anxiety and loneliness are positively correlated (e.g., Down, Javidi, & Nussbaum, 1987; Solano & Koester, 1989; Zakahi & Duran, 1982, 1985).

Protective Self-Presentation

This last category includes behaviors that serve to present socially anxious individuals in a relatively positive manner (Leary, 1982, 1983c). According to Schlenker and Leary's (1982) self-presentation theory, socially anxious individuals are motivated to make a particular impression but doubt their ability to do so. Partial or total withdrawal from a social situation can serve to protect a fragile self-image. When withdrawal from the situation is impossible, anxious individuals often engage in a protective self-presentational style to minimize losses in social approval and/or to avoid social disapproval (Arkin, 1981; Bruch, Hamer, & Heimberg, 1995; Chen, 1994; Greenberg, Pyszcyznski, & Stine, 1985; Langston & Cantor, 1989; Wolfe, Lennox, & Cutler, 1986). Instead of maximizing a positive impression, the focus is on minimizing a negative impression. For example, socially anxious individuals may try to project an image of being polite and interested by being innocuously sociable, conveying impressions of similarity, and presenting cautious self-descriptions (Leary, 1982, 1983c).

On the other hand, it should be noted that self-protective strategies deprive individuals of necessary and informative social feedback (Arkin, 1981). Adopting self-protective strategies may elicit negative interpersonal reactions and maintain self-defeating interpersonal patterns of behavior (Alden, 1992; Meleshko & Alden, 1993). If this is the case, the biased self-perceptions of anxious subjects may be a result of their habitual self-protection (Meleshko & Alden, 1993).

One technique of managing self-presentation is *innocuous sociability,* defined as behaving in ways that indicate interest in and agreement with what others are saying while not getting actively involved in the interaction (Leary, 1983c; Schlenker & Leary, 1982). In situations where individuals feel socially anxious, they may appear innocuously sociable and convey interest in others by (a) smiling, (b) head nodding, (c) using back-channel responses, (d) not interrupting others, and (e) asking questions. Compared with nonanxious individuals, socially anxious individuals smile and nod their heads more frequently (as if in agreement) in interacting with others (Arkowitz, Lichtenstein, McGovern, & Hines, 1975; Pilkonis, 1977; Slivken & Buss, 1984) and also use more back-channel responses (e.g., "uh-huh," "hmm") to indicate greater attention to speakers (Natale, Jaffe, & Entin, 1979). Socially anxious individuals also use more rhetorical interrogatives (e.g., "you know?") (Powers, 1977). Furthermore, socially anxious individuals interrupt their partners less frequently (Arntson, Mortensen, & Lustig, 1980; Leary, Knight, & Johnson, 1987). Initiating back-channel responses and avoiding interruptions conveys the image of friendliness and interest, yet permits individuals to maintain minimal involvement in interactions.

If the behavior of anxious individuals encourages others to talk more, then anxious individuals have fewer opportunities to disclose information about themselves (e.g., Bruch, Kaflowitz, & Pearl, 1988; McCroskey & Richmond, 1977; Post, Wittmaier, & Radin, 1978). Making fewer self-disclosures can also be a protective device by preventing the anxious person from being drawn further into the conversation (Post et al., 1978; Wheeless, Nesser, & McCroskey, 1986). In addition, anxious individuals may permit others to dominate the conversation by asking questions. Questioning others reduces the need to self-disclose, prompts others to speak, and maintains the focus on other individuals (Efran & Korn, 1969; Hill, 1989; Leary, 1983c; Leary et al., 1987). Socially anxious individuals also use more question intonations (i.e., rising intonations with declarative statements) (McMullen & Pasloski, 1992).

Although innocuous sociability can serve as an image protection device for socially anxious individuals, those employing such a strategy are not always perceived as friendly (e.g., Jones & Briggs, 1984). Furthermore, innocuous sociability, or passivity, if carried to an extreme, may convey a total lack of assertiveness (Alden & Phillips, 1990; Dow et al., 1985; Leary, 1983c) and create negative impressions. This, in turn, exacerbates the plight of socially anxious individuals.

Another way socially anxious individuals may try to present themselves in a favorable manner is to convey an impression of *similarity* (Leary, 1983c). Similarity is one of the key components to interpersonal attraction (Byrne, 1971), because people tend to like others whom they judge as similar to themselves in values, attitudes, and behaviors. Conformity is a specific way that socially anxious individuals can appear similar to others (Santee & Maslach, 1982; Turner, 1977). Pilkonis and Zimbardo (1979) discuss unpublished data showing that socially anxious individuals conform more than do non-socially anxious individuals (Maslach & Solomon, 1977; Souz e Silva, 1977).

When socially anxious individuals are in situations that demand some type of self-disclosure, they typically present cautious, less positive descriptions of themselves to others than do non-socially anxious persons (Leary, 1983c; Schlenker & Leary, 1985). This cautious self-description apparently reflects, in part, their own self-views and low self-esteem (Leary et al., 1987). Cautious self-presentations also serve to lower others' expectations of what these individuals might accomplish and so minimize the risks that they will fail to meet those expectations (Schlenker & Leary, 1985).

Because socially anxious individuals worry that others view their actions negatively, they may also use *disclaimers* (Leary, 1983c). Disclaimers are statements that people make in advance of their actions to help dispel any unfavorable impressions that may be created (Hewit & Stokes, 1975). The disclaimers to which Hewit and Stokes (1975) refer can also be described as self-handicapping strategies (Jones & Berglas, 1978).

Self-handicapping is the use of self-invoked impediments to performance in evaluative settings (Jones & Berglas, 1978). This provides an individual with a ready excuse for possible failure and avoids negative implications of a failed performance by controlling the causal attribution of failure. In this way, self-handicapping enables the person to control and externalize the causal attributions related to failure. To the extent that symptoms of anxiety provide an explanation for poor social performance or a reason to avoid potentially difficult social situations, social anxiety or shyness may often have a self-serving function (Leary & Schlenker, 1981; Snyder & Smith, 1986; Snyder, Smith, Augelli, & Ingram, 1985). Shyness may serve as a self-handicap because it is often viewed as an understandable reason to avoid difficult social situations (Snyder & Smith, 1986; Snyder et al., 1985).

Summary

The behaviors that accompany social anxiety are quite diverse and serve different psychological and social functions (Leary, 1983c). For example, some behaviors are involuntary (e.g., stuttering) and some are strategic responses to social situations (e.g., withdrawal). First, arousal-mediated behaviors (e.g, self-manipulations, speech disfluencies) are involuntary behaviors that signal to others that individuals are nervous. Second, if individuals are sufficiently anxious, they can withdraw from social encounters or, if necessary, completely avoid them. If they remain in the interactions, anxious individuals often attempt to reduce the amount of social contact by decreasing verbal and nonverbal involvement (Leary, 1983c). Finally, socially anxious individuals may engage in self-presentational behaviors that serve to create a relatively positive impression or, at least, serve to minimize a negative impression. To project an image of being polite and interested, socially anxious individuals may smile, nod their heads, and use back-channel responses (e.g., innocuous sociability) (Leary, 1983c). Nevertheless, such patterns may still create negative impressions if the individuals are seen as too passive.

COGNITIVE CORRELATES OF SOCIAL ANXIETY

Although the behaviors of socially anxious individuals are somewhat variable, their cognitions are fairly consistent. Hartman (1983, 1986) argues that all socially anxious people are similar at the metacognitive level of psychological function. Metacognition describes a person's awareness, knowledge, and active monitoring of cognitive processes and strategies (Flavell, 1979). Hartman (1986) states that socially anxious people become "preoccupied with metacognition: thoughts about their physiological arousal, ongoing performance, and others' perceptions of them as socially incompetent, inappropriately nervous, or physiologically inadequate" (p. 269). The effects of social anxiety on cognitive reactions are pervasive and, with one exception (self-attribution), quite large in size (mean $d = 1.05$). The effects discussed in this section include excessive self-focused attention, negative thoughts and self-ratings, evaluation apprehension, self-efficacy concerns, evaluation by others, self-attributions, irrational beliefs, and memory effects.

Self-Focused Attention

Self-focused attention involves an awareness of self-referent, internally generated information (Buss, 1980; Carver & Scheier, 1981; Duval & Wicklund, 1972). Characteristic of this self-focus is *anxious self-preoccupation,* that is, heightened concern over one's inadequacies and shortcomings (Sarason, 1975). Numerous studies have found that socially anxious individuals focus attention toward themselves (e.g., Alden & Phillips, 1990; Arnold & Cheek, 1986; Bates, Campbell, & Burgess, 1990; Ickes, Robertson, Tooke, & Teng, 1986; Ingram, 1990). In general, self-focused attention diverts attention from environmental cues, hampers information processing, and affects performance (Comadena & Prusank, 1988; DePaulo & Tang, 1994; Sarason, 1975; Sarason & Sarason, 1986; Sarason, Sarason, & Pierce, 1990).

In particular, in social situations increased self-focus reduces attention both to the partner and to critical social information. In turn, this may result in individuals' initiating inappropriate or awkward behaviors (Crozier, 1979; Hartman, 1983; Jones & Briggs, 1984; Patterson, 1995; Sarason et al., 1990). The self-focus of attention may also result in impaired ability to decode nonverbal information about others (Winton, Clark, & Edelmann, 1995).

Self-focused attention can also lead to increased negative affect about the self (Duval & Wicklund, 1972), often because the individual cannot achieve the internalized standards of an ideal behavior. Self-focused attention may, however, also be the product of negative affect. That is, negative affect or the anticipation of negative affect may mediate self-focused attention (Gibbons, 1990, 1991). Regardless of how self-focused attention is related to negative affect, the result is typically increased difficulty in interpersonal behavior. That is, self-focused attention and negative affect can inhibit important social behaviors.

Negative Thoughts and Self-Ratings

The most frequently cited and most consistent cognitive correlate of social anxiety is the report of fewer positive thoughts and/or more negative thoughts in social situations (e.g., Ayres, 1988; Bruch et al., 1989; Glass, Merluzzi, Biever, & Larsen, 1982; Hartman, 1984; Ickes et al., 1986; Zweig & Brown, 1985). As part of the negative thought processes, socially anxious individuals generally rate themselves more negatively than do non-socially anxious persons (e.g., Alden, 1987; Arkin & Appelman, 1983; Booth-Butterfield, 1989; Burgio, Glass, & Merluzzi, 1981; Pelias & Pelias, 1988). Among the specific self-judgments that are most characteristic of socially anxious individuals are the following: (a) feeling more tense, anxious, and nervous (e.g., Arnold & Cheek, 1986; Asendorpf, 1987; Britt & Blumenthal, 1993; Greenberg et al., 1985); (b) feeling less competent and confident (e.g., Curran, Wallander, & Fischetti, 1980; Halford & Foddy, 1982; Leary & Kowalski, 1993; Leary, Kowalski, & Bergen, 1988; Neer, 1982; Rubin & Rubin, 1989); (c) feeling less involved, comfortable, and assertive in interactions (e.g., Alden & Phillips, 1990; Burgoon, Pfau, Birk, & Manusov, 1987; Cheek & Buss, 1981; Pilkonis, 1977); (d) feeling less friendly and open (Jones & Briggs, 1984; Patterson, Churchill, & Powell, 1991); and even (c) feeling less physically attractive (e.g., Bruch, Giordan, & Pearl, 1986; Lord & Zimbardo, 1985; Montgomery, Haemmerlie, & Edwards, 1991; Prisbell, 1982).

These negative self-descriptions of socially anxious individuals may arise as (a) valid expressions of low self-esteem, (b) protective strategies to lower the expectations of others, and (c) reactions upon failing to meet excessively high standards (Leary, 1983c; Schlenker & Leary, 1985). The pervasiveness of negative thoughts in socially anxious individuals is apparently related to evaluation apprehension and self-efficacy concerns. That is, in social situations, anxious people are particularly concerned about the evaluations of others and concerned about their ability to "perform" successfully (Leary, 1983b). Below, we review the research on these two important characteristics of social anxiety.

Evaluation Apprehension

Socially anxious individuals typically employ excessively high standards for social comparisons and have high needs for social approval. Not surprisingly, they are also extremely concerned about the evaluations of others (Goldfried & Sobocinski, 1975; Leary, 1983c; Leary & Kowalski, 1993). Socially anxious individuals typically believe that others are disinterested, critical, and hard to impress (Ayres, 1989; Ingram, Cruet, Johnson, & Wisnicki, 1988; Jones & Briggs, 1984; Jones & Carpenter, 1986; Leary, Kowalski, & Campbell, 1988) and also doubt their own abilities to make the desired impression (Schlenker & Leary, 1982).

Numerous studies have demonstrated that socially anxious individuals are concerned that others will evaluate them negatively (e.g., Clark & Arkowitz, 1975; DePaulo, Kenny, Hoover, Webb, & Oliver, 1987; DePaulo, Epstein, & LeMay, 1990; Goldfried, Padawer, & Robins, 1984; Gregorich, Kemple, & Leary, 1985; Pozo, Carver, Wellens, & Scheier, 1991). This concern over evaluation by others contributes to self-focused attention, which may in turn inhibit appropriate behavior and lead to still greater anxiety.

Self-Efficacy

Socially anxious individuals are also skeptical about their abilities to perform and particularly doubt their impression management skills (e.g., low self-efficacy expectations). A large number of studies have consistently shown that socially anxious individuals have low self-efficacy expectations (e.g., Alden, 1987; Alden, Bieling, & Wallace, 1994; Chesebro et al., 1992; Goldfried et al., 1984; Halford & Foddy, 1982; Leary, Atherton, Hill, & Hur, 1986; Maddux, Norton, & Leary, 1988; Proctor, Douglas, Garera-Izquierdo, & Wartman, 1994). In fact, the effect of social anxiety on self-efficacy is by far the largest specific effect ($d = 1.56$) found in the meta-analysis.

Furthermore, studies of thoughts before and during interactions reveal that anxious individuals expect to perform more poorly during interactions, feel less capable of controlling the impressions others form of them, and characterize themselves as less socially skilled than do less anxious individuals (Cacioppo, Glass, & Merluzzi, 1979; Clark & Arkowitz, 1975; Glass et al., 1982; Leary et al., 1987).

Novel and ambiguous situations may provide additional problems for anxious individuals, because such circumstances increase the likelihood of their behaving inappropriately. In turn, behaving inappropriately can increase social anxiety levels and lower self-efficacy expectations (Leary & Atherton, 1986). Also, when people have low self-efficacy expectations, they are likely to become anxious about interaction outcomes and enter into a self-focus and self-evaluation cycle from which it is difficult to escape (Carver & Scheier, 1981; Gibbons, 1990; Greenberg & Pyszczynski, 1986).

As people experience more anxiety, they are more likely to assume that they are handling the situation poorly and, subsequently, withdraw from the interaction (Leary & Miller, 1986). Thus, the relationship between social anxiety and self-efficacy is bidirectional. First, low self-efficacy expectations heighten social anxiety with ruminations about impending negative outcomes. Second, the experience of anxiety can lower self-efficacy by serving as a cue that the individual is not in control. In turn, this leads the individual to expect that his or her performance will be less than optimal (Leary & Atherton, 1986).

In summary, anxious individuals are concerned about the impressions they make and about their social skills in relating to others. But how do others actually view them? We next review the evidence on this question as a check on the consistency between self-evaluations and others' evaluations.

Evaluations by Others

The concern that socially anxious individuals have about evaluations by others is not unwarranted. People who are socially anxious often do create negative impressions. This includes being judged as (a) less socially and interpersonally skilled (e.g., Dow et al., 1985; McCroskey, Daly, Richmond, & Cox, 1975; Meleshko & Alden, 1993; O'Bannion & Arkowitz, 1977); (b) less credible and trustworthy (McCroskey & Richmond, 1976; Mulac & Sherman, 1975; Richmond, 1978); (c) less assertive, responsive, expressive, and open (Kearney & McCroskey, 1980; Reno & Kenny, 1992); (d) less confident and competent (e.g., Arntson et al., 1980; DePaulo et al., 1989; Gough & Thorne, 1986; Jones & Briggs, 1986); (e) less friendly, attentive, and relaxed (Burgoon & Koper, 1984; Jones & Briggs, 1984; Richmond, Beatty, & Dyba, 1985; Zimbardo, 1977); and even (f) less physically attractive (e.g., Cheek & Buss, 1981; Mandel & Shrauger, 1980; Steffen & Redden, 1977; Zakahi, Duran, & Adkins, 1994).

Self-Attributions

When socially anxious people are asked to make attributions for their own behavior, they tend to reinforce already existing social concerns. Specifically, socially anxious individuals tend to make internal attributions (e.g., lack of intelligence or ability) for failures and external attributions (e.g., luck or an easy task) for successes (e.g., Alfano, Joiner, & Perry, 1994; Anderson & Arnoult, 1985; Booth-Butterfield, 1989; Lake & Arkin, 1985). When socially anxious individuals make internal attributions for failures, they are more likely to experience interaction problems and avoid difficult social situations (Bandura, 1977; Leary & Atherton, 1986; Storms & McCaul, 1976). In contrast, if interactions are positive and successful, anxious individuals do not take credit for such outcomes and, consequently, do not alter their negative expectancy.

When feedback is given to anxious individuals about their performances, they more readily accept negative feedback and tend to ignore, resist, or doubt the accuracy of positive evaluations (e.g., Asendorpf, 1987; Greenberg et al., 1985; Smith & Sarason, 1975; Teglasi & Fagin, 1984). Thus, socially anxious individuals are more accepting of feedback congruent with their negative self-perceptions (McFarlin & Blascovich, 1981). When individuals ignore positive feedback and accept negative feedback, they are also deprived of opportunities to experience social success and to receive approval from others (Arkin, Lake, & Baumgardner, 1986; Cheek, Melchior, & Carpentieri, 1986; Lake & Arkin, 1985).

Irrational Beliefs

Consistent with the patterns of evaluation apprehension, self-efficacy concerns, and biased attributions is the presence of irrational beliefs in anxious individuals. Ellis (1962) identifies a number of such beliefs, including the following: (a) it is essential to be liked and approved of by everyone, (b) it is essential to be competent and successful in all situations, (c) everyone should attain perfection in order to be considered worthwhile, and (d) a person's worth is solely dependent on and determined by the opinions of others. According to Ellis, these beliefs are irrational and self-defeating because they constitute unattainable goals and result in insecurity and unhappiness. Thus, individuals who place extreme emphasis on social approval often feel insecure and socially anxious when interacting with others because they believe that they cannot achieve the full acceptance that they desire (Leary, 1983c).

In fact, research shows that, compared with nonanxious individuals, socially anxious individuals hold more irrational beliefs (e.g., Alden et al., 1994; Bates et al., 1990; Deffenbacher et al., 1986; Johnson & Glass, 1989). Only one study, conducted by Burgio et al. (1981) with a sample of college females, failed to find a significant relationship between social anxiety and irrational beliefs.

Memory Effects

In addition to the various effects related to both self-evaluations and evaluations by others, socially anxious individuals tend to report more negative than positive self-traits (Breck & Smith, 1983; Claeys, 1989; O'Bannion & Arkowitz, 1977). This is consistent with individuals' tendency to remember information about themselves more easily when it converges with self-schemata (Markus, 1977, 1980). Furthermore, once people view themselves and their social abilities negatively, they are more likely to recall circumstances in which they performed negatively and in which they received unfavorable rather than favorable reactions from others (Markus, 1980). This selective memory may, in turn, increase the interpersonal difficulties of socially anxious individuals (Leary, 1983c).

People who are socially anxious also tend to recall fewer characteristics of their interaction partners (Hope, Heimberg, & Klein, 1990; Kimble & Zehr, 1982) and fewer details of the interactions (Clark, 1989; Lord, Saenz, & Godfrey, 1987; Pelias & Pelias, 1988; Ryan, Plant, & Kuczkowjski, 1991), remember classroom materials less effectively (Booth-Butterfield, 1988; McCroskey, Booth-Butterfield, & Payne, 1989), and suffer from the "next-in-line effect," or the inability to recall what happened immediately prior to their turn to perform (Bond & Omar, 1990). Thus, high self-focused attention not only impedes attention to other people but reduces the cognitive resources necessary to process information about others (Crozier, 1979; Patterson, 1995).

Summary

The cognitive component of social anxiety includes personal beliefs, assumptions, and expectations about how the world works and one's role in the world (Sarason & Sarason, 1986). In general, the cognitions of socially anxious individuals are quite consistent. The overall pattern is that anxious individuals experience increased self-focused attention and anxious self-preoccupation (Sarason, 1975). This heightened attention to the self diverts attention from environmental cues, hampers information processing, and disrupts behavior (Sarason et al., 1990; Patterson, 1995).

More specifically, socially anxious individuals also tend to (a) report fewer positive thoughts in social situations (e.g., Asendorpf, 1987), (b) experience more concern about evaluations by others (e.g., Glass & Furlong, 1990), (c) have low self-efficacy (e.g., Alden, 1987), (d) be evaluated negatively by others (e.g., Jones & Carpenter, 1986), (e) make negative self-attributions (e.g., Teglasi & Fagin, 1984), (f) hold irrational beliefs (e.g., Bates et al., 1990), and (g) have impaired memory abilities (e.g., Bond & Omar, 1990).

THEORETICAL MODELS

Although our review clearly indicates that distinct physiological, behavioral, and cognitive reactions are characteristic of social anxiety, specifying the causal relationships among these components and the experience of social anxiety is a more complicated issue. In fact, a number of different dynamic links have been offered to account for the relationships among social anxiety, arousal, behavior, and cognitions (e.g., Beatty, Dobos, Balfantz, & Kuwabara, 1991; Leary, 1986a, 1990; Richmond & McCroskey, 1992, pp. 93-96).

Because numerous subtle variations in the specific links among these components are possible, we will not attempt to discuss each one. Instead, we suggest that the various dynamic links may be broadly classified in terms of the primacy of arousal, cognitions, or behavior in initiating the experience of social anxiety. Within each category, we describe a representative causal model.

Three general assumptions across the models offered here should be made explicit. First, although trait social anxiety predisposes an individual to experience the state of social anxiety, the trait itself is not a sufficient cause of the experience of social anxiety. A second and related assumption is that the development of social anxiety is dependent upon the anticipation or initiation of a social encounter that is relevant for self-presentation and/or self-evaluation. That is, the experience of social anxiety occurs in an actual or anticipated social context. Third, the relationships among the various components are recursive. That is, feedback across the component processes continually shapes the experience of social anxiety and its arousal, cognitive, and behavioral correlates.

Primacy of Arousal

The first approach emphasizes the importance of arousal in the initiation of social anxiety. One suggestion is that excessive arousal or activation may be experienced as social anxiety in the context of an important meeting, a speech, or other significant social event (Richmond & McCroskey, 1992, pp. 93-94). Presumably, if arousal and its related bodily disturbances (e.g., dry mouth, trembling hands, and shortness of breath) are sufficiently intense, social anxiety may result, without any cognitive input. The experience of social anxiety can, however, precipitate both cognitive reactions and behavioral adjustments.

This sequence would not, however, adequately explain the experience of social anxiety when arousal is not intense. In the latter circumstance, arousal may serve as a signal to initiate a "meaning analysis" or evaluation of the arousal (Mandler, 1975, chap. 4). In a similar fashion, Richmond and McCroskey (1992, pp. 94-95) describe a sequence in which arousal is inappropriately processed (i.e., a misattribution process), leading to the experience of social anxiety.

Figure 8.1 illustrates a simple version of a causal model in which arousal is primary in the development of social anxiety. In this model, when the trait anxious individual enters in, or anticipates, a social situation, physiological arousal precipitates a meaning analysis or attribution process (i.e., a cognitive evaluation) that leads to the experience of social anxiety. Next, behavioral

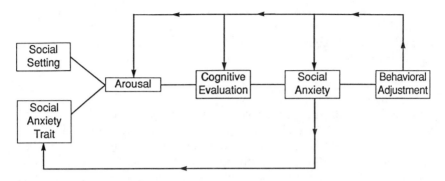

Figure 8.1. An Arousal Primacy Model of Social Anxiety

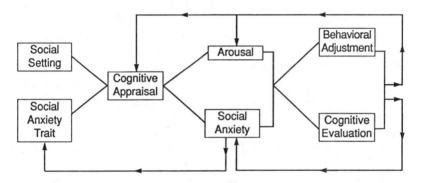

Figure 8.2. A Cognitive Primacy Model of Social Anxiety

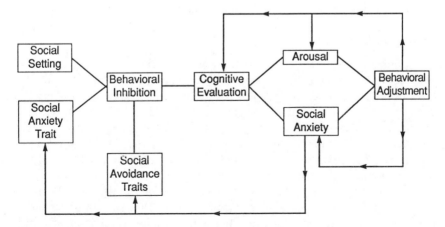

Figure 8.3. A Behavioral Primacy Model of Social Anxiety

adjustments are initiated as a means of adapting to the anxiety. In turn, the behavioral adjustments can moderate social anxiety and the accompanying arousal and cognitive reactions. Finally, it is assumed that the residue of the anxiety experience can influence the subsequent level of trait anxiety.

Primacy of Cognitions

A second general approach emphasizes the primacy of cognitions. According to Leary (1990), social anxiety may be the product of the individual's assessing the likely outcome, costs, and rewards of getting involved in a particular social setting. If the individual judges the likelihood of success as low and the relative costs (including the experience of anxiety) as high, then anxiety can result. Nevertheless, avoidant behavior, or partial withdrawal from the interaction, can feed back and limit the experience of anxiety. Thus, one tactic for limiting self-presentational concerns and the resulting social anxiety may be to do little or nothing at all (Leary, 1986a).

An emphasis on the primacy of cognitions is also consistent with appraisal theories of emotion (e.g., Lazarus & Smith, 1988; Scherer, 1993). In general, appraisal theories propose that emotions are the product of an evaluation (appraisal) of the significance of an event for one's personal well-being. According to this approach, appraisal of the adaptive significance of the event would precipitate the experience of social anxiety and its related arousal and behavioral reactions. In fact, increased arousal may actually prepare the individual for the effort required in initiating an adaptive response (Smith, 1989).

In this model, seen in Figure 8.2, the initial and rapid appraisal represents only one type of cognitive response. More elaborate cognitions may be engaged later and, in combination with the behavioral adjustments, feed back to affect the other component processes. Finally, the experience of social anxiety can also affect the subsequent trait anxiety.

Primacy of Behavior

The third general path emphasizes the importance of habitual patterns of behavioral avoidance or withdrawal in precipitating social anxiety. That is, the chronic behavioral inhibition of individuals in social situations sets the stage for the development of social anxiety. In this model, as individuals recognize their own inhibition and its effect on impressions formed by their partners, they become aroused and anxious (see Kenny & DePaulo, 1993, on the origin of these metaperspective judgments). Furthermore, additional behavioral adjustments may then follow the experience of social anxiety.

In a variant of this path, Patterson (1995) proposes that the habitual behavior and cognitive patterns of dispositionally anxious individuals contribute to the interaction difficulties. In particular, a low level of gaze toward partners and an increase in self-focused thoughts limit the individuals' opportunity to gather and process information about their partners. In turn, the reduced attention to and processing of information about the partners lead to less accurate judgments of partners' momentary reactions, decreased behavioral coordination, and, eventually, increased social anxiety. The disruption of interactive behavior and its accompanying anxiety will, of course, be accelerated by increased arousal.

Finally, because a number of other characteristics (e.g., introversion, low sociability, low self-esteem, loneliness, and depression) are all moderately correlated with trait social anxiety and predictive of behavioral inhibition (Ritts, 1994), trait anxiety is not the only antecedent of the behavior patterns contributing to the experience of social anxiety. That is, a larger category of traits, reflecting a more general pattern of social avoidance, may lead to the inhibited behavior that precipitates the experience of social anxiety. This particular sequence in the behavioral model is represented in Figure 8.3 in the path from the social avoidance traits to behavioral inhibition.

In general, initial behavioral inhibition increases the likelihood of interaction difficulties. In turn, the recognition of these difficulties (i.e., cognitive evaluation) precipitates social anxiety, arousal, and behavioral adjustments. As in the other models, it is assumed that feedback affects the ongoing reactions and subsequent levels of trait anxiety and other social avoidance traits.

Synthesis

From this overview of theoretical models, it seems likely that the experience of social anxiety can develop in a number of different ways. Furthermore, although trait social anxiety predisposes an individual to experience social anxiety in an appropriate social setting, the trait is not a necessary antecedent. If we assume that the alternative models described here have merit, what factors might affect the initiation of one or another causal path? The two variables identified at the start of each model—trait social anxiety and the social setting—seem to be the most promising determinants.

In general, with higher levels of trait anxiety and situations that are perceived to be more important for self-evaluation, increased arousal and/or more pervasive negative self-focused cognitions are more likely to precipitate social anxiety, even before the start of the interaction. Furthermore, the intensity of the arousal, negative cognitions, and social anxiety are likely to increase with increased proximity to the social event. If complete avoidance of the setting is not possible, then behavioral withdrawal may serve to limit the experience of anxiety while at the same time introducing other interaction problems that may exacerbate subsequent social anxiety.

In contrast, individuals with low to moderate levels of trait social anxiety and those engaging in social settings where evaluational concerns are low are less likely to experience arousal, negative cognitions, and social anxiety in anticipation of the interaction. To the extent that the social anxiety trait, or other social avoidance traits, contributes to inhibited behavior, social anxiety is still a possible consequence. That is, as individuals become aware of the consequences of their inhibited behavior, they become anxious. Thus, different causal paths may develop as a function of different levels of trait anxiety and different evaluational pressures.

CONCLUSIONS

The extensive research on social anxiety indicates that dispositional social anxiety, as measured by a variety of scales, is reliably related to increased physiological arousal, avoidant and inhibited behavior, and negative, self-focused cognitions in social settings. The results of the meta-analysis show that virtually all of the specific measures are highly related to trait measures of social anxiety. Nevertheless, the cognitive measures, especially judgments of self-efficacy, are more strongly related to social anxiety than are the physiological and behavioral measures.

Finally, we have discussed and analyzed different theoretical perspectives on the development of social anxiety. Specifically, we have considered different causal models identifying arousal, behavior, and cognitive processes as primary in the experience of social anxiety. Given the complexity of social life and the variability in individual reactions in social settings, it seems likely that there are multiple paths to the experience of social anxiety. Future research might well focus on the circumstances contributing to the activation of these different causal paths to social anxiety.

REFERENCES

Note: Asterisks indicate studies included in the meta-analysis.

*Ahern, D. K., Wallander, J. L., Abrahms, D. M., & Monti, P. M. (1983). Bimodal assessment in a stressful encounter: Individual differences, lead-lag relationships, and response styles. *Journal of Behavioral Assessment, 5,* 317-326.
*Alden, L. (1987). Attributional responses of anxious individuals to different patterns of social feedback: Nothing succeeds like improvement. *Journal of Personality and Social Psychology, 52,* 100-106.
Alden, L. (1992). Cognitive-interpersonal therapy for avoidant personality disorder. In L. Vandecreek (Ed.), *Innovations in clinical practice* (11th ed., pp. 5-22). Indiana, PA: Professional Resources Exchange.
*Alden, L., Bieling, P. J., & Wallace, S. T. (1994). Perfectionism in an interpersonal context: A self-regulation analysis of dysphoria and social anxiety. *Cognitive Therapy and Research, 18,* 297-316.
Alden, L., & Phillips, N. (1990). An interpersonal analysis of social anxiety and depression. *Cognitive Therapy and Research, 14,* 499-513.

*Alden, L. E., Teschuk, M., & Tee, K. (1992). Public self-awareness and withdrawal from social interactions. *Cognitive Therapy and Research, 16,* 249-267.

*Alden, L. E., & Wallace, S. T. (1995). Social phobia and social appraisal in successful and unsuccessful social interactions. *Behavior Research and Therapy, 5,* 497-505.

Alfano, M. S., Joiner, T. E., & Perry, M. (1994). Attributional style: A mediator of the shyness-depression relationship? *Journal of Research in Personality, 28,* 287-300.

Amies, P. L., Gelder, M. G., & Shaw, P. M. (1983). Social phobia: A comparative clinical study. *British Journal of Psychiatry, 142,* 174-179.

Anderson, C. A., & Arnoult, L. H. (1985). Attributional style and everyday problems in living: Depression, loneliness, and shyness. *Social Cognition, 3,* 16-35.

Anderson, C. A., & Harvey, R. J. (1988). Discriminating between problems in living: An examination of measures of depression, loneliness, shyness, and social anxiety. *Journal of Social and Clinical Psychology, 6,* 482-491.

Anderson, D. A., & Coussoule, A. R. (1980). The perceptual world of the communication apprehensive: The effect of communication anxiety and interpersonal gaze on interpersonal perception. *Communication Quarterly, 28,* 44-54.

Argyle, M., & Dean, J. (1965). Eye contact, distance, and affiliation. *Sociometry, 28,* 289-304.

Arkin, R. M. (1981). Self-presentation styles. In J. T. Tedeschi (Ed.), *Impression management theory and social psychological research* (pp. 311-333). New York: Academic Press.

*Arkin, R. M., & Appelman, A. J. (1983). Social anxiety and receptivity to interpersonal evaluation. *Motivation and Emotion, 7,* 11-18.

*Arkin, R. M., Appelman, A. J., & Burger, J. M. (1980). Social anxiety, self-presentation and the self-serving bias in causal attribution. *Journal of Personality and Social Psychology, 38,* 23-35.

*Arkin, R. M., & Grove, T. (1990). Shyness, sociability, and patterns of everyday affiliation. *Journal of Social and Personal Relationships, 7,* 273-281.

Arkin, R. M., Lake, E. A., & Baumgardner, A. H. (1986). Shyness and self-presentation. In W. H. Jones, J. M. Cheek, & S. R. Briggs (Eds.), *Shyness: Perspectives on research and treatment* (pp. 189-204). New York: Plenum.

Arkowitz, H., Hinton, R., Perl, J., & Himadi, W. (1978). Treatment strategies for dating in college men based on real life practices. *Counseling Psychologist, 7,* 41-46.

*Arkowitz, H., Lichtenstein, E., McGovern, K., & Hines, P. (1975). The behavioral assessment of competence in males. *Behavioral Therapy, 6,* 3-13.

Arnold, A. P., & Cheek, J. M. (1986). Shyness, self-preoccupation, and the Stroop color and word test. *Personality and Individual Differences, 7,* 571-573.

*Arntson, P. H., Mortensen, C. D., & Lustig, M. W. (1980). Predispositions toward verbal behavior in task-oriented interactions. *Human Communication Research, 6,* 239-252.

Asendorpf, J. (1986). Shyness in middle and late childhood. In W. H. Jones, J. M. Cheek, & S. R. Briggs (Eds.), *Shyness: Perspectives on research and treatment* (pp. 91-104). New York: Plenum.

*Asendorpf, J. B. (1987). Videotape reconstruction of emotions and cognitions related to shyness. *Journal of Personality and Social Psychology, 53,* 542-549.

*Asendorpf, J. B. (1990). Beyond social withdrawal: Shyness, unsociability, and peer avoidance. *Human Development, 33,* 250-259.

*Asendorpf, J. B. (1992). A Brunswikean approach to trait continuity: Application to shyness *Journal of Personality, 60,* 53-77.

*Ayres, J. (1986). Perceptions of speaking ability: An experiment for stage fright. *Communication Education, 35,* 275-287.

*Ayres, J. (1988). Coping with speech anxiety. *Communication Education, 37,* 289-296.

*Ayres, J. (1989). The impact of communication apprehension and interaction structure on initial interactions. *Communication Monographs, 56,* 75-88.

*Ayres, J. (1992). An examination of the impact of anticipated communication and communication apprehension on negative thinking, task relevant thinking, and recall. *Communication Research Reports, 20,* 3-11.

*Ayres, J. (1992). Personal ads: An exploratory investigation into the relationships among ad characteristics, communication apprehension, and contact. *Communication Reports, 5,* 67-72.

*Ayres, J., Ayres, D. M., & Sharp, D. (1993). A progress report on the development of an instrument to measure communication apprehension in employment interviews. *Communication Research Reports, 10,* 87-94.

*Ayres, J., & Ratis, S. M. (1992). The impact of evaluation and preparation time on high public speaking anxious speakers' thoughts, behavior, and state-communication apprehension. *Southern Communication Journal, 57,* 323-327.

Bandura, A. (1977). Self-efficacy: Toward a unifying theory of behavioral change. *Psychological Review, 84,* 191-215.

Barlow, D. H. (1986). Causes of sexual dysfunction: The role of anxiety and cognitive interference. *Journal of Consulting and Clinical Psychology, 54,* 140-148.

Bates, G. W., Campbell, I. M., & Burgess, P. M. (1990). Assessment of articulated thoughts in social anxiety: Modification of the ATSS procedure. *British Journal of Clinical Psychology, 29,* 91-98.

*Baumgardner, A. H., & Brownlee, E. A. (1987). Strategic failure in social interaction: Evidence for expectancy disconfirmation processes. *Journal of Personality and Social Psychology, 52,* 525-535.

Beatty, M. (1984). Physiological assessment. In J. A. Daly & J. C. McCroskey (Eds.), *Avoiding communication: Shyness, reticence, and communication apprehension* (pp. 95-106). Beverly Hills, CA: Sage.

*Beatty, M. J. (1987). Communication apprehension as a determinant of avoidance, withdrawal, and performance anxiety. *Communication Quarterly, 35,* 202-217.

*Beatty, M. J. (1988). Public speaking apprehension, decision-making errors in the selection of speech introduction strategies, and adherence to strategy. *Communication Education, 37,* 297-311.

*Beatty, M. J., Balfantz, G. L., & Kuwabara, A. Y. (1989). Trait-like qualities of selected variables assumed to be transient causes of performance state anxiety. *Communication Education, 38,* 277-289.

*Beatty, M. J., & Behnke, R. R. (1991). Effects of public speaking trait anxiety and intensity of speaking task on heart rate during performance. *Human Communication Research, 18,* 147-176.

*Beatty, M. J., Behnke, R. R., & McCallum, K. (1978). Situational determinants of communication apprehension. *Communication Monographs, 45,* 187-191.

Beatty, M. J., Dobos, J. A., Balfantz, G. L., & Kuwabara, A. Y. (1991). Communication apprehension, state anxiety, and behavioral disruption: A causal analysis. *Communication Quarterly, 39,* 48-57.

*Beatty, M. J., Forst, E. C., & Stewart, R. A. (1986). Communication apprehension and motivation as predictors of public speaking duration. *Communication Education, 35,* 143-146.

*Beatty, M. J., Springhorn, R. G., & Kruger, M. W. (1976). Toward the development of cognitively experienced speech anxiety scales. *Central States Speech Journal, 27,* 181-185.

Beck, A. T., & Emery, G. (1985). *Anxiety disorders and phobias.* New York: Basic.

Behnke, R. R. (1971). An analysis of psychophysiological research in communication. *Central States Speech Journal, 22,* 16-20.

*Behnke, R. R., & Beatty, M. (1981). A cognitive-physiological model of speech anxiety. *Communication Monographs, 48,* 158-163.

*Behnke, R. R., & Carlile, L. W. (1971). Heart rate as an index of speech anxiety. *Speech Monographs, 38,* 65-69.

*Behnke, R. R., Carlile, L. W., & Lamb, D. H. (1974). A psychophysiological study of state and trait anxiety in public speaking. *Central States Speech Journal, 25,* 249-253.

*Behnke, R. R., Sawyer, C. R., & King, P. E. (1987). The communication of public speaking anxiety. *Communication Education, 36,* 138-141.

Beidel, D. C., Borden, J. W., Turner, S. M., & Jacob, R. G. (1989). The social phobia and anxiety inventory: Concurrent validity with a clinic sample. *Behavioral Research and Therapy, 27,* 573-576.

Beidel, D. C., Turner, S. M., & Cooley, M. R. (1993). Assessing reliable and clinically significant change in social phobia: Validity of the social phobia and anxiety inventory. *Behavioral Research and Therapy, 31,* 331-337.

*Beidel, D. C., Turner, S. M., & Dancu, C. V. (1985). Physiological, cognitive and behavioral aspects of social anxiety. *Behavioral Research and Therapy, 23,* 109-117.

*Biggers, T., & Masterson, J. T. (1984). Communication anxiety as a personality trait: An emotional defense of a concept. *Communication Monographs, 51,* 381-390.

*Bond, C. F., & Omar, A. S. (1990). Social anxiety, state dependence, and the next-in-line effect. *Journal of Experimental Social Psychology, 26,* 185-198.

*Boohar, R. K., & Seiler, W. J. (1982). Speech communication anxiety: An impediment to academic achievement in the university classroom. *Journal of Classroom Interaction, 18,* 23-27.

*Booth-Butterfield, M. (1986). Stifle or stimulate? The effects of communication task structure on apprehensive and non-apprehensive students. *Communication Education, 35,* 337-348.

*Booth-Butterfield, M. (1989). The interpretation of classroom performance feedback: An attributional approach. *Communication Education, 38,* 119-131.

*Booth-Butterfield, M., & Booth-Butterfield, S. (1986). Effects of evaluation, task structure, trait-CA, and reticence on state-CA and behavioral disruption in dyadic settings. *Communication Monographs, 53,* 144-159.

*Booth-Butterfield, S. (1987). Action assembly theory and communication apprehension. *Human Communication Research, 13,* 386-398.

Booth-Butterfield, S. (1988). Inhibition and student recall of instructional messages. *Communication Education, 37,* 312-324.

Booth-Butterfield, S., & Gould, M. (1986). The communication inventory: Validation of state and context communication apprehension. *Communication Quarterly, 34,* 194-205.

Borkovec, T. D., Fleischman, D. J., & Caputo, J. A. (1973). The measurement of anxiety in an analogue social situation. *Journal of Consulting and Clinical Psychology, 41,* 157-161.

*Borkovec, T. D., Stone, N., O'Brien, G., & Kaloupek, D. (1974). Identification and measurement of a clinically relevant target behavior for analogue outcome research. *Behavior Therapy, 5,* 503-513.

*Breck, B. E., & Smith, S. H. (1983). Selective recall of self-descriptive traits by socially anxious and nonsocially anxious females. *Social Behavior and Personality, 11,* 71-76.

Britt, T. W., & Blumenthal, T. D. (1993). Social anxiety and latency of response to startle stimuli. *Journal of Research in Personality, 27,* 1-14.

*Brockner, J. (1979). Self-esteem, self-consciousness, and task performance: Replications, extensions, and possible expectancies. *Journal of Personality and Social Psychology, 37,* 447-461.

*Brodt, S. E., & Zimbardo, P. G. (1981). Modifying shyness-related social behavior through misattribution. *Journal of Personality and Social Psychology, 41,* 437-449.

*Brownell, W. W., & Katula, R. A. (1986). The communication anxiety graph: A classroom tool for managing speech anxiety. *Communication Research, 13,* 243-249.

*Bruch, M. A., Giordan, S., & Pearl, L. (1986). Differences between fearful and self-conscious shy subtypes in background and adjustment. *Journal of Research in Personality, 20,* 172-186.

*Bruch, M. A., Gorsky, J. M., Collins, T. M., & Berger, P. A. (1989). Shyness and sociability reexamined: A multicomponent analysis. *Journal of Personality and Social Psychology, 57,* 904-915.

*Bruch, M. A., Hamer, R. J., & Heimberg, R. G. (1995). Shyness and public self-consciousness: Additive or interactive relation with social interaction? *Journal of Personality, 63,* 47-63.

Bruch, M. A., Kaflowitz, N. G., & Pearl, L. (1988). Mediated and nonmediated relationships of personality components to loneliness. *Journal of Social and Clinical Psychology, 6,* 346-355.

*Bruch, M. A., Mattia, J. I., Heimberg, R. G., & Holt, C. S. (1993). Cognitive specificity in social anxiety and depression: Supporting evidence and qualifications due to affective confounding. *Cognitive Therapy and Research, 17,* 1-21.

*Bruch, M. A., & Pearl, L. (1995). Attributional style and symptoms of shyness in a heterosocial interaction. *Cognitive Therapy and Research, 19,* 91-107.

*Buhr, T. A., Pryor, B., & Sullivan, M. (1991). A further examination of communication apprehension and information processing. *Cognitive Therapy and Research, 15,* 303-317.

*Buller, D. B. (1987). Communication apprehension and reactions to proxemic violations. *Journal of Nonverbal Behavior, 11,* 13-25.

*Burgio, K. L., Glass, C. R., & Merluzzi, T. V. (1981). The effects of social anxiety on videotape performance feedback on cognitions and self-evaluations. *Behavioral Counseling Quarterly, 1,* 288-301.

*Burgoon, J. K. (1976). The unwillingness to communicate scale: Development and validation. *Communication Monographs, 43,* 60-69.

*Burgoon, J. K. (1977). Unwillingness to communicate as a predictor of small group discussion behaviors and evaluations. *Central States Speech Journal, 28,* 122-133.

*Burgoon, J. K., & Burgoon, M. (1974). Unwillingness to communicate, anomia-alienation, and communication apprehension as predictors of small group communication. *Journal of Psychology, 88,* 31-38.

*Burgoon, J. K., & Hale, J. L. (1983). Dimensions of communication reticence and their impact on verbal encoding. *Communication Quarterly, 31,* 302-312.

*Burgoon, J. K., & Koper, R. J. (1984). Nonverbal and relational communication associated with reticence. *Human Communication Research, 10,* 601-626.

Burgoon, J. K., Pfau, M., Birk, T., & Manusov, V. (1987). Nonverbal communication performance and perceptions associated with reticence: Replication and classroom implications. *Communication Education, 36,* 119-130.

Buss, A. H. (1980). *Self-consciousness and social anxiety.* San Francisco: Freeman.

*Butler, J. F. (1986). Personality characteristics of subjects high and low in apprehension about communication. *Perceptual and Motor Skills, 62,* 895-898.

Byrne, D. (1971). *The attraction paradigm.* New York: Academic Press.

*Cacioppo, J. T., Glass, C. R., & Merluzzi, T. V. (1979). Self-statements and self-evaluations: A cognitive-response analysis of heterosocial anxiety. *Cognitive Therapy and Research, 3,* 249-262.

Campbell, D. T., & Fiske, D. W. (1959). Convergent and discriminant validation by the multitrait-multimethod matrix. *Psychological Bulletin, 56,* 81-105.

*Cappella, J. N. (1985). Production principles for turn-taking rules in social interaction: Socially anxious vs. socially secure persons. *Journal of Language and Social Psychology, 4,* 195-212.

*Carducci, B. J., & Webber, A. W. (1979). Shyness as a determinant of interpersonal distance. *Psychological Reports, 44,* 1075-1078.

Carver, C. S., & Scheier, M. F. (1981). *Attention and self-regulation: A control theory approach to human behavior.* New York: Springer-Verlag.

Castelfranchi, C., & Poggi, I. (1990). Blushing as discourse: Was Darwin wrong? In W. R. Crozier (Ed.), *Shyness and embarrassment: Perspectives from social psychology* (pp. 230-254). Cambridge: Cambridge University Press.

Cheek, J. M. (1982, August). Shyness and self-esteem: A personological perspective. In M. R. Leary (Chair), *Recent research in social anxiety.* Symposium conducted at the annual meeting of the American Psychological Association, Washington, DC.

*Cheek, J. M., & Buss, A. H. (1981). Shyness and sociability. *Journal of Personality and Social Psychology, 41,* 330-339.

Cheek, J. M., & Melchior, L. A. (1990). Shyness, self-esteem, and self-consciousness. In H. Leitenberg (Ed.), *Handbook of social and evaluation anxiety* (pp. 47-82). New York: Plenum.

Cheek, J. M., Melchior, L. A., & Carpentieri, A. M. (1986). Shyness and self-concept. In L. M. Hartman & K. R. Blankstein (Eds.), *Perception of self in emotional disorder and psychotherapy* (pp. 113-131). New York: Plenum.

Cheek, J. M., & Watson, A. K. (1989). The definition of shyness: Psychological imperialism or construct validity? *Journal of Social Behavior and Personality, 4,* 85-95.

Chen, G. M. (1994). Social desirability as a predictor of argumentativeness and communication anxiety. *Journal of Psychology, 128,* 433-438.

*Chesebro, J. W., McCroskey, J. C., Atwater, D. F., Bahrenfuss, R. M., Cawelti, G., Gaudino, J. L., & Hodges, H. (1992). Communication apprehension and self-perceived communication competence of at-risk students. *Communication Education, 42,* 345-360.

*Claeys, W. (1989). Social anxiety, evaluative threat and incidental recall of trait words. *Anxiety Research, 2,* 27-43.

*Clark, A. J. (1989). Communication confidence and listening competence: An investigation of the relationships of willingness to communicate, communication anxiety, and receiver apprehension to comprehension of emotional meaning in spoken messages. *Communication Education, 38,* 118-125.

*Clark, J. V., & Arkowitz, H. (1975). Social anxiety and self-evaluation of interpersonal performance. *Psychological Reports, 36,* 211-221.

Clevenger, T., & King, T. R. (1961). A factor analysis of the visible symptoms of stage fright. *Speech Monographs, 28,* 296-298.

Cohen, J. (1977). *Statistical power analyses for the behavioral sciences.* New York: Academic Press.

*Colby, N., Hopf, T., & Ayres, J. (1993). Nice to meet you? Inter/intrapersonal perceptions of communication apprehension in initial interaction. *Communication Quarterly, 41,* 221-230.

Comadena, M. E., & Prusank, D. T. (1988). Communication anxiety and academic achievement among elementary and middle school students. *Communication Education, 37,* 270-277.

*Conger, J. C., & Farrell, A. D. (1981). Behavioral components of heterosocial skills. *Behavior Therapy, 12,* 41-55.

Crozier, W. R. (1979). Shyness as anxious self-preoccupation. *Psychological Reports, 44,* 959-962.

*Curran, J. P., Wallander, J. L., & Fischetti, M. (1980). The importance of behavioral and cognitive factors in heterosexual-social anxiety. *Journal of Personality, 48,* 287-292.

Daly, J. A. (1978). The assessment of social-communication anxiety via self reports: A comparison of measures. *Communication Monographs, 45,* 204-218.

*Daly, J. A., & McCroskey, J. C. (1975). Occupational desirability and choice as a function of communication apprehension. *Journal of Counseling Psychology, 22,* 309-313.

*Daly, J. A., Richmond, V. P., & Leth, S. (1979). Social communicative anxiety and the personnel selection process: Testing the similarity effect in selection decisions. *Human Communication Research, 6,* 18-32.

Daly, J. A., & Stafford, L. (1984). Correlates and consequences of social-communicative anxiety. In J. A. Daly & J. C. McCroskey (Eds.), *Avoiding communication: Shyness, reticence, and communication anxiety* (pp. 125-144). Beverly Hills, CA: Sage.

*Daly, J. A., Vangelisti, A. L., Neel, H. L., & Cavanaugh, P. D. (1989). Pre-performance concerns associated with public speaking anxiety. *Communication Quarterly, 37,* 39-53.

*Daly, S. (1978). Behavioral correlates of social anxiety. *British Journal of Social and Clinical Psychology, 17,* 117-120.

Darwin, C. (1955). *The expression of emotions in man and animals.* New York: Philosophical Library. (Original work published 1872)

*Davison, G. C., Feldman, P. M., & Osborn, C. E. (1984). Articulated thoughts, irrational beliefs, and fear of negative evaluations. *Cognitive Therapy and Research, 8,* 349-362.

*Deffenbacher, J. L., Zwemer, W. A., Whisman, M. A., Hill, R. A., & Sloan, R. D. (1986). Irrational beliefs and anxiety. *Cognitive Therapy and Research, 10,* 281-292.

*DePaulo, B. M., Dull, W. R., Greenberg, J. M., & Swaim, G. W. (1989). Are shy people reluctant to ask for help? *Journal of Personality and Social Psychology, 56,* 834-844.

*DePaulo, B. M., Epstein, J. A., & LeMay, C. S. (1990). Responses of the socially anxious to the prospect of interpersonal evaluation. *Journal of Personality, 58,* 623-640.

DePaulo, B. M., Kenny, D. A., Hoover, C. W., Webb, W., & Oliver, P. V. (1987). Accuracy of person perception: Do people know what kinds of impressions they convey? *Journal of Personality and Social Psychology, 52,* 303-315.

DePaulo, B. M., & Tang, J. (1994). Social anxiety and social judgment: The example of detecting deception. *Journal of Research in Personality, 28,* 142-153.

*Dodge, C. S., Heimberg, R. G., Nyman, D., & O'Brien, G. T. (1987). Daily heterosocial interactions of high and low socially anxious college students. *Behavior Therapy, 18,* 90-96.

*Dow, M. G., Biglan, A., & Glaser, S. R. (1985). Multimethod assessment of socially anxious and socially nonanxious women. *Behavioral Assessment, 7,* 273-282.

*Down, V. C., Javidi, M., & Nussbaum, J. F. (1987). Communication apprehension and loneliness in older adults: An empirical test of socio-environmental theory. *Communication Research Reports, 4,* 38-42.

Duval, S., & Wicklund, R. A. (1972). *A theory of objective self-awareness.* New York: Academic Press.

Edelmann, R. J. (1985). Dealing with embarrassing events: Socially anxious and nonsocially anxious groups compared. *British Journal of Clinical Psychology, 24,* 281-288.

Edelmann, R. J. (1987). *The psychology of embarrassment.* New York: John Wiley.

*Edelmann, R. J. (1990). Chronic blushing, self-consciousness, and social anxiety. *Journal of Psychopathology and Behavioral Assessment, 12,* 119-127.

*Edelmann, R. J. (1991). Correlates of chronic blushing. *British Journal of Clinical Psychology, 30,* 177-178.

*Edelmann, R. J., & Skov, V. (1993). Blushing propensity, social anxiety, anxiety sensitivity and awareness of bodily sensations. *Personality and Individual Differences, 14,* 495-498.

*Efran, J. S., & Korn, P. R. (1969). Measurement of social caution: Self-appraisal, role playing, and discussion behavior. *Journal of Consulting and Clinical Psychology, 33,* 78-83.

*Eisenberg, N., Fabes, R., & Murphy, B. C. (1995). Relations of shyness and low sociability to regulation and emotionality. *Journal of Personality and Social Psychology, 68,* 505-517.

Ellis, A. (1962). *Reason and emotion in psychotherapy.* New York: Lyle Stuart.

*Ellis, K. (1995). Apprehension, self-perceived competency, and teacher immediacy in the laboratory-supported public speaking course: Trends and relationships. *Communication Education, 44,* 64-78.

*Ericson, P. M., & Gardner, J. W. (1992). Two longitudinal studies of communication apprehension and its effects in college students' success. *Communication Quarterly, 40,* 127-137.

Evans, M. A. (1993). Communicative competence as a dimension of shyness. In K. H. Rubin & J. B. Asendorpf (Eds.), *Social withdrawal, inhibition, and shyness in childhood* (pp. 189-214). Hillsdale, NJ: Lawrence Erlbaum.

Exline, R. V., & Fehr, B. J. (1978). Applications of semiosis to the study of visual interaction. In A. W. Siegman & S. Feldstein (Eds.), *Nonverbal behavior and communication* (pp. 117-152). Hillsdale, NJ: Lawrence Erlbaum.

*Falcione, R. L., McCroskey, J. C., & Daly, J. A. (1979). Job satisfaction as a function of employees' communication apprehension, self-esteem, and perceptions of their immediate supervisors. In B. D. Ruben (Ed.), *Communication yearbook 1* (pp. 57-72). New Brunswick, NJ: Transaction.

*Farabee, D. J., Holcom, M. L., Ramsey, S. L., & Cole, S. G. (1993). Social anxiety and speaker gaze in a persuasive atmosphere. *Journal of Research in Personality, 27,* 365-376.

*Fatis, M. (1983). Degree of shyness and self-reported physiological, behavior, and cognitive reaction. *Psychological Reports, 52,* 351-354.

Fenigstein, A., Scheier, M. F., & Buss, A. H. (1975). Public and private self-consciousness: Assessment and theory. *Journal of Consulting and Clinical Psychology, 43,* 522-527.

*Fischetti, M., Curran, J. P., & Wessberg, H. W. (1977). Sense of timing: A skill deficiency in heterosexually-socially anxious males. *Behavior Modification, 1,* 179-194.

*Fisher, J. Y., & Infante, D. A. (1973). The relationship between communication anxiety and human motivation variables. *Central States Speech Journal, 24,* 246-252.

Flavell, J. H. (1979). Metacognition and cognitive monitoring: A new area of cognitive developmental inquiry. *American Psychologist, 34,* 906-911.

*Franzoi, S. L. (1983). Self-concept differences as a function of private self-consciousness and social anxiety. *Journal of Research in Personality, 17,* 275-287.

*Freimuth, V. S. (1976). The effects of communication apprehension on communication effectiveness. *Human Communication Research, 2,* 289-295.

*Garcia, S., Stinson, L., Ickes, W., Bissonnette, V., & Briggs, S. R. (1991). Shyness and physical attractiveness in mixed sex dyads. *Journal of Personality and Social Psychology, 61,* 35-49.

*Gatchel, R. J., & Proctor, J. D. (1976). Effectiveness of voluntary heart rate control in reducing speech anxiety. *Journal of Consulting and Clinical Psychology, 44,* 381-389.

Gibbons, F. X. (1990). Self-evaluation and self-perception: The role of attention in the experience of anxiety. *Anxiety Research, 2,* 153-163.

Gibbons, F. X. (1991). Self-attention and behavior: A review and theoretical approach. In M. Zanna (Ed.), *Advances in experimental social psychology* (Vol. 23, pp. 249-303). San Diego, CA: Academic Press.

*Giffin, K., & Gilham, S. M. (1971). Relationship between speech anxiety and motivation. *Speech Monographs, 38,* 65-69.

*Girodo, M., Dotzenroth, S. E., & Stein, S. J. (1981). Causal attribution bias in shy males: Implications for self-esteem and self-confidence. *Cognitive Therapy and Research, 5,* 325-338.

*Glasgow, R. E., & Arkowitz, H. (1975). The behavioral assessment of male and female social competence in dyadic heterosexual interactions. *Behavior Therapy, 6,* 488-498.

*Glass, C. R., & Furlong, M. (1990). Cognitive assessment of social anxiety: Affective and behavioral correlates. *Cognitive Therapy and Research, 14,* 365-380.

*Glass, C. R., Gottman, J. M., & Shmurak, S. (1976). Response acquisition and cognitive self-statement modification approaches to dating skills training. *Journal of Counseling Psychology, 23,* 520-526.

*Glass, C. R., Merluzzi, T. V., Biever, J. L., & Larsen, K. H. (1982). Cognitive assessment of social anxiety: Development and validation of a self-statement questionnaire. *Cognitive Therapy and Research, 6,* 37-55.

*Goldfried, M. R., Padawer, W., & Robins, C. (1984). Social anxiety and the semantic structure of heterosocial interactions. *Journal of Abnormal Psychology, 93,* 87-97.

*Goldfried, M. R., & Sobocinski, D. (1975). The effect of irrational beliefs on emotional arousal. *Journal of Consulting and Clinical Psychology, 43,* 504-510.

*Gormally, J., Sipps, G., Raphael, R., Edur, D., & Varvil-Weld, D. (1981). The relationship between maladaptive cognitions and social anxiety. *Journal of Consulting and Clinical Psychology, 49,* 300-301.

Gough, H. G., & Thorne, A. (1986). Positive, negative, and balanced shyness: Self-definitions and the reactions of others. In W. H. Jones, J. M. Cheek, & S. R. Briggs (Eds.), *Shyness: Perspectives on research and treatment* (pp. 205-225). New York: Plenum.

*Greenberg, J., & Pyszczynski, T. (1986). Persistent high self-focus after failure and low self-focus after success: The depressive self-focusing style. *Journal of Personality and Social Psychology, 50,* 1039-1044.

*Greenberg, J., Pyszczynski, T., & Stine, P. (1985). Social anxiety and anticipation of future interaction as determinants of the favorability of self-presentation. *Journal of Research in Personality, 19,* 1-11.

*Greene, J. O., & Sparks, G. G. (1983). The role of outcome expectations in the experience of state communication anxiety. *Communication Quarterly, 31,* 212-219.

*Gregorich, S. E., Kemple, K., & Leary, M. R. (1985). Fear of negative evaluation and reactions to information regarding others' performances. *Representative Research in Social Psychology, 16,* 15-26.

*Haemmerlie, F. M. (1983). Heterosocial anxiety in college females: A biased interactions treatment. *Behavior Modification, 7,* 611-623.

*Haemmerlie, F. M., Montgomery, R. L., & Melchers, J. (1988). Social support, perceptions of attractiveness, weight, and the CPI in socially anxious males and females. *Journal of Clinical Psychology, 44,* 435-440.

*Halford, K., & Foddy, M. (1982). Cognitive and social skills correlates of social anxiety. *British Journal of Clinical Psychology, 21,* 17-28.

Hall, R., & Goldberg, D. G. (1977). The role of social anxiety in social interaction difficulties. *British Journal of Psychiatry, 131,* 610-615.

*Hansford, B. C. (1988). Self-reports and observations of dominant communicator style and communication apprehension. *Communication Research Reports, 5,* 44-51.

Hansson, R. O. (1986). Shyness and the elderly. In W. H. Jones, J. M. Cheek, & S. R. Briggs (Eds.), *Shyness: Perspectives on research and treatment* (pp. 117-132). New York: Plenum.

*Hart, E. A., Leary, M. R., & Rejeski, W. J. (1989). The measurement of social physique anxiety. *Journal of Sport and Exercise Psychology, 11,* 94-104.

Hartman, L. (1983). A metacognitive model of social anxiety: Implications for treatment. *Clinical Psychology Review, 3,* 435-456.

Hartman, L. (1984). Cognitive components of social anxiety. *Journal of Clinical Psychology, 40,* 137-139.

Hartman, L. (1986). Social anxiety, problem drinking, and self-awareness. In L. M. Hartman & K. R. Blankstein (Eds.), *Perceptions of self in emotional disorders and psychotherapy* (pp. 265-281). New York: Plenum.

*Hawkins, K., & Stewart, R. A. (1991). Effects of communication apprehension on perceptions of leadership and intragroup attraction in small task-oriented groups. *Southern Communication Journal, 57,* 1-10.

*Heimberg, R. G., Acerra, M. C., & Holstein, A. (1985). Partner similarity mediates interpersonal anxiety. *Cognitive Therapy and Research, 9,* 443-445.

*Heimberg, R. G., Harrison, D. F., Montgomery, D., Madsen, C. H., & Sherfey, J. A. (1980). Psychiatric behavioral analysis of a social anxiety inventory: The situation questionnaire. *Behavioral Assessment, 2,* 403-415.

Heimberg, R. G., Madsen, C. H., Montgomery, D., & McNabb, C. E. (1980). Behavioral treatments for heterosocial problems. *Behavior Modification, 4,* 147-172.

Hewit, J. P., & Stokes, R. (1975). Disclaimers. *American Sociological Review, 40,* 1-11.

*Hill, G. J. (1989). An unwillingness to act: Behavioral appropriateness, situational constraint, and self-efficacy in shyness. *Journal of Personality, 57,* 871-890.

*Hoffman, M. A., & Teglasi, H. (1982). The role of causal attributions in counseling shy subjects. *Journal of Counseling Psychology, 29,* 132-139.

*Hope, D. A., & Heimberg, R. G. (1988). Public and private self-consciousness and social phobia. *Journal of Personality Assessment, 52,* 626-639.

Hope, D. A., & Heimberg, R. G. (1990). Dating anxiety. In H. Leitenberg (Ed.), *Handbook of social and evaluation anxiety* (pp. 217-245). New York: Plenum.

*Hope, D. A., Heimberg, R. G., & Klein, J. F. (1990). Social anxiety and recall of interpersonal information. *Journal of Cognitive Psychotherapy, 4,* 185-195.

*Hopf, T., & Colby, N. (1992). The relationship between interpersonal communication apprehension and self-efficacy. *Communication Research Reports, 9,* 131-135.

Hunter, J. E., Schmidt, F., & Jackson, G. B. (1982). *Meta-analysis: Cumulating research findings across studies.* Beverly Hills, CA: Sage.

Hunter, J. E., Schmidt, F., & Jackson, G. B. (1990). *Advanced meta-analysis.* Newbury Park, CA: Sage.

*Hurt, H. T., & Preiss, R. (1978). Silence isn't necessarily golden: Communication apprehension, desired social choice, and academic success among middle school students. *Human Communication Research, 4,* 315-328.

*Ickes, W., Robertson, E., Tooke, W., & Teng, G. (1986). Naturalistic social cognition: Methodology, assessment, and validation. *Journal of Personality and Social Psychology, 51,* 66-82.

*Iizuka, Y. (1994). Gaze during speaking as related to shyness. *Perceptual and Motor Skills, 78,* 1259-1264.

*Ingram, R. E. (1989). Unique and shared cognitive factors in social anxiety and depression: Automatic thinking and self-appraisal. *Journal of Social and Clinical Psychology, 8,* 198-208.

Ingram, R. E. (1990). Attentional nonspecificity in depressive and generalized anxious affective states. *Cognitive Therapy and Research, 14,* 25-35.

Ingram, R. E., Cruet, D., Johnson, B. R., & Wisnicki, K. S. (1988). Self-focused attention, gender, gender role, and vulnerability to negative affect. *Journal of Personality and Social Psychology, 55,* 967-978.

*Ishiyama, F. I. (1984). Shyness: Anxious social sensitivity and self-isolating tendency. *Adolescence, 19,* 903-911.

Johnson, K. A., Johnson, J. E., & Petzel, T. P. (1992). Social anxiety, depression, and distorted cognitions in college students. *Journal of Social and Clinical Psychology, 11,* 181-195.

*Johnson, R. L., & Glass, C. R. (1989). Heterosocial anxiety and direction of attention in high school boys. *Cognitive Therapy and Research, 13,* 509-526.

Jones, E., & Berglas, S. (1978). Control of attributions about the self through self-handicapping strategies: The appeal of alcohol and the role of underachievement. *Personality and Social Psychology Bulletin, 4,* 200-206.

Jones, W. H., & Briggs, S. R. (1984). The self-other discrepancy in social shyness. In R. Schwarzer (Ed.), *The self in anxiety, stress, and depression* (pp. 93-107). New York: Elsevier Science.

Jones, W. H., & Briggs, S. R. (1986). *A manual for the social reticence scale: A measure of shyness.* Palo Alto, CA: Consulting Psychologists Press.

Jones, W. H., Briggs, S. R., & Smith, T. G. (1986). Shyness: Conceptualization and measurement. *Journal of Personality and Social Psychology, 51,* 629-639.

Jones, W. H., & Carpenter, B. V. (1986). Shyness, social behavior, and relationships. In W. H. Jones, J. M. Cheek, & S. R. Briggs (Eds.), *Shyness: Perspectives on research and treatment* (pp. 227-238). New York: Plenum.

Jones, W. H., & Russell, D. (1982). The social reticence scale: An objective instrument to measure shyness. *Journal of Personality Assessment, 46,* 629-631.

Jordan, W. J., & Powers, W. G. (1978). Verbal behavior as a function of apprehension and social contact. *Human Communication Research, 4,* 294-300.

*Kearney, P., & McCroskey, J. C. (1980). Relationships among teacher communication style, trait and state communication apprehension, and teacher effectiveness. In D. Nimmo (Ed.), *Communication yearbook 4* (pp. 533-552). New Brunswick, NJ: Transaction.

Kelly, L. (1982). A rose by any other name is still a rose: A comparative analysis of reticence, communication anxiety, unwillingness to communicate, and shyness. *Human Communication Research, 8,* 99-113.

Kelly, L., & Keaton, J. (1992). A test of the effectiveness of the reticence program at the Pennsylvania State University. *Communication Education, 41,* 361-374.

Kendon, A. (1967). Some functions of gaze-direction in social interactions. *Acta Psychologica, 26,* 22-63.

Kenny, D. A., & DePaulo, B. M. (1993). Do people know how others view them? An empirical and theoretical account. *Psychological Bulletin, 102,* 390-402.

*Kimble, C. E., & Zehr, D. (1982). Self-consciousness, information load, self-presentation, and memory in a social situation. *Journal of Social Psychology, 118,* 39-46.

*Kondo, D. S. (1994). A comparative analysis of interpersonal communication motives between high and low communication apprehensives. *Communication Research Reports, 11,* 53-58.

Lacey, J. I. (1967). Somatic response patterning and stress: Some revisions of activation theory. In M. H. Appley & R. Trumbull (Eds.), *Psychological stress.* New York: Appleton-Century-Crofts.

LaFrance, M., & Mayo, C. (1978). *Moving bodies.* Monterey, CA: Brooks/Cole.

*Lake, E. A., & Arkin, R. M. (1985). Reactions to objective and subjective interpersonal evaluation: The influence of social anxiety. *Journal of Social and Clinical Psychology, 3,* 143-160.

Langston, C. A., & Cantor, N. (1989). Social anxiety and social constraint: When making friends is hard. *Journal of Personality and Social Psychology, 56,* 649-661.

Lazarus, R. S., & Smith, C. A. (1988). Knowledge and appraisal in the cognition-emotion relationship. *Cognition and Emotion, 2,* 281-300.

Leary, M. R. (1982). Social anxiety. In L. Wheeler (Ed.), *Review of personality and social psychology* (Vol. 3, pp. 97-120). Beverly Hills, CA: Sage.

Leary, M. R. (1983a). The conceptual distinctions are important: Another look at communication apprehension and related constructs. *Human Communication Research, 10,* 305-312.

Leary, M. R. (1983b). Social anxiousness: The construct and its measurement. *Journal of Personality Assessment, 47,* 66-75.

Leary, M. R. (1983c). *Understanding social anxiety: Social, personality, and clinical perspectives.* Beverly Hills, CA: Sage.

Leary, M. R. (1986a). Affective and behavioral components of shyness: Implications for theory, measurement, and research. In W. H. Jones, J. M. Cheek, & S. R. Briggs (Eds.), *Shyness: Perspectives on research and treatment* (pp. 27-38). New York: Plenum.

*Leary, M. R. (1986b). The impact of interactional impediments on social anxiety and self-presentation. *Journal of Experimental Social Psychology, 22,* 122-135.

Leary, M. R. (1987). Socially-based anxiety: A review of measures. In C. Tardy (Ed.), *A handbook for the study of human communication: Methods and instruments for observing, measuring, and assessing communication processes* (pp. 365-384). Norwood, NJ: Ablex.

Leary, M. R. (1990). Anxiety, cognition, and behavior: In search of a broader perspective. *Journal of Social Behavior and Personality, 5,* 39-44.

Leary, M. R. (1991). Social anxiety, shyness, and related constructs. In J. P. Robinson, P. R. Shaver, & L. S. Wrightsman (Eds.), *Measures of personality and social psychological attitudes* (pp. 161-194). San Diego, CA: Academic Press.

Leary, M. R., & Atherton, S. C. (1986). Self-efficacy, social anxiety, and inhibition in interpersonal encounters. *Journal of Social and Clinical Psychology, 4,* 256-267.

*Leary, M. R., Atherton, S. C., Hill, S., & Hur, C. (1986). Attributional mediators of social inhibition and avoidance. *Journal of Personality, 54,* 704-716.

Leary, M. R., Britt, T. W., Cutlip, W. D., & Templeton, J. L. (1992). Social blushing. *Psychological Bulletin, 112,* 446-460.

Leary, M. R., & Dobbins, S. E. (1983). Social anxiety, sexual behavior, and contraceptive use. *Journal of Personality and Social Psychology, 45,* 1347-1354.

*Leary, M. R., Knight, P. D., & Johnson, K. A. (1987). Social anxiety and dyadic conversation: A verbal response analysis. *Journal of Social and Clinical Psychology, 5,* 34-50.

*Leary, M. R., & Kowalski, R. M. (1993). The interaction anxiousness scale: Construct and criterion-related validity. *Journal of Personality Assessment, 61,* 136-146.

Leary, M. R., Kowalski, R. M., & Bergen, D. J. (1988). Interpersonal information acquisition and confidence in first encounters. *Personality and Social Psychology Bulletin, 14,* 68-77.

*Leary, M. R., Kowalski, R. M., & Campbell, C. D. (1988). Self-presentational concerns and social anxiety: The role of generalized impression expectancies. *Journal of Research in Personality, 22,* 308-321.

*Leary, M. R., & Meadows, S. (1991). Predictors, elicitors, and concomitants of social blushing. *Journal of Personality and Social Psychology, 60,* 254-262.

Leary, M. R., & Miller, R. S. (1986). *Social psychology and dysfunctional behavior: Origins, diagnosis, and treatment.* New York: Springer-Verlag.

Leary, M. R., & Schlenker, B. R. (1981). The social psychology of shyness: A self-presentation model. In J. T. Tedeschi (Ed.), *Impression management theory and social psychological research* (pp. 335-358). New York: Academic Press.

Lederman, L. C. (1983). High communication apprehensives talk about communication anxiety and its effects on their behavior. *Communication Quarterly, 31,* 233-237.

*Lord, C. G., Saenz, D. S., & Godfrey, D. K. (1987). Effects of perceived scrutiny on participant memory for social interaction. *Journal of Experimental Social Psychology, 23,* 498-517.

*Lord, C. G., & Zimbardo, P. G. (1985). Actor-observer differences in perceived stability of shyness. *Social Cognition, 3,* 250-265.

*Maddux, J. E., Norton, L. W., & Leary, M. R. (1988). Cognitive components of social anxiety: An investigation of the integration of self-presentation theory and self-efficacy theory. *Journal of Social and Clinical Psychology, 6,* 180-190.

*Mahone, E. M., Bruch, M. A., & Heimberg, R. G. (1993). Focus of attention and social anxiety: The role of negative self-thoughts and perceived positive attributes of the other. *Cognitive Therapy and Research, 17,* 209-224.

*Mandel, N. M., & Shrauger, J. S. (1980). The effects of self-evaluative statements on heterosocial approach in shy and nonshy males. *Cognitive Therapy and Research, 4,* 369-381.

Mandler, G. (1975). *Mind and emotion.* New York: John Wiley.

Markus, H. (1977). Self-schemata and processing information about the self. *Journal of Personality and Social Psychology, 35,* 63-78.

Markus, H. (1980). The self in thought and memory. In D. M. Wegner & R. R. Valacher (Eds.), *The self in social psychology* (pp. 102-130). New York: Oxford University Press.

*Maroldo, G. K. (1981). Shyness and loneliness among college men and women. *Psychological Reports, 48,* 885-886.

Maslach, C., & Solomon, T. (1977). *Pressures toward dehumanization from within and without.* Unpublished manuscript, University of California, Berkeley.

McCroskey, J. C. (1970). Measures of communication-bound anxiety. *Speech Monographs, 37,* 269-277.

McCroskey, J. C. (1976). The effects of communication apprehension on nonverbal behavior. *Communication Quarterly, 24,* 39-44.

McCroskey, J. C. (1977). Oral communication: Assumption of recent theory and research. *Human Communication Research, 4,* 78-96.

McCroskey, J. C. (1978). Validity of the PRCA as an index of oral communication apprehension. *Communication Monographs, 45,* 192-203.

McCroskey, J. C. (1982). Oral communication apprehension: A reconceptualization. In M. Burgoon (Ed.), *Communication yearbook 6* (pp. 136-170). Beverly Hills, CA: Sage.

McCroskey, J. C. (1984). The communication perspective. In J. A. Daly & J. C. McCroskey (Eds.), *Avoiding communication: Shyness, reticence, and communication anxiety* (pp. 13-38). Beverly Hills, CA: Sage.

*McCroskey, J. C., & Andersen, J. F. (1976). Relationship between communication apprehension and academic achievement. *Human Communication Research, 3,* 73-81.

McCroskey, J. C., Booth-Butterfield, S., & Payne, S. K. (1989). The impact of communication apprehension on college students' retention and success. *Communication Quarterly, 37,* 100-107.

*McCroskey, J. C., & Daly, J. A. (1976). Teachers' expectations of communication apprehensive children in the elementary school. *Human Communication Research, 3,* 67-72.

*McCroskey, J. C., Daly, J. A., Richmond, V. P., & Cox, B. G. (1975). The effects of communication apprehension on interpersonal attraction. *Human Communication Research, 2,* 51-65.

*McCroskey, J. C., Daly, J. A., & Sorensen, G. (1976). Personality correlates of communication apprehension: A research note. *Human Communication Research, 2,* 376-380.

*McCroskey, J. C., & Richmond, V. P. (1976). The effects of communication apprehension on the perception of peers. *Western Journal of Speech Communication, 40,* 14-21.

McCroskey, J. C., & Richmond, V. P. (1977). Communication apprehension as a predictor of self-disclosure. *Communication Quarterly, 25,* 40-43.

*McCroskey, J. C., & Sheahan, M. E. (1978). Communication apprehension, social preference, and social behavior in a college environment. *Communication Quarterly, 26,* 41-50.

McEwan, K. L., & Devins, G. M. (1983). Is increased arousal in social anxiety noticed by others? *Journal of Abnormal Psychology, 92,* 417-421.

McFarlin, D. B., & Blascovich, J. (1981). Effects of self-esteem and performance on future affective preferences and cognitive expectations. *Journal of Personality and Social Psychology, 40,* 521-531.

McMullen, L. M., & Pasloski, D. D. (1992). Effects of communication apprehension, familiarity of partner, and topic on selected "women's language" features. *Journal of Psycholinguistic Research, 21,* 17-30.

*Melchior, L. A., & Cheek, J. M. (1990). Shyness and anxious self-preoccupation during a social interaction. *Journal of Social Behavior and Personality, 5,* 117-130.

*Meleshko, K. G. A., & Alden, L. E. (1993). Anxiety and self-disclosure: Toward a motivational model. *Journal of Personality and Social Psychology, 64,* 1000-1009.

*Miller, M. D. (1987). The relationship of communication reticence and negative expectations. *Communication Education, 36,* 228-235.

*Miller, R. S. (1995). On the nature of embarrassability: Shyness, social evaluation, and social skill. *Journal of Personality, 62,* 315-339.

*Miller, W. R., & Arkowitz, H. (1977). Anxiety and perceived causation in social success and failure experiences: Disconfirmation of an attribution hypothesis. *Journal of Abnormal Psychology, 86,* 665-668.

*Modigliani, A. (1971). Embarrassment, facework, and eye contact: Testing a theory of embarrassment. *Journal of Personality and Social Psychology, 17,* 15-24.

Monroe, C., & Borzi, M. G. (1988). Communication apprehension and avoidance of postsecondary education. *School Counselor, 36,* 118-123.

*Montgomery, R. L., Haemmerlie, F. M., & Edwards, M. (1991). Social, personal, and interpersonal deficits in socially anxious people. *Journal of Social Behavior and Personality, 6,* 859-872.

*Monti, P. M., Boice, R., Fingeret, A. L., Zwick, W. R., Kolko, D., Munroe, S. M., & Grunberger, A. (1984). Mid-level measurement of social anxiety in psychiatric and non-psychiatric samples. *Behavioral Research and Therapy, 22,* 651-660.

*Monti, P. M., Kolko, D. J., Fingeret, A. L., Zwick, W. R. (1984). Three levels of measurement of social skill and social anxiety. *Journal of Nonverbal Behavior, 8,* 187-194.

*Monti, P. M., Wallander, J. L., Ahern, D. K., Abrahms, D. B., & Munroe, S. M. (1983). Multi-modal measurement of anxiety and social skills in a behavioral role-play test: Generalizability and discriminant validity. *Behavioral Assessment, 6,* 15-25.

*Morris, L. W., Harris, E. W., & Rovins, D. S. (1981). Interactive effects of generalized and situational expectancies on the arousal of cognitive and emotional components of social anxiety. *Journal of Research in Personality, 15,* 302-311.

*Mulac, A., & Sherman, A. R. (1974). Behavioral assessment of speech anxiety. *Quarterly Journal of Speech, 60,* 134-143.

*Mulac, A., & Sherman, A. R. (1975). Relationships among four parameters of speaker evaluation: Speech skill, source credibility, subjective speech anxiety, and behavioral speech anxiety. *Speech Monographs, 42,* 302-310.

Natale, M., Jaffe, J., & Entin, E. (1979). Vocal interruptions in dyadic communication as a function of speech and social anxiety. *Journal of Personality and Social Psychology, 37,* 865-878.

Neer, M. R. (1982). Enrolling students in communication apprehension laboratories. *Communication Education, 31,* 205-210.

Nichols, K. A. (1974). Severe social anxiety. *British Journal of Medical Psychology, 47,* 301-306.

*O'Bannion, K., & Arkowitz, H. (1977). Social anxiety and selective memory for affective information about the self. *Social Behavior and Personality, 5,* 321-328.

O'Hair, D., Cody, M. J., & Behnke, R. R. (1985). Communication apprehension and vocal stress as indices of deception. *Western Journal of Speech Communication, 49,* 286-300.

*Parks, M. R. (1980). A test of cross-situational consistency of communication apprehension. *Communication Monographs, 47,* 220-236.

*Parks, M. R., Dindia, K., Adam, J., Berlin, E., & Larson, K. (1980). Communication apprehension and student dating patterns: A replication and extension. *Communication Quarterly, 28,* 3-9.

*Patterson, M. L. (1973). Stability of nonverbal immediacy behaviors. *Journal of Experimental Social Psychology, 9,* 97-109.

*Patterson, M. L. (1977). Interpersonal distance, affect, and equilibrium theory. *Journal of Social Psychology, 101,* 205-214.

Patterson, M. L. (1983). *Nonverbal behavior: A functional perspective.* New York: Springer-Verlag.

Patterson, M. L. (1995). A parallel process model of nonverbal communication. *Journal of Nonverbal Behavior, 19,* 3-29.

*Patterson, M. L., Churchill, M. E., & Powell, J. L. (1991). Interpersonal expectancies and social anxiety in anticipating interactions. *Journal of Social and Clinical Psychology, 10,* 414-423.

Paul, G. (1966). *Insight versus desensitization in psychotherapy.* Stanford, CA: Stanford University Press.

Pearson, J. C., & Turner, L. H. (1984). *The PRCA: Predictive validity and behavior correlates.* Paper presented at the annual meeting of the Eastern Communication Association, Philadelphia.

Pelias, M. H., & Pelias, R. J. (1988). Communication anxiety in the basic course in performance of literature. *Communication Education, 37,* 118-126.

Peterson, J., Fischetti, M., Curran, J. P., & Arland, S. (1981). Sense of timing: A skill deficit in heterosocially anxious women. *Behavior Therapy, 12,* 195-201.

Phillips, G. M. (1968). Reticence: Pathology of the normal speaker. *Speech Monographs, 35,* 39-49.

*Pilkonis, P. (1977). The behavioral consequences of shyness. *Journal of Personality, 45,* 596-611.

Pilkonis, P., & Zimbardo, P. G. (1979). The personal and social dynamics of shyness. In C. E. Izard (Ed.), *Emotions in personality and psychopathology* (pp. 133-160). New York: Plenum.

*Porter, D. T. (1974). Self-report scales of communication apprehension and autonomic arousal: A test of construct validity. *Speech Monographs, 41,* 267-276.

*Porter, D. T. (1982). Communication style perceptions as a function of communication apprehension. *Communication Quarterly, 30,* 237-244.

Post, A. L., Wittmaier, B. C., & Radin, M. E. (1978). Self-disclosure as a function of state and trait anxiety. *Journal of Consulting and Clinical Psychology, 46,* 12-19.

*Powers, W. G. (1977). The rhetorical interrogative: Anxiety or control? *Human Communication Research, 4,* 44-47.

*Pozo, C., Carver, C. S., Wellens, A. R., & Scheier, M. F. (1991). Social anxiety and social perception: Construing others' reactions to the self. *Personality and Social Psychology Bulletin, 17,* 355-362.

*Prisbell, M. (1982). Heterosocial communication behavior and communication anxiety. *Communication Quarterly, 30,* 251-258.

Proctor, R. F., Douglas, A. T., Garera-Izquierdo, T., & Wartman, S. L. (1994). Approach, avoidance, and apprehension: Talking with high communication apprehensive students about getting help. *Communication Education, 43,* 312-321.

*Ragsdale, J. D. (1976). Relationships between hesitation phenomena anxiety and self-control in a normal communication situation. *Language and Speech, 19,* 257-265.

*Remland, M. S., & Jones, T. S. (1989). The effects of nonverbal involvement and communication apprehension on state anxiety, interpersonal attraction, and speech duration. *Communication Quarterly, 37,* 170-183.

*Reno, R. R., & Kenny, D. A. (1992). Effects of self-consciousness and social anxiety on self-disclosure among unacquainted individuals: An application of the social relations model. *Journal of Personality, 60,* 79-94.

*Richmond, V. P. (1978). The relationship between trait and state communication apprehension and interpersonal perceptions during acquaintance stages. *Human Communication Research, 4,* 338-349.

Richmond, V. P., Beatty, M. J., & Dyba, P. (1985). Shyness and popularity: Children's views. *Western Journal of Speech Communication, 49,* 116-125.

Richmond, V. P., & McCroskey, J. C. (1985). *Communication: Apprehension, avoidance, and effectiveness.* Scottsdale, AZ: Gorsuch Scarisbrick.

Richmond, V. P., & McCroskey, J. C. (1992). *Communication: Apprehension, avoidance, and effectiveness* (3rd ed.). Scottsdale, AZ: Gorsuch Scarisbrick.

*Richmond, V. P., McCroskey, J. C., & McCroskey, L. L. (1989). An investigation of self-perceived communication competence and personality orientation. *Communication Research Reports, 6,* 28-36.

Ritts, V. (1994). *Social anxiety and action identification in social interactions.* Unpublished doctoral dissertation, University of Missouri, St. Louis.

*Rosenfeld, L. B., Grant, C. H., & McCroskey, J. C. (1995). Communication apprehension and self-perceived communication competence of academically gifted students. *Communication Education, 44,* 79-86.

*Rosenfeld, L. B., & Plax, T. G. (1976). Personality discriminants of reticence. *Western Speech Communications, 36,* 22-31.

*Rubin, R. B., & Graham, E. (1988). Communication correlates of college success: An exploratory investigation. *Communication Education, 37,* 14-27.

Rubin, R. B., & Rubin, A. M. (1989). Communication apprehension and satisfaction in interpersonal relationships. *Communication Research Reports, 6,* 13-20.

Ryan, R. M., Plant, R. W., & Kuczkowjski, R. J. (1991). Relation of self-projection processes to performance, emotion, and memory in a controlled interaction setting. *Personality and Social Psychology Bulletin, 17,* 427-434.

Samter, W., & Burleson, B. R. (1984). Cognitive and motivational influences on spontaneous comforting behavior. *Human Communication Research, 11,* 231-260.

*Santee, R. T., & Maslach, C. (1982). To agree or not to agree: Personal dissent amid social pressure to conform. *Journal of Personality and Social Psychology, 42,* 690-700.

*Sanz, J., & Avia, M. D. (1994). Cognitive specificity in social anxiety and depression: Self-statements, self-focused attention, and dysfunctional attitudes. *Journal of Social and Clinical Psychology, 13,* 105-137.

Sarason, I. G. (1975). Anxiety and self-preoccupation. In I. G. Sarason & C. D. Spielberger (Eds.), *Stress and anxiety* (Vol. 2, pp. 165-187). New York: Hemisphere.

Sarason, I. G., & Sarason, B. R. (1986). Anxiety and interfering thoughts: Their effect on social interaction. In W. H. Jones, J. M. Cheek, & S. R. Briggs (Eds.), *Shyness: Perspectives on research and treatment* (pp. 253-264). New York: Plenum.

Sarason, I. G., Sarason, B. R., & Pierce, G. R. (1990). Anxiety, cognitive interference, and performance. *Journal of Social Behavior and Personality, 5,* 1-18.

Scherer, K. R. (1993). Studying the emotion-antecedent appraisal process: An expert systems approach. *Cognition and Emotion, 7,* 325-355.

Schlenker, B. R., & Leary, M. R. (1982). Social anxiety and self-presentation: A conceptualization and model. *Psychological Bulletin, 92,* 641-669.

Schlenker, B. R., & Leary, M. R. (1985). Social anxiety and communication about the self. *Journal of Language and Social Psychology, 4,* 171-196.

*Scott, M. D., McCroskey, J. C., & Sheahan, M. E. (1978). Measuring communication apprehension. *Journal of Communication, 28*(1), 104-111.

*Scott, M. D., & Wheeless, L. R. (1977a). Communication anxiety, student attitudes, and level of satisfaction. *Western Journal of Speech Communication, 41,* 188-198.

*Scott, M. D., & Wheeless, L. R. (1977b). The relationship of three types of communication anxiety to classroom achievement. *Southern Speech Communication Journal, 42,* 246-255.

*Scott, M. D., Wheeless, L. R., Yates, M. P., & Randolph, F. L. (1977). The effects of communication apprehension and test anxiety on three indicants of achievement in an alternative system of instruction: A follow-up study. In B. D. Ruben (Ed.), *Communication yearbook 1* (pp. 543-556). New Brunswick, NJ: Transaction.

*Shahidi, S., & Baluch, B. (1991). False heart-rate feedback, social anxiety, and self-attribution of embarrassment. *Psychological Reports, 69,* 1024-1026.

*Slivken, D. E., & Buss, A. H. (1984). Misattribution and speech anxiety. *Journal of Personality and Social Psychology, 47,* 396-402.

Smith, C. A. (1989). Dimensions of appraisal and physiological response in emotion. *Journal of Personality and Social Psychology, 56,* 339-353.

*Smith, R. E., & Sarason, I. G. (1975). Social anxiety and the evaluation of negative interpersonal feedback. *Journal of Consulting and Clinical Psychology, 43,* 429.

*Smith, T. W., Ingram, R. E., & Brehm, S. S. (1983). Social anxiety, anxious self-preoccupation, and recall of self-relevant information. *Journal of Personality and Social Psychology, 44,* 1276-1283.

*Smythe, M. J., & Powers, W. G. (1978). When Galatea is apprehensive: The effect of communication apprehension on teacher expectations. In B. D. Ruben (Ed.), *Communication yearbook 2* (pp. 487-491). New Brunswick, NJ: Transaction.

Snyder, C. R., & Smith, T. W. (1986). On being "shy like a fox": A self-handicapping analysis. In W. H. Jones, J. M. Cheek, & S. R. Briggs (Eds.), *Shyness: Perspectives on research and treatment* (pp. 161-172). New York: Plenum.

Snyder, C. R., Smith, T. W., Augelli, R., & Ingram, R. E. (1985). On the self-serving function of social anxiety: Shyness as a self-handicapping strategy. *Journal of Personality and Social Psychology, 48,* 970-980.

Solano, C. H., & Koester, N. H. (1989). Loneliness and communication problems: Subjective anxiety or objective skills? *Personality and Social Psychology Bulletin, 15,* 126-133.

Souz e Silva, M. C. (1977). *Social and cognitive dynamics of shyness.* Unpublished master's thesis, Stanford University.

*Steffen, J. T., & Reckman, R. F. (1978). Selective perception and interpretation of interpersonal cues in dyadic interactions. *Journal of Psychology, 99,* 245-248.

*Steffen, J. T., & Redden, J. (1977). Assessment of social competence in an evaluation-interaction analogue. *Human Communication Research, 4,* 30-37.

*Steptoe, A., Malik, F., Pay, C., Pearson, P., Price, C., & Win, Z. (1995). The impact of stage fright on student actors. *British Journal of Psychology, 86,* 27-39.

Storms, M. D., & McCaul, K. D. (1976). Attributional processes and the emotional exacerbation of dysfunctional behavior. In J. H. Harvey, W. J. Ickes, & R. F. Kidd (Eds.), *New directions in attribution research* (Vol. 1, pp. 143-164). Hillsdale, NJ: Lawrence Erlbaum.

Strauman, T. J., & Higgins, E. T. (1988). Self-discrepancies as predictors of vulnerability to distinct syndromes of chronic emotional distress. *Journal of Personality, 56,* 685-707.

*Sutton-Simon, K., & Goldfried, M. R. (1979). Faulty thinking patterns in two types of anxiety. *Cognitive Therapy and Research, 3,* 193-203.

*Tardy, C. H., Allen, M. T., Thompson, W. R., & Leary, M. R. (1991). Social anxiety and cardiovascular responses to interpersonal communication. *Southern Communication Journal, 57,* 25-34.

*Teglasi, H., & Fagin, S. S. (1984). Social anxiety and self-other biases in causal attribution. *Journal of Research in Personality, 18,* 64-80.

*Teglasi, H., & Hoffman, M. A. (1982). Causal attributions of shy subjects. *Journal of Research in Personality, 16,* 376-385.

Trower, P., & Gilbert, P. (1989). New theoretical conceptions of social anxiety and social phobia. *Clinical Psychology Review, 9,* 19-35.

*Turner, R. G. (1977). Self-consciousness and anticipatory belief change. *Personality and Social Psychology Bulletin, 3,* 438-441.

*Turner, S. M., Beidel, D. C., & Larkin, K. T. (1986). Situational determinants of social anxiety in clinical and nonclinical samples. *Journal of Consulting and Clinical Psychology, 54,* 523-527.

*Twentyman, C. T., & McFall, R. M. (1975). Behavioral training of social skills in shy males. *Journal of Consulting and Clinical Psychology, 43,* 384-395.

*Wallace, S. T., & Alden, L. E. (1991). A comparison of social standards and perceived ability in anxious and nonanxious men. *Cognitive Therapy and Research, 15,* 237-254.

*Watson, A. K., & Monroe, E. E. (1990). Academic achievement: A study of relationships of IA, communication apprehension, and teacher perception. *Communication Reports, 3,* 28-36.

*Watson, D., & Friend, R. (1969). Measurement of social-evaluative anxiety. *Journal of Consulting and Clinical Psychology, 33,* 448-457.

Wheeless, L. R., Nesser, K., & McCroskey, J. C. (1986). The relationships of self-disclosure and disclosiveness to high and low communication apprehension. *Communication Research Reports, 3,* 129-134.

*Wheeless, L. R., & Williamson, A. M. (1992). State communication apprehension and uncertainty in continuing initial interactions. *Southern Communication Journal, 57,* 249-255.

Winton, E. C., Clark, D. M., & Edelmann, R. J. (1995). Social anxiety, fear of negative evaluation, and the detection of negative emotion in others. *Behavior Research and Therapy, 33,* 193-196.

Wolfe, R. N., Lennox, R. D., & Cutler, B. L. (1986). Getting along and getting ahead: Empirical support for a theory of protective and acquisitive self-presentation. *Journal of Personality and Social Psychology, 50,* 356-361.

Zakahi, W. R., & Duran, R. L. (1982). All the lonely people: The relationship among loneliness, communicative competence, and communication anxiety. *Communication Quarterly, 30,* 203-209.

Zakahi, W. R., & Duran, R. L. (1985). Loneliness, communicative competence, and communication apprehension: Extension and replication. *Communication Quarterly, 33,* 50-60.

*Zakahi, W. R., Duran, R. L., & Adkins, M. (1994). Social anxiety, only skin deep? The relationship between physical attractiveness and social anxiety. *Communication Research Reports, 11,* 23-31.

*Zakahi, W. R., Jordan, F. F., & Christophel, D. (1992). Social adjustment to college: Communication apprehension and social network development among college students. *Communication Research Reports, 10,* 39-46.

*Zakahi, W. R., & McCroskey, J. C. (1989). Willingness to communicate: A potential confounding variable in communication research. *Communication Reports, 2,* 96-103.

Zimbardo, P. G. (1977). *Shyness: What it is, what to do about it.* Reading, MA: Addison-Wesley.

Zweig, D. R., & Brown, S. D. (1985). Psychometric evaluation of a written stimulus presentation format for the social interaction self-statement test. *Cognitive Therapy and Research, 9,* 285-295.

CHAPTER CONTENTS

9 The Development of Social and Communicative Competence in Childhood: Review and a Model of Personal, Familial, and Extrafamilial Processes

CRAIG H. HART
SUSANNE FROST OLSEN
CLYDE C. ROBINSON
BARBARA L. MANDLECO
Brigham Young University

The purpose of this chapter is to explicate a conceptual model that illustrates how extrafamilial (e.g., sources of stress and support), personal (e.g., inherent psychological child and parent resources), and familial (e.g., parenting, family interactions) processes work together to affect social/communicative peer group outcomes in young children. It is traditionally assumed that proximal factors (e.g., parenting, sibling/family interactions) have the greatest influence on child outcomes. In this review the authors discuss how these proximal factors work in combination with a host of personal and extrafamilial variables in ways that are linked to child social/communicative competence with peers. In addition to explaining possible mechanisms responsible for linkages within and between model components, the authors recommend directions for future research in areas of the framework that have weak empirical support.

SPECTS of children's behavioral, communicative, and social-cognitive skills have been of central interest to students of child-peer competence for several decades (see Hart, McGee, & Hernandez, 1993). Recently, attention has turned to linkages between family communi-

AUTHORS' NOTE: We are grateful for the suggestions of anonymous reviewers for insightful comments that helped clarify the nature of our model.

Correspondence and requests for reprints: Craig H. Hart, Department of Family Sciences, 1239-B SFLC, Brigham Young University, Provo, UT 84602; e-mail craig_hart@byu.edu

Communication Yearbook 20, pp. 305-373

cative and interactive processes and children's social/communicative competence with peers (e.g., Applegate, Burleson, & Delia, 1992; Black & Logan, 1995; Burleson, Delia, & Applegate, 1995; Burleson & Kunkel, 1996; Parke & Kellam, 1994; Parke & Ladd, 1992; Stafford & Bayer, 1993). These studies have been invigorated by longitudinal evidence suggesting that children having peer relations problems in childhood are at risk for many social/psychological difficulties throughout their lives (see DeRosier, Kupersmidt, & Patterson, 1994; Parker, Rubin, Price, & DeRosier, 1995; Rubin, Bukowski, & Parker, in press).

Many inquiries into the familial origins of social/communicative child outcomes focus on ways parenting beliefs and behaviors are related to children's competencies in peer groups (e.g., Black & Logan, 1995; Burleson, Delia, & Applegate, 1992; Hart, DeWolf, & Burts, 1993; Ladd & Le Sieur, 1995; Mize, Pettit, & Brown, 1995; Rubin, Stewart, & Chen, 1995). Other work focuses on predictors of parenting practices and parent-child interaction quality, emphasizing that parenting is multiply determined (Belsky, 1984; Das Eiden, Teti, & Corns, 1995). In a recent comprehensive synthesis of relevant literature, Stafford and Bayer (1993) illustrate a surprising amount of convergence across disciplines. However, less effort has been made to integrate knowledge across various literatures that explain how extrafamilial, personal, and familial processes may work through (or in conjunction with) parenting behaviors to link up with social/communicative outcomes in young children.

Our purposes in this chapter are to review the literature and to organize possible linkages in a conceptual model of social/communicative competence for early and middle childhood. Our assumptions and concepts are drawn, in part, from other models providing a foundation for our conceptual organization (e.g., Belsky, 1984; Chen & Rubin, 1994; Conger, Ge, Elder, Lorenz, & Simons, 1994; Hinde, 1987; Ladd, 1989; Lerner, Castellino, Terry, Villarruel, & McKinney, 1995; Parke & Kellam, 1994; Patterson, DeBaryshe, & Ramsey, 1989; Rollins & Thomas, 1979; Rubin, LeMare, & Lollis, 1990; Rubin & Mills, 1991; Shonkoff, Hauser-Cram, Krauss, & Upshur, 1992). We owe a considerable debt to ecological systems theory (e.g., Bronfenbrenner, 1986). Within this perspective, family and peer systems are not viewed as isolated from but as enmeshed within societal, cultural, and historical influences (see Moen, Elder, & Luscher, 1995).

We begin our literature review by briefly defining general component terms, providing an overview of the need for conceptual organization, discussing possible directions of effects, and previewing direct, mediating, and moderating linkages. Next, we define child-peer group outcomes associated with social/communicative competence and move backward through the conceptual model, specifying linkages within and between components. Throughout the review, we address connections that are lacking empirical support. In the concluding sections we touch upon implications for intervention and indicate directions for future empirical study.

CONCEPTUAL MODEL OVERVIEW

Component Definitions

In our proposed model, proximal factors include parenting and familial patterns of functioning (see Figure 9.1 and Table 9.1). Personal factors are defined as innate personal/psychological characteristics of children and parents derived from trait-oriented views (see Stafford & Bayer, 1993). For parents, learned characteristics, such as beliefs and cognitions, also are included to encompass life experiential factors. Experiential factors for children are reflected in peer group outcomes. Distal factors include extrafamilial (non-nuclear family) conditions such as sources of stress and support. All components will be defined in sections following the model overview. The primary purpose of this review is to explore relations among proximal influences (e.g., parenting, familial interactions), distal variables (e.g., economic stress), and personal factors (e.g., personality characteristics). We will then describe ways these factors may be linked to child-peer social/communicative competence, as reflected in internalizing, externalizing, and sociable child behaviors.

Because the literature is generally unclear as to causal linkages and directions of effects, it should be recognized that Figure 9.1 is not a formal causal model, but rather a pictorial representation of the interrelationships among model components. Figure 9.1 is not a formal causal model for at least three reasons. First, the bidirectional relationships specified by many model components are not testable because we have not specified the time frame under which causal effects flow in each direction; research designs geared toward testing causal relationships (e.g., longitudinal; cross-lagged correlations) will be needed to ferret out the nature of these relationships (see Gardner, 1992). Second, the model parts, as diagrammed, are overspecified (interconnected), leaving no unspecified paths for testing predicted against observed effects. Third, moderated relationships are not represented differently from mediated relationships in the diagram.

Need for Conceptual Organization

We organize the literature on peer social/communicative competence with an eye toward future research efforts complementing and extending prior work. Our conceptual model emphasizes fine levels of peer social/communicative variables and their linkages with specific proximal, personal, and distal features. These are typically unaddressed in more macrosystemic life-span approaches (e.g., Lerner et al., 1995). For example, macrosystemic models often collapse across personal child factors (e.g., temperament) and child-peer behaviors (e.g., sociable communication styles) in ways that conceptually mask linkages between inherent child characteristics and child social/communicative outcomes of interest here. Although there is some overlap

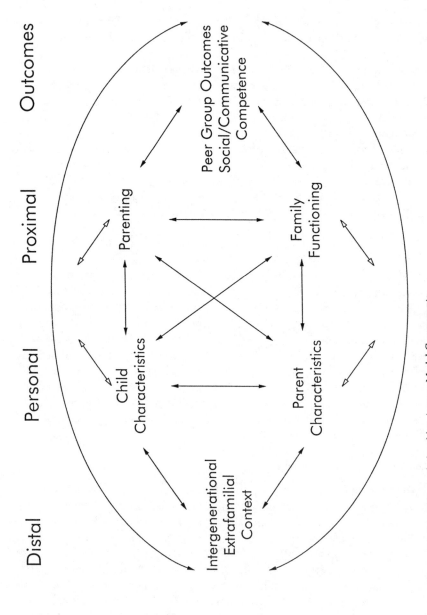

Figure 9.1. Representation of Interrelationships Among Model Components

TABLE 9.1
Model Components

Social communicative competence/peer group outcomes
 1. Internalizing disorders
 2. Externalizing disorders
 3. Sociable behaviors
 4. Peer acceptance and rejection
Proximal factors
 1. Parenting
  a. parent-child interactions
  b. parents as managers
  c. parents as educators
 2. Family functioning
  a. marital relationship
  b. sibling relationships
  c. family relationships
Personal factors
 1. Parent characteristics
  a. cognitions and emotions
  b. personal/psychological resources
  c. negative affect/depression
 2. Child characteristics
  a. genetic factors
  b. developmental level
  c. gender
Distal factors
 1. Intergenerational
 2. Employment/role strain
 3. Socioeconomic status
 4. Stress and support
 5. Culture

with nonsystemic models referenced above, our model reflects updated supporting literature and includes factors not typically addressed in some other frameworks. Some factors include sibling/familial interactions, communication processes, and parental arrangement of extrafamilial social environments. In addition, many models focus on singular child outcomes (withdrawal, aggression, delinquency, school adjustment, and so on) and do not reflect the multiple aspects of social/communicative competence explored here. It should be recognized, however, that some of the specificity and precision demonstrated in other models focusing on singular aspects of child behavior (e.g., Rubin et al., 1990) may be lost in the broader view presented here. Therefore, readers are encouraged to examine other cited sources to consider deeper levels of specificity. Finally, our model is unique in linking together child social and communicative competencies (see Fujiki & Brinton, 1994) and factors impinging upon them, and, we hope, will provide a framework for future research.

Most current empirical research focusing on early and middle childhood lends itself to unidirectional interpretations. Philosophical controversies and empirical inadequacies concerning "who affects whom" in the parent-child dyad and family system are cogently articulated by Stafford and Bayer (1993). We may further understand the intricacies of human development by investigating unidirectional, bidirectional, and systemic linkages across proximal, personal, and distal factors. To accommodate the complexity of these relationships, arrows in our model are drawn bidirectionally, which allows for possible mutual influences (e.g., Sameroff, 1983), most requiring further investigation. Extant data in early and middle childhood supporting bidirectional understandings of mutually influential child/parent effects will be explicated where possible (see Dishion, Duncan, Eddy, Fagot, & Fetrow, 1994; Stafford & Bayer, 1993; Vuchinich, Bank, & Patterson, 1992).

Although they are not highlighted in this review, it is important to recognize the substantial theoretical contributions of systemic and transactional viewpoints (see Lerner et al., 1995; Minuchin, 1985; Sameroff, 1983; Werner & Baxter, 1994). Concepts driving these views are drawn from clinical research and therapeutic applications as well as from research exploring the effects of relationships in linear or bidirectional fashion (Stafford & Bayer, 1993). Although not typically supported empirically, systemic models should be prime movers of future investigations extending linkages introduced in this chapter (see Rubin, Stewart, & Chen, 1995). This could include spirals of recursive feedback loops across various aspects of the framework. Describing a transactive system from this perspective is a daunting task and "would theoretically encompass the universe" (Minuchin, 1985, p. 290). Given that little empirical research supports the possible transactional linkages in our model, the potential for further scholarly examination of such relationships is enormous.

Linkage Specifications Overview

We will describe below the direct, mediating, and moderating linkages fully and partially supported by research, and we will identify gaps in the literature. We assume that personal and proximal factors may mediate, partially mediate, or moderate relationships between distal ecological variables (see Booth, Rose-Krasnor, McKinnon, & Rubin, 1994) and child-peer outcomes. Direct relations between child-peer outcomes and distal factors (e.g., socioeconomic, intergenerational influences) may be attenuated when personal and/or proximal factors are controlled for in statistical applications of the model (Baron & Kenny, 1986). Similarly, proximal factors may mediate or moderate relations between personal factors and child outcomes.

Before discussing individual components, we will provide an overview of the conceptual model by illustrating the complexity of how factors may be linked. We will explain component linkages carefully in later sections. Although proximal features have traditionally been assumed to have the most direct influence on child social/communicative competence, recent evidence suggests that distal, personal, and proximal factors all work in combination to influence peer group outcomes (Rubin, Stewart, & Chen, 1995). Distal, personal, and proximal factors also may moderate negative and positive effects of other variables. For example, negative child characteristics (e.g., difficult temperament) may be heightened by harsh parenting/family interactions that, in turn, may lead to aggressive/disruptive peer group behavior (see Lerner et al., 1995). In contrast, difficult temperamental factors within children also may be diminished by nurturing/responsive familial interactions, resulting in lower levels of negative peer group behaviors. Given that recent evidence suggests that many parenting cognitions, behaviors, and affective responses may be a function of perceived (or actual) child characteristics (e.g., Bell & Chapman, 1986; Bugental, Blue, & Lewis, 1990; Profilet & Ladd, 1994; Rubin, Stewart, & Chen, 1995; Sanson & Rothbart, 1995), the latter scenario probably would not occur unless moderated by positive familial interactions and factors within the parents (e.g., strong beliefs about nurturant child-rearing, positive self-regard, low-conflict marital relations). Such factors may override inclinations to be unresponsive or to respond negatively to child difficulties (see Belsky, Fish, & Isabella, 1991; Washington, Minde, & Goldberg, 1986). Likewise, emotional stability and other personal factors of parents may serve to override aversive parenting or conflictual familial interactions that commonly occur in the face of negative distal events such as economic stress (see Benasich & Brooks-Gunn, 1996; Conger et al., 1994; Hoff-Ginsberg & Tardif, 1995). Such conjecture begs further empirical scrutiny.

Similarly, family interactions and parenting may be moderated by child personal characteristics and behavioral outcomes. For example, mothers of children with highly active dispositions are likely to display higher levels of stress than mothers of less active children, and may feel socially isolated and depressed. They also may be more prone to marital conflict and to vacillate among avoidant, harsh, and permissive parenting (see Dix, 1991; Lerner et al., 1995). Depression and higher maternal anger accompanied by erratic patterns of avoidant and controlling parenting behaviors may also be associated with mothers of children who consistently display aggressive behavioral outcomes (see Downey & Coyne, 1990; Rubin & Mills, 1990; Rubin, Stewart, & Chen, 1995). Future research should explore whether such negative relations are buffered by more positive maternal perceptions of parenting capability and lower attributions of child difficulty (personal factors). These may be moderated by support from others within (proximal) and outside (distal) the nuclear family (e.g., Ladd & Le Sieur, 1995; Melson, Ladd, & Hsu, 1993).

To complicate matters further, multiple linkages with individual child outcomes become more challenging to disentangle when siblings are considered. We hope our brief synthesis will guide future inquiry by suggesting how several factors in our conceptual model might be connected to differential parental treatment of siblings, to sib-sib influences, to linkages with parenting behaviors, and to other familial interactions. For example, aversive parent-child interactions appear to extend to siblings as well, supporting the notion that the whole family system is disrupted in such cases (Patterson, Dishion, & Bank, 1984). Considering sibling effects is critical, because 80% of families include more than one child (Plomin, 1994).

Finally, parent and child characteristics may mediate and/or moderate ways parents respond to and organize distal extrafamilial environments in terms of parenting, lending themselves to more or less competent social/communicative peer group interactions. As will be seen, parents tend to arrange and manage social environments for their children differentially based on beliefs, child perceptions, and knowledge of what activities and socialization strategies may be important for facilitating optimal social development (e.g., Ladd & Hart, 1992; Ladd & Le Sieur, 1995; Mize, Pettit, & Brown, 1995; Profilet & Ladd, 1994). However, distal factors such as socioeconomic status, employment, choice of neighborhood, schools, and availability of desirable peers may all serve to enhance or constrain the degree to which parents can effectively arrange and manage their children's social lives (Ladd, Profilet, & Hart, 1992).

In summary, it has traditionally been assumed that there are rather direct linkages between child outcomes and proximal parenting behaviors or family interactions. However, proximal influences appear to be mediated and/or moderated by the personal characteristics of parent and child (e.g., temperament, gender). The bidirectional arrows in the conceptual model also imply that inherent and noninherent personal parental characteristics (e.g., temperament, personality, education, experience) may influence how parents respond to and/or arrange extrafamilial factors (e.g., economic circumstances, children's peers, support); these factors, in turn, may relate to child-peer group outcomes. Similarly, children's inherent characteristics (temperament, resilience, gender) resulting from a shared genetic pool with parents may also affect the ways children respond to many distal factors (e.g., day care, peers, school, media, other adults), also reflected in child-peer group behavior. Distal factors, in turn, may impinge on more proximal domains. For example, children's social difficulties in distal settings (e.g., school) may be communicated (e.g., by teachers) to parents, who might adjust their parenting behaviors accordingly to deal with problematic behavior. The effects of other distal factors (e.g., economic stress) may also be related to child outcomes but are likely filtered through parenting and family interactions buffered by personal factors within parents and children. Given this general overview, we now turn to more detailed discussion of each component of the conceptual model.

PEER GROUP BEHAVIORAL/COMMUNICATIVE OUTCOMES

To achieve parsimony, we will discuss peer group outcomes associated with social/communicative competence (defined below) in broad terms of externalizing, internalizing, and sociable behavior. Each of these individualistic behavioral tendencies has implications for children's social interactions that occur in relationships (e.g., friendship interactions between two individuals) that are embedded within groups or networks of relationships. Groups are governed by norms that serve as criteria for group acceptance or rejection by peers (e.g., Newcomb, Bukowski, & Pattee, 1993). Events and processes within each level of social complexity (individual, interactions, relationships, groups) are enhanced or constrained by events and processes at other levels (see Asher, Parker, & Walker, 1996; Hinde, 1987; Rubin, Bukowski, & Parker, in press).

Although there are many subdomains within externalizing, internalizing, and sociable behavior, much of the current literature exploring parent-child and family interactions as related to social outcomes does not clearly delineate these forms of the broader behavioral categories. However, a few exceptions have been noted recently in the communication literature with regard to sociable behavior as defined below (Burleson et al., 1995; Burleson & Kunkel, 1996).

Externalizing disorders. Externalizing disorders are behavioral reflections of psychological undercontrol. These typically include aggressive, impulsive/disruptive, and nonconforming behaviors linked to peer rejection (Campbell, 1995; Coie, Dodge, & Kupersmidt, 1990; Fantuzzo et al., 1995; Olson & Brodfeld, 1991; Rubin, Stewart, & Chen, 1995) and are relatively stable across contexts and time (Campbell, Pierce, March, Ewing, & Szumowski, 1994).

Much of the research on externalizing disorders focuses on aggression. This construct comprises many forms, including relational aggression that involves exclusionary or ostracizing tactics (e.g., Crick & Grotpeter, 1995; Crick, Casas, & Mosher, in press; McNeilly-Choque, Hart, Robinson, Nelson, & Olsen, in press); proactive instrumental aggression enacted for the purpose of acquiring objects, territory, or privilege (e.g., Hartup, 1974); proactive bullying for the purpose of intimidating or dominating others (e.g., Olweus, 1993; Perry, Perry, & Kennedy, 1992; Slee & Rigby, 1993); and reactive aggression in response to peer provocations (e.g., Dodge & Coie, 1987; Price & Dodge, 1989; Schwartz, Dodge, & Coie, 1993). However, beyond global definitions of aggression, relatively little is known about how these specific forms are linked to other aspects of our model (e.g., parenting). Even less is known about the ways impulsive/disruptive behaviors are delineated from and linked to forms of aggression (e.g., Halperin et al., 1995). Such linkages need to be explored in future research before they can be integrated into this type of conceptual framework. Hence, for current purposes, we will refer to these behavioral subtypes within the broader category of externalizing disorders. Specific behavioral manifestations of externalizing disorders will be noted for clarification.

Internalizing disorders. Internalizing disorders are rooted in psychological overcontrol and are typically manifested in withdrawn forms of behavior (e.g., Rubin, Stewart, & Chen, 1995). These forms are currently conceptualized and empirically defined as reticence (e.g., shy, anxious, wary, behaviorally inhibited), solitary-passive (object versus person orientation), and solitary-active or immature play (e.g., solitary-functional, immature pretend play). These may be more or less maladaptive in terms of isolation from or rejection by peers, depending on child age and other considerations (e.g., Coplan, Rubin, Fox, Calkins, & Stewart, 1994; Rubin & Asendorpf, 1993). As with aggression, relatively little is known about how these specific forms of withdrawal are linked to proximal patterns of family interaction, parenting behaviors, and distal aspects of the model shown in Figure 9.1 (Rubin, Stewart, & Coplan, 1995). Thus, we will discuss in our model only general internalizing disorders as reflected in withdrawn behavior, with an eye toward facilitating future research on linkages with withdrawn behavioral subtypes.

Sociable behavior. For our purposes, we will refer to behaviors leading to positive psychosocial outcomes, such as acceptance by peers, as sociable behavior (see East, 1991). Behavioral/communicative manifestations of sociable behavior include conforming and friendly/amicable behavior, impulse control, leadership/assertiveness, rough-and-tumble cooperative play, prosocial behavior (helping, sharing, comforting—emotional supportiveness), and person-centered communication (see Burleson & Kunkel, 1996; Eisenberg et al., 1995; Hart, McGee, & Hernandez, 1993; Masten, Morison, & Pellegrini, 1985; Radke-Yarrow, Zahn-Waxler, & Chapman, 1983; Smith, 1989; Stafford & Bayer, 1993; Tremblay, Vitaro, Gagnon, Piche, & Royer, 1992). Hence, as with internalizing and externalizing disorders, we will discuss sociable behavior as a general category accompanied by specific definitions.

Behavioral and Communicative Indicators of Social Competence

Externalizing and internalizing difficulties reflect social skill and communication deficits not conducive to normative social/emotional growth and well-being (Rubin, Stewart, & Chen, 1995). In contrast, sociable behavior is desirable and adaptive and involves skillful verbal communication (e.g., Black & Logan, 1995; Burleson et al., 1995; Kemple, Speranza, & Hazen, 1992). After a presentation of our working definitions of social/communicative competence, we will offer our theoretical view about how these behaviors are acquired.

McFall (1982) portrays social competence as a "judgment call" based on how an audience views an actor's behavioral repertoire. A review of definitions of child social competence indicates that communicative competence, as a vital part of social competence, has generally been implied rather than explicitly stated (see Dodge, 1985; Fujiki & Brinton, 1994; Gresham, 1986; Odom & McConnell, 1992). Whether by verbal or nonverbal means (e.g., Burgoon, 1994), communication competence (or the lack thereof) is the essence of social competence, particularly in relationship development (Duck, 1989). As Burleson et al. (1995) put it, functional communication competence is "the ability to use communicative resources strategically to accomplish personal and social goals—to persuade, inform, console, appease, compromise, or the like" (p. 36). It is the primary process by which children make their internal states accessible to others (Burleson et al., 1995).

Social competencies are displayed through verbal and/or nonverbal means (e.g., gaze aversion, smiling, sharing, pushing) and are closely tied to social-cognitive (e.g., social problem solving skills) and emotional regulative (e.g., anger regulation) processes (see Applegate et al., 1992; Eisenberg et al., 1996). Rubin and Rose-Krasnor (1992) define social competence as "the ability to achieve personal goals in social interaction while simultaneously maintaining positive relationships with others over time and across situations" (p. 285). Mills and Rubin (1993) further state that social competence "encompasses skills and abilities relating to all aspects of interpersonal problem solving, from the self-regulation of emotions aroused in social interaction, to the negotiation of solutions to interpersonal conflicts" (p. 98).

In support of this view (see Rubin, Bukowski, & Parker, in press), more sociable children better discern emotional states of others and are more adept at regulating their own emotions (e.g., Denham, Renwick-DeBardi, & Hewes, 1994; Eisenberg et al., 1996). They also verbally communicate in relevant and socially contingent ways during social interaction (Black & Logan, 1995; Fujiki & Brinton, 1994; Guralnick, Connor, Hammond, Gottman, & Kinnish, 1996; Kemple et al., 1992; Steinkamp, 1989) and expect that sociable behavior will lead to instrumental gains and enhanced relations with peers in interpersonal conflict situations (Hart, DeWolf, & Burts, 1992; Hart, Ladd, & Burleson, 1990). In contrast, externalizing children tend to communicate their desires verbally in a less skillful, noncontingent manner (e.g., Black & Logan, 1995; Kemple et al., 1992) and envision externalizing, antisocial behaviors as means for achieving desirable goals to the exclusion of relationship considerations during interpersonal conflicts (see Chung & Asher, 1996; Dodge & Price, 1994; Hart, McGee, & Hernandez, 1993; Murphy & Eisenberg, 1996). Children with internalizing difficulties who display a consistent pattern of social reticence or unassertive social and communicative strategies to meet social goals may lead others to view them as less socially competent (Giles & Street, 1994; Rubin, Stewart, & Chen, 1995).

Many verbal and nonverbal behavioral/communicative outcomes associated with sociable, externalizing, and internalizing behaviors can be linked to the extrafamilial, personal, and familial communicative and interactive processes described shortly. We now turn our attention to these factors by briefly discussing theoretical viewpoints of how these linkages might occur; we then move on to a discussion of parenting.

Theoretical Foundations

Traditional theoretical explanations for how child behavioral and communicative competencies are acquired are many. Because they have been well described elsewhere (e.g., Rubin, Bukowski, & Parker, in press; Stafford & Bayer, 1993), we will not take the space to explicate them here. Briefly summarized, our view is closely aligned with constructivist perspectives on development (e.g, Piaget, 1983; Vygotsky, 1978). Simply put, we believe that children differentially exert personal characteristics on proximal and distal features of their environments in ways that allow them to extract information from stimulation occurring in the context of interpersonal interactions with significant others. This stimulation can come as reinforcements or punishments, modeled behavior, more or less warm and responsive interactions, and verbally communicated adaptive and maladaptive forms of social functioning (see Putallaz & Heflin, 1990). Through these stimulations, children gather information to build repertoires of social strategy knowledge that guide their behavior and communication in peer group interactions (see Applegate, Burke, Burleson, Delia, & Kline, 1985; Hart, DeWolf, & Burts, 1993).

Although modeling may be a source for information gathering in marital and other family interactions (e.g., Wilson & Gottman, 1995), parent communications in family interactions set the primary environmental parameters from which children extract information in social/communicative schema-constructive processes (see Burleson et al., 1995). These interactions are buttressed by more or less warm and responsive parenting and familial relationships (see below). As will be seen, evidence suggests that more complex forms of parental and familial communications (e.g., induction, problem solving, conflict resolution) draw children's attention toward certain features of interpersonal situations in ways that do not focus the child on a specific set of scripted, routine responses, but rather facilitate more sophisticated social cognitions guiding sociable behavior (see Applegate et al., 1992). As Burleson et al. (1995) suggest, behaviorally complex messages provide children with "a generalized interpretive orientation and set of constructs that guide [their] emergent assessment and management of situations" (p. 62). In contrast, behaviorally simple, authoritarian, and hostile messages allow children to focus only on rigid and conflictual interactional styles as an efficacious means of resolving interpersonal issues (Eisenberg & Miller, 1990; Hart, DeWolf, & Burts, 1993), whereas permissive parenting provides little or no information at all.

PARENTING AS A PROXIMAL INFLUENCE ON CHILD OUTCOMES AND DISTAL FACTORS

Parenting behaviors are not only directly related to child social/communicative competence, but serve to enhance or constrain distal factors including peer group, media, schooling/child care, and other extrafamilial influences. Socialization factors revolve around ways that parents provide access to distal social opportunities and how parents interact with and instruct their children about the social milieu (e.g., Ladd & Le Sieur, 1995; Parke, Burks, Carson, Neville, & Boyum, 1994; Putallaz & Heflin, 1990). In conjunction with the notion that children build repertoires of social strategy knowledge through interactions with significant others, three non-mutually exclusive pathways have been conceptualized through which children gather information about their social world via verbal and nonverbal communications with parents: parent-child interactions or *styles*, managerial functions, and educational strategies. The latter two highlight *practices* focusing on parental facilitation and arrangement of distal factors that entail interactions with extrafamilial adults and peers. Recent evidence suggests both parenting style (aggregates or constellations of parenting behaviors) and goal-directed practices for facilitating peer competence uniquely contribute to social-communicative competence (Mize & Pettit, in press).

Parent-Child Interactions/Styles

The first pathway for information gathering is that of parent-child interactions. Within the interaction and relationship context, many competencies necessary for social interaction develop. This is where children begin to develop expectations and assumptions about interactions and relationships with others as well as experience the freedom to explore features of the social universe (Hartup, 1985).

Paths of linkages between parent-child interactions and child social/communicative competence can take several forms and may be indirect, because the parent's goal is not explicitly to modify the child's relationships with peers (Ladd, 1992). To achieve parsimony and clarity in our discussion, we will use a typological approach to parenting. Although the use of typologies is diminishing in popularity because of concerns regarding cultural generalizability (e.g., Nucci, 1994) and the nonspecificity of which behavioral components within each typology are related to specific child outcomes (e.g., Darling & Steinberg, 1993; Smetana, 1994), we still find them useful for organizing relevant literature. Of the typologies available (see Maccoby & Martin, 1983), we will focus on Baumrind's (1971, 1989) authoritative, authoritarian, and permissive parenting styles, which have been used frequently in past research.

Individual behavioral/communicative components of these typologies have recently been empirically defined for parents of young children (Robinson, Mandleco, Olsen, & Hart, 1995), and we will specify and/or elaborate these as needed in the review that follows. Based on this recent empirical work, features of authoritative parenting practice include warmth and responsiveness, induction (reasoning), democratic participation, and good natured/easygoing parent-child interactions (e.g., the parent patiently responds to the child's demands; the parent jokes and plays with child). Authoritarian parenting includes power-assertive or coercive forms of verbal hostility, corporal punishment, nonreasoning punitive strategies, and directiveness. Permissiveness is empirically defined as lack of follow-through and the ignoring of misbehavior, and is associated with a lack of self-confidence in parenting. Although parenting behaviors appear to vary according to affective arousal due to situational contexts (e.g., nature of child misdeed) that are moderated by a host of personal parent and child characteristics (e.g., Chamberlain & Patterson, 1995; Dix, 1991; Grusec & Goodnow, 1994; Smetana, 1994), how parents regulate their children's behavior using these styles in disciplinary and other interactive contexts has been consistently related to children's peer interaction (e.g., Baumrind, 1971; 1989; Burleson et al., 1995; Hart, DeWolf, & Burts, 1993; Maccoby & Martin, 1983). This transfer from home to peer environments likely happens through communicative, cognitive, and emotional mechanisms (e.g., MacDonald, 1987; Parke et al., 1994).

Authoritative Interactions and Sociable Behavior

The literature shows clear linkages between child social/communicative competence and authoritative parenting. Specifically, the investigation of person-centered communication (which is akin to inductive and democratic parenting components of the authoritative style) has been a fruitful area of inquiry. As Burleson et al. (1995) point out, reflection-enhancing messages help children to understand situations "in a broadened way and see that courses of action should follow from consideration of relevant situational features and enduring values" (p. 62). For example, reasoning with children about consequences of their actions and possible solutions to interpersonal conflict should focus children on the perspectives, feelings, attitudes, motivations, needs, and other psychological qualities affecting their behavior (e.g., Bearson & Cassel, 1975). Other-oriented forms of induction have been consistently linked to sociable (i.e., prosocial) behavior with peers, particularly when accompanied by positive parental affect (McGrath, Wilson, & Frassetto, 1995).

Recent findings suggest that more complex and sophisticated forms of parent-child communications are related to flexible and socially adept consequential thinking styles in preschool and school-age children (e.g., children's envisioning friendly-assertive sociable behavior as leading to instrumental gains and enhancing relations with peers) (Hart, DeWolf, & Burts, 1992; Hart, Ladd, & Burleson, 1990). As noted earlier, these social cognitions have also been linked to sociable behavior and peer acceptance. Authoritative reflection-enhancing parenting also may be linked to sociable, emotionally supportive behavior in children (Burleson & Kunkel, 1996). Related findings suggest that authoritative parenting (e.g., responsiveness to child cues, reflective listening) is positively related to how "easy" children perceive it is to enact sociable behavior with peers and to perform such behavior (Pettit, Harrist, Bates, & Dodge, 1991). Authoritative parenting demands placed on children during toddlerhood (e.g., emphasizing dos rather than don'ts in communicative exchanges) are also related to lower levels of internalizing and externalizing behavior at age 5 (Kuczynski & Kochanska, 1995).

Alternative mechanisms suggested earlier may also have effects on children's sociable behavior apart from or in conjunction with authoritative induction (Burleson et al., 1995; Putallaz & Heflin, 1990; Rubin & Sloman, 1984). For example, mothers of more socially competent children appear to model and thus communicate a more easygoing authoritative style with their children that is positive, synchronous, and agreeable (e.g., Harrist, Pettit, Dodge, & Bates, 1994). In a related vein, Black and Logan (1995) recently demonstrated that authoritative (responsive) parent-child communication, in turn-taking style and utterance type, is related to more sociable, responsive interactions and higher peer acceptance for children in the peer group. In contrast, nonresponsive communications with parents (i.e., irrelevant turns, simultaneous turns, and turns that fail to leave time for a response following a request) are linked to similar communication patterns with and rejection by peers (see Kahen, Katz, & Gottman, 1994). These findings highlight similarities among parent-parent, parent-child, and child-peer communication found in the literature (see Putallaz & Heflin, 1990).

Authoritative warm and responsive parenting also appears to provide an emotionally secure relationship that gives the child the confidence and self-efficacy he or she needs to explore unfamiliar social environments and seek out emotional ties with others, including peers (Mueller & Silverman, 1989; Putallaz & Heflin, 1990). Sociable children tend to have parents who exhibit warmth and responsive interactions with them (Chen & Rubin, 1994; East, 1991). Such interactions appear to facilitate the development of "working models" that children can use as a basis for expectations about other interpersonal relationships (e.g., Bowlby, 1973; Elicker, Egeland, & Sroufe, 1992). For example, children may expect positive reciprocal interpersonal outcomes when caregivers are available and responsive (Elicker et al., 1992). Conversely, children may expect nonreciprocal and negative outcomes from others when parents are unavailable and display low levels of responsiveness (Cicchetti, Lynch, Shonk, & Manly, 1992).

Children who do not have "felt security" generally lack social confidence, hold negative expectations for social outcomes, and are less likely to engage in sociable interactions with unfamiliar peers, thus diminishing opportunities for developing functional social skills (e.g., Rubin, Booth, Rose-Krasnor, & Mills, 1995; Sroufe, 1983). Indeed, warm and responsive parenting promotes secure attachments with caregivers and has been linked concurrently and longitudinally to more sociable behavior and fewer internalizing and externalizing problems with peers (e.g., Booth et al., 1994; Elicker et al., 1992; Russell & Russell, 1996; Shaw, Keenan, & Vondra, 1994; Sroufe & Fleeson, 1986). In contrast, early insecure attachments are related to later internalizing problems. Negative maternal interaction style (e.g., low warmth, hostile interactions) is more strongly linked to later externalizing difficulties (Booth et al., 1994). This suggests that interactive behavior and attachment security are important for social/communicative competence but are differentially related to a child's later social development (see Rose-Krasnor, Rubin, Booth, & Coplan, 1996; Rothbaum, Rosen, Pott, & Beatty, 1995).

Authoritarian Interactions and
Externalizing/Internalizing Disorders

Externalizing and internalizing disorders have been linked to authoritarian parenting styles. Recent evidence suggests that consistent authoritarian interactions with children (e.g., directiveness, verbal hostility, corporal punishment) diminish children's emotional functioning skills (e.g., encoding emotional signals and decoding others' emotional states) and cognitive representational processes (e.g., less attention to relevant social cues, more misattributions of hostile intent, fewer adaptive solutions generated for interpersonal conflict, and greater expectations of positive consequences for hostile behavior). The attenuation of the functional development of these emotional skills and social-cognitive processes appears to coincide with externalizing (e.g., aggressive/disruptive) interactions with and rejection by peers (see Crick & Dodge, 1994; Hart, DeWolf, & Burts, 1993; Parke et al., 1994). In addition, such deficiencies have been linked to authoritarian parent-child interactions when measured as part of overall maladaptive social information processing styles (Weiss, Dodge, Bates, & Pettit, 1992).

More externalizing children (particularly boys) also appear to have authoritarian mothers who display more negative affect accompanied by nonsynchronous, coercive, directive, and controlling behaviors (e.g., Barth & Parke, 1993; Dishion et al., 1994; Kuczynski & Kochanska, 1995; LaFreniere & Dumas, 1992; Pettit, Clawson, Dodge, & Bates, 1996; Pettit & Harrist, 1993; Putallaz & Heflin, 1990). Similar findings have been obtained separately for fathers (e.g., Dekovic & Janssens, 1992; East, 1991; Hart, DeWolf, Wozniak, & Burts, 1992; Parke, Cassidy, Burks, Carson, & Boyum, 1992) and for father and mother scores combined (Vuchinich et al., 1992). Such parenting interactions also appear to impede communication competencies in children (Stafford & Bayer, 1993) and may be systemically maintained through mutually coercive parent-child exchanges (e.g., Dishion et al., 1994; Vuchinich et al., 1992).

Authoritarian parenting style linkages with internalizing disorders reflected in withdrawn behavior are less clear, although progress is being made in understanding the mechanisms, particularly for those who are *extremely* withdrawn (Rubin & Mills, 1990). Overcontrol through authoritarian means coupled with overprotective and less warm and responsive parenting appear to be the operative mechanisms (East, 1991; Rubin & Mills, 1990; Rubin & Stewart, in press; Rubin, Stewart, & Chen, 1995). Overprotective parents actively encourage dependency by restricting their children's behavior to low risk-taking activities. Such restrictions may deprive children of opportunities to interact spontaneously with peers, thus inhibiting their opportunities to explore the social milieu. Overcontrolling parents (who may also be overprotective) tend to display negative affects and to be more authoritarian (i.e., coercive and commanding) in helping their child become more responsive to social expectations (LaFreniere & Dumas, 1992). In addition, although low authoritativeness (lack of warmth and responsiveness) has also been linked to children's internalizing behaviors, this appears particularly true for father-daughter relationships (East, 1991).

Whether or not, and under what conditions, overcontrolling and overprotective parenting behaviors are interrelated is not yet clearly understood (Rubin, Stewart, & Chen, 1995). Moreover, whether parents respond to personal factors of child inhibition (e.g., temperament) or are the cause of it is still in question. As Rubin, Stewart, and Coplan (1995) point out, regardless of the direction of effect, parental overcontrol and overprotection are likely to exacerbate and/or maintain rather than ameliorate social inhibition in children. A similar point could also be made pertaining to authoritarian parenting and childhood externalizing behaviors. Until further research clarifies some of these issues, the current literature supports the idea that parents who use authoritarian commands combined with constraints on exploration and independence tend to raise more shy, dependent, anxious/fearful, and reserved children (Rubin & Sloman, 1984; Rubin, Stewart, & Chen, 1995). Taken together, these findings support the view that behaviorally simple, authoritarian parenting not only predisposes children toward externalizing difficulties, but, when combined with other factors, may also be related to internalizing disorders.

Permissive Parenting and Externalizing Disorders

Permissive parents are characterized as allowing children to express their impulses without asserting authority or imposing controls or restrictions that are either authoritative or authoritarian in nature (Maccoby & Martin, 1983). Parents who are permissive are generally classified as indulgent (i.e., warm but nondemanding) or indifferent (i.e., less warm and uninvolved). Permissive parenting has been linked with externalizing, emotional/impulsive, and nonconforming behaviors discussed earlier (Attili, 1989; Baumrind, 1967, 1971; Maccoby & Martin, 1983; Olweus, 1980). This parenting style has also been associated with lower levels of parental monitoring of child behavior and whereabouts, as well as higher levels of delinquent or deviant behavior in children later on (see Chamberlain & Patterson, 1995; Ladd & Le Sieur, 1995; Parke et al., 1994). Such child outcomes are to be expected when parents do not communicate behavioral expectations to their children in ways that help them to build social cognitions that facilitate social/communicative competence.

Parents as Managers

The second pathway for information gathering entails opportunities parents provide for children to learn by arranging interactions with peers in the distal environment (e.g., Ladd & Hart, 1992; Ladd et al., 1992; Parke & Kellam,

1994). During the early and middle childhood years, parents (particularly mothers) are in the best position to facilitate peer contacts. They do this by enrolling children in organized activities, chauffeuring them from one house or social event to another, exposing them to playmates who are children of parents in the parents' own adult social networks, and scheduling play interactions for their children with peers (Ladd et al., 1992; Rubin & Sloman, 1984). Although siblings also play an important role in the proximal environment (see below), contacts with siblings are less likely to be arranged by parents. Children take in communicated information from a variety of others (peers and adults) in peer interaction contexts that allow them to further construct repertoires of social strategy knowledge and to practice social/communicative behaviors learned in the home.

Parental facilitation of contacts with peers is important for several reasons. Although parenting and other familial interactions appear to set the stage for social/communicative competencies in the peer group (e.g., Hart, DeWolf, & Burts, 1993), peers become increasingly important as children grow older (see Berndt & Ladd, 1989; Rubin, Bukowski, & Parker, in press; Rubin & Coplan, 1992). Friendships with peers and peer social status (e.g., acceptance/rejection) are separate and unique predictors of children's psychosocial adjustment (e.g., Asher et al., 1996; Buhrmester, 1996; Parker & Asher, 1993; Vandell & Hembree, 1994). Close relationships with siblings and friends may ameliorate the negative effects (e.g., loneliness) of lower acceptance by peers (East & Rook, 1992; Parker & Asher, 1993). Peers, siblings, and friends may enhance or diminish children's social/communicative competencies (Sharabany & Hertz-Lazarowitz, 1981). They also provide security, social support, and impetus for more or less sociable conflict resolutions. However, these functions may vary according to age and gender differences, how conflictual the friendship relationships are, as well as whether or not peers are perceived as friends or acquaintances (e.g., Hartup & Laursen, 1993; Ladd, Kochenderfer, & Coleman, 1996; Parker & Gottman, 1989; Shaffer, 1994).

Whether they intend to or not, parents "manage" how much contact children have with peers and adults in the distal environment (Ladd et al., 1992). This is considered a direct path of influence because how parents organize/arrange these experiences may have direct bearing on children's development of social/communicative competence (Ladd, Le Sieur, & Profilet, 1993). In the managerial function, parents play an active role by (a) designing the child's social world, and (b) mediating the process of the child's meeting peers and facilitating his or her interactions with them.

Designing

Parents act as designers when they provide settings where children meet and interact with peers and other adults (Ladd & Le Sieur, 1995). The stage for these interactions provides access to and facilitates participation in a variety of neighborhood (e.g., schoolyard, playground, and backyard) and community settings (e.g., day care, Cub Scouts, 4-H, Little League, church-sponsored activities). For example, socialization is a major concern for parents enrolling their children in preschool and child care (see Ladd et al., 1992). Participation in child-care or preschool environments can have positive and negative ramifications for children's social/communicative competence (e.g., Bates et al., 1994; Field, 1994; Haskins, 1989; Howes, Phillips, & Whitebook, 1992), but has only recently been examined in combination with a host of other factors (e.g., Burchinal, Ramey, Reid, & Jaccard, 1995). The success of this facilitation appears to depend on many distal, personal, and proximal factors, including the family's socioeconomic status, parents' employment factors, child temperament, child friendships, parents' marital relationship, parent-child interactions and involvement, parental beliefs and/or reasons for enrollment (e.g., Hagekull & Bohlin, 1995; Ladd et al., 1992; Roopnarine, Bright, & Riegraf, 1994; Taylor & Machida, 1994), as well as quality of curriculum, peer influences, and teacher guidance factors within the school (e.g., Hart, Burts, & Charlesworth, in press; Howes et al., 1992; Jacobs & White, 1994; Volling & Feagans, 1995). Overall, this research suggests that low-quality environments (e.g., low caregiver authoritative warmth and responsiveness; high teacher/child ratio; developmentally inappropriate curriculum) coupled with high amounts of early child care and troubled familial interactions are associated with higher levels of internalizing and externalizing disorders in children. The converse appears to be true for sociable behaviors.

Mediating

Beyond providing access to particular social settings, a parent may serve as a "bridge" between the child and playmates by actively helping the child to meet peers and by orchestrating child-peer engagements (Ladd & Le Sieur, 1995). For example, parental creation of informal play opportunities with peers may enhance sociable behavior and peer status in early (e.g., Ladd & Golter, 1988; Ladd & Hart, 1992) and middle childhood (Krappman, 1986). Parents who encourage and coach their children in how to initiate contacts and how to interact with peers help children learn to take responsibility for peer activities and relationships (Ladd & Hart, 1992). As a result, children become empowered to initiate, communicate, and manage their own peer relationships in informal and classroom contexts. This moves our discussion into the educational role that parents may play.

Parents as Educators

The third pathway for information gathering in distal domains involves the parent in a direct instructional role, including supervision and advising/consulting (e.g., Bhavnagri & Parke, 1991; Ladd et al., 1993; Lollis, Ross, &

Tate, 1992). This is also considered a direct path of influence because parents are more or less engaged in educating their children about ways to negotiate the peer system, using interactions with peers as teaching opportunities.

Supervision

The supervision role includes interactive and directive interventions (Lollis et al., 1992) and also incorporates monitoring (Ladd & Le Sieur, 1995). Parents who are active participants in their toddlers' play with peers often employ *interactive interventions,* in which they successfully enhance sociable play by proactively regulating or "scaffolding" social interactions (Bhavnagri & Parke, 1985). *Directive interventions,* on the other hand, involve parents' operating from outside the context of children's play, typically as observers. Although directive interventions may be used with toddlers, they are more likely to be geared toward older preschool children (see Lollis et al., 1992) and to be reactive to events that occur in children's play (Ladd & Le Sieur, 1995). Research suggests that high levels of maternal involvement coupled with less skilled directive interventions involving irrelevant or power-assertive communications are related to less competent child behavior with peers (Finnie & Russell, 1988; Mize, Pettit, & Brown, 1995).

Parents' awareness or knowledge of children's play activities, partners, and whereabouts when these do not include direct parental involvement is referred to as *monitoring.* This is generally employed with older children (e.g., late grade-schoolers or adolescents), as they are more capable than younger children of supervising themselves and tend to play in settings less accessible to parents. It appears that the link between lack of parental monitoring and child behavior problems (e.g, delinquency, externalizing) becomes stronger as children age (see Ladd & Le Sieur, 1995; Parke et al., 1994).

Advising/Consulting

Much of the educational role that parents play in fostering peer relationships occurs in contexts where peers are not present. Parents who are successful in this role communicate advice, support, and directions about ways to negotiate the peer culture. These "decontextualized discussions" may occur during dinner, after school, before bedtime, during travel in a car, or in a variety of other settings (Lollis et al., 1992). Consulting may be proactive, designed to prepare children for future social activities, or reactive, taking the form of advice to children about how to cope with new or unfamiliar peer situations (Ladd & Le Sieur, 1995).

For preschoolers, most discussions with parents appear to occur within the first few hours after the preschool ends (Laird, Pettit, Mize, Brown, & Lindsey, 1994). During these talks, parents may advise their children about how to initiate friendships, manage conflicts, identify solutions to interpersonal problems, deflect teasing, repel bullies, and so on (Ladd et al., 1992).

Parents may also act as sounding boards for children's self-generated solutions and assessments in this role (Kuczynski, 1984). Research concerning this involvement indicates that higher levels of quantity (e.g., number of conversations) and quality (e.g., of advice offered, warmth and positivity) are linked to positive social/communicative peer group outcomes (Laird et al, 1994; Mizet & Pettit, in press; Profilet & Ladd, 1996; Russell & Finnie, 1990). Alternatively, blaming-oriented maternal consulting has been associated with childhood withdrawal (Profilet & Ladd, 1996)

In sum, proximal parent-child interactions, parental management practices, and educational strategies all appear to play significant roles in the socialization of child social/communicative competence. We now turn our attention to other proximal variables.

FAMILY FUNCTIONING AS A PROXIMAL INFLUENCE

Much of the research addressed to this point has focused on proximal family influences in dyads (e.g., parent-child interactions). However, the family system encompasses a broad range of persons (e.g., mothers, fathers, siblings, grandparents, and others). Given this, some investigators have stressed the need to study family influences at broader levels of analysis (e.g., Kreppner, 1992; Parke, 1992). As with parenting styles (e.g., induction), more complex and positive forms of family problem solving and conflict resolution reflected in marital, sibling, and other family interactions may lend themselves to more sophisticated social cognitions that guide child social/communicative behavior. Hostile interactions may focus children on behaviorally simple and rigid interaction styles as an efficacious means of resolving interpersonal issues (see Burleson et al., 1995). However, unlike the parenting literature, the investigation of such mechanisms has not yet occurred. With this in mind, we next review three proximal factors: the marital relationship, sibling relationships, and family relationships.

The Marital Relationship

Using longitudinal, prospective, and retrospective designs, researchers continue to discover linkages between parents' marital relationship and children's social/communicative competence with peers. Specific aspects of the marital relationship, including marital adjustment/satisfaction and conflict, have been investigated. For example, lower levels of marital adjustment are more strongly related to externalizing than to internalizing disorders and are correlated more consistently with boys' behavior problems than with girls' (Jouriles et al., 1991). In addition, children with parents in unhappy marriages are more likely to experience externalizing problems such as fighting at school (Bryant & DeMorris, 1992).

Marital Conflict

Marital conflict seems to be a better predictor of child externalizing and internalizing behaviors than global marital satisfaction (Cummings, 1994a, 1994b). In fact, some consider marital conflict to be the best familial predictor of childhood behavior problems (Gottman & Katz, 1989). Marital conflict is related to externalizing behaviors (e.g., antisocial behavior, delinquency, and aggression), internalizing behaviors (social withdrawal), and poor social competence (Katz & Gottman, 1994). Marital conflict is also a better predictor of children's functioning than is change in family structure or separation from parents (Cummings, 1994a, 1994b). Different types of marital conflict are related to various child behavior problems. Longitudinal research conducted over 3 years revealed that an observed mutually hostile pattern of marital interaction during conflict resolution predicted children's externalizing behavior, whereas in marriages where husbands were angry and withdrawn in conflict, children had higher levels of internalizing behavior (Katz & Gottman, 1993).

Four possible mechanisms link marital conflict and child outcomes: (a) modeling, (b) children's maladaptive information processing, (c) stress, and (d) parenting (Rutter, 1994; Wilson & Gottman, 1995). First, children may model interparental aggression, believing it is acceptable. On the other hand, parents who are successful in resolving conflict may provide positive models of problem solving, and their children may respond to conflict with less distress, thus increasing mature coping skills and social competence (Grych & Fincham, 1993). Second, children who see parents fighting may develop hostile attributional biases and, as a result, behave more aggressively (Rutter, 1994). Third, parental conflict may contribute to a family context that includes background anger as a family stressor. For example, angry and argumentative adult interactions have been linked to internalizing and externalizing childhood problems (Bryant & DeMorris, 1992; Grych & Fincham, 1993). Fourth, parenting may mediate marital relationships and child's peer social/ communicative outcomes (Belsky, 1984). For example, satisfactory marital relationships predict parenting outcomes consistent with authoritative styles, whereas poor marital adjustment or conflict is associated with authoritarian styles (see Cowan & Cowan, 1992; Vondra & Belsky, 1993; Wilson & Gottman, 1995).

Marital conflict may be associated with increases in child behavior problems because parents are absorbed in their own conflicts and become less effective or consistent in discipline. Parental conflict may also drain emotional energy from parent-child relationships. Marriage partners who experience high levels of marital conflict may also lose an important source of support in parenting, their spouses (Wilson & Gottman, 1995).

It is not clear from the literature, however, whether marital conflict is directly or indirectly related to children's social/communicative competence with peers (Rutter, 1994). Some studies support a direct relationship. For example, Jenkins and Smith (1991) found that marital conflict was positively related with children's externalizing and internalizing behavior problems. Although authoritative parenting behaviors also were negatively related to behavior problems, direct effects of marital conflict were not eliminated.

Other studies support indirect linkages. Marital conflict may contribute to negative changes in parent-child relationships and may be an important pathway through which familial discord contributes to child behavior problems (see Cummings, 1994a). For example, Gottman and Katz (1989) found that maritally distressed couples interacted with their children permissively and unresponsively, resulting in higher levels of externalizing (noncompliant) behaviors in their children; these behaviors were linked to negative interactions with peers.

Additional factors related to marital conflict and its influence on parenting and children's social/communicative competence include how the conflict is resolved; its content, frequency, and intensity; and whether it is overt or covert (see Bryant & DeMorris, 1992; Cummings, 1994a). The degree to which children are exposed to marital conflict may also be a moderating factor (Katz & Gottman, 1993). More work is needed to determine how children's appraisals of marital conflict influence their behavior (see Crockenberg & Forgays, 1996; Grych & Fincham, 1990, 1993). Further investigations of reciprocal relationships among marriage, parenting, and children's behavior are also warranted (Emery & Tuer, 1993).

Sibling Relationships

Sibling relationships are unique among relationships because of their duration, common cultural milieu, and highly egalitarian nature. Sibling roles are ascribed rather than earned, and they endure regardless of circumstances (Stocker, Dunn, & Plomin, 1989). However, for most traits, siblings are not very similar, in part because of nonshared environments (Plomin, 1994). Therefore, it is not surprising that siblings would have different influences on each other and experience different patterns of family interaction and parenting.

Sibling Influences on Other Siblings

Children may learn sociable/communicative discourse patterns and externalizing behaviors while interacting with siblings as well as with peers (Dunn, 1983; Martin & Ross, 1995; Stafford & Bayer, 1993; Stormshak, Bellanti, & Bierman, 1996; Youngblade & Dunn, 1995). Sibling influences on siblings may be examined in relation to gender, age, or position within the family (Fitzpatrick & Badzinski, 1994; Piotrowski, 1995). Although evidence of gender-based differences between siblings is conflicting, the literature generally indicates greater amounts of sociable behavior in same-sex sibling pairs as they develop, maintain friendly interactions, and demonstrate more companionship and similarity. Older siblings initiate more prosocial and externalizing behaviors and tend to dominate younger siblings. Closely spaced siblings also display more externalizing disorders (Buhrmester & Furman, 1990; Dunn, 1983). For preschoolers, children displaying externalizing behavior (aggression) and internalizing behavior (withdrawal) with siblings also tend to display similar behavior with peers (Berndt & Bulleit, 1985). Similar findings have been reported for 7- to 8-year-olds (Vandell, Minnet, Johnson, & Santrock, 1990; cited in Dunn, 1992). Finally, recent evidence suggests that warm and less conflictual sibling relationships (as opposed to highly conflictual ones) serve to enhance aggressive children's social competencies with peers (Stormshak et al., 1996).

Sibling Influences on Parenting/Family Functioning

Sibling characteristics also may influence parenting behaviors and interactions of other family members (Bryant & DeMorris, 1992). For example, when mothers perceive older daughters as selfish, they control them more by authoritarian means; mothers' authoritative responsiveness to children's needs is associated with decreased levels of sibling externalizing behavior and increased levels of sociable behaviors (Bryant & Crockenberg, 1980). Mothers also use more authoritative child-rearing practices when their older children demonstrate sociable behavior toward their younger children (Martin & Ross, 1995). In addition, maternal encouragement of curiosity and openness to experiences is positively related to the amount of sociable/conforming behaviors older siblings direct toward younger siblings (Martin & Ross, 1995).

Differential Treatment of Siblings

Differential treatment of children in parenting (e.g., authoritative interactions) occurs often (Dunn & McGuire, 1994; Furman, 1995) and may have long-term effects (Volling & Belsky, 1992). Typically, parents are congruent in their differential treatment of siblings (Deal, Halverson, & Wampler, 1989; McHale, Crouter, McGuire, & Updegraff, 1995). Differential treatment influences sibling/peer relations because it often creates feelings of inequity, anger, and rivalry, which in turn are linked to negative relationships manifested in externalizing (hostile/aggressive, emotional/impulsive) behaviors (Collins, Harris, & Sussman, 1995; Fitzpatrick & Badzinski, 1994; Martin & Ross, 1995).

Parental differential treatment of children occurs for several reasons. First, emotional demands created by parental conflict may compromise parents' ability to foster positive relationships with each child (Brody, Stoneman, & McCoy, 1992). Second, the birth of a second child may result in differential treatment; the firstborn may receive less maternal attention and sensitivity (Stafford & Bayer, 1993). Third, parents tend to be harsher toward sons than toward daughters in disciplinary practices (Greenberger, O'Neil, & Nagel, 1994). Fourth, birth order may influence treatment, with parents displaying more tolerance toward later-born siblings (Martin, 1995). Fifth, gender of parent may influence differential treatment, as mothers usually are more available to their children than are fathers (Brody & Stoneman, 1994; Stocker, 1995). Finally, differential treatment may be linked to differences in family cooperation, rule and chore expectations, and sibling friendliness (Daniels, Dunn, Furstenberg, & Plomin, 1985; Furman, 1995).

Family Relationships

Experiences in families, where rules and roles concerning group membership are learned, may affect children's functioning in group settings such as play groups (Parke, 1994). Within the family, children learn competencies and skills that may, in turn, be generalized or transferred to peer groups. In addition, distressed family relations and circumstances may become "staging areas" for child maladjustment or incompetence (Ladd, 1992). The overall functioning of the family is an important construct that should be examined. It includes the complex interplay among all family members (Feldman & Weinberger, 1994). Thus, for our purposes, *family relationships* refers to interactions and processes experienced by the family as a whole. The aspects we will review include cohesiveness, interaction quality, organization, communication, and conflict. We will also discuss the influence of family structure.

Family Cohesiveness, Interaction Quality, and Organization

Family harmony (lack of conflict), cohesiveness (support, affection, caring), and interaction quality are aspects of family relationships associated with positive social/communicative outcomes for children. For example, in families referred for clinical services, those with moderate amounts of cohesion and adaptability have been shown to have children with fewer problem behaviors (Smets & Hartup, 1988). Popular and sociable children also come from cohesive families that are lacking in tension (Bryant & DeMorris, 1992). Family cohesion is negatively related to adolescents' internalizing and externalizing problem behaviors (Barber & Buehler, 1996), and positive family relationships are negatively associated with adolescent boys' delinquent behavior (Feldman & Weinberger, 1994). In contrast, lack of cohesion has been linked to externalizing (bullying) behavior in middle childhood (Bowers, Smith, & Binney, 1994). Similar relations have been found between younger children's behavior problems and less cohesive family relationships (Crnic & Greenberg, 1990).

A general atmosphere of family harmony buffers the family against stress, allowing family members to be more effective in the negotiation of daily hassles (Garmezy, 1983). Harmony, partially reflected in positive emotional expressiveness exhibited by family members (Halberstadt, Cassidy, Stifter,

Parke, & Fox, 1995), also is linked to children's sociable behavior and acceptance by peers (e.g., Boyum & Parke, 1995; Denham et al., 1994).

Interaction models (see Kreppner, 1992) and organization structures observed in families may help children create specific interaction patterns as they continue to develop. For example, families with more structured organization (e.g., activity planning, responsibility assignments) have been found to have children who exhibit fewer externalizing problems and more responsible behavior (Hardy, Power, & Jaedicke, 1993).

Family Communication

Typically, family communication patterns have not been directly linked to child behavioral outcomes (see family expressiveness for an exception, e.g., Cassidy, Parke, Butkovsky, & Braungart, 1992; Denham & Grout, 1992); however, they may serve as mediators between other family processes and child social/communicative competence. For instance, individuals who score negatively on verbal aggressiveness and positively on verbal argumentativeness report behaviors that are consistent with authoritative parenting (Bayer & Cegala, 1992). Marital communication patterns are related to family communication patterns, indicating an underlying "family communication schema" (Fitzpatrick & Ritchie, 1994) that we hypothesize may indirectly influence children's externalizing or internalizing behaviors. Other research indicates that children's perceptions of communication in the family change as the children mature (Ritchie & Fitzpatrick, 1990). Thus, communication patterns may influence children's behavior more or less, depending on their ages.

Family Conflict

For the most part, family conflict has been associated with negative peer outcomes in children. For example, families of rejected children have higher levels of adult aggression than do families of popular or average children. Parental aggression is related to children's aggression (Patterson et al., 1984), which predicts less acceptance by peers (Strassberg, Dodge, Bates, & Pettit, 1992). Longitudinal research with adolescents also demonstrates negative effects of family conflict. Hostile behavior by parents (getting angry, yelling, threatening) is related to externalizing and internalizing symptoms (Conger et al., 1994). Little is known about similar longitudinal relationships for younger children.

Alternatively, Bryant and DeMorris (1992) suggest that conflict is a normal part of interpersonal relationships, and when children are exposed to conflicts that are resolved effectively, they may better understand their social worlds as well as learn communication and problem-solving skills. Research by Garner, Jones, and Miner (1994) indicates that the relationship between family conflict and child behavior may be curvilinear. In their study of low-income preschoolers, family conflict was positively correlated with children's knowledge about sad situations, suggesting that moderate levels of family conflict may foster the acquisition of emotional knowledge. Clearly, more research is needed to identify the ways in which family conflict affect children's social/communicative competence.

Family Structure and Transitions

Living in a single-parent household, as well as negotiating the transition from two-parent to single-parent household or from one-parent to two-parent household, may have disruptive short-term effects for parents and children (see Hetherington & Stanley-Hagan, 1995). For example, single-parent and blended families experience more severe parenting and child problems (Hoge, Andrews, & Robinson, 1990). Children from divorcing families are more externalizing and less sociable (e.g., compliant) than are children from intact families (Dix, 1991) and may experience more internalizing problems when they reach adolescence (Hetherington, Stanley-Hagan, & Anderson, 1989). In addition, boys in two-parent families are less externalizing (aggressive) than are those in single-parent families (Vaden-Kiernan, Ialongo, Pearson, & Kellam, 1995).

Longitudinal research also has found relationships between family transitions and externalizing (bullying) and internalizing (social anxiety) disorders (Kurtz, Vitaro, & Tremblay, 1995). Children from families in which the parents divorced when the children were in kindergarten and then either remained divorced or remarried during the children's elementary school years showed high levels of bullying in a school context and were the most at risk for social anxiety.

Typically, marital transitions are characterized by an initial period of disequilibrium, a reorganization of some sort, and eventual restabilization, a process that may place children at risk. However, complex interactions among many factors may influence whether or not children in these circumstances experience negative peer outcomes. Lack of an effective support system, household disorganization, children's involvement in parental conflict, and disrupted parenting may contribute to children's risk for developing problems. On the other hand, the presence of an authoritative, responsible, caring, and involved adult may protect children from possible adverse effects and promote children's social well-being (Hetherington & Stanley-Hagan, 1995).

In sum, proximal family interactions involving the marital dyad, sibling relations, and the family as a whole all set the stage for the development of social/communicative competence in children. However, it should be noted that little empirical research has addressed the transactional (Rubin, Stewart, & Chen, 1995; Stafford & Bayer, 1993) and dialectical nature (Cissna, Cox, & Bochner, 1990; Stamp & Banski, 1992) of family interactions. Notable exceptions are studies examining the dialectical nature of stepfamilies (Cissna et al., 1990) and the transition to parenthood (Stamp & Banski, 1992) as well as the work of Patterson and Dishion (1988), who emphasize the transactional nature of coercive family patterns (see Gardner, 1992).

Ladd and Le Sieur (1995) also point out that few studies have investigated the relationships among various types of family influences and how combinations of influences may affect children's peer relationships. As noted above, family factors (e.g., marital and sibling relations) may interact with processes such as parenting style. However, little effort has been made to examine whether these and other family variables (e.g., cohesion, conflict) are related to each other and to parent management or education practices (see Ladd et al., 1992). Because familial processes may influence child-rearing styles and parents' efforts to manage children's peer relationships, researchers need to understand which family processes, in what combinations, affect children's social/communicative competence with peers and how these processes are orchestrated (Ladd & Le Sieur, 1995; Parke, 1992).

PERSONAL FACTORS

Personal characteristics of parents and children may influence parenting, family interactions, and children's social/communicative competence. We begin by discussing the parents' contribution, followed by a discussion of children.

Characteristics of Parents

This subsection introduces issues in our model addressing the influence of parent characteristics that are learned and inherent. We include parental cognitions and emotions, parental psychological resources, and negative affect/depression.

Parental Cognitions and Emotions

Much of what guides how parents socialize their children's social/communicative competence is thought to be influenced by parental cognitions and emotions (e.g., Ladd et al., 1993; Ladd & Price, 1986; McGillicuddy-DeLisi & Sigel, 1995; Rubin, Mills, & Rose-Krasnor, 1989). Of the many conceptualizations of cognitions available (Holden, 1995; McGillicuddy-DeLisi & Sigel, 1995), those receiving recent attention in the socialization literature include beliefs, perceptions, and knowledge, which represent empirically distinct domains (e.g., Mize et al., 1995). In addition, how parents enact child-rearing strategies may be linked to cognitive and affective processes that are influenced by sociological and personal-social circumstances (e.g., Goodnow, 1995; Rubin, Rose-Krasnor, Bigras, Mills, & Booth, 1996).

Parents possess varying *beliefs* about the nature of children, child-rearing influences, developmental timetables, attributions about causality, opinions about modifiability, and degrees of importance attached to different aspects of behavior (e.g., Goodnow, 1988; Miller, 1995; Rubin et al., 1989). Parents also vary in their *perceptions* of children's behavioral dispositions (e.g., aggressive, withdrawn, sociable) as well as in views about themselves, their own parenting abilities, and relationships with their children (see Holden, 1995; Janssens, 1994). *Knowledge* of socialization strategies may be associated with parenting behaviors linked to children's peer relations. For example, reports of parental behavior in hypothetical child-rearing situations are reflections of underlying knowledge and indicate the most sophisticated strategies available in the parents' repertoires (e.g., Applegate et al., 1985; Finnie & Russell, 1988; Hart, DeWolf, Wozniak, & Burts, 1992; Mize & Ladd, 1988; Mize et al., 1995).

Preschool-age children whose mothers attach greater importance to social skills and believe social skills are modifiable through factors external to the child (e.g., parental arrangements of the social environment) are more sociable in peer group interactions (Rubin et al., 1989). As noted by Ladd and Le Sieur (1995), success in socialization tasks takes on a "positivity bias" by often being attributed to positive factors in the child, such as child sociability (see Gretarsson & Gelfand, 1988). In addition, mothers who perceive their preschoolers as more sociable not only tend to believe social skills are important, but also believe that mothers should play an active role in furthering socialization of these competencies (Mize et al., 1995). One way mothers accomplish this is by facilitating their children's informal activities with peers (Profilet & Ladd, 1994). These parenting behaviors may be additionally reinforced by their children's further acquisition of social skills (Rubin et al., 1989). In a related vein, Mize et al. (1995) recently reported that quality of maternal supervision during informal play activities is another important variable linked to more sophisticated levels of social strategy knowledge (i.e., more induction). This knowledge appears to guide more skillful supervision of peer play, particularly when mothers strongly believe that social skills are important and modifiable.

The picture is quite different for parents of children prone to internalizing or externalizing behavior (see Rubin & Mills, 1990). Mothers of preschoolers who display less competent behavior tend to believe that once acquired, poor social skills are difficult to change (Rubin et al., 1989). They also tend to attribute difficulty or failure in socialization tasks to factors within themselves, such as parental incompetence (Ladd & Le Sieur, 1995). Mills and Rubin (1990) found that mothers further attribute the general nature of externalizing (i.e., aggressive) and withdrawn behavior more to transient factors such as mood swings, stages, or fatigue than to stable dispositions or traits, although aggressive behavior is more often assumed than withdrawal to be attributed to age-related factors (e.g., skills not yet acquired or passing stages). However, in extreme cases of aggression and withdrawal, mothers tend to attribute these to traits in the child (Mills & Rubin, 1993; Rubin & Mills, 1990). In addition, mothers who perceive their preschoolers as more interpersonally delayed appear less inclined to encourage their children's play contacts with peers (Profilet & Ladd, 1994), are more intrusive in supervising their children's peer play (Ladd & Golter, 1988), and are more likely to be authoritarian in dealing with aggression (Mills & Rubin, 1990). However, they are less sure how to intervene with withdrawal, mainly using indirect techniques such as asking a child what is wrong or, at times, even resorting to peer contact initiations (Mills & Rubin, 1990). As noted earlier, however, parents of extremely withdrawn children appear to respond with overcontrolling, authoritarian parenting behaviors during early childhood (Rubin & Mills, 1990), perhaps as a direct measure to change or control their children's inept or inhibited behavior styles (Mills & Rubin, 1993).

Complementary findings on emotional reactions to these behaviors indicate that mothers and fathers of preschoolers report that aggressive behavior elicits anger, disappointment, and embarrassment (as does extreme withdrawal), whereas withdrawn behavior in general evokes more surprise and puzzlement (Mills & Rubin, 1990, 1993; Rubin & Mills, 1990). Given these emotional reactions, it is not surprising that parents are more likely to use authoritarian parenting strategies to deal with their children's aggression than with their social withdrawal (see Janssens, 1994). However, when withdrawn behavior is extreme in nature, it becomes more prone to authoritarian parenting as well (Rubin & Mills, 1990).

Personal/Psychological Resources

The influence of personal/psychological resources on parenting also has been examined. However, across studies there has been a lack of consistency concerning the personality types, psychological characteristics, and disorders related to specific types of parenting (Vondra & Belsky, 1993). Indeed, psychological resources may include a variety of factors, including adult temperament, personality variables, and states such as psychological well-being. However, most studies have focused on personal/psychological problems, such as depression, and less empirical research has explored the relationships among other personal psychological resources, parenting, and child-peer outcomes. We summarize results under two patterns: (a) the influence of psychological resources in the form of psychological well-being and integration, and (b) the effect of high negative affect associated with anxiety or depression (see Vondra & Belsky, 1993).

Belsky (1984) underscores the importance of psychological resources as predictors of competent parenting, and some empirical research has supported this linkage. For example, psychological well-being is positively related to authoritative warm and supportive parenting (Vermulst, DeBrock, & Van Zutphen, 1990). In addition, psychological integration is associated with mothers' sensitivity and mothers' and fathers' authoritative warmth and sensitivity with their infants. Interpersonal trust, self-efficacy, and an active coping style are other personal characteristics positively related to quality of parenting among mothers of infants (Vondra & Belsky, 1993).

Negative Affect/Depression

Much work has explored the associations among negative affect, parenting, and children's social/communicative competence. *Negative affect* can refer to a wide range of behaviors, including impulsivity, anxiety, depression, hostility, and emotional instability (Vondra & Belsky, 1993). Although parental personality disorders may have a stronger influence than parental depression on children's adjustment (Rutter & Quinton, 1984), more attention has been paid to relationships among depression, parenting/family functioning, and children's social/communicative outcomes.

Depressed individuals often have difficulties in close interpersonal relationships, higher rates of marital conflict, and higher divorce rates (Downey & Coyne, 1990). Rubin, Stewart, and Chen (1995) note that families with depressed parents are less emotionally expressive and cohesive (see Billings & Moos, 1985). Depressed mothers also tend to be less authoritative and more authoritarian and permissive (Dix, 1991). As a result, their children are more likely to exhibit higher levels of internalizing and externalizing disorders (Dix, 1991; Downey & Coyne, 1990; Field, 1995), although this may vary by child gender (Wall & Holden, 1994). Children with a manic-depressive parent tend to have a difficult time maintaining social interactions with peers and controlling aggressive behaviors. In addition, they show lower levels of sociable (prosocial) behaviors in their interactions with playmates (Zahn-Waxler, Cummings, McKnew, & Radke-Yarrow, 1984) and also seem to be at risk for school adjustment problems as well as social withdrawal (Ladd, 1992).

A number of explanations have been posed to explain children's internalizing disorders. Some place the blame on parents, suggesting that problems are inherited or that continuous exposure and interaction with a depressed parent may influence children to adopt negative emotions. Another view is that other factors, such as poverty and marital conflict, may be linked to depression in parents and children (Downey & Coyne, 1990; Zahn-Waxler et al., 1984). Finally, children's depression-related difficulties (e.g., inability to carry out peer interaction) may be related to dysfunctions within the children themselves, such as negative self-concept or attributional styles. Such outcomes might be influenced by a number of factors, such as spousal relationship and parental communicative style and behavior. The extent of the influence depends on other risk and/or protective factors the child experiences (Zahn-Waxler, Denham, Iannotti, & Cummings, 1992). Downey and Coyne (1990) suggest that it would be helpful to develop a more contextual view of depressed parents and their children, examining how personal genetic factors, biological vulnerabilities, and distal contextual factors interact to influence children's adjustment. The transactional nature of these relationships also warrants investigation (see Gardner, 1992).

In sum, more is known about relations between personal parent characteristics and parenting styles than about other factors in the model impinging on child-peer outcomes. Future research should focus on the ways in which parent cognitions, emotions, psychological resources, and depression are linked to parent management and educational practices as well as to patterns of family functioning (e.g., cohesion, conflict, sibling relationships).

Characteristics of Children

This subsection addresses the portion in our model that treats the influences of child characteristics (e.g., genetic influences on the family environment, temperament, age, gender, and resilience). We assume that genetic influences are universal among all members of the species and also unique to individuals.

Genetic Influences on the Family Environment

Parents' behavior and family interactions are thought to affect children's social/communicative development, but within the constraints of genetics. Likewise, children's genetic characteristics may affect parenting behaviors and familial functioning. All possibilities should be considered in the effort to achieve a complete understanding of familial/child interactive behaviors.

Currently, a provocative nature/nurture debate is in progress in the socialization literature; there is some disagreement among researchers concerning how extensively or rigidly heredity determines childhood behaviors and how extensively or to what degree parents influence childhood outcomes (see Baumrind, 1993; Rowe, 1994; Scarr, 1992, 1993). Some prominent behavioral geneticists maintain that there is a species-specific "average expectable environment" that ensures being reared in one family rather than another makes few differences in children's personality and intellectual development, and that the ordinary differences between families have little effect on children's development, unless a family is outside of a normal developmental range (Rowe, 1994; Scarr, 1992, 1993). This range is apparently viewed as being quite broad, with only very dysfunctional, abusive (emotional, physical, sexual), and/or poverty-stricken families falling outside of it. Critics of this rather genetically deterministic position claim that the heritability analyses used to support this view are limited by the improbability of their fundamental assumptions, their use of underdeveloped constructs, their reliance on inadequate measures of family environments (typically self-report versus more reliable behavioral observations), and their use of unrepresentative populations (typically middle-class adoptive families) (see Baumrind, 1993; Jackson, 1993). Cross-cultural studies (within and outside the United States) that measure family environments are needed to help settle this debate.

Measures of family environments generally used in child development research do appear to show some genetic effects when treated as phenotypes in twin and adoption studies. For example, Plomin and Bergeman (1991) found that measures of parental closeness (warmth and cohesion) tend to indicate a greater role of genetics than do measures of parental control. They cite several studies showing that environmental measures yield heritability estimates of sufficient magnitude to indicate that more than a quarter of the variance in environmental measures can be accounted for by genetic differences. In addition, Plomin, Reiss, Hetherington, and Howe (1994) report significant genetic effects for 15 of 18 diverse measures of the family environment.

Child responses to distal social environment effects outside the family, such as peer groups (Baker & Daniels, 1990), life events (Plomin, Lichtenstein, Pedersen, McClearn, & Nesselroade, 1990), and social support (Bergeman, Plomin, Pedersen, McClearn, & Nesselroade, 1990), may also be moderated by children's genetic factors. Plomin et al. (1994) conclude that understanding how genetic factors are involved in the ways children interact with their environments is important for helping us to understand how nature and nurture transact to affect development (see also Ge et al., 1996).

Child's Genotype Effects on the Environment

It is hypothesized that a child's genotype may influence his or her familial and nonfamilial environment in three ways: passively, evocatively, and actively (Scarr & McCartney, 1983). For example, in the active role, children increasingly select, modify, and even create their environments as they mature (see Plomin et al., 1994). The tendency actively to choose environments that complement heredity is referred to as *niche picking* (see Scarr & McCartney, 1983). Children may actively search for, select, or build environments that they find stimulating or congenial. For example, children who may be genetically predisposed to be extroverted or gregarious may actively seek the association of others and thus become involved in a wide range of social activities. These experiences, in turn, enhance the expression of the child's genotype to be sociable.

Child's Temperament Effects

Temperament is also genetically influenced and appears to predict important variations in children's social behavior and parent-child interactions (see Sanson & Rothbart, 1995). It may also moderate the influence of socialization (see Kochanska, 1995). Recent research on temperament suggests that children differ not only in the ease with which their positive and negative emotions are aroused, but also in how well they can regulate their emotions (see Rubin, Bukowski, & Parker, in press). Emotional regulation (or dysregulation) appears to lay the foundation for how children approach and interact with peers in sociable, aggressive/disruptive, or withdrawn fashion (see Eisenberg et al., 1995; Rubin, Coplan, Fox, & Calkins, 1995).

Recent studies demonstrate biological linkages with temperamental dispositions. A series of studies have found that resting frontal asymmetry, as measured by electroencephalogram (EEG), may be a marker for certain temperamental dispositions. For example, children exhibiting right frontal EEG asymmetry have been found to be more likely (a) to cry during maternal separation as newborns (Fox, Bell, & Jones, 1992), (b) to display signs of negative affect and distress over separation at 10 months of age, and (c) to display this pattern during face-to-face interactions with depressed mothers (Dawson, Grofer-Klinger, Panagiotides, Spieker, & Frey, 1992). Likewise, Fox et al. (1995) found that 4-year-olds who displayed sociability (high degree of social initiation and positive affect) exhibited greater relative left frontal activation attending to visual stimuli, whereas children who displayed social withdrawal (isolated, on looking, and unoccupied behavior) during play exhibited greater relative right frontal activation.

It has been argued that individual differences stemming from temperament are pervasive across situations and relatively stable over time. There is a growing body of evidence suggesting that individual traits identified in infancy and toddlerhood (e.g., difficult/active or inhibited temperament) are related to corresponding externalizing and internalizing behavioral orientations in early and middle childhood (see Rothbart, Ahadi, & Hershey, 1994; Rubin, Booth, et al., 1995). Such stylistic differences are thought to affect the types of interactions children establish with their environments, and the children are in turn modified by those environments (Thomas & Chess, 1977). For example, internalizing (withdrawn) children tend to watch classmates and engage in behaviors that discourage interaction, such as pushing other children away and speaking to them less often (Broberg, Lamb, & Hwang, 1990). Rubin and Stewart (in press) postulate that behavioral inhibition, coupled with insecure attachment status (likely associated with parental insensitivity, overprotection, and/or overcontrol), accounts for why some children preclude themselves from social exploration and peer play (see Rubin, Bukowski, & Parker, in press).

In some cases, a child's social/communicative behavior seems to be a direct result of temperament (Rubin et al., 1990); in other instances, it may be due to the way parents and others respond to the child's emotional style (see Eisenberg et al., 1995). Thus, the behavior of children may dispose parents to enact certain child-rearing strategies, may selectively reinforce certain parent behaviors, or may create expectations that then guide the parents' behaviors (see Bell & Chapman, 1986). For example, Lee and Bates (1985) found that infants rated as having difficult temperaments were more resistant to their mothers' efforts to control them. Early difficult temperament also correlated with later use of authoritarian strategies by mothers. In addition, early high activity level and emotional reactivity in infants has also been found to be predictive of aggression in adolescence, but the relationship seems to result from the tendency of many mothers to be permissive of antisocial, externalizing behavior in their children who have these characteristics (Olweus, 1980).

Thomas and Chess (1977) have proposed a goodness-of-fit model to describe how temperament and environmental pressures combine to affect the course of development. When the child's style of responding and environmental demands are in harmony, or achieve a "good fit," development is optimal. When dissonance, or a "poor fit" between temperament and environment, exists, the outcome is maladjustment and distorted development. To ensure goodness of fit, parents/adults must create child-rearing environments that recognize each child's temperament while encouraging more adaptive functioning.

At least in middle-class Caucasian American families, children with difficult temperaments frequently experience parenting that fits poorly with their dispositions. As infants, they are far less likely to receive sensitive caregiving (Crockenberg, 1986). By these children's second year, their parents often resort to authoritarian discipline styles. In response, the children react with defiance and disobedience. This in turn causes parents to behave inconsistently, rewarding the children's noncompliant behavior by giving in, although they resisted at first (Lee & Bates, 1985). Thus, the difficult child's temperament combined with harsh, authoritarian, and inconsistent child rearing forms a poor fit that maintains and may increase the child's irritable, conflict-ridden style. Temperament may also influence marital interactions (Stafford & Bayer, 1993). However, less is known about linkages among temperament, other features of parenting (e.g., authoritative, management practices), and family interaction.

Child's Developmental Effects

There is ample evidence suggesting that parental behaviors may vary with the age or maturity level of the child. As children grow older, parents expect and/or observe developmental advances and adjust their standards according to perceived social behavior norms that change with age (Dix, Ruble, & Zambarano, 1989). These adjustments, in turn, may prompt subtle or dramatic changes in parental beliefs/behaviors over time (Mills & Rubin, 1992).

The developmental picture for children with externalizing and internalizing disorders is complex. With regard to internalizing disorders, the temperament literature suggests that age moderates the association between parenting and child temperament. For example, parents may begin by investing greater effort in their children with internalizing problems (e.g., distress prone), but may not be able to sustain this effort over time (Crockenberg, 1986). Peters-

Martin and Wachs (1984) report similar findings. At 6 months, infant withdrawal was related to more maternal authoritative emotional and verbal
responsiveness. By 12 months, however, intensity (another negative affect
temperament dimension) was related to less maternal involvement and more
authoritarian parenting.

Regarding externalizing disorders in early development, longitudinal studies following children from 6 months to 2 years (e.g., Lee & Bates, 1985)
found that at 6 and 13 months, infants with high "fussy/difficult" ratings
received more authoritative (warm and responsive) stimulations from their
mothers. At 24 months, however, more difficult children resisted their mothers' efforts at control and received more authoritarian control from their
mothers. This pattern appears to persist until at least age 4 (Mulhern &
Passman, 1981).

Examining internalizing and externalizing problems with older children,
Dix et al. (1989) found that parent ratings of authoritarian parenting became
more favorable, whereas ratings of authoritative induction became less favorable as parents adjusted their practices in accordance with attributions toward
age-specific child behavioral competencies. This pattern became more apparent across the 4- to 12-year age span as mothers of older children inferred that
the children were more capable of understanding the rules they had violated,
acting appropriately, and being more responsible for their negative behavior.
Dix et al. (1989) also suggest that as children grow older, parents expect their
social skills to mature with age, and therefore are prone to hold their children
more responsible for negative behaviors (see Geller & Johnston, 1995; Rubin
& Mills, 1992).

In other longitudinal work following children from 4 to 6 years of age,
Mills and Rubin (1992) found that over time general displays of aggression
and withdrawal were less likely to be viewed as reflecting immaturity or as
being caused by sources external to the child (e.g., "Other children began the
fight"; "Other children would not let my child play with them"). Mothers
came to attribute these behaviors to internal dispositional characteristics of
their children (see Rubin, Stewart, & Chen, 1995). Mothers also continued
predominantly to choose more authoritarian strategies in dealing with aggression. However, for withdrawal, mothers tended to respond less to the behavior. These findings, coupled with those covered earlier, suggest that parents
may actively intervene for children who are withdrawn during early childhood. In time, however, parents may judge that these efforts have fallen short,
and they may choose to ignore or to avoid the problem (see Mills & Rubin,
1993).

There is some evidence suggesting that sociable behavior (e.g., socially
contingent communication strategies, friendly/amicable behavior) increases
in complexity and sophistication with age (see Hart, DeWolf, & Burts, 1993;
Hartup, 1983). However, less is known about how child temperament and
parenting/familial influences are related to emerging sociable behaviors across

the early and middle childhood age span. Children with varying sociability levels verbally communicate in more or less relevant and socially contingent ways linked to similar parent communication patterns (e.g., Black & Logan, 1995). Research suggests that these competencies increase with age (e.g., Giles & Street, 1994; Snow, Pan, Imbens-Bailey, & Herman, 1996). It is widely believed that these skills are facilitated (or diminished) in the context of reciprocal parent-child turn-taking activities from birth, providing a discourse structure from which children learn communicative rules of social engagement (Lamb, Ketterlinus, & Fracasso, 1992; Stafford & Bayer, 1993). Early child sociability (e.g., compliance, cooperation) also appears to breed later sociability, resulting from mutually contingent parent-child authoritative interactions (Stafford & Bayer, 1993). However, little is known about specific ways that person-centered communications in the context of parenting/familial interactions accompanied by exposure to siblings and peers across time lend themselves to the development of these capabilities (see Baudonniere, Garcia-Werebe, Michel, & Liegeois, 1989).

Child Gender Effects

Sex or gender is another child characteristic that affects various components in the model. Sex is typically defined as the biological difference between boys and girls, and gender as the construction that society has imposed on sex. Work from anthropology (Whiting & Edwards, 1988) shows that in most cultures young boys and girls live in similar worlds. However, in many cultures, by adolescence the activities of boys and girls overlap very little. Despite anthropological evidences, the influence of differential socialization by parents on determining the roles taken by boys and girls has been debated in developmental psychology since the 1970s (see Grusec & Lytton, 1988). Two major reviews have concluded that there is little evidence to suggest that boys and girls in the United States are socialized differently (Lytton & Romney, 1991; Maccoby & Jacklin, 1974). For example, Maccoby and Jacklin (1974) maintain that the only consistent differences in children's socialization are found in the shaping of sex-typed play, and that boys receive more physical punishment than do girls. Block (1976) questions these conclusions, because few studies included in Maccoby and Jacklin's review examined fathers and most were biased toward younger children. This point is relevant because cross-cultural studies suggest that socialization of children into gender roles does not occur in most cultures until later childhood or adolescence.

In the temperament literature there is ample evidence supporting bidirectional gender effects on children's socialization, if one examines gender-by-temperament interactions (Sanson & Rothbart, 1995). For example, mothers are more demanding with their 3- to 4-year-old daughters who are identified as difficult than with daughters identified as easy, whereas for sons the opposite pattern is found (Gordon, 1983). In addition, mothers have better authoritative interactions with shy girls than with nonshy girls, but the opposite pattern holds for boys (Simpson & Stevenson-Hinde, 1985). Also, longitudinal work shows that early child inflexibility is related to later maternal authoritarian parenting (i.e., punishment) for girls only, suggesting less maternal acceptance of negativity in girls than in boys (Sanson, Smart, Prior, & Oberklaid, 1993). Similarly, fathers are more authoritatively involved (generally and in social activities) with difficult (externalizing) sons than with easy or less difficult daughters (Lamb, Frodi, Hwang, Forstromm, & Corry, 1982; Redina & Dicker-scheid, 1976). The main pattern emerging from the sex-by-temperament interaction data is one of more positive responses to boys' difficultness and lower acceptance of difficultness in girls, especially on the part of fathers.

Similar to the temperament literature, the parenting literature displays evidence supporting gender effects. Baumrind and Black (1967) have shown that boys and girls react differently to parenting styles; for example, among their sample, in conditions of low structure with high emotional warmth (i.e., permissiveness) girls appeared to be very competent, whereas boys seemed much less socially competent. Fagot and Hagan (1991) examined behavioral differences in mothers' and fathers' reactions toward boys and girls at three different ages (12 months, 18 months, and 5 years). They found that mothers used more authoritarian directives than did fathers, and fathers spent more time in positive play interactions. Also, boys received more negative comments from mothers for attempts to communicate than did girls. Lastly, mothers responded in more authoritarian fashion to aggression in girls than in boys and reported more negative emotional reactions to withdrawal for girls than for boys (Rubin & Mills, 1992).

Prior work also suggests that girls, compared with boys, are more likely to seek proximity to others and to emphasize interpersonal relations and proso-cial behavior with peers. Boys tend to exhibit less affiliative and more externalizing behavior (e.g., impulsive/disruptive) in peer group interactions (Grusec & Lytton, 1988). However, Maccoby (1990) argues that behavioral differentiation of the sexes is minimal when children are observed or tested individually, and that sex differences emerge primarily in social situations with same-sex peers. Much of parental gender socialization follows from these gender-specific interactions as children grow older. Early on, mothers respond similarly to younger sons and daughters and fathers tend to treat children in a more gendered way. As children grow older and have more extensive interactions with peers, they develop interactive styles typical of their sex, and both parents begin interacting with them as they have done with opposite-sex or same-sex others (Maccoby, 1990).

Resilience

Resilience refers to the common core of dispositions and situations ena-bling children to modify their responses to risk and to maintain a sense of control and competence in their lives (see Werner, 1989; Zimmerman & Arunkumar, 1994). Operationalizing resilience, however, is difficult because researchers often consider it either a predisposing child characteristic or an outcome variable. Even though we agree that resilience may be either (Kaplan, 1994), we will treat it as a predisposing child characteristic that may be partially composed of facilitating genetic/temperamental characteristics (for descriptions, see Luther & Zigler, 1991; Masten, Best, & Garmezy, 1990; Rolf, Masten, Cicchetti, Nuechterlein, & Weintraub, 1990). In summary of child personal factors, more is known about relations involving parenting styles and the variables noted above. Relatively little is known concerning how child characteristics of development, gender, genetics, temperament, and resilience influence family interactions, marital relations, and other components of our model, and how each of these may serve to mediate or moderate linkages with child-peer outcome variables.

DISTAL FACTORS

We define distal factors as influences outside the immediate family context that have direct or indirect impacts on parenting and children's social/communicative competence. Peers, discussed earlier, may be considered a distal factor. In this section we review intergenerational relationships, employment/role strain, socioeconomic status, social support/stress, and culture.

Family of Origin/Intergenerational Relationships

Patterns of parenting in the family of origin may be linked intergenerationally. Transmission may be direct from one generation to the next or mediated by personal or proximal variables such as personality, negative affect, and the marital relationship (Caspi & Elder, 1988; Covell, Grusec, & King, 1995; Olsen, 1993; Whitbeck et al., 1992). Mechanisms used to explain the intergenerational transmission of parenting have included social learning and attachment theories (Van IJzendoorn, 1992).

Few studies have examined the intergenerational transmission of authoritative parenting. More have focused on the transmission of authoritarian aspects of parenting and on spousal and child abuse. Generally, findings indicate that the cycle of abuse associated with authoritarian parenting may be broken when an individual has high levels of support from a spouse or from an emotionally supportive, nonabusive adult. Such relationships may be corrective for persons involved in problematic relationships in the family of origin (Belsky & Pensky, 1988). Research on siblings also supports the view that unhealthy patterns in families can be altered. For example, Kramer and Baron (1995) found that mothers who reported negative sibling histories were more likely to have children who interacted positively with each other. These mothers apparently selected child-rearing strategies that included less differential treatment of siblings.

In a related vein, mothers' peer relationships during childhood may also play a role in how they socialize their children. For example, mothers who recollect anxious/lonely (withdrawn) peer relations appear to be more active in orchestrating their children's social experiences, resulting in more socially competent children (Putallaz, Costanzo, & Klein, 1993; Putallaz, Costanzo, & Smith, 1991).

Employment/Role Strain

Maternal employment has increased dramatically over the past 40 years, resulting in greater involvement and independence training of children and increased father involvement in household responsibilities, such as child care and division of household labor (Gottfried, Gottfried, & Bathurst, 1995). However, even when maternal employment and socioeconomic factors are taken into account (Cherlin, 1996), wives spend more time per week than husbands in household chores and child care, although the time husbands spend has increased (Hochschild, 1989; Shelton, 1990; Spitze, 1991). The amount and quality of a husband's help is related to how he was raised (Melson & Fogel, 1988), sex role expectations, his wife's attitude about his involvement, timing of parenthood, and the value he places on marital and family stability (Cherlin, 1996; Parke, 1995). Role strain or satisfaction associated with maternal employment and division of household labor for both mothers and fathers may also be influenced by the number of children in the family, their ages and dispositions, and the work situation itself, such as inconvenient schedules, job pressures, or long hours (Crouter, 1994; Gottfried et al., 1995; Parke, 1995).

Satisfaction with the division of household labor associated with maternal employment may be an important contributor to marital quality (Hochschild, 1989; Suitor, 1991). Maternal employment also has an impact on family relationships, depending upon other factors. For example, although there are few direct effects of maternal employment on marital relationships, marital quality decreases with sex role traditionalism or employment resentment. It increases when the mother is educated, if the mother works for personal rather than economic reasons, and if the mother's work is part-time (Chase-Lansdale, 1994; Gottfried et al., 1995). Taking these factors into account, there are different perspectives on the effects of maternal employment. One viewpoint is that employment can enhance a woman's life and be a buffer against stress. Another is that fulfilling the dual roles of worker and mother is stressful and increases role strain, which in turn may be linked to maternal depression, diminishment in the quality of parenting, and negative impacts on child outcomes (Gottfried et al., 1995; Hoffman, 1989).

Evidence supporting either view is complicated and depends on the variables studied. With regard to child outcomes associated with parenting, maternal employment seems to be beneficial for daughters in terms of their having less restricted views of sex roles (Crouter, 1994; Gottfried et al., 1995). On the downside, more hours of work may be related to less parental monitoring of children's activities and whereabouts (Crouter & McHale, 1993), which, as noted above, is linked to childhood externalizing behavior. Other effects of maternal employment on child-peer outcomes are mediated by the quality of child-care arrangements, as noted earlier. In addition, parenting behaviors associated with maternal employment are mediated or moderated by other influences within (e.g., role strain, marital relationships) and outside the family (e.g., network support, economic stress) as well as by personal factors such as commitment to parenting (see Borge & Melhuish, 1995; Gottfried et al., 1995). For example, employed mothers often compensate for their absence from the home by spending more time with their children during nonworking hours (Easterbrooks & Goldberg, 1985). Working mothers committed to work and parenting also interact more with their children, are more likely to use authoritative parenting styles, and focus on positive rather than negative qualities in their children (Greenberger et al., 1994). Clearly, additional research is warranted to disentangle the complicated linkages among maternal/paternal employment, personal and proximal variables, and child-peer outcomes (Hoffman, 1989).

Socioeconomic Influences

A consistent relationship between socioeconomic status (SES) and child-peer outcomes (e.g., Duncan, Brooks-Gunn, & Klebanov, 1994; Hart, McGee, & Hernandez, 1993; Pettit et al., 1991, 1996; Ramsey, 1988) has emerged in the literature. Low-SES family backgrounds have been directly linked to less social/communicative competence in children, and this relationship is probably mediated by factors more proximal to child outcomes. Economic deprivation presents challenges to the coping resources of families and the individuals within them (Garbarino & Kostelny, 1993). Although little is known about relations between SES variables and patterns of family functioning, linkages of SES with peer group outcomes, marital relationships, and parenting styles have been studied extensively (Hoff-Ginsberg & Tardif, 1995; Patterson, Griesler, Vaden, & Kupersmidt, 1992).

Chronic stressors associated with poverty can directly influence children's peer group outcomes (Garner et al., 1994). For example, family income and poverty are related to externalizing and internalizing behaviors (Duncan et al., 1994) and rejection (Patterson et al., 1992) in early and middle childhood. The effects of persistent poverty on internalizing and externalizing behaviors are substantially greater than the effects of transient poverty (Duncan et al., 1994). Duration of poverty has been related to antisocial behavior (Dubow & Ippolito, 1994), conduct problems, and difficulties in peer relations (Bolger, Patterson, Thompson, & Kupersmidt, 1995) in elementary-age children.

Poverty also is directly related to the ways in which children interact with peers in the distal environment. Children from economically deprived families seek the advice of friends and prefer the company of peers more than do children whose families are nondeprived. The need for group inclusion may make them more sensitive and emotionally vulnerable to their peers' reactions (Elder, 1974). A positive outcome, therefore, may be that their increased sensitivity may influence children to try to obtain social skills valued by peers (Bryant & DeMorris, 1992).

Direct linkages between SES and peer outcomes may be mediated by marital interactions or parenting style. For example, economic hardship is related to marital conflict (Bryant & DeMorris, 1992), which, as noted earlier, is linked to internalizing and externalizing disorders in children (Cummings, 1994a, 1994b). Research examining the relationship between SES and parenting styles has documented that middle-class parents are more authoritative and less authoritarian (see Hart, Lawrence, Thomasson, & Wozniak, 1990). Lower-SES parents, on the other hand, have been found to be more authoritarian and more oriented toward maintaining obedience and order (Hoff-Ginsberg & Tardif, 1995; Pettit et al., 1996).

The stress associated with economic hardship is viewed as one mechanism accounting for the relationship between SES and parenting. Economic disadvantage in families may create stress that interferes with authoritative (sensitive and responsive) parenting. Distressing financial conditions and the stress that may accompany them are related to authoritarian parenting features, including anger, conflict, inconsistency, insensitivity, and punitiveness (Rubin & Mills, 1991), as well as child maltreatment (Coulton, Korbin, Su, & Chow, 1995).

Applegate et al. (1985) provide evidence that greater differentiation of parents' interpersonal construct system (i.e., cognitive structure for interpreting, evaluating, and anticipating the thoughts and behaviors of others) also mediates the effects of higher levels of SES on authoritative (reason-oriented) parenting (see Applegate et al., 1992). Parental belief systems are thought to be yet another mechanism by which SES and parenting are related (Kohn, 1969; McLoyd, 1990). For example, research in the United States and other countries (Hoffman, 1989; Kohn, 1969) focusing on occupational roles has found that where the father has a blue-collar occupation, parents stress conforming to rules in their child rearing and are more authoritarian. This contrasts with parents who have professional and managerial occupations, who tend to be more authoritative and encourage their children's initiative and independence. These traits are valued because in professional and managerial occupations, initiative and independence are believed to pay off, whereas in blue-collar occupations, obedience and sticking to the rules are believed to be beneficial (Kohn, 1969). McLoyd (1990) extended Kohn's ideas beyond occupational roles to broader SES factors. In the United States, ethnic minorities are overrepresented in lower-SES populations; this may account for some minority group parents' being viewed as more authoritarian (see Garcia Coll, Meyer, & Brillon, 1995; Patterson, Kupersmidt, & Vaden, 1990).

In sum, socioeconomic status and poverty influence parenting behaviors, family interactions (including marital relationships), and social/communicative outcomes. It is most likely that socioeconomic status indirectly influences social/communicative outcomes, its effects being mediated through stress on parenting and marital/familial interactions as well as through parental interpersonal construct and belief systems (see Baldwin, Baldwin, & Cole, 1990; Dodge, Pettit, & Bates, 1994). Finally, it should be remembered that poverty does not operate in a vacuum. In families with scarce financial resources, stress and marital conflict may be high or support may be inadequate. These and other factors may operate in a cumulative fashion to influence children's functioning (Shaw & Emery, 1988).

Social Support and Stress

Other factors impinging on parenting and family relationships include social support and stress. Families experiencing economic hardship are more likely to experience negative life events (e.g., job loss, illness) and marital disruptions/transitions that may negatively affect peer group outcomes (Bryant & DeMorris, 1992). Stressful life events have been related to authoritarian (coercive) parent-child interactions and to both internalizing and externalizing (aggressive) behavior with peers (e.g., MacKinnon-Lewis et al., 1994). However, cohesive family interactions may mitigate these negative effects (Quamma & Greenberg, 1994). Although life stress and minor daily hassles (e.g., irritating child whining, sibling conflicts) are predictive of lower parenting satisfaction, authoritarian and controlling parent-child interactions appear to be related more to daily hassles than to major life stressors (Crnic & Greenberg, 1990). In addition, greater daily hassles are related to spousal differences in coparenting (Belsky, Crnic, & Gable, 1995) and to externalizing behavior in children (Creasey, Mitts, & Catanzaro, 1995).

As Rubin, Stewart, and Chen (1995) point out, social support from extended family, neighborhood, and community structures may enhance or buffer the effects of stress on parenting and childhood behavior problems. For example, recent findings indicate that stressful life events are strong predictors of childhood aggression only under conditions of high neighborhood disadvantage (Attar, Guerra, & Tolan, 1994). In contrast, life stressors related to childhood aggression appear to be mitigated by advantaged neighborhood settings (Kupersmidt, Griesler, DeRosier, Patterson, & Davis, 1995). The positive or negative effects of this type of support may vary according to distal (e.g., socioeconomic status, culture) and personal factors such as parent personality and parenting (Cochran, 1993) that can be enhanced by supportive neighborhoods and community structures. Through formal and informal social networks, parents become exposed to new ideas about child development and parenting (see Goodnow, 1995; Okagaki & Divecha, 1993) and receive emotional support that helps them feel more competent in coping with stressors associated with parenting.

Support network characteristics have been shown to predict peer acceptance indirectly through effects on less perceived difficulty in helping children socially (Melson et al., 1993). However, families lacking such support may be prone to problems. For example, preschool children whose mothers report less social support receive higher aggression ratings. Also, children who have stable behavior problems by the time they enter school have been found to come from families that have had more stressful events and lower levels of social support (see Campbell, 1995).

Culture-Specific Influences

In the broader community, the communication of normative cultural standards about child rearing occurs through advice from relatives and experts and through parents' witnessing of interactions within families other than their own (e.g., Bronfenbrenner, 1986; Goodnow, 1995; Goodnow, Miller, & Kessel, 1995). Each culture, and to some extent each subculture, supplies models for parent-child interaction patterns that result in specific behaviors that, when implemented under local conditions, become culture-specific styles (LeVine & White, 1986).

Research on parenting has revealed evidence of universals and cultural variations in parenting (Harkness & Super, 1995). For example, similar social/communicative child-peer outcomes associated with authoritarian and permissive parenting behaviors have been found in the United States, Russia, and China (Chen, Dong, & Zhou, 1996; Nelson, 1995). These findings suggest that there may be developmental universals at work that are somewhat varied in terms of cross-cultural meanings or nuances involving other parenting variables such as child training in culture-specific conventions (Chao, 1994).

Our proposed model is intended to explain extrafamilial, familial, and individual influences on child social/communicative outcomes within a predominant cultural context, not between cultures (cross-culture influences). Subculture-specific nuances embedded within a predominant culture, however, do come into play in the dynamics of the model and need to be taken into consideration. A number of researchers and theorists have criticized the use of middle-class Caucasian American models for explaining the socialization of minority group children (e.g., Darling & Steinberg, 1993; Nucci, 1994). For example, it has been suggested that the greater frequency of physical punishment among African American families than among Caucasian American families (see Maccoby, 1984) may be normative for survival in neighborhoods where violence and risk associated with antisocial activities are relatively commonplace. Thus, authoritarian parenting may be less negative for an African American child raised under these circumstances (see Garcia Coll et al., 1995). Maccoby's (1984) work highlights the "dangers of generalizing the findings" concerning parent-child compliance strategies from one culture to another (p. 215). In this view, the issue becomes what is "normal" for each culture/subculture and what route is best for children within that social milieu. How far this argument goes is not well understood due to limited parent-child interaction data from African American and other minority groups (Garcia Coll et al., 1995; Socha, Sanchez-Hucles, Bromley, & Kelly, 1995).

Also addressing this issue, Ogbu (1988) has proposed that the parenting styles observed among minority families are geared toward the development of instrumental competencies unique to particular subcultures or environments. As a consequence, the socialization goals of minority families are likely to be different from or at odds with the goals espoused by the dominant Caucasian American culture. For example, Harrison, Wilson, Rine, Chan, and Buriel (1990) have identified two socialization goals of ethnic minorities that are different from goals accepted by the dominant American culture: positive identification with the ethnic group and socialization toward interdependence. Socialization toward interdependence is common among ethnic minority families (Lin & Fu, 1990). Likewise, ethnic minority children are instructed to behave cooperatively, as opposed to the competitive, individualistic style favored by Caucasian middle-class parents (Harrison et al., 1990).

In extending the body of literature involving distal variables, future investigations should concentrate on the parenting attitudes, values, and behaviors of successful ethnic and minority families (Harrison et al., 1990; Lamberty & Garcia Coll, 1994) to contribute to our understanding of family process when race is not confounded with socioeconomic status. The subcultural examination of "successful" parenting against all odds (e.g., of recent poor immigrants) may shed light on whether there are universal norms in parenting.

In addition, our review of distal factors suggests that little is known about how SES, work, and culture variables influence other aspects of familial functioning and parenting (parental management and education practices) discussed earlier. For example, economic circumstances and parent work schedules may influence flexibility in arranging peer contacts (e.g., ability to transport children). The quality of interactions with peers as facilitated by adult supervision practices and access to community resources (e.g., parks) in more or less dangerous neighborhoods may also be influenced by the location in which the family resides. Also, parents' beliefs concerning the value of informal peer contacts may vary by culture/subculture (see Ladd, Hart, Wadsworth, & Golter, 1988; Ladd & Hart, 1992).

IMPLICATIONS FOR INTERVENTION

It is important for interventionists to understand the complexity of relationships among factors impinging on social/communicative competence as set forth in our conceptual model. This should help them determine the best variable(s) to consider when intervening with internalizing/externalizing disorders. Traditionally, social skills training has targeted problematic child behavior using cognitive behavioral models such as coaching, modeling, rehearsal, feedback, and reinforcement (see Asher et al., 1996; Lochman, Coie, Underwood, & Terry, 1993; Mize & Ladd, 1990; Zarazoga, Vaughn, & McIntosh, 1991). Other interventions could focus on factors sustaining lower levels of social/communicative competence as well. For example, social skills training could be enhanced by being coupled with early childhood interventions or parenting programs (e.g., van den Boom, 1995). Moreover, many community-based family strengthening programs offer a range of services, including parenting programs, day care (respite), and social support groups for parents. In concert, these could be effective for reducing the risk associated with distal factors (e.g., economic stress) and personal or proximal factors such as negative parent cognitions (e.g., Cunningham, Bremner, & Boyle, 1995; Reynolds, 1994). Finally, the enhancement of communication skills should be a focal point in intervention (Applegate et al., 1992). It is particularly important that effective interventions focus on the interplay between social and communicative competence, not only for normative communicative deficiencies, but also for specific language impairments (Fujiki & Brinton, 1994; Guralnick et al., 1996).

CONCLUSION

Paths in our conceptual model have both strong and weak empirical support, and throughout this review we have noted where empirically based knowledge is incomplete. For example, more is known about mechanisms linking maternal parenting styles to other proximal, personal, distal, and child-peer outcomes than about specific mechanisms linking other proximal parenting variables (e.g., management, education practices, fathering) and familial interactions (e.g., cohesion, sibling interactions).

With specific regard to proximal parenting and family interaction variables, little empirical work has assessed child outcomes associated with (a) the additive effects or the interaction of family functioning and parenting variables or (b) the interactions of parenting style components across typological domains. For example, what child-peer outcomes might be expected for cohesive family relationships and harmonious marital interactions coupled with authoritarian parenting (if there is such a combination)? What is the additive effect of either positive or negative familial and parenting variables on children's social/communicative competence? Is it possible that some parents who use corporal punishment (authoritarian) also display high levels of warmth and/or reasoning (authoritative) control strategies with their children as well (see Larzelere, 1986)? What types of child outcomes might be associated with such combinations of parenting variables? In addition, current adolescent research on parenting suggests that psychological control impacts both internalizing and externalizing behavior, whereas behavioral control is related to externalizing behavior only (Barber, in press). How might these types of parental control relate to social/ communicative outcomes in early and middle childhood?

Somewhat related questions concern understanding thresholds, or critical points, where parenting and family interaction variables have dramatic impacts on child outcomes (Burr, Beutler, Yorgason, & Olsen, 1995; Burr, Dollahite, & Draper, 1995; Burr, Hill, Nye, & Reiss, 1979). As Rowe (1994) argues in his analysis of nature/nurture issues, many family processes do not appear to make much difference in most of their range of variation. It is only when conditions are fairly extreme that the impact becomes important. This view lends itself to a variety of possible inquiries. For example, how much or at what point does parental reasoning make a difference in children's social/communicative competence? Might the relationship between parental reasoning (or reflection-enhancing strategies) and children's sociable behavior be curvilinear? In other words, might the power of the relationship decrease (or increase) dramatically after some threshold? These are difficult questions to answer because most research is based on linear assumptions. Similar questions could be asked about other proximal aspects of parenting and patterns of family functioning as well as personal and distal variables explored in our model. Identifying critical points also has practical implications. For example, if parents are only moderately conflictual in their marital relationship, and supposing research indicates that conflict above the 75th percentile is what is linked to chronic childhood behavioral problems, then it might be best to focus on other areas of the model for interventions.

In addition to other questions raised throughout this review, future queries could include the following: Which features of the distal environment (e.g., culture, economics) and/or personal parent factors (e.g., psychological resources) are linked to parent management/education practices or family interaction patterns? What specifically do children learn about social/communicative competence from siblings, and how are these competencies transferred to social/communicative behavior with peers (see Berndt & Bulleit, 1985)? How might sibling temperament and communicative behaviors interact with a child's social/communicative competencies, and how are these related to other proximal or distal factors? Why do siblings from the same family vary so much in their social/communicative competencies (see Plomin, 1994) and not so much in other areas, such as political and religious beliefs (Bower, 1991)?

Additional questions include the following: Why is family cohesion or organization linked to positive social/communicative outcomes, and which distal or personal factors also are related to these variables? How might changes occurring over the family life cycle impinge on these factors over time? How do parent and child characteristics influence the relationship between family functioning and child-peer outcomes, and how are these also related to sibling interactions? What is the additive effect of different parenting behaviors and family interactions on children's social/communicative competence in both friendship and group acceptance domains (see Rubin, Bukowski, & Parker, in press)? Such questions provide a fruitful field for inquiry.

Although our model is quite comprehensive, it has limitations. As previously noted, few empirical studies examine the transactional nature of the system shown in Figure 9.1. As our understanding increases, other components and new ways of conceptualizing these relationships could be added. It is evident that relatively little is known about many model linkages, especially in relation to communicative features of child-peer outcomes. For instance, how do children acquire nonverbal social/communication strategies (e.g., gaze aversion, smiling), and how are these strategies linked to other model components (see Burgoon, 1994)? Moreover, relatively little is known about the ways distal factors not included in the model affect child social/communicative behavior and are mediated by personal and/or proximal variables. For example, childhood externalizing behavior may be related to aggressive behavior seen on television when coupled with authoritarian parenting and parents' failings to monitor their children's viewing (Singer & Benton, 1989). However, it is not well understood how relationships involving the media are moderated by personal parenting variables (e.g., beliefs) and child factors such as temperamental disposition (Bushman, 1995). Linkages between religious subcultural influences and some components of our model are just beginning to be understood (e.g., Brody, Stoneman, & Flor, 1996; Heaton, Goodman, & Holman, 1994), as are the effects of ethnic and political violence on children's social/behavioral outcomes (e.g., Ladd & Cairns, 1996). However, little empirical knowledge exists to explain how changes in political and government support structures, cultural values and beliefs, historical events, and natural disasters impinge on model components over time (e.g., Lerner et al., 1995). In addition, little is known about how these processes operate in atypical families, such as families in which children or other members have disabilities or suffer from chronic illness (e.g., Turnbull et al., 1993).

Taken together, our model demonstrates that parenting and family interactions related to children's peer group outcomes do not occur in a vacuum. Understanding how these components are connected will be beneficial for our understanding of the ways extrafamilial, personal, and familial processes serve to enhance or inhibit social/communicative competence in young children. As Rutter (1989) cogently illustrates in his review of pathways from childhood to adult life, understanding linkages among the enhancing or diminishing effects of different early life experiences will help us better recognize the multiplicity of pathways and diversity of end points that are evident across the human life span.

REFERENCES

Applegate, J. L., Burke, J. A., Burleson, B. R., Delia, J. G., & Kline, S. L. (1985). Reflection enhancing parental communication. In I. E. Sigel (Ed.), *Parental belief systems: The psychological consequences for children* (pp. 107-142). Hillsdale, NJ: Lawrence Erlbaum.

Applegate, J. L., Burleson, B. R., & Delia, J. G. (1992). Reflection-enhancing parenting as an antecedent to children's social-cognitive and communicative development. In I. E. Sigel, A. V. McGillicuddy-DeLisi, & J. J. Goodnow (Eds.), *Parental belief systems: The psychological consequences for children* (2nd ed., pp. 3-39). Hillsdale, NJ: Lawrence Erlbaum.

Asher, S. R., Parker, J. G., & Walker, D. L. (1996). Distinguishing friendship from acceptance: Implications for intervention and assessment. In W. M. Bukowski, A. F. Newcomb, & W. W. Hartup (Eds.), *The company they keep: Friendship during childhood and adolescence* (pp. 366-405). New York: Cambridge University Press.

Attar, B. K., Guerra, N. G., & Tolan, P. H. (1994). Neighborhood disadvantage, stressful life events, and adjustment in urban elementary-school children. *Journal of Clinical Child Psychology, 23,* 391-400.

Attili, G. (1989). Social competence versus emotional security: The link between home relationships and behavior problems at school. In B. H. Schneider, G. Attili, J. Nadel, & R. P. Weissberg (Eds.), *Social competence in developmental perspective* (pp. 293-311). Dordrecht, Netherlands: Kluwer.

Baker, L. A., & Daniels, D. (1990). Nonshared environmental influences and personality differences in adult twins. *Journal of Personality and Social Psychology, 58,* 103-110.

Baldwin, A. L., Baldwin, C., & Cole, R. E. (1990). Stress-resistant families and stress-resistant children. In J. Rolf, A. S. Masten, D. Cicchetti, K. H. Nuechterlein, & S. Weintraub (Eds.), *Risk and protective factors in the development of psychopathology* (pp. 257-280). New York: Cambridge University Press.

Barber, B. K. (in press). Parental psychological control: Revisiting a neglected construct. *Child Development.*

Barber, B. K., & Buehler, C. (1996). Family cohesion and psychological control: Different constructs, different effects. *Journal of Marriage and the Family, 58,* 433-441.

Baron, R. M., & Kenny, D. A. (1986). The moderator-mediator variable distinction in social psychological research: Conceptual, strategic, and statistical considerations. *Journal of Personality and Social Psychology, 51,* 1173-1182.

Barth, J. M., & Parke, R. D. (1993). Parent-child relationship influences on children's transition to school. *Merrill-Palmer Quarterly, 39,* 173-195.

Bates, J. E., Marvinney, D., Kelly, T., Dodge, K. A., Bennett, D. S., & Pettit, G. S. (1994). Child-care history and kindergarten adjustment. *Developmental Psychology, 30,* 690-700.

Baudonniere, P., Garcia-Werebe, M., Michel, J., & Liegeois, J. (1989). Development of communicative competencies in early childhood: A model and results. In B. H. Schneider, G. Attili, J. Nadel, & R. P. Weissberg (Eds.), *Social competence in developmental perspective* (pp. 175-193). Dordrecht, Netherlands: Kluwer.

Baumrind, D. (1967). Child care practices anteceding three patterns of preschool behavior. *Genetic Psychology Monographs, 75,* 43-88.

Baumrind, D. (1971). Current patterns of parental authority. *Developmental Psychology Monograph, 4,* 1-103.

Baumrind, D. (1989). Rearing competent children. In W. Damon (Ed.), *Child development today and tomorrow* (pp. 349-378). San Francisco: Jossey-Bass.

Baumrind, D. (1993). The average expectable environment is not good enough: A response to Scarr. *Child Development, 64,* 1299-1317.

Baumrind, D., & Black, A. E. (1967). Socialization practices associated with dimensions of competence in preschool boys and girls. *Child Development, 38,* 291-327.

Bayer, C. L., & Cegala, D. J. (1992). Trait verbal aggressiveness and argumentativeness: Relations with parenting style. *Western Journal of Communication, 56,* 301-310.

Bearson, D. J., & Cassel, T. Z. (1975). Cognitive decentration and social codes: Communicative effectiveness in young children from different family contexts. *Developmental Psychology, 11,* 29-36.

Bell, R. Q., & Chapman, M. (1986). Child effects in studies using experimental or brief longitudinal approaches to socialization. *Developmental Psychology, 22,* 595-603.

Belsky, J. (1984). The determinants of parenting: A process model. *Child Development, 55,* 83-96.

Belsky, J., Crnic, K., & Gable, S. (1995). The determinants of coparenting in families with toddler boys: Spousal differences. *Child Development, 66,* 629-642.

Belsky, J., Fish, M., & Isabella, R. (1991). Continuity and discontinuity in infant negative and positive emotionality: Family antecedents and attachment consequences. *Developmental Psychology, 27,* 421-431.

Belsky, J., & Pensky, E. (1988). Developmental history, personality, and family relationships: Toward an emergent family system. In R. A. Hinde & J. Stevenson-Hinde (Eds.), *Relationships within families: Mutual influences* (pp. 193-217). Oxford: Oxford University Press.

Benasich, A. A., & Brooks-Gunn, J. (1996). Maternal attitudes and knowledge of child-rearing: Association with family and child outcomes. *Child Development, 67,* 1186-1205.

Bergeman, C. S., Plomin, R., Pedersen, N. L., McClearn, G. E., & Nesselroade, J. R. (1990). Genetic and environmental influences on social support: The Swedish Adoption/Twin Study of Aging (SATA). *Journal of Gerontology: Psychological Sciences, 45,* 101-106.

Berndt, T. J., & Bulleit, T. N. (1985). Effects of sibling relationships on preschoolers' behavior at home and at school. *Developmental Psychology, 21,* 761-767.

Berndt, T. J., & Ladd, G. W. (Eds.). (1989). *Peer relationships in child development.* New York: John Wiley.

Bhavnagri, N., & Parke, R. D. (1985, April). *Parents as facilitators of preschool children's peer relationships.* Paper presented at the biennial meeting of the Society for Research in Child Development, Toronto.

Bhavnagri, N., & Parke, R. D. (1991). Parents as direct facilitators of children's peer relationships: Effects of age of child and sex of parent. *Journal of Social and Personal Relationships, 8,* 423-440.

Billings, A. G., & Moos, R. H. (1985). Children of parents with unipolar depression: A controlled 1 year follow-up. *Journal of Abnormal Child Psychology, 14,* 149-166.

Black, B., & Logan, A. (1995). Links between communication patterns in mother-child, father-child, and child-peer interactions and children's social status. *Child Development, 66,* 255-271.

Block, J. H. (1976). Issues, problems and pitfalls in assessing sex differences: A critical review of the psychology of sex differences. *Merrill-Palmer Quarterly, 22,* 283-308.

Bolger, K. E., Patterson, C. J., Thompson, W. W., & Kupersmidt, J. B. (1995). Psychosocial adjustment among children experiencing persistent and intermittent family economic hardship. *Child Development, 66,* 1107-1129.

Booth, C. L., Rose-Krasnor, L., McKinnon, J., & Rubin, K. H. (1994). Predicting social adjustment in middle childhood: The role of preschool attachment security and maternal style. *Social Development, 3,* 189-204.

Borge, A., & Melhuish, E. (1995). A longitudinal study of childhood behavior problems, maternal employment, and day care in a rural Norwegian community. *International Journal of Behavioral Development, 18,* 23-42.

Bower, B. (1991, December). Same family, different lives. *Science News,* pp. 376-378.

Bowers, L., Smith, P. K., & Binney, V. (1994). Perceived family relationships of bullies, victims, and bully/victims in middle childhood. *Journal of Personal and Social Relationships, 11,* 215-232.

Bowlby, J. (1973). *Attachment and loss: Vol. 2. Separation.* New York: Basic Books.

Boyum, L. A., & Parke, R. D. (1995). The role of family emotional expressiveness in the development of children's social competence. *Journal of Marriage and the Family, 57,* 593-608.

Broberg, A., Lamb, M. E., & Hwang, P. (1990). Inhibition: Its stability and correlates in 16- to 40-month-old children. *Child Development, 61,* 1153-1163.

Brody, G. H., & Stoneman, Z. (1994). Sibling relationships and their associations with parental differential treatment. In E. M. Hetherington, D. Reiss, & R. Plomin (Eds.), *Separate social worlds of siblings: The impact of nonshared environment on development* (pp. 129-142). Hillsdale, NJ: Lawrence Erlbaum.

Brody, G. H., Stoneman, Z., & Flor, D. (1996). Parental religiosity, family processes, and youth competence in rural, two-parent African American families. *Developmental Psychology, 32,* 696-706.

Brody, G. H., Stoneman, Z., & McCoy, J. K. (1992). Associations of maternal and paternal direct and differential behavior with sibling relationships: Contemporaneous and longitudinal analyses. *Child Development, 63,* 82-92.

Bronfenbrenner, U. (1986). Ecology of the family as a context for human development: Research perspectives. *Developmental Psychology, 22,* 723-742.

Bryant, B., & Crockenberg, S. (1980). Correlates and dimensions of prosocial behavior: A study of female siblings and their mothers. *Child Development, 51,* 529-544.

Bryant, B. K., & DeMorris, K. A. (1992). Beyond parent-child relationships: Potential links between family environments and peer relations. In R. D. Parke & G. W. Ladd (Eds.), *Family-peer relationships: Modes of linkage* (pp. 159-189). Hillsdale, NJ: Lawrence Erlbaum.

Bugental, D. B., Blue, J., & Lewis, J. (1990). Caregiver beliefs and dysphoric affect directed to difficult children. *Developmental Psychology, 26,* 631-638.

Buhrmester, D. (1996). Need fulfillment, interpersonal competence, and the developmental contexts of friendship. In W. M. Bukowski, A. F. Newcomb, & W. W. Hartup (Eds.), *The company they keep: Friendship during childhood and adolescence* (pp. 158-185). New York: Cambridge University Press.

Buhrmester, D., & Furman, W. (1990). Perceptions of sibling relationships during middle childhood and adolescence. *Child Development, 61,* 1387-1398.

Burchinal, M. R., Ramey, S. L., Reid, M. K., & Jaccard, J. (1995). Early child care experiences and their association with family and child characteristics during middle childhood. *Early Childhood Research Quarterly, 10,* 33-61.

Burgoon, J. K. (1994). Nonverbal signals. In M. L. Knapp & G. R. Miller (Eds.), *Handbook of interpersonal communication* (2nd ed., pp. 229-285). Thousand Oaks, CA: Sage.

Burleson, B. R., Delia, J. G., & Applegate, J. L. (1992). Effects of maternal communication and children's social-cognitive and communication skills on children's acceptance by the peer group. *Family Relations, 41,* 264-272.

Burleson, B. R., Delia, J. G., & Applegate, J. L. (1995). The socialization of person-centered communication: Parents' contributions to their children's social-cognitive and communication skills. In M. A. Fitzpatrick & A. L. Vangelisti (Eds.), *Explaining family interactions* (pp. 34-76). Thousand Oaks, CA: Sage.

Burleson, B. R., & Kunkel, A. W. (1996). The socialization of emotional support skills in childhood. In G. R. Pierce, B. S. Sarason, & I. G. Sarason (Eds.), *Handbook of social support and the family* (pp. 105-140). New York: Plenum.

Burr, W. R., Beutler, I. F., Yorgason, F., & Olsen, J. A. (1995, November). *Toward more pragmatic family science theories: Part II. Loving in families as an example.* Paper presented at the annual meeting of the National Council on Family Relations, Portland, OR.

Burr, W. R., Dollahite, D. C., & Draper, T. W. (1995, November). *Toward more pragmatic family science theories: Part I. Philosophical and methodological issues.* Paper presented at the annual meeting of the National Council on Family Relations, Portland, OR.

Burr, W. R., Hill, R., Nye, F. I., & Reiss, I. L. (Eds.). (1979). *Contemporary theories about the family: Vol. 1. Research-based theories.* New York: Free Press.

Bushman, B. J. (1995). Moderating role of trait aggressiveness in the effects of violent media on aggression. *Journal of Personality and Social Psychology, 69,* 950-960.

Campbell, S. B. (1995). Behavior problems in preschool children: A review of recent research. *Journal of Child Psychology and Psychiatry, 36,* 113-149.

Campbell, S. B., Pierce, E. W., March, C. L., Ewing, L. J., & Szumowski, E. K. (1994). Hard-to-manage preschool boys: Symptomatic behavior across contexts and time. *Child Development, 65,* 836-851.

Caspi, A., & Elder, G. H., Jr. (1988). Emergent family patterns: The intergenerational construction of problem behaviour and relationships. In R. A. Hinde & J. Stevenson-Hinde (Eds.), *Relationships within families: Mutual influences* (pp. 218-240). Oxford: Oxford University Press.

Cassidy, J., Parke, R. D., Butkovsky, L., & Braungart, J. M. (1992). Peer-family connections: The roles of emotional expressiveness within the family and children's understanding of emotion. *Child Development, 63,* 603-618.

Chamberlain, P., & Patterson, G.R. (1995). Discipline and child compliance in parenting. In M. H. Bornstein (Ed.), *Handbook of parenting: Vol. 4. Applied and practical parenting* (pp. 205-225). Mahwah, NJ: Lawrence Erlbaum.

Chao, R. K. (1994). Beyond parental control and authoritarian parenting style: Understanding Chinese parenting through the cultural notion of training. *Child Development, 65,* 1111-1119.

Chase-Lansdale, P. (1994). Families and maternal employment during infancy: New linkages. In R. D. Parke & S. G. Kellam (Eds.), *Exploring family relationships within other social contexts* (pp. 29-47). Hillsdale, NJ: Lawrence Erlbaum.

Chen, X., Dong, Q., & Zhou, H. (1996). *Authoritative and authoritarian parenting practices and school performance in Chinese children.* Manuscript submitted for publication.

Chen, X., & Rubin, K. H. (1994). Family conditions, parental acceptance, social competence and aggression in Chinese children. *Social Development, 3,* 269-290.

Cherlin, A. (1996). *Public and private families.* New York: McGraw-Hill.

Chung, T., & Asher, S. R. (1996). Children's goals and strategies in peer conflict situations. *Merrill-Palmer Quarterly, 42,* 125-147.

Cicchetti, D., Lynch, M., Shonk, S., & Manly, J. T. (1992). An organizational perspective on peer relations in maltreated children. In R. D. Parke & G. W. Ladd (Eds.), *Family-peer relationships: Modes of linkage* (pp. 345-384). Hillsdale, NJ: Lawrence Erlbaum.

Cissna, K. N., Cox, D. E., & Bochner, A. P. (1990). The dialectic of marital and parental relationships within the stepfamily. *Communication Monographs, 57,* 44-61.

Cochran, M. (1993). Parenting and personal social networks. In T. Luster & L. Okagaki (Eds.), *Parenting: An ecological perspective* (pp. 149-178). Hillsdale, NJ: Lawrence Erlbaum.

Coie, J. D., Dodge, K. A., & Kupersmidt, J. B. (1990). Peer group behavior and social status. In S. R. Asher & J. D. Coie (Eds.), *Peer rejection in childhood: Origins, consequences, and intervention* (pp. 17-59). Cambridge: Cambridge University Press.

Collins, W. A., Harris, M. L., & Sussman, A. (1995). Parenting during middle childhood. In M. H. Bornstein (Ed.), *Handbook of parenting: Vol. 1. Children and parenting* (pp. 65-89). Mahwah, NJ: Lawrence Erlbaum.

Conger, R. D., Ge, X., Elder, G. H., Jr., Lorenz, F. O., & Simons, R. L. (1994). Economic stress, coercive family process, and developmental problems of adolescents. *Child Development, 65,* 541-561.

Coplan, R. J., Rubin, K. H., Fox, H. A., Calkins, S. D., & Stewart, S. L. (1994). Being alone, playing alone, and acting alone: Distinguishing among reticence and passive and active solitude in young children. *Child Development, 65*, 129-137.

Coulton, C. J., Korbin, J. E., Su, M., & Chow, J. (1995). Community level factors and child maltreatment rates. *Child Development, 66*, 1262-1276.

Covell, K., Grusec, J. E., & King, G. (1995). The intergenerational transmission of maternal discipline and standards for behavior. *Social Development, 4*, 32-43.

Cowan, C. P., & Cowan, P. A. (1992). *When partners become parents: The big life change for couples.* New York: Basic Books.

Creasey, G., Mitts, N., & Catanzaro, S. (1995). Associations among daily hassles, coping, and behavior problems in nonreferred kindergartners. *Journal of Clinical Child Psychology, 24*, 311-319.

Crick, N. R., Casas, J. F., Mosher, M. (in press). Relational and overt aggression in preschool. *Developmental Psychology.*

Crick, N. R., & Dodge, K. A. (1994). A review and reformulation of social information-processing mechanisms in children's social adjustment. *Psychological Bulletin, 115*, 74-101.

Crick, N. R., & Grotpeter, J. K. (1995). Relational aggression, gender, and social-psychological adjustment. *Child Development, 66*, 710-722.

Crnic, K. A., & Greenberg, M. T. (1990). Minor parenting stresses with young children. *Child Development, 61*, 1628-1637.

Crockenberg, S. B. (1986). Are temperamental differences in babies associated with predictable differences in care-giving? In J. V. Lerner & R. M. Lerner (Eds.), *Temperament and social interaction in infants and children* (pp. 75-88). San Francisco: Jossey-Bass.

Crockenberg, S. B., & Forgays, D. K. (1996). The role of emotion in children's understanding and emotional reactions to marital conflict. *Merrill-Palmer Quarterly, 42*, 22-47.

Crouter, A. C. (1994). Processes linking families and work: Implications for behavior and development in both settings. In R. D. Parke & S. G. Kellam (Eds.), *Exploring family relationships within other social contexts* (pp. 9-28). Hillsdale, NJ: Lawrence Erlbaum.

Crouter, A. C., & McHale, S. M. (1993). The long arm of the job: Influences of parental work on childrearing. In T. Luster & L. Okagaki (Eds.), *Parenting: An ecological perspective* (pp. 179-202). Hillsdale, NJ: Lawrence Erlbaum.

Cummings, E. M. (1994a). *Children and marital conflict: The impact of family dispute and resolution.* New York: Guilford.

Cummings, E. M. (1994b). Marital conflict and children's functioning. *Social Development, 3*, 16-36.

Cunningham, C. E., Bremner, R. B., & Boyle, M. (1995). Large group community-based parenting programs for families of preschoolers at risk for disruptive behavior disorders: Utilization, cost effectiveness, and outcome. *Journal of Child Psychology and Psychiatry, 36*, 1111-1159.

Daniels, D., Dunn, J., Furstenberg, F. F., Jr., & Plomin, R. (1985). Environmental differences within the family and adjustment differences within pairs of adolescent siblings. *Child Development, 56*, 764-774.

Darling, N., & Steinberg, L. (1993). Parenting style as context: An integrative model. *Psychological Bulletin, 113*, 487-496.

Das Eiden, R., Teti, D. M., & Corns, K. M. (1995). Maternal working models of attachment, marital adjustment, and the parent-child relationship. *Child Development, 66*, 1504-1518.

Dawson, G., Grofer-Klinger, L., Panagiotides, H., Spieker, S., & Frey, K. (1992). Infants of mothers with depressive symptoms: Electroencephalographic and behavioral findings related to attachment status. *Development and Psychopathology, 4*, 67-80.

Deal, J. E., Halverson, C. F., Jr., & Wampler, K. S. (1989). Parental agreement on child-rearing orientations: Relations to parental, marital, family, and child characteristics. *Child Development, 60,* 1025-1034.

Dekovic, M., & Janssens, J. A. M. (1992). Parents' child-rearing style and child's sociometric status. *Developmental Psychology, 28,* 925-932.

Denham, S. A., & Grout, L. (1992). Mothers' emotional expressiveness and coping: Relations with preschoolers' social-emotional competence. *Genetic, Social, and General Psychology Monographs, 118,* 75-101.

Denham, S. A., Renwick-DeBardi, S., & Hewes, S. (1994). Emotional communication between mothers and preschoolers: Relations with emotional competence. *Merrill-Palmer Quarterly, 40,* 488-508.

DeRosier, M. E., Kupersmidt, J. B., & Patterson, C. J. (1994). Children's academic and behavioral adjustment as a function of the chronicity and proximity of peer rejection. *Child Development, 65,* 1799-1813.

Dishion, T. J., Duncan, T. E., Eddy, J. M., Fagot, B. I., & Fetrow, R. (1994). The world of parents and peers: Coercive exchanges and children's social adaption. *Social Development, 3,* 255-268.

Dix, T. (1991). The affective organization of parenting: Adaptive and maladaptive processes. *Psychological Bulletin, 110,* 3-25.

Dix, T., Ruble, D. N., & Zambarano, R. J. (1989). Mothers' implicit theories of discipline: Child effects, parent effects, and the attribution process. *Child Development, 60,* 1373-1391.

Dodge, K. A. (1985). Facets of social interaction and the assessment of social competence. In B. H. Schneider, K. H. Rubin, & J. Ledingham (Eds.), *Children's peer relations: Issues in assessment and intervention* (pp. 3-22). New York: Springer-Verlag.

Dodge, K. A., & Coie, J. D. (1987). Social information processing factors in reactive and proactive aggression in children's peer groups. *Journal of Personality and Social Psychology, 53,* 1146-1158.

Dodge, K. A., Pettit, G. S., & Bates, J. E. (1994). Socialization mediators of the relation between socioeconomic status and child conduct problems. *Child Development, 65,* 649-665.

Dodge, K. A., & Price, J. M. (1994). On the relation between social information processing and socially competent behavior in early school-aged children. *Child Development, 65,* 1385-1397.

Downey, G., & Coyne, J. C. (1990). Children of depressed parents: An integrative review. *Psychological Bulletin, 108,* 50-76.

Dubow, E. F., & Ippolito, M. F. (1994). Effects of poverty and quality of the home environment on changes in the academic and behavioral adjustment of elementary school-age children. *Journal of Clinical Child Psychology, 23,* 401-412.

Duck, S. (1989). Socially competent communication and relationship development. In B. H. Schneider, G. Attili, J. Nadel, & R. P. Weissberg (Eds.), *Social competence in developmental perspective* (pp. 91-106). Dordrecht, Netherlands: Kluwer.

Duncan, G. J., Brooks-Gunn, J., & Klebanov, P. K. (1994). Economic deprivation and early childhood development. *Child Development, 65,* 296-318.

Dunn, J. (1983). Sibling relationships in early childhood. *Child Development, 54,* 787-811.

Dunn, J. (1992). Sisters and brothers: Current issues in developmental research. In F. Boer & J. Dunn (Eds.), *Children's sibling relationships: Developmental and clinical issues* (pp. 1-17). Hillsdale, NJ: Lawrence Erlbaum.

Dunn, J., & McGuire, S. (1994). Young children's nonshared experiences: A summary of studies in Cambridge and Colorado. In E. M. Hetherington, D. Reiss, & R. Plomin (Eds.), *Separate social worlds of siblings: The impact of nonshared environment on development* (pp. 111-128). Hillsdale, NJ: Lawrence Erlbaum.

East, P. L. (1991). The parent-child relationships of withdrawn, aggressive, and sociable children: Child and parent perspectives. *Merrill-Palmer Quarterly, 37,* 425-444.

East, P. L., & Rook, K. S. (1992). Compensatory patterns of support among children's peer relationships: A test using school friends, nonschool friends, and siblings. *Developmental Psychology, 28,* 163-172.

Easterbrooks, M., & Goldberg, W. (1985). Effects of early maternal employment on toddlers, mothers, and fathers. *Developmental Psychology, 4,* 774-783.

Eisenberg, N., Fabes, R. A., Karbon, M., Murphy, B. C., Wosinski, M., Polazzi, L., Carlo, G., & Juhnke, C. (1996). The relations of children's dispositional prosocial behavior to emotionality, regulation, and social functioning. *Child Development, 67,* 974-992.

Eisenberg, N., Fabes, R. A., Murphy, B., Maszk, P., Smith, M., & Karbon, M. (1995). The role of emotionality and regulation in children's social functioning: A longitudinal study. *Child Development, 66,* 1360-1384.

Eisenberg, N., & Miller, P. A. (1990). The development of prosocial behavior versus nonprosocial behavior in children. In M. Lewis & S. M. Miller (Eds.), *Handbook of developmental psychopathology* (pp. 181-188). New York: Plenum.

Elder, G. H., Jr. (1974). *Children of the great depression.* Chicago: University of Chicago Press.

Elicker, J., Egeland, B., & Sroufe, L. A. (1992). Predicting peer competence and peer relationships in childhood from early parent-child relationships. In R. D. Parke & G. W. Ladd (Eds.), *Family-peer relationships: Modes of linkage* (pp. 77-106). Hillsdale, NJ: Lawrence Erlbaum.

Emery, R. E., & Tuer, M. (1993). Parenting and the marital relationship. In T. Luster & L. Okagaki (Eds.), *Parenting: An ecological perspective* (pp. 121-148). Hillsdale, NJ: Lawrence Erlbaum.

Fagot, B. I., & Hagan, R. (1991). Observations of parent reactions to sex-stereotyped behaviors: Age and sex effects. *Child Development, 62,* 617-628.

Fantuzzo, J., Sutton-Smith, B., Coolahan, K. C., Manz, P. H., Canning, S., & Debnam, D. (1995). Assessment of preschool play interaction behaviors in young low-income children: Penn Interactive Peer Play Scale. *Early Childhood Research Quarterly, 10,* 105-120.

Feldman, S. S., & Weinberger, D. A. (1994). Self-restraint as a mediator of family influences on boys' delinquent behavior: A longitudinal study. *Child Development, 65,* 195-211.

Field, T. (1995). Psychologically depressed parents. In M. H. Bornstein (Ed.), *Handbook of parenting: Vol. 4. Applied and practical parenting* (pp. 85-99). Mahwah, NJ: Lawrence Erlbaum.

Field, T. M. (1994). Infant day care facilitates later social behavior and school performance. In H. Goelman & E. V. Jacobs (Eds.), *Children's play in child care settings* (pp. 69-84). Albany: State University of New York Press.

Finnie, V., & Russell, A. (1988). Preschool children's social status and their mothers' behavior and knowledge in the supervisory role. *Developmental Psychology, 24,* 789-801.

Fitzpatrick, M. A., & Badzinski, D. (1994). All in the family: Interpersonal communication in kin relationships. In M. L. Knapp & G. R. Miller (Eds.), *Handbook of interpersonal communication* (2nd ed., pp. 726-771). Thousand Oaks, CA: Sage.

Fitzpatrick, M. A., & Ritchie, L. D. (1994). Communication schemata within the family: Multiple perspectives on family interaction. *Human Communication Research, 20,* 275-301.

Fox, N. A., Bell, M. A., & Jones, N. A. (1992). Individual differences in response to stress and cerebral asymmetry. *Developmental Neuropsychology, 8,* 161-184.

Fox, N. A., Rubin, K. H., Calkins, S. D., Marshall, T. R., Coplan, R. J., Porges, S. W., Long, J. M., & Stewart, S. (1995). Frontal activation asymmetry and social competence at four years of age. *Child Development, 66,* 1770-1784.

Fujiki, M., & Brinton, B. (1994). Social competence and language impairment in children. In R. V. Watkins & M. L. Rice (Eds.), *Specific language impairments in children* (pp. 123-143). Baltimore: Paul H. Brooks.

Furman, W. (1995). Parenting siblings. In M. H. Bornstein (Ed.), *Handbook of parenting: Vol. 1. Children and parenting* (pp. 143-162). Mahwah, NJ: Lawrence Erlbaum.

Garbarino, J., & Kostelny, K. (1993). Neighborhood and community influences on parenting. In T. Luster & L. Okagaki (Eds.), *Parenting: An ecological perspective* (pp. 203-226). Hillsdale, NJ: Lawrence Erlbaum.

Garcia Coll, C. T., Meyer, E. C., & Brillon, L. (1995). Ethnic and minority parenting. In M. H. Bornstein (Ed.), *Handbook of parenting: Vol. 3. Status and social conditions of parenting* (pp. 189-209). Mahwah, NJ: Lawrence Erlbaum.

Gardner, F. E. M. (1992). Parent-child interaction and conduct disorder. *Educational Psychology Review, 4,* 135-163.

Garmezy, N. (1983). Stressors of childhood. In N. Garmezy & M. Rutter (Eds.), *Stress, coping, and development in children* (pp. 17-51). New York: McGraw-Hill.

Garner, P. W., Jones, D. C., & Miner, J. L. (1994). Social competence among low-income preschoolers: Emotion socialization practices and social cognitive correlates. *Child Development, 65,* 622-637.

Ge, X., Conger, R. D., Cadoret, R. J., Neiderhiser, J. M., Yates, W., Troughton, E., & Stewart, M. A. (1996). The developmental interface between nature and nurture: A mutual influence model of child antisocial behavior and parent behaviors. *Developmental Psychology, 32,* 574-589.

Geller, J., & Johnston, C. (1995). Predictors of mothers' responses to child noncompliance: Attributions and attitudes. *Journal of Clinical Child Psychology, 24,* 272-278.

Giles, H., & Street, R. L., Jr. (1994). Communicator characteristics and behavior. In M. L. Knapp & G. R. Miller (Eds.), *Handbook of interpersonal communication* (2nd ed., pp. 103-161). Thousand Oaks, CA: Sage.

Goodnow, J. J. (1988). Parents' ideas, actions and feelings: Models and methods from developmental and social psychology. *Child Development, 59,* 286-320.

Goodnow, J. J. (1995). Parents' knowledge and expectations. In M. H. Bornstein (Ed.), *Handbook of parenting: Vol. 3. Status and social conditions of parenting* (pp. 305-332). Mahwah, NJ: Lawrence Erlbaum.

Goodnow, J. J., Miller, P. J., & Kessel, F. (Eds.). (1995). Cultural practices as contexts for development. *New Directions for Child Development, 67,* 1-126.

Gordon, B. (1983). Maternal perception of child temperament and observed mother-child interaction. *Child Psychiatry and Human Development, 13,* 153-167.

Gottfried, A., Gottfried, A., & Bathurst, K. (1995). Maternal and dual-earner employment status and parenting. In M. H. Bornstein (Ed.), *Handbook of parenting: Vol. 2. Biology and ecology of parenting* (pp. 139-160). Mahwah, NJ: Lawrence Erlbaum.

Gottman, J. M., & Katz, L. F. (1989). Effects of marital discord on young children's peer interactions and health. *Developmental Psychology, 25,* 373-381.

Greenberger, E., O'Neil, R., & Nagel, S. K. (1994). Linking workplace and homeplace: Relations between the nature of adults' work and their parenting behaviors. *Developmental Psychology, 30,* 990-1002.

Gresham, F. M. (1986). Conceptual issues in the assessment of social competence in children. In P. S. Strain, M. J. Guralnick, & H. M. Walker (Eds.), *Children's social behavior: Development, assessment, and modification* (pp. 143-180). Orlando, FL: Academic Press.

Gretarsson, S. J., & Gelfand, D. M. (1988). Mothers' attributions regarding their children's social behavior and personality characteristics. *Developmental Psychology, 24,* 264-269.

Grusec, J. E., & Goodnow, J. J. (1994). Impact of parental discipline methods on the child's internalization of values: A reconceptualization of current points of view. *Developmental Psychology, 30,* 4-19.

Grusec, J. E., & Lytton, H. (1988). *Social development: History, theory, and research.* New York: Springer-Verlag.

Grych, J. H., & Fincham, F. D. (1990). Marital conflict and children's adjustment: A cognitive-contextual framework. *Psychological Bulletin, 108,* 267-290.

Grych, J. H., & Fincham, F. D. (1993). Children's appraisals of marital conflict: Initial investigations of the cognitive-contextual framework. *Child Development, 64,* 215-230.

Guralnick, M. J., Connor, R. T., Hammond, M. A., Gottman, J. M., & Kinnish, K. (1996). The peer relations of preschool children with communication disorders. *Child Development, 67,* 471-489.

Hagekull, B., & Bohlin, G. (1995). Day care quality, family and child characteristics, and socioemotional development. *Early Childhood Research Quarterly, 10,* 505-526.

Halberstadt, A. G., Cassidy, J., Stifter, C. A., Parke, R. D., & Fox, N. A. (1995). Self-expressiveness within the family context: Psychometric support for a new measure. *Psychological Assessment, 7,* 93-103.

Halperin, J. M., Newcorn, J. H., Matier, K., Bedi, G., Hall, S., & Sharma, V. (1995). Impulsivity and the initiation of fights in children with disruptive behavior disorders. *Journal of Child Psychology and Psychiatry, 36,* 1199-1211.

Hardy, D. F., Power, T. G., & Jaedicke, S. (1993). Examining the relation of parenting to children's coping with everyday stress. *Child Development, 64,* 1829-1841.

Harkness, S., & Super, C. (1995). Culture and parenting. In M. H. Bornstein (Ed.), *Handbook of parenting: Vol. 3. Status and social conditions of parenting* (pp. 211-234). Mahwah, NJ: Lawrence Erlbaum.

Harrison, A. O., Wilson, M. N., Rine, C. J., Chan, S. Q., & Buriel, R. (1990). Family ecologies of minority children. *Child Development, 61,* 347-362.

Harrist, A. W., Pettit, G. S., Dodge, K. A., & Bates, J. E. (1994). Dyadic synchrony in mother-child interaction: Relation with children's subsequent kindergarten adjustment. *Family Relations, 43,* 417-424.

Hart, C. H., Burts, D. C., & Charlesworth, R. (in press). Integrated developmentally appropriate curriculum: From theory and research to practice. In C. H. Hart, D. C. Burts, & R. Charlesworth (Eds.), *Integrated curriculum and developmentally appropriate practice: Birth to age 8.* Albany: State University of New York Press.

Hart, C. H., DeWolf, M. D., & Burts, D. C. (1992). Linkages among preschoolers' playground behavior, outcome expectations, and parental disciplinary strategies. *Early Education and Development, 3,* 265-283.

Hart, C. H., DeWolf, M. D., & Burts, D. C. (1993). Parental disciplinary strategies and preschoolers' play behavior in playground settings. In C. H. Hart (Ed.), *Children on playgrounds: Research perspectives and applications* (pp. 271-313). Albany: State University of New York Press.

Hart, C. H., DeWolf, M. D., Wozniak, P., & Burts, D. C. (1992). Maternal and paternal disciplinary styles: Relations with preschoolers' playground behavioral orientations and peer status. *Child Development, 63,* 879-892.

Hart, C. H., Ladd, G. W., & Burleson, B. R. (1990). Children's expectations of the outcomes of social strategies: Relations with sociometric status and maternal disciplinary styles. *Child Development, 61,* 127-137.

Hart, C. H., Lawrence, F., Thomasson, R., & Wozniak, P. (1990). Measuring socioeconomic status in child development research. *Psychological Reports, 67,* 457-458.

Hart, C. H., McGee, L., & Hernandez, S. (1993). Themes in the peer relations literature: Correspondence to playground interactions portrayed in children's literature. In C. H. Hart (Ed.), *Children on playgrounds: Research perspectives and applications* (pp. 371-416). Albany: State University of New York Press.

Hartup, W. W. (1974). Aggression in childhood: Developmental perspectives. *American Psychologist, 29,* 336-341.

Hartup, W. W. (1983). Peer relations. In E. M. Hetherington (Ed.), *Handbook of child psychology: Vol. 4. Socialization, personality, and social development* (4th ed., pp. 103-196). New York: John Wiley.

Hartup, W. W. (1985). Relationships and their significance in cognitive development. In R. A. Hinde, A. Perret-Clermont, & J. Stevenson-Hinde (Eds.), *Social relationships and cognitive development* (pp. 66-82). Oxford: Clarendon.

Hartup, W. W., & Laursen, B. (1993). Conflict and context in peer relations. In C. H. Hart (Ed.), *Children on playgrounds: Research perspectives and applications* (pp. 44-84). Albany: State University of New York Press.

Haskins, R. (1989). Beyond metaphor: The efficacy of early childhood education. *American Psychologist, 44,* 274-282.

Heaton, T. B., Goodman, K. L., Holman, T. B. (1994). In search of a peculiar people: Are Mormon families really different? In M. Cornwall, T. B. Heaton, & L. A. Young (Eds.), *Contemporary Mormonism: Social science perspectives* (pp. 87-117). Urbana: University of Illinois Press.

Hetherington, E. M., & Stanley-Hagan, M. M. (1995). Parenting in divorced and remarried families. In M. H. Bornstein (Ed.), *Handbook of parenting: Vol. 3. Status and social conditions of parenting* (pp. 233-254). Mahwah, NJ: Lawrence Erlbaum.

Hetherington, E. M., Stanley-Hagan, M. M., & Anderson, E. R. (1989). Marital transitions: A child's perspective. *American Psychologist, 44,* 303-312.

Hinde, R. A. (1987). *Individuals, relationships and culture: Links between ethology and the social sciences.* New York: Cambridge University Press.

Hochschild, A. (1989). *The second shift: Working parents and the revolution at home.* New York: Viking.

Hoff-Ginsberg, E., & Tardif, T. (1995). Socioeconomic status and parenting. In M. H. Bornstein (Ed.), *Handbook of parenting: Vol. 2. Biology and ecology of parenting* (pp. 161-188). Mahwah, NJ: Lawrence Erlbaum.

Hoffman, L. W. (1989). Effects of maternal employment in the two-parent family. *American Psychologist, 44,* 283-292.

Hoge, R. D., Andrews, D. A., & Robinson, D. (1990). Patterns of child and parenting problems within six family types. *Canadian Journal of Behavioural Science, 22,* 99-109.

Holden, G. W. (1995). Parental attitudes toward childrearing. In M. H. Bornstein (Ed.), *Handbook of parenting: Vol. 3. Status and social conditions of parenting* (pp. 359-392). Mahwah, NJ: Lawrence Erlbaum.

Howes, C., Phillips, D. A., & Whitebook, M. (1992). Thresholds of quality: Implications for the social development of children in center-based child care. *Child Development, 63,* 449-460.

Jackson, J. F. (1993). Human behavioral genetics, Scarr's theory, and her views on interventions: A critical review and commentary on their implications for African American children. *Child Development, 64,* 1318-1332.

Jacobs, E. V., & White, D. R. (1994). The relationship of child-care quality and play to social behavior in the kindergarten. In H. Goelman & E. V. Jacobs (Eds.), *Children's play in child care settings* (pp. 85-101). Albany: State University of New York Press.

Janssens, J. M. A. M. (1994). Authoritarian child rearing, parental locus of control, and the child's behavior style. *International Journal of Behavioral Development, 17,* 485-501.

Jenkins, J. M., & Smith, M. A. (1991). Marital disharmony and children's behavior problems: Aspects of a poor marriage that affect children adversely. *Journal of Child Psychology and Psychiatry, 32,* 793-810.

Jouriles, E. N., Murphy, C. M., Farris, A. M., Smith, D. A., Richters, J. E., & Waters, E. (1991). Marital adjustment, parental disagreements about child rearing, and behavior problems in boys: Increasing the specificity of the marital assessment. *Child Development, 62,* 1424-1433.

Kahen, V., Katz, L. F., & Gottman, J. M. (1994). Linkages between parent-child interaction and conversations of friends. *Social Development, 3,* 238-254.

Kaplan, H. B. (1994). *Toward an understanding of resilience: A critical review of definitions and models.* Paper presented at the National Conference on the Role of Resilience in Drug Abuse, Alcohol Abuse, and Mental Illness, Department of Health and Human Services, Washington, DC.

Katz, L. F., & Gottman, J. M. (1993). Patterns of marital conflict predict children's internalizing and externalizing behaviors. *Developmental Psychology, 29,* 940-950.

Katz, L. F., & Gottman, J. M. (1994). Patterns of marital interaction and children's emotional development. In R. D. Parke & S. G. Kellam (Eds.), *Exploring family relationships within other social contexts* (pp. 49-74). Hillsdale, NJ: Lawrence Erlbaum.

Kemple, K., Speranza, H., & Hazen, N. (1992). Cohesive discourse and peer acceptance: Longitudinal relations in the preschool years. *Merrill-Palmer Quarterly, 38,* 364-381.

Kochanska, G. (1995). Children's temperament, mothers' discipline, and security of attachment: Multiple pathways to emerging internalization. *Child Development, 66,* 597-615.

Kohn, M. L. (1969). *Class and conformity: A study in values.* Homewood, IL: Dorsey.

Kramer, L., & Baron, L. A. (1995). Intergenerational linkages: How experiences with siblings relate to the parenting of siblings. *Journal of Social and Personal Relationships, 12,* 67-87.

Krappman, L. (1989). Family relationships and peer relationships in middle childhood. In K. Kreppner & R. M. Lerner (Eds.), *Family systems and lifespan development* (pp. 93-104). Hillsdale, NJ: Erlbaum.

Kreppner, K. (1992). Development in a developing context: Rethinking the family's role for children's development. In L. T. Winegar & J. Valsiner (Eds.), *Children's development within social context: Vol. 1. Metatheory and theory* (pp. 161-182). Hillsdale, NJ: Lawrence Erlbaum.

Kuczynski, L. (1984). Socialization goals in mother-child interaction: Strategies for long-term and short-term compliance. *Developmental Psychology, 20,* 1061-1073.

Kuczynski, L., & Kochanska, G. (1995). Function and content of maternal demands: Developmental significance of early demands for competent action. *Child Development, 66,* 616-628.

Kupersmidt, J. B., Griesler, P. C., DeRosier, M. E., Patterson, C. J., & Davis, P. W. (1995). Childhood aggression and peer relations in the context of family and neighborhood factors. *Child Development, 66,* 360-375.

Kurtz, L., Vitaro, F., & Tremblay, R. (1995). *Bullying and social anxiety in children from families in transition: A longitudinal study.* Paper presented at the annual meeting of the Society for Research in Child Development, Indianapolis.

Ladd, G. W. (1989). Children's social competence and social supports: Precursors of early school adjustment? In B. H. Schneider, G. Attili, J. Nadel, & R. P. Weissberg (Eds.), *Social competence in developmental perspective* (pp. 277-291). Dordrecht, Netherlands: Kluwer.

Ladd, G. W. (1992). Themes and theories: Perspectives on processes in family-peer relationships. In R. D. Parke & G. W. Ladd (Eds.), *Family-peer relationships: Modes of linkage* (pp. 3-34). Hillsdale, NJ: Lawrence Erlbaum.

Ladd, G. W., & Cairns, W. (1996). Children: Ethnic and political violence. *Child Development, 67,* 14-18.

Ladd, G. W., & Golter, B. (1988). Parents' management of preschoolers' peer relations: Is it related to children's social competence? *Developmental Psychology, 24,* 109-117.

Ladd, G. W., & Hart, C. H. (1992). Creating informal play opportunities: Are parents' and preschoolers' initiations related to children's competence with peers? *Developmental Psychology, 28,* 1179-1187.

Ladd, G. W., Hart, C. H., Wadsworth, E. M., & Golter, B. S. (1988). Preschoolers' peer networks in nonschool settings: Relationship to family characteristics and school adjustment. In S. Salzinger, J. Antrobus, & M. Hammer (Eds.), *Social networks of children, adolescents, and college students* (pp. 61-92). Hillsdale, NJ: Lawrence Erlbaum.

Ladd, G. W., Kochenderfer, B. J., & Coleman, C. C. (1996). Friendship quality as a predictor of young children's early school adjustment. *Child Development, 67,* 1103-1118.

Ladd, G. W., & Le Sieur, K. D. (1995). Parents' and children's peer relationships. In M. H. Bornstein (Ed.), *Handbook of parenting: Vol. 4. Applied and practical parenting* (pp. 377-410). Hillsdale, NJ: Lawrence Erlbaum.

Ladd, G. W., Le Sieur, K. D., & Profilet, S. M. (1993). Direct parental influences of young children's peer relations. In S. Duck (Ed.), *Learning about relationships* (pp. 152-183). London: Sage.

Ladd, G. W., & Price, J. M. (1986). Promoting children's cognitive and social competence: The relations between parent's perceptions of task difficulty and children's perceived and actual competence. *Child Development, 57,* 446-460.

Ladd, G. W., Profilet, S. M., & Hart, C. H. (1992). Parents' management of children's peer relations: Fostering and supervising children's activities in the peer culture. In R. D. Parke & G. W. Ladd (Eds.), *Family-peer relationships: Modes of linkage* (pp. 215-253). Hillsdale, NJ: Lawrence Erlbaum.

LaFreniere, P. J., & Dumas, J. E. (1992). A transactional analysis of early childhood anxiety and social withdrawal. *Development and Psychopathology, 4,* 385-402.

Laird, R. D., Pettit, G. S., Mize, J., Brown, E. G., & Lindsey, E. (1994). Mother-child conversations about peers: Contributions to competence. *Family Relations, 43,* 425-432.

Lamb, M. E., Frodi, M., Hwang, C., Forstromm, B., & Corry, T. (1982). Stability and change in parental attitudes following an infant's birth into traditional and nontraditional Swedish families. *Scandinavian Journal of Psychology, 23,* 53-62.

Lamb, M. E., Ketterlinus, R. D., & Fracasso, M. P. (1992). Parent-child relationships. In M. H. Bornstein & M. E. Lamb (Eds.), *Developmental psychology: An advanced textbook* (pp. 465-518). Hillsdale, NJ: Lawrence Erlbaum.

Lamberty, G., & Garcia Coll, C. T. (1994). Expanding on what is known about the health and development of Puerto Rican mothers and children. In G. Lamberty & C. T. Garcia Coll (Eds.), *Puerto Rican women and children: Issues in health, growth and development* (pp. 302-327). New York: Plenum.

Larzelere, R. E. (1986). Moderate spanking: Model or deterrent of children's aggression in the family? *Journal of Family Violence, 1,* 27-36.

Lee, C. L., & Bates, J. E. (1985). Mother-child interaction at age two years and perceived difficult temperament. *Child Development, 56,* 1314-1325.

Lerner, R. M., Castellino, D. R., Terry, P. A., Villarruel, F. A., McKinney, M. H. (1995). Developmental contextual perspective on parenting. In M. H. Bornstein (Ed.), *Handbook of parenting: Vol. 2. Biology and ecology of parenting* (pp. 285-309). Mahwah, NJ: Lawrence Erlbaum.

LeVine, R., & White, M. I. (1986). *Human conditions: The cultural basis of educational development.* London: Routledge & Kegan Paul.

Lin, C. C., & Fu, V. R. (1990). A comparison of child-rearing practices among Chinese, immigrant Chinese, and Caucasian-American parents. *Child Development, 61,* 429-433.

Lochman, J. E., Coie, J. D., Underwood, M. K., & Terry, R. (1993). Effectiveness of a social relations intervention program for aggressive and nonaggressive, rejected children. *Journal of Consulting and Clinical Psychology, 61,* 1053-1058.

Lollis, S. P., Ross, H. S., & Tate, E. (1992). Parents' regulation of children's peer interactions: Direct influences. In R. D. Parke & G. W. Ladd (Eds.), *Family-peer relationships: Modes of linkage* (pp. 255-284). Hillsdale, NJ: Lawrence Erlbaum.

Luther, S., & Zigler, E. (1991). Vulnerability and competence: A review of research on resilience in childhood. *American Journal of Orthopsychiatry, 61,* 6-22.

Lytton, H., & Romney, D. M. (1991). Parents' sex-related differential socialization of boys and girls: A meta-analysis. *Psychological Bulletin, 109,* 267-296.

Maccoby, E. E. (1984). Middle childhood in the context of the family. In W. A. Collins (Ed.), *Development during middle childhood: The years from six to twelve* (pp. 184-239). Washington, DC: National Academy.

Maccoby, E. E. (1990). Gender and relationships: A developmental account. *American Psychologist, 45,* 513-520.

Maccoby, E. E., & Jacklin, C. N. (1974). *The psychology of sex differences.* Stanford, CA: Stanford University Press.

Maccoby, E. E., & Martin, J. A. (1983). Socialization in the context of the family: Parent-child interaction. In E. M. Hetherington (Ed.), *Handbook of child psychology: Vol. 4. Socialization, personality, and social development* (4th ed., pp. 1-101). New York: John Wiley.

MacDonald, K. B. (1987). Parent-child physical play with rejected, neglected, and popular boys. *Developmental Psychology, 23,* 705-711.

MacKinnon-Lewis, C., Volling, B. L., Lamb, M. E., Dechman, K. R., Abiner, D., & Curtner, M. E. (1994). A cross-contextual analysis of boys' social competence: From family to school. *Developmental Psychology, 30,* 325-333.

Martin, J. L. (1995). *Sibling physical aggression: A different experience for girls and boys?* Paper presented at the annual meeting of the Society for Research in Child Development, Indianapolis.

Martin, J. L., & Ross, H. S. (1995). The development of aggression within sibling conflict. *Early Education and Development, 6,* 335-358.

Masten, A. S., Best, K., & Garmezy, N. (1990). Resilience and development: Contributions from the study of children who overcome adversity. *Development and Psychopathology, 2,* 425-444.

Masten, A. S., Morison, P., & Pellegrini, D. S. (1985). A revised class play method of peer assessment. *Developmental Psychology, 3,* 523-533.

McFall, R. M. (1982). A review and reformulation of the concept of social skills. *Behavioral Assessment, 4,* 1-33.

McGillicuddy-DeLisi, A. V., & Sigel, I. E. (1995). Parental beliefs. In M. H. Bornstein (Ed.), *Handbook of parenting: Vol. 3. Status and social conditions of parenting* (pp. 333-358). Mahwah, NJ: Lawrence Erlbaum.

McGrath, M. P., Wilson, S. R., & Frassetto, S. J. (1995). Why some forms of induction are better than others at encouraging prosocial behavior. *Merrill-Palmer Quarterly, 41,* 347-360.

McHale, S. M., Crouter, A. C., McGuire, S. A., & Updegraff, K. A. (1995). Congruence between mothers' and fathers' differential treatment of siblings: Links with family relations and child well-being. *Child Development, 66,* 116-128.

McLoyd, V. C. (1990). The impact of economic hardship on black families and children: Psychological distress, parenting, and socioemotional development. *Child Development, 61,* 311-346.

McNeilly-Choque, M. K., Hart, C. H., Robinson, C. C., Nelson, L. J., & Olsen, S. F. (in press). Overt and relational aggression on the playground: Correspondence among different informants. *Journal of Research in Childhood Education.*

Melson, G. F., & Fogel, A. (1988, January). Learning to care. *Psychology Today, 22,* 38-45.

Melson, G. F., Ladd, G. W., & Hsu, H. (1993). Maternal support networks, maternal cognitions, and young children's social and cognitive development. *Child Development, 64,* 1401-1417.

Miller, S. A. (1995). Parents' attributions for their children's behavior. *Child Development, 66,* 1557-1584.

Mills, R. S. L., & Rubin, K. H. (1990). Parental beliefs about problematic social behaviors in early childhood. *Child Development, 61,* 138-151.

Mills, R. S. L., & Rubin, K. H. (1992). A longitudinal study of maternal beliefs about children's social behavior. *Merrill-Palmer Quarterly, 38,* 494-512.

Mills, R. S. L., & Rubin, K. H. (1993). Socialization factors in the development of social withdrawal. In K. H. Rubin & J. B. Asendorpf (Eds.), *Social withdrawal, inhibition, and shyness in childhood* (pp. 117-148). Hillsdale, NJ: Lawrence Erlbaum.

Minuchin, P. (1985). Families and individual development: Provocations from the field of family therapy. *Child Development, 56,* 289-302.

Mize, J., & Ladd, G. W. (1988). Predicting preschoolers' peer behavior and status from their interpersonal strategies: A comparison of verbal and enactive responses to hypothetical social dilemmas. *Developmental Psychology, 24,* 782-788.

Mize, J., & Ladd, G. W. (1990). Toward the development of successful social skills training for preschool children. In S. R. Asher & J. D. Coie (Eds.), *Peer rejection in childhood: Origins, consequences, and intervention* (pp. 338-361). Cambridge: Cambridge University Press.

Mize, J., & Pettit, G. S. (in press). Mothers' social coaching, mother-child relationship style, and children's peer competence: Is the medium the message? *Child Development.*

Mize, J., Pettit, G. S., & Brown, E. G. (1995). Mothers' supervision of their children's peer play: Relations with beliefs, perceptions and knowledge. *Developmental Psychology, 31,* 311-321.

Moen, P., Elder, G. H., & Luscher, K. (1995). *Examining lives in context: Perspectives on the ecology of human development.* Washington, DC: American Psychological Association.

Mueller, E., & Silverman, N. (1989). Peer relations in maltreated children. In D. Cicchetti & V. Carlson (Eds.), *Child maltreatment: Theory and research on the causes and consequences of child abuse and neglect* (pp. 529-578). New York: Cambridge University Press.

Mulhern, R. K., Jr., & Passman, R. H. (1981). Parental discipline as affected by the sex of the parent, the sex of the child, and the child's apparent responsiveness to discipline. *Developmental Psychology, 17,* 604-613.

Murphy, B. C., & Eisenberg, N. (1996). Provoked by a peer: Children's anger-related responses and their relations to social functioning. *Merrill-Palmer Quarterly, 42,* 103-124.

Nelson, D. (1995). *Parenting practices and children's social competence in contemporary Russia: An exploratory study.* Unpublished honors thesis, Brigham Young University.

Newcomb, A. F., Bukowski, W. M., & Pattee, L. (1993). Children's peer relations: A meta-analytic review of popular, rejected, neglected, controversial, and average sociometric status. *Psychological Bulletin, 113,* 99-128.

Nucci, L. (1994). Mothers' beliefs regarding the personal domain of children. *New Directions for Child Development, 66,* 81-97.

Odom, S. L., & McConnell, S. R. (1992). Improving social competence: An applied behavior analysis perspective. *Journal of Applied Behavior Analysis, 25,* 239-244.

Ogbu, J. (1988). Cultural diversity and human development. In D. Slaughter (Ed.), *Black children and poverty: A developmental perspective* (pp. 11-28). San Francisco: Jossey-Bass.

Okagaki, L., & Divecha, D. J. (1993). Development of parental beliefs. In T. Luster & L. Okagaki (Eds.), *Parenting: An ecological perspective* (pp. 35-67). Hillsdale, NJ: Lawrence Erlbaum.

Olsen, S. F. (1993, November). *Intergenerational transmission of parenting and family relationships.* Paper presented at the annual meeting of the Gerontological Society of America, New Orleans.

Olson, S. H., & Brodfeld, P. L. (1991). Assessment of peer rejection and externalizing behavior problems in preschool boys: A short-term longitudinal study. *Journal of Abnormal Child Psychology, 19,* 493-503.

Olweus, D. (1980). Familial and temperamental determinants of aggressive behavior in adolescent boys: A causal analysis. *Developmental Psychology, 16,* 644-666.

Olweus, D. (1993). Bullies on the playground: The role of victimization. In C. H. Hart (Ed.), *Children on playgrounds: Research perspectives and applications* (pp. 85-128). Albany: State University of New York Press.

Parke, R. D. (1992). Epilogue: Remaining issues and future trends in the study of family-peer relationships. In R. D. Parke & G. W. Ladd (Eds.), *Family-peer relationships: Modes of linkage* (pp. 425-438). Hillsdale, NJ: Lawrence Erlbaum.

Parke, R. D. (1994). Epilogue: Unresolved issues and future trends in family relationships within other contexts. In R. D. Parke & S. G. Kellam (Eds.), *Exploring family relationships within other social contexts* (pp. 215-229). Hillsdale, NJ: Lawrence Erlbaum.

Parke, R. D. (1995). Fathers and families. In M. H. Bornstein (Ed.), *Handbook of parenting: Vol. 3. Status and social conditions of parenting* (pp. 27-64). Mahwah, NJ: Lawrence Erlbaum.

Parke, R. D., Burks, V. M., Carson, J. L., Neville, B., & Boyum, L. A. (1994). Family-peer relationships: A tripartite model. In R. D. Parke & S. G. Kellam (Eds.), *Exploring family relationships within other social contexts* (pp. 115-145). Hillsdale, NJ: Lawrence Erlbaum.

Parke, R. D., Cassidy, J., Burks, V. M., Carson, J. L., & Boyum, L. A. (1992). Familial contributions to peer competence among young children: The role of interactive and affective processes. In R. D. Parke & G. W. Ladd (Eds.), *Family-peer relationships: Modes of linkage* (pp. 107-134). Hillsdale, NJ: Lawrence Erlbaum.

Parke, R. D., & Kellam, S. G. (Eds.). (1994). *Exploring family relationships within other social contexts.* Hillsdale, NJ: Lawrence Erlbaum.

Parke, R. D., & Ladd, G. W. (Eds.). (1992). *Family-peer relationships: Modes of linkage.* Hillsdale, NJ: Lawrence Erlbaum.

Parker, J. G., & Asher, S. R. (1993). Friendship and friendship quality in middle childhood: Links with peer group acceptance and feelings of loneliness and social dissatisfaction. *Developmental Psychology, 29,* 611-621.

Parker, J. G., & Gottman, J. M. (1989). Social and emotional development in a relational context: Friendship interaction from early childhood to adolescence. In T. J. Berndt & G. W. Ladd (Eds.), *Peer relationships in child development* (pp. 95-132). New York: John Wiley.

Parker, J. G., Rubin, K. H., Price, J. M., & DeRosier, M. E. (1995). Peer relationships, child development and adjustment: A developmental psychopathological perspective. In D. Cicchetti & E. Cohen (Eds.), *Developmental psychopathology: Vol 2. Risk, disorder, and adaptation* (pp. 96-161). New York: John Wiley.

Patterson, C. J., Griesler, P. C., Vaden, N. A., & Kupersmidt, J. B. (1992). Family economic circumstances, life transitions, and children's peer relations. In R. D. Parke & G. W. Ladd (Eds.), *Family-peer relationships: Modes of linkage* (pp. 385-424). Hillsdale, NJ: Lawrence Erlbaum.

Patterson, C. J., Kupersmidt, J. B., & Vaden, N. A. (1990). Income level, gender, ethnicity, and household composition as predictors of children's school based competence. *Child Development, 61,* 485-494.

Patterson, G. R., DeBaryshe, B. D., & Ramsey, E. (1989). A developmental perspective on antisocial behavior. *American Psychologist, 44,* 329-335.

Patterson, G. R., & Dishion, T. J. (1988). Multilevel family process models: Traits, interactions, and relationships. In R. A. Hinde & J. Stevenson-Hinde (Eds.), *Relationships within families: Mutual influences* (pp. 283-310). Oxford: Oxford University Press.

Patterson, G. R., Dishion, T. J., & Bank, L. (1984). Family interaction: A process model of deviancy training. *Aggressive Behavior, 10,* 253-267.

Perry, D., Perry, L., & Kennedy, E. (1992). Conflict and the development of antisocial behavior. In C. Shantz & W. W. Hartup (Eds.), *Conflict in child and adolescent development* (pp. 301-329). New York: Cambridge University Press.

Peters-Martin, P., & Wachs, T. (1984). A longitudinal study of temperament and its correlates in the first 12 months. *Infant Behavior and Development, 7,* 285-298.

Pettit, G. S., Clawson, M. A., Dodge, K. A., & Bates, J. E. (1996). Stability and change in peer-rejected status: The role of child behavior, parenting, and family ecology. *Merrill-Palmer Quarterly, 42,* 267-294.

Pettit, G. S., & Harrist, A. W. (1993). Children's aggressive and socially unskilled playground behavior with peers: Origins in early family relations. In C. H. Hart (Ed.), *Children on playgrounds: Research perspectives and applications* (pp. 240-270). Albany: State University of New York Press.

Pettit, G. S., Harrist, A. W., Bates, J. E., & Dodge, K. A. (1991). Family interaction, social cognition, and children's subsequent relationships with peers at kindergarten. *Journal of Social and Personal Relationships, 8*, 383-402.

Piaget, J. (1983). Piaget's theory. In P. H. Mussen (Ed.), *Handbook of child psychology* (Vol. 4, pp. 103-128). New York: John Wiley.

Piotrowski, C. C. (1995). Children's interventions into family conflict: Links with the quality of sibling relationships. *Early Education and Development, 6*, 377-403.

Plomin, R. (1994). Nature, nurture and social development. *Social Development, 3*, 37-53.

Plomin, R., & Bergeman, C. S. (1991). The nature of nurture: Genetic influence on "environmental" measures. *Behavior and Brain Sciences, 14*, 373-386.

Plomin, R., Lichtenstein, P., Pedersen, N. L., McClearn, G. E., & Nesselroade, J. R. (1990). Genetic influence on life events during the last half of the life span. *Psychology and Aging, 5*, 25-30.

Plomin, R., Reiss, D., Hetherington, E. M., & Howe, G. W. (1994). Nature and nurture: Genetic contributions to measures of the family environment. *Developmental Psychology, 30*, 32-43.

Price, J. M., & Dodge, K. A. (1989). Reactive and proactive aggression in childhood: Relations to peer status and social context dimensions. *Journal of Abnormal Child Psychology, 17*, 455-471.

Profilet, S. M., & Ladd, G. W. (1994). Do mothers' perceptions and concerns about preschoolers' peer competence predict their peer-management practices? *Social Development, 3*, 205-221.

Profilet, S. M., & Ladd, G. W. (1996). *Relations between maternal consulting about kindergarten children's peer relationships and children's peer competence.* Paper presented at the annual meeting of the American Educational Research Association, New York.

Putallaz, M., Costanzo, P. R., & Klein, T. P. (1993). Parental ideas as influences on children's social competence. In S. Duck (Ed.), *Learning about relationships* (pp. 63-97). London: Sage.

Putallaz, M., Costanzo, P. R., & Smith, R. B. (1991). Maternal recollections of childhood peer relationships: Implications for their children's social competence. *Journal of Social and Personal Relationships, 8*, 403-422.

Putallaz, M., & Heflin, A. H. (1990). Parent-child interaction. In S. R. Asher & J. D. Coie (Eds.), *Peer rejection in childhood: Origins, consequences, and intervention* (pp. 274-305). Cambridge: Cambridge University Press.

Quamma, J. P., & Greenberg, M. T. (1994). Children's experience of life stress: The role of family social support and social problem-solving skills as protective factors. *Journal of Clinical Child Psychology, 23*, 295-305.

Radke-Yarrow, M., Zahn-Waxler, C., & Chapman, M. (1983). Children's prosocial dispositions and behavior. In E. M. Hetherington (Ed.), *Handbook of child psychology: Vol. 4. Socialization, personality, and social development* (pp. 469-545). New York: John Wiley.

Ramsey, P. G. (1988). Social skills and peer status: A comparison of two socioeconomic groups. *Merrill-Palmer Quarterly, 32*, 185-202.

Redina, I., & Dickerscheid, J. D. (1976). Father involvement with first-born infants. *Family Coordinator, 25*, 373-378.

Reynolds, A. J. (1994). Effects of a preschool plus follow-on intervention for children at risk. *Developmental Psychology, 30*, 787-804.

Ritchie, L. D., & Fitzpatrick, M. A. (1990). Family communication patterns: Measuring intrapersonal perceptions of interpersonal relationships. *Communication Research, 17*, 523-544.

Robinson, C. C., Mandleco, B., Olsen, S. F., & Hart, C. H. (1995). Authoritative, authoritarian, and permissive parenting practices: Development of a new measure. *Psychological Reports, 77*, 819-830.

Rolf, J., Masten, A. S., Cicchetti, D., Nuechterlein, K. H., & Weintraub, S. (Eds.). (1990). *Risk and protective factors in the development of psychopathology.* New York: Cambridge University Press.

Rollins, B. C., & Thomas, D. L. (1979). Parental support, power, and control techniques in the socialization of children. In W. R. Burr, R. Hill, F. I. Nye, & I. L. Reiss (Eds.), *Contemporary theories about the family: Vol. 1. Research-based theories* (pp. 317-364). New York: Free Press.

Roopnarine, J. L., Bright, J. A., & Riegraf, N. B. (1994). Family dynamics and day care children's peer group participation. In H. Goelman & E. V. Jacobs (Eds.), *Children's play in child care settings* (pp. 53-68). Albany: State University of New York Press.

Rose-Krasnor, L., Rubin, K. H., Booth, C. L., & Coplan, R. J. (1996). Maternal directiveness and child attachment security as predictors of social competence in preschoolers. *International Journal of Behavioral Development, 14,* 309-325.

Rothbart, N. K., Ahadi, S. A., & Hershey, K. L. (1994). Temperament and social behavior in childhood. *Merrill Palmer Quarterly, 40,* 21-39.

Rothbaum, F., Rosen, K. S., Pott, M., & Beatty, M. (1995). Early parent-child relationships and later problem behavior: A longitudinal study. *Merrill-Palmer Quarterly, 41,* 133-151.

Rowe, D. C. (1994). *The limits of family influence: Genes, experience, and behavior.* New York: Guilford.

Rubin, A., & Sloman, J. (1984). How parents influence their children's friendships. In M. Lewis (Ed.), *Beyond the dyad* (pp. 223-250). New York: Plenum.

Rubin, K. H., & Asendorpf, J. B. (Eds.). (1993). *Social withdrawal, inhibition, and shyness in childhood.* Hillsdale, NJ: Lawrence Erlbaum.

Rubin, K. H., Booth, C. L., Rose-Krasnor, L., & Mills, R. S. L. (1995). Social relationships and social skills: A conceptual and empirical analysis. In S. Shulman (Ed.), *Close relationships and socio-emotional development.* Norwood, NJ: Ablex.

Rubin, K. H., Bukowski, W., & Parker, J. G. (in press). Peer interactions, relationships, and groups. In N. Eisenberg (Ed.), *Handbook of child psychology: Vol 4. Social, emotional, and personality development.* New York: John Wiley.

Rubin, K. H., & Coplan, R. J. (1992). Peer relationships in childhood. In M. H. Bornstein & M. E. Lamb (Eds.), *Developmental psychology: An advanced textbook* (pp. 519-578). Hillsdale, NJ: Lawrence Erlbaum.

Rubin, K. H., Coplan, R. J., Fox, N. A., & Calkins, S. D. (1995). Emotionality, emotion regulation, and preschoolers' social adaptation. *Development and Psychopathology, 7,* 49-62.

Rubin, K. H., LeMare, L. J., & Lollis, S. (1990). Social withdrawal in childhood: Developmental pathways to peer rejection. In S. R. Asher & J. D. Coie (Eds.), *Peer rejection in childhood: Origins, consequences, and intervention* (pp. 217-249). Cambridge: Cambridge University Press.

Rubin, K. H., & Mills, R. S. L. (1990). Maternal beliefs about adaptive and maladaptive social behaviors in normal, aggressive, and withdrawn preschoolers. *Journal of Abnormal Child Psychology, 18,* 419-435.

Rubin, K. H., & Mills, R. S. L. (1991). Conceptualizing developmental pathways to internalizing disorders in childhood. *Canadian Journal of Behavioural Science, 23,* 300-317.

Rubin, K. H., & Mills, R. S. L. (1992). Parent's thoughts about children's socially adaptive and maladaptive behaviors: Stability, change and individual differences. In I. E. Sigel, A. V. McGillicuddy-DeLisi, & J. J. Goodnow (Eds.), *Parental belief systems: The psychological consequences for children* (2nd ed., pp. 41-68). Hillsdale, NJ: Lawrence Erlbaum.

Rubin, K. H., Mills, R. S. L., & Rose-Krasnor, L. (1989). Parental beliefs and children's social competence. In B. H. Schneider, G. Atilli, J. Nadel, & R. P. Weissberg (Eds.), *Social competence in developmental perspective* (pp. 313-331). Dordrecht, Netherlands: Kluwer.

Rubin, K. H., & Rose-Krasnor, L. (1992). Interpersonal problem solving and social competence in children. In V. B. Van Hasselt & M. Hersen (Eds.), *Handbook of social development: A lifespan perspective* (pp. 283-323). New York: Plenum.

Rubin, K. H., Rose-Krasnor, L., Bigras, M., Mills, R. S. L., & Booth, C. L. (1996). Predicting parental behavior: The influences of setting conditions, psychosocial factors, and parental beliefs. In G. M. Tarabulsy & R. Tessier (Eds.), *Social-emotional development of children.* Quebec: University of Quebec Press.

Rubin, K. H., & Stewart, S. L. (in press). Social withdrawal in childhood. In E. Mash & R. Barkley (Eds.), *Child psychopathology.* New York: Guilford.

Rubin, K. H., Stewart, S. L., & Chen, X. (1995). Parents of aggressive and withdrawn children. In M. H. Bornstein (Ed.), *Handbook of parenting: Vol. 1. Children and parenting* (pp. 255-284). Mahwah, NJ: Lawrence Erlbaum.

Rubin, K. H., Stewart, S. L., & Coplan, R. J. (1995). Social withdrawal in childhood: Conceptual and empirical perspectives. In T. Ollendick & R. Prinz (Eds.), *Advances in clinical child psychology* (Vol. 17, pp. 157-196). New York: Plenum.

Russell, A., & Finnie, V. (1990). Preschool children's social status and maternal instructions to assist group entry. *Developmental Psychology, 26,* 603-611.

Russell, A., & Russell, G. (1996). Positive parenting and boys' and girls' misbehavior during a home observation. *International Journal of Behavioral Development, 19,* 291-307.

Rutter, M. (1989). Pathways from childhood to adult life. *Journal of Child Psychiatry, 30,* 23-51.

Rutter, M. (1994). Family discord and conduct disorder: Cause, consequence, or correlate? *Journal of Family Psychology, 8,* 170-186.

Rutter, M., & Quinton, D. (1984). Parental psychiatric disturbance: Effects on children. *Psychological Medicine, 14,* 853-880.

Sameroff, A. J. (1983). Developmental systems: Contexts and evolution. In W. Kessen (Ed.), *Handbook of child psychology: Vol. 1. History, theory, and methods* (pp. 238-294). New York: John Wiley.

Sanson, A., & Rothbart, M. K. (1995). Child temperament and parenting. In M. H. Bornstein (Ed.), *Handbook of parenting: Vol. 4. Applied and practical parenting* (pp. 299-321). Mahwah, NJ: Lawrence Erlbaum.

Sanson, A. V., Smart, D. F., Prior, M., & Oberklaid, F. (1993). *Interactions between parenting and temperament among 3- to 7-year-old children.* Unpublished manuscript.

Scarr, S. (1992). Developmental theories for the 1990s: Development and individual differences. *Child Development, 63,* 1-19.

Scarr, S. (1993). Biological and cultural diversity: The legacy of Darwin for development. *Child Development, 64,* 1333-1353.

Scarr, S., & McCartney, K. (1983). How people make their own environments: A theory of genotype → environment effects. *Child Development, 54,* 424-435.

Schwartz, D., Dodge, K. A., & Coie, J. D. (1993). The emergence of chronic peer victimization in boys' play groups. *Child Development, 64,* 1755-1772.

Shaffer, D. R. (1994). *Social and personality development.* Pacific Grove, CA: Brooks/Cole.

Sharabany, R., & Hertz-Lazarowitz, R. (1981). Do friends share and communicate more than non-friends? *International Journal of Behavioral Development, 4,* 45-59.

Shaw, D. S., & Emery, R. E. (1988). Chronic family adversity and school-age children's adjustment. *Journal of the American Academy of Child and Adolescent Psychiatry, 27,* 200-206.

Shaw, D. S., Keenan, K., & Vondra, J. I. (1994). Developmental precursors of externalizing behavior: Ages 1 to 3. *Developmental Psychology, 30,* 355-364.

Shelton, B. (1990). The distribution of household tasks. *Journal of Family Issues, 11,* 115-135.

Shonkoff, J. P., Hauser-Cram, P., Krauss, M. W., & Upshur, C. C. (1992). Development of infants with disabilities and their families: Implications for theory and service delivery. *Monographs of the Society for Research in Child Development, 57,* 1-88.

Simpson, A. E., & Stevenson-Hinde, J. (1985). Temperamental characteristics of three- to four-year-old boys and girls and child-family interactions. *Journal of Child Psychology and Psychiatry, 2,* 43-53.

Singer, D. G., & Benton, W. (1989). Caution: Television can be hazardous to a child's mental health. *Development and Behavioral Pediatrics, 10,* 259-261.

Slee, P. T., & Rigby, K. R. (1993). Australian school children's self appraisal of interpersonal relations: The bullying experience. *Child Psychiatry and Human Development, 23,* 273-281.

Smetana, J. G. (1994). Parenting styles and beliefs about parental authority. *New Directions for Child Development, 66,* 21-36.

Smets, A. C., & Hartup, W. W. (1988). Systems and symptoms: Family cohesion/adaptability and childhood behavior problems. *Journal of Abnormal Child Psychology, 16,* 233-246.

Smith, P. K. (1989). The role of rough-and-tumble play in the development of social competence: Theoretical perspectives and empirical evidence. In B. H. Schneider, G. Attili, J. Nadel, & R. P. Weissberg (Eds.), *Social competence in developmental perspective* (pp. 239-255). Dordrecht, Netherlands: Kluwer.

Snow, C. E., Pan, B. A., Imbens-Bailey, A., & Herman, J. (1996). Learning how to say what one means: A longitudinal study of children's speech act use. *Social Development, 5,* 56-84.

Socha, T. J., Sanchez-Hucles, J., Bromley, J., & Kelly, B. (1995). Invisible parents and children: Exploring African-American parent-child communication. In T. J. Socha & G. H. Stamp (Eds.), *Parents, children, and communication: Frontiers of theory and research* (pp. 127-145). Mahwah, NJ: Lawrence Erlbaum.

Spitze, G. (1991). Women's employment and family relations: A review. In A. Booth (Ed.), *Contemporary families: Looking forward, looking back* (pp. 381-404). Minneapolis: National Council on Family Relations.

Sroufe, L. A. (1983). Infant-caregiver attachment and patterns of adaptation in preschool: The roots of maladaptation. In M. Perlmutter (Ed.), *Minnesota Symposia on Child Psychology* (Vol. 16, pp. 41-83). Hillsdale, NJ: Lawrence Erlbaum.

Sroufe, L. A., & Fleeson, J. (1986). Attachment and the construction of relationships. In W. W. Hartup & Z. Rubin (Eds.), *Relationships and development* (pp. 51-72). Hillsdale, NJ: Lawrence Erlbaum.

Stafford, L., & Bayer, C. L. (1993). *Interaction between parents and children.* Newbury Park, CA: Sage.

Stamp, G. H., & Banski, M. A. (1992). The communicative management of constrained autonomy during the transition to parenthood. *Western Journal of Communication, 56,* 281-300.

Steinkamp, M. W. (1989). Factors mediating the relationships between preschool children's play patterns and peer ratings: Verbal communication styles. *Journal of Applied Developmental Psychology, 10,* 505-525.

Stocker, C. (1995). Differences in mothers' and fathers' relationships with siblings: Links with children's behavior problems. *Development and Psychopathology, 7,* 499-513.

Stocker, C., Dunn, J., & Plomin, R. (1989). Sibling relationships: Links with child temperament, maternal behavior, and family structure. *Child Development, 60,* 715-727.

Stormshak, E. A., Bellanti, C. J., & Bierman, K. L. (1996). The quality of sibling relationship and the development of social competence and behavioral control in aggressive children. *Developmental Psychology, 32,* 79-89.

Strassberg, Z., Dodge, K. A., Bates, J. E., & Pettit, G. S. (1992). The longitudinal relation between parental conflict strategies and children's sociometric standing in kindergarten. *Merrill-Palmer Quarterly, 38,* 477-493.

Suitor, J. J. (1991). Marital quality and satisfaction with the division of household labor across the family life cycle. *Journal of Marriage and the Family, 53,* 221-230.

Taylor, A. R., & Machida, S. (1994). The contribution of parent and peer support to Head Start children's early school adjustment. *Early Childhood Research Quarterly, 9,* 387-405.

Thomas, A., & Chess, S. (1977). *Temperament and development.* New York: Brunner/Mazel.

Tremblay, R. E., Vitaro, F., Gagnon, C., Piche, C., & Royer, N. (1992). A prosocial scale for the Preschool Behaviour Questionnaire: Concurrent and predictive correlates. *International Journal of Behavioral Development, 15,* 227-245.

Turnbull, A. P., Patterson, J. M., Behr, S. K., Murphy, D. L., Marquis, J. G., & Blue-Banning, M. J. (1993). *Cognitive coping, families, and disability.* Baltimore: Paul H. Brooks.

Vaden-Kiernan, N., Ialongo, N. S., Pearson, J., & Kellam, S. G. (1995). Household family structure and children's aggressive behavior: A longitudinal study of urban elementary school children. *Journal of Abnormal Child Psychology, 23,* 553-568.

Vandell, D. L., & Hembree, S. E. (1994). Peer social status and friendship: Independent contributors to children's social and academic adjustment. *Merrill-Palmer Quarterly, 40,* 461-477.

Vandell, D. L., Minnet, A. M., Johnson, B. S., & Santrock, J. W. (1990). *Siblings and friends: Experiences of school-aged children.* Unpublished manuscript, University of Texas at Dallas.

van den Boom, D. C. (1995). Do first-year intervention effects endure? Follow-up during toddlerhood of a sample of Dutch irritable infants. *Child Development, 66,* 1798-1816.

Van IJzendoorn, M. H. (1992). Intergenerational transmission of parenting: A review of studies in nonclinical populations. *Developmental Review, 12,* 76-99.

Vermulst, A. A., DeBrock, A. J. L. L., & Van Zutphen, R. A. H. (1990). Transmission of parenting across generations. In P. K. Smith (Ed.), *The psychology of grandparenthood: An international perspective* (pp. 100-122). New York: Routledge.

Volling, B. L., & Belsky, J. (1992). The contribution of mother-child and father-child relationships to the quality of sibling interaction: A longitudinal study. *Child Development, 63,* 1209-1222.

Volling, B. L., & Feagans, L. V. (1995). Infant day care and children's social competence. *Infant Behavior and Development, 18,* 177-188.

Vondra, J., & Belsky, J. (1993). Developmental origins of parenting: Personality and relationship factors. In T. Luster & L. Okagaki (Eds.), *Parenting: An ecological perspective* (pp. 1-33). Hillsdale, NJ: Lawrence Erlbaum.

Vuchinich, S., Bank, L., & Patterson, G. R. (1992). Parenting, peers, and the stability of antisocial behavior in preadolescent boys. *Developmental Psychology, 28,* 510-521.

Vygotsky, L. S. (1978). *Mind in society: The development of higher psychological processes* (M. Cole, V. John-Steiner, S. Scribner, & E. Souberman, Eds. & Trans.). Cambridge, MA: Harvard University Press.

Wall, J. E., & Holden, E. W. (1994). Aggressive, assertive, and submissive behaviors in disadvantaged, inner-city preschool children. *Journal of Clinical Child Psychology, 23,* 382-390.

Washington, J., Minde, K., & Goldberg, S. (1986). Temperament in preterm infants: Style and stability. *Journal of the American Academy of Child Psychiatry, 25,* 493-502.

Weiss, B., Dodge, K. A., Bates, J. E., & Pettit, G. S. (1992). Some consequences of early harsh discipline: Child aggression and a maladaptive social information processing style. *Child Development, 63,* 1321-1335.

Werner, C. M., & Baxter, L. A. (1994). Temporal qualities of relationships: Organismic, transactional, and dialectical views. In M. L. Knapp & G. R. Miller (Ed.), *Handbook of interpersonal communication* (2nd ed., pp. 323-379). Thousand Oaks, CA: Sage.

Werner, E. E. (1989). High risk children in young adulthood: A longitudinal study from birth to 32 years. *American Journal of Orthopsychiatry, 59,* 72-81.

Whitbeck, L. B., Hoyt, D. R., Simons, R. L., Conger, R. D., Elder, G. H., Jr., Lorenz, F. O., & Huck, S. (1992). Intergenerational continuity of parental rejection and depressed affect. *Journal of Personality and Social Psychology, 63,* 1036-1045.

Whiting, B. B., & Edwards, C. P. (1988). *Children of different worlds: The formation of social behavior.* Cambridge, MA: Harvard University Press.

Wilson, B. J., & Gottman, J. M. (1995). Marital interaction and parenting. In M. H. Bornstein (Ed.), *Handbook of parenting: Vol. 4. Applied and practical parenting* (pp. 33-56). Hillsdale, NJ: Lawrence Erlbaum.

Youngblade, L. M., & Dunn, J. (1995). Individual differences in young children's pretend play with mother and sibling: Links to relationships and understanding of other people's feelings and beliefs. *Child Development, 66,* 1472-1492.

Zahn-Waxler, C., Cummings, E. M., McKnew, D. H., & Radke-Yarrow, M. (1984). Altruism, aggression, and social interactions in young children with a manic-depressive parent. *Child Development, 55,* 112-122.

Zahn-Waxler, C., Denham, S., Iannotti, R. J., & Cummings, E. M. (1992). Peer relations in children with a depressed caregiver. In R. D. Parke & G. W. Ladd (Eds.), *Family-peer relationships: Modes of linkage* (pp. 317-344). Hillsdale, NJ: Lawrence Erlbaum.

Zarazoga, N., Vaughn, S., & McIntosh, R. (1991). Social skills interventions and children with behavior problems: A review. *Behavioral Disorders, 16,* 260-275.

Zimmerman, M. A., & Arunkumar, R. (1994). Resiliency research: Implications for schools and policy. *Social Policy Report: Society for Research in Child Development, 8,* 1-17.

CHAPTER CONTENTS

10 Communication and Cross-Sex Friendships Across the Life Cycle: A Review of the Literature

MICHAEL MONSOUR
University of Colorado at Denver

This chapter reviews the literature on cross-sex friendships and communication across the life cycle. It begins by establishing the importance and historical relevance of cross-sex friendships and the relative neglect of these relationships by the scholarly community. It then offers a delineation of conceptual and methodological issues involved in the study of male-female friendships. Next, with a focus on communication, studies are reviewed on cross-sex friendships in early childhood, middle and late childhood, adolescence, young and middle adulthood, and old age. Finally, the author makes some summarizing observations concerning the lack of theory in cross-sex friendship studies, the adoption of a "heterosexist" worldview in cross-sex friendship investigations, and the relative neglect of communication topics pertinent to those friendships. The central observation in the chapter is that cross-sex friendships have a protean quality that makes them significantly different in each stage of the life cycle, and that those differences are manifested in communication.

C ROSS-SEX friendships occupy an unusual place in the relational fabric of society. Because they lack the prominence and notoriety of same-sex friendships and romantic relationships, they have had to struggle for recognition in the scholarly and lay communities. Cross-sex friendships have been relegated to second-class status in a society where romantic relationships and same-sex friendships are given higher priority (O'Meara, 1989).

Adult cross-sex friendships are fairly common, although they are fewer than same-sex friendships. In his summary of noncollege adult samples,

Correspondence and requests for reprints: Michael Monsour, Department of Communication, Box 176, University of Colorado, P.O. Box 173364, Denver, CO 80217-3364; e-mail wmonsour@castle.cudenver.edu

Communication Yearbook 20, pp. 375-414

Wright (1989) found that roughly 40% of the men and 30% of the women had close cross-sex friends. The percentages are considerably higher in college samples (e.g., Monsour, 1988; Rose, 1985), but significantly lower in samples of the elderly (e.g., Adams, 1985), adolescents (e.g., Gottman, 1986), and children of all ages (Rawlins, 1992).

Cross-sex friendships serve important functions and provide unique advantages (O'Meara, 1989). Simply put, people need friends (Duck, 1983; Solano, 1986). Assuming individuals need the companionship and emotional support that friends provide, it is puzzling why so many people overlook members of the opposite sex as possible friends (Cassel, 1989). Viewing cross-sex friendship as a "viable interpersonal option" doubles an individual's potential for establishing friendships (Rawlins, 1982). Cross-sex friends give one another "insider information" on how members of the opposite sex think, feel, and behave (Bell, 1981; Hacker, 1981; Sapadin, 1988). Obtaining insider perspectives from cross-sex friends makes the behavior of opposite-sex others less mysterious (Rubin, 1985). Cross-sex friends also give one another cross-sex validation as attractive members of the opposite sex (Bell, 1981; Rubin, 1985); such validation is particularly important for adolescents and young adults (Monsour, 1988; Rice, 1978). Another advantage of cross-sex friendships is that they improve understanding and communication between the sexes (McWilliams & Howard, 1993). Men and women live in different worlds, making communication between the sexes problematic—and, at times, incomprehensible (Tannen, 1990). Cross-sex friends help overcome gender differences by supplying insider information and opposite-sex companionship. Males and females learn to understand and accept their similarities and differences when they spend time together as friends (Monsour, 1988; Rubin, 1980).

The functions and unique advantages of cross-sex friendships establish a rationale for investigation of those relationships. However, there is additional justification for such an investigation based on changes occurring in society. Cross-sex friendship is clearly a twentieth-century phenomenon. Prior to 1900, friendships were almost exclusively same-sex in nature (Smith-Rosenberg, 1975), and although same-sex friendships have been empirically investigated for almost 100 years (Newcomb & Bagwell, 1995), the scientific study of cross-sex friendship did not begin until 1974 (Booth & Hess, 1974). Since that date, society has changed in ways that make the study of cross-sex friendship more imperative. With the advent of AIDS in the past 15 years, the growing number of pregnancies among teenagers, and the increasing proportion of women in the workplace, it has become more important for males and females to recognize that their relationships do not need to be romantic or sexual in order to be fulfilling.

Despite the documented advantages and historical relevance of cross-sex friendships, they have been ignored and de-emphasized by the scholarly community (Allan, 1989; Hays, 1988; O'Meara, 1989; Werking, 1994). For example, in an otherwise impressive meta-analytic review of childhood friendship studies, Newcomb and Bagwell (1995) made no attempt to differentiate cross-sex friendships from their same-sex counterparts. Scholarly neglect is further illustrated by the fact that there have been no comprehensive reviews of the cross-sex friendship literature. As this review will illustrate, that literature is young, fragmented, and meager. A review of the literature is needed to determine what is known and not known about cross-sex friendships, to identify methods and research programs that hold promise, and to pinpoint problems in the study of these relationships.

The scarcity of cross-sex friendship studies in the general scientific community is equally apparent in the field of communication. With the exception of a few noteworthy endeavors (e.g., Rawlins, 1982; Werking, 1992; Yingling, 1994), communication scholars have mostly neglected the investigation of cross-sex friendships. However, individuals from other disciplines have directly and indirectly studied cross-sex friendship communication in various stages of the life cycle (e.g., Adams, 1985; Whaley & Rubenstein, 1994). Although there have been cross-sex friendship studies, and some have focused on communication, there is still much that is not known about these friendships and their communication patterns. A review of the cross-sex friendship literature is needed that highlights the role of communication in the study and development of cross-sex friendships.

I have two objectives in this chapter. The first is to summarize, critique, and integrate the literature on cross-sex friendships. The second is to examine how scholars have studied communication across the life cycle in these relationships and to explain the role of communication in the development of cross-sex friendships. The central observation of this review is that friendships between males and females are significantly different in each stage of the life cycle, and that those differences are manifested in communication (Gottman, 1986). Although I will show in this review how cross-sex friendships in different life stages are distinct from one another, I will also note their similarities.

The chapter is divided into three sections. In the first, I delineate conceptual and methodological issues pertaining to the investigation of cross-sex friendships and identify key elements in defining those relationships. In the second section, I review the cross-sex friendship literature. Among other things, this review emphasizes how researchers study communication in cross-sex friendships and how communication affects the development of these relationships. I take a life-cycle approach in the review of literature, which is a common strategy in the organization of friendship studies (see Dickens & Perlman, 1981; Rawlins, 1992; Tesch, 1983). In the final section of the chapter I present summarizing observations concerning the cross-sex friendship literature and the future role of communication scholars in the expansion of that literature.

CONCEPTUAL AND METHODOLOGICAL ISSUES
IN THE STUDY OF CROSS-SEX FRIENDSHIPS

There are many intricately related methodological and conceptual issues in the study of cross-sex friendship. Some of these issues are depicted in this section as problems in the way cross-sex friendships are conceptualized and studied, whereas others are portrayed as areas worthy of scholarly attention.

Conceptual Issues

There are three interrelated crucial conceptual conundrums in the investigation of male-female friendships: (a) What are cross-sex friendships? (b) How do they differ from same-sex friendships and romantic relationships? (c) What conceptual problems do scholars face when trying to define cross-sex friendships?

Friendship researchers believe that cross-sex friendship is a type of friendship similar in many respects to other varieties of friendship (Monsour, 1988). Defining friendship is therefore a necessary, but possibly not sufficient, condition for defining cross-sex friendship. Defining friendship is problematic because of its protean quality and the variations in how people conceptualize it (Blieszner & Adams, 1992; Hays, 1988). Additional difficulties arise because friendships may be described in many ways—as casual friendships, close friendships, good friendships, best friendships, and so on. Each type of friendship may bring to mind a different set of defining characteristics. It is also necessary to draw a distinction between studies whose main purpose is to define friendship and studies that start with a working definition of friendship and then investigate some feature of the friendship relation.

Scholars use a number of methods to define friendship. One common approach is to interview subjects and ask them to describe what they mean by the term *friendship* (e.g., LaGaipa, 1977). Another method is to restrict in some way the definition of friendship in the design of the study (Adams, 1989). Alternatively, some researchers do not define friendship for their respondents (Winstead & Derlega, 1986). Researchers have also defined friendship through paradigm case formulations (e.g., Davis & Todd, 1982; Roberts, 1982), by reviewing empirical and theoretical research on friendship (e.g., Hays, 1988; Newcomb & Bagwell, 1995), and by developing their own theoretical frameworks (e.g., Wright, 1984). I briefly review each of these approaches to defining friendship below.

Interviews with adults have revealed an extensive list of defining characteristics of friendship. Friends share common interests and activities; are understanding, accepting, and helpful; have positive regard for one another; and engage in ritualistic social exchange (LaGaipa, 1977; Weiss & Lowenthal, 1975). In interviews with more than 300 adults, Rubin (1985) found that friendships were described as involving trust, honesty, respect, commitment, safety, support, generosity, loyalty, mutuality, constancy, understanding, and acceptance. Definitions that children give for friendship are usually obtained indirectly. Rather than asking a child, "What is a friend?" a researcher might ask the child to write an essay about what he or she expects from a best friend. In Bigelow's (1977) study of 480 children ages 6 to 12, ego reinforcement and reciprocity of liking were central expectations of a best friendship. Other indirect techniques reveal that children define friendship as spending a lot of time together (Mannarino, 1980), engaging in self-disclosures, and playing together (Gottman, 1986).

The majority of researchers restrict friendship in some way by specifying type of friendship to their respondents (such as "good friend" or "close friend") or by identifying defining features of those relationships (Adams, 1989). For example, Bell (1981) asked respondents why they identified certain people as friends. Based upon those interviews, Bell defined cross-sex and same-sex friendships as being voluntary, enduring, and exemplifying an appreciation of the unique qualities of the friend. O'Meara (1989) defined cross-sex friendship for his adult respondents as a nonromantic, nonfamilial, personal relationship between a man and a woman. I define cross-sex friendships for my respondents as friendships with members of the opposite sex that do not include family or dating relationships (e.g., Monsour, 1988; Monsour, Betty, & Kurzweil, 1993).

Restricting the definition of friendship has advantages and disadvantages for researchers (Adams, 1989). A central advantage is that restrictions make possible comparisons with other studies that have similarly narrowed the conceptualization of friendship (Hays, 1988). A potential disadvantage is that by limiting respondents' definition of friendship, researchers are studying subtypes of friendship rather than friendship in general (Adams, 1989). For example, in their definition, Booth and Hess (1974) restricted friendship to relationships in which people are predisposed to engage in a wide range of activities together. That definition excludes friendships in which individuals do only a few things together but enjoy those things and each other immensely.

Many researchers assume that individuals know the meaning of friendship, and therefore do not define it for respondents (Winstead & Derlega, 1986). There are two major difficulties with this approach. First, any comparisons between studies may be flawed because there is no way of determining if friendship meant the same thing for all the respondents. Further, the lack of a definition makes it difficult to interpret findings, because subjects may have different meanings for friendship. However, an advantage of this research technique is that it does not impose the researcher's worldview on the respondents, but instead allows them to define friendship according to their own experience (Hays, 1988).

Scholars also define friendship and cross-sex friendship through utilization of paradigm case formulations (e.g., Davis & Todd, 1982, 1985; Roberts, 1982). Paradigm case formulations are generated by use of theory, by relying on past research, or by researcher intuition (Davis & Todd, 1985). There is variety among paradigm cases, such as genuine cases, or first cases, but the variant used by Davis and Todd (1982, 1985) is referred to as a *fundamental* or *archetypal case*. This is a case that best exemplifies the essence of the concept, but does not need to be statistically frequent. A paradigm case formulation involves the construction of a complex paradigm case of the concept under investigation, against which other cases can be recognized as variations of the paradigm case (Davis & Todd, 1982; Ossorio, 1981). Alternative paradigm case formulations of the same concept are "possible because of legitimate differences in purposes and focus" (Davis & Todd, 1982, p. 83).

Scholars also define friendship by reviewing empirical and theoretical work on friendship or by developing their own theoretical frameworks. For example, in a recent meta-analytic review of childhood friendship studies, Newcomb and Bagwell (1995) conclude that those friendships can be differentiated from peer relationships by more intense interaction, equality, more frequent conflict resolution, and more effective task management. In his review of empirical and theoretical work on mostly adult friendships, Hays (1988) defines friendship as "voluntary interdependence between two persons over time, that is intended to facilitate social-emotional goals of the participants, and may involve varying types and degrees of companionship, intimacy, affection, and mutual assistance" (p. 395). Wright (1984) developed his own theoretical framework, labeled a "self-referent model of friendship"; he defines friendship as "a relationship involving voluntary or unconstrained interaction in which the participants respond to one another personally, that is, as unique individuals rather than as packages of discrete attributes or mere role occupants" (p. 119). Rawlins (1982) gives a detailed delineation of cross-sex friendships in his presentation of a typology designed to display the interaction between friendship and romantic love. He defines friendship, platonic love, friendship-love, physical love, and romantic love, and argues that although male-female relationships can have different combinations of all these categories, cross-sex friendship is a relationship without overt sexuality. Adler and Furman (1988) conclude that children's friendships are characterized by warmth and closeness, exclusivity, and conflict.

In summary, let me return to the first conceptual issue presented at the beginning of this section: What is a cross-sex friendship? At the most fundamental level, a cross-sex friendship is a type of friendship, sharing many of the characteristics of all friendships (Duck, Miell, & Gaebler, 1980; O'Meara, 1989). Cross-sex friendships are also defined by spontaneity and support (Davis & Todd, 1982), acceptance and understanding (Monsour et al., 1993), and sexual energy (Rubin, 1985). A defining feature of cross-sex friendship is that participants provide one another with opposite-sex companionship and insider perspectives (Sapadin, 1988). Additionally, in many cross-sex friendships relational partners must negotiate underlying sexual and romantic undertones that generally do not plague same-sex friendships (O'Meara,

1989). Another defining feature of cross-sex friendships is their relative lack of social acceptance and understanding (Nardi, 1992). Though this lack of acceptance is changing, many individuals who do not have cross-sex friendships view such friendships with suspicion (Rawlins, 1992).

Given that cross-sex friendships are different in various life stages (Gottman, 1986) and vary within specific stages, a paradigm case formulation is a profitable approach to defining cross-sex friendships, because this approach is so flexible. Roberts (1982) has already laid the groundwork for a paradigm case approach to the conceptualization of cross-sex friendships, and concludes that cross-sex friendships are characterized by symmetrical eligibility, intimacy, respect, trust, and liking. From a paradigm case approach, a researcher has the freedom to argue that cross-sex friendships may or may not involve sexual attraction, that they may or may not involve spontaneity, that they may or may not have any other feature characterizing friendship. Nevertheless, if a relationship is missing a key feature of friendship, one could legitimately question whether that relationship is actually a friendship. For example, at a minimum, a cross-sex friendship is a relationship between a male and a female in which both individuals label the relationship as a friendship. However, even the requirement that friendship be reciprocal, rather than unilateral, is hotly debated in the friendship literature (Newcomb & Bagwell, 1995).

A caveat needs to be offered in reference to the preceding depiction of cross-sex friendships. The description given of cross-sex friendship is largely based on research findings and conceptual speculations concerning adult cross-sex friendships. However, the functions and appearances of cross-sex friendships depend upon the stage of the life cycle in which those friendships occur (Gottman, 1986). The picture becomes even more complex if individuals are in different developmental stages (O'Connor, 1993). Cross-sex friendship scholars, some of them communication researchers (e.g., Rawlins, 1994), have called for the development of a typology of cross-sex friendships. Such a typology would identify variations of cross-sex friendship and stipulate how those variations display different communication patterns and serve different functions throughout the life cycle.

A second conceptual issue in the study of cross-sex friendships is the differentiation of these relationships from romantic relationships (e.g., Lin & Rusbult, 1995) and same-sex friendships (Monsour, 1988). Romantic relationships and cross-sex friendships are similar because both involve members of the opposite sex. However, unlike cross-sex friendships, romantic relationships are characterized by exclusivity and fascination (Roberts, 1982). Cross-sex friendships can be distinguished from romantic relationships by the absence of overt sexuality—at least in the vast majority of cross-sex friendships (Monsour, 1988; Rawlins, 1982). There is also evidence suggesting that adolescents and young adults feel more freedom to be themselves in cross-sex friendships than they do in romantic relationships (Rawlins, 1992; Rubin, 1985).

Several researchers have documented differences between same-sex and cross-sex friendships in various stages of the life cycle (e.g., Gottman, 1986; Monsour, 1988; Rubin, 1985; Wright, 1989). The greatest difference is the opposite-sex companionship and insider perspectives that are provided by cross-sex friends (Cassel, 1989; Furman, 1986; Rubin, 1985; Sapadin, 1988). When studying differences between cross-sex and same-sex friendships, researchers usually choose some construct of interest and compare how that construct is manifested in same-sex and cross-sex friendships (e.g., Monsour, 1992). Rose (1985) compared the functions, formation, and maintenance characteristics of same-sex and cross-sex friendships. Some studies compare the relative importance to participants of same-sex and cross-sex friendships (e.g., Davis & Todd, 1982, 1985; Leibowitz & Rawlins, 1980). Werking (1994) argues in her review of the adult cross-sex friendship literature that researchers have devoted too much attention to comparing same-sex and cross-sex friendships.

Scholars face a number of conceptual problems when trying to identify defining features of cross-sex friendships. For example, though some scholars implicitly treat them as such, not all cross-sex friendships are the same. Such friendships differ in each stage of the life cycle and within life stages (Gottman, 1986; Rawlins, 1992). What might be a defining feature of cross-sex friendship in one stage of the life cycle may be unimportant in another. In like fashion, a defining feature of cross-sex friendship in a specific life stage may not be relevant to all cross-sex friendships in that life stage. For example, sexual tensions that characterize young adult cross-sex friendships are usually absent in early childhood friendships. However, not all young adult cross-sex friendships are characterized by the same type of sexual tension. Among other things, the sexual orientations of the participants have impacts on the expression and experience of sexuality in a cross-sex friendship (Rubin, 1985).

Another conceptual problem occurs when researchers neglect to define cross-sex friendship for participants in their studies. Though there are legitimate reasons for not defining cross-sex friendship for respondents, serious problems arise when the absence of a definition reflects a conceptual or methodological oversight. Researchers' failure to define cross-sex friendship for participants has led to a confounding of cross-sex friendships with romantic relationships, because some participants consider their romantic partners to be friends also (e.g., Aukett, Ritchie, & Mill, 1988; Banikiotes, Neimeyer, & Lepkowsky, 1981; Derlega, Durham, Gockel, & Sholis, 1981; Fitzpatrick & Bochner, 1981; Komarovsky, 1976; Snell, 1989; Won-Doornink, 1985). According to one study, 41% of young adults consider their dating partners to be their friends, which means that participants might describe romantic relationships when asked to report on cross-sex friendships (Hendrick & Hendrick, 1993). Compounding the problem, friendship scholars routinely cite these studies as if they fall squarely within the friendship literature (e.g., Blieszner & Adams, 1992, who cite Won-Doornink, 1985, and Snell, 1989; and Monsour, 1988, and Rawlins, 1992, who cite Komarovsky, 1976).

Another potential problem in conceptualizing cross-sex friendships is the protean quality of these relationships. Like most friendships, cross-sex friendships change as they appear in each stage of an individual's life (Hays, 1988). The cross-sex friendships that people experience in specific developmental epochs differ in the functions they serve for the relational partners and in the tensions and challenges that characterize the friendships (Gottman, 1986; Rawlins, 1992). Cross-sex friendship also has different meanings for participants as they go through the life cycle. The meaning of cross-sex friendship is not the same for 2-year-olds as it is for adolescents or middle-aged adults (Rawlins, 1992). Same-sex friendships also have a protean quality, but this presents less of a conceptual problem to researchers because developmental milestones such as puberty and marriage have less impact on same-sex friendships than they do on cross-sex ones (Booth & Hess, 1974; Gottman, 1986).

A final conceptual problem presents itself when researchers make decisions concerning the relative impacts of structural and psychological variables on cross-sex friendships (Blieszner & Adams, 1992; Wright, 1989). Too much reliance on one perspective limits understanding of cross-sex friendships. Psychological perspectives emphasize individual characteristics, such as motives for being in the friendship and personal preferences concerning interactional styles (Blieszner & Adams, 1992). For example, Rose (1985) argues that males and females have different expectations for friendship, which causes problems in cross-sex friendships. Sociological perspectives focus more heavily on societal and structural factors. From a sociological perspective, cross-sex friendships are not as voluntary as traditional conceptualizations portray them. Although a defining characteristic of friendship is its voluntary nature (Allan & Adams, 1989), structural opportunities and constraints frequently force people apart or together. Structural approaches also emphasize how the structure of society gives men and women access to different types of power and privileges. Researchers should combine sociological and psychological perspectives in their conceptualizations of friendship (Blieszner & Adams, 1992; Werking, 1994; Wright, 1989).

I should make one final observation before moving on to a discussion of methodological issues in the study of cross-sex friendships. Throughout this chapter, I refer to male-female friendships as *cross-sex friendships* rather than *cross-gender friendships*. My use of *cross-sex* rather than *cross-gender* should not be taken to mean that social and cultural factors have less impact on male-female friendships than do biological factors. *Cross-sex* simply means that these relationships occur between members of different sexes, which encompasses social differences as well.

Methodological Issues

There are four interrelated methodological issues that have special relevance for the study of cross-sex friendships: (a) the heavy reliance on
cross-sectional data and the relative neglect of longitudinal designs, (b) the
tendency to utilize only one method within an investigation, (c) the comparative lack of qualitative research, and (d) the practice of obtaining the perspective of only one participant in each cross-sex friendship.

The vast majority of research on cross-sex friendship has been cross-sectional. Despite general agreement among personal relationship scholars and
friendship researchers that longitudinal research is desirable (Duck & Perlman,
1985; Griffin & Sparks, 1990), it is seldom conducted in the area of cross-sex
friendship. However, to a limited degree, longitudinal designs have been
employed in the investigation of cross-sex friendships among toddlers (Whaley
& Rubenstein, 1994), the elderly (Adams, 1987), and young adults (Griffin
& Sparks, 1990). The protean nature of cross-sex friendships make them
ideally suited for longitudinal designs. Such research can follow a cross-sex
friendship as it changes within and between stages of the life cycle. For example,
sometimes a cross-sex friendship will change into a romantic relationship
(Metts, Cupach, & Bejlovec, 1989). As another example, Gottman (1986)
notes that little is known about the interactional dynamics of cross-sex
friendships that begin in preschool and continue through the elementary
school years. A longitudinal design would enable researchers to study these
interactional dynamics. Longitudinal designs would also be productive for
tracking cross-sex friendships through developmental milestones. For instance, what happens to a cross-sex friendship as the participants enter
puberty? In order to study this phenomenon adequately, one must follow the
friendship from preadolescence through adolescence.

A second methodological issue is the common practice of employing only
one method in a given cross-sex friendship study, typically quantitative
retrospective self-reports (Monsour, 1988). In only a few studies has communication between adult cross-sex friends been recorded and analyzed (Monsour, 1988). Most studies that have examined actual communication have
focused on friendships in early and middle childhood (e.g., Gottman, 1986;
Yingling, 1994). Many scholars have extolled the virtues of methodological
triangulation (Chaffee & Berger, 1987; Harvey, Christensen, & McClintock,
1983; McCarthy, 1981). Through the strategic and complementary employment of multiple methods, investigators can make sure the strengths of one
method make up for the weaknesses of another (Denzin, 1978). Observational
methods coupled with self-reports can ensure a more comprehensive description and understanding of cross-sex friendships. For example, if cross-sex
friends report that they never engage in flirting behavior in public, that report
could be observationally verified by members of their social network. There
is evidence that self-reports of cross-sex friendships do not always match the

actual communication behavior in those relationships (e.g., Monsour, 1988). Self-reports are also subject to social desirability effects (Watt & Van Den Berg, 1995). Because cross-sex friendships are frowned upon by large segments of society, research participants may be particularly prone to give socially desirable responses to questions concerning frequency and dynamics of cross-sex friendships.

Though quantitative methods have a place in the study of cross-sex friendships, researchers should utilize qualitative approaches more frequently than they currently do. The use of qualitative research methods is becoming more common in the field of communication (Watt & Van Den Berg, 1995), and cross-sex friendship researchers have begun to employ these methods (e.g., O'Connor, 1993). Qualitative research has particular relevance for the study of cross-sex friendship because it often entails the accumulation of considerable amounts of descriptive data, which are necessary for the development of theory (Berscheid & Peplau, 1983). The study of cross-sex friendship is still in its infancy, a fact partly reflected in a relatively small database. Strategic use of appropriate qualitative methods could increase the size of that database. Additionally, increasing numbers of researchers are acknowledging that investigations of friendship should employ qualitative techniques that involve intensive interviewer probing (Blieszner & Adams, 1992). In-depth interviewing of cross-sex friends could augment our understanding of how males and females view such relationships.

The overwhelming majority of cross-sex friendship studies at every stage of the life cycle have investigated the perspective of only one member of each friendship pair (but see Monsour et al., 1993). Personal relationship researchers stress the importance of obtaining the perspectives of both partners in order to determine whether or not they experience a shared reality (Duck & Sants, 1983). The necessity of acquiring both friends' perspectives is dramatically illustrated by Rubin's (1985) work. In her study of cross-sex friendships, more than two-thirds of the females who were identified by a male friend as a "close friend" denied that definition of the relationship. In my own research, I have found that it is common for one partner in a friendship to perceive significant problems in the relationship while the other partner perceives the relationship to be problem free (Monsour, 1995).

CROSS-SEX FRIENDSHIPS ACROSS THE LIFE CYCLE

Classifying investigations according to participants' developmental stages is a profitable approach for systematizing studies on cross-sex friendships. Life-cycle milestones such as puberty and marriage (or not getting married) have tremendous impacts on the frequency, meaning, and viability of cross-sex friendships (Booth & Hess, 1974; Rawlins, 1992). Additionally, as individuals move through the different stages of their lives, the functions, expectations, and centrality of friendships for them change (Dickens & Perlman, 1981).

There is a noticeable lack of consensus in the developmental literature concerning the best way to divide the life cycle chronologically, with disagreement on such fundamental points as what the phases of the life cycle are and when they occur (Rogers, 1982; Santrock, 1983). Nevertheless, based on a review of the life-cycle literature, the following segmentation of the life cycle seems reasonable. A survey of the literature on cross-sex friendships from a life-cycle perspective reveals that these friendships occur during early childhood, middle and late childhood, adolescence, young adulthood, middle adulthood, and old age.

A version of Santrock's (1983) life-cycle stages was utilized for the purpose of organizing cross-sex friendship studies. Early childhood encompasses ages 2 through 6 (preschool years), middle and late childhood includes ages 7 through 11 (elementary school years), adolescence spans ages 12 through 17 (middle school and high school), young adulthood covers ages 18 through 35, middle adulthood encompasses ages 36 through 64, and old age is any age 65 years and above. This organizational scheme facilitates categorization of cross-sex friendship research because it parallels common patterns for entering and leaving the educational system and the workplace, which are the most common locations for cross-sex friendship studies.

Early Childhood (Ages 2 to 6)

> It is my impression that, up to about age 7, cross-sex best friendships are very intense emotional relationships, not unlike some marriages. (Gottman, 1986, p. 156)

The preceding quotation has numerous implications for the study of cross-sex friendships in early childhood, especially considering Gottman's widely acknowledged expertise and research on marital relationships (e.g., Gottman, 1979). I will discuss some of those implications in this part of the chapter, but first, a preview of how this subsection is organized. I begin with an overview of the importance of early childhood friendships and what is involved in these relationships. I then examine the explanations given for same-sex preferences among children ages 2 to 6, preferences that persist throughout the life cycle. This is followed by a review of investigations of toddler cross-sex friendships and a discussion of research on the cross-sex friendships of children between the ages of 3 and 6. This subsection, like those that follow, concludes with a description of a typical cross-sex friendship, how that typicality is manifested in communication behavior, and identification of relevant developmental milestones.

Children have a rudimentary understanding of friendship when they are about 2 years old (Rubin, 1980). By the time they are 3 or 4, the word *friend* has become part of their working vocabulary (Mannarino, 1980). Early childhood friendships involve sharing toys, engaging in mutual activities, self-disclosure, playing, helping one another, and carrying on conversations (Gottman, 1986; Rubenstein & Howes, 1976). Peer friendships in early childhood provide companionship, stimulation, physical and ego support, social comparison, and intimacy (Ginsberg, Gottman, & Parker, 1986). Early childhood friendships also affect later development and social adjustment (Roopnarine & Field, 1984). A number of the functions provided by friends in this life stage are made possible by verbal and nonverbal communication (Ginsberg et al., 1986; Gottman, 1986).

Cross-sex friendships in early childhood are extremely rare compared with the frequency of their same-sex counterparts (Gottman, 1986; Karweit & Hansell, 1983; Rubin, 1980), though they are more common than cross-sex friendships in middle childhood and adolescence. The majority of children after about the age of 2 or 3 prefer to spend time with members of their own sex (Eder & Hallinan, 1978; Roopnarine & Field, 1984; Rubin, 1980). There are same-sex preferences even before the age of 3 (for a review, see Maccoby, 1988). The preference for same-sex interaction also occurs in cultures outside the United States (Edwards & Whiting, 1988; Serbin, Tonick, & Sternglanz, 1977).

A number of explanations have been offered for same-sex preferences among individuals in early childhood, and thus the rarity of cross-sex friendships. These include biological accounts (e.g., Omark, Omark, & Edelman, 1975), psychoanalytic interpretations (e.g., Rubenstein & Rubin, 1984), and explanations focusing on the distribution of resources (e.g., Lipman-Blumen, 1976). Additionally, some researchers argue that young children prefer to play with same-sex others because children tend to group according to sex-typed play preferences (e.g., Rubin, Fein, & Vandenberg, 1983). Others adopt a social-cognitive explanation of same-sex preferences, contending that as children grow older they develop an understanding of gender and begin to value members of their own gender category (e.g., Maccoby, 1988). Rubin (1980) believes that same-sex playmate preferences among young children are partially a product of adult-engineered gender segregation, which precludes the opportunity for cross-sex interaction.

There are no definitive and commonly agreed-upon explanations for same-sex playmate preferences (Rubenstein, 1984). In a study investigating the impact of gender labels and play styles in playmate selection among 4- to 5-year-olds, Alexander and Hines (1994) conclude that no single theory can adequately explain same-sex preferences and that some combination of theoretical approaches is warranted. Their recommendation for theoretical pluralism is a valid one, especially considering that same-sex preferences have an "on-off" character as individuals go through the life cycle (Gottman, 1986). Epstein (1986) explains the on-off nature of same-sex preferences when he observes, "The literature suggests a curvilinear, developmental pattern of cross-sex choices of friends. Very young children make frequent cross-sex (sociometric) choices, children in elementary and middle school grades make almost no cross-sex choices, and adolescents increase their cross-sex choice of friends" (p. 137). This observation is supported by findings that some toddlers prefer cross-sex friendships to same-sex friendships (Epstein, 1986; Gottman, 1986; Rickleman, 1981; Rubin, 1980), but as they grow older their preferences change (Rawlins, 1992).

There is growing agreement among childhood friendship experts that toddlers are capable of forming and maintaining friendships and are willing to do so. However, there have been few investigations of the friendships of children between the ages of 2 and 3 (Whaley & Rubenstein, 1994). One reason for the paucity of studies conducted with this age group is the methodological proclivity of friendship researchers to employ interviewing techniques in their investigations (Whaley & Rubenstein, 1994). Even precocious toddlers lack sufficient linguistic skills to be interviewed about friendship, leaving researchers to study those friendships through observational techniques (e.g., Gottman, 1986; Howes, 1987; Whaley & Rubenstein, 1994). Unlike the majority of investigations in later stages of the life cycle, early childhood cross-sex friendship studies frequently involve longitudinal observation of communication between friends.

The studies that have been conducted have shown that toddlers in friendships are capable of displaying intimacy, loyalty, sharing, and constructing similarity through modeling of one another's play styles (Whaley & Rubenstein, 1994). Some toddlers grieve when separated from friends, with their grief usually manifested as antisocial behavior (Whaley & Rubenstein, 1994). Toddler friendships are also characterized by the friends' seeking one another out, maintaining close proximity, and displaying positive emotions for one another (Howes, 1987). Whaley and Rubenstein (1994) observed that toddlers create similarity nonverbally by imitating one another's behavior. Personal relationship scholars have recognized the importance of similarity in building intimacy (e.g., Duck, 1989; Monsour, 1994).

Toddler friendship studies have not occurred in a theoretical vacuum. One of the more appealing theoretical explanations of friendship formation among toddlers is based on social constructivism (Corsaro, 1985; Vygotsky, 1978). Social constructivists contend that children initially gain knowledge and experience within an interpersonal context, then they internalize those experiences. From this perspective, toddler friendships develop as a product of toddlers' interacting with peers. Yingling (1994) makes a similar point when she adopts a relational perspective on the development of toddler friendships. She observes: "A relational perspective on children's developing friendships focuses on spoken symbolic interaction rather than on thoughts alone. The interaction we observe in talk does not merely express thought but shapes it to some extent, thus the interaction in relationships shapes the cognitive model of that relationship" (p. 414).

Friendships of children between the ages of 3 and 6 have received more scholarly attention than those occurring at earlier ages. Friendships during this period are primarily ones of convenience, with children playing with others who are in close physical proximity (Selman, 1981). Rawlins (1992) notes that friendships exist while children are playing together, but once separated, the children tend to forget each other. The idea that friendships among the very young are matters of convenience is challenged by Whaley and Rubenstein's (1994) finding that toddlers miss one another and grieve when cross-sex friends are gone.

Coordinated play is the central manifestation of peer interaction among children approximately 3 to 7 years old (Gottman, 1986). Coordinated play among cross-sex and same-sex friends involves self-disclosure, often done in the context of fantasy play (Gottman, 1986). Gottman (1986) concludes that cross-sex friendships among preschoolers have a uniquely intimate character. Like many marriages, they contain a wide range of negative and positive emotions, and a common fantasy theme for young cross-sex friends is to pretend they are married. The closeness exhibited in these friendships lends credence to the contention of some theorists that 3-year-olds often have friendship preferences for opposite-sex others (e.g., Gesell, 1945). Gottman bolsters his argument regarding the uniqueness of cross-sex friendships by citing Sherman's (1975) research on "glee." Glee is almost exclusively a cross-sex phenomenon among preschoolers.

Friendships between the ages of 3 and 6 are characterized by the formation of groups and by attempts to include others in and exclude others from those groups (Corsaro, 1981). Young children who are not already part of an established group may "hover" outside the perimeter of the group, looking for an opportunity to become part of it (Putallaz & Gottman, 1981). Some researchers argue that boys at this age enjoy interacting in groups more than in dyads, and that girls display the opposite preference (e.g., Benenson, 1993). Group membership is also illustrated by the dialectical principle of judgment and acceptance (Rawlins, 1992). The dialectic of judgment and acceptance involves choices made by young children concerning who will be included within or excluded from their groups. Choosing a cross-sex person as a friend might entail the cost of being excluded from other friendships and groups (Rawlins, 1992).

Though group membership is not always determined by sex, it is frequently dictated by obvious physical similarities among group members and potential group members (Rubin, 1980). The most apparent physical characteristic is an individual's sex. In addition, boys and girls quickly learn that certain activities, behaviors, and interests are more appropriate for one sex than the other. This enculturation encourages a kind of in-group/out-group mentality among young children barely out of diapers (Rubenstein & Rubin, 1984). The same-sex friendship and playmate preferences expressed by young boys and girls are a precursor to attitudes toward members of the opposite sex displayed in later stages of the life cycle.

Part of the typicality of cross-sex friendship at this stage of the life cycle is its relative rarity, its atypicality. Like cross-sex friendships that occur in other stages of the life cycle, male-female friendships among preschoolers are less common than same-sex friendships. Nevertheless, even the youngest of cross-sex friends demonstrate loyalty, intimacy, social support, and helping behavior and show signs of missing one another when separated (Whaley & Rubenstein, 1994). Some of these characteristics, such as intimacy, have previously been considered as probably not important for toddlers (e.g., Vandell & Mueller, 1980).

Although the cross-sex friendships of preschoolers are similar in many respects to those of older individuals, there are also significant differences. Perhaps the most important difference is that preschoolers have little control over opportunities for cross-sex interaction. Unlike their adult counterparts, and more so than older children, preschoolers are at the mercy of parents and day-care providers, who may structure their environments so that the children have little opportunity to interact with members of the opposite sex. The opportunity or lack of opportunity to interact with opposite-sex others can be a major facilitator or impediment to cross-sex friendship formation for individuals of any age (O'Meara, 1994; Rubin, 1980). When preschoolers are given opportunities to play with members of both sexes, they are exposed to a wider range of behavioral practices and activities and learn to appreciate the similarities and differences between boys and girls (Rubin, 1980). Exposure to members of the opposite sex makes children's subsequent interaction in elementary school smoother and more inclusive. Interactions in these early relationships can be instrumental in teaching toddlers how to be friends with members of the other sex (Whaley & Rubenstein, 1994; Yingling, 1994).

Early childhood friendship studies clearly establish the centrality of communication in the emergence of cross-sex friendships. *Emergence* means the first communicative manifestation of what relationship scholars would label as friendship. It also refers to the first cognitive realization on the part of preschoolers that they are in a different relationship from the kind they have with their parents. Toddlers and preschoolers initially learn what friendship means through the verbal and nonverbal communication that occurs during coordinated play (Gottman, 1986; Whaley & Rubenstein, 1994; Yingling, 1994). Young children create friendships in a sophisticated fashion through communication, while at the same time internalizing what it means to be a friend (Corsaro, 1985). Communication in early childhood takes both verbal and nonverbal forms, molding and reflecting the child's conceptualization of friendship. Young cross-sex friends engage in gossip, usually in the form of "we against others," fantasy talk, and self-disclosure (Gottman, 1986). The function of gossip changes as the life cycle progresses, but in early childhood its main function is to build solidarity (Gottman, 1986). In Gottman's (1986) research, 4-year-old cross-sex friends engaged in more self-disclosure than either 8-year-old cross-sex friends or 4-year-old same-sex friends.

In closing this section, I want to identify a seldom acknowledged developmental milestone that occurs in early childhood, because of its relevance to initial perception of cross-sex interaction and potential friendship. There has been no attempt to study systematically the first occasion for extended cross-sex interaction between infants or toddlers—that is, what happens the first time a preschooler has an opportunity to interact with a nonfamilial member of the opposite sex. Nor has there been any attempt to study the first cross-sex friendship that an individual makes during the preschool years. From a social constructivist and relational perspective, the first cross-sex interactions and/or friendships that individuals experience could have significant impacts on how they initially perceive peer members of the opposite sex and on the relational schemata they subsequently develop. As defined by Planalp (1985), relational schemata are "coherent frameworks of relational knowledge which are used to derive relational implications of messages and are modified in accord with ongoing experiences with relationships" (p. 9). When individuals first interact with members of the opposite sex, they begin to develop a cross-sex friendship schema, a schema that directs communication with cross-sex friends but is also modified by that communication. The developing cross-sex friendship schema helps to guide future interaction and provides a framework for understanding communication and other events that occur within that relationship and other cross-sex friendships.

Middle and Late Childhood (Ages 7 to 11)

> Gender is the most potent psychological determinant of friendship choice in middle childhood. . . . whatever the origins, it is clear that as a result of the tendency for children to select same-sex friends boys and girls operate in very different reference groups throughout middle childhood. (Gottman, 1986, p. 140)

As the above quotation makes clear, same-sex playmate preferences exhibited by preschoolers continue through middle childhood and may be even more pronounced than they were in early childhood. There is ample evidence that cross-sex friendships at any level of closeness are rare in middle and late childhood (Gottman, 1986; Hallinan, 1977; Kupersmidt, DeRosier, & Patterson, 1995; Rawlins, 1992; Rubin, 1980). In a door-to-door survey of parents, Rickleman (1981) found that best cross-sex friendships were nonexistent among their 7- and 8-year-olds. Additional research has shown that there is a steady and statistically significant increase in selection of same-sex playmates from kindergarten to the fourth grade (Gottmann & Benson, reported in Gottman, 1986). Rickleman (1981) was able to find only five older pairs of cross-sex friends, and those five had "gone underground," meaning that the friends played with each other at home but ignored one another at school.

The relative rarity of cross-sex friendships during the elementary school years is accompanied by an equal scarcity of cross-sex friendship studies. The studies that have been conducted have shown that there are more adventure and domestic fantasy themes in the conversations of middle-aged cross-sex friends than in the conversations of preschoolers (Gottman, 1986), and that these friendships emphasize similarity (Rizzo, 1989). The importance of similarity in social skills to interpersonal attraction between elementary school children has received very little attention (but see Burleson, 1994; Kupersmidt et al., 1995). Gottman has also discovered that middle-aged cross-sex friends engage in more conflict than either younger cross-sex friends or younger and older same-sex friends. Gottman (1986) observes, "One of the purposes of older cross-sex friendships may be to make it possible for children both to fantasize and to fight at high levels" (p. 188).

Boys and girls who associate with members of the opposite sex run the risk of being teased by their same-sex friends (Rubin, 1980; Thorne, 1987), forcing those friendships underground (Gottman, 1986). When public interaction does take place, it is often strained and interferes with friendship development (Schofield & Sagar, 1977). In middle childhood, individuals are very concerned with peer group acceptance, and cross-sex friends engage in a considerable amount of gossip trying to decide what the norms are for such acceptance (Gottman, 1986). Whereas coordination of play is the goal in early childhood, not being rejected by same-sex peer groups is the goal in middle childhood. Few children are willing to risk fraternizing with opposite-sex others because it jeopardizes peer group acceptance (Rawlins, 1992; Rubin, 1980). Also, fraternizing with members of the opposite sex is not easy. Some researchers have documented hostility between boys and girls at this stage of the life cycle (e.g., Howe, 1993). On the other hand, heterosexual boys and girls in late childhood find themselves romantically attracted to members of the opposite sex (Rawlins, 1992). In fact, most of the empirical and scholarly interest in cross-sex relationships during the elementary school years focuses on how that interaction might be a precursor to adolescence and later romantic stirrings.

Another barrier to the development of cross-sex friendships in middle and late childhood, in addition to the fear of being ostracized, is the well-documented preference of boys and girls to interact in groups and dyads, respectively (for a review of those preferences, see Belle, 1989). It is difficult for a girl to gain admittance into a group of boys for the purpose of establishing a friendship with one of its members. Not only will the group probably not accept her as a member (Rubin, 1980), but she might find it hard to interact outside of the dyadic context (Belle, 1989). In a similar fashion, because boys are more accustomed to group interaction, they may find dyadic interaction for the purposes of forming a friendship particularly demanding.

Sullivan's (1953) model of personality development is relevant to this review because it ignores cross-sex friendship potential in middle and late childhood and because Sullivan's concept of "chums" is frequently referenced by friendship researchers (e.g., Buhrmester & Furman, 1986). According to Sullivan's theory, preadolescence is the period in which a child has begun to reach his or her full potential to have and be a friend. Because at this age the child is looking to form a friendship with someone very similar to him- or herself, an isophilic choice, the friend the child seeks is a same-sex other, that is, a chum. One's chum must be a member of one's own sex. Chums provide consensual validation and meet mutual needs for interpersonal intimacy, frequently manifested as extensive and deep self-disclosure (Sullivan, 1953).

Sullivan does not allow for the possibility that a chum could be a member of the opposite sex. The exclusion of opposite-sex others limits the explanatory utility of Sullivan's theory, but opens up avenues for research activity and questions. For example, can cross-sex friends be chums? If preadolescent children are looking for similar others to form chumships, what precludes a member of the opposite sex from being perceived as a similar other? Whaley and Rubenstein (1994) have established that toddlers in cross-sex friendships create similarity. If children engage in cross-sex interaction in early childhood, when it comes time to establish chumships they might have a basis for determining similarity other than gender-specific physical traits (Rubin, 1980). The potential to establish friendships with members of the opposite sex is important because it widens the pool of possible friends. One study found that 10% of children in grades 3 through 6 report feelings of loneliness and not having anyone to play with (Asher, Hymel, & Renshaw, 1984), and loneliness for children of this age can have serious psychological consequences (Page, Scanlan, & Deringer, 1994).

The typical cross-sex friendship in middle and late childhood is significantly different from the typical cross-sex friendship in early childhood. An interesting developmental milestone occurs during the elementary school years. To a greater extent than in the preschool years, boys and girls notice they are different. In a dialectical manner, boys and girls are simultaneously drawn to and repelled by members of the opposite sex. The deliberate avoidance of opposite-sex others in the early elementary school years is contradicted by a growing inclination to be attracted to opposite-sex others for romantic reasons (Rawlins, 1992; Rubin, 1980). Children in elementary school begin to form sex-segregated groups, with peer acceptance into these groups being of primary importance. Individuals who form cross-sex friendships run the risk of being teased, ostracized, and excluded from these groups.

It is difficult for boys and girls to form friendships with one another during the elementary school years, but once such friendships are established they are often quite extraordinary (Gottman, 1986). Cross-sex friendships become even more complex and special if they can be traced back to early childhood. However, as Gottman (1986) notes, "We have no idea what functions such rare and special relationships serve" (p. 190). This observation is a succinct summary of what we currently know about specific cross-sex friendships that span middle to late childhood.

Communication plays a dominant role in cross-sex friendships in middle and late childhood. Cross-sex friendships during the elementary school years display less fantasy play and more gossip than do cross-sex friendships between preschoolers. Cross-sex friends engage in a considerable amount of gossip, but it serves a different function than it does for early childhood cross-sex friends. Based upon Gottman's (1986) work, it is reasonable to conclude that cross-sex friends might gossip about others who ridicule them for being friends. Girls and boys also engage in moderate amounts of intimate self-disclosures that involve revealing fears and making direct verbal expressions of affection (Gottman, 1986). Cross-sex friends also have definite ideas about how friends are supposed to be and are willing to correct one another's behavior verbally when it strays from expectations (Rizzo, 1989).

Adolescence (Ages 12 to 17)

> Cross-sex relationships during adolescence are inherently ambiguous. Societal expectations, personal values, degrees of emerging sexuality, peer group pressures, and coordinated or clashing assumptions and perceptions all combine in shaping the dynamics of given relationships. Whatever occasions the shift, romantic involvement apparently alters adolescents' cross-sex friendships. (Rawlins, 1992, p. 93)

Adolescence is a significant stage of the life cycle that occurs between childhood and adulthood and encompasses physical, emotional, intellectual, spiritual, and sexual maturation (Rice, 1978). Individuals in adolescence are no longer children, nor are they adults. Because of the multifaceted nature of the metamorphosis from childhood to adulthood, the choice of a chronological time frame in which adolescence occurs is arbitrary. Individuals mature in different areas at different rates, and though general patterns can be identified, there is considerable room for individual variation (Gottman & Mettetal, 1986; Rice, 1978).

Despite the fact that there are reportedly more studies of adolescent friendships than of friendships in any other life stage (Kon, 1981), studies examining adolescent cross-sex friendships are rare (Rawlins, 1992). Some empirical investigations have not even differentiated between same-sex and cross-sex friendships (e.g., Shulman, 1993), and other investigations have been restricted to same-sex friendships (e.g., Windle, 1995). The small number of studies reflects the reality that cross-sex friendships among adolescents are the exception rather than the rule, no doubt a continuation of the pattern of sex segregation established in earlier life stages (Karweit & Hansell, 1983; Kon, 1981; Rawlins, 1992; Rice, 1978; Schofield, 1981).

Adolescent boys and girl spend more time together than do children in early and middle childhood, but primarily they interact for dating purposes. Furthermore, some adolescents practically apologize when admitting that a particular cross-sex partner is "just a friend" (Rawlins, 1992). The reluctance of some adolescents, particularly males, to admit having platonic cross-sex friends is surprising given the finding that male high school juniors report their best female friends give them more emotional support than their parents or best male friends (Wright & Keple, 1981). Furthermore, other studies show that cross-sex friends engage in communication on a wider range of intimate topics than do dating partners (e.g., Werebe, 1987).

The most salient aspect of adolescence as it pertains to cross-sex relationships is sexual maturation, or puberty. The onset of puberty signals a turning point in the way girls and boys view one another (Rawlins, 1982). Intimacy needs before puberty are generally met by parents and same-sex others, but during puberty cross-sex relationships take the place of same-sex ones for fulfillment of intimacy needs (Berndt, 1982). Individuals begin to view members of the opposite sex as sexual beings, and there is considerable peer pressure, especially among boys, to try to convert cross-sex relationships into romantic or sexual encounters. As observed by Rawlins (1992), "Cultural expectations of 'real men' and concerns about peer status may persuade boys to enact sex-typed scenarios with cross-sex friends who are quite happy with the status quo" (p. 92). For example, high school girls reported in one study that their male friends would try to change the relationship into a dating arrangement, which would often hurt the friendship (Rawlins, 1989).

Despite biological changes and social norms encouraging heterosexual adolescents to view one another as potential dating partners, boys and girls in adolescence do manage to initiate and maintain cross-sex friendships (Buhrmester & Furman, 1986; Kon & Losenkov, 1978). These friendships can be differentiated from romantic relationships through self-reported communication behavior. Adolescents report that becoming a boyfriend or girlfriend restrains communication in ways that platonic cross-sex relationships do not, with cross-sex friendships providing greater freedom to be oneself than most dating relationships (Rawlins, 1992).

Communication between adolescent cross-sex friends involves considerable self-disclosure and gossip, both employed in the service of self-exploration and defining the relationship (Gottman & Mettetal, 1986). Some of these self-disclosures probably involve telling one another what it is like to be a guy or a girl. These insider perspectives are particularly valuable because they help individuals to establish gender identity and to recognize similarities and differences between themselves and their cross-sex friends. The primary goal of conversations with peers during adolescence is to understand the self in relation to others, and the major function of friendship is to aid in that self-exploration (Gottman & Mettetal, 1986). Gossip and self-disclosure in adolescent friendships concentrate on relationship problems, with intimacy development secondary to self-understanding.

In the typical adolescent cross-sex friendship, both individuals are searching for self-identity and are using one another as cross-sex guides in their exploration of self. Cross-sex friendships of heterosexual adolescents are complicated by emerging sexual and social needs for a romantic dimension to opposite-sex encounters, though cross-sex friendships in which one or both participants are not heterosexual are equally complex. For example, Zera (1992) contends that some gay and lesbian adolescents date members of the opposite sex to keep up the appearance of being heterosexual. This means that these relationships are essentially cross-sex friendships, even though the heterosexual partner may not know the sexual orientation of his or her partner. Because adolescents are just beginning to understand the intricacies of cross-sex intimacy, individuals in heterosexual cross-sex relationships cannot always determine if the feelings they have for each other are romantic or friendly (Rawlins, 1992). Although this feeling of ambiguity continues into young adulthood (O'Meara, 1989), it is usually more pronounced in adolescence. It is reasonable to conjecture that part of the conversations of cross-sex friends would involve self-disclosures about the feelings they have for one another. These self-disclosures would help participants better understand themselves and their cross-sex relationships. In a similar fashion, positive gossip between cross-sex friends about the cross-sex friendships of others might validate their own relationship.

A major distinction between adolescent cross-sex friendships and those that occur earlier in life is the degree to which gender differences appear in these relationships. For example, boys tend to seek emotional gratification in their cross-sex friendships, more so than in their same-sex ones. However, this pattern does not hold true for young girls, who are equally adept at obtaining emotional gratification in both kinds of relationships (Rawlins, 1992). Another gender difference is that boys are under greater peer pressure than girls to convert cross-sex friendships into romantic relationships (Bell, 1981; Rawlins, 1992).

The central developmental milestone occurring during adolescence is puberty. The impact of puberty on cross-sex friendships is determined in large part by the individuals' sexual orientations. If an individual is beginning to view him- or herself as gay or lesbian, that view will influence his or her perspective on members of the opposite sex. Once a cross-sex friend discovers that his or her friend is not heterosexual, communication with that friend may have different characteristics. Whether there are important differences between heterosexual adolescent cross-sex friendships and those in which one or both partners are not heterosexual is open to empirical investigation.

Young and Middle Adulthood (Ages 18 to 64)

Can men and women really be just friends? That is the tricky and timeless question the movie, *When Harry Met Sally,* has posed once again. Part of the reason this issue never seems to be put to rest is that while the idea of man and woman as lovers may be fertile ground for sociologist, songwriter, and poet, it is undeniably familiar turf. However, the concept of man and woman as friends, pals, buddies, and chums is still uncharted territory. It might well be the final frontier in human relationships—the one realm of social experience where few people of either sex have gone before. (Cassel, 1989, p. 19)

Cross-sex friendships in young and middle adulthood have received considerably more empirical and conceptual attention than those in other stages of the life cycle, undoubtedly because young adults in college are readily available as research participants. Studies covering young and middle adulthood have been placed in this section for practical purposes. There has been only one study pertaining solely to cross-sex friendships among middle-aged adults (Booth & Hess, 1974), and two in which the samples span both life stages (Rubin, 1985; Sapadin, 1988). In this section I divide adult cross-sex friendship investigations into three categories. First, there are conceptual and empirical pieces detailing the struggles some adults endure in defining the nature of their cross-sex friendships. Second, there are studies that compare cross-sex friendships with same-sex friendships. Finally, there are studies that explore the existence and dynamics of cross-sex friendships in the workplace.

Although Cassel overstates the scarcity of cross-sex friendships in the quotation above, she makes an interesting reference to the film *When Harry Met Sally*. The movie is a romantic comedy about a young couple struggling to answer the question, Can a man and woman be friends, or will romantic and sexual urges always get in the way? The movie reinforces the notion that male-female friendships are simply precursors to romantic relationships, and is a classic illustration of the enigma concerning whether mass media are shapers of societal views, reflections of those views, or some combination of the two.

Researchers have devoted attention to the question of whether a man and a woman can be friends without becoming romantic partners. Their work has explored the societal, dyadic, and individual pressures to convert cross-sex friendships into romantic encounters, pressures manifested as "challenges" that cross-sex friends must overcome. Rawlins, the first communication scholar to take serious interest in cross-sex friendships, introduced the challenges line of research in his landmark 1982 study. He conceptualizes cross-sex friendship as a "rhetorical challenge," contending that cross-sex friendships are characterized by rhetorical issues that must be negotiated in the friendship. In part, a woman and a man must communicatively establish a shared definition of their relationship in which romance is avoided, overt sexuality is de-emphasized, equality is fostered, and personal freedom is permitted.

O'Meara (1989) restructures the communicative challenges enumerated by Rawlins into four obstacles, or challenges, that cross-sex friends face: Women and men in cross-sex friendships must (a) determine the kind of emotions they feel for one another, (b) confront the issue of sexuality, (c) present the correct picture of the relationship to relevant audiences, and (d) grapple with questions of equality in a society where men frequently have more power in cross-sex relationships. The challenges identified by O'Meara, though intriguing, have received marginal support. My associates and I have employed self-report data in the form of surveys and diaries and have concluded that these challenges are not salient to most participants in cross-sex friendships, though for some individuals they are of central importance (Monsour, Beard, Harris, & Kurzweil, 1994).

Of the four challenges identified by O'Meara, the sexual challenge faced by some cross-sex friends has received the most research attention. Some writers argue that society conditions males and females to view one another as potential sexual partners rather than as potential friends (e.g., Chafetz, 1974; Monsour, 1988; Pankin, 1973). This assumed conditioning has led investigators to argue that sexual dynamics underlie all cross-sex relationships (e.g., Buhrmester & Furman, 1986). However, research indicates that this conditioning presents a sexual challenge in only a small percentage of young adult friendships (Monsour et al., 1994). The challenge is typically manifested as a subjective impression of sexual tension in the relationship.

Although the issue of sexuality may not present a significant problem in most cross-sex friendships, it is still a salient component of many male-female friendships. Interviews with cross-sex friends reveal that some participants enjoy the sexual tension, believing that it adds zest to the friendship, whereas others are concerned that sexual overtones threaten the integrity of the friendship (Bell, 1981; Rubin, 1985; Sapadin, 1988). There is also evidence of gender differences in perception of the sexual dimension of cross-sex friendships. Women are generally less motivated by sexual attraction to formulate cross-sex friendships than are men (Rose, 1985), men are more likely than women to define intimacy in cross-sex friendships as involving sexual contact (Monsour, 1992), and women are less inclined than men to attribute friendly behavior as a sign of sexual interest (Abbey, 1982; Shotland & Craig, 1988). Finally, some men may approach cross-sex friendships with a hidden "sexual agenda," giving these friendships a "Trojan horse" quality (Rawlins, 1982).

The majority of empirical inquiries into cross-sex friendships have compared those relationships with same-sex friendships (Werking, 1994). Researchers pick a construct of interest, usually intimacy, and then compare that construct in both types of friendships (e.g., Gaines, 1994). Comparing intimacy or closeness in cross-sex and same-sex friendships is a common strategy, sometimes leading to the neglect of other equally important relational phenomena in cross-sex friendships (Werking, 1994).

There is conflicting evidence concerning the comparative intimacy of same-sex and cross-sex friendships. Some studies have found that males and females are closer to their same-sex friends than they are to their cross-sex ones (Bell, 1981; Griffin & Sparks, 1990). Other investigations have revealed that women are closer to their same-sex friends than they are to their cross-sex ones, but with men the pattern is reversed (e.g., Rose, 1985; Rubin, 1985). Hacker (1981) found that men confide almost as much to their male friends as they do to their female friends, but women confide more in their same-sex friendships than in their cross-sex ones. In my own research, I discovered through self-reports that women self-disclose more frequently to same-sex friends than to cross-sex ones, but men disclose equally in both types of friendships (Monsour, 1988). However, when videotaped conversations between cross-sex friends were analyzed, men were found to be considerably less emotionally expressive in their same-sex friendships than in their cross-sex ones. On the other hand, women were more expressive and disclosed more in their same-sex friendships than in their cross-sex ones (Monsour, 1988).

It is difficult to reconcile conflicting findings concerning comparative intimacy in cross-sex and same-sex friendships. One explanation is that men and women have different ideas concerning intimacy and closeness in relationships, with women emphasizing self-disclosure and men placing more importance on shared activities (Caldwell & Peplau, 1982; Nardi, 1992). This position is supported by Rubin's (1985) finding, cited above, that two-thirds of the women who were identified by male friends as close friends disagreed with the men's definitions of their relationships, suggesting that men and women may have different ideas about what makes a relationship close. However, men and women defined intimacy similarly in my research on the meaning of intimacy in cross-sex friendships (Monsour, 1992). In a more recent investigation, I found that women were just as likely as men to view their friendships as more intimate than they were viewed by their friends (Monsour, 1995).

Within-gender differences in the ways males and females view intimacy are another reason researchers arrive at different conclusions concerning intimacy in cross-sex and same-sex friendships. For example, Bell (1981) divided his sample of men and women on the basis of *conventionality* versus *nonconventionality*. Nonconventional women had a more positive attitude toward their cross-sex friends than did conventional women, and nonconventional men reported more positive experiences and attitudes toward their cross-sex friends than did conventional men. In my own research, some men identified physical contact as a component of cross-sex friendship intimacy, some did not (Monsour, 1992). In like fashion, some women defined intimacy as involving flirting behavior and others did not. Hacker (1981) found that some women are hesitant to reveal strengths in cross-sex friendships, whereas others reveal them willingly. Some of Rubin's (1985) female respondents reported feeling as close to their male friends as to their female friends because those males were different from most men. As one woman put it, "His feminine side is the most highly developed of any man I've ever known" (p. 159). This statement suggests that sex role orientation has a pronounced effect on cross-sex interactions. In a different study, males who were categorized as feminine according to Bem's Sex-Role Inventory (Bem, 1974) reported higher levels of emotional expressiveness and self-disclosure in their cross-sex friendships than males who were categorized as masculine, and had three times as many cross-sex friendships (Monsour, 1988).

Werking (1994) posits the emergence of a "cross-sex friendship deficit model" in her critique of studies comparing same-sex friendships to cross-sex ones. She argues that her cross-sex friendship deficit model is a variation of the "male deficit model." In the male deficit model, men and their friendships are relegated to second-class status in the area of intimacy because they do not disclose as frequently as women (Tavris, 1992; Wood, 1994). Some researchers have implicitly embraced a cross-sex friendship deficit model by arguing that cross-sex friendships are less emotionally fulfilling for women than for men (e.g., Rose, 1985; Rubin, 1985). Although I agree with Werking's assessment as it applies to adult cross-sex friendship research, there is little evidence that researchers examining cross-sex friendships in other life stages have adopted a cross-sex friendship deficit model.

Only a few studies have examined cross-sex friendships in the workplace. Most work in the area of male-female organizational friendships has involved theoretical speculations about those relationships (e.g., Fine, 1986; O'Meara, 1994; Safilios-Rothschild, 1981). O'Meara (1994) gives a fairly detailed analysis of how the workplace offers an opportunity structure for cross-sex friendships to flourish (also see Booth & Hess, 1974). Fine (1986) contends that the workplace is an especially fertile area for cross-sex friendships to develop because of forced proximity of workers. Forced proximity can lead to problems because sexual attraction between coworkers is inevitable (Eyler & Baridon, 1992), but as organizational romances are generally frowned upon (Collins, 1983), there is incentive for women and men to restrict their social relationships to the friendship arena. As Fine (1986) so colorfully puts it, "If the company is a family, an organizational romance is incest" (p. 197).

Sapadin (1988) studied the same-sex and cross-sex friendships of 156 professional women and men in a variety of organizations in a rare empirical investigation of organizational cross-sex friendships. Professional women rated their same-sex friendships higher than their cross-sex ones in overall quality, intimacy, nurturance, and enjoyment, whereas professional men rated their cross-sex friends higher in all areas except intimacy. A unique benefit of cross-sex friendship, reported by both women and men, is that it provides an insider's perspective on how members of the opposite sex think, feel, and behave.

The effect of structural opportunities on the formation of cross-sex friendships has clear applications in organizational communication. Commonly researched areas of organizational communication, such as superior-subordinate communication, have obvious links to the existence of cross-sex friendships in the workplace. For example, what happens to the relational dynamics of superior-subordinate communication when the superior and subordinate are also cross-sex friends, and are those dynamics different from what they would be if the two individuals involved were same-sex friends?

A typical cross-sex friendship in young adulthood is less conspicuous than cross-sex friendships occurring in other stages of the life cycle, primarily because such friendships are considerably more common in young adulthood. Most cross-sex friendship researchers draw from college populations for their samples, and students have greater opportunities than individuals in other life stages to form male-female friendships because of forced proximity. There is little information available concerning the frequency of cross-sex friendships among young adults who have fewer opportunities for cross-sex interaction because they are not attending college. However, Booth and Hess (1974) found that middle-aged blue-collar workers have fewer cross-sex friendships than do their white-collar counterparts, a situation that might also be true of younger blue-collar workers.

Depending upon what study is examined, approximately 30% to 90% of young and middle-aged adults have cross-sex friendships (Bell, 1981; Monsour, 1988; Wright, 1989). Many of these individuals see cross-sex friendships as significant additions to their world of relationships (Rubin, 1985). To the question posed at the beginning of this section—Can women and men be friends without sexual and romantic undertones getting in the way?—I respond with a resounding yes (Monsour et al., 1994). Though unmarried men and women sometimes have difficulty negotiating the relational definition of their friendships, as a general rule they do not. However, men often place more emphasis on the sexual undertones in cross-sex friendships than do women, but generally not to the point of causing significant interpersonal problems. In fact, women and men in cross-sex friendships value those friendships because they provide insider perspectives and opposite-sex companionship without the pressures that normally accompany romantic relationships (Swain, 1992).

Communication in adult cross-sex friendships has been the focus of some research attention, usually in studies on self-disclosure (e.g., Hacker, 1981; Monsour, 1988) and other manifestations of intimacy (e.g., Bell, 1981; Griffin & Sparks, 1990; Monsour, 1988; Rose, 1985; Rubin, 1985). Intimate communication in cross-sex friendships is an important topic to explore, but researchers have overemphasized it and neglected other equally important communication phenomena, such as deception, conflict management, and compliance gaining (Werking, 1994). Other topics need to be investigated if we are to gain a comprehensive view of the interactional dynamics in cross-sex friendships. Communication is also the means through which cross-sex friends negotiate the definition of their relationships (Rawlins, 1982, 1992). Unfortunately, other than the ongoing research program of Bill Rawlins, communication strategies and techniques used to define cross-sex friendship have been understudied.

The most important developmental milestone occurring in young and middle adulthood is whether an individual gets married or remains single.

Studies show that married individuals have fewer cross-sex friendships than do single individuals (Booth & Hess, 1974; Monsour, 1988). There is a strong taboo against the initiation of cross-sex friendships by married individuals (Bell, 1981), though married men are apparently given greater freedom by society to pursue cross-sex friendships than are their female counterparts (Rawlins, 1992). It is generally believed that once an individual gets married he or she should no longer need to have friendships with members of the opposite sex (Leefeldt & Callenbach, 1979). Married individuals do have cross-sex friendships, but usually within the safe confines of marriage, and these involve only superficial interactions between the cross-sex friends (Bell, 1981; Booth & Hess, 1974; Rawlins, 1982).

Old Age (Age 65 to Death)

> In yet another approach to conceptions of friendship, Adams (1985) explored older women's views of cross-sex friendships. Only about 4% of the friendships described by respondents were with men, and only 17% of the women had any male friends. When asked why they did not have any or more male friends, the women expressed the belief that cross-sex friendships were preludes to romance, and they cited strong norms against courtship among older adults. (Blieszner & Adams, 1992, p. 80)

The choice of age 65 as the beginning of the final stage of the life cycle is somewhat arbitrary. As Rogers (1982) notes, 65 is often chosen as the starting point of old age for practical reasons, because it is the normal age of retirement and when social security payments begin. Some experts differentiate the young-old, ages 65 to 75 or 80, from the old-old, who are above 80 years of age and whose physical decline is more obvious (Rogers, 1982).

The final stage of the life cycle has received even less research attention from cross-sex friendship researchers than have other parts of the life cycle. Some studies that might be included in the cross-sex friendship literature are problematic because the researchers did not ask respondents to indicate whether they were reporting on same-sex friendships or cross-sex friendships (e.g., Gupta & Korte, 1994; O'Connor, 1995). There are several explanations for the neglect of cross-sex friendships in this age group as an area of study. One reason is that cross-sex friendships among the elderly are rather rare. The inclination to associate primarily with members of one's own sex stretches into the twilight years of an individual's life. Like their younger counterparts, elderly men and women typically select members of their own sex to spend time with, though this pattern is more pronounced for women than it is for men (Nussbaum, Thompson, & Robinson, 1989).

The rarity of cross-sex friendships in old age is partly due to normal developmental changes. Friendships in general are unavoidably affected by the developmental changes that accompany old age (Nussbaum et al., 1989).

Physical illnesses such as rheumatism, bronchitis, and circulatory problems limit mobility, lessening the opportunity for the initiation of new friendships and the continuation of old ones (Blieszner & Adams, 1992; Chown, 1981). O'Connor (1993) notes that structural factors such as living in the same place or having previously been neighbors are important to same-age elderly cross-sex friends, and that those who are housebound are more likely to have cross-sex friendships. Another developmental factor that has a direct impact on the frequency of cross-sex friendships is that women live about 7 years longer than men (Rogers, 1982). Because they have a larger pool to choose from, older men usually have more cross-sex friends than do older women (Nussbaum et al., 1989). Another reason for the paucity of investigations into cross-sex friendship among the elderly is the relative difficulty involved in getting research participants. Individuals in other stages of the life cycle can be found in large numbers at schools or in workplaces. Outside of nursing homes, however, there are few centralized places where large numbers of old people congregate.

Lack of structural opportunities and the developmental changes that accompany old age are not the only inhibitors of cross-sex friendship formation among older individuals; there are also dispositional factors at work. Adams (1985) discovered that the vast majority of elderly women prefer same-sex friends to cross-sex ones because they believe cross-sex friendships are the first step toward romantic encounters, which are considered taboo among older individuals. Additional research has shown that societal norms more heavily discourage older women than older men from forming cross-sex friendships (Usui, 1984).

Compared with other stages of the life cycle, cross-sex friendships in the final stage of the life cycle are more likely to be intergenerational. In a qualitative investigation of the frail elderly, O'Connor (1993) discovered that one-third of the cross-sex friends named by her 22 respondents (19 females, 3 males) were young adults, and those friendships were more likely for individuals who were housebound. Intergenerational cross-sex friendships present interesting theoretical issues. From a traditional social exchange perspective, older individuals may avoid intergenerational friendships with young people because such friendships are perceived as one-sided, with the younger friend doing most of the giving and the older friend most of the taking (O'Connor, 1993). This situation may make an individual feel overly rewarded, which is an uncomfortable arrangement from a social exchange perspective. Similarly, young people may feel as if the costs of such relationships are too great (Chown, 1981). The motive to have equity in relationships is partly due to older persons' desires to be independent and needed in some way (Nussbaum et al., 1989). Although some intergenerational cross-sex friendships are based on social exchange principles, same-age cross-sex friendships among the elderly are more communal in nature. One study found that a communal orientation in peer elderly cross-sex friendships is more directly related to increased friendship satisfaction than is an exchange orientation (Jones & Vaughan, 1990).

The typical cross-sex friendship of an older person is characterized by many of the same qualities that define cross-sex friendships in earlier life stages. These friendships are sometimes challenged by sexual and romantic undertones (Adams, 1985) and are subject to the same public scrutiny that face male-female friendships in other life stages. The main differences between cross-sex friendships of older individuals and those that occur among younger individuals are that elderly cross-sex friendships are more likely to be intergenerational in nature and are more severely curtailed by opportunity structures that are often related to the limited mobility of the elderly.

Although communication between elderly friends has received some research attention (Nussbaum et al., 1989), cross-sex friendship communication has been relatively ignored. There are many fascinating areas awaiting exploration. For example, research has shown that reminiscing with friends among the elderly is a common communication behavior that provides important benefits, such as enabling an individual to cope with the fear of death (McMahon & Rhudick, 1964; Nussbaum et al., 1989) and helping the individual to defend his or her self-esteem and beliefs (Priefer & Gambert, 1984). The act of reminiscence is a fertile area for cross-sex friendship and communication researchers. For instance, cross-sex friends whose spouses have died may spend considerable time recalling what their marital relationships were like and trying to reconcile unresolved problems. An insider's perspective provided by a cross-sex friend could be valuable for helping an individual to understand the perspective of his or her departed spouse.

The central developmental milestone for the elderly has already been discussed in some detail. Individuals are beset by the indignities of old age as they enter the final stage of the life cycle. They become increasingly less mobile, and with that loss of mobility the opportunity to pursue friendships, cross-sex and otherwise, declines. Like any friendship, cross-sex friendship has the potential of making the ravages of old age more tolerable.

CONCLUSIONS

This is a propitious time for communication scholars to expand their participation and instigate pioneering work in the continuing exploration of cross-sex friendships. The number of cross-sex friendships is bound to increase as more women enter the workplace and traditional attitudes about cross-sex relationships begin to fade (Monsour, 1988). Changing attitudes about appropriate cross-sex relationships will have impacts not only on the potential friendships of adults, but also on the children and parents of those adults. In concluding this chapter, I present five summarizing observations concerning the study of cross-sex friendships and the potential role of com-

munication scholars in the investigation of these relationships. These observations focus on (a) the lack of theory in cross-sex friendship investigations,
(b) the adoption of a "heterosexist" worldview concerning cross-sex friendships (Rawlins, 1994), (c) the need for a typology of cross-sex friendships,
(d) a summary of what we do not know about cross-sex friendships, and
finally (e) a summary of common themes that run through the findings of
cross-sex friendship studies spanning stages of the life cycle.

Most of the research on cross-sex friendships throughout the life cycle has
been narrowly focused and bereft of theory. With few exceptions, cross-sex
friendship researchers have conducted their investigations without the benefit
of a theoretical framework to guide their explorations (but see Gaines, 1994;
McWilliams & Howard, 1993; Monsour et al., 1993). Well-articulated theories suggest important research questions and are linked to the methodological designs employed in the study of relational phenomena (Poole & McPhee,
1985).

Communication scholars can make valuable theoretical contributions to the
understanding of cross-sex friendships by applying existing communication
theories to these relationships. A comprehensive detailing and application of
these theories would entail another chapter. However, it is easy to speculate
how speech accommodation theory (Giles, Mulac, Bradac, & Johnson, 1987)
and uncertainty reduction theory (Berger & Calabrese, 1975) can be applied
to cross-sex friendships. For example, one could argue from a speech accommodation theory framework that women and men in cross-sex friendships
attempt to accommodate the friendship expectations and communicative
styles of their partners in order to gain social approval. Uncertainty reduction
theory could explain how cross-sex friends in every stage of the life cycle go
about reducing their levels of uncertainty about one another concerning
relational intentions. Neither of these theories has been applied to cross-sex
friendships.

Communication researchers can also contribute insights to a much ignored
variety of cross-sex friendship: that in which one or both partners are not
heterosexual (but see Rubin, 1985). Most cross-sex friendship researchers
adopt what Rawlins (1994) astutely refers to as a heterosexist worldview. This
is illustrated by their tendency to focus on sexual and romantic dimensions
of cross-sex friendships in nearly every stage of the life cycle and to forget
that heterosexuality is not universal. The neglect of cross-sex friendships in
which one or both partners are not heterosexual is unfortunate, especially
considering that such friendships exist. Though no one really knows how
common these friendships are (Rubin, 1985), one study reported that two-
thirds of the gay men interviewed said they had a close female friend (Bell &
Weinberg, 1978). Half the gay men and one-fifth of the lesbians in Rubin's
(1985) research reported having a cross-sex friend. Communication researchers can help chart this unexplored territory and answer many important
questions. For example, what impact does the initial disclosure of one friend's

nonheterosexual orientation have on a cross-sex friendship? How do gay and lesbian adolescents explore their identities through communication with their cross-sex friends? Do gay men and lesbians who form cross-sex friendships with one another communicate in different ways from heterosexual cross-sex friends?

A serious limitation of the existing cross-sex friendship literature is the lack of a clear delineation of the different types of cross-sex friendship (Rawlins, 1982, 1994). The development of a typology of cross-sex friendships is needed if we are to understand fully the intricacies of these relationships as they are manifested throughout the life cycle. Close inspection and study of communication occurring in various types of cross-sex friendships is perhaps the best way to differentiate these relationships from one another, and thus increase our understanding of them all. A communication-based typology would need to identify distinguishing communication patterns from one life stage to the next, but also within life stages. For example, adolescent cross-sex friends might communicate in different ways and for different reasons compared with elderly cross-sex friends, and yet there are probably differences within varieties of adolescent and elderly cross-sex friendships.

Though great progress has been made in our understanding of cross-sex friendships, there are still many important things about those friendships we do not know. We know nothing about the first cross-sex friendship an individual forms as a toddler or young child and how that initial friendly contact with a member of the opposite sex affects subsequent interaction and friendship formation. The first cross-sex friendship may occur for some in early childhood; for others it may occur, if at all, in later life stages. The question of whether cross-sex friends can be chums has not been addressed. We also know very little about cross-sex friendships in which one or both partners are not heterosexual, nor do we have even the beginnings of a typology of cross-sex friendships. There is also a noticeable lack of knowledge concerning how long-term cross-sex friendships change as the involved participants go from one life stage to the next, with the accompanying developmental milestones.

Many communication topics have not been explored as they relate to cross-sex friendships. For example, we know nothing about deception and equivocation in cross-sex friendships, little about how similarity in communication styles might facilitate the formation of such friendships, little about how mass media portrayals of cross-sex friendships affect these relationships, and almost nothing about the role of reminiscing in old age among cross-sex friends. Finally, although gossip between adolescent cross-sex friends has received some research attention, it has been ignored as a cross-sex friendship research topic in other stages of the life cycle.

Though cross-sex friendships in each stage of the life cycle display characteristics that are unique to that stage, this review of the literature has revealed that there are also noticeable similarities among all or most of the stages of the life cycle. First, in every stage of the life cycle the opportunity to form cross-sex friendships is the major factor in whether such friendships will be initiated or maintained (O'Meara, 1994). Opportunity factors include such things as parents and day-care providers separating toddlers and young children based on sex, the increased opportunities for cross-sex interaction that the workplace and college provide, the decreased opportunities that married individuals, particularly women, have for cross-sex friendships, and the fact that elderly individuals have fewer opportunities to initiate and maintain cross-sex friendships because of decreased mobility. Without the opportunity for cross-sex interaction, cross-sex friendships cannot be formed or maintained. A second theme permeating the cross-sex friendship literature is that in nearly every stage of the life cycle there are individual and societal expectations that cross-sex interaction is primarily for romantic or sexual purposes. These expectations begin before puberty and extend throughout the twilight years of an individual's life. A third theme is that in every stage of the life cycle, cross-sex friendships provide advantages that same-sex friendships cannot. The most important of these advantages, and the best documented, is the insider perspective that cross-sex friends give one another concerning how members of the opposite sex think, feel, and behave. A final theme is that communication is vital to the initiation, formation, negotiation, and maintenance of cross-sex friendships in every stage of the life cycle.

This chapter has been a call to arms and a plea for participation. Cross-sex friendships and communication have a protean quality that makes these relationships special at every juncture of the life cycle. Communication scholars need to join the interdisciplinary attempt to understand these important relationships more fully. Possibly more than any other social science discipline, the field of communication can offer unique contributions to the ongoing investigation of cross-sex friendships.

REFERENCES

Abbey, A. (1982). Sex differences in attributions for friendly behavior: Do males misperceive females' friendliness? *Journal of Personality and Social Psychology, 42,* 830-838.

Adams, R. G. (1985). People would talk: Normative barriers to cross-sex friendship for elderly women. *Gerontologist, 25,* 605-611.

Adams, R. G. (1987). Patterns of network change: A longitudinal study of friendships of elderly women. *Gerontologist, 27,* 222-227.

Adams, R. G. (1989). Conceptual and methodological issues in studying friendships of older adults. In R. G. Adams & R. Blieszner (Eds.), *Older adult friendships* (pp. 17-41). Newbury Park, CA: Sage.

Adler, T. F., & Furman, W. (1988). A model of children's relationships and relationship dysfunctions. In S. W. Duck (Ed.), *Handbook of personal relationships* (pp. 211-229). New York: John Wiley.

Alexander, G., & Hines, M. (1994). Gender labels and play styles: Their relative contributions to children's selection of playmates. *Child Development, 65,* 869-879.

Allan, G. (1989). *Friendship: Developing a sociological perspective.* Boulder, CO: Westview.

Allan, G., & Adams, R. G. (1989). Aging and the structure of friendship. In R. G. Adams & R. Blieszner (Eds.), *Older adult friendships* (pp. 45-64). Newbury Park, CA: Sage.

Asher, S. R., Hymel, S., & Renshaw, P. D. (1984). Loneliness in children. *Child Development, 55,* 1456-1464.

Aukett, R., Ritchie, J., & Mill, K. (1988). Gender differences in friendship patterns. *Sex Roles, 19,* 57-66.

Banikiotes, P. G., Neimeyer, G. J., & Lepkowsky, C. (1981). Gender and sex-role orientation effects on friendship choice. *Personality and Social Psychology Bulletin, 7,* 605-610.

Bell, A. P., & Weinberg, M. S. (1978). *Homosexualities: A study of diversities among men and women.* New York: Simon & Schuster.

Bell, R. R. (1981). Friendships of women and men. *Psychology of Women Quarterly, 5,* 402-417.

Belle, D. (1989). Gender differences in children's social networks and support. In D. Belle (Ed.), *Children's social networks and social supports* (pp. 173-188). New York: John Wiley.

Bem, S. L. (1974). The measurement of psychological androgyny. *Journal of Consulting and Clinical Psychology, 42,* 155-162.

Benenson, J. E. (1993). Greater preferences among females than males for dyadic interaction in early childhood. *Child Development, 64,* 544-555.

Berger, C. R., & Calabrese, R. J. (1975). Some explorations in initial interaction and beyond: Toward a developmental theory of interpersonal communication. *Human Communication Research, 1,* 99-112.

Berndt, T. J. (1982). The features and effects of friendship in early adolescence. *Child Development, 53,* 1447-1460.

Berscheid, E., & Peplau, L. A. (1983). The emerging science of relationships. In H. Kelley, E. Berscheid, A. Christensen, J. Harvey, T. Huston, G. Levinger, E. McClintock, L. Peplau, & D. Peterson (Eds.), *Close relationships* (pp. 1-19). New York: W. H. Freeman.

Bigelow, B. J. (1977). Children's friendship expectations: A cognitive developmental study. *Child Development, 48,* 246-253.

Blieszner, R., & Adams, R. G. (1992). *Adult friendship.* Newbury Park, CA: Sage.

Booth, A., & Hess, E. (1974). Cross-sex friendships. *Journal of Marriage and the Family, 36,* 38-47.

Buhrmester, D., & Furman, W. (1986). The changing functions of friends in childhood: A neo-Sullivanian perspective. In V. J. Derlega & B. A. Winstead (Eds.), *Friendship and social interaction* (pp. 41-62). New York: Springer-Verlag.

Burleson, B. R. (1994). Friendship and similarities in social-cognitive and communication abilities: Social skills bases of interpersonal attraction in childhood. *Personal Relationships, 1,* 371-389.

Caldwell, M. A., & Peplau, L. A. (1982). Sex differences in same-sex friendships. *Sex Roles, 8,* 721-732.

Cassel, C. (1989, October/November). The final frontier: Other-gender friendship. *SIECUS Report,* pp. 19-20.

Chafetz, J. S. (1974). *Masculine/feminine or human?* Itasca, IL: Peacock.

Chaffee, S. H., & Berger, C. R. (1987). What communication scientists do. In C. R. Berger & S. H. Chaffee (Eds.), *Handbook of communication science* (pp. 99-122). Newbury Park, CA: Sage.

Chown, S. M. (1981). Friendships in old age. In S. W. Duck & R. Gilmour (Eds.), *Personal relationships 2: Developing personal relationships* (pp. 231-246). New York: Academic Press.

Collins, N. W. (1983). *Professional women and their mentors.* Englewood Cliffs, NJ: Prentice Hall.

Corsaro, W. A. (1981). Friendship in the nursery school: Social organization in a peer environment. In S. R. Asher & J. M. Gottman (Eds.), *The development of children's friendships* (pp. 207-241). New York: Cambridge University Press.

Corsaro, W. (1985). *Friendship and peer culture in the early years.* Norwood, NJ: Ablex.

Davis, K. E., & Todd, M. J. (1982). Friendship and love relationships. In K. E. Davis & T. O. Mitchell (Eds.), *Advances in descriptive psychology* (Vol. 2, pp. 79-122). Greenwich, CT: JAI.

Davis, K. E., & Todd, M. J. (1985). Assessing friendship: Prototypes, paradigm cases, and relationship descriptions. In S. W. Duck & D. Perlman (Eds.), *Understanding personal relationships: An interdisciplinary approach* (pp. 17-38). London: Sage.

Denzin, N. (1978). *The research act: A theoretical introduction to sociological methods.* Chicago: Aldine.

Derlega, V. J., Durham, B., Gockel, M., & Sholis, D. (1981). Sex differences in self-disclosure: Effects of topic content, friendship, and partner's sex. *Sex Roles, 7,* 433-447.

Dickens, W. J., & Perlman, D. (1981). Friendships over the life-cycle. In S. W. Duck & R. Gilmour (Eds.), *Personal relationships 2: Developing personal relationships* (pp. 91-122). New York: Academic Press.

Duck, S. W. (1983). *Friends for life: The psychology of close relationships.* New York: St. Martin's.

Duck, S. W. (1989). Socially competent communication and relationship development. In B. H. Schneider, G. Attili, J. Nadel, & R. P. Weissberg (Eds.), *Social competence in developmental perspective* (pp. 91-106). Dordrecht, Netherlands: Kluwer.

Duck, S. W., Miell, D. K., & Gaebler, H. C. (1980). Attraction and communication in children's interactions. In H. C. Foot, A. J. Chapman, & R. J. Smith (Eds.), *Friendships and social relations in children* (pp. 89-115). Chichester: John Wiley.

Duck, S. W., & Perlman, D. (1985). The thousand islands of personal relationships: A prescriptive analysis for future explorations. In S. W. Duck & D. Perlman (Eds.), *Understanding personal relationships: An interdisciplinary approach* (pp. 1-15). London: Sage.

Duck, S. W., & Sants, H. K. A. (1983). On the origin of the species: Are personal relationships really interpersonal states? *Journal of Social and Clinical Psychology, 1,* 27-41.

Eder, D., & Hallinan, M. T. (1978). Sex differences in children's friendships. *American Sociological Review, 43,* 237-250.

Edwards, C. P., & Whiting, B. B. (1988). *Children of different worlds.* Cambridge, MA: Harvard University Press.

Epstein, J. L. (1986). Friendship selection: Developmental and environmental influences. In E. Mueller & C. Cooper (Eds.), *Process and outcome in peer relations.* New York: Academic Press.

Eyler, D., & Baridon, A. (1992, May/June). Far more than friendship. *Psychology Today, 25,* 60-67.

Fine, G. A. (1986). Friendships in the workplace. In V. J. Derlega & B. A. Winstead (Eds.), *Friendship and social interaction* (pp. 185-206). New York: Springer-Verlag.

Fitzpatrick, M. A., & Bochner, A. (1981). Perspectives on self and other: Male-female differences in perception of communication behavior. *Sex Roles, 7,* 523-535.

Furman, L. G. (1986). Cross-gender friendships in the workplace: Factors and components (Doctoral dissertation, Fielding Institute, 1986). *Dissertation Abstracts International,* DEU87-03955.

Gaines, S. O. (1994). Exchange of respect-denying behaviors among male-female friendships. *Journal of Social and Personal Relationships, 11,* 5-24.

Gesell, A (1945). *The embryology of behavior.* New York: Harper.

Giles, H., Mulac, A., Bradac, J., & Johnson, P. (1987). Speech accommodation theory: The first decade and beyond. In M. McLaughlin (Ed.), *Communication yearbook 10* (pp. 13-48). Newbury Park: Sage.

Ginsberg, D., Gottman, J. M., & Parker, J. G. (1986). The importance of friendship. In J. M. Gottman & J. G. Parker (Eds.), *Conversations of friends: Speculations on affective development* (pp. 3-48). Cambridge: Cambridge University Press.

Gottman, J. M. (1979). *Marital interactions: Experimental investigations.* New York: Academic Press.

Gottman, J. M. (1986). The world of coordinated play: Same- and cross-sex friendship in young children. In J. M. Gottman & J. G. Parker (Eds.), *Conversations of friends: Speculations on affective development* (pp. 139-191). Cambridge: Cambridge University Press.

Gottman, J. M., & Mettetal, G. (1986). Speculations about social and affective development: Friendship and acquaintance through adolescence. In J. M. Gottman & J. G. Parker (Eds.), *Conversations of friends: Speculations on affective development* (pp. 192-237). Cambridge: Cambridge University Press.

Griffin, E., & Sparks, G. G. (1990). Friends forever: A longitudinal exploration of intimacy in same-sex and platonic pairs. *Journal of Social and Personal Relationships, 7,* 29-46.

Gupta, V., & Korte, C. (1994). The effects of a confidant and a peer group on the well-being of single elders. *International Journal of Aging and Human Development, 39,* 293-302.

Hacker, H. M. (1981). Blabbermouths and clams: Sex differences in self-disclosure in same-sex and cross-sex friendship dyads. *Psychology of Women Quarterly, 5,* 385-401.

Hallinan, M. T. (1977). *The development of children's friendship cliques.* Paper presented at the annual meeting of the American Sociological Association, Chicago.

Harvey, J., Christensen, A., & McClintock, E. (1983). Research methods. In H. Kelley, E. Berscheid, A. Christensen, J. Harvey, T. Huston, G. Levinger, E. McClintock, L. Peplau, & D. Peterson (Eds.), *Close relationships* (pp. 449-485). New York: W. H. Freeman.

Hays, R. B. (1988). Friendship. In S. W. Duck (Ed.), *Handbook of personal relationships* (pp. 391-408). New York: John Wiley.

Hendrick, S. S., & Hendrick, C. (1993). Lovers as friends. *Journal of Social and Personal Relationships, 10,* 459-466.

Howe, F. C. (1993). The child in elementary school. *Child Study Journal, 24*(4).

Howes, C. (1987). Peer interaction of young children. *Monographs of the Society for Research in Child Development, 217*(53).

Jones, D. C., & Vaughan, K. (1990). Close friendships among senior adults. *Psychology and Aging, 5,* 451-457.

Karweit, N., & Hansell, S. (1983). Sex differences in adolescent relationships: Friendship and status. In J. L. Epstein & N. Karweit (Eds.), *Friends in school* (pp. 115-130). New York: Academic Press.

Komarovsky, M. (1976). *Dilemmas of masculinity: A study of college youth.* New York: W. W. Norton.

Kon, I. S. (1981). Adolescent friendship: Some unanswered questions for future research. In S. W. Duck & R. Gilmour (Eds.), *Personal relationships 2: Developing personal relationships* (pp. 187-204). New York: Academic Press.

Kon, I. S., & Losenkov, V. A. (1978). Friendships in adolescence: Values and behavior. *Journal of Marriage and Family, 40,* 143-157.

Kupersmidt, J. B., DeRosier, M. E., & Patterson, P. C. (1995). Similarity as the basis for children's friendships: The roles of sociometric status, aggressive and withdrawn behavior, academic achievement and demographic characteristics. *Journal of Social and Personal Relationships, 12,* 439-452.

LaGaipa, J. J. (1977). Testing a multidimensional approach to friendship. In S. W. Duck (Ed.), *Theory and practice in interpersonal attraction* (pp. 249-270). New York: Academic Press.

Leefeldt, C., & Callenbach, E. (1979). *The art of friendship.* New York: Berkeley.

Leibowitz, K., & Rawlins, W. K. (1980, May). *The relationship of gender to patterns of self-disclosure.* Paper presented at the annual meeting of the International Communication Association, Acapulco.

Lin, W., & Rusbult, C. E. (1995). Commitment to dating relationships and cross-sex friendships in America and China. *Journal of Social and Personal Relationships, 12,* 7-26.

Lipman-Blumen, J. (1976). Toward a homosocial theory of sex-roles: An explanation of the sex segregation of social institutions. In M. M. Blaxall & B. Reagan (Eds.), *Women and the workplace* (pp. 15-32). Chicago: University of Chicago Press.

Maccoby, E. E. (1988). Gender as a social category. *Developmental Psychology, 24,* 755-765.

Mannarino, A. P. (1980). The development of children's friendships. In H. C. Foot, A. J. Chapman, & J. R. Smith (Eds.), *Friendship and social relations in children* (pp. 45-63). New York: John Wiley.

McCarthy, B. (1981). Studying personal relationships. In S. W. Duck & R. Gilmour (Eds.), *Personal relationships 1: Studying personal relationships* (pp. 23-46). New York: Academic Press.

McMahon, A. W., & Rhudick, P. J. (1964). Reminiscing: Adaptational significance in the aged. *Archives of General Psychiatry, 10,* 292-298.

McWilliams, S., & Howard, J. A. (1993). Solidarity and hierarchy in cross-sex friendships. *Journal of Social Issues, 49,* 191-202.

Metts, S., Cupach, W. R., & Bejlovec, R. A. (1989). "I love you too much to ever start liking you": Redefining romantic relationships. *Journal of Social and Personal Relationships, 6,* 259-274.

Monsour, M. (1988). *Cross-sex friendships in a changing society: A comparative analysis of cross-sex friendships, same-sex friendships, and romantic relationships.* Unpublished doctoral dissertation, University of Illinois, Champaign.

Monsour, M. (1992). Meanings of intimacy in cross- and same-sex friendships. *Journal of Social and Personal Relationships, 9,* 277-295.

Monsour, M. (1994). Similarities and dissimilarities in personal relationships: Constructing meaning and building intimacy through communication. In S. W. Duck (Ed.), *Understanding relationship processes: Vol. 4. Dynamics of relationships* (pp. 112-134). Thousand Oaks, CA: Sage.

Monsour, M. (1995). *Termination of cross-sex friendships: Differing relational definitions.* Manuscript in preparation.

Monsour, M., Beard, C., Harris, B., & Kurzweil, N. (1994). Challenges confronting cross-sex friendships: "Much ado about nothing"? *Sex Roles, 31,* 55-77.

Monsour, M., Betty, S., & Kurzweil, N. (1993). Levels of perspectives and the perception of intimacy in cross-sex friendships: A balance theory explanation of shared perceptual reality. *Journal of Social and Personal Relationships, 10,* 529-550.

Nardi, P. M. (Ed.). (1992). *Men's friendships.* Newbury Park, CA: Sage.

Newcomb, A. F., & Bagwell, C. L. (1995). Children's friendship relations: A meta-analytic review. *Psychological Bulletin, 117,* 306-347.

Nussbaum, J. F., Thompson, T., & Robinson, J. D. (1989). *Communication and aging.* New York: Harper & Row.

O'Connor, B. (1995). Family and friendship relationships among older and younger adults: Interaction motivation, mood, and quality. *International Journal of Aging and Human Development, 40,* 9-29.

O'Connor, P. (1993). Same-gender and cross-gender friendships among the frail elderly. *Gerontologist, 33,* 24-30.

Omark, D. R., Omark, M., & Edelman, M. S. (1975). Formation of dominance hierarchies in young children: Action and perception. In T. R. Williams (Ed.), *Psychological anthropology.* The Hague: Mouton.

O'Meara, D. (1989). Cross-sex friendship: Four basic challenges of an ignored relationship. *Sex Roles, 21,* 525-543.

O'Meara, D. (1994). Cross-sex friendship opportunity challenge: Uncharted terrain for exploration. *Personal Relationship Issues, 2*(1).

Ossorio, P. G. (1981). Conceptual-notational devices: The PCF and related types. In K. E. Davis (Ed.), *Advances in descriptive psychology* (Vol. 1). Greenwich, CT: JAI.

Page, R. M., Scanlan, A., & Deringer, N. (1994). Childhood loneliness and isolation: Implications and strategies for childhood educators. *Child Study Journal, 24,* 107-118.

Pankin, R. M. (1973, May). *The romantic myth, sexism, and the bureaucratic property system.* Paper presented at the annual meeting of the North Central Sociological Association, Cincinnati, OH.

Planalp, S. (1985). Relational schemata: A test of alternative forms of relational knowledge as guides to communication. *Human Communication Research, 12,* 1-29.

Poole, S., & McPhee, R. (1985). Methodology in interpersonal communication. In M. L. Knapp & G. R. Miller (Eds.), *Handbook of interpersonal communication* (pp. 100-170). Beverly Hills, CA: Sage.

Priefer, B. A., & Gambert, S. R. (1984). Reminiscence and life review in the elderly. *Psychiatric Medicine, 2,* 91-100.

Putallaz, M., & Gottman, J. M. (1981). Social skills and group acceptance. In S. R. Asher & J. M. Gottman (Eds.), *The development of children's friendships* (pp. 116-149). Cambridge: Cambridge University Press.

Rawlins, W. K. (1982). Cross-sex friends and the communicative management of sex-role expectations. *Communication Quarterly, 30,* 343-352.

Rawlins, W. K. (1989). *Boys and girls as friends versus boyfriends and girlfriends: Adolescents' conceptions of cross-sex relationships.* Paper presented at the annual meeting of the Speech Communication Association, San Francisco.

Rawlins, W. K. (1992). *Friendship matters: Communication, dialectics, and the life course.* New York: Walter de Gruyter.

Rawlins, W. K. (1994). Reflecting on (cross-sex) friendship: De-scripting the drama. *Personal Relationship Issues, 2*(1), 4-7.

Rice, F. P. (1978). *The adolescent: Development, relationships, and culture.* Boston: Allyn & Bacon.

Rickleman, K. E. (1981). *Childhood cross-sex friendships: An investigation of trends and possible explanatory theories.* Unpublished manuscript, University of Illinois, Champaign.

Rizzo, T. A. (1989). *Friendship development among young children.* Norwood, NJ: Ablex.

Roberts, M. K. (1982). Men and women: Partners, lovers, friends. In K. E. Davis & T. O. Mitchell (Eds.), *Advances in descriptive psychology* (Vol. 2, pp. 57-78). Greenwich, CT: JAI.

Rogers, D. (1982). Life-span development. Monterey, CA: Brooks/Cole.

Roopnarine, J. L., & Field, T. M. (1984). Play interactions of friends and acquaintances in nursery school. In T. M. Field, J. L. Roopnarine, & M. Segal (Eds.), *Friendships in normal and handicapped children* (pp. 89-98). Norwood, NJ: Ablex.

Rose, S. (1985). Same- and cross-sex friendships and the psychology of homosociality. *Sex Roles, 12,* 63-74.

Rubenstein, J. (1984). Friendship development in normal children: A commentary. In T. M. Field, J. L. Roopnarine, & M. Segal (Eds.), *Friendships in normal and handicapped children* (pp. 125-135). Norwood, NJ: Ablex.

Rubenstein, J., & Howes, C. (1976). The effects of peers on toddler interaction with mother and toys. *Child Development, 47,* 597-605.

Rubenstein, J., & Rubin, C. (1984). Children's fantasies of interaction with same and opposite-sex peers. In T. M. Field, J. L. Roopnarine, & M. Segal (Eds.), *Friendships in normal and handicapped children* (pp. 99-124). Norwood, NJ: Ablex.

Rubin, K. H., Fein, G. G., & Vandenberg, B. (1983). Play. In E. M. Hetherington (Ed.), *Handbook of child psychology: Vol. 4. Socialization, personality, and social development* (pp. 694-774). New York: John Wiley.

Rubin, L. B. (1985). *Just friends: The role of friendship in our lives.* New York: Harper & Row.

Rubin, Z. (1980). *Children's friendships.* Cambridge, MA: Harvard University Press.

Safilios-Rothschild, C. (1981). Toward a social psychology of relationships. *Psychology of Women Quarterly, 5,* 377-384.

Santrock, J. W. (1983). *Life-span development.* Dubuque, IA: William C. Brown.

Sapadin, L. A. (1988). Friendship and gender: Perspectives of professional men and women. *Journal of Social and Personal Relationships, 5,* 387-403.

Schofield, J. W. (1981). Complementary and conflicting identities: Images and interaction in an interracial school. In S. R. Asher & J. M. Gottman (Eds.), *The development of children's friendships* (pp. 53-90). Cambridge: Cambridge University Press.

Schofield, J. W., & Sagar, H. (1977). Peer interaction patterns in an integrated middle school. *Sociometry, 40,* 130-138.

Selman, R. (1981). The child as a friendship philosopher. In S. R. Asher & J. M. Gottman (Eds.), *The development of children's friendships* (pp. 242-272). Cambridge: Cambridge University Press.

Serbin, L. A., Tonick, I. J., & Sternglanz, S. H. (1977). Shaping cooperative cross-sex play. *Child Development, 48,* 924-929.

Sherman, L. W. (1975). An ecological study of glee in small groups of preschool children. *Child Development, 46,* 53-61.

Shotland, R. L., & Craig, J. M. (1988). Can men and women differentiate between friendly and sexually interested behavior? *Social Psychology Quarterly, 51,* 66-73.

Shulman, S. (1993). Close relationships and coping behavior in adolescence. *Journal of Adolescence, 16,* 267-283.

Smith-Rosenberg, C. (1975). The female world of love and ritual: Relations between women in 19th century America. *Signs, 1*(1), 1-29.

Snell, W. E. (1989). Willingness to self-disclose to female and male friends as a function of society anxiety and gender. *Personality and Social Psychology Bulletin, 15,* 113-125.

Solano, C. H. (1986). People without friends: Loneliness and its alternatives. In V. J. Derlega & B. A. Winstead (Eds.), *Friendship and social interaction* (pp. 227-246). New York: Springer-Verlag.

Sullivan, H. S. (1953). *The interpersonal theory of psychiatry.* New York: W. W. Norton.

Swain, S. O. (1992). Men's friendships with women: Intimacy, sexual boundaries, and the informant role. In P. M. Nardi (Ed.), *Men's friendships* (pp. 153-171). Newbury Park, CA: Sage.

Tannen, D. (1990). *You just don't understand: Women and men in conversation.* New York: William Morrow.

Tavris, C. (1992). *The mismeasure of woman.* New York: Simon & Schuster.

Tesch, S. A. (1983). Review of friendship development across the lifespan. *Human Development, 26,* 266-276.

Thorne, B. (1987). Girls and boys together . . . but mostly apart: Gender arrangement in elementary schools. In W. W. Hartup & Z. Rubin (Eds.), *Relationships and development* (pp. 167-184). Hillsdale, NJ: Lawrence Erlbaum.

Usui, W. M. (1984). Homogeneity of friendship networks of elderly blacks and whites. *Journal of Gerontology, 39,* 350-356.

Vandell, D. L., & Mueller, E. C. (1980). Peer play and friendships during the first two years. In H. C. Foot, A. J. Chapman, & J. R. Smith (Eds.), *Friendships and social relations in children* (pp. 181-208). New York: John Wiley.

Vygotsky, L. S. (1978). *Mind in society: The development of higher psychological processes.* Cambridge, MA: Harvard University Press.

Watt, J. H., & Van Den Berg, S. (1995). *Research methods for communication science.* Boston: Allyn & Bacon.

Weiss, L., & Lowenthal, M. (1975). Life-course perspectives on friendship. In M. Lowenthal, M. Thurnher, & D. Chiriboga (Eds.), *Four stages of life* (pp. 48-61). San Francisco: Jossey-Bass.

Werebe, M. J. G. (1987). Friendship and dating relationships among French adolescents. *Journal of Adolescence, 10,* 269-289.

Werking, K. J. (1992). *The communicative management of cross-sex friendship.* Unpublished doctoral dissertation, Purdue University.

Werking, K. J. (1994). Hidden assumptions: A critique of existing cross-sex friendship research. *Personal Relationship Issues 2*(1), 8-10.

Whaley, K. L., & Rubenstein, T. S. (1994). How toddlers "do" friendship: A descriptive analysis of naturally occurring friendships in a group child care center. *Journal of Social and Personal Relationships, 11,* 383-400.

Windle, M. (1995). A study of friendship characterization and problem behaviors among middle adolescents. *Child Development, 65,* 1764-1777.

Winstead, B. A., & Derlega, V. J. (1986). Friendship and social interaction: An introduction. In V. J. Derlega & B. A. Winstead (Eds.), *Friendship and social interaction* (pp. 1-7). New York: Springer-Verlag.

Won-Doornink, M. J. (1985). Self-disclosure and reciprocity in conversation. *Social Psychology Quarterly, 48,* 97-107.

Wood, J. T. (1994). *Gendered lives: Communication, gender, and culture.* Belmont, CA: Wadsworth.

Wright, P. H. (1984). Self-referent motivation and the intrinsic quality of friendship. *Journal of Social and Personal Relationships, 1,* 115-130.

Wright, P. H. (1989). Gender differences in adults' same- and cross-gender friendships. In R. G. Adams & R. Blieszner (Eds.), *Older adult friendships* (pp. 197-221). Newbury Park, CA: Sage.

Wright, P. H., & Keple, T. W. (1981). Friends and parents of a sample of high school juniors: An exploratory study of relationship intensity and interpersonal rewards. *Journal of Marriage and the Family, 43,* 559-570.

Yingling, J. (1994). Constituting friendship in talk and metatalk. *Journal of Social and Personal Relationships, 11,* 411-426.

Zera, D. (1992). Coming of age in a heterosexist world: The development of gay and lesbian adolescents. *Adolescence, 27,* 849-854.

AUTHOR INDEX

SUBJECT INDEX

Abuse, child, 343
Accommodation in public relations,
    contingency model of, 143-144
Action:
    attitudes influencing, 215
    deliberating before taking, 211
    descriptive norms motivating, 167
    fear appeals motivating, 205
    reasoned, 212, 215
    spontaneous, 212, 215
    symbolic interactionism perspective and, 79
Activation:
    frequency of, and attitude accessibility,
        209-210, 213, 216
    recency of, and attitude accessibility,
        207-208, 213, 216
Activities:
    early childhood cross-sex friendships, 387
    friends sharing, 378, 379
    group participation and, 247-249
Actual opinions, 176-179
Adolescence, cross-sex friendships in, 388,
    394-396
Adoption studies, 337
Adulthood, cross-sex friendships in, 396-404
Adversarial role, reporters and, 142
Advertising:
    fashion, 91
    gendered decoding and, 91-99, 100-101
    gender images in, 71-103
    realism in, 75
    semiology of, 84
    symbolic potential of images, 79
Advising, parental role in, 324-325
Advocacy function:
    public relations and, 123-124
    reporters and, 142
Aesthetic value, female body and, 86-87
Affect:
    group participation and, 244-245
    parents', 335-336
Affective arousal, parenting practices and,
    317-318
Affective beliefs, foreign television impact
    on, 57
Affective responses:
    attitudes and, 191-192
    to messages, 194
    parental, 311

social anxiety and, 264
Affiliation, effects of social anxiety on,
    271-273
Affluence perceptions, television viewing
    and, 14-15
African Americans, advertising and, 98-99
Age:
    cultivation analysis of television viewing
        and, 30
    foreign television impact and, 61
    small group participation and, 233
Aggregation of results, 21
Aggressive behavior in children, 311, 313
    authoritarian parenting and, 320
    marital conflict and, 326
    parental attribution and, 334
    parental depression and, 335
    parenting practices and, 340
    rejected children and, 330
    stressful life events and, 347
Ambiguous information:
    interpreting, 197, 202
    social anxiety and, 279
Anorexia, 97-98
ANOVA, cultivation analysis of television
    viewing and, 24-25
Anthropology, gender/advertising
    relationship and, 72
Antisocial behavior in children, 315
    emotional reactivity and, 339
    marital effects on, 326
Anxiety:
    children's, 314
    communicative, 263-286
    fear appeals and, 205-206
    parenting effects, 335
    small group participation and, 231
    social, 263-286
    state, 264-266
Anxious self-preoccupation, 276
Appraisal theories of emotion, 284
Archetypal case, 380
Arguments, strength of, 193
Arousal:
    child's emotions, 337-338
    social anxiety and, 267, 282-284
Arousal-mediated behaviors, 270-271
Ascendancy, small group participation and,
    231

437

ABOUT THE EDITOR

BRANT R. BURLESON (Ph.D., University of Illinois at Urbana-Champaign, 1982) is a Professor in the Department of Communication at Purdue University, where he teaches courses in communication theory, interpersonal communication, and the philosophy of the social sciences. His research interests center on communication skills acquisition and development, social-cognitive foundations of strategic communication, effects of communication skills on relationship formation and development, and supportive forms of communication, such as comforting. His research has appeared in edited volumes and journals, including the *American Journal of Family Therapy, Child Development, Communication Monographs, Communication Research, Family Relations, Human Communication Research, Journal of Language and Social Psychology,* and *Quarterly Journal of Speech.* He has held several offices in both the International Communication Association and the Speech Communication Association and has served on the editorial boards of more than a dozen major journals. Recently, he coedited (with Terrance Albrecht and Irwin Sarason) *Communication of Social Support: Messages, Interactions, Relationships, and Community* (1994).

ABOUT THE AUTHORS

JOSEPH A. BONITO (Ph.D., University of Illinois at Urbana-Champaign, 1996) is Visiting Assistant Professor of Communication at the University of Arizona. His research interests focus on distribution of floor time, achievement of coordination, and the construction of common ground through face-to-face interaction. He is currently studying participation in small groups, with emphasis on how structures of knowledge and structures of interaction combine to produce participation hierarchies. He recently served on the review board for *Research on Language and Social Interaction.*

GLEN T. CAMERON (Ph.D., University of Texas at Austin, 1989) is Associate Professor of Public Relations in the Henry W. Grady College of Journalism and Mass Communication at the University of Georgia in Athens. He serves as Director of Research in the James M. Cox, Jr. Institute for Newspaper Management Studies, most recently leading a two-year study of electronic newspapers. He researches public relations management issues, new media technologies, sources of information pollution in news media, and information processing of media messages. His recent publications include an article on information pollution in *Journalism and Mass Communication Quarterly* and articles on professional standards in the *Journal of Public Relations Research* and *Public Relations Review.* A book chapter on measurement of memory response latencies appeared in *Measures of the Psychological Processing of Television.*

PATRICIA A. CURTIN (Ph.D., University of Georgia, 1996) is Assistant Professor of Public Relations at the University of North Carolina in Chapel Hill. Her research interests include media relations and agenda building, and her recent publications include articles on information pollution in *Journalism and Mass Communication Quarterly* and a historical case study of agenda building in *American Journalism.*

MICHEL G. ELASMAR (Ph.D., Michigan State University, 1993) is Assistant Professor of Communication and Director of the Communication Research Center at Boston University. His research interests include the adoption patterns and effects of new communication technologies at home and in the workplace, and the impact of cross-border communication. His publications include a study of news source selection during the Persian Gulf War (in *Desert Storm and the Mass Media,* edited by B. Greenberg and W. Gantz, 1993) and an assessment of the direct broadcast industry in the United States (in *Journal of Broadcasting and Electronic Media,* 1995). His current research on new communication technologies focuses on the development of a methodologically adequate and practically useful strategy to measure the usage patterns of World Wide Web sites. His current research on cross-border communication focuses on the measurement of the impact of foreign TV on young adults abroad. Data have so far been collected in Israel, Lebanon, Turkey, Japan, and Taiwan.

CARROLL J. GLYNN (Ph.D., University of Wisconsin—Madison, 1983) is Associate Professor and Department Chair in the Department of Communication at Cornell University. Her research interests center on the formation and change of public opinion and include the study of the relationships among communication, social norms, and other factors in opinion formation and expression. She has published articles in *Public Opinion Quarterly, Journal of Social Psychology, Social Science Research, Journalism Quarterly,* and *Communication Research,* as well as chapters in *Communication Yearbook* and a number of other books. She is currently in the process of writing a textbook on public opinion with several coauthors.

CRAIG H. HART (Ph.D., Purdue University, 1987) is Associate Professor in the Department of Family Sciences at Brigham Young University, where he teaches courses in human development and early childhood education. His research interests include children's social/communicative development and peer relations in the context of parenting/familial variables, as well as the impact of quality indices in early childhood education programs on developmental outcomes in young children. His research has appeared in several edited volumes and journals, including *Child Development, Developmental Psychology,* and the *Early Childhood Research Quarterly.* Recently, he edited *Children on Playgrounds: Research Perspectives and Applications* and coedited a volume titled *Integrated Developmentally Appropriate Curriculum: Birth Through Age Eight.* He currently serves as associate editor for *Early Childhood Research Quarterly.*

ANDREA B. HOLLINGSHEAD (Ph.D., University of Illinois at Urbana-Champaign, 1993) is Assistant Professor of Speech Communication and Psychology at the University of Illinois at Urbana-Champaign. Her research investigates the cognitive and social processes that lead to effective decision making and collaboration in work groups. She is also interested in the impact of communication technologies that support group communication in work settings. Her recent publications include a book, *Groups Interacting with Technology* (coauthored with Joe McGrath), and articles in *Organizational and Human Decision Making Processes, Human Communication Research,* and *Journal of Personality and Social Psychology.*

JOHN E. HUNTER (Ph.D., University of Illinois, 1964) is Professor of Psychology at Michigan State University. He is coauthor of three books: *Meta-Analysis, Mathematical Models of Attitude Change,* and *Methods of*

Meta-Analysis. He is a Fellow of the Society of Industrial and Organizational Psychology, the American Psychological Society, and the American Psychological Association. He has published more than 150 articles on a wide variety of topics, including personnel selection, organizational interventions, attitude change, psychometric theory, personality, group dynamics, other social processes, and oddities such as dust bathing in quail. His current research in meta-analysis focuses on the extension of meta-analysis methods to correct for artifacts not yet handled. His research in psychometric theory currently has three foci: the use of path analysis to analyze experiments and interventions, the relationship between static and dynamic causal models, and nonlinear and hierarchical measurement models. His current foci in personality research are shame, the inner voice, and authoritarianism. He is also working in several areas of persuasion and interpersonal communication.

BARBARA L. MANDLECO (Ph.D., Brigham Young University, 1991) is Assistant Professor in the College of Nursing at Brigham Young University, where she is also an associate member of the Graduate Faculty in the Department of Family Sciences. Her research interests include stress, coping, and resilience in children and family adaptation to a disabled child. She has published articles in psychology and nursing journals, and she is currently authoring a nursing text titled *Dimensions, Characteristics, and Roles Used in Client Care.*

MICHAEL MONSOUR (Ph.D, University of Illinois at Urbana-Champaign, 1988) is Associate Professor in the Department of Communication at the University of Colorado at Denver. His current research interests focus primarily on cross-sex friendships; the impact of similarity on relationship initiation, development, and breakdown; and interpersonal perception as it relates to relationship development. He has published articles and book chapters in the areas of cross-sex friendships, intimacy, interpersonal perception, and similarity in relationships.

MICHAEL MORGAN (Ph.D., University of Pennsylvania, 1980) is Professor in the Department of Communication at the University of Massachusetts. His research interests include the social and cultural impacts of media in the United States and internationally. Recently, he and James Shanahan published *Democracy Tango,* a work about television's cultivation of political beliefs in Argentina. He is also coeditor, with Nancy Signorielli, of *Cultivation Analysis: New Directions in Media Effects Research* (1990) and, with Susan Leggett, *Mainstream(s) and Margins: Cultural Politics in the 90s* (1996).

SUSANNE FROST OLSEN (Ph.D., University of Georgia, 1992) is Assistant Professor in the Department of Family Sciences at Brigham Young University, where she teaches courses in human development and research methods.

Her research interests include parent-child relationships across the life span and the intergenerational transmission of parenting. She has published articles in psychology and gerontology journals.

MILES L. PATTERSON (Ph.D., Northwestern University, 1968) is Professor of Psychology at the University of Missouri-St. Louis. His present research interests include the study of the interface between behavior management and social cognition, and patterns of nonverbal cues in pedestrian behavior. He is the author of two books and more than 50 other publications on nonverbal communication, including "A Parallel Process Model of Nonverbal Communication," in the *Journal of Nonverbal Behavior* (1995); the article on nonverbal communication in *The Blackwell Encyclopedia of Social Psychology* (1995); and "Social Behavior and Social Cognition: A Parallel Process Approach," in *What's Social About Social Cognition: Social Cognition in Small Groups,* edited by J. L. Nye and A. M. Brower (1996). From 1986 to 1991 he served as editor of the *Journal of Nonverbal Behavior.*

VICKI RITTS (Ph.D., University of Missouri at St. Louis, 1994) is Instructor of Psychology at St. Louis Community College-Meramec. Her current research interests include social anxiety in social interactions, nonverbal behavior in the instructional process, and physical attractiveness in the educational setting. Her recent publications include "Verification and Commitment in Marital Relationships: An Exploration of Self-Verification Theory in Community College Students," in *Psychological Reports* (1995); "Effects of Social Anxiety and Action Identification on Impressions and Thoughts in Interaction," in the *Journal of Social and Clinical Psychology* (1996); "Expectations, Impressions, and Judgments of Physically Attractive Students: A Review," in *Review of Educational Research* (1992); and "Nonverbal Teaching Tips," in *Intervention: In School and Clinic* (1994).

CLYDE C. ROBINSON (Ph.D., University of North Carolina at Greensboro, 1982) is Associate Professor in the Department of Family Sciences at Brigham Young University, where he teaches courses in early childhood education, human development, and research methods. His research interests include parenting practices and styles and their relationships to child socialization outcomes. He has directed university laboratory preschools for 7 years. He is a consulting editor for and has published articles in early childhood education and psychology journals.

DAVID R. ROSKOS-EWOLDSEN (Ph.D., Indiana University, 1990) is Associate Professor in the Department of Speech Communication at the University of Alabama. His research focuses on the transactive relationship between attitudes and persuasion—how attitudes influence the processing of persuasive messages and how various persuasive strategies influence the accessibility of attitudes from memory. In addition, he examines the impact of media portrayals of information on people's implicit theories of probability. His work has appeared in several journals, including *Journal of Personality and Social Psychology, Personality and Social Psychology Bulletin,* and *Cognition and Emotion,* and in *The Heart's Eye: Emotional Influences in Perception and Attention,* edited by P. M. Niedenthal and S. Kitayama.

LYNNE M. SALLOT (Ph.D., University of Florida, 1993) is Assistant Professor of Public Relations in the Henry W. Grady College of Journalism and Mass Communication at the University of Georgia in Athens. Her research interests include effective teaching and impression management in public relations, and effects of public relations on news content. Her recent publications include articles on professional standards in *Journal of Public Relations Research* and *Public Relations Review,* and on how the campaigns course can build better relationships for public relations in and out of the university setting in *Journalism & Mass Communication Educator.*

JAMES SHANAHAN (Ph.D., University of Massachusetts, 1991) is Assistant Professor in the Department of Communication at Cornell University. His research interests include environmental communication and media impacts upon political beliefs and ideologies. Recently, he and Michael Morgan published *Democracy Tango,* a work about television's cultivation of political beliefs in Argentina.

VICKIE RUTLEDGE SHIELDS (Ph.D., Ohio State University, 1994) is Assistant Professor of Telecommunications and Women's Studies at Bowling Green State University. Her research interests focus on critical/cultural approaches to the study of gender representations in popular media, cultural studies theory and research, media audience reception, and feminist criticism. She has published her work on gender and advertising in *The Journal of Communication Inquiry* and *The Women's Studies Encyclopedia.* She has published her work on feminist research methodologies in *Women's Studies International Forum* (with Brenda Dervin).